The Sundance Reader

Seventh Edition

Mark Connelly

Milwaukee Area Technical College

CENGAGE
Learning·

Australia • Brazil • Japan • Korea • Mexico • Singapore • Spain • United Kingdom • United States

CENGAGE
Learning·

The Sundance Reader,
Seventh Edition
Mark Connelly

Product Director:
Monica Eckman

Product Manager:
Kate Derrick

Content Developer:
Kathy Sands-Boehmer

Content Coordinator:
Danielle Warchol

Media Developer:
Janine Tangney

Marketing Manager:
Lydia Lestar

Content Project Manager:
Dan Saabye

Art Director: Marissa Falco

Manufacturing Planner:
Betsy Donaghey

Rights Acquisition Specialist:
Ann Hoffman

Production Service:
MPS Limited

Text Designer: Bill Reuter

Cover Designer: Bill Reuter

Cover Image: MIXA/Getty
Images

Compositor: MPS Limited

For product information and technology assistance, contact us at **Cengage Learning Customer & Sales Support, 1-800-354-9706**

For permission to use material from this text or product, submit all requests online at **www.cengage.com/permissions** Further permissions questions can be e-mailed to **permissionrequest@cengage.com**

Library of Congress Control Number: 2013950395

ISBN-13: 978-1-285-42720-1

ISBN-10: 1-285-42720-3

Cengage Learning
200 First Stamford Place, 4th Floor
Stamford, CT 06902
USA

Cengage Learning is a leading provider of customized learning solutions with office locations around the globe, including Singapore, the United Kingdom, Australia, Mexico, Brazil and Japan. Locate your local office at **international.cengage.com/region**

Cengage Learning products are represented in Canada by Nelson Education, Ltd.

For your course and learning solutions, visit **www.cengage.com**

Purchase any of our products at your local college store or at our preferred online store **www.cengagebrain.com**

Instructors: Please visit **login.cengage.com** and log in to access instructor-specific resources.

Printed in the United States of America
1 2 3 4 5 6 7 17 16 15 14 13

To Stanley Felber

Contents

12 Argument and Persuasion 431

Thematic Contents

Psychology and Human Behavior

Science and Technology

Sociology

Values

Women and Men

Work and Career

Writing

Preface

Why Write?

Few students plan to become writers. You may think of writers only as people who write for a living—journalists, novelists, and playwrights. But all professionals—all educated men and women, in fact—write to achieve their goals. Lawyers write motions and draft appeals. Doctors record a diagnosis and plan a course of treatment on a patient's chart. Police officers file reports about accidents and criminal investigations. Salespeople, administrators, and managers send streams of email to announce new products, respond to questions, and inform employees, customers, and investors. Men and women entering any profession soon realize that they depend on writing to share ideas, express opinions, and influence others.

Thinking about your future career, you probably imagine yourself in action—an engineer working in a test lab, a contractor walking through a construction site, or a restaurant owner supervising a banquet. But whether your goal is teaching children or owning your own business, writing will be critical to your success. In the information age nearly all jobs involve exchanging data. The ability to write not only will help you complete academic assignments but accomplish tasks and solve problems in any vocation you may enter.

Learning to write well sharpens your critical thinking skills, improving your ability to locate information, examine evidence, solve problems, and persuade others. The strategies you learn in a writing course can enhance your performance in oral presentations, job interviews, meetings, and conference calls. By learning to think more clearly, analyze your audience, and organize your ideas, you will be a more effective communicator in any situation.

The Sundance Reader

The Sundance Reader, Seventh Edition, contains over sixty readings drawn from a range of academic disciplines and professions. The collection of essays and articles, organized by rhetorical modes, includes both classic and contemporary authors such as Mark Twain, Ellen Goodman, Joe Klein, Fouad Ajami, William Safire, Martin Luther King, Sarah Chayes, and Jessica Valenti. In addition to writing from the disciplines of law, economics, and science by writers such as Robert Reich and Rachel Carson, *The Sundance Reader* offers students practical advice on résumé writing and job interviews. Applied readings at the end of each chapter demonstrate how writers use the rhetorical modes beyond the classroom. Entries such as a résumè, a website, and an incident report illustrate writing tasks students will face in future courses and in their careers.

The Sundance Reader's wide variety of topics on the environment, culture, social issues, the media, and business make the textbook suitable for thematic courses.

Individual chapters include self-contained units on current issues, and the thematic table of contents lists topics that can be explored in depth.

With its wealth of readings and four-part questioning strategy following each entry, *The Sundance Reader* provides students a unique perspective on how writing is shaped in different contexts.

The Sundance Reader has several features that make it a useful teaching tool for college instructors:

- **A range of readings** Each chapter opens with brief, readable entries that clearly demonstrate the rhetorical mode, followed by longer, more challenging essays. Each chapter highlights a model "blending" the modes showing how writers often use several methods of development to tell a story or explain a process. Samples of applied writing appear at the end, illustrating how writers use the mode in different professions. Instructors have flexibility in assigning readings best suited to their student populations.

- **Brief entries suitable for in-class reading** Many of the essays are short enough to be read in class and used as writing prompts, reducing the need for handouts.

- **An emphasis on writing** *The Sundance Reader* moves students from reading to writing. Chapters open with reading questions and conclude with writing strategies and lists of suggested topics. Each chapter ends with a checklist of common writing problems.

- **An emphasis on critical thinking** *The Sundance Reader* stresses critical thinking by including essays such as James Austin's article about the role of chance in scientific research. Samuel Scudder's essay "Take This Fish and Look at It" dramatizes the importance of detailed observation. Benjamin Radford's "How Television Distorts Reality" demonstrates how the media shapes perceptions and influences public opinion.

- **Pro and con entries** Instructors have found that presenting essays with opposing viewpoints can stimulate class discussions and prompt writing activities. *The Sundance Reader* presents pairs of pro and con articles on four critical issues: motherhood, the minimum wage, free speech and censorship, and ethnic identity.

- **Focus on diversity** Over a third of the selections are written by women and minorities. African American, Hispanic, and Asian writers are represented. These essays cover diverse issues, including business and technology.

- **Writing across the curriculum** *The Sundance Reader* demonstrates how each mode is developed by writers working in several disciplines, including law, medicine, psychology, history, economics, media, and business.

- **Writing beyond the classroom** Each chapter includes a section illustrating how writers use the modes in "the real world." Websites, brochures, government documents, reports, and a résumé introduce elements of business and technical writing to composition students.

- **Collaborative writing** Writing suggestions following the readings include directions for collaborative writing activities. The introduction provides useful guidelines for successful group writing.

- *Advice on the job search* The Sundance Reader contains articles offering students practical advice on writing résumés and succeeding in job interviews.
- *An annotated essay in each chapter* The first essay used to introduce each mode is annotated to guide students through its construction.
- *Writer's Guide to Documenting Sources* The Sundance Reader provides examples on how to apply both MLA and APA rules for documenting sources. The guide includes an MLA documented essay with its original sources, demonstrating the use of direct quotations and paraphrases.

Above all, *The Sundance Reader* has been designed to encourage students to read critically and develop confidence as writers.

New in this Edition

- *Thirty-one new essays*
  "How the Teachers Killed a Dream," **Joel Klein**
  "The Rise of Pancho Villa," **John Reed**
  "Returning to Southie," **Michael Patrick MacDonald**
  "The San Francisco Earthquake," **Jack London**
  "The Sounds of the City," **James Tuite**
  "A Jerk," **Sydney Harris**
  "Liberal and Conservative," **William Safire**
  "Who Counts as Rich?," **Bruce Bartlett**
  "How Poor is 'Poor'?," **Robert Rector**
  "Two Ways of Seeing A River," **Mark Twain**
  "Impressions of America," **Oscar Wilde**
  "How the Lawyers Stole Winter," **Christopher Daly**
  "Don't Blame Wal-Mart," **Robert Reich**
  "How to Grade Teachers: Lessons from the Teachers Strike," **Harold Meyerson**
  "Why is the Arab World so Easily Offended?," **Fouad Ajami**
  "I'm a Mom," **Jenny Allen**
  "Are All Women Born to be Mothers?," **Jessica Valenti**
  "Four Sides to Every Story," **Stewart Brand**
  "Stuck in the Middle," **Florence King**
  "Death and Justice: How Capital Punishment Affirms Life," **Edward Koch**
  "Modifying Your Résumé for Computer Selection," **Walter C. Vertreace**
  "How to Recover From a Bad Interview," **Donna Farrugia**
  "Syria's Cyberwars: Using Social Media Against Dissent," **Mark Clayton**
  "In the Facebook Era, Students Tell You Everything," **Stephen Winzenburg**
  "We Can't Wish Away Climate Change," **Al Gore**
  "Are We Losing Our Memory?," **Alexander Stille**
  "Why We Must Raise the Minimum Wage," **Alexander Cockburn**
  "A Starter Wage for Teenagers," **Phil Kerpen and Nicole Kaeding**
  "Five Reasons to Stop Fearing China," **Rick Newman.**
  "There's No Place for Censorship-by-Riot," **Charles Lane**
  "Anti-Muslim Movie May Not Meet the Free Speech Test," **Sarah Chayes**
- *Revised discussion of the modes* provides students with greater instruction in understanding, writing, and organizing essays.
- *A new feature, Writing Techniques,* in each chapter provides students with practical tools to improve essays and overcome common problems.

- **Additional documented student papers** illustrate how to introduce and cite outside sources to support a thesis.
- **Revised MLA and APA guidelines** expand coverage of online sources and explain DOI numbers.
- **Critical Issues** offers students online readings and research guides for four issues: immigration, the American Dream, America's role in the world, and privacy in the electronic age.

Accompanying English CourseMate Resources

 Visit English CourseMate at **www.cengagebrain.com** to find many helpful resources and study tools for this chapter.

Acknowledgments

I would like to thank the following reviewers for their valuable suggestions to this edition of *The Sundance Reader:*

Anthony Booker, Fayetteville State University

Katawna Caldwell, Eastfield College

Sheryl Chisamore, SUNY Ulster

Zana Easley, Pima Community College

Sarah Etlinger, Rock Valley College

Jane Gamber, Hutchinson Community College

Loren Gruber, Missouri Valley College

Amy Hander, Austin Community College

Karen Jackson, North Carolina Central University

Amelia Keel, Lone Star College,Kingwood

Erica Lara, Southwest Texas Junior College

Susan Latta, Indiana State University

Julie Long, College of the Albermarle

Quentin Miller, Suffolk University

Kelly Moffatt, Northern Kentucky University

Michele Singletary, Nashville State Community College

Andrew Tomko, Bergen Community College

Robert Williams, Radford University

All books are a collaborative effort. My special thanks go to Monica Eckman, Publisher; Kate Derrick, Sponsoring Editor; Kathy Sands-Boehmer, Senior Development Editor; and Daniel Saabye, Content Project Manager, for their continued support, vision, and enthusiasm for *The Sundance Reader.*

The Writing Context

How We Write

In the summer of 1939, scientist Leo Szilard was worried. As Americans enjoyed the New York World's Fair, the exiled physicist followed events in Europe with growing anxiety. His experiments proved that a nuclear chain reaction could create an atomic bomb. German scientists had split the atom, and the Nazis had seized rich deposits of uranium in Czechoslovakia. As a Jew who had escaped on the last train out of Nazi Germany, Szilard was horrified at the prospect of Hitler obtaining nuclear weapons. Now living in New York, he tried to warn the American government, but officials in Washington were unwilling to fund atomic research. A refugee without resources or political contacts, Szilard sought help from his old friend Albert Einstein, a Nobel Prize winner with an international reputation. Szilard hoped the government would listen to Einstein. Although the idea of a nuclear chain reaction had never occurred to him, Einstein quickly grasped its implications and suggested writing to President Roosevelt. Einstein dictated a letter and asked Szilard to revise it. Szilard wrote a new version, and then telephoned Einstein, who requested another meeting. Accompanied by fellow physicist Edward Teller, Szilard met Einstein at a summer cottage to discuss the letter. The scientists soon became frustrated. Einstein realized their abstract theories would be difficult to explain to a nonscientist. Equally frustrating was the fact that English was a second language to all three scientists. Einstein dictated a new draft to Edward Teller in German. Leo Szilard wrote two more letters in English and mailed them to Einstein. After reviewing them carefully, Einstein selected the longer version and signed it. Just eight paragraphs long, the letter was presented to President Roosevelt and helped launch the Manhattan Project and the nuclear age.

The story behind Einstein's letter demonstrates important elements about writing. Writing is a complex process and does not occur in a vacuum. It takes place in a context formed by four factors:

1. The writer's purpose and role
2. The knowledge base, attitudes, needs, expectations, and biases of the reader
3. The conventions, history, and culture of a particular discipline, profession, organization, publication, situation, or community
4. The nature of the document

Writing, as the creation of Einstein's letter shows, is often collaborative—the product of a group activity. Writing may reflect the ideas of more than one person. Einstein's letter also illustrates a common problem writers face in a technological society. Experts frequently have to communicate with readers outside their discipline—people with little understanding or appreciation of the writers' subjects.

Context explains why a newspaper article about an airplane crash differs from a Federal Aviation Administration (FAA) report or the airline's condolence letter to the victims' families. Stated simply and printed in narrow columns for easy skimming, a newspaper account briefly describes the accident for general readers. An FAA report examining the causes of a plane crash contains hundreds of pages and includes extensive data, test results, and testimony of witnesses. Directed to aviation experts, the report is stated in technical language largely incomprehensible to the average reader. The airline's letter to victims' families addresses people experiencing confusion, grief, and anger. Carefully worded, it attempts to inform readers without appearing falsely sympathetic or admitting responsibility.

You may have noticed how context affects your own writing. The notes you take in class for personal use look very different from the in-class essay you submit for a grade. The words you choose when adding a line to a birthday card for your seven-year-old cousin differ from those you use on a job application or in a tweet to a friend. Almost unconsciously, you alter the way you write depending on your purpose, reader, and circumstances.

To be an effective writer in college and in your future career, it is important to increase your understanding of the four elements that form a writing context.

QUESTIONS

1. Can you recall writing situations where you had difficulty expressing your ideas because you were unsure how your reader would react? Did you have problems finding the right words or just "getting your thoughts on paper"?

2. Have you noticed that instructors have different attitudes about what constitutes "good writing"? How is writing a paper for an English literature class different from writing a report for a psychology or economics course?

3. Have you observed that magazines, websites, and blogs often have different writing styles? What do articles in *Cosmopolitan*, *Car and Driver*, *TMZ*, or *The Wall Street Journal* reveal about their intended readers? What does the wording of a Facebook page suggest about its creator?

The Writer

All writing has a goal. A shopping list refreshes your memory. A company email informs employees of a policy change. Research papers demonstrate students' knowledge and skills. Résumés encourage employers to call applicants for job interviews. Even essays written for self-expression contain more than random observations. To be effective, an essay must arouse interest, provide readers with information they can understand, and offer proof to support the writer's thesis.

The Writer's Purpose

Students and professionals in all fields face similar writing tasks. The way they present their ideas, the language they use, and even the physical appearance of their finished documents are determined in part by their purpose. Although every writing assignment forms a unique context, most writing tasks can be divided into basic *modes* or types:

Narration *relates a series of events, usually in chronological order.* Biographies, newspapers, and novels use narration to tell stories. Doctors write narration to record patient histories, and police officers use narration to fill out accident reports. Narration can be fictional or factual and can be written in first or third person.

Description *creates a picture or impression of a person, place, object, or condition. Objective description* presents factual details, such a building's height and cost. *Subjective description* shares personal impressions of a subject, such as a building's style or atmosphere.

Definition *explains a term, condition, topic, or issue.* Definitions may be precise and standard, such as a state's definition of second-degree murder or a biology book's definition of a virus. Other definitions, such as those of a good parent or an ideal teacher, may be based on a writer's personal observation, experience, and opinion.

Comparison and contrast *examines the similarities and differences between subjects.* Textbooks compare African and Indian elephants, bacterial and viral infections, or film and digital cameras. Comparison can be used to explain differences or recommend that one subject is superior to others. Comparison can also explain the advantages and disadvantages of a single subject or present a "before and after" description to show how something has changed.

Analysis *evaluates a subject and identifies its essential elements, impact, effectiveness, or qualities.* Writers of a formal analysis may follow a standard method. Stockbrokers, medical examiners, building inspectors, archaeologists, and criminologists use uniform methods of studying subjects and presenting their conclusions. Essayists and newspaper columnists, on the other hand, often analyze issues from a personal perspective, relying on anecdotal evidence and individual observation to review a movie, discuss a football team, or explain the popularity of a political candidate.

Division *names subgroups or divisions in a broad class.* Writers can make a complex topic easier to understand by separating it into smaller units. Insurance can be divided into life, health, home, and auto policies. A zoology text divides animals into fish, birds, mammals, and reptiles. Divisions can be officially established by professional organizations, corporations, or governments. Writers can also invent their own divisions, often creating names for each type or category.

Classification *places subjects into classes or ranks according to a single measurement.* Homicides are classified as first, second, or third degree according to circumstances and premeditation. Burns are classified as first, second, or third degree based on the severity of tissue damage. Like division, classification can be based on professional standards or personal evaluation. A financial adviser might rate mutual funds by risk and performance using commonly accepted criteria. A movie critic, however, could grade films on a one- to five-star scale based solely on his or her tastes.

Process *explains how something occurs or demonstrates how to accomplish a specific task.* A nuclear power plant, the human heart, and inflation can be explained by breaking the process into stages. A recipe, a repair manual, and a first-aid book, may present step-by-step instructions to bake a cake, replace a hard drive, or treat an injury.

Cause and effect *examines the reasons for or results of an occurrence.* A writer can list causes for an increase in crime, the return of an endangered species, or the success or failure of an advertising campaign. Similarly, he or she can list the effects crime has on a community, the response to rescued wildlife, or the impact of television commercials. Physicians refer to medical books that explain the causes of disease and the effects of drugs.

Argument and persuasion *influence reader opinion, attitudes, and actions.* Writers persuade people to accept their ideas using *logical* appeals based on factual evidence, *ethical* appeals based on values or beliefs, and *emotional* appeals that arouse feelings. A fund-raising letter persuades readers to donate money to a charity. An engineer's report argues that a building should be condemned or an engine redesigned. Bloggers and columnists influence readers to accept their opinions on topics ranging from globalization to immigration.

QUESTIONS

1. Consider how you have organized papers in the past. Did any assignments lend themselves to using a particular mode? Could following one of these methods make it easier to present and organize your ideas?
2. Do you use modes such as *comparison, classification,* or *cause and effect* to organize your thoughts and solve problems? Do you *compare* apartments before deciding which one to rent, or *classify* courses you want to take next semester by difficulty or desirability?

A Note about Modes

Modes refer to the writer's basic goal. Often writing cannot be neatly labeled. Few writing tasks call for the use of a single mode. A dictionary entry is pure definition, and a parts catalog offers simple product descriptions. But a movie review *analyzing* a new release will first *describe* the film and possibly *compare* it to the director's previous work. It might use *narration* to explain the plot and *classification* to rank it among other films. Some writing can easily fit two or more categories. The Declaration of Independence, for instance (page 418), is an example of both *cause and effect* and *persuasive writing*.

The Writer's Role

As a student, your role is much like that of a freelance writer. Your essays, reports, and research papers are expected to reflect only your own efforts. In general, each piece of your work is judged independently. A low grade on a first paper should not affect your chances of earning a higher grade later in the semester. What you write in psychology class has no influence on your grades in English. Comments made on controversial issues in college papers are not likely to be raised at future job interviews.

Outside of college, however, your role is more complicated. Often you represent an organization, corporation, or profession. Business letters, emails, and reports are assumed to express the views of the employer, not those of a single employee. Expressing personal views that conflict with corporate practices or administrative policy can jeopardize your position. Frequently, you will have an ongoing relationship with your readers. Comments made in one letter or report affect how readers will respond to your ideas in the future.

Probably the most obvious aspect of a writer's role concerns *perspective,* or the writer's position. Writing in a newspaper's sports section, a columnist may be free to offer personal opinion: "Given poor ticket sales and the age of the stadium, I predict this town will lose its ball club within two years." A front-page article, however, would be weakened by the use of the first person. A reporter would express the same view in more objective terms: "The decline in ticket sales and the age of the stadium indicate the city is in danger of losing its baseball team."

When writing as an employee or a member of a group, remember that the ideas you express will be considered the ideas of the group. Refrain from stating anything that would alienate other members or expose your organization to liability. If you state personal views, make sure you clearly identify them as being your opinions.

In many instances, your profession will dictate a role that determines what is expected in your writing. Police officers and nurses, for example, are required to provide objective and impersonal records of their observations. Fashion consultants, decorators, and advertising executives are esteemed for their creativity and are more likely to offer personal insights and make first-person statements.

QUESTIONS

1. Consider the jobs you may have had and the organizations you have done business with. What writing style would be appropriate for professionals in these fields? Is objective reporting required, or are employees free to offer personal impressions and suggest ideas?

2. What type of writing do you expect to encounter in your career? How does writing in engineering and accounting differ from writing in public relations, sales, or non-profit management? Does your future profession demand adherence to government regulations or industry standards, or does it encourage individual expression?

The Reader

Writing is more than self-expression; it is an act of communication. To be effective, your message must be understood. The content, form, and tone of your writing are shaped by the needs and expectations of your readers. A medical researcher announcing a new treatment for AIDS would word an article for *Immunology* very differently from one for *Newsweek* or *Redbook*.

Each magazine represents a different audience, a different knowledge base, and a different set of concerns. Fellow immunologists would be interested in the author's research methods and demand detailed proof of his or her claims. Readers of *Immunology* would expect to see extensive data and precise descriptions of experiments and testing methods. Most readers of nonmedical publications would require definitions of scientific terms and would expect brief summaries of data that they could not evaluate on their own. Readers of *Newsweek* could be concerned with issues such as cost, government policy, and insurance coverage. Subscribers to a women's magazine such as *Redbook* might wonder if the treatment works equally well for both sexes or if it is safe for pregnant women.

Audiences often differ within a discipline. The medical researcher writing for the *New England Journal of Medicine* would be addressing practicing physicians, not laboratory researchers. Doctors would be interested in the practical aspects of the treatment. What drugs does it interact with? What are the side effects? Which patients should receive the drug and in what doses? An article in *Nursing* would focus on the concerns of nurses, who closely monitor patients for reactions. What effect does the treatment have on a patient's physical and psychological well-being? Are there special considerations for patients with unrelated disorders, such as hypertension and diabetes?

As a writer, you have to determine how much knowledge your readers have about your subject. Should you define technical terms? Does your writing include historical or biographical references requiring explanation? Do you use concepts that general readers might misunderstand or find confusing? In addition to your readers' level of understanding, you must consider your readers' needs and expectations in relation to your goal. What information do your readers want from you? Is your audience reading for general interest, curiosity, or entertainment, or do they demand specific information in order to make decisions or plan future actions?

It is also important to take into account how your readers will respond to your ideas. Is your audience likely to be favorably inclined or hostile to you, your ideas, or the organization you represent? Defense attorneys and prosecutors have different attitudes toward illegally obtained evidence. Environmentalists and real estate developers have conflicting philosophies of land use. Liberals and conservatives have opposing views of the role of government. When presenting ideas to audiences with undefined or differing attitudes, you will have to work hard to overcome their natural resistance, biases, and suspicions.

Individual Readers

The papers you write in college are usually read by a single instructor who evaluates your work in the context of a particular course. Instructors form a special audience because they are expected to read your papers objectively. Beyond the classroom, however, you may have to persuade someone to read your résumé or proposal. Few of these readers will even attempt objectivity. Unlike the papers you write for instructors, your reports and email seek more than a grade. They ask an employer for a job or try to persuade a client to buy a product. In accepting your ideas, your reader may invest substantial resources on your behalf, conceivably placing his or her career in your hands. In writing to these individuals, you will have to carefully analyze their needs, concerns, and objections.

Extended Readerships

Many contexts involve two audiences: the immediate person or persons who receive your document and a second, extended readership. When you write as a student, your work is returned to you. In most jobs, your email, reports, and publications are retained for future reference. The safety inspection report you write in April may be routinely skimmed by your supervisor, filed, and forgotten. But if a serious accident occurs in May, this report will be retrieved and closely examined by state inspectors, insurance investigators, and attorneys. If you have a dispute with a customer or another employee, your correspondence may be reviewed by a supervisor or, in the case of litigation, introduced into court as evidence. Many professionals practice "defensive writing," precisely wording their thoughts and observations, understanding that whatever they write may be examined by adversaries. In court, police officers and physicians are often asked to explain and defend comments they wrote months or years before.

When you write outside of college, consider who else may see your writing. Think carefully before making remarks that might be misunderstood out of context.

The Perceptual World

To learn how readers respond to ideas, it is helpful to understand what communications researchers call the *perceptual world*—the context in which people perceive and react to new information and experiences. As individuals or groups, readers base their reactions on a number of factors that have varying significance and often operate simultaneously.

- **Social roles,** such as being a parent or a civic leader, influence how people evaluate ideas and respond to events. A thirty-year-old with two small children has different concerns from someone of the same age without children. Coaches, clergy members, shop stewards, and elected officials represent the interests of other people and often consider more than their personal opinions in making judgments.

- **Reference groups** include people or institutions readers respect and to whom they defer. A physician who is unsure about prescribing a new drug may base his or her decision on recommendations from the American Medical Association. A student thinking of changing his or her major might seek advice from parents and friends.

- **Past experiences** influence how people respond to new information and events. Readers who have lost money in the stock market will be more skeptical of an investment offer than those who have enjoyed substantial returns.

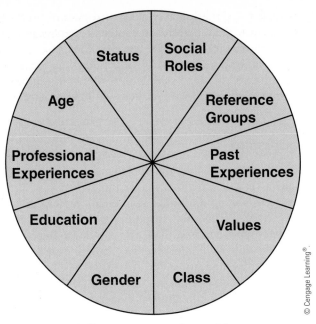

© Cengage Learning®

The perceptual world

A labor union with a harmonious relationship with management will view contract offers differently from a union with a history of stalled talks, bitter negotiations, and strikes.

- **Values** whether religious, political, or cultural, shape readers' responses. People's attitudes about money, sexual conduct, drug use, abortion, gun control, and many other issues affect how they react to new ideas.

- **Class** can shape the way people respond to political and economic issues. Those with wealth may have different attitudes about the role of government or taxes than do working people or the poor.

- **Gender** influences the way people respond to many issues. Polls consistently show a "gender gap" between men and women about topics such as national defense, health care spending, divorce laws, and child support.

- **Education,** both formal and informal, affects people's reading ability, background knowledge, and understanding of terminology. Training in specific disciplines influences how readers evaluate the evidence writers present as support. Scientists and mathematicians, for example, may be more skeptical than the general public of advertising claims using statistics.

- **Professional experience,** along with training and job responsibilities, shapes people's attitudes. An economics professor with tenure may exhibit a greater ability to be objective about a new tax policy than a small business owner struggling to meet a weekly payroll. Police officers and emergency room doctors may be less sympathetic to drunken drivers than people who rarely see the harm these drivers cause.

■ **Age** affects reader attitudes in two ways. People are products of the times they have lived through. Young people growing up during a severe recession have different attitudes about credit cards from their older brothers and sisters, raised in an era of greater prosperity. Older readers have more invested in existing institutions than younger readers and may be more cautious about accepting change.

■ **Status** or amount of investment influences people's response to new ideas or policies. An entry-level employee is less likely to be concerned about a change in pension plans than someone nearing retirement. Homeowners have more invested in their neighborhoods than renters, and may show greater interest in crime or pollution.

Other aspects of the perceptual world include ethnicity and geography. In determining your readers' perceptual world, it is important to avoid basing assumptions on common stereotypes. Not all older people are conservative, and not all African Americans favor affirmative action. Many elements of the perceptual world are unconscious and cannot be easily ascertained. No doubt you have been surprised by the reactions of friends you believed you knew very well.

QUESTIONS

1. How would you describe the perceptual world of your parents, coworkers, or friends? How do their common experiences, values, roles, and education affect their attitudes? How would they respond to a letter urging them to donate money to the homeless, support a handgun ban, or picket an abortion clinic? Which issues would be difficult to present to them? Why?

2. Have you ever tried to understand someone you hoped to influence? In practicing a presentation, preparing for a job interview, or seeking the right words to discuss a difficult issue with a friend or family member, did you consider how that person might react? Is understanding people's perceptual worlds something we engage in every day?

The Discipline

The communication between writer and reader occurs within a particular discipline, setting, culture, profession, or situation. Each academic discipline has a unique history. Some disciplines, such as literature and mathematics, have slowly evolved over thousands of years. Students still read *Oedipus* and study Euclid's principles of geometry. In contrast, the Internet and bioengineering are so new that many of their founders are still actively developing the nature of the discipline.

Every discipline has its own communications style and methods of measuring data, weighing results, and presenting conclusions. In the humanities, research generally examines specific works. Whether the researcher is studying Bach, Shakespeare, or Georgia O'Keeffe, the artist's work is the central focus. Disciplines often contain several schools of thought or types of criticism. In literature, for example, some scholars interpret a novel in light of the author's life and thoughts. Other critics will analyze the book in terms of its historical position or political message. Some critics specialize in feminist or Marxist interpretations of literature. But no matter what their approach, literary critics aim to present an educated opinion based on interpretations of the text.

In the sciences, such as biology, chemistry, and physics, writers base their evaluations on the principles of laboratory research and experiments. Scholars making new assertions in these fields must demonstrate where they obtained their data and prove that other scientists can repeat their experiments and obtain the same results. Although the sciences can seem exact, personal opinion can play a significant role in setting up experiments and interpreting data.

The social sciences of psychology, sociology, criminology, political science, and economics blend some of the features of the humanities and sciences. Although psychologists and criminologists conduct experiments and often use scientific evidence, many of their conclusions are based on data that can be collected and interpreted in a number of ways.

As a college student, you can understand the nature of each discipline by examining your textbooks, particularly introductory chapters, which often provide a history of the field.

Each profession forms its own context of historical experience, technical training, areas of concern, responsibilities, and political and social outlooks. Corporate executives seeking investor capital for expansion and research have different attitudes toward income taxes than social workers assisting low-income families. The medical profession has a strict tradition of relying on standardized treatment and research methods. Physicians tend to be skeptical of anyone claiming to have a cure for a disease unless the claims can be clearly supported by scientific research, rather than personal testimonials alone. Professions measure success differently, praising creativity, sales, or communications skills. Law enforcement officers approach a case of suspected child abuse with the goal of determining if evidence indicates that a crime has been committed. A mental health professional is more interested in the child's well-being, whether the situation meets the legal definition of abuse or not. A therapist would take even a trivial incident seriously if it caused the child distress.

The discipline, profession, or situation creates different methods of using and looking at writing. David Ogilvy, a noted advertising executive, devoted his career to writing ad copy, coming up with snappy, creative, innovative ways of grabbing consumers' attention and boosting sales of his clients' products. For him, writing was a tool to project an image, gain attention, and, above all, sell:

> Always try to inject *news* into your headlines, because the consumer is always on the lookout for new products, or new ways to use an old product, or new improvements in an old product. The two most powerful words you can use in a headline are FREE and NEW. You can seldom use FREE, but you can almost always use NEW—if you try hard enough.

Fran Martin, a nurse who serves as an expert witness in medical malpractice trials, offers a very different kind of writing advice to nurses. Unlike ad writers, whose success depends on creativity, nurses are expected to maintain precise records:

> You communicate with other health care providers through the chart and, obviously, incorrect data doesn't give an accurate picture of your

patient's condition. That could lead to life-threatening errors. It also raises the specter of fraud, which could make your actions appear not just negligent, but also criminal.

The Document

The nature of the document influences the way you write to meet your readers' expectations. Tweets, memos, and emails may include slang and informal abbreviations that would be unacceptable in a business report or a research paper. A literature instructor would expect a book report to briefly summarize a novel and express the student's opinion. The same instructor would demand that a research paper present a more thorough analysis and refer to outside sources that are clearly documented.

In your career, you may be required to write résumés, draft legal briefs, fill out sales reports, or create websites. Each document forms a unique context that determines the appropriate content, style, tone, and wording. To communicate effectively and appear professional, make sure you understand the nature of all the documents you write.

Writing Contexts

The contexts in which writers operate are limitless, but there are general patterns:

1. **Expert to general reader.** Most books and articles are written by experts to people reading for information or enjoyment. An attorney preparing a university brochure on drunk driving might anticipate that most students' understanding of the law has been shaped by movies and television. He or she might have to dispel common misconceptions and explain legal terms and procedures.

2. **Expert to expert within a discipline.** Law reviews, medical journals, and trade magazines are read by professionals within a specific field. Writers for these periodicals assume readers understand basic concepts and terminology. Similarly, advanced textbooks in biology or criminal law rarely provide the introductory material found in first-year books. The email, reports, and documents generated within a corporation or government agency may adopt a unique style and format that almost becomes a code few outsiders can understand. But writers in these situations should always keep an extended readership in mind. An audit, budget review, or investigation could circulate as an email or be available online to a wider audience.

3. **Expert to expert in another discipline.** This is perhaps one of the most challenging contexts writers face. Einstein's letter to Roosevelt is a classic example of this context—a world-famous scientist attempting to explain a discovery to a powerful political leader with minimal knowledge of physics. How does an engineer explain the practical difficulties of construction to a designer interested in style and creativity? How does an economist persuade a governor facing re-election to raise taxes or cut benefits? In communicating with professionals in another discipline, it is important for writers to establish trust, address their readers' concerns, and explain unfamiliar concepts clearly.

Whenever you write, it is important to consider the context—your goals, your reader, the discipline, and the nature of the document. Context will determine how you should state your ideas, which supporting details to include, and which words you should choose.

Accompanying English CourseMate Resources

 Visit English CourseMate at **www.cengagebrain.com** to find many helpful resources and study tools for this chapter.

The Writing Process

2

What Is Writing?

Writing is a process as well as a product. Good writing respects each of the four elements of context. When you plan a writing project, determine your purpose, evaluate your readers, follow the conventions of your discipline, and understand the nature of the document. Many college instructors provide requirements for writing assignments. At work, study examples of patient charts, websites, sales reports, or other documents you are required to write.

Critical Thinking

Good writing is never "about" a topic—it has a purpose and makes a point. An essay about your summer vacation can be simply a list of places you visited and things you did, or it can focus on something deeper and more significant—how visiting Mount Rushmore made you contemplate American values, how traveling together helped you appreciate your family, or how spending a weekend in a cabin without electricity led you to discover how lost you feel without the Internet. A good paper shares more than facts and dates, first impressions, or immediate reactions. Good writing goes beyond the obvious to explore people, ideas, and events.

For example, if you decide to write an essay about your first apartment, your first thought might be to record every detail you can remember, trying to capture on paper what the apartment looked like:

On August 12, 2013, I moved into my first apartment. It was a flat on Newhall Street on the top floor of a 100-year-old house. The living room was massive and had wood paneling and antique brass chandeliers. The dining room had a huge built-in buffet and china cabinets with glass doors I used as bookcases. The kitchen was L-shaped and narrow, but there was a pantry with lots of shelves. The battered refrigerator was old but spacious.

There were two big bedrooms. I planned to use the front bedroom for my study. The back bedroom was a bit smaller, but it had a great advantage. It was away from the street and shielded from the noise of traffic. In addition, there were awnings that blocked the morning sun, so I could sleep late on weekends. The bedrooms did not have any closets. Instead, there were large two-door wardrobes with built-in drawers. There was a spacious balcony off the front bedroom. It was covered by a redwood deck and had new patio furniture and an outdoor grill.

I had little money and had to get furniture from Goodwill and the Salvation Army. The floors were bare, but I covered them with old carpeting from my parents' house.

This approach simply lists physical details, which may be of little interest to anyone else. Before beginning to write, think about the topic and ask yourself key questions:

Why did you choose this topic? Of all the possible subjects, why did you decide to write about your first apartment? What made you think of that, rather than your first car, your last boss, a trip to Mexico, or a recent job interview? Clearly, something about that apartment made it significant. What did it represent to you? What events took place there that changed your life? Are your memories of this place happy or sad? Why? What did you learn there? What is the most important thing you want your readers to know?

What are the most significant details? Instead of listing everything you can remember about your subject, select the most memorable details. Is the date you moved or the number of bedrooms really important? What do you want readers to remember about your topic?

How can you share your thoughts and feelings with readers? Readers may not be interested in a room-by-room description of an apartment, but they may be able to identify with more universal experiences, thoughts, or emotions. How did you feel about moving? What change did it make in your life? Are there larger issues that other people can relate to?

What is the dominant impression you want to give readers? Focusing on a single theme or message will help you select details. If you concentrate on describing your excitement about getting your first apartment, you can ignore irrelevant details such as dates, furnishings, and parking.

Considering these questions can help you create an essay that has greater meaning for both you and your reader.

> In August I moved into my first apartment, a great flat on Newhall Street. Although I could only afford to furnish it with battered items from Goodwill and the Salvation Army, I was excited. I was finally going to be on my own, free of my parents, my cramped room, my sisters' fighting, my brother's stereo. I spent two weeks cleaning, painting, and transforming the old flat into my home. I hung up posters of my favorite bands, stocked the kitchen with my favorite foods, and set the radio to my favorite stations. I was finally on my own, free at last.
>
> But coming home from class, I was struck by the silence. Instead of hearing the drone of my brother's stereo, my sisters' laughing and fighting, I heard the hum of the refrigerator and the nervous tick-tick of an electric clock. I always hated that my mother watched soap operas, but now I found myself turning the television on in the afternoon to hear the hated but familiar voices while I labored over algebra or ironed clothes.
>
> On weekends I went home—but not to raid the kitchen or borrow money. I had been an adult. I had been responsible. I had saved money over the summer and budgeted carefully. I could easily afford my new apartment. I had hungered for a place of my own all through high school. But I never imagined how lonely it would feel to go home to an empty house.

By thinking in more detail about a subject, you can probe its depth, developing writing that does more than simply report obvious facts and record simple observations.

Critical thinking involves moving beyond first impressions by carefully examining subjects, people, and ideas. Too often we rush to judgment, making instant assumptions based on what we think we know rather than what we can prove. We confuse opinions with facts, accept statistics without question, and let stereotypes distort our evaluations. We allow what we "feel" to short-circuit how we think.

> Pete Wilson was a great quarterback—he'll make a great coach.
> Nancy's driving a BMW—her new travel agency must be a success.
> Alabama improved reading scores 12 percent using this program—our schools should use it, too.
> Jersey Lube ruined my car—two days after I went there for an oil change my transmission went out.

All these statements make a kind of sense at first glance. But further analysis will lead you to question their validity:

Does a skilled quarterback necessarily know how to coach—how to inspire, manage, and teach other players, especially those on defense?

Does Nancy even own the BMW she was seen driving? Did she get it as a gift, pay for it with existing savings, borrow it from a friend, or lease it at a low rate? Does the car really prove anything about the success or failure of her travel agency?

Alabama may have improved reading scores with a particular program, but does that really prove the program will work in Nevada or Minnesota? Could children in other states have low reading scores caused by other reasons than those in Alabama?

Did Jersey Lube ruin your transmission? The mechanics may have only changed the oil and never touched the transmission, which was due to fail in two days. Had you driven through a car wash the day before, could you just as easily have blamed it?

Errors like these are easy to make. Unless you develop critical thinking skills, you can be impressed by evidence that at first glance seems reliable and convincing.

Avoiding Errors in Critical Thinking

Lapses in critical thinking are called *logical fallacies*. In reading the works of others and developing your own ideas, avoid these common mistakes:

- **Hasty generalizations.** If your dorm is robbed, a friend's car stolen from a student parking lot, and a classmate's purse snatched on her way to class, you might assume that the campus is experiencing a crime wave. The evidence is compelling because it is immediate and personal. But it does not prove there is an increase in campus crime. In fact, crime could be dropping, and you and your friends may simply belong to the declining pool of victims. Only a review of police reports would prove if crime is increasing. *Resist jumping to conclusions.*

- **Absolute statements.** Although it is important to convince readers by making strong assertions, avoid absolute claims that can be dismissed with a single exception. If you write, "All professional athletes are irresponsible," readers only need to think of a single exception to dismiss your argument. A qualified remark, however, is harder to disprove. The claim that "Many professional athletes are irresponsible" acknowledges that exceptions exist.

- ***Non sequitur* (it does not follow).** Avoid making assertions based on irrelevant evidence: "Jill Klein won an Oscar for best actress last year—she'll be great on Broadway." Although an actress might succeed on film, she may lack the ability to perform on stage before a live audience.

- **Begging the question.** Do not assume what has to be proved: "These needless math classes should be dropped because no one uses algebra and geometry after they graduate." This statement makes an assertion, but it fails to prove that the courses are needless or that "no one" uses mathematics outside of academic settings.

- **False dilemma.** Do not assume there are only two solutions to resolve a problem: "Either employees must take a 20 percent wage cut, or the company will go bankrupt." This statement ignores other possible solutions such as raising prices, lowering production costs, selling unused assets, or increasing sales. If a wage cut is needed, does it have to be 20 percent? Could it be 15 percent or 10 percent? Before accepting what appears to be the better of two bad choices, determine if other options exist.

■ **False analogy.** Comparisons make weak arguments: "Marijuana should be legalized since Prohibition did not work." Marijuana and alcohol are different substances. Humans have consumed alcohol legally for thousands of years. Marijuana, however, remains illegal throughout much of the world. The fact that Prohibition failed could be used to justify legalizing anything that is banned, including automatic weapons, child pornography, or crack cocaine.

■ **Red herring.** Resist the temptation to dodge the real issue by making emotionally charged or controversial statements: "How can you justify spending money on a new football stadium when homeless people are sleeping in the streets and terrorists are threatening to destroy us?" Homelessness and terrorism are genuine concerns but have little to do with the merits of a proposed stadium. The same argument could be used to attack building a park, a zoo, or an art gallery.

■ **Borrowed authority.** Avoid assuming that an expert in one field can be accepted as an authority in another: "Senator Goode claims Italy will win the World Cup." A respected senator may have no more insight into soccer than a cab driver or a hairdresser. Celebrity endorsements are common examples of borrowed authority.

■ *Ad hominem* **(attacking the person).** Attack ideas, not the people who advocate them: "How can you accept a budget proposed by an alderman accused of domestic violence?" The merits of the budget have to be examined, not the person who proposed it.

■ **Assuming past events will predict the future.** The 2008 recession was caused, in part, because mortgage brokers believed that real estate prices would continue to rise 6 percent annually. When home values fell as much as 50 percent, millions of homeowners faced foreclosure and investors lost billions of dollars. *Past trends cannot be assumed to continue into the future.*

■ **Ignoring alternative interpretations.** Even objective facts can be misleading. If research shows that reports of child abuse have jumped 250 percent in the last ten years, does that mean that child abuse is on the rise? Could those numbers instead reflect stricter reporting methods or an expanded definition of abuse, so that previously unrecorded incidents are now counted?

■ **Filtering data.** If you begin with a preconceived thesis, you may consciously or unconsciously select evidence that supports your view and ignore evidence that contradicts it. Good analysis is objective; it does not simply collect facts to support a previously held conviction. A list of high-school dropouts who became celebrities does not disprove the value of a diploma.

■ **Assuming that parts represent the whole.** Just because one or more patients with a given disease respond favorably to a new drug does not mean that it will cure all people suffering from the same disease.

■ **Assuming the whole represents each part.** If 50 percent of students on campus receive financial aid, it does not mean you can assume that half the English majors receive aid. The student population in any given department may be less or more than the college average.

■ **Mistaking a time relationship for a cause** *(post hoc, ergo propter hoc).* Can the president take credit for a drop in unemployment six months after signing a jobs bill? Because events occur in time, it can be easy to assume an action that precedes another is a cause. A drop in unemployment, however, could be caused by a decline in interest rates, fewer people looking for work, or an upsurge in exports, and may have nothing to do with the president's bill. *Do not assume events were caused by preceding events.*

■ **Mistaking an effect for a cause.** Early physicians saw fever as a cause of disease rather than as an effect or symptom. If you observe that children with poor reading skills watch a lot of television, you might easily assume that television interferes with their reading. In fact, excessive viewing could be a symptom. Because they have trouble reading, they watch television.

Strategies FOR IMPROVING CRITICAL THINKING

You can improve your college papers by engaging in critical thinking. Before you start to write, ask yourself these questions:

1. How much do you really know about this subject? Do you fully understand the history, depth, and character of the topic? Are you basing your assumptions on objective facts or only on what you have read on blogs or heard on talk radio? Should you research your topic more fully before making judgments?

2. Have you looked at your topic closely? First impressions can be striking but misleading. Examine your subject closely, ask questions, and probe beneath the surface. Look for patterns; measure similarities and differences.

3. Have you rushed to judgment? Collect evidence but avoid drawing conclusions until you have analyzed your findings and observations.

4. Do you separate facts from opinions? Don't confuse facts, evidence, and data with opinions, claims, and assertions. Opinions are judgments or inferences, not facts. Facts are reliable pieces of information that can be verified by studying other sources:

   > FACT: This semester a laptop, petty cash, and a cell phone were taken from the tutoring lab while Sue Harper was on duty.
   >
   > OPINION: Sue Harper is a thief.

   The factual statement can be proven. Missing items can be documented. The assumption that Sue Harper is responsible remains unproven.

5. Are you aware of your assumptions? Assumptions are ideas we accept or believe to be true. It is nearly impossible to separate ourselves from what we have been taught, but you can sharpen your critical thinking skills if you acknowledge your assumptions. Avoid relying too heavily on a single theory—that IQ tests measure intelligence, that poverty causes crime, that video games are a bad influence on children.

6. **Have you collected enough evidence?** A few statistics and quotations taken out of context may seem convincing, but they may not be adequate proof. Make sure you collect enough evidence from a variety of sources before making judgments.

7. **Do you evaluate evidence carefully?** Do you apply consistent standards to evaluate the data you collect? Do you question the source of statistics or the validity of an eyewitness? The fact that you can find dozens of books about alien abductions does not prove they occur.

WRITING ACTIVITY

1. Review this list of topics and select one that you have strong opinions about.

the president	the war on terrorism	gun control
reality TV shows	gay marriage	NFL players
high school	your boss	homelessness
health insurance	landlords	online dating
cable news	lotteries	hybrid cars
global warming	welfare reform	job interviews

2. After selecting a topic, write a statement summarizing your attitudes about it. Write a full paragraph or list ideas or even words you associate with this subject.

3. Examine your comments carefully and consider these questions:

   What do I really know about this topic?

   Why do I feel this way?

   Would other people call my views unfair or biased?

   Are my views based on facts or assumptions?

   Can I provide sufficient evidence to support my opinion?

   Do I detect any logical fallacies in my response—hasty generalizations, red herrings, or mistaking a time relationship for a cause?

   Do I need to conduct additional research before I can make a valid judgment?

   Are there alternative opinions? Do they have any merit?

   Could I organize a logical and convincing argument to persuade others to accept my point of view?

Examining and challenging your values, ideas, and opinions improves your ability to express yourself to others and anticipate their questions and objections.

Prewriting

Writing is not only a means to produce a document but is also a way to explore ideas. Prewriting puts critical thinking into action to discover a topic, develop a thesis, and organize details. You can use a number of techniques to get started.

Freewriting records memories, thoughts, facts, and impressions without interruption and without any concern for spelling, grammar, or punctuation. Freewriting should not be confused with writing a rough draft. It may have no direction, skip from topic to topic, and contradict itself. The goal of freewriting is not writing a "paper" but exploring ideas, like an artist who makes sketches before starting a painting.

Overhearing a claim that the government was behind the influx of drugs in the inner city, a student sat at her computer and rapidly recorded a stream of thoughts on the topic of conspiracy theories:

> The CIA is behind the drug epidemic. The US government pays South Koreans to set up grocery stores in the ghetto. Every president since Nixon has lied about MIA's held captive in Southeast Asia. The Air Force lies about UFO sitings. The number of conspiracy theories is limitless. The lumber industry is against legalizing marijuana because hemp makes better paper than wood pulp. Roosevelt knew the Japanese were going to bomb Pearl Harbor but let it happen. The government either planned or knew about 9/11 but let it happen so that Bush could attack Iraq and grab their oil. Obama was born in Kenya. Conspiracies are endless. They are popular. They light up the blogosphere, create a lot of TV shows, and employ an army of theorists who move from talk show to talk show touting their books and their latest proof that the CIA or ilegal immigrants or the Fortune 500 is responsible for some horrible deed or social threat. No doubt some mad scientist in a govenment laboratory created AIDS and loosed it on the world. No doubt someone has cured cancer and has been kidnapped or killed so that millions of doctors and thousands of drug companies won't go out of business. Why? Why do people love these theories?
>
> Some people do need to believe that no lone asassin could have killed JFK. They cling to this belief, no matter what the evidence. Why? Maybe we need to believe in conspiracy theories. It makes the evil in the world less frightening. We are not victims of random choas, but of evil people who can theoretically be located and exposed. To abandon conspiracy theories means accepting chaos. Also it allows us to escape blame. If we put the blame for all our problems on mysterious forces beyond our control, then we can dodge personal responsiblity.

Although this freewriting is loose, repetitive, and misspelled, it moves from listing conspiracy theories to speculating about why people need to believe in them. The student now has something to focus on and a possible title: "Why We Need Conspiracy Theories."

Brainstorming is a prewriting process that can generate ideas and identify possible topics for further writing. As in freewriting, list ideas as quickly as possible. Do not worry if your ideas are repetitive or irrelevant. Again, your purpose is not to outline a paper but rather to develop ideas.

Brainstorming can be used to discover a topic for an essay or to help a professional identify details needed in a business report. A composition student assigned a comparison/contrast essay might list as many ideas as possible to find a topic:

high school teachers/college professors
male/female attitudes about first dates
American/Japanese ideas about privacy
Puerto Ricans vs. Mexican Americans
Mexican-born vs. 1st generation Mex-Americans
English only vs. bilingual
Mexican-born English/1st generation Mex-American English

Through brainstorming or listing, the student runs through a number of ideas before focusing on a topic suited for a short paper: comparing the attitudes of Mexican-born Americans and their children toward English.

Even when the topic is defined, brainstorming can help identify important details. The supervisor of a warehouse writing a report following a forklift accident could use brainstorming to make sure he or she produces a complete account that managers can use to examine the firm's legal liability, safety policies, employee training, and equipment use:

time/date/location of accident
injured personnel—Alex Bolton, Sara Lopez (medical status)
911 call—get time from dispatcher
Bolton's forklift—last inspection (service log)
forklift load—stability (check manual)
use of helmets
surveillance cameras (tapes)
accident witnesses

WRITING ACTIVITY

1. *Freewriting:* Select one of the following topics, and write for at least ten minutes. Do not worry about making sense or maintaining logical connections between ideas. Remember, this is not the rough draft of a paper but instead is an attempt to develop ideas and discover topics.

downloading music	blind dates	camera phones and privacy
prisons	binge drinking	capital punishment
recycling	road rage	student loans
family values	car repair	media images of women

2. *Brainstorming:* Select one of the columns of topics and build on it, adding your own ideas. Jot down your thoughts as quickly as possible. Do not worry if some of your ideas are off the topic.

men/women	success/money	vacation plans
dating	careers	plane/car
expectations	salary/income	hotel/meals
conflicts	risk/reward	budget/costs

Clustering is a visual method of developing ideas. Instead of writing complete sentences or listing ideas, the writer groups topics in circles and boxes. Visual markers such as arrows, question marks, and ink color can be used to organize and link ideas. Thinking about his sister's decision to adopt a baby from China, a student clustered a series of observations and questions:

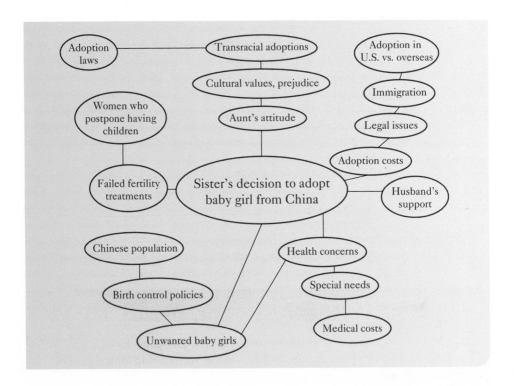

In this case, clustering charts the positive and negative elements of transracial adoption.

Asking questions is a method used by reporters and investigators to collect critical information. For generations, newspaper reporters have been trained to ask the "five W's": *Who? What? When? Where? Why?* Asking questions can identify topics and narrow your focus. A student considering writing a paper about Arthur Miller's play *Death of a Salesman* might list questions to discover a topic:

Death of a Salesman

What are Willy's values?

Is Willy a victim of society or of his own delusions?

What role does Uncle Ben play?

Is Willy's suicide caused by despair or a last attempt at success?

What impact does Willy's infidelity have?

Biff steals a suit and a fountain pen. What do these objects represent?

Linda knows Willy has lost his salary but does not confront him about it. Why?

Why does Miller compare Willy and Biff to Charlie and Bernard?

Is the play an attack on the American dream?

Why does Willy refuse to take a job from Charlie?

This play is world famous but the hero is abusive, selfish, and short-tempered. Why is the play so popular?

What is the purpose of the requiem at the end? How would the play be different without it?

WRITING ACTIVITY

1. *Clustering:* Select one of the following topics. Use a large piece of paper to arrange your ideas. Group related items within circles or squares. Use arrows to connect ideas. You may use different colors, switch from pen to pencil, or mark major ideas with a highlighter. Whatever method you use, do not allow your artwork to overshadow your goal of developing ideas for a paper.

year-round school	identity theft	diets
child support	the American dream	women in combat
airport security	working out	teenage obesity
aging	Internet scams	outsourcing jobs

2. *Asking questions:* Select one of the following topics, and write a list of questions. Try to ask as many questions as you can to explore as many avenues as possible.

recent hit movie	gangs	credit cards
unions	suburbs	role models
teen pregnancy	rap music	bloggers' impact
nightclubs	spring break	on politics

Moving from Topic to Thesis

Good writing has a purpose. A paper is never "about" something; it must make a clear statement. Whether the topic is global warming, a first job, terrorism, or a high school football game, your writing should state a point or express an opinion. The **thesis** is the paper's main or controlling idea. A **thesis statement** presents the writer's position in a sentence or two and serves as the document's mission statement. **A thesis is more than a limited or narrowed topic—it expresses a point of view. It is a declaration stating your purpose.**

Topic	Narrowed Topic	Thesis Statement
gun control	handgun ban	*The city's proposed handgun ban will not prevent gang violence.*
online crime	consumer fraud	*Consumers will resist shopping on the Internet unless credit card security is assured.*
campus housing	rehabbing dorms	*Because of increased demand for on-campus housing, the fifty-year-old men's dorm should be rehabbed.*
terrorism	cyberterrorism	*Homeland Security must take greater steps to protect sensitive computer networks from cyberattacks.*

Elements of a Thesis Statement

Effective thesis statements share common characteristics:

They are generally stated in a single sentence. This statement forms the core of the paper and clearly and concisely states the writer's point of view.

They express an opinion or point of view, not a topic or a fact. A thesis statement does more than announce what the paper is about; it makes a declaration. The statement *This paper is about teenage obesity* announces a topic. The sentence *One out of four teenagers is obese* presents a fact. A thesis expresses a point: *We must curb teenage obesity because it is responsible for the epidemic of juvenile diabetes, early heart disease, and misuse of diet pills.*

They limit the topic. A thesis statement can focus the paper by limiting the scope of the writer's concentration. *Television is bad for children* states an opinion but fails to target the paper and can lead a writer to list only superficial observations. A defined thesis statement such as *Television action heroes teach children that violence is an acceptable method of resolving conflicts* guides the writer to develop a more engaging and original paper.

They indicate the kind of support that follows. Opinions require proof. The thesis *Because of declining enrollments, the costly film course should be canceled* indicates an argument based on factual support, leading readers to expect enrollment and budget figures.

They organize supporting material. The thesis statement *Exercise is essential to control weight, prevent disease, and reduce stress* suggests the body of the paper will be presented in three parts.

Effective thesis statements are precisely worded. Because they express a writer's main idea in a single sentence, thesis statements must be accurately worded. General words like *good, bad, serious,* and *important* are vague and weak. The thesis statement *The college should improve dorm security to prevent crime* is not as effective as *The college should install deadbolt locks to deter break-ins,* which is both more accurate and easier to support.

Supporting the Thesis

Once you determine your thesis, select supporting details. Because each type of evidence has limitations, writers often present a blend:

Personal observations are descriptive details and sensory impressions about a person, place, object, or condition. Writers can support a thesis by supplying readers with specific details. The thesis "Westwood High School must be renovated" can be supported with observations about leaking roofs, faulty wiring, unsafe elevators, and peeling paint.

Personal experiences can provide convincing support. As a college student, you have direct insight into higher education. An Iraq War veteran has insights about combat and greater credibility than a commentator relying on media reports. Because personal observations and experiences are individual, writers often add objective evidence such as facts or statistics to give their writing greater authority.

Examples are specific events, persons, or situations that represent a general trend, condition, or concept. A writer supporting the right to die might relate the story of a single terminal patient. The story of one small business could illustrate an economic trend. Because examples are isolated, they are often supplemented with facts and statistics to provide additional support.

Testimony consists of observations and statements by witnesses, participants, and experts. A paper about global warming might include quotations by environmentalists citing scientific studies and farmers reporting personal observations.

Facts are objective details that can be gathered or observed. The need for greater airport security can be demonstrated by counting security officers, noting defective surveillance cameras, and reviewing inspection reports.

Statistics are factual data expressed in numbers. A paper about identity theft might include statistics about the number of victims, the amount of money stolen, or the time it takes a person to restore his or her credit rating. Statistics can be easily manipulated or misinterpreted and should be used carefully.

Whatever evidence you use to support your thesis, make sure it is *relevant, accurate,* and *reliable.* Avoid taking facts, statistics, or quotations out of context. Make sure your evidence truly supports your thesis. Readers will only be persuaded by your support if you present it clearly and indicate where you obtained facts, quotations, and statistics.

Developing Outlines

Once you have assembled supporting details, create an outline to organize your ideas. Consider an outline a rough sketch or road map to guide your writing. A student familiar with life insurance might need only an informal outline to list or his or her ideas:

Whole Life and Term Insurance

Whole life
— explain premiums
— savings and loan options

Term
— no savings
— lower rates

Conclusion — last point

A formal outline, however, includes more detail, so prewriting can be refined into a clear framework for the first draft. Outlines should address the goals of the three main parts of any essay:

The introduction grabs attention, states the writer's goal, and indicates the kind of support to follow. Avoid introductions that simply announce a topic: *This paper is about life insurance* or *Life insurance is very important.* Writers use several techniques to create effective introductions.

Open with a thesis statement:
Life insurance should form the core of any investment portfolio.

Begin with a fact or statistic:
Two-thirds of 2,500 business owners surveyed only had enough life insurance to support their families for six months.

Use a quotation:
Addressing consumers last month, Andrea Hernandez announced, "With the collapse of real estate values, couples can no longer consider the equity in their homes as a source of income in the event of a spouse's death."

Open with a brief narrative:
Frank Monroe planned to leave his children a thriving software company. But without life insurance to cover the expenses of Frank's final illness and make up for lost income, his son was forced to sell the family business at a loss.

The body presents supporting details in a logical manner. Depending on the kind of paper you are writing, you can use a variety of methods to organize details:

Chronological order arranges details by time. Personal narratives, biographies, and historical events are usually presented as a chain of events.

Spatial order breaks details into major parts or types. An essay about alternative energy might be organized into three sections: wind, solar, and biofuels. A paper about life insurance could discuss insurance options for single adults, couples with small children, and people nearing retirement.

Degree of importance opens with the most important details and concludes with the least important, or begins with a minor detail and concludes with the most important. Your most significant ideas should open or close an essay, because that is where readers' attention is highest. Do not place important ideas in the middle of a document where readers may overlook them.

The conclusion brings the paper to a logical end and makes a final impression on the reader. Avoid simply repeating the introduction: *In conclusion, insurance should form the core of any investment portfolio.* There are several methods of creating an effective conclusion.

Present a call to action:
When you do your taxes this year, take time to review your life insurance needs.

End with a question to provoke thought:
How long could your family pay its bills in the event of your death?

Conclude with a quotation:
Speaking at a convention last month, Janet Liebling told investment counselors, "All the media coverage of real estate and the stock market has led too many of us to overlook what should be the bedrock of our clients' investments—life insurance."

End with a final fact, statistic, claim, or prediction:
With an unpredictable stock market and falling housing prices, more investors are buying life insurance to provide security for their families.

In the next example, a student develops a formal outline using spatial order to compare two forms of life insurance:

Whole Life and Term Insurance
I. Introduction: Whole life and term insurance
II. Whole life insurance
  A. General description
    1. History
    2. Purpose
      a. Protection against premature death
      b. Premium payments include savings
  B. Investment feature
    1. Cash value accrual
    2. Loans against cash value
III. Term insurance
  A. General description
    1. History
    2. Purpose
      a. Protection against premature death
      a. Premium payments lower than whole life insurance
  B. Investment feature
    1. No cash accrual
    2. No loans against cash value
  C. Cost advantage
    1. Lower premiums
    2. Affordability of greater coverage

IV. Conclusion
    A. Insurance needs of consumer
        1. Income
        2. Family situation
        3. Investment goals and savings
        4. Obligations
    B. Investment counselors' advice about insurance coverage

How to Write an Essay

Many writers use a five-stage process to improve their writing and save time. As a beginning writer, you can benefit from following these guidelines. With experience, you can personalize your method of writing.

1. **Plan—establish context.** Once you have established your thesis, determine how you will develop your paper based on your readers' needs, the discipline, and the nature of the document. Develop an outline listing your main ideas. Make sure the introduction and conclusion are effective and that the body of the paper is clearly organized.

2. **Write—get your ideas on paper.** After reviewing your plans, write as much as possible without stopping. Writing the first draft can be considered controlled freewriting. As you write, new ideas may occur to you. Record *all* your thoughts. Do not break your train of thought to check spelling or look up a fact. Instead, underline misspelled words and leave space for missing details. Place question marks next to items you want to double-check. If writing on a computer, use bold or colored fonts to highlight areas needing further attention.

3. **Cool—put your writing aside.** It is difficult to evaluate your work immediately after writing because much of what you wish to say is still fresh in your mind. Set your work aside. Work on other assignments, read, watch television, or take a walk to clear your mind. Afterward, you can return to your writing with greater objectivity.

4. **Revise—review your writing in context.** Before searching your paper for misspelled words or grammatical errors, examine it holistically. Review your goal and plan. Examine any instructions you have received. Then read your paper. Does it clearly express your goal and support your thesis? Is it properly directed to your audience? Does it violate any principles in the discipline? Revision can mean rewriting the entire paper or merely reworking details.

5. **Edit—correct mechanical errors and polish style.** When you have a completed paper, examine your writing for grammatical errors and missing and misspelled words. In addition, review your diction. Eliminate wordy phrases and reduce repetition. Make sure ideas flow evenly and smoothly. *Reading a paper aloud can help identify errors and awkward sentences.*

These five stages are not neatly isolated. Writing, according to current research, is *recursive*—the steps overlap and occur simultaneously. As you write, you will find yourself brainstorming, editing, correcting spelling, and freewriting.

Each writing assignment is unique. For example, a narrative requires attention to chronology, while a division paper demands clear organization, and persuasion depends on the skillful use of logic. You may find some papers more challenging than others. Because it is often difficult to determine how hard a particular assignment may be, it is advisable to start writing as soon as possible. Just ten minutes of prewriting will quickly reveal how much time and effort you need to devote to an assignment.

Strategies FOR CREATING A COMPOSING STYLE

1. **Review past writing.** Consider how you have written in the past. Which of your papers received the highest and lowest grades in high school? Why? What can you recall about writing them? What mistakes did you make? What comments have teachers made about your work? Have you had trouble organizing or wording emails or reports you wrote at work?

2. **Experiment with methods of composing.** Write at different times and places, using pen and paper or a computer. See what conditions improve your writing.

3. **Study returned papers for clues.** Read your instructors' comments carefully. If your papers lack a clear thesis, devote more attention to prewriting and planning. If instructors fill your papers with red ink—circling misspelled words and underlining fragments—spend more time editing.

Writing the Whole Composition

The stages of the writing process are illustrated by a student developing a paper for a freshman composition class.

Prewriting

The student begins by exploring topics through prewriting. Note that her work blends several techniques, including brainstorming, freewriting, and clustering.

Topics: criminal justice (issues)
capital punishment
pro/con gun control
courtroom TV
What is the impact of televised trials?
Do TV trials educate the public?
How does media attention affect juries?
Victims and crime—are they forgotten?
Who speaks for victims?
Do prosecutors properly speak for victims?

Victim impact statements are increasingly a feature of modern trials as people are allowed to state their feelings about the crime and the criminal after he/she is convicted. Judges can consider the impact of the crime on the victim in sentencing.

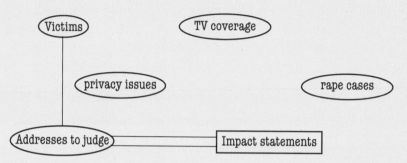

Sometimes victims ask for harsh punishment and sometimes they even ask for leniency and give the criminal, especially a young person, a second chance...
Who is most impressive?
What about victims who can't speak well or don't know English?
What about families of homicide victims?
Victims without mourners? Less important?

Topic: Victim impact statements
Thesis: Although victim impact statements are supposed to empower the victims of crime, they may serve only to further marginalize the most helpless among us.

Planning

Once the student selects a topic and develops a thesis, she creates a plan to organize her main ideas:

Victim Impact Statements
INTRO: Background of impact statements
         Definition
PRO: — empowers victims who feel forgotten
         — helps heal victims by addressing criminals
         — helps people regain control over their lives and move on
         — makes the human cost of a crime part of the sentencing decision
CON: Question?
         Whose impact is more effective?
         Middle-class professional vs. welfare mom
END: Question, helpful or hurtful to victims?

First Draft with Revision Notes

Using the plan as a guide, the student writes a first draft to get her ideas on paper, then notes sentences and paragraphs needing improvement or corrections:

In America today more and more victims of crime are being allowed to address the court in terms of making what is called a victim impact <u>statment</u>. These statements are very important in making changes in the way people, the public, the media, and judges look at crime and criminals. These statements can be written or delivered orally.

Awkward, revise

Advocates of victim impact statements point to advantages. First, these statements give people voices. For years people have felt helpless. Prosecutors represent the state, not the individual. They have been upset when <u>prosacuters</u> have arranged <u>plee</u> bargains without their OK. Some victims are still recovering from their injuries when they learn the guy who hurt them is walking off with probation.

Sp

Wordy

Therapists who work with victims also have been known to say that being able to <u>adress</u> the court helps with the healing process. Victims of violent crime can feel powerless and vulnerable. So instead of suffering in silence, they are given the chance to talk to the criminal, to clear their chests, and get on with the rest of their lives. These statements allow judges to consider what sentences are appropriate. But giving victims a chance to speak raises some issues. What about the victims who cannot present themselves?

Sp

Add idea?

[Victim impact statements may help victims who are smart to begin with but not help those who are not.]

Expand ideas?

Revision Notes
— Need stronger opening
— Check spelling
— Add examples

Revised Draft with Instructor's Annotations

The student's instructor reads the essay, noting mechanical errors, missing details, and unclear sentences, and suggests revisions to improve the essay:

Across America today more and more victims of crime are being allowed to address the court in terms of making what is called a victim impact statement. These statements are very important and are changing the way the public, the media, and judges look at criminals. These statements can be written or delivered orally.

Be specific. What is the purpose of these statements? Provide clear definition.

This written or oral presentation to the court allows victims to express their feelings to the judge after someone has been convicted of a crime.

Add examples

Advocates of victim impact statements point to key advantages. <u>First</u>, these statements give victims a voice. For years, victims have felt helpless. Prosecutors represent the state, not the crime victim.

Use with only more than one point

Victims have been dismayed when <u>prosacuters</u> have arranged plea bargains without their knowledge. Some victims are still recovering from their injuries when they learn the person who hurt them pled to a lesser charge and received probation. *Sp*

Therapists who work with victims also say that being able to address the court helps with the healing process. Victims of violent crime can feel powerless and vulnerable. Instead of suffering in silence, they are given the chance to address the criminal, to <u>clear their chests</u>, and get on with the rest of their lives. *Informal, delete*

Impact statements allow judges to consider what sentences are appropriate. In one case, a judge who planned to fine a teenager for shoplifting accepted the storeowner's suggestion of <u>waving</u> the fine if the defendant completed his GED. *Sp*

But giving victims a chance to speak raises some issues. What about the victim who is not articulate, who doesn't even speak English? *Expand this final point.*

Comments

A good topic, but the essay needs further development:

—Add a stronger attention getter at the opening to dramatize impact statements.

— Define what an impact statement is. You state they are important but do not fully explain what they are.

— You mention the advantages and disadvantages of impact statements but do not provide enough examples.

— The ending could raise more than one question. Reading your paper aloud can help you detect weak, awkward, and repetitive phrases.

Final Draft

After reviewing the instructor's comments and her own notes, the student writes a final draft, improving the introduction, adding details, refining points, and correcting mechanical errors:

The courtroom scene was riveting. One by one, the survivors of a deadly commuter-train shooting took the stand and addressed the man who had maimed them. Their voices quivering with emotion, they told the court how the gunman's actions changed their lives forever. Spouses and parents of the dead spoke of loss. There were tears, moments of intense anger, and quiet despair. Victim impact statements have become a common feature of criminal proceedings. Spoken in court or submitted in writing, these statements provide an opportunity for victims to be heard before judges sentence those who harmed them.

Advocates of victim impact statements believe these declarations give victims a voice, an opportunity to be heard. Traditionally, victims have appeared in court only as witnesses subject to cross-examination. Prosecutors, victims soon learn, represent the state and not individuals. Still hospitalized after a brutal beating, a New Jersey restaurant owner learned from reading a newspaper that his assailants had plea-bargained to a lesser charge and received probation. Joining with other victims, he became an advocate for victims' rights, including impact statements.

Therapists who counsel victims of crime believe that addressing the court and taking an active role in the legal process instead of remaining passive witnesses helps people recover from a sense of helplessness and regain a measure of self-respect.

Impact statements allow judges to consider appropriate sentences. In a Florida case, a judge who intended to fine a teenager for shoplifting agreed with the storeowner's suggestion that the fine be waived if the defendant completed his GED.

But giving victims a chance to speak has led to ugly courtroom scenes that seem inappropriate in a democracy. In Milwaukee a sister of a young man murdered by Jeffrey Dahmer wailed and shrieked in contortions of pure rage. The relative of another murder victim shouted that he would execute the killer himself. Bailiffs had to restrain him as he begged the judge, "Just gimme five minutes with him!" Defense attorneys argue these harangues are unnecessary. What need is there to heap abuse upon a person about to lose his or her life or liberty? Can anger and harassment be considered healing?

But even restrained, well-reasoned impact statements raise troubling questions. What about the victim who is too impaired, too frightened, or too wounded to speak? Is his or her absence judged as indifference? What about those whose English is limited? What of those without friends or family? Should the drunk driver who kills a young professional missed by friends, family, and colleagues receive a tougher sentence than the drunk driver who kills a homeless man who dies unmourned, unmissed, and uncounted? Do we really want our courts and society to suggest that some lives are more significant than others?

Victim impact statements may help empower victims, especially the educated, the personally impressive, and the socially prominent. But these statements, unintentionally, may also further marginalize the most helpless among us, allowing forgotten victims to remain voiceless.

QUESTIONS

1. What have you found most challenging or difficult about writing? Discovering ideas? Getting started? Revising?

2. What comments have instructors made about your writing? Does a pattern exist? Have they suggested areas for improvement?

3. What are your writing habits? What could improve your work and help you meet deadlines? What ideas in this chapter could help you write more effectively?

Writing on a Computer

If you have never written on a computer, take advantage of whatever opportunities your campus offers to learn word processing. Many colleges offer one-credit courses or free tutorials. If no course is available, ask a friend or classmate to show you how he or she uses a computer to write.

Strategies FOR WRITING ON A COMPUTER

1. **Appreciate the advantages and limitations of using a computer.** Computers speed up the writing process and correct spelling, but they will not make you a better writer. They cannot refine a thesis, improve your logic, or enhance critical thinking. *Don't confuse the neatness of the finished product with good writing.*

2. **Learn the features of your program.** If you are unfamiliar with writing on a computer, make sure you learn how to move blocks of text, change formats, check spelling, and, most importantly, master the print and save functions. *Find out if your program has an undo function. This can save the day if you accidentally delete or "lose" some of your text.* This function simply undoes your last action, restoring deleted text or eliminating what you just added.

3. **Write in single space.** Most instructors require that papers be double-spaced, but you may find it easier to compose your various drafts in single space so that you can see more of your essay on the screen. You can easily change to double space when you print the final version.

4. **Date and color-code your drafts.** To make sure you do not accidentally turn in an earlier, unedited draft of a paper, always put today's date in the header to identify the most recent version. In writing and editing a longer paper, highlight passages and change colors. You might highlight passages needing grammatical editing in red and those needing fact checking or additional details in blue. Marking up drafts in this way can make final editing easier. When you complete editing a section, change the color to black. When the entire document is free of red or blue paragraphs, you know you have fully edited the paper.

5. **Save your work.** If your program has an automatic save function, use it. Save your work to a flash drive. If you are writing on a college or library computer and do not have a flash drive, email your work to yourself, or print a hard copy. Don't let a power outage or a keystroke error make you lose your work!

6. **Print drafts of your work as you write.** Computer screens usually only allow you to view less than a page of text at a time. Although it is easy to scroll up and down through the text, it can be difficult to revise on the screen. You may find it easier to work with a hard copy of your paper. Double- or triple-space printed copies to make room for notes and comments.

7. **Keep backup copies of your work.** Flash drives can be damaged or lost. *Store important data on more than one device or save printed copies.*

8. **Make use of special features.** Most word processing applications allow you to count the number of words, check spelling, and use a built-in thesaurus. Some programs will aid you with grammar and usage rules.

9. **Use spell- and grammar checkers but recognize their limitations.** A spell-checker will go through your document and flag words it does not recognize, quickly locating many mistakes you might overlook on your own. *Spell-checkers do not locate missing words or recognize errors in usage, such as confusing* there *and* their *or* adopt *and* adapt. *Grammar checkers sometimes offer awkward suggestions and flag correct expressions as errors.* Reading your text aloud is still the best method of editing.

10. **Follow your instructor's guidelines when emailing papers.** Make sure to include your name and course information on any attachments you send.

Collaborative Writing

Writing often occurs in groups. Even when produced by a single person, writing may have to reflect the views of many people. Thomas Jefferson wrote the Declaration of Independence, but a committee including Jefferson, John Adams, Benjamin Franklin, and two others made forty-seven changes. Franklin replaced Jefferson's original phrase (in italics) "we hold these rights to be *sound and undeniable*" with "*self-evident.*" More changes occurred when the document was presented to the entire Continental Congress. Jefferson's impassioned attack on slavery was eliminated to appease Southern representatives. In all, eighty-seven alterations were made to Jefferson's declaration before it was accepted. By the time John Hancock stepped forward to sign the Declaration of Independence, a quarter of Jefferson's original draft had been changed or deleted.

As a college student, you may be called on to work in a writing group. More and more professors assign collaborative writing projects because writing in groups is common in business and industry. Most professionals work in committees to write reports, draft letters, develop proposals, respond to complaints, or create websites.

Working in groups adds challenges to the writing process. Viewpoints and personalities may clash. Because people regard their writing as personal expression and are accustomed to working alone, it can be difficult for them to accept criticism.

But whether you are writing alone or in a group, the basic process remains the same. The writing must address the issue, meet the needs of the readers, and respect the conventions of the discipline or discourse community. To be effective, writing groups must achieve the "three Cs" of group dynamics: *cohesion, cooperation,* and *compromise.* Members must have a clearly defined goal or task. They must be willing to meet and to work outside the group. Finally, and often most difficult, individuals must be willing to accept that their opinions may not prevail and be willing to drop or modify ideas they greatly value.

Strategies FOR COLLABORATIVE WRITING

1. **Establish cohesion by stressing the goals, intended readers, and requirements of the writing project.** It is important for members of a writing group to feel trust so they can share ideas and offer and accept criticism.

2. **Keep the group focused by creating a timeline.** Discussions can easily become generalized forums for spirited debate or the latest gossip. A target timeline can keep the group on track by outlining expected outcomes and reminding members of the deadline. The timeline should reflect stages in the writing process.

3. **Make meetings productive by setting goals and assigning tasks.** Members should be given specific responsibilities: gathering research, conducting interviews, or writing sample drafts. Each meeting should open with a goal statement of what is to be achieved and end with a summary of what has been completed and an announcement of what must be accomplished at the next meeting.

4. **Designate one member to serve as a moderator or recorder.** One member of the group should document the progress of the group and serve as secretary to exchange messages between meetings.

5. **Avoid personalizing disagreements.** It is important to discuss opposing viewpoints in neutral terms. Avoid "us-against-them" conflicts.

6. **Take advantage of technology.** Students often have trouble finding common times to meet for social activities, let alone assignments. Consider how the group can maintain links through email and telephone conferences.

7. **Acknowledge contributions made by others by noting quotations and paraphrases or listing their names as co-authors.**

Writer's Block

At some time almost everyone experiences writer's block—the inability to write. With a paper due in a few days, you may find yourself incapable of coming up with a single line or even unable to sit at your desk. You can feel frustrated, nervous, bored, tired, or anxious. The more time passes, and the more you think about the upcoming assignment, the more frustrated you can become.

There is no magic cure for writer's block, but there are tactics that can help.

Strategies FOR OVERCOMING WRITER'S BLOCK

1. **Recognize that writer's block exists.** When you have the time to write, write. Get as much writing as possible done when you can. If you delay work, you may find yourself unable to write as the deadline nears.

2. **Review your assignment carefully and turn the instructions into a series of questions to spark critical thinking.**

3. If you are having trouble selecting a topic, use key words from the assignment as search terms. See what web pages these key words produce. Even unrelated references can spark your imagination and help develop ideas.

4. Write anything. The longer you delay writing, the harder it will be to start. If you have trouble focusing on your assignment, get into the mood for writing by emailing a friend.

5. Discuss your assignment with others. Talking with a friend can boost your confidence and reduce your anxiety about an assignment. A spirited discussion may generate free associations about your topic, helping you to view your subject from new angles.

6. Force yourself to write for five minutes. Let one idea run into another. If you have trouble writing about your topic, write about anything that comes to mind. Even writing nonsense will help you break the physical resistance you may have to sitting down and working with a pen or keyboard. Try to steer your experimental writing to the assigned task. If your draft is going nowhere, save your work and stop after five minutes. Take a walk or run some errands, then return to your writing. Sometimes seeing a word or phrase out of context will lead to significant associations.

7. Lower your standards. Don't be afraid to write poorly. Don't expect your first draft to be perfect. Badly written drafts can form the foundation of a good paper.

8. Don't feel obligated to start at the beginning. If you find yourself unable to develop a convincing opening line or a satisfactory introduction, begin writing the body or conclusion of the paper. Get your ideas flowing.

9. Switch subjects. If you are bogged down on your English paper, start work on the history project due next month. Writing well on a different subject may help you gain the confidence you need to return to a difficult assignment.

10. Record your thoughts on tape or note cards. If you find writing frustrating, consider talking into a voice recorder or listing ideas on index cards. You may find working with different materials an effective method of getting started.

11. Try writing in a different location. If you can't work at home because of distractions, go to the library or a quiet room. If the library feels stifling and intimidating, move to a less formal environment. You may discover yourself doing your best work while drinking coffee in a noisy student union.

12. If you still have problems with your assignment, talk to your instructor.

WRITING ACTIVITIES

1. Choose one of the following topics and use the five-step method described in this chapter to draft a short essay. As you write, note which stages of the process pose the greatest challenges. Alter your composing style in any way that improves your writing.

divorce	mandatory courses	televised trials
stepparents	charter schools	alternative energy
hate speech	volunteering	racial profiling
the insanity defense	college sports	minimum wage

2. Select an upcoming assignment and write a rough draft. Use this experience to identify topic areas that require the most attention. *Save your notes and draft for future use.*

3. Write an email to a friend about a recent experience. Before sending it, set it aside, letting it "cool." After two or three days, examine your draft for missing details, awkward or confusing phrases, misspelled words, and repetitious statements. *Notice how revision and editing can improve your writing.*

Avoid Plagiarism

In writing college papers, you may often include ideas, facts, and information from outside sources. Whenever you copy material or restate the ideas of others in your own words, you must indicate the source. Presenting the words or ideas of others as your own is called *plagiarism*, a serious academic offense. Students who submit plagiarized papers are frequently failed or expelled.

Strategies FOR AVOIDING PLAGIARISM

1. When you copy a source word for word, indicate it as a direct quote with quotation marks:

   Original source
   The airbag is not the most important automotive safety device. It is a sober driver.
   —William Harris, address before National Safety Council

   Quotation used in student paper:
   Speaking before the National Safety Council, William Harris said, "The air bag is not the most important safety device. It is a sober driver."

2. When you state the ideas of others in your own words, you still must acknowledge their source:

   Paraphrase used in student paper:
   William Harris has noted that a sober driver is a better safety device than an air bag.

3. When working on drafts, color-code quotations and paraphrases to distinguish them from your own words. In writing a paper over several days, you may forget where you used outside sources. Whenever you cut and paste material into a paper, color-code it or place it in bold as a reminder that it needs to be treated as a quotation or a paraphrase in final editing.

4. Always record the source of outside material. When you cut and paste or paraphrase material, always copy the information needed to cite the source: the author, title, website or publication, dates, and page numbers.

Refer to *A Writer's Guide to Documenting Sources* in the appendix for information on using and citing outside sources.

Accompanying English CourseMate Resources

 Visit English CourseMate at **www.cengagebrain.com** to find many helpful resources and study tools for this chapter.

Critical Reading

Reading Critically

As a student you read for information. Cramming for a history exam, you study a textbook to find the names, dates, and facts you expect to appear on the test. Reading a novel for entertainment, you become absorbed by the writer's plot, style, and characters. As a writer, however, you need to read critically. You need to read with a "writer's eye." While most diners savor a new dessert, a chef wants to know the recipe. Tourists marvel at a new high-rise, but an architect analyzes its support structure. Moviegoers gasp at an exciting car chase as film students review the director's editing technique. As a writer, you need to look at writing in much the same way. In addition to determining *what* an essay says, it is important to note *how* it is organized, *how* the writer overcame problems, and *how* language and detail contribute to its effect. You can improve your writing skills by critically reading the works of others.

Strategies FOR CRITICAL READING

First Reading

1. **Look ahead and skim selections.** Do not wait until the night before a class discussion to read assigned essays. Check your syllabus and skim through upcoming readings to get a general impression.

2. **Study the headnote and introduction.** Consider the author, the issue, the writing context. What readers does the writer seem to be addressing? What can you observe about the discourse community?

3. **Suspend judgment.** Put your personal views aside as you read. Even if you disagree with the author's choice of topic, tone, or opinion, read the essay objectively. Remember, your goal is to understand *how* the writer states his or her point. Even if you reject an author's thesis, you can still learn useful techniques.

4. **Consider the title.** Titles often provide clues about the author's attitude toward his or her subject. Does the title label the essay, state a thesis, pose a question, or use a creative phrase to attract attention?

5. **Read the entire work.** Do not pause to look up an unfamiliar word at this stage. Instead, try to get the "big picture."

6. **Focus on understanding the writer's main point.** If possible, summarize the writer's thesis in your own words.

7. **Jot down your first impressions.** What do you think of this work? Do you like it? If so, why? If you find it dull, disturbing, or silly, ask why: What is lacking? How did the author fail in your eyes?

Put the essay aside, allowing it to cool. If possible, let two or three days pass before returning to the assignment. If the assignment is due the next day, read the selection early in the day and then turn to other work or run an errand so that you can come back to it with a fresh outlook.

Second Reading

1. **Review your first impressions.** Determine if your attitudes are based on personal biases rather than the writer's ability. If you disagree with the author's thesis, try to put your opinions aside to evaluate objectively how well the writer presented his or her point of view. Don't allow personal views to cloud your critical thinking. Appreciating an author's writing ability does not require you to accept his or her opinion.

2. **Read with a pen in your hand.** Make notes and underline passages that strike you as interesting, meaningful, offensive, or disturbing. Reading with a pen will prompt you to write—to be an active reader rather than a passive consumer of words.

3. **Look up unfamiliar words.** Paying attention to words can increase your vocabulary and enhance your appreciation of word choices.

4. **Analyze passages you found difficult or confusing during the first reading.** In many instances, a second reading can help you understand complex passages. If you still have difficulty understanding the writer's point, ask why. Would other readers also have problems comprehending the meaning? Could ideas be stated more directly?

5. **Review the questions at the end of the selection.** Considering the questions can help you focus on a closer, more analytical reading of the work. The questions are arranged in three groups:

Understanding Meaning

1. What is the writer's purpose?
2. What is the thesis?
3. What audience is the writer addressing?
4. What is the writer trying to share with his or her readers?

Evaluating Strategy

1. How effective is the title?
2. How does the writer introduce the essay?
3. What evidence supports the thesis?
4. How does the writer organize ideas?
5. Where does the writer use paragraph breaks?
6. What role does the writer play?
7. Is the writer's approach subjective or objective?
8. How does the writer address possible objections or differing opinions?
9. How does the writer conclude the essay?
10. Does the writer use any special techniques?

Appreciating Language

1. How does the writer use words?
2. What does the language reveal about the intended readers?
3. What emotional impact do the words have?
4. How do the words establish the writer's tone?

6. **Summarize your responses in a point or two for class discussion.** Be prepared to back up your remarks by citing passages in the text.

7. **Most importantly, focus on what this essay can teach you about writing.** How can this writer's style, way of organizing ideas, or word choice enrich your own writing?

8. **Think of how writers resolve problems you have encountered.** If you have trouble making an outline and organizing ideas, study how the essays in this book are arranged. If your instructor returns papers with comments about vague thesis statements and lack of focus, examine how the writers in this book develop controlling ideas.

Before-Class Discussion

1. **Before class, review the reading and your notes.** Identify your main reactions to the piece. What do you consider the essay's strongest or weakest points?

2. **Ask other students about their reactions to the assignment.** Determine whether their responses to the writer's thesis, tone, approach, and technique match yours. If their reactions differ from yours, review your notes to get a fresh perspective.

3. **Be prepared to ask questions.** Ask your instructor about unfamiliar techniques or passages you find confusing.

Above All, Read to Learn

Read the following essay by Cornel West and study how it has been marked during a critical reading. West is a highly organized writer who blends the use of several modes in this comparison essay on the current state of African American political leadership.

CORNEL WEST

Cornel West was a religion professor and Director of Afro-American Studies at Princeton University before he was appointed to the faculty at Harvard University. The author of *Keeping Faith, Prophetic Fragments,* and other books, West has specialized in writing on race in America. In 2012 he co-authored *The Rich and the Rest of Us: A Poverty Manifesto* with Tavis Smiley.

Black Political Leadership

CONTEXT: *"Black Political Leadership" appeared in West's best-selling 1994 book,* Race Matters. *In this section, West compares the current generation of black political leaders with leaders of the Civil Rights era.*

WRITER'S NOTE: *Although West's purpose is to compare, he uses a number of modes to develop his ideas.*

<u>Black political leadership reveals the tame and genteel face of the black middle class.</u> The black dress suits with white shirts worn by Malcolm X and Martin Luther King Jr. signified the seriousness of their deep commitment to black freedom, whereas today the expensive tailored suits of black politicians symbolize their personal success and individual achievement. Malcolm and Martin called for the realization that black people are somebodies with which America has to reckon, whereas black politicians tend to turn our attention to *their* somebodiness owing to *their* "making it" in America.

1
thesis/ opening

clothes as symbolic

comparison

note use of italics

   This crude and slightly unfair comparison <u>highlights two distinctive features of black political leaders in the post–Civil Rights era: the relative lack of authentic anger and the relative absence of genuine humility.</u> What stood out most strikingly about Malcolm X, Martin Luther King Jr., Ella Baker, and Fannie Lou Hamer was that they were almost always visibly upset about the condition of black America. When one saw them speak or heard their voices, they projected on a gut level that the black situation was urgent, in need of immediate attention. One even gets the impression that their own stability and sanity rested on how soon the black predicament could be improved. Malcolm, Martin, Ella, and Fannie were angry about the state of black America, and this anger fueled their boldness and defiance.

2
division

examples

   <u>In stark contrast,</u> most present-day black political leaders appear <u>too hungry for status</u> to be angry, <u>too eager</u> for acceptance to be bold, <u>too self-invested</u> in advancement to be defiant. And when they do drop their masks and try to get mad (usually in the presence of black audiences), their bold rhetoric is more performance than personal, more play-acting than heartfelt. Malcolm, Martin, Ella, and Fannie made sense of the black plight in a poignant and powerful

3
shift/ transition

repetitive wording for emphasis

manner, <u>whereas</u> most contemporary black political leaders' oratory appeals to black people's sense of the sentimental and sensational.

contrast

4

Similarly, Malcolm, Martin, Ella, and Fannie were examples of humility. Yes, even Malcolm's aggressiveness was accompanied by a common touch and humble disposition toward ordinary black people. <u>Humility is the fruit of inner security and wise maturity.</u> To be humble is to be so sure of one's self and one's mission that one can forego calling excessive attention to one's self and status. And, even more pointedly, to be humble is to revel in the accomplishments or potential of others—especially those with whom one identifies and to whom one is linked organically. The relative absence of humility in most black political leaders today is a symptom of the status-anxiety and personal insecurity pervasive in black middle-class America. In this context, even a humble vesture is viewed as a cover for some sinister motive or surreptitious ambition.

supplies personal definition

cause and effect

<u>Present-day black political leaders can be grouped under three types: race-effacing managerial leaders, race-identifying protest leaders, and race-transcending prophetic leaders.</u> The <u>first type</u> is growing rapidly. The Thomas Bradleys and Wilson Goodes of black America have become a model for many black leaders trying to reach a large white constituency and keep a loyal black one. This type survives on sheer political savvy and thrives on personal diplomacy. This kind of candidate is the lesser of two evils in a political situation where the only other electoral choice is a conservative (usually white) politician. Yet this type of leader tends to stunt progressive development and silence the prophetic voices in the black community by casting the practical mainstream as the only game in town.

5.

division definition

The <u>second type</u> of black political leader—race-identifying protest leaders—often view themselves in the tradition of Malcolm X, Martin Luther King Jr., Ella Baker, and Fannie Lou Hamer. Yet they are usually self-deluded. They actually operate more in the tradition of Booker T. Washington, by confining themselves to the black turf, vowing to protect their leadership status over it, and serving as power brokers with powerful nonblack elites (usually white economic or political elites, though in Louis Farrakhan's case it may be Libyan) to "enhance" this black turf. It is crucial to remember that even in the fifties, Malcolm X's vision and practice were international in scope, and that after 1964 his project was transracial—though grounded in the black turf. King never confined himself to being solely the leader of black America—even though the white press attempted to do so. And Fannie Lou Hamer led the National Welfare Rights Organization, not the Black Welfare Rights Organization. In short, race-identifying protest leaders in the post–Civil Rights era function as figures who white Americans must appease so that the plight of the black poor is overlooked and forgotten. When such leaders move successfully into elected office—as with Marion Barry—they usually become managerial types with large black constituencies, flashy styles, flowery rhetoric, and Booker T. Washington–like patronage operations within the public sphere.

6

analysis

Race-transcending prophetic leaders are rare in contemporary   7
black America. Harold Washington was one. The Jesse Jackson of   *examples*
1988 was attempting to be another—yet the opportunism of his
past weighed heavily on him. To be an elected official and prophetic leader requires personal integrity and political savvy, moral
vision and prudential judgment, courageous defiance and organizational patience. The present generation has yet to produce such
a figure. We have neither an Adam Clayton Powell Jr., nor a Ronald
Dellums. This void sits like a festering sore at the center of the crisis   *final effects*
of black leadership—and the predicament of the disadvantaged in
the United States and abroad worsens.

Using *The Sundance Reader*

The Sundance Reader is organized into nine chapters focusing on writers' goals.
The readings in each section illustrate how writers achieve their purpose in different contexts. Each chapter opens with an explanation of the goal or mode.
The first few readings in each chapter are brief, clear-cut examples of the mode
and can serve as models for many of your composition assignments. The middle readings are longer and more complex and demonstrate writing tasks in a
range of disciplines and writing situations. Each chapter ends with samples of
applied writings taken from business, industry, and government to illustrate how
writing is used beyond the classroom. Student papers provide models for your
own assignments.

When reading entries, keep these general questions in mind:

1. **What is the writer's purpose—to share an experience, raise questions,
   state a position, or motivate readers to take action?**

2. **What is the writer's thesis?** Does the essay contain a clear thesis statement,
   or is it implied? Can you restate the thesis in your own words?

3. **Who are the intended readers?** Note the source of the article. What does
   it tell you about the readers? Does the writer direct it to a specific group or
   a general audience? What assumptions does the writer seem to make about
   the reader? What terms or references are defined? What knowledge does the
   writer expect his or her audience to possess?

4. **What evidence does the writer use to support the thesis?** Does the
   writer provide personal observation, statistics, facts, or the testimony of others to support his or her views?

5. **What is the nature of the discipline, profession, or writing situation?** Is
   the writer working within a discipline or addressing readers in another discipline? Do special circumstances guide the way the writer develops the
   thesis, presents ideas, and designs the physical appearance of the writing?

6. **How successful is this writing in its context?** Does the writer achieve his or
   her goals while respecting the needs of the reader and the conventions of the discipline or situation? Do special circumstances explain why the author appears
   to "break" the rules of what most English courses consider "good writing"?

Writing Techniques

In addition to reading entire essays, you can improve your writing by studying paragraphs that accomplish specific tasks:

Making Introductions

Klein, "How the Teachers Killed a Dream," page 66, par. 1
Tuite, "The Sounds of the City," page 110, par. 1
Sherry, "In Praise of the F Word," page 442, par. 1
Malveaux, "Still Hyphenated Americans," page 463, par. 1

Stating a Thesis

Tuan, "Chinese Space, American Space," page 185, par. 1
Valenti, "Are All Women Born to be Mothers?" page 276, par. 22
Gatto, "Why Schools Don't Educate," page 383, par. 1
Koch, "Death and Justice: How Capital Punishment Affirms Life,"page 320, par. 15

Defining Terms

Simpson, "Dyslexia," page 145, par. 1
Harris, "A Jerk," page 150, par. 6
Safire, "Liberal and Conservative," page 155, par. 1, and page 156, par. 13
Austin, "Four Kinds of Chance," page 303, par. 1

Presenting Quotations and Statistics as Support

Klein, "How the Teachers Killed a Dream," page 66, par. 2
Rector, "How Poor is 'Poor'"? page 164, par. 6
Radford, "How Television Distorts Reality" page 263, par. 2
Cockburn, "Why We Must Raise the Minimum Wage," page 412, par. 4

Using Dialogue

Scudder, "Take This Fish and Look at It," page 61, pars. 2–6
Pérez, "The Fender-Bender," page 73, pars. 8–12
Rowan, "Unforgettable Miss Bessie,"page 117, pars. 2–7

Stating Conclusions

Gansberg, "Thirty-Eight Who Saw Murder and Didn't Call the Police," page 80, par. 31
Burciaga, "My Ecumenical Father," page 115, par. 23
Lane, "There's No Place for Censorship-by-Riot," page 454, par. 14
Sherry, "In Praise of the F Word," page 444, par. 12

Analyzing Visual Images

We increasingly communicate in images. We are bombarded daily with advertisements in print, online, on television, and billboards. College textbooks, which thirty years ago consisted of only text, now feature graphs and photographs on nearly every page. Websites, once blocks of words, now include streaming video. Satellites allow journalists to broadcast from remote parts of the world. Cable news networks provide images of breaking events twenty-four hours a day. The personal computer and desktop publishing enable students and small-business owners to develop sophisticated multimedia presentations rivaling those created by major corporations. Digital cameras allow people to transmit photos and video instantly worldwide.

Images can be used to grab attention, evoke an emotional response, record events, document conditions, record evidence, illustrate an idea or condition, establish a mood, or develop a context for discussion. Visual images command attention. They can be presented without comment or woven into the text of a written message.

Photographs, Film, and Video

Photographs, film, and video are compelling. There is a belief that "the camera does not lie." A written description of a person or a place never seems as objective or as accurate as a photograph. The camera, we think, hides nothing. It tells the whole truth. It leaves nothing out. People writing reports about a car accident

Charles Fenno Jacobs/Hulton-Deutsch Collection/Corbis

Image vs. reality

can exaggerate or minimize the damage, but a photograph, we assume, provides us with irrefutable evidence. Nevertheless, visuals can be highly subjective and often misleading. They require careful analysis to determine their meaning and reliability.

The impression a photograph or video makes is shaped by a number of factors: *perspective and contrast, context, timing and duplication, manipulation,* and *captions.*

Perspective and Contrast

How large is a group of a hundred? How tall is a twenty-story building? The impression we get of events, objects, and people depends on perspective, the angle, and distance of the camera and the subject. A hundred protesters photographed in close-

Charles Lindbergh, 1927

up will look like an overwhelming force. Fists raised, faces twisted in emotion, lunging toward the camera, they can appear all-powerful and unstoppable. Photographed from a distance, the crowd can seem small against a landscape of multi-story buildings or acres of empty pavement. In contrast to large fixed objects, the protest can appear futile and weak. If ordinary people going about routine business are shown in the foreground, the protesters, in contrast, may appear abnormal, ephemeral, even pathetic. A twenty-story building in a suburban neighborhood of two-story structures will loom over the landscape. Located in midtown Manhattan, dwarfed by skyscrapers, the same structure will seem undersized, less formidable, even homey in contrast. A luxury car photographed in front of a stately country home can appear as a desirable symbol of style, elegance, and taste. Parked next to a migrant farmworker's shack, the same car can appear oppressive, a symbol of tasteless greed, exploitation, and injustice. A mime shown entertaining small children will look wholesome, joyful, and playful. Posed next to a homeless man taking shelter in a cardboard box, a mime will look irrelevant, inane, even insulting.

An individual can appear large or small, weak or powerful, depending on perspective. Charles Lindbergh is shown in close-up. His face fills the frame. No other people, structures, or objects detract from his larger-than-life presence. In addition, he is photographed wearing his flight helmet and goggles, emblems of his famous 1927 transatlantic flight. His clear eyes look upward as if gazing to the horizon and the future. This photograph depicts a human being as powerful, in command of his environment. It is the type of image seen on movie posters and postage stamps, in official portraits and celebrity stills. Shown in isolation, any subject can appear dominant because there is nothing else to compare it to.

In contrast to Lindbergh's picture, the photograph of James Dean in Times Square was shot at some distance. Unlike Lindbergh, Dean is shown not in isolation but within an environment. Though he is at the center of the photograph, his stature is diminished by the urban landscape. Tall buildings rise above him. The iron fence on the right restricts his freedom of movement. In addition, the environment is hostile—dark, cold, and wet. Dean is hunched forward, his collar turned up against the wind, his hands buried in his pockets against the cold. The picture creates an image of brooding loneliness and alienation, suited to Dean's Hollywood image as a loner and troubled rebel.

James Dean in Times Square, 1955

The impression created of Lee Harvey Oswald is shaped by perspective. In the press photo taken shortly after his arrest, Oswald looks weak, subdued, cowardly. He is literally cornered, shown offcenter at the edge of the frame. Though he is the subject of the photograph, he is markedly smaller in relation to

Lee Harvey Oswald under arrest, Dallas, 1963

the officers. The angle of the camera distorts the relative sizes of the figures so that the uniformed men in the foreground are oversized, their power and authority emphasized. The officer's badge appears larger than Oswald's head. The room is blank and featureless. Handcuffed and still disheveled from his arrest, Oswald is depicted as a disarmed menace, an assassin rendered harmless.

Context

Photographs and video images are isolated glimpses of larger events. A camera captures a split second of reality, but it does not reveal what happened before or after the image was taken. The photograph of a baseball player hitting a home run shows a moment of athletic triumph, but it does not reveal the player's batting average or who won the game. Photographs taken during a melee between police and demonstrators can capture a protester hurling a rock at a police officer or the officer striking back with a nightstick. A single striking image may distort our impressions of a larger event.

Motion picture and video cameras offer us a window onto the world, bringing world events into our homes—but it is a narrow window. During the hostage crisis in Iran in 1979, for example, television cameras continually showed violent demonstrations outside the American embassy, creating the impression that the entire nation was swept by a wave of anti-Americanism. American journalists, however, reported that only a block away they could walk through crowded streets and chat with passers-by without incident. Aware of the power of image, protest groups around the world stage demonstrations for cameras to gain maximum media exposure.

Watching an evening of cable news creates the illusion that you are being well informed about world events. In thirty minutes, you see a conflict in the Middle East, a White House spokesperson, a senator commenting on the economy, a high-speed car chase in San Diego. But to a great extent cable news is limited to covering visual stories. Stories that are more complicated may not provide gripping visuals or may require too much explanation to make good television. Stories that break in developed countries within easy reach of media crews receive more coverage than events that occur in remote areas. Recent conflicts in the Middle East and Northern Ireland that claimed a few hundred lives a year received more coverage than a genocidal rebellion that killed hundreds of thousands in Rwanda or the ethnic cleansing that destroyed hundreds of villages in Sudan.

Juries have acquitted people caught on videotape buying drugs or engaged in violent assaults. Whereas the public only sees a dramatic segment, juries are often shown a videotape in its entirety. Defense attorneys place the tape in context by providing additional information about the people and events depicted. By raising doubts, they can persuade a jury to rethink what it has seen, questioning the tape's meaning and reliability.

Visual Connotations

Like words, images have connotations. They create emotional responses. Politicians are interviewed with flags and bookshelves in the background to demonstrate patriotism and indicate knowledge. Campaign commercials show candidates with their families, visiting the elderly, shaking hands with firefighters, or visiting veterans to link themselves with positive images. Ads and commercials will use provocative images of sex and violence to draw people's attention. Book covers and movie posters only vaguely associated with World War II often feature a swastika because it is a symbol bound to attract attention.

Certain images become icons—symbols of an event, culture, attitude, or value. Reproduced in books and films, on murals and T-shirts, they serve to communicate a message with a single image. Marilyn Monroe's upswirled skirt symbolizes sex. The photograph of two African American athletes raising gloved fists at the 1968 Olympic Games became an icon of Black Power. The World Trade Center attack has become an international symbol of terrorism. Often the icon takes on a meaning of its own, so that fiction can become reality. Although John Wayne never served in the military, his picture is often hung in Pentagon offices because his Hollywood image expresses values embraced by the military.

Timing and Duplication

Timing and duplication can enhance an image's impact and distort perceptions. If two celebrities meet briefly at a special event and photographs of them shaking hands are widely reproduced over several months, it can create the impression they are close friends. The two figures become a single image repeatedly imprinted on the public, with few viewers recognizing that they are simply seeing the same moment from different angles. Stalin, Roosevelt, and Churchill only met on a few occasions during the World War II, but the continual reproduction of photographs of them together helped create the image of the Big Three as a solid alliance against Hitler. Cable news reports of a suicide bombing, a shooting spree, or a car chase will recycle scenes over and over, often creating an exaggerated sense of their significance.

Manipulating Images

Just as painters in a king's court often depicted royalty in flattering poses without blemishes, photographers and filmmakers can use lighting, perspective, and contrast to alter perceptions of reality. Short actors can be made to seem taller on screen by lowering cameras or placing taller people in the background. Makeup and lighting can magnify or diminish facial features, improving someone's appearance. Even candid images can be carefully selected to show a subject in a positive light. Portraits of Kaiser Wilhelm and Joseph Stalin camouflaged the fact that both men had one arm that was noticeably shorter than the other. Wishing to project power and authority, both leaders wished to disguise their physical disability. Although most Americans knew that President Roosevelt had been stricken with polio, few were aware of how severely handicapped he actually was. The media did not release films of him in motion. Photographs and newsreels showed him standing or seated. The fact that he often had to be lifted out of cars or carried up steps was not made public. Although suffering from a painful back injury and Addison's disease, President Kennedy projected an image of youth and vigor by being shown in athletic contexts: playing touch football, swimming, or boating. Only a handful of photographs show Kennedy wearing the eyeglasses he needed for reading.

US Army Signal Corps/Time & Life Pictures/Getty Images

President Wilson and General Pershing. A retoucher has partially erased a figure walking behind the two famous men, altering viewers' perception of a historical event. Frequently, negative or distracting images are removed from photographs to enhance their effect.

Photographs and film can be edited, revised, cut, or altered after the fact. A group photo can be reduced to focus on a single person. People and objects can be added or removed to alter the record of actual events. Leon Trotsky was once a powerful Soviet leader, and was often photographed standing next to Lenin. Wishing to obliterate his rival's role in the Russian Revolution, Stalin had thousands of pictures retouched to remove Trotsky from group photographs.

Today, with digital technology, images can be easily removed and inserted. Photographs, motion pictures, and videos now have an increasing power to create their own reality, which may exaggerate, minimize, or distort actual events.

Gender and Cultural Issues

Images, like language, affect our perceptions. Historically, images have reflected prevailing attitudes and biases. Words like *policeman, mankind,* and *mailman,* and the universal use of *he* as a single pronoun, gave English a distinct sexist stance. Advertising historically presented women as sexual objects or in a secondary role to men. Automobile ads show men standing next to or driving a car, while women are draped across the hood as ornaments. Soap ads depict men taking showers; women are posed lying in tubs. As gender roles change, popular culture and advertising alter our perceptions of men and women.

Perception and Analysis

Our analysis of images is shaped by our perceptions, both personal and cultural. A photograph taken in Iran depicts a male professor lecturing female seminary students from behind a screen. To Western eyes, this image can seem a shocking example of oppression and exclusion. To many Iranians, however, the image of women studying Islam represents inclusion and empowerment.

Eitan Abramovich/AFP/Getty Images

Libyan female soldier. Social change is reflected by a clash of traditional gender images. Makeup and jewelry are decidedly feminine, in contrast to the masculine uniform.

Lise Sarfati/Magnum Photos

In Iran, a male professor lectures female students from behind a screen.

Strategies FOR ANALYZING VISUAL IMAGES

1. **Examine the image holistically.** What does it represent? What is your initial reaction? Does it convey a message?

2. **Consider the nature of the image.** Is this a professional portrait or a candid press shot? Was this video taken at a prepared ceremony or a spontaneous event? Were people, images, or objects deliberately posed to make a statement?

3. **Examine perspective.** Is the subject depicted in close-up or at a distance? Does the subject appear in control of the environment, or does the background dominate the frame?

4. **Analyze contrasts and contexts.** Is the background supportive, neutral, or hostile to the subject? Does the image depict conflict or harmony?

5. **Examine poses and body language of human figures.** How are human figures depicted? What emotions do they seem to express?

6. **Look for bias.** Do you sense that the photographers were trying to manipulate the people or events depicted, casting them in either a favorable or negative light?

7. **Consider the larger context.** Does the image offer a fair representation of a larger event, or is it an isolated exception?

8. **Review the image for possible manipulation.** Could camera angles, digital editing, or retouching have altered what appears to be a record of actual events?

9. **Consider the story the image seems to tell.** What is the thesis of this image? What visual details or symbols help tell the story?

Accompanying English CourseMate Resources

 Visit English CourseMate at **www.cengagebrain.com** to find many helpful resources and study tools for this chapter.

Narration: Relating Events

What Is Narration?

Narration answers the basic question "What happened?" The goal of narration is to tell a story. Narratives can be fact or fiction, and they can be written in first or third person. The Bible, accident reports, Greek myths, novels, news stories, diaries, blogs, autobiographies, and history books are examples of narration. Physicians write narration to record a patient's history and outline a course of treatment. Attorneys use narrative writing to relate the details of a crime or explain the rationale for a lawsuit. Government reports, grant proposals, and business plans generally include a narrative section that provides the history of an organization or summarizes a current problem or project.

The Writer's Purpose

Narration can be **subjective** or **objective**, depending on the writer's goal and context. **Subjective narration** focuses on personal impressions, thoughts, insights, and feelings. Often the writer is at the center of the narrative, either as a principal character or as a key witness. In "Returning to Southie" (pages 84–85), Michael Patrick MacDonald uses first person to recall the emotions he felt visiting his old neighborhood:

> I agreed to take the reporter on a tour through Southie. We stayed in the car, because I was too nervous to walk around with an "outsider" in a suit. It was bad enough that I was driving his rented sports car. People in Southie usually drove big Chevys, or when they were in with "the boys," as we called our revered gangsters, they'd upgrade to an even bigger Caddy or Lincoln Continental. I wore sunglasses and a scally cap, the traditional local cap once favored by hard-working Irish immigrants and longshoremen, and more recently made popular by tough guys and wannabes. I disguised myself so I wouldn't be identified collaborating with outsiders.

Objective narration, in contrast, is usually stated in the third person to give the writer's views a sense of neutrality. In objective narration, the author is not a participant but a collector and presenter of evidence. In "Thirty-Eight Who Saw Murder and Didn't Call the Police" (page 78), Martin Gansberg presents a factual account of a murder victim's last movements:

> Twenty-eight-year-old Catherine Genovese, who was called Kitty by almost everyone in the neighborhood, was returning home from her job as manager of a bar in Hollis. She parked her red Fiat in a lot adjacent to the Kew Gardens Long Island Rail Road Station, facing Mowbray Place. Like many residents of the neighborhood, she had parked there day after day since her arrival from Connecticut a year ago, although the railroad frowns on the practice.
>
> She turned off the lights of her car, locked the door, and started to walk the 100 feet to the entrance of her apartment at 82-70 Austin Street, which is in a Tudor building with stores on the first floor and apartments on the second.
>
> The entrance to the apartment is in the rear of the building because the front is rented to retail stores. At night the quiet neighborhood is shrouded in the slumbering darkness that marks most residential areas.

Chronology

Chronology, or time, is a central organizing element in narrative writing. Writers do not always relate events in a straight timeline. A biography, for instance, does not have to begin with birth and childhood. Writers often alter the time sequences of their stories to dramatize events or limit their topic. A biographer of Franklin D. Roosevelt might choose to highlight a key event or turning point in his life. The narrative might open with his polio attack, flash back to his childhood and early political career, then flash forward to his recovery and election to the presidency. Other writers find it more dramatic to begin a narrative at the end and then explain what led to this final event. The first chapter of a book about Czar Nicholas II could describe his execution and then flash back to the events leading to his downfall and death.

Each method of organizing a narrative has distinct advantages and disadvantages:

- **Beginning at the beginning** creates an open-ended narrative, providing readers with little hint of later events. Writers who relate complex stories with many possible causes can use a straight chronology to avoid highlighting a single event. Using a direct beginning-to-end approach is the most traditional method of telling a story. One of the difficulties with this method can be determining exactly when the narrative should start. Often the beginning of a story consists of incidental background information that readers may find uninteresting.

- **Beginning at the middle or at a turning point** can arouse reader interest by opening with a dramatic scene. This method of organization can focus on the chain of events, persuading readers to concentrate on a particular issue. This is a common pattern in nonfiction articles, biographies, and histories written for a general readership. Critics, however, can view this alteration of chronology as distorting. Not all historians, for instance, may agree that Roosevelt's illness was the "turning point" of his life. Some biographers might feel that focusing on his physical disability ignores his intellectual development or downplays his political role.

- **Beginning at the end** serves to dramatize the final event. When everything is presented in flashback, readers see events, actions, and thoughts in hindsight. The elements of suspense and randomness are removed, providing a stronger sense of cause and effect. Some readers will object to this method because it implies the final outcome was inevitable, when, in fact, events just as easily could have led to alternative endings.

Writing Techniques: NARRATION

Focus

The goal of narration is not always to record "everything that happened." Although narratives may not contain a thesis statement, they have a purpose. In "Take This Fish and Look at It" (page 61) Samuel Scudder focuses on the most important lesson he learned during his first days in college. Joel Klein uses a single incident (page 66) to illustrate the challenges of school reform. Focus leads writers to highlight significant events, people, and statements and ignore unimportant details.

Dialogue

Writers use direct quotations to record conversations. Including people's actual words reveals their tone, character, and attitude. In "The Fender-Bender" Ramon Pérez (page 73) uses dialogue to dramatize the attitudes of people involved in a minor accident. Dialogue is often compressed and edited to dramatize the writer's main point.

Tense

Most narratives are written in past tense. Narratives explaining ongoing events, however, may use present tense to remind readers that the action is still occurring. Some writers, like Ramon Pérez (page 73), relate a past incident in present tense to dramatize the action and give their writing a sense of immediacy.

Strategies FOR READING NARRATION

When reading the narratives in this chapter, keep these questions in mind.

Understanding Meaning

1. What is the author's narrative purpose—to inform, enlighten, share a personal experience, or provide information?
2. What is the writer's role? Is the author a participant, a witness, or a reporter? Is he or she expressing personal opinions and reactions or objective facts?
3. What readership is the narration directed toward—general or specific? How much knowledge does the author assume readers have?
4. What is the nature of the discipline, discourse community, or writing situation? Is the narration objective or subjective? Does the original source of the narrative (news magazine, scientific journal, or government document) reveal anything about the context?

Evaluating Strategy

1. What details does the writer select to highlight? Are some items summarized or ignored?
2. What kind of support does the writer use—personal observation or factual documentation?
3. What is the sequence of events? How is the narration organized? Does the writer begin at the beginning, the end, or a midpoint?
4. Does the writer use flashbacks and flash-forwards?
5. What transitional devices does the writer use to advance the narrative? Does the author use time references such as "later that day" or "two months later"?

Appreciating Language

1. What does the level of language suggest about the writer's role, the intended readers, and the nature of the discipline or writing situation?
2. How does the writer use words to create tone and style? What do word choices suggest about the writer's attitude toward the subject?

SAMUEL SCUDDER

Samuel Scudder (1837–1911) was born in Boston and attended Williams College. In 1857, he entered Harvard, where he studied under the noted professor Louis Agassiz. Scudder held various positions and helped in founding the Cambridge Entomological Club. He published hundreds of papers and developed a comprehensive catalog of three centuries of scientific publications in mathematics and the natural and physical sciences. While working for the United States Geological Survey, he named more than a thousand species of fossil insects. Although later scientists would question some of his conclusions, much of Scudder's work is still admired for its attention to detail.

Take This Fish and Look at It

CONTEXT: *Today educators stress critical thinking, which begins with close observation. In this famous essay, Scudder relates the lesson in observation he learned under Professor Agassiz, whose teaching method was simple. Instead of lecturing, he directed his young student to "look again, look again."*

WRITER'S NOTE: *Scudder omits unnecessary details such as dates, addresses, and even Professor Agassiz's appearance.*

It was more than fifteen years ago that I entered the laboratory of Professor Agassiz, and told him I had enrolled my name in the Scientific School as a student of natural history. He asked me a few questions about my object in coming, my antecedents generally, the mode in which I afterwards proposed to use the knowledge I might acquire, and, finally, whether I wished to study any special branch. To the latter I replied that, while I wished to be well grounded in all departments of zoology, I purposed to devote myself specially to insects.

"When do you wish to begin?" he asked.

"Now," I replied.

This seemed to please him, and with an energetic "Very well!" he reached from a shelf a huge jar of specimens in yellow alcohol. "Take this fish," he said, "and look at it; we call it a haemulon; by and by I will ask what you have seen."

With that he left me, but in a moment returned with explicit instructions as to the care of the object entrusted to me.

"No man is fit to be a naturalist," said he, "who does not know how to take care of specimens."

I was to keep the fish before me in a tin tray, and occasionally moisten the surface with alcohol from the jar, always taking care to replace the stopper tightly. Those were not the days of ground-glass stoppers and elegantly shaped exhibition jars; all the old students will recall the huge neckless glass bottles with their leaky,

intro sets time

brief summary

uses dialogue

1

2

3

4

gives directions

5

6

7

Take this Fish and Look at It (annotated) from 'In the Laboratory with Agassiz,' by Samuel H. Scudder, from Every Saturday (April 4, 1874) 16, 369–370.

wax-besmeared corks, half-eaten by insects and begrimed with cellar dust. Entomology was a cleaner science than ichthyology, but the example of the Professor, who had unhesitatingly plunged to the bottom of the jar to produce the fish, was infectious; and though this alcohol had a "very ancient and fishlike smell," I really dared not show any aversion within these sacred precincts, and treated the alcohol as though it were pure water. Still I was conscious of a passing feeling of disappointment, for gazing at a fish did not commend itself to an ardent entomologist. My friends at home, too, were annoyed when they discovered that no amount of eau-de-Cologne would drown the perfume which haunted me like a shadow.

In ten minutes I had seen all that could be seen in that fish, and started in search of the Professor—who had, however, left the Museum; and when I returned, after lingering over some of the odd animals stored in the upper apartment, my specimen was dry all over. I dashed the fluid over the fish as if to resuscitate the beast from a fainting fit, and looked with anxiety for a return of the normal sloppy appearance. This little excitement over, nothing was to be done but to return to a steadfast gaze at my mute companion. Half an hour passed—an hour—another hour; the fish began to look loathsome. I turned it over and around; looked it in the face— ghastly; from behind, beneath, above, sideways, at three-quarters' view—just as ghastly. I was in despair; at an early hour I concluded that lunch was necessary; so, with infinite relief, the fish was carefully replaced in the jar, and for an hour I was free.

8
first impression

emphasizes boredom

On my return, I learned that Professor Agassiz had been at the Museum, but had gone, and would not return for several hours. My fellow students were too busy to be disturbed by continued conversation. Slowly I drew forth that hideous fish, and with a feeling of desperation again looked at it. I might not use a magnifying glass; instruments of all kinds were interdicted. My two hands, my two eyes, and the fish: it seemed a most limited field. I pushed my finger down its throat to feel how sharp the teeth were. I began to count the scales in the different rows, until I was convinced that was nonsense. At last a happy thought struck me—I would draw the fish; and now with surprise I began to discover new features in the creature. Just then the Professor returned.

9

discovers by drawing

"That is right," said he; "a pencil is one of the best of eyes. I am glad to notice, too, that you keep your specimen wet, and your bottle corked."

10

With these encouraging words, he added: "Well, what is it like?"

11

He listened attentively to my brief rehearsal of the structure of parts whose names were still unknown to me: the fringed gill-arches and movable operculum; the pores of the head, fleshy lips, and lidless eyes; the lateral line, the spinous fins, and forked tail; the compressed and arched body. When I finished, he waited as if expecting more, and then, with an air of disappointment:

12

"You have not looked very carefully; why," he continued more earnestly, "you haven't even seen one of the most conspicuous

13

features of the animal, which is plainly before your eyes as the fish itself; <u>look again, look again!"</u> and he left me to my misery.

<u>I was piqued; I was mortified. Still more of that wretched fish!</u> But now I set myself to my task with a will and discovered one new thing after another, until I saw how just the Professor's criticism had been. The afternoon passed quickly; and when, towards its close, the Professor inquired: **14** *initial reaction*

"Do you see it yet?"   **15**

<u>"No," I replied, "I am certain I do not, but I see how little I saw before."</u>   **16**

"That is next best," said he, earnestly, "but I won't hear you now; put away your fish and go home; perhaps you will be ready with a better answer in the morning. I will examine you before you look at the fish."   **17**

This was disconcerting. Not only must I think of my fish all night, studying, without the object before me, what this unknown but most visible feature might be; but also, without reviewing my discoveries, I must give an exact account of them the next day. I had a bad memory; so I walked home by Charles River in a distracted state, with my two perplexities.   **18**

The cordial greeting from the Professor the next morning was reassuring; here was a man who seemed to be quite as anxious as I that I should see for myself what he saw.   **19**

"Do you perhaps mean," I asked, "that the fish has symmetrical sides with paired organs?"   **20**

His thoroughly pleased "Of course! Of course!" repaid the wakeful hours of the previous night. After he had discoursed most happily and enthusiastically—as he always did—upon the importance of this point, I ventured to ask what I should do next.   **21** *asks for help*

"Oh, look at your fish!" he said, and left me again to my own devices. In a little more than an hour he returned and heard my new catalogue.   **22**

"That is good, that is good!" he repeated; "but that is not all; go on"; and so for three long days he placed that fish before my eyes, forbidding me to look at anything else, or to use any artificial aid. <u>"Look, look, look," was his repeated injunction.</u>   **23** *repeated command*

<u>This was the best entomological lesson I ever had—a lesson whose influence has extended to the details of every subsequent study; a legacy the Professor had left to me, as he has left it to so many others, of inestimable value which we could not buy, with which we cannot part.</u>   **24** *thesis/value of lesson*

A year afterward, some of us were amusing ourselves with chalking outlandish beasts on the Museum blackboard. We drew prancing starfishes; frogs in mortal combat; hydra-headed worms; stately crawfishes, standing on their tails, bearing aloft umbrellas; and grotesque fishes with gaping mouths and staring eyes. The Professor came in shortly after, and was as amused as any at our experiments. He looked at the fishes.   **25** *flash-forward to humorous episode*

"Haemulons, every one of them," he said. "Mr. ——————— drew   26
them."

True; and to this day, if I attempt a fish, I can draw nothing but   27
haemulons.

The fourth day, a second fish of the same group was placed   28
beside the first, and I was bidden to point out the resemblances
and differences between the two; another and another followed,
until the entire family lay before me, and a whole legion of jars
covered the table and surrounding shelves; the odor had become
a pleasant perfume; and even now, the sight of an old, six-inch
worm-eaten cork brings fragrant memories.

The whole group of haemulons was thus brought in review; and,   29
whether engaged upon the dissection of the internal organs, the
preparation and examination of the bony framework, or the description of the various parts, Agassiz's training in the method of
observing facts and their orderly arrangement was ever accompanied by the urgent exhortation not to be content with them.

"Facts are stupid things," he would say, "until brought into con-   30
nection with some general law."   *conclusion*

At the end of eight months, it was almost with reluctance that I   31
left these friends and turned to insects; but what I had gained by
this outside experience has been of greater value than years of
later investigation in my favorite groups.

Understanding Meaning

1. What is the purpose of Scudder's narrative? What is he trying to impress on his reader? What makes this essay more than a simple "first day of school" story?

2. Why did the professor prevent Scudder from using a magnifying glass? What did Professor Agassiz mean when he said "a pencil is one of the best of eyes"?

3. What did Scudder find frustrating about Dr. Agassiz's teaching method?

4. *Critical Thinking:* How effective was Professor Agassiz's nineteenth-century teaching method? By directing a new student to "look again, look again," did he accomplish more than if he had required Scudder to attend a two-hour lecture on the importance of observation? Is close observation a discipline most of us lack? Can you consider detailed observation the first level of critical thinking?

Evaluating Strategy

1. How does Scudder focus his narrative? What details does he leave out?

2. Do his personal reactions to the smell and his frustrations dramatize an extremely passive event? How can a writer create action in a story where the events are mental or emotional?

3. How does Scudder recreate his sense of boredom and frustration?

4. *Blending the Modes:* How does Scudder use *description* of the fish, the specimen bottles, and the smells to provide readers with a clear impression of the laboratory?

Appreciating Language

1. Review Scudder's narrative. How much scientific language does he use in relating his story? What does this say about his readers?

2. This story has little action. Essentially, it is a story about a man interacting with a dead fish. What words add drama or humor to the narrative?

WRITING SUGGESTIONS

1. Apply Professor Agassiz's technique to a common object you might use every day. Spend five minutes carefully examining a clock radio, your watch, or a can of your favorite soft drink. Then write a brief description of what you have observed. List the features you have never noticed before.

2. Professor Agassiz gave his student little direction beyond a simple command. Write an essay relating an experience in which a parent, teacher, superior officer, or boss left you to act on your own. What problems did you encounter? Were you frustrated, afraid, or angry? Was it a learning experience?

3. *Collaborative Writing:* Working with three or four other students, select an object unfamiliar to the group. Allow each member to study the object and make notes. *Compare* your findings, and work to create a single *description* of it. Pay attention to the words you select to create an accurate, objective picture of the object. Notice the details you overlooked that others observed.

JOE KLEIN

Joe Klein (1946–) began his journalism career in the early 1970s. He has been a regular columnist for both *Time* and *Newsweek* and is currently Washington correspondent for *The New Yorker*. His books include *Payback: Five Marines after Vietnam* (1984), *Primary Colors: A Novel of Politics* (1996), and *The Natural: The Misunderstood Presidency of Bill Clinton* (2003). Originally published anonymously, Klein's *Primary Colors* became a best seller and a motion picture starring John Travolta.

How the Teachers Killed a Dream

CONTEXT: *Klein's article, which appeared in* Time *in 2003, explains what happened when a philanthropist tried to endow charter schools in Detroit, an effort opposed by the teachers union.*

WRITER'S NOTE: *Klein briefly summarizes Bob Thompson's business career to focus on the events of the "story that deserves telling."*

In 1999, an unassuming Michigan road builder named Bob 1
Thompson sold his construction company for $442 million, an amount he and his wife Ellen believed was far more than they needed for retirement. His first act, which received national attention, was to distribute $128 million to his employees; about 80 became instant millionaires. Then Thompson decided to donate most of the rest of his money to public education, preferably in Detroit. After doing some research, he offered $200 million to build 15 small, independent public high schools in the inner city. A few weeks ago, Thompson withdrew his offer after the Detroit Federation of Teachers (DFT) led a furious, and scurrilous, campaign against his generosity. The philanthropist is in seclusion now—friends say he is stunned and distressed—but his is a story that deserves telling.

Thompson's research led him to Doug Ross, founder of University 2
Preparatory Academy in Detroit. Ross is a prominent New Democrat policy wonk who served in Bill Clinton's Labor Department, then went home to Michigan and ran unsuccessfully for Governor in 1998. "I learned during the campaign there was one overpowering issue for inner-city parents: to get their kids a college education," Ross told me. "I was tired of theoretical policy junk; I wanted to do something that really mattered. It was clear that urban kids were not responding to the industrial-age assembly-line education model— and there were people around the country who had figured out how to educate kids in a more humane, customized way."

Indeed, recent studies indicate that small schools with special- 3
ized curriculums have much lower dropout rates and higher college-admission rates than traditional education factories. "The cost per pupil is a bit higher," says Patty Stonesifer of the Gates

Foundation, which has become a major supporter of the small-school movement. "But the cost per graduate is much lower—and that really should be our goal."

Ross decided to tackle the toughest education problem: middle school. He started in 2000 with 112 sixth-graders and has added a new grade each year. He had been in business two years when Thompson came to visit. "I had him sit in on some classes," Ross says. "He liked what he saw and asked how he could help. I asked him to build me a high school. He said he'd build one to my specifications and lease it to me for $1 per year—but there had to be accountability. How would he know if I was succeeding or not? I told him my goals—a 90% graduation rate and 90% of graduates going on to college. If I didn't meet those benchmarks after three graduating classes, he could take the school away and let someone else give it a try. He accepted, and I got my high school."   4

This was, essentially, the same deal that Thompson offered Detroit. He didn't specify curriculum or who should run the 15 independent charter schools. Theoretically, any organization—including the teachers' union—was eligible to propose its own system if it presented a plausible plan for a 500-student campus and agreed to Thompson's 90–90 yardstick. New state legislation would be needed to establish the schools. But both Detroit Mayor Kwame Kilpatrick and Governor Jennifer Granholm were thrilled by Thompson's offer—at least until the Detroit Federation of Teachers made plain its opposition. On Sept. 25 the DFT held a work stoppage, which closed the public schools, and staged a rally at the state capitol in Lansing. The mayor withdrew his support, and Thompson withdrew his offer soon after.   5

"The Thompson schools would devastate the critical mass of students who remained in our traditional schools," Janna Garrison, president of the DFT, told me last week. She was referring to the $7,100 per pupil that would travel with each student who chose to go to a charter school (although the state offered the Detroit schools $15 million to compensate for the lost funds). This is a familiar union song—similar to the argument against school vouchers—that grows less powerful as urban schools grow worse. The fact that charter-school teachers in Detroit are not union members probably had something to do with the union's stand too (Ross said he would accept a union if his teachers wanted one). But Garrison took the argument a step further: "If someone from the outside came to Bob Thompson's suburban town and said, 'I'm gonna give you a lot of money for education, but we spend it my way,' they just wouldn't tolerate it."   6

This was thinly veiled racial politics. "You've got a lot of poison in the air," Mayor Kilpatrick told me. "People here are sensitive about white people bossing them around." Kilpatrick insisted he wasn't opposed to more charter schools; his own children go to one. And he was not pleased by the union's role, even though   7 he's a former teacher. "The teachers' union once was a progressive force, but that day has passed," he says. "And it's not coming back until the union realizes that we're going to have to make dramatic changes to improve education here."

Understanding Meaning

1. What agreement did Bob Thompson make with Doug Ross? How did it influence Thompson's later gift to Detroit?
2. What requirements did Thompson establish for his proposed schools?
3. Why did the teachers union oppose Thompson's donation?
4. *Critical Thinking:* Why do you think Klein considered this "a story that deserves telling"? Do the objections of the teachers' union seem valid? Have attitudes toward teachers' unions changed since this article was published in 2003? Would today's politicians and parents demand that their city accept a $200 million donation to their schools?

Evaluating Strategy

1. How does Klein describe Bob Thompson?
2. How does Klein use paired quotations from Detroit's mayor and the president of the teachers' union to make his point?
3. How does Klein use paragraph breaks to advance the narrative?

Appreciating Language

1. Define Doug Ross's phrase "industrial-age assembly-line education model" in your own words. Do you believe it is an accurate description of current schools? Would any of the schools you attended fit this model?
2. What does Klein suggest with the phrase "thinly veiled racial politics"?
3. How would you describe the tone Klein creates? Does his narrative favor one side in this dispute?

WRITING SUGGESTIONS

1. Thompson stipulated that the charter schools achieve a 90% graduation rate and that 90% of the graduates go on to college. Is this a realistic goal for an urban high school? Write an essay that supports or questions the "90–90" rule Thompson required.

2. *Collaborative Writing:* Discuss Klein's essay with a group of students. Do they believe that a donor has the right to establish guidelines for how his or her money is used? Do they think Thompson's plan encouraged excellence or threatened to drain resources from the remaining public schools? Write a short essay stating your group's views. If students have conflicting opinions, consider developing opposing statements.

JOHN REED

John Reed (1887–1920) was born in Portland, Oregon, and graduated from Harvard University in 1910. After touring Europe, Reed settled in New York City, where he pursued a career as a journalist and social activist. He joined the staff of *The Masses* in 1913 and became involved in the labor movement. Later that year *Metropolitan Magazine* sent him to cover the Mexican Revolution. His collected dispatches were published in *Insurgent Mexico* in 1914. Reed reported on the Russian Revolution, which he described in *Ten Days That Shook the World*. An active supporter of the Bolshevik government, he participated in party congresses. Reed died of typhus in Russia and was buried near the Kremlin.

The Rise of Pancho Villa

CONTEXT: *In this passage from* Insurgent Mexico *Reed provides an eyewitness account of Pancho Villa at an awards ceremony then traces his origins and emergence as a revolutionary hero.*

WRITER'S NOTE: *Reed contrasts Villa's appearance with that of his officers and comments on the difficulty in obtaining accurate sources about Villa's past.*

1 It was while Villa was in Chihuahua City, two weeks before the advance on Torreon, that the artillery corps of his army decided to present him with a gold medal for personal heroism on the field.

2 The officers of artillery, in smart blue uniforms faced with black velvet and gold, were solidly banked across one end of the audience hall, with flashing new swords and their gilt-braided hats stiffly held under their arms. From the door of that chamber, around the gallery, down the state staircase, across the grandiose inner court of the palace, and out through the imposing gates to the street, stood a double line of soldiers, with their rifles at present arms. Four regimental bands grouped in one wedged in the crowd. The people of the capital were massed in solid thousands on the Plaza de Armas before the palace.

3 "*Ya viene!*" "Here he comes!" "Viva Villa!" "Viva Madero!" "Villa, the Friend of the Poor!"

4 The roar began at the back of the crowd and swept like fire in heavy growing crescendo until it seemed to toss thousands of hats above their heads. The band in the courtyard struck up the Mexican national air, and Villa came walking down the street.

5 He was dressed in an old plain khaki uniform, with several buttons lacking. He hadn't recently shaved, wore no hat, and his hair had not been brushed. He walked a little pigeon-toed, humped over, with his hands in his trousers pockets. As he entered the aisle between the rigid lines of soldiers he seemed slightly embarrassed, and grinned and nodded to a *compadre* here and there in the ranks. At the foot of the grand staircase, Governor Chao

John Reed, *Insurgent Mexico.* D. Appleton & Co., New York 1914.

and Secretary of State Terrazzas joined him in full-dress uniform. The band threw off all restraint, and, as Villa entered the audience chamber, at a signal from someone in the balcony of the palace, the great throng in the Plaza de Armas uncovered, and all the brilliant crowd of officers in the room saluted stiffly.

It was Napoleonic! 6

Villa hesitated for a minute, pulling his mustache and looking 7 very uncomfortable, finally gravitated toward the throne, which he tested by shaking the arms, and then sat down, with the Governor on his right and the Secretary of State on his left.

Señor Bauche Alcalde stepped forward, raised his right hand to 8 the exact position which Cicero took when denouncing Catiline, and pronounced a short discourse, indicting Villa for personal bravery on the field on six counts, which he mentioned in florid detail. He was followed by the Chief of Artillery, who said: "The army adores you. We will follow you wherever you lead. You can be what you desire in Mexico." Then three other officers spoke in the high-flung, extravagant periods necessary to Mexican oratory. They called him "The Friend of the Poor," "The Invincible General," "The Inspirer of Courage and Patriotism," "The Hope of the Indian Republic." And through it all Villa slouched on the throne, his mouth hanging open, his little shrewd eyes playing around the room. Once or twice he yawned, but for the most part he seemed to be speculating, with some intense interior amusement, like a small boy in church, what it was all about. He knew, of course, that it was the proper thing, and perhaps felt a slight vanity that all this conventional ceremonial was addressed to him. But it bored him just the same.

Finally, with an impressive gesture, Colonel Servin stepped for- 9 ward with the small pasteboard box which held the medal. General Chao nudged Villa, who stood up. The officers applauded violently; the crowd outside cheered; the band in the court burst into a triumphant march.

Villa put out both hands eagerly, like a child for a new toy. He 10 could hardly wait to open the box and see what was inside. An expectant hush fell upon everyone, even the crowd in the square. Villa looked at the medal, scratching his head, and, in a reverent silence, said clearly: "This is a hell of a little thing to give a man for all that heroism you are talking about!" And the bubble of Empire was pricked then and there with a great shout of laughter.

Villa was an outlaw for twenty-two years. When he was only a 11 boy of sixteen, delivering milk in the streets of Chihuahua, he killed a government official and had to take to the mountains. The story is that the official had violated his sister, but it seems probable that Villa killed him on account of his insufferable insolence. That in itself would not have outlawed him long in Mexico, where human life is cheap; but once a refugee he committed the unpardonable crime of stealing cattle from the rich *hacendados*. And from that time to the outbreak of the Madero revolution the Mexican government had a price on his head.

Villa was the son of ignorant peons. He had never been to school. He hadn't the slightest conception of the complexity of civilization, and when he finally came back to it, a mature man of extraordinary native shrewdness, he encountered the twentieth century with the naïve simplicity of a savage. 12

It is almost impossible to procure accurate information about his career as a bandit. There are accounts of outrages he committed in old files of local newspapers and government reports, but those sources are prejudiced, and his name became so prominent as a bandit that every train robbery and holdup and murder in northern Mexico was attributed to Villa. But an immense body of popular legend grew up among the peons around his name. There are many traditional songs and ballads celebrating his exploits—you can hear the shepherds singing them around their fires in the mountains at night, repeating verses handed down by their fathers or composing others extemporaneously. For instance, they tell the story of how Villa, fired by the story of the misery of the peons on the Hacienda of Los Alamos, gathered a small army and descended upon the Big House, which he looted, and distributed the spoils among the poor people. He drove off thousands of cattle from the Terrazzas range and ran them across the border. He would suddenly descend upon a prosperous mine and seize the bullion. When he needed corn he captured a granary belonging to some rich man. He recruited almost openly in the villages far removed from the well-traveled roads and railways, organizing the outlaws of the mountains. Many of the present rebel soldiers used to belong to his band and several of the Constitutionalist generals, like Urbina. His range was confined mostly to southern Chihuahua and northern Durango, but it extended from Coahuila right across the Republic to the State of Sinaloa. 13

His reckless and romantic bravery is the subject of countless poems. They tell, for example, how one of his band named Reza was captured by the *rurales* and bribed to betray Villa. Villa heard of it and sent word into the city of Chihuahua that he was coming for Reza. In broad daylight he entered the city on horseback, took ice cream on the Plaza—the ballad is very explicit on this point— and rode up and down the streets until he found Reza strolling with his sweetheart in the Sunday crowd on the Paseo Bolivar, where he shot him and escaped. In time of famine he fed whole districts, and took care of entire villages evicted by the soldiers under Porfirio Diaz's outrageous land law. Everywhere he was known as The Friend of the Poor. He was the Mexican Robin Hood. 14

In all these years he learned to trust nobody. Often in his secret journeys across the country with one faithful companion he camped in some desolate spot and dismissed his guide; then, leaving a fire burning, he rode all night to get away from the faithful companion. That is how Villa learned the art of war, and in the field today, when the army comes into camp at night, Villa flings the bridle of his horse to an orderly, takes a serape over his shoulder, and sets out for the hills alone. He never seems to sleep. In the dead of night 15 he will appear somewhere along the line of outposts to see if the sentries are on the job; and in the morning he returns from a totally different direction. No one, not even the most trusted officer of his staff, knows the last of his plans until he is ready for action.

From that time to the outbreak of the last revolution, Villa lived   16
in El Paso, Texas, and it was from there that he set out, in April, 1913, to conquer Mexico with four companions, three led horses, two pounds of sugar and coffee, and a pound of salt.

Understanding Meaning

1. What does Villa's physical appearance and behavior reveal about his background and personality?
2. How did his life as a bandit prepare Villa to become a revolutionary?
3. Why did the people see Villa as a hero? How do their songs and legends portray him?
4. *Critical Thinking*: Reed traveled with Villa for four months and came to admire the man he was writing about. Does this narrative portray Villa objectively in your view? Should a journalist attempt to be neutral or openly declare his or her opinion?

Evaluating Strategy

1. How does Reed shift roles from eyewitness to biographer?
2. *Blending the Modes*: How does Reed use contrast to describe Villa's appearance and attitudes?
3. *Critical Thinking*: Reed comments on the difficulty of finding reliable information about Villa's past, questioning the objectivity of press and government reports and the veracity of legendary tales of his bravery. Why is it important for writers to inform readers about the quality of their sources?

Appreciating Language

1. What words and phrases does Reed use to describe Villa? What images do they create?
2. *Critical Thinking*: Look up the word "savage." Has its connotation changed since 1913? Would the term be seen as negative or insulting today?

WRITING SUGGESTIONS

1. Conduct a brief online search of sources about Pancho Villa and write a short objective narrative of his life. How is he portrayed today? If sources provide conflicting accounts, briefly summarize their main points.
2. *Collaborative Writing*: Working with a group of students write a brief biography of a current political figure or celebrity. Note conflicting opinions. Do Democrats and Republicans view this person differently? Has this person developed fans and critics? Your group can decide to write a brief objective summary or develop opposing viewpoints.

RAMON "TIANGUIS" PÉREZ

Ramon "Tianguis" Pérez is an undocumented immigrant and does not release biographical information.

The Fender-Bender

CONTEXT: *This narrative, taken from Pérez's book* Diary of an Undocumented Immigrant, *illustrates how even a minor incident can affect the precarious existence of an undocumented worker. For Pérez, a few pieces of paper stand between a life in America and deportation.*

WRITER'S NOTE: *Pérez omits unimportant details such as the date, intersection, or type of car he was driving.*

One night after work, I drive Rolando's old car to visit some friends, and then head towards home. At a light, I come to a stop too late, leaving the front end of the car poking into the crosswalk. I shift into reverse, but as I am backing up, I strike the van behind me. Its driver immediately gets out to inspect the damage to his vehicle. He's a tall Anglo-Saxon, dressed in a deep blue work uniform. After looking at his car, he walks up to the window of the car I'm driving.   1

"Your driver's license," he says, a little enraged.   2

"I didn't bring it," I tell him.   3

He scratches his head. He is breathing heavily with fury.   4

"Okay," he says. "You park up ahead while I call a patrolman."   5

The idea of calling the police doesn't sound good to me, but the accident is my fault. So I drive around the corner and park at the curb. I turn off the motor and hit the steering wheel with one fist. I don't have a driver's license. I've never applied for one. Nor do I have with me the identification card that I bought in San Antonio. Without immigration papers, without a driving permit, and having hit another car, I feel as if I'm just one step away from Mexico.   6

I get out of the car. The white man comes over and stands right in front of me. He's almost two feet taller.   7

"If you're going to drive, why don't you carry your license?" he asks in an accusatory tone.   8

"I didn't bring it," I say, for lack of any other defense.   9

I look at the damage to his car. It's minor, only a scratch on the paint and a pimple-sized dent.   10

"I'm sorry," I say. "Tell me how much it will cost to fix, and I'll pay for it; that's no problem." I'm talking to him in English, and he seems to understand.   11

"This car isn't mine," he says. "It belongs to the company I work for. I'm sorry, but I've got to report this to the police, so that I don't have to pay for the damage."   12

"That's no problem," I tell him again. "I can pay for it."   13

After we've exchanged these words, he seems less irritated. But   14
he says he'd prefer for the police to come, so that they can report
that the dent wasn't his fault.

While we wait, he walks from one side to the other, looking down   15
the avenue this way and that, hoping that the police will appear.

Then he goes over to the van to look at the dent.   16

"It's not much," he says. "If it was my car, there wouldn't be any   17
problems, and you could go on."

After a few minutes, the long-awaited police car arrives. Only   18
one officer is inside. He's a Chicano, short and of medium com-
plexion, with short, curly hair. On getting out of the car, he walks
straight towards the Anglo.

The two exchange a few words.   19

"Is that him?" he asks, pointing at me.   20

The Anglo nods his head.   21

Speaking in English, the policeman orders me to stand in front   22
of the car and to put my hands on the hood. He searches me and
finds only the car keys and my billfold with a few dollars in it. He
asks for my driver's license.

"I don't have it," I answered in Spanish.   23

He wrinkles his face into a frown, and casting a glance at the   24
Anglo, shakes his head in disapproval of me.

"That's the way these Mexicans are," he says.   25

He turns back towards me, asking for identification. I tell him I   26
don't have that, either.

"You're an illegal, eh?" he says.   27

I won't answer.   28

"An illegal," he says to himself.   29

"Where do you live?" he continues. He's still speaking in English.   30

I tell him my address.   31

"Do you have anything with you to prove that you live at that   32
address?" he asks.

I think for a minute, then realize that in the glove compartment is   33
a letter that my parents sent to me several weeks earlier.

I show him the envelope and he immediately begins to write   34
something in a little book that he carries in his back pocket. He
walks to the back of my car and copies the license plate number.
Then he goes over to his car and talks into his radio. After he talks,
someone answers. Then he asks me for the name of the car's owner.

He goes over to where the Anglo is standing. I can't quite hear what   35
they're saying. But when the two of them go over to look at the dent
in the van, I hear the cop tell the Anglo that if he wants, he can file
charges against me. The Anglo shakes his head and explains what he
had earlier explained to me, about only needing for the police to cer-
tify that he wasn't responsible for the accident. The Anglo says that he
doesn't want to accuse me of anything because the damage is light.

"If you want, I can take him to jail," the cop insists.   36

The Anglo turns him down again.   37

"If you'd rather, we can report him to Immigration," the cop 38
continues.

Just as at the first, I am now almost sure that I'll be making a 39
forced trip to Tijuana. I find myself searching my memory for my
uncle's telephone number, and to my relief, I remember it. I am waiting for the Anglo to say yes, confirming my expectations of the trip.
But instead, he says no, and though I remain silent, I feel appreciation for him. I ask myself why the Chicano is determined to harm
me. I didn't really expect him to favor me, just because we're of the
same ancestry, but on the other hand, once I had admitted my guilt,
I expected him to treat me at least fairly. But even against the white
man's wishes, he's trying to make matters worse for me. I've known
several Chicanos with whom, joking around, I've reminded them
that their roots are in Mexico. But very few of them see it that way.
Several have told me how, when they were children, their parents
would take them to vacation in different states of Mexico, but their
own feeling, they've said, is, "I am an American citizen!" Finally, the
Anglo, with the justifying paper in his hands, says goodbye to the
cop, thanks him for his services, gets into his van, and drives away.

The cop stands in the street in a pensive mood. I imagine that 40
he's trying to think of a way to punish me.

"Put the key in the ignition," he orders me. 41

I do as he says. 42

Then he orders me to roll up the windows and lock the doors. 43

"Now, go on, walking," he says. 44

I go off taking slow steps. The cop gets in his patrol car and stays 45
there, waiting. I turn the corner after two blocks and look out for my
car, but the cop is still parked beside it. I begin looking for a coat
hanger, and after a good while, find one by a curb of the street. I keep
walking, keeping about two blocks away from the car. While I walk, I
bend the coat hanger into the form I'll need. As if I'd called for it, a
speeding car goes past. When it comes to the avenue where my car
is parked, it makes a turn. It is going so fast that its wheels screech as
it rounds the corner. The cop turns on the blinking lights of his patrol
car and leaving black marks on the pavement beneath it, shoots out
to chase the speeder. I go up to my car and with my palms force a
window open a crack. Then I insert the clothes hanger in the crack and
raise the lock lever. It's a simple task, one that I'd already performed.
This wasn't the first time that I'd been locked out of a car, though
always before, it was because I'd forgotten to remove my keys.

Understanding Meaning

1. How serious is the accident?
2. Why does the van driver insist on calling the police?
3. What makes this incident a dangerous one for Pérez?
4. How does Pérez attempt to prevent the van driver from summoning the police?
5. Pérez answers the Chicano patrolman in Spanish. Was this a mistake? How did the officer treat Pérez?

6. *Critical Thinking:* Pérez implies that Chicanos have been offended when he has alluded to their Mexican roots; they insist on being seen as American citizens. What does this say about assimilation and identity? Does the Chicano officer's comments about Mexicans reveal contempt for immigrants? Have other ethnic groups—Jews, Italians, Irish—resented the presence of unassimilated new arrivals from their homelands?

Evaluating Strategy

1. Why is a minor incident like a fender-bender a better device to explain the plight of the undocumented immigrant than a dramatic one?
2. How does Pérez use dialogue to advance the narrative? Are direct quotations more effective than paraphrases? Why or why not?

Appreciating Language

1. What words does Pérez use to minimize the damage caused by the accident?
2. What word choices and images stress the importance of paper documents in the lives of aliens?

WRITING SUGGESTIONS

1. Write a short narrative essay detailing a minor event that provided insight into your life or social conditions. Perhaps you discovered your dependence on energy when your apartment lost power and you could not use your computer, watch television, or even open the garage door to get your car. A simple interaction with a homeless person may have caused you to question your assumptions about the poor.

2. *Collaborative Writing:* Working with a group of students, discuss your views on immigration and "undocumented workers" or "illegal aliens." Take notes and write a brief statement outlining your views. If students disagree, draft opposing statements.

MARTIN GANSBERG

Martin Gansberg (1920–1995) grew up in Brooklyn and worked as a reporter, editor, and book reviewer for the New York Times for over forty years. His 1964 article about a woman who was fatally stabbed while her neighbors watched but failed to call the police stunned readers and caused a national outrage. Psychologists blamed the impact of television for causing what they called "the bystander effect." Editorials cited the incident as sign of urban alienation and social apathy. Critics later claimed that Gansberg's article exaggerated events, and that his dramatic opening line created the false impression that the neighbors passively watched the entire incident from beginning to end. In fact, most witnesses only heard what they thought was a late-night argument, and the most vicious part of the attack occurred out of sight of many neighbors. The man convicted of the 1964 murder of Kitty Genovese, Winston Moseley, remains in prison. He was denied parole for the fifteenth time in November 2011.

Thirty-Eight Who Saw Murder and Didn't Call the Police

CONTEXT: *This article appeared four months after the assassination of President Kennedy, when many commentators and most of the public were troubled by social unrest, crime, violence, and a growing sense that America was, as some put it, a "sick society." Consider how today's cable news commentators and bloggers would react to a similar event.*

WRITER'S NOTE: *Gansberg follows the standard short sentence, short paragraph style used in newspaper articles designed for skimming rather than reading.*

For more than half an hour 38 respectable, law-abiding citizens in Queens watched a killer stalk and stab a woman in three separate attacks in Kew Gardens. 1

Twice their chatter and the sudden glow of their bedroom lights interrupted him and frightened him off. Each time he returned, sought her out, and stabbed her again. Not one person telephoned the police during the assault; one witness called after the woman was dead. 2

That was two weeks ago today. 3

Still shocked is Assistant Chief Inspector Frederick M. Lussen, in charge of the borough's detectives and a veteran of 25 years of homicide investigations. He can give a matter-of-fact recitation on many murders: But the Kew Gardens slaying baffles him—not because it is a murder, but because the "good people" failed to call the police. 4

"As we have reconstructed the crime," he said, "the assailant 5 had three chances to kill this woman during a 35-minute period. He returned twice to complete the job. If we had been called when he first attacked, the woman might not be dead now."

This is what the police say happened beginning at 3:20 A.M. in 6 the staid, middle-class, tree-lined Austin Street area:

Twenty-eight-year-old Catherine Genovese, who was called Kitty 7 by almost everyone in the neighborhood, was returning home from her job as manager of a bar in Hollis. She parked her red Fiat in a lot adjacent to the Kew Gardens Long Island Rail Road Station, facing Mowbray Place. Like many residents of the neighborhood, she had parked there day after day since her arrival from Connecticut a year ago, although the railroad frowns on the practice.

She turned off the lights of her car, locked the door, and started 8 to walk the 100 feet to the entrance of her apartment at 82-70 Austin Street, which is in a Tudor building with stores in the first floor and apartments on the second.

The entrance to the apartment is in the rear of the building be- 9 cause the front is rented to retail stores. At night the quiet neighborhood is shrouded in the slumbering darkness that marks most residential areas.

Miss Genovese noticed a man at the far end of the lot, near a 10 seven-story apartment house at 82-40 Austin Street. She halted. Then, nervously, she headed up Austin Street toward Lefferts Boulevard, where there is a call box to the 102nd Police Precinct in nearby Richmond Hill.

She got as far as a streetlight in front of a bookstore before 11 the man grabbed her. She screamed. Lights went on in the 10-story apartment house at 82-67 Austin Street, which faces the bookstore. Windows slid open and voices punctuated the early-morning stillness.

Miss Genovese screamed: "Oh, my God, he stabbed me! Please 12 help me! Please help me!"

From one of the upper windows in the apartment house, a man 13 called down: "Let that girl alone!"

The assailant looked up at him, shrugged, and walked down 14 Austin Street toward a white sedan parked a short distance away. Miss Genovese struggled to her feet.

Lights went out. The killer returned to Miss Genovese, now try- 15 ing to make her way around the side of the building by the parking lot to get to her apartment. The assailant stabbed her again.

"I'm dying!" she shrieked. "I'm dying!" 16

Windows were opened again, and lights went on in many apart- 17 ments. The assailant got into his car and drove away. Miss Genovese staggered to her feet. A city bus, 0–10, the Lefferts Boulevard line to Kennedy International Airport, passed. It was 3:35 A.M.

The assailant returned. By then, Miss Genovese had crawled to 18 the back of the building, where the freshly painted brown doors to the apartment house held out hope for safety. The killer tried the first door; she wasn't there. At the second door, 82-62 Austin Street, he saw her slumped on the floor at the foot of the stairs. He stabbed her a third time—fatally.

It was 3:50 by the time the police received their first call, from a 19 man who was a neighbor of Miss Genovese. In two minutes they were at the scene. The neighbor, a 70-year-old woman, and another woman were the only persons on the street. Nobody else came forward.

The man explained that he had called the police after much de- 20 liberation. He had phoned a friend in Nassau County for advice, and then he had crossed the roof of the building to the apartment of the elderly woman to get her to make the call.

"I didn't want to get involved," he sheepishly told police. 21

Six days later, the police arrested Winston Moseley, a 29-year- 22 old business machine operator, and charged him with homicide. Moseley had no previous record. He is married, has two children and owns a home at 133-19 Sutter Avenue, South Ozone Park, Queens. On Wednesday, a court committed him to Kings County Hospital for psychiatric observation.

When questioned by the police, Moseley also said that he 23 had slain Mrs. Annie May Johnson, 24, of 146-12 133rd Avenue, Jamaica, on Feb. 29 and Barbara Kralik, 15, of 174-17 140th Avenue, Springfield Gardens, last July. In the Kralik case, the police are holding Alvin L. Mitchell, who is said to have confessed to that slaying.

The police stressed how simple it would have been to have got- 24 ten in touch with them. "A phone call," said one of the detectives, "would have done it." The police may be reached by dialing "0" for operator or SPring 7-3100.

Today witnesses from the neighborhood, which is made up of 25 one-family homes in the $35,000 to $60,000 range with the exception of the two apartment houses near the railroad station, find it difficult to explain why they didn't call the police.

A housewife, knowingly if quite casually, said, "We thought it 26 was a lovers' quarrel." A husband and wife both said, "Frankly, we were afraid." They seemed aware of the fact that events might have been different. A distraught woman, wiping her hands in her apron, said, "I didn't want my husband to get involved."

One couple, now willing to talk about that night, said they heard 27 the first screams. The husband looked thoughtfully at the bookstore where the killer first grabbed Miss Genovese.

"We went to the window to see what was happening," he said, 28 "but the light from our bedroom made it difficult to see the street." The wife, still apprehensive, added: "I put out the light and we were able to see better."

Asked why they hadn't called the police, she shrugged and re- 29 plied: "I don't know."

A man peeked out from a slight opening in the doorway to his 30 apartment and rattled off an account of the killer's second attack.

Why hadn't he called the police at the time? "I was tired," he said without emotion. "I went back to bed."

It was 4:25 A.M. when the ambulance arrived to take the body 31 of Miss Genovese. It drove off. "Then," a solemn police detective said, "the people came out."

Understanding Meaning

1. What details of this murder transformed it from a local crime story into an event that captured national attention?
2. How did the duration of the attack add to the significance of the neighbors' failure to call the police?
3. What reasons did the residents of Kew Gardens give for not taking action?
4. Gansberg mentions that William Moseley was a married homeowner with two children. Would these details surprise readers? Do most people have stereotyped notions about violent criminals?
5. Gansberg describes the neighborhood as being middle class. Is this significant? Why or why not?
6. *Critical Thinking:* Do you think this article describes an isolated event or captures commonplace attitudes and behaviors? Would most people call 911 today? Have you or anyone you know reported a crime in progress? Do you believe that urban life and television violence have desensitized people to crime and led them to passively watch rather than help? Do you think the same situation could occur in a small town? Is it a fact of modern life or human nature that leads people to avoid getting involved?

Evaluating Strategy

1. What impact does the first line have? Although it states facts and not a point of view, can you consider it a thesis statement? Why or why not?
2. Gansberg includes details such as times and addresses. Why is this expected in a newspaper article? Does the author's inclusion of objective facts give the article greater authority?
3. Gansberg includes several direct quotations by neighbors explaining their actions that night. Are direct quotes more effective than paraphrases? Why?
4. *Critical Thinking:* Does the opening line imply that all the witnesses passively watched the attack from beginning to end? Do writers, especially reporters, have an ethical responsibility to be accurate? Do you believe some journalists distort or exaggerate events to make their stories more dramatic?

Appreciating Language

1. Gansberg uses passive voice to describe the actions of neighbors that night, stating "lights went out" and "windows opened." What impact does this have?
2. What verbs does Gansberg use to describe the victim's calls for help? What effect do they have?
3. What words does Gansberg use to describe the witnesses after the attack?
4. Gansberg uses the word "shrugged" to describe both the killer and a witness. Do you think this was deliberate? Why or why not?

WRITING SUGGESTIONS

1. Write an objective narrative about a recent incident you observed and reconstruct an accurate timeline of events. Include details suited for a newspaper report about times, dates, locations, and participants.

2. *Collaborative Writing:* Discuss Gansberg's article with a group of students. Are they aware of similar incidents? Have they observed people's reaction to the plight of a person in distress? Do they believe most people are apathetic to victims of violence? Why or why not? Use division to organize your group's responses. If the group comes up with opposing viewpoints, consider using comparison to prepare contrasting statements.

Blending the Modes
MICHAEL PATRICK MACDONALD

Michael Patrick MacDonald (1966–) was born in Boston and grew up in South Boston's Old Colony housing project, located in one of the country's poorest white urban communities. He helped launch Boston's gun buyback program, founded the South Boston Vigil Group, and worked with several anti-violence organizations. In 1999 he published his autobiography *All Souls*, which received the American Book Award.

Returning to Southie

CONTEXT: *In this section from* All Souls, *MacDonald explains how returning to his violence-scarred neighborhood reminded him both of the deaths of his brothers and his love for Southie, the "best place in the world."*

WRITER'S NOTE: *MacDonald uses direct quotations to highlight his statements to the reporter who is "horrified" by his remarks.*

I was back in Southie, "the best place in the world," as Ma used 1 to say before the kids died. That's what we call them now, "the kids." Even when we want to say their names, we sometimes get confused about who's dead and who's alive in my family. After so many deaths, Ma just started to call my four brothers "the kids" when we talked about going to see them at the cemetery. But I don't go anymore. They're not at the cemetery; I never could find them there. When I accepted the fact that I couldn't feel them at the graves, I figured it must be because they were in heaven, or the spirit world, or whatever you want to call it. The only things I kept from the funerals were the mass cards that said, "Do not stand at my grave and weep, I am not there, I do not sleep. I am the stars that shine through the night," and so on. I figured that was the best way to look at it. There are seven of us kids still alive, and sometimes I'm not even sure if that's true.

I came back to Southie in the summer of 1994, after everyone in 2 my family had either died or moved to the mountains of Colorado. I'd moved to downtown Boston after Ma left in 1990, and was pulled one night to wander through Southie. I walked from Columbia Point Project, where I was born, to the Old Colony Project where I grew up, in the "Lower End," as we called it. On that August night, after four years of staying away, I walked the streets of my old neighborhood, and finally found the kids. In my memory of that night I can see them clear as day. *They're right here,* I thought, and it was an ecstatic feeling. I cried, and felt alive again myself. I passed by the outskirts of Old Colony, and it all came back to me—the kids were joined in my mind by so many others I'd last seen in caskets at Jackie

O'Brien's Funeral Parlor. They were all here now, all of my neighbors and friends who had died young from violence, drugs, and from the other deadly things we'd been taught didn't happen in Southie.

We thought we were in the best place in the world in this neighbor- 3 hood, in the all-Irish housing projects where everyone claimed to be Irish even if his name was Spinnoli. We were proud to be from here, as proud as we were to be Irish. We didn't want to own the problems that took the lives of my brothers and of so many others like them: poverty, crime, drugs those were black things that happened in the ghettos of Roxbury. Southie was Boston's proud Irish neighborhood.

On this night in Southie, the kids were all here once again—I 4 could feel them. The only problem was no one else in the neigh- borhood could. My old neighbors were going on with their nightly business—wheeling and dealing on the corners, drinking on the stoops, yelling up to windows, looking for a way to get by, or something to fight for. Just like the old days in this small world within a world. It was like a family reunion to me. That's what we considered each other in Southie—family. There was always this feeling that we were protected, as if the whole neighborhood was watching our backs for threats, watching for all the enemies we could never really define. No "outsiders" could mess with us. So we had no reason to leave, and nothing ever to leave for. It was a good feeling to be back in Southie that night, surrounded by my family and neighbors; and I remember hating having to cross over the Broadway Bridge again, having to leave the peninsula neigh- borhood and go back to my apartment in downtown Boston.

Nor long after, I got a call at Citizens for Safety, where I'd been 5 working on antiviolence efforts across Boston since 1990. It was a reporter from *U.S. News & World Report* who was working on an article about what they were calling "the white under class." The re- porter had found through demographic studies that Southie showed three census tracts with the highest concentration of poor whites in America. The part of Southie he was referring to was the Lower End, my own neighborhood at the bottom of the steep hills of City Point, which was the more middle-class section with nicer views of the har- bor. The magazine's findings were based on rates of joblessness and single-parent female-headed households. Nearly three-fourths of the families in the Lower End had no fathers. Eighty-five percent of Old Colony collected welfare. The reporter wasn't telling me anything new—I was just stunned that someone was taking notice. No one had ever seemed to believe me or to care when I told them about the amount of poverty and social problems where I grew up. Liberals were usually the ones working on social problems, and they never seemed to be able to fit urban poor whites into their world view, which tended to see blacks as the persistent dependent and their own white selves as provider. Whatever race guilt they were holding onto, Southie's poor couldn't do a thing for their consciences. After our violent response to court-ordered busing in the 1970s, Southie was labeled as the white racist oppressor. I saw how that label worked to take the blame away from those able to leave the city and drive back to all-white suburban towns at the end of the day.

Outsiders were also used to the image, put out by our own poli-   6
ticians, that we were a working-class and middle-class community with the lowest rates of social problems anywhere, and that we wanted to keep it that way by not letting blacks in with all their problems. Growing up, I felt alone in thinking this attitude was an injustice to all the Southie people I knew who'd been murdered. Then there were all the suicides that no one wanted to talk about. And all the bank robberies and truck hijackings, and the number of addicts walking down Broadway, and the people limping around or in wheelchairs, victims of violence.

The reporter asked me if I knew anyone in Southie he could   7
talk to. He wanted to see if the socioeconomic conditions in the neighborhood had some of the same results evident in the highly concentrated black ghettos of America. I called some people, but most of them didn't want to talk. We were all used to the media writing about us only when something racial happened, ever since the neighborhood had erupted in antibusing riots during the seventies. Senator Billy Bulger, president of the Massachusetts Senate, had always reminded us of how unfair the media was with its attacks on South Boston. He told us never to trust them again. No news was good news. And his brother, neighborhood drug lord James "Whitey" Bulger, had liked it better that way. Whitey probably figured that all the shootings in the nearby black neighborhood of Roxbury, and all the activists willing to talk over there, would keep the media busy. They wouldn't meddle in Southie as long as we weren't as stupid and disorganized as Roxbury's drug dealers. And by the late eighties, murders in Southie had started to be less visible even to us in the community. Word around town was that Whitey didn't allow bodies to be left on the streets anymore; instead, people went missing, and sometimes were found hogtied out in the suburbs, or washed up on the shores of Dorchester Bay. The ability of our clean-cut gangsters to keep up appearances complemented our own need to deny the truth. Bad guy stuff seemed to happen less often within the protected turf of South Boston. Maybe a few suicides here and there, or maybe an addict "scumbag," but that was the victim's own problem. Must have come from a bad family—nothing to do with "Our Beautiful World," as the South Boston Tribune was used to calling it, above pictures of church bazaars, bake sales, christenings, and weddings.

I agreed to take the reporter on a tour through Southie. We   8
stayed in the car, because I was too nervous to walk around with an "outsider" in a suit. It was bad enough that I was driving his rented sports car. People in Southie usually drove big Chevys, or when they were in with "the boys," as we called our revered gangsters, they'd upgrade to an even bigger Caddy or Lincoln Continental. I wore sunglasses and a scally cap, the traditional local cap once favored by hard-working Irish immigrants and longshoremen, and

more recently made popular by tough guys and wannabes. I disguised myself so I wouldn't be identified collaborating with an outsider. Everyone knew I was an activist working to reduce violence and crime. Bur when they saw me on the news, I was usually organizing things over in Roxbury or Dorchester, the black places that my neighbors thanked God they didn't live in. "That stuff would never happen in Southie," a mother in Old Colony once told me. Her own son had been run over by gangsters for selling cocaine on their turf without paying up.

When I rode around the Lower End with the reporter, I pointed   9
to the landmarks of my childhood: St. Augustine's grammar school, where Ma struggled to keep up with tuition payments so we wouldn't be bused to black neighborhoods; the Boys and Girls Club, where I was on the swim team with my brother Kevin; Darius Court, where I played and watched the busing riots; the liquor store with a giant green shamrock painted on it, where Whitey Bulger ran the Southie drug trade; the sidewalk where my sister had crashed from a project rooftop after a fight over drugs; and St. Augustine's Church, down whose front steps I'd helped carry my brothers' heavy caskets. "I miss this place," I said to him. He looked horrified but kept scribbling notes as I went on about this being the best place in the world. "I always had a sense of security here, a sense of belonging that I've never felt anywhere else," I explained. "There was always a feeling that someone would watch your back. Sure, bad things happened to my family, and to so many of my neighbors and friends, but there was never a sense that we were victims. This place was ours, it was all we ever knew, and it was all ours."

Talking to this stranger, driving through the streets of Southie,   10
and saying these things confused me. I thought about how much I'd hated this place when I'd learned that everything I'd just heard myself say about Southie loyalty and pride was a big myth, one that fit well into the schemes of career politicians and their gangster relatives. I thought about how I'd felt betrayed when my brothers ended up among all the other ghosts in our town who were looked up to when they were alive, and shrugged off when they were dead, as punks only asking for trouble.

I didn't know now if I loved or hated this place. All those beauti-   11
ful dreams and nightmares of my life were competing in the narrow littered streets of Old Colony Project. Over there, on my old front stoop at 8 Patterson Way, were the eccentric mothers, throwing their arms around and telling wild stories. Standing on the corners were the natural-born comedians making everyone laugh. Then there were the teenagers wearing their flashy clothes, "pimp" gear, as we called it. And little kids running in packs, having the time of their lives in a world that was all theirs. But I also saw the junkies, the depressed and lonely mothers of people who'd died, the wounded, the drug dealers, and a known murderer accepted by everyone as warmly as they accepted anything else in the familiar landscape. "I'm thinking of moving back," I told the reporter.

Understanding Meaning

1. How does MacDonald describe his boyhood neighborhood? Why did his mother proclaim it to be the "best place in the world"?
2. What happened to MacDonald's brothers and sister?
3. Why did MacDonald feel uncomfortable being seen with a stranger in Southie? What does this suggest about the residents?
4. What positive elements did MacDonald see in Southie?
5. *Critical Thinking*: What does this story have to do with race? Does a white ghetto indicate that problems of poverty, drugs, and crime cannot be blamed on racism? Do the residents in Southie engage in denial, refusing to see how much they have in common with poor African Americans?

Evaluating Strategy

1. What impact does the first line have?
2. How does MacDonald use touring the neighborhood with a reporter as device to advance the narrative?
3. What does MacDonald's final statement reveal about his attitude toward the community? What draws him back to a neighborhood that claimed the lives of four brothers and a sister?

Appreciating Language

1. Why does MacDonald's family refer to four lost brothers as "the kids"?
2. Residents of Southie call local gangsters "the boys." What does this suggest about their attitude toward criminals?
3. MacDonald tells the reporter he always felt a sense of security in Southie. How does he appear to define this term? How can "security" be associated with a neighborhood ravaged by crime, violence, and drugs?

WRITING SUGGESTIONS

1. Write a brief narrative about a place that shaped your life—a home, a school, your first workplace, a military base, or your first apartment. Rather than describe physical details, focus on what you learned there or how it influenced your values.

2. *Collaborative Writing:* Discuss this essay with a group of students and list reasons why society appears to overlook the plight of poor whites. Why do both liberals and conservatives appear to deny that white neighborhoods share many of the problems that plague minority communities?

Writing Beyond the Classroom

ROISIN REARDON

Roisin Reardon is a special events coordinator in charge of booking, organizing, and supervising business meetings, conventions, receptions, and exhibitions for a major hotel in midtown Manhattan. Like many professionals who deal with the public, she has been trained to document events that might lead to legal actions against her employer.

Incident Report

CONTEXT: *Following a disturbance requiring a call to the police, Reardon documented her observations and actions for a report sent to the hotel's legal department.*

WRITER'S NOTE: *Reardon attempts to establish an objective timeline to explain the event and present herself as a responsible professional.*

Metro Hotel
New York

INCIDENT REPORT
July 23, 2011
Sandra Berman
Legal Department

RE: Disturbance at Central Assurance Annual Meeting, Continental Ballroom 7/22/11 7:30–7:45 P.M.

At approximately 7:30 last evening I left my office and encountered a disturbance outside the Continental Ballroom, where Central Assurance was holding its annual meeting. A woman was shouting at a female security guard, insisting she be allowed into the ballroom. I approached this woman and asked her to identify herself. She refused and demanded entry into the meeting. I politely asked her to show a pass or a room key. Central Assurance required that security only allow invited guests with passes into the meeting. This woman, who finally identified herself as Sharon Engleman, never produced any credentials.

I politely asked that she lower her voice and leave the premises unless she could produce either a pass to the meeting or a hotel key. At this point George Muir of Central Assurance came from the ballroom, identified himself, and explained to me that Ms. Engleman had been part of a class action lawsuit and was demanding to address the shareholders. He stated that their attorneys had told both her and her attorneys that she had no legal right to appear at a shareholders' meeting because she was neither an employee of Central Assurance nor a stockholder.

At this point Ms. Engleman began screaming obscenities and demanded to distribute flyers to the shareholders. I told her she could leave her flyers on the table outside the ballroom. She then pushed both Mr. Muir and myself.

The security guard called for assistance. Ted Wilson of hotel security arrived and immediately asked Ms. Engleman to leave the hotel. When she refused, he called the police. At approximately 7:45 P.M. two NYPD officers arrived and escorted Ms. Engleman from the building. On her way out she shouted obscenities at me and threatened to sue the hotel.

I reported this incident to Frank Canon, Vice President of Central Assurance, when the meeting ended at 10:35 P.M.

Please contact me for further information on this matter.

Roisin Reardon
Special Events Coordinator

Understanding Meaning

1. What is the purpose of Reardon's narrative?
2. What role does Reardon play in her narrative?
3. Who is the immediate and potential extended audience for this document?
4. *Critical Thinking:* How might the threat of a lawsuit compel a professional to document his or her actions?

Evaluating Strategy

1. How can a writer deal with events that do not have a clearly established time reference?
2. Are there missing details that you believe should be included? Does this narrative leave you with questions about the incident?

Appreciating Language

1. Why is word choice important in reports that might be read by judges and juries?
2. Why do you think Reardon repeats the word "politely" to describe her actions? What words does she use to characterize Sharon Engleman?
3. Is the language largely objective or subjective in your view?

WRITING SUGGESTIONS

1. Create an objective report of a dramatic situation you witnessed, such as a car accident, demonstration, rally, athletic event, or live concert.
2. *Collaborative Writing:* Working with a group of students, read the incident report and discuss your impressions. Did the hotel employee appear to act professionally and responsibly? What image does she project in her report? Do you see anything in the tone or style of the report that seems inappropriate? Why or why not? Write a brief report using comparison to organize the positive and negative comments of your group.

Responding to Images

New Orleans following Hurricane Katrina, September 2005

1. What are your first reactions to this photograph? Do you recall seeing images like this one on television following Hurricane Katrina? How did you and those around you respond to them?
2. How do you interpret the people's expressions and gestures?
3. Would this image be better suited to accompany an objective or a subjective narrative about the aftermath of the hurricane? Why?
4. *Visual Analysis:* How does the distress in the faces in the foreground contrast with the Superdome looming behind them? What image did the Superdome have? What did it represent? Did it become an ironic image following the hurricane?
5. Write a short narrative about two people in this picture. Add dialogue, inventing a conversation between the pair.
6. *Collaborative Writing:* Work with a group of students to create a caption for this photograph. Have each member write a caption, and then discuss each one. Note how word choices imply different meanings or interpretations of the event. What words do students use to describe the people and the situation?

Strategies FOR WRITING NARRATION

1. **Determine your purpose.** Does your narrative have a goal beyond simply telling a story? What details or evidence do readers need to accept your point of view? Before writing down a list of events, ask yourself why this experience was important. What do you want your readers to learn? What do you want them to remember?

2. **Define your role.** As a narrator, you can write in first person, either as the major participant in or as a witness to events. Alternatively, you can use third person for greater objectivity, inserting personal opinions if desired.

3. **Consider your audience.** What are your readers' needs and expectations? How much background material will you have to supply? Which events will the audience find most impressive?

4. **Review the discipline or writing situation.** If you are writing a narrative report as an employee or agent of an organization, study samples to determine how you should present your story.

5. **Identify the beginning and end of your narrative.** You may find it helpful to place background information in a separate foreword or introduction, and limit comments on the ending to an afterword. This can allow the body of the paper to focus on a specific chain of events.

6. **Narrow the focus of your narrative if needed.** Your goal is not to tell readers everything that happened during a particular experience. If you are writing about the day your grandmother died, for instance, do not feel obligated to summarize the entire day, which might simply produce a list of events. You might develop a more interesting paper by selecting one episode, such as breaking the news to a relative or driving to the hospital. Think of your narrative as a clip from a movie, not the entire film.

7. **Select a chronological pattern.** After reviewing the context of the narrative, determine which pattern would be most effective for your purpose—using a straight chronology, opening with a mid- or turning point, or presenting the final events first.

8. **Include dialogue to dramatize interactions between people.**

Revising and Editing

1. **Make use of transitional statements.** In revising your paper, make sure you have included clear transitional statements to advance the narrative and prevent confusion. Statements such as "later that day" or "two weeks later" can help readers follow the passage of time. Clear transitions are important if you alter chronological order with flashbacks and flash-forwards.

2. **Use consistent tense in narrating events.** Stories can be related in past or present tense. Avoid illogical shifts between past and present tense, as in "I *woke* up late and *see* it is snowing."

Suggested Topics for Writing Narration

General Assignments

Write a narrative on any of the following topics. Your narrative may contain passages making use of other modes, such as definition or comparison. Choose your narrative structure carefully, and avoid including minor details that add little to the story line. Use flashbacks and flash-forwards carefully. Transitional statements, paragraphing, and line breaks can help clarify changes in the chronology. Remember, a narrative can include dialogue, which can dramatize a conversation.

1. A job interview
2. Moving into your first dorm room or apartment
3. The events that led you to take a major action—quit a job, end a relationship, or join an organization
4. A sporting event you played in or observed (you may wish to limit the narrative to a single play)
5. A brief history of an organization you belong to or a company you work for
6. An event that placed you in danger
7. An experience that led you to change your opinion about a friend or family member
8. A brief biography of a person you admire or the history of a musical group
9. The worst day of your high school or college career
10. An accident or medical emergency—focus on creating a clear, minute-by-minute chronology

Writing in Context

1. Imagine you are participating in an experiment in which psychologists ask you to write a journal recording your experiences in college. Specifically, the researchers are interested in measuring stressors students face—deadlines, lack of sleep, conflicts with jobs, financial pressures. Write a diary for a week, detailing instances when you experience stress. Be as objective as possible.
2. Write an email to a friend relating the events of a typical day in college. Select details your friend will find humorous or interesting.
3. Preserve on paper a favorite story told by your grandparents or other relatives. Include background details and identify characters.
4. You are accused of committing a crime last Tuesday. To establish an alibi, create a detailed log to the best of your recollection of the day's events and your movements.

Student Paper: Narration

This paper was written in response to the following assignment:

> Write a 350- to 500-word narrative essay based on personal experience or observation. Limit your topic, select details, and use figurative language to recreate the sights, sounds, smells, and moods you experienced.

First Draft with Instructor's Comments

Intro. is weak, the second paragraph makes a stronger opening.

This paper is about a trip I made last spring to San Diego to visit my aunt and uncle. I saw a lot during that week but the most meaningful part I remember was a one day trip to Mexico. I think it really changed the whole way I think about things. Sometimes <u>its</u> the minor things you remember as important. | *Run-on* / *it's*

I got off the San Diego Trolley and I knew that I was going to start an adventure. Tijuana. As I neared the entrance to cross the <u>boarder</u> there is a priest with a plastic bowl. With a picture of some kids saying "feed Tijuana's homeless children." Yeah, right, I think to myself, just another scam, this guy probably isn't even a priest. | *Run-on/This would make a better opening* / *Avoid shift from past to present*

Tijuana. Just the name of the city brings back a special smell. A smell that you will only know if you have been there. It only takes one time and you can relate to what I am trying to say to you. A smell that will permeate your olfactory senses forever. The smell was terrible. | *Fragment* / *Fragment*

As I cross the <u>boarder</u> the first thing that hits you is the smell I just mentioned. Then you witness the terrible suffering and horrible poverty. It makes you realize how terrible many people have it in this world. | *Avoid shift from "I" to "you"* / *Add details*

Once I get past the few blocks of poverty and handed out all I can, I wandered upon a busy little plaza where <u>you</u> could see all kinds of people having fun and partying. | *Avoid shift from "I" to "you"*

As I continued my journey, I reached a bridge. The bridge was horrible. | *Add details*

Toward the midspan of the bridge, I experienced one of the most touching moments in my whole life, one of those happy ones where it's not clear <u>weather</u> you should laugh or cry. There was this little child playing the accordion and another one playing a guitar. | *Sp*

It was getting to be late, and I <u>started to get ready</u> to leave. But this time as I passed the priest I filled his plastic bowl with the rest of my money. | *Wordy*

Like I stated, this one afternoon is what I remember from my whole trip. I still think about those people and the way they lived their lives. We as Americans take way too much for granted and never realize how bad other people have it in this world today. | *Good image for the ending* / *Wordy, delete last paragraph, repetitive*

Revised Draft

Spare Change

As I stepped off the San Diego Trolley, I knew I was going to embark on a great adventure. Tijuana. As I neared the entrance to the border, I saw a priest with a plastic bowl next to a picture of sad-looking kids. The caption of the picture said, "Feed Tijuana's homeless children." Yeah, right, I thought, just another scam. This man, I was convinced, probably was not even a priest.

Tijuana. Just the name of the city brings back a distinct smell, one that will permeate my olfactory senses forever. A thousand different scents compounded into one. It was the overwhelming smell of fast food, sweat, sewage, and tears.

As I crossed the border the first thing that hit me was the smell. Then I witnessed countless victims of unforgettable poverty and suffering. A man without legs sat on a worn cushion begging for money. A ragged woman with her children huddled around her stood on the corner and waved an old grease-stained paper cup at passersby. When I paused to put a dollar bill in her cup, I was immediately surrounded by dirty-faced children dressed in Salvation Army hand-me-downs, ripped pants, and mismatched shoes begging for money. Their hands searched my pockets for change, anything to buy food for the night.

Once I got past the few blocks of human suffering and handed out all I could, I wandered upon a busy little plaza. This place was reasonably clean and clear of trash. Deafening music poured from a row of flashy clubs, and I saw dozens of drunken young Americans stumbling around. Tourists, who had spent the day in the numerous outlet stores, trudged past, distressed and exhausted from a day of hard shopping. They lugged huge plastic bags jammed with discount jeans, shoes, purses, and blouses. A score of children held out little packs of colored Chiclets, a local gum they sold to Americans at whatever price the tourists could haggle them down to. It is pathetic to think tourists feel the need to haggle over the price of gum with a child, but this is Tijuana.

Tourists come from all over the world to drink, to shop, to haggle 5 with children. This is just the way it is, the way it will always be. As I continued my journey, I reached a bridge. The bridge was horrible. Along the sides there was trash and rubbish. Toward the midspan of the bridge, I experienced one of the most touching moments of my life, one of those happy ones where I didn't know if I should shed a tear from happiness or out of despair. A small boy played an accordion and another played a guitar. He was singing a Spanish song, well actually, it sounded like he was screaming as his compadre strummed a guitar. He had a little cup in front of him, and I threw a coin into it. He just smiled and kept singing. I turned around and left, but as I passed the priest at the border, I filled his plastic bowl with the rest of my change.

Questions for Review and Revision

1. This student was assigned a 350- to 500-word narrative in a composition class. How successfully does this paper meet this goal?

2. How does the student open and close the narrative? Does the opening grab attention? Does the conclusion make a powerful statement?

3. What devices does the student use to advance the chronology?

4. Most writers focus on visual details. This student includes the senses of sound and smell as well. How effective is this approach?

5. Did the student follow the instructor's suggestions? Do you see habitual errors the student should identify to improve future assignments?

6. Read the paper aloud. What changes would you make? Can you detect passages that would benefit from revision or rewording?

WRITING SUGGESTIONS

1. Using this essay as a model, write a short narrative about a trip that exposed you to another culture. Try to recapture the sights, sounds, and smells that characterized the experience.

2. *Collaborative Writing:* Ask a group of students to assign a grade to this essay and then explain their evaluations. What strengths and weaknesses does the group identify?

EVALUATING NARRATION CHECKLIST

Before submitting your paper, review these points:

1. Does the narrative have a clear focus?
2. Can readers follow the chronology of events?
3. Do you write in a consistent tense or time? Does your paper contain illogical shifts from past to present?
4. Does the narrative flow evenly, or is it bogged down with unnecessary detail?
5. Does your narrative maintain a consistent point of view? Do you switch from first to third person without reason?
6. Does your narrative suit your purpose, reader, discipline, and situation?

Accompanying English CourseMate Resources

Visit English CourseMate at **www.cengagebrain.com** to find many helpful resources and study tools for this chapter.

Description: Presenting Impressions

5

What Is Description?

Description captures the essence of a person, place, object, or condition through sensory details. Nearly all writing requires description. Before you can narrate events, compare, classify, or analyze, you must provide readers with a clear picture of your subject. Dramatists open plays with set and character descriptions. Homicide detectives begin reports with descriptions of crime scenes. Before proposing expanding an airport, the writers of a government study must first describe congestion in the existing facility.

The way writers select and present details depends on context. Carl T. Rowan's article "Unforgettable Miss Bessie" (page 117), published in *Reader's Digest*, describes an influential teacher to a general audience reading for human interest:

> She was only about five feet tall and probably never weighed more than 110 pounds, but Miss Bessie was a towering presence in the classroom. She was the only woman tough enough to make me read *Beowulf* and think for a few foolish days that I liked it. From 1938 to 1942, when I attended Bernard High School in McMinnville, Tenn., she taught me English, history, civics—and a lot more than I realized.

Rowan's description includes facts about the teacher's height and weight, the courses she taught, and the name of the school. But Rowan's focus is her "towering presence" and the impact she had in shaping his life. Writing in the first person, Rowan places himself in the essay to build rapport with his readers.

This intimate portrait contrasts sharply with the description of Lee Harvey Oswald included in an FBI report:

> OSWALD was advised questions were intended to obtain his complete physical description and background. Upon repetition of the question as to his present employment, he furnished the same without further discussion.

RACE	White
SEX	Male
DATE OF BIRTH	October 18, 1939
PLACE OF BIRTH	New Orleans, Louisiana
HEIGHT	5'9"
WEIGHT	140 pounds
HAIR	Medium brown, worn medium length, needs haircut
EYES	Blue-gray

Aside from noting that Oswald needed a haircut, the FBI agent never offers personal impressions and presents his observations in cold, factual statements. Unlike Rowan, who is writing to a general audience reading for entertainment, the FBI agent is preparing a report for specialized readers collecting evidence for a criminal investigation. The writer's statements will be scrutinized by investigators and attorneys. The inclusion of any personal impressions or colorful phrases would be unprofessional and subject to challenge.

The differences between the descriptions of Miss Bessie and Lee Harvey Oswald illustrate the differences between **subjective** and **objective description**.

Objective and Subjective Description

The purpose of **objective description** is to inform readers by accurately reporting factual details. Its language attempts to provide a realistic photograph of what people, places, things, and conditions are like. Research papers, business and government reports, and newspaper articles are objective. Objective description is effective when the writer's purpose is to present readers with information required to make an evaluation or decision. In many instances, it does not attempt to arouse a reader's interest since it is often written in response to reader demand.

Objective description focuses on data and observable detail. A business website provides a fact-based description of Chicago:

> Chicago is the seat of Cook County in NE Illinois on Lake Michigan. The city encompasses an area of 237 square miles with 26 miles of lake front. It is the third largest city in the United States with 2.7 million residents

and a metropolitan population of ten million. Incorporated in 1837, Chicago is the largest city in the Midwest and a major communications, transportation, commercial, and financial center. For over a century it has been the most important rail hub in North America. Chicago's O' Hare Airport is the second busiest airport in the United States. The central business district, known as the Loop, includes the Merchandise Mart, once the largest building in the world. The 110-story Willis Tower (formerly the Sears Tower) is the tallest building in the Western Hemisphere.

In contrast to objective description, **subjective description** creates impressions through sensory details and imagery. Short stories, novels, essays, and opinion pieces use highly personal sensory details to create an individual sense of the subject. Instead of presenting photographic realism, subjective description paints scenes, creates moods, or generates emotional responses. Providing accurate information is less important than giving readers a "feel" for the subject.

Attempting to capture his impression of Chicago, novelist John Rechy compares the city to an expectant mother:

> You get the impression that once Chicago was like a constantly pregnant woman, uneasy in her pregnancy because she has miscarried so often. After its rise as a frontier town, plush big time madams, adventurers, and soon the titanic rise of the millionaires, the city's subsequent soaring population—all gave more than a hint that Chicago might easily become America's First City. But that title went unquestionably to New York. Brazenly, its skyscrapers, twice as tall as any in the Midwest city, symbolically invaded the sky. Chicago, in squat self-consciousness, bowed out. It became the Second City....

Rechy uses imagery and unconventional syntax to create a highly personalized view of the city. In the context of this essay written for a literary magazine, impression is more important than accuracy. Exact numbers, dates, and statistics are irrelevant to his purpose. The writer's goal in subjective description is to share a feeling, not provide information.

Many writers blend the realism of objective description with the impressionistic details of subjective description to create striking portraits, such as Russell Miller's depiction of Chicago's State Street:

> Summer 1983. State Street, "that great street," is a dirty, desolate, and depressing street for most of its length. It runs straight and potholed from the Chicago city line, up through the black ghettos of the South Side, an aching wasteland of derelict factories pitted with broken windows, instant slum apartment blocks, vandalized playgrounds encased in chain-linked fencing, and vacant lots where weeds sprout gamely from the rubble and from the rusting hulks of abandoned automobiles. Those shops that remain open are protected by barricades of steel mesh. One or two men occupy every doorway, staring sullenly onto the street, heedless of the taunting cluster of skyscrapers to the north.

In this passage, details such as "vandalized playgrounds" are interwoven with expressions granting human emotions to inanimate objects, so wastelands are "aching" and skyscrapers "taunting." Blended descriptions such as this one are useful in strengthening subjective views with factual details. This style of writing is used by

From "Chicago, Savage City" by John Rechy in The Moderns, ed. Leroi Jones, New York: Corinth Books, 1963, p. 141.
From Bunny: The Real Story of Playboy by Russell Miller, New York: New American Library, 1984, p 1.

journalists and freelance authors writing to audiences who may be reading for both enjoyment and information.

Whether objective or subjective, all descriptive writing communicates through a careful selection and clear presentation of facts or impressions that serve the writer's purpose and impress readers.

The Language of Description

Words have power. The impact of descriptive writing depends on diction, the writer's choice of words. Whether your description is objective, subjective, or a blend, the words you select should be *accurate, effective,* and *appropriate.* In choosing words, consider your purpose, readers, and discipline.

USE WORDS ACCURATELY

Many words are easily confused. Should a patient's heart rate be monitored "continually," meaning at regular intervals such as once an hour, or "continuously," meaning without interruption? Is the city council planning to "adapt" or "adopt" a handgun ban? Some of the numerous pairs of frequently misused words follow:

EASILY CONFUSED WORDS

allusion	An indirect reference
illusion	A false or imaginary impression
infer	To interpret
imply	To suggest
conscience	A sense of moral or ethical conduct
conscious	To be awake or aware of something
principle	Basic law, rule, or concept
principal	Something or someone important, as in school principal
affect	To change or influence
effect	A result; to achieve

When writing, consult a dictionary or review the usage section of a handbook to make sure you are using the correct word.

USE WORDS EFFECTIVELY

You can improve the impact of your writing by using specific words, eliminating unnecessary words and diluted verbs, and avoiding clichés and inflated phrases. Reading a paper aloud can help you "hear" wordy and ineffective sentences.

USE SPECIFIC WORDS

Specific words are direct and understandable. They communicate more information and make clearer impressions than do vague, abstract words:

ABSTRACT	**SPECIFIC**
motor vehicle	pickup truck
modest suburban home	three-bedroom colonial

human resources	employees
protective headgear	helmet
residential rental unit	studio apartment

ELIMINATE UNNECESSARY WORDS

Avoid cluttering your description with words that add little or no meaning:

WORDY	IMPROVED
at this point in time	now
few in number	few
consensus of opinion	consensus
thunderstorm activity	thunderstorms
winter months	winter
went to go to the store	went to the store
there are good jobs out there	there are good jobs
my favorite game to play	my favorite game
started to clean my room	cleaned my room
round-shaped	round

AVOID DILUTED VERBS

Verbs convey action. Do not dilute their meaning by turning them into wordy phrases that weaken their impact and obscure the action they describe:

DILUTED VERB	IMPROVED
achieve purification	purify
render an examination of	examine
are found to be in agreement	agree
conduct an analysis	analyze

AVOID CLICHÉS AND INFLATED PHRASES

Description uses figurative language such as *similes* (comparisons using *like* or *as*) and *metaphors* (direct comparisons). To be effective, figurative language should create fresh and appropriate impressions. Avoid *clichés* (overly used expressions) and inflated phrases that distort through exaggeration:

CLICHÉ/INFLATED	IMPROVED
back in the day	in the past
pretty as a picture	attractive

straight from the shoulder	direct
as plain as day	obvious
terrible disaster	disaster
in the whole world today	today

Use Words Appropriately

Understand the Roles of Denotation and Connotation

Denotation refers to a word's basic meaning. The words *home, residence*, and *domicile* all refer to where a person lives. Each has the same basic meaning or denotation. **Connotation** refers to a word's implied or suggested meanings. The word *home* evokes thoughts of family, friends, and favorite belongings. *Domicile*, on the other hand, has a legalistic sound devoid of personal associations.

Connotations often reflect the writer's purpose and opinion. A resort cabin can be called a "rustic cottage" or a "seedy shack" depending on a person's point of view. Someone who shops for bargains can be praised for being "frugal" or ridiculed for being "cheap." A developer can be applauded for "draining a swamp to build homes" or condemned for "destroying a wetland to construct a subdivision." The Supreme Court's *Roe v. Wade* decision on abortion can be labeled a "*protection* that assures women's rights" or a "*restriction* that prevents states from passing laws." The following pairs of words and phrases have the same basic meaning or denotation, but their connotations create different impressions:

young	inexperienced
traditional	old-fashioned
brave	reckless
casual	sloppy
illegal aliens	undocumented workers
residential care facility	nursing home
unintended landing	plane crash
lied	misspoke
drilling for oil	exploring for energy
tax break	tax relief
low wages	competitive wages

BE CONSCIOUS OF ETHICAL ISSUES WITH CONNOTATION

Words can be selected to dramatize or minimize an event or situation. This raises ethical issues. Because words such as *accident* and *explosion* might alarm the public, nuclear regulations substitute the terms *event* and *rapid disassembly*. When the space shuttle *Challenger* exploded in mid-air, the National Aeronautics and Space

Administration (NASA) referred to a *major malfunction*. Writers in all disciplines have to weigh the moral implications of the words they choose.

Writing Techniques: DESCRIPTION

Dominant Impressions

The goal of description is not always to record every fact. Writers highlight significant features and delete minor details to create dominant impressions that give their essays focus. In "The Bomb" (page 105), Lansing Lamont captures the fearful nature of the first atomic bomb by describing it as a "monster" that terrifies its creators. To emphasize the devastation of the San Francisco earthquake, Jack London uses repetition, telling readers, "Its industrial section is wiped out. Its business section is wiped out. Its social and residential section is wiped out" (page xxx). In description writers sometimes omit a thesis statement, instead using dominant impressions to express their views.

Action and Dialogue

Descriptions can become a dull list of facts and observations, so writers portray their subjects in action and bring people to life by having them speak. In "My Ecumenical Father" (page 113) Jose Burciaga describes his father's values, then demonstrates them through a series of brief narratives. Carl Rowan reveals the impact a teacher had on his life by including her words in direct quotations (page 117). Readers are more engaged when writers "show" rather than simply "tell."

Organization

To prevent a description from becoming a collection of random facts, writers organize details to give an essay a sense of direction. In "Sounds of the City" (page 110), James Tuite arranges details on a time line, showing how the sounds of New York vary throughout the day.

Strategies FOR READING DESCRIPTIONS

While reading the descriptions in this chapter, keep these questions in mind.

Understanding Meaning

1. What is the author's goal—to inform, enlighten, share personal observations, or provide information demanded by others? What is the writer's role? Is he or she writing from a personal or professional perspective?

2. What is the intended audience—general or specific readers? How much knowledge does the author assume his or her readers have? Are technical terms defined? Does the description appear to have a special focus?

3. What is the nature of the discipline, discourse community, or writing situation? Is the description objective or subjective? Does the original source of the description (newsmagazine, scientific journal, or government document) reveal something about context?

Evaluating Strategy

1. What details does the writer select? Does he or she seem to ignore or minimize some details?

2. Does the description establish a dominant impression? Which details support this impression?

3. How are details organized? Does the author use a particular method of grouping observations?

Appreciating Language

1. What level of language does the writer employ? Are technical terms used without explanation?

2. Does the language include connotations that shape reader reaction to the subject?

LANSING LAMONT

Lansing Lamont was born in New York City and was educated at Harvard College and the Columbia School of Journalism. He was a national political correspondent for *Time* magazine from 1961 to 1968. He became deputy chief of *Time*'s London bureau and later served as the magazine's Ottawa bureau chief. His best-selling book *Day of Trinity* (1965) told the story behind the development of the atom bomb during World War II. His second book, *Campus Shock* (1979), examined American college life in the 1970s.

The Bomb

CONTEXT: *In this section from* Day of Trinity *Lamont describes the first atomic bomb before its detonation in the New Mexico desert in July 1945.*

WRITER'S NOTE: *Lamont includes both objective facts and subjective impressions to characterize the bomb as a "monster."*

The bomb rested in its cradle. 1

It <u>slept</u> upon a steel-supported oakwood platform, inside a sheet-metal shack 103 feet above the ground: a <u>bloated black squid girdled with cables and leechlike detonators</u>, each tamped with enough explosive to spark simultaneously, within a millionth of a second, the final conflagration. <u>Tentacles</u> emerged from the <u>squid</u> in a harness of wires connecting the detonators to a shiny aluminum tank, the firing unit. 2 *subjective animal imagery*

Stripped of its coils, the bomb weighed 10,000 pounds. Its teardrop dimensions were 4½ feet wide by 10½ feet long. Its guts contained two layers of wedge-shaped high-explosive blocks surrounding an inner core of precisely machined nuclear ingots that lay, as one scientist described them, like diamonds in an immense wad of cotton. These ingots were made from a metal called plutonium. 3 *objective facts*

At the <u>heart</u> of the bomb, buried inside the layers of explosive and plutonium, lay the ultimate key to its success or failure, a metallic sphere no bigger than a ping-pong ball that even twenty years later would still be regarded a state secret: the initiator. 4

Within five seconds the initiator would trigger the sequence that hundreds of shadows had gathered to watch that dawn. The bomb would either fizzle to a premature death or shatteringly christen a new era on earth. 5

Weeks, months, years of toil had gone into it. 6

The nation's finest brains and leadership, the cream of its scientific and engineering force, plus two billion dollars from the taxpayers had built the squat monster on the tower for this very moment. Yet it had been no labor of love. There was not the mildest affection for it. 7

Other instruments of war bore dashing or maidenly names: Britain's "Spitfires"; the "Flying Tigers"; the "Gravel Gerties" and "Gypsy Rose Lees" that clanked across North Africa or blitzed 8

"The Bomb" from THE DAY OF TRINITY by Lansing Lamont pp 11–12 (Antheneum, 1985 copyright Lansing Lamont. Reprinted by permission.

bridgeheads on the Rhine; even the Germans' "Big Bertha" of World War I; and, soon, the Superfortress "Enola Gay" of Hiroshima, deliverer of an atomic bundle called "Little Boy."

The test bomb had no colorful nickname. One day its spawn would be known as "Fat Man" (after Churchill). But now its identity was cloaked in a welter of impersonal terms: "the thing," "the beast," "the device" and its Washington pseudonym, "S-1." The scientists, most of whom called it simply "the gadget," had handled it gently and daintily, like the baby it was—but out of respect, not fondness. One wrong jolt of the volatile melon inside its Duralumin frame could precipitate the collision of radioactive masses and a slow, agonizing death from radiation. Or instant vaporization. **9**

The <u>monster</u> engendered the sort of fear that had caused one young scientist to break down the evening before and be escorted promptly from the site to a psychiatric ward; and another, far older and wiser, a Nobel Prize winner, to murmur, as he waited in his trench, "I'm scared witless, absolutely witless." **10** *use of witness quotation*

Understanding Meaning

1. What dominant impression does Lamont make?
2. How did the scientists feel about the bomb they created?
3. What impact does the final quotation have?
4. *Critical Thinking*: Lamont notes that, unlike other weapons of WWII, the bomb was not given a colorful nickname. What does this imply? How does it set this weapon apart from the others that bore heroic or even whimsical names?

Evaluating Strategy

1. How does Lamont blend objective details and subjective impressions?
2. How does Lamont demonstrate how the scientists felt about the weapon?

Appreciating Language

1. What words create Lamont's dominant impression?
2. What role does animal imagery play in the description? How does it make the bomb appear as a living "monster"?

WRITING SUGGESTIONS

1. Write a short description of an object like a car, house, or computer and use subjective impressions to bring it to life by comparing it to a person or animal. You might describe an old car as a "beast" or a guitar as a "best friend."

2. *Collaborative Writing*: Work with a group of students and write a short essay describing the threat of nuclear terrorism. What would happen if terrorists were able to place a nuclear weapon in a large American city? How would the nation and the public respond to a sudden, unexpected explosion that claimed a hundred thousand lives?

JACK LONDON

Jack London (1876–1916) was born in San Francisco and worked a number of jobs before going to sea in 1893. Returning to California, London became a reporter, novelist, and social activist. In 1897 he traveled to the Klondike to prospect for gold. His experiences in the Yukon inspired his best known books *Call of the Wild* and *White Fang*. After reporting on the 1905 Russo-Japanese War, London wrote an eyewitness account of the 1906 San Francisco earthquake for *Collier's* magazine. His later books include *The Iron Heel*, *The Cruise of the Snark*, and *The Valley of the Moon*.

The San Francisco Earthquake

CONTEXT: *On April 18, 1906, San Francisco was devastated by an earthquake. Fires from broken gas mains erupted throughout the city and burned over 25,000 buildings, including Jack London's boyhood home. Further destruction was caused by the dynamiting of surviving structures to create fire breaks. Historians estimate that 700 to 3,000 people were killed, and nearly three-fourths of the residents were made homeless.*

WRITER'S NOTE: *London uses graphic visual details to convey the scope of the disaster and repeats words and phrases for dramatic emphasis.*

1 The earthquake shook down in San Francisco hundreds of thousands of dollars worth of walls and chimneys. But the conflagration that followed burned up hundreds of millions of dollars' worth of property. There is no estimating within hundreds of millions the actual damage wrought. Not in history has a modern imperial city been so completely destroyed. San Francisco is gone. Nothing remains of it but memories and a fringe of dwelling-houses on its outskirts. Its industrial section is wiped out. Its business section is wiped out. Its social and residential section is wiped out. The factories and warehouses, the great stores and newspaper buildings, the hotels and the palaces of the nabobs, are all gone. Remains only the fringe of dwelling houses on the outskirts of what was once San Francisco.

2 Within an hour after the earthquake shock the smoke of San Francisco's burning was a lurid tower visible a hundred miles away. And for three days and nights this lurid tower swayed in the sky, reddening the sun, darkening the day, and filling the land with smoke.

3 On Wednesday morning at a quarter past five came the earthquake. A minute later the flames were leaping upward. In a dozen different quarters south of Market Street, in the working-class ghetto, and in the factories, fires started. There was no opposing the flames. There was no organization, no communication.

Jack London, "The Story of an Eye-Witness" *Collier's* May 6, 1906.

All the cunning adjustments of a twentieth century city had been smashed by the earthquake. The streets were humped into ridges and depressions, and piled with the debris of fallen walls. The steel rails were twisted into perpendicular and horizontal angles. The telephone and telegraph systems were disrupted. And the great water-mains had burst. All the shrewd contrivances and safeguards of man had been thrown out of gear by thirty seconds' twitching of the earth-crust.

The Fire Made its Own Draft

By Wednesday afternoon, inside of twelve hours, half the heart 4 of the city was gone. At that time I watched the vast conflagration from out on the bay. It was dead calm. Not a flicker of wind stirred. Yet from every side wind was pouring in upon the city. East, west, north, and south, strong winds were blowing upon the doomed city. The heated air rising made an enormous suck. Thus did the fire of itself build its own colossal chimney through the atmosphere. Day and night this dead calm continued, and yet, near to the flames, the wind was often half a gale, so mighty was the suck.

Wednesday night saw the destruction of the very heart of the 5 city. Dynamite was lavishly used, and many of San Francisco's proudest structures were crumbled by man himself into ruins, but there was no withstanding the onrush of the flames. Time and again successful stands were made by the fire-fighters, and every time the flames flanked around on either side or came up from the rear, and turned to defeat the hard-won victory.

An enumeration of the buildings destroyed would be a directory 6 of San Francisco. An enumeration of the buildings undestroyed would be a line and several addresses. An enumeration of the deeds of heroism would stock a library and bankrupt the Carnegie medal fund. An enumeration of the dead will never be made. All vestiges of them were destroyed by the flames. The number of the victims of the earthquake will never be known. South of Market Street, where the loss of life was particularly heavy, was the first to catch fire.

Remarkable as it may seem, Wednesday night while the whole 7 city crashed and roared into ruin, was a quiet night. There were no crowds. There was no shouting and yelling. There was no hysteria, no disorder. I passed Wednesday night in the path of the advancing flames, and in all those terrible hours I saw not one woman who wept, not one man who was excited, not one person who was in the slightest degree panic stricken.

Before the flames, throughout the night, fled tens of thousands 8 of homeless ones. Some were wrapped in blankets. Others carried bundles of bedding and dear household treasures. Sometimes a whole family was harnessed to a carriage or delivery wagon that was weighted down with their possessions. Baby buggies, toy wagons, and go-carts were used as trucks, while every other person was dragging a trunk. Yet everybody was gracious. The most perfect courtesy obtained. Never in all San Francisco's history, were her people so kind and courteous as on this night of terror.

Understanding Meaning

1. How extensive was the damage to San Francisco?
2. How did failed infrastructure–ruptured gas and water mains–contribute to the disaster?
3. Why were firefighting efforts futile?
4. Why, in London's view, will the death toll never be known?
5. How does London describe the reactions of the survivors?

Evaluating Strategy

1. In paragraphs 1 and 6 London repeats phrases several times for emphasis. Is this an effective way for writers to drive home their points? Can too much repetition become monotonous?
2. What role does London play in the description? In observing the destruction of his hometown, is he an objective observer or subjective participant?
3. *Critical Thinking*: London was writing when most people got their news from print journalism. Was it more important in that era to provide readers with visual details? Do print reporters and bloggers today focus more on facts and analysis, assuming their readers have seen video coverage of major events?

Appreciating Language

1. How would you characterize the tone and style of London's article? Does it seem suited for a popular magazine? Why or why not?
2. What words and phrases does London use to demonstrate the extent of the damage?
3. *Critical Thinking*: Would it more accurate to name this disaster "The San Francisco Fire"? Why or why not?

WRITING SUGGESTIONS

1. Using London's article as a model, describe a neighborhood or other area that has been altered by an natural, economic, or demographic change or event.
2. *Collaborative Writing*: Working with a group of students select a recent dramatic event and write a one paragraph description for an audience with no access to visual images. What details can you include to demonstrate the size or significance of the incident? Read the passage aloud and ask members to comment on the accuracy and impact of word choices.

JAMES TUITE

James Tuite (1921–2012) was born in the Greenpoint neighborhood of Brooklyn, New York, and began writing as a teenager, working for the *Greenpoint Weekly Star.* While serving in World War II, he edited two army newspapers. After the war he worked for the *Providence Journal* and founded *The Catholic War Veteran.* From 1948 until his retirement in 1984, he worked for the *New York Times,* writing thousands of news stories and serving as the newspaper's sports editor for many years. His books include *Snowmobiles and Snowmobiling* (1969) and *How to Watch Sports on TV* (1976).

The Sounds of the City

CONTEXT: *Originally published in* The New York Times *in 1966, Tuite's soundscape of New York City has become a classic description essay, building impressions through sounds rather than sights.*

WRITER'S NOTE: *Tuite demonstrates the variety of New York sounds through verbs—rattle, growl, screech, bellow, chirp.*

New York is a city of sounds: muted sounds and shrill sounds; shattering sounds and soothing sounds; urgent sounds and aimless sounds. The cliff dwellers of Manhattan—who would be racked by the silence of the lonely woods—do not hear these sounds because they are constant and eternally urban. 1

The visitor to the city can hear them, though, just as some animals can hear a high-pitched whistle inaudible to humans. To the casual caller to Manhattan, lying restive and sleepless in a hotel twenty or thirty floors above the street, they tell a story as fascinating as life itself. And back of the sounds broods the silence . . . 2

There are few sounds so exciting in Manhattan as those of fire apparatus dashing through the night. At the outset there is the tentative hint of the first-due company bullying its way through midtown traffic. Now a fire whistle from the opposite direction affirms that trouble is, indeed, afoot. In seconds, other sirens converging from other streets help the skytop listener focus on the scene of excitement. 3

But he can only hear and not see, and imagination takes flight. Are the flames and smoke gushing from windows not far away? Are victims trapped there, crying out for help? Is it a conflagration, or only a trash-basket fire? Or, perhaps, it is merely a false alarm. 4

The questions go unanswered and the urgency of the moment dissolves. Now the mind and the ear detect the snarling, arrogant bickering of automobile horns. People in a hurry. Taxicabs blaring, insisting on their checkered priority. 5

Even the taxi horns dwindle down to a precocious few in the gray and pink moments of dawn. Suddenly there is another sound, a morning sound that taunts the memory for recognition. The 6 growl of a predatory monster? No, just garbage trucks that have begun a day of scavenging.

Trash cans rattle outside restaurants. Metallic jaws on sanitation trucks gulp and masticate the residue of daily living, then digest it with a satisfied groan of gears. 7

The sounds of the new day are businesslike. The growl of buses, so scattered and distant at night, becomes a demanding part of the traffic bedlam. An occasional jet or helicopter injects an exclamation point from an unexpected quarter. When the wind is right, the vibrant bellow of an ocean liner can be heard. 8

The sounds of the day are as jarring as the glare of a sun that outlines the canyons of midtown in drab relief. A pneumatic drill frays countless nerves with its rat-a-tat-tat, for dig they must to perpetuate the city's dizzy motion. After each screech of brakes there is a moment of suspension, of waiting for the thud or crash that never seems to follow. 9

The whistles of traffic policemen and hotel doormen chirp from all sides, like birds calling for their mates across a frenzied aviary. And all of these sounds are adult sounds, for childish laughter has no place in these canyons. 10

Night falls again, the cycle is complete, but there is no surcease from sound. For the beautiful dreamers, perhaps, the "sounds of the rude world heard in the day, lulled by the moonlight have all passed away," but this is not so in the city. 11

Too many New Yorkers accept the sounds about them as bland parts of everyday existence. They seldom stop to listen to the sounds, to think about them, to be appalled or enchanted by them. In the big city, sounds are life. 12

Understanding Meaning

1. How do visitors respond differently to the sounds of the city than New Yorkers do?
2. What activities do various sounds indicate?
3. How does the sound of a siren affect a listener's imagination? Do sounds have greater impact than sights? Do people invent images to match the sounds they hear?
4. *Critical Thinking*: What does Tuite suggest by stating, "all these sounds are adult sounds, for childish laughter has no place in these canyons"? What does this imply about Manhattan and the children who live there?

Evaluating Strategy

1. How does Tuite organize details?
2. Tuite compares trash trucks to animals in paragraph 9, referring to machines with "metallic jaws" that "gulp" and "digest." Is this an effective device? Can colorful or clever imagery become distracting?
3. Tuite states that the "sounds of the day are as jarring as the glare of a sun that outlines the canyons of midtown in drab relief." Is it effective to compare a sound to a visual image? Why or why not?

Appreciating Language

1. Tuite uses the word "sounds" seven times in the first sentence. Does repeating a word or phrase add emphasis or does it risk boring or irritating readers?

2. *Critical Thinking*: Most writers provide visual images. How is word choice different when the sensory impressions come from sound, taste, or touch? Are there fewer words to express these senses?

WRITING SUGGESTIONS

1. Using Tuite's essay as a model, create a soundscape for your campus, neighborhood, home, or workplace. Consider organizing the sounds by revealing how they change throughout the day or season or from room to room or street to street.

2. *Collaborative Writing:* Working with a group of students, select a location everyone is familiar with and have each person focus on a single sense— sight, sound, touch, smell. Compare lists of details, and then write a brief description that blends the most significant sensory details. Consider if writers too often rely on visual details alone to describe a subject.

JOSÉ ANTONIO BURCIAGA

José Antonio Burciaga *(1940–1996)* grew up in a synagogue in El Paso, where his father worked as a custodian. Burciaga served in the U.S. Air Force and then attended the University of Texas, where he earned a fine arts degree. Pursuing both art and litera-ture, Burciaga was also active in Chicano affairs. His artwork was first exhibited in 1974. Two years later he published a collection of poetry called *Restless Serpents*, followed by a variety of other publications.

My Ecumenical Father

CONTEXT: *This essay, which first appeared in* Drink Cultura, *describes Burciaga's father, a man who maintained his ties to Mexi-can culture while taking pride in his American citizenship and devel-oping a fierce devotion to the Jewish faith.*

WRITER'S NOTE: *Burciaga ignores details about his father's appearance to focus on his values.*

1 ¡Feliz Navidad! Merry Christmas! Happy Hanukkah! As a child, my season's greetings were tricultural—Mexicano, Anglo, and Jewish.

2 Our devoutly Catholic parents raised three sons and three daughters in the basement of a Jewish synagogue, Congregation B'nai Zion in El Paso, Texas. José Cruz Burciaga was the custodian and *shabbat goy*. A shabbat goy is Yiddish for a Gentile who, on the Sabbath, performs certain tasks forbidden to Jews under or-thodox law.

3 Every year around Christmas time, my father would take the menorah out and polish it. The eight-branched candleholder symbolizes Hanukkah, the commemoration of the first recorded war of liberation in that part of the world.

4 In 164 B.C., the Jewish nation rebelled against Antiochus IV Epiphanes, who had attempted to introduce pagan idols into the temples. When the temple was reconquered by the Jews, there was only one day's supply of oil for the Eternal Light in the temple. By a miracle, the oil lasted eight days.

5 My father was not only in charge of the menorah, but for ten years he also made sure the Eternal Light remained lit.

6 As children we were made aware of the differences and joys of Hanukkah, Christmas and Navidad. We were taught to respect each celebration, even if they conflicted. For example, the Christ-mas carols taught in school. We learned the song about the twelve days of Christmas, though I never understood what the hell a par-tridge was doing in a pear tree in the middle of December.

7 We also learned a German song about a boy named Tom and a bomb—*O Tannenbaum*. We even learned a song in the obscure

language of Latin, called "Adeste Fideles," which reminded me of, *Ahh! d'este fideo*, a Mexican pasta soup. Though 75 percent of our class was Mexican American, we never sang a Christmas song in *Español*. Spanish was forbidden.

So our mother—a former teacher—taught us "Silent Night" in 8 Spanish: *Noche de paz, noche de amor*. It was so much more po-etic and inspirational.

While the rest of El Paso celebrated Christmas, Congregation 9 B'nai Zion celebrated Hanukkah. We picked up Yiddish and learned a Hebrew prayer of thanksgiving. My brothers and I would help my father hang the Hanukkah decorations.

At night, after the services, the whole family would rush across 10 the border to Juarez and celebrate the *posadas*, which take place for nine days before Christmas. They are a communal re-enactment of Joseph and Mary's search for shelter, just before Jesus was born.

To the *posadas* we took candles and candy left over from the 11 Hanukkah celebrations. The next day we'd be back at St. Patrick's School singing, "I'm dreaming of a white Christmas."

One day I stopped dreaming of the white Christmases depicted 12 on greeting cards. An old immigrant from Israel taught me Jesus was born in desert country just like that of the West Texas town of El Paso.

On Christmas Eve, my father would dress like Santa Claus and 13 deliver gifts to his children, nephews, godchildren and the little kids in orphanages. The next day, minus his disguise, he would take us to Juarez, where we delivered gifts to the poor in the streets.

My father never forgot his childhood poverty and forever sought 14 to help the less fortunate. He taught us to measure wealth not in money but in terms of love, spirit, charity and culture.

We were taught to respect the Jewish faith and culture. On 15 the Day of Atonement, when the whole congregation fasted, my mother did not cook, lest the food odors distract. The respect was mutual. No one ever complained about the large picture of Jesus in our living room.

Through my father, leftover food from B'nai B'rith luncheons, Bar 16 Mitzvahs, and Bat Mitzvahs found its way to Catholic or Baptist churches or orphanages. Floral arrangements in the temple that surrounded a Jewish wedding *huppah* canopy many times found a second home at the altar of St. Patrick's Cathedral or San Juan Convent School. Surplus furniture, including old temple pews, found their way to a missionary Baptist Church in *El Segundo Barrio*.

It was not uncommon to come home from school at lunchtime 17 and find an uncle priest, an aunt nun, and a Baptist minister visit-ing our home at the same time that the Rabbi would knock on our door. It was just as natural to find the president of B'nai Zion eating beans and tortillas in our kitchen.

My father literally risked his life for the Jewish faith. Twice he was 18 assaulted by burglars who broke in at night. Once he was stabbed in the hand.

Another time he stayed up all night guarding the sacred Torahs 19
after anti-Semites threatened the congregation. He never philoso-
phized about his ecumenism; he just lived it.

Cruz, as most called him, was a man of great humor, a hot 20
temper, and a passion for dance. He lived the Mexican Revolution and rode the rails during the Depression. One of his proudest moments came when he became a U.S. citizen.

On September 23, 1985, sixteen months after my mother passed 21
away, my father followed. Like his life, his death was also ecumenical. The funeral was held at Our Lady of Peace, where a priest said
the mass in English. My cousins played mandolin and sang in Spanish. The president of B'nai Zion Congregation said a prayer in Hebrew. Members of the congregation sat with Catholics and Baptists.

Observing Jewish custom, the cortege passed by the synagogue 22
one last time. Fittingly, father was laid to rest on the Sabbath. At
the cemetery, in a very Mexican tradition, my brothers, sisters, and
I each kissed a handful of dirt and threw it on the casket.

I once had the opportunity to describe father's life to the late, 23
great Jewish American writer Bernard Malamud. His only comment
was, "Only in America!"

Understanding Meaning

1. What is a *shabbat goy?*
2. How did the author's family show respect to the congregation?
3. How did the author's family manage to blend respect for several cultures?
4. Burciaga points out that though he learned German and Latin songs in school, he was not allowed to sing in Spanish. What does this reveal about the educational system?
5. Why is the description of his father's funeral central to Burciaga's story?
6. *Critical Thinking:* What values does the ecumenical father represent? Are these values rare in our society? What lesson could this essay teach?

Evaluating Strategy

1. Would Bernard Malamud's comment, "Only in America," make a good title for this essay? Why or why not?
2. Burciaga offers an explanation of Hanukkah. What does this suggest about his intended audience?
3. *Blending the Modes:* Can this description be seen as an extended definition of "ecumenical"?

Appreciating Language

1. How did Burciaga's father define "wealth"?
2. Read through Burciaga's description and highlight his use of non-English words and phrases. How does he define them? What impact do all these unfamiliar words have?

WRITING SUGGESTIONS

1. Burciaga builds his description largely through details about his father's actions and behavior. Write a few paragraphs describing a person you know well. Try to capture what you consider the person's principal attributes by describing actions that reveal his or her values.

2. *Collaborative Writing:* Discuss this essay with a group of students. What do readers find most striking about this Mexican immigrant? Are his attitudes valuable to society? Is multiculturalism a trend today? Have each member write a few paragraphs explaining the significance of this essay. Read the responses aloud, and work to blend as many as possible in a short analysis of this essay.

CARL T. ROWAN

Carl T. Rowan (1925–2000) was born in Tennessee and received degrees from Oberlin College and the University of Minnesota. He worked for years as a columnist for the *Minneapolis Tribune* and the *Chicago Sun Times*, expressing his views on a variety of issues, especially race relations. Rowan also served as the director of the United States Information Agency and was the ambassador to Finland.

Unforgettable Miss Bessie

CONTEXT: *This article describing a schoolteacher originally appeared in* Reader's Digest, *where Rowan served as an editor. Rowan's account is personal, and much of his description focuses on the impact this teacher had on him and other disadvantaged students.*

WRITER'S NOTE: *Rowan's comment that Miss Bessie was "a blessing to children and an asset to the nation" (paragraph 8) serves as a thesis summarizing the goal of his essay.*

1   She was only about five feet tall and probably never weighed more than 110 pounds, but Miss Bessie was a towering presence in the classroom. She was the only woman tough enough to make me read *Beowulf* and think for a few foolish days that I liked it. From 1938 to 1942, when I attended Bernard High School in McMinnville, Tenn., she taught me English, history, civics—and a lot more than I realized.

2   I shall never forget the day she scolded me into reading *Beowulf*.

3   "But Miss Bessie," I complained, "I ain't much interested in it."

4   Her large brown eyes became daggerish slits. "Boy," she said, "how dare you say 'ain't' to me! I've taught you better than that."

5   "Miss Bessie," I pleaded, "I'm trying to make first-string end on the football team, and if I go around saying 'it isn't' and 'they aren't,' the guys are gonna laugh me off the squad."

6   "Boy," she responded, "you'll play football because you have guts. But do you know what *really* takes guts? Refusing to lower your standards to those of the crowd. It takes guts to say you've got to live and be somebody 50 years after all the football games are over."

7   I started saying "it isn't" and "they aren't," and I still made first-string end—and class valedictorian—without losing my buddies' respect.

8   During her remarkable forty-four-year career, Mrs. Bessie Taylor Gwynn taught hundreds of economically deprived black youngsters—including my mother, my brother, my sisters, and me. I remember her now with gratitude and affection—especially in this era when Americans are so wrought-up about a "rising

tide of mediocrity" in public education and the problems of finding competent, caring teachers. Miss Bessie was an example of an informed, dedicated teacher, a blessing to children and an asset to the nation.

Born in 1895, in poverty, she grew up in Athens, Ala., where there was no public school for blacks. She attended Trinity School, a private institution for blacks run by the American Missionary Association, and in 1911 graduated from the Normal School (a "super" high school) at Fisk University in Nashville. Mrs. Gwynn, the essence of pride and privacy, never talked about her years in Athens; only in the months before her death did she reveal that she had never attended Fisk University itself because she could not afford the four-year course. 9

At Normal School she learned a lot about Shakespeare, but most of all about the profound importance of education—especially for people trying to move up from slavery. "What you put in your head, boy," she once said, "can never be pulled out by the Ku Klux Klan, the Congress or anybody." 10

Miss Bessie's bearing of dignity told anyone who met her that she was "educated" in the best sense of the word. There was never a discipline problem in her classes. We didn't dare mess with a woman who knew about the Battle of Hastings, the Magna Carta and the Bill of Rights—and who could also play the piano. 11

This frail-looking woman could make sense of Shakespeare, Milton, Voltaire, and bring to life Booker T. Washington and W. E. B. DuBois. Believing that it was important to know who the officials were that spent taxpayers' money and made public policy, she made us memorize the names of everyone on the Supreme Court and in the President's Cabinet. It could be embarrassing to be unprepared when Miss Bessie said, "Get up and tell the class who Frances Perkins is and what you think about her." 12

Miss Bessie knew that my family, like so many others during the Depression, couldn't afford to subscribe to a newspaper. She knew we didn't even own a radio. Still, she prodded me to "look out for your future and find some way to keep up with what's going on in the world." So I became a delivery boy for the Chattanooga *Times*. I rarely made a dollar a week, but I got to read a newspaper every day. 13

Miss Bessie noticed things that had nothing to do with school-work, but were vital to a youngster's development. Once a few classmates made fun of my frayed, hand-me-down overcoat, calling me "Strings." As I was leaving school, Miss Bessie patted me on the back of that old overcoat and said, "Carl, never fret about what you *don't* have. Just make the most of what you *do* have—a brain." 14

Among the things that I did not have was electricity in the little frame house that my father had built for $400 with his World War I bonus. But because of her inspiration, I spent many hours squinting beside a kerosene lamp reading Shakespeare and Thoreau, Samuel Pepys and William Cullen Bryant. 15

No one in my family had ever graduated from high school, so 16 there was no tradition of commitment to learning for me to lean on. Like millions of youngsters in today's ghettos and barrios, I needed the push and stimulation of a teacher who truly cared. Miss Bessie gave plenty of both, as she immersed me in a wonderful world of similes, metaphors, and even onomatopoeia.

She led me to believe that I could write sonnets as well as Shake- 17 speare, or iambic-pentameter verse to put Alexander Pope to shame.

In those days the McMinnville school system was rigidly "Jim 18 Crow," and poor black children had to struggle to put anything in their heads. Our high school was only slightly larger than the once-typical little red schoolhouse, and its library was outrageously in-adequate—so small, I like to say, that if two students were in it and one wanted to turn a page, the other one had to step outside.

Negroes, as we were called then, were not allowed in the town 19 library, except to mop floors or dust tables. But through one of those secret Old South arrangements between whites of con-science and blacks of stature, Miss Bessie kept getting books smuggled out of the white library. That is how she introduced me to the Brontës, Byron, Coleridge, Keats, and Tennyson. "If you don't read, you can't write, and if you can't write, you might as well stop dreaming," Miss Bessie once told me.

So I read whatever Miss Bessie told me to, and tried to remember 20 the things she insisted that I store away. Forty-five years later, I can still recite her "truths to live by," such as Henry Wadsworth Longfel-low's lines from "The Ladder of St. Augustine":

The heights by great men reached and kept
Were not attained by sudden flight.
But they, while their companions slept,
Were toiling upward in the night.

Years later, her inspiration, prodding, anger, cajoling, and almost 21 osmotic infusion of learning finally led to that lovely day when Miss Bessie dropped me a note saying, "I'm so proud to read your col-umn in the Nashville *Tennessean*."

Miss Bessie was a spry 80 when I went back to McMinnville and 22 visited her in a senior citizens' apartment building. Pointing out proudly that her building was racially integrated, she reached for two glasses and a pint of bourbon. I was momentarily shocked, because it would have been scandalous in the 1930s and '40s for word to get out that a teacher drank, and nobody had ever raised a rumor that Miss Bessie did.

I felt a new sense of equality as she lifted her glass to mine. Then 23 she revealed a softness and compassion that I had never known as a student.

"I've never forgotten that examination day," she said, "when Buster 24 Martin held up seven fingers, obviously asking you for help with ques-tion number seven, 'Name a common carrier.' I can still picture you looking at your exam paper and humming a few bars of 'Chattanooga Choo Choo.' I was so tickled, I couldn't punish either of you."

Miss Bessie was telling me, with bourbon-laced grace, that I never fooled her for a moment.   25

When Miss Bessie died in 1980, at age 85, hundreds of her for-mer students mourned. They knew the measure of a great teacher: love and motivation. Her wisdom and influence had rippled out across generations.   26

Some of her students who might normally have been doomed to poverty went on to become doctors, dentists and college pro-fessors. Many, guided by Miss Bessie's example, became public-school teachers.   27

"The memory of Miss Bessie and how she conducted her classroom did more for me than anything I learned in college," recalls Gladys Wood of Knoxville, Tenn., a highly respected English teacher who spent 43 years in the state's school system. "So many times, when I faced a difficult classroom problem, I asked myself, *How would Miss Bessie deal with this?* And I'd remember that she would handle it with laughter and love."   28

No child can get all the necessary support at home, and mil-lions of poor children get *no* support at all. This is what makes a wise, educated, warmhearted teacher like Miss Bessie so vital to the minds, hearts and souls of this country's children.   29

Understanding Meaning

1. What is Rowan's purpose in describing Miss Bessie? What makes this teacher significant to a middle-aged man?
2. What qualities of Miss Bessie does Rowan admire?
3. Does Rowan offer Miss Bessie as a role model? How does he demonstrate that she is an "asset to the nation"?

Evaluating Strategy

1. Rowan opens his essay with a physical description of Miss Bessie. Why are these details important to his purpose?
2. Why would this article appeal to readers of *Reader's Digest*? What values does it reinforce?
3. *Critical Thinking:* Would some people object to Rowan's article as being senti-mental? Why or why not? Does this article suggest simple solutions to complex problems? Would a Miss Bessie be able to succeed in a modern urban high school?

Appreciating Language

1. Study the words Rowan uses in describing Miss Bessie. Which words have the most impact?
2. Rowan includes dialogue in his article. What do you notice about Miss Bessie's language? What does this add to the description?

WRITING SUGGESTIONS

1. Write a brief description of a teacher, employer, or coworker who greatly influenced your development. Provide specific examples of the lessons you learned.

2. *Collaborative Writing:* Working with three or four other students, discuss Miss Bessie's statement, "What you put in your head, boy, can never be pulled out by the Ku Klux Klan, the Congress or anybody." Use this quote as the headline of a poster urging people to read. Keep your message short. Read it aloud to hear how it sounds.

Blending the Modes
PAUL M. BARRETT

Paul M. Barrett has been a reporter and editor at the *Wall Street Journal* for over eighteen years and now directs the investigating reporting team at *Business Week*. His books include *The Good Black: A True Story of Race in America* (1999) and *American Islam: The Struggle for the Soul of a Religion* (2007).

American Islam

CONTEXT: *In this section from* American Islam, *Barrett provides readers with a general description of American Muslims.*

WRITER'S NOTE: *Barrett presents objective details to counter commonly held misconceptions about Islam in the United States. As you read the essay, notice how Barrett uses* definition, comparison, *and* cause and effect *to develop his description.*

Most American Muslims are not Arab, and most Americans of 1 Arab descent are Christian, not Muslim. People of South Asian descent—those with roots in Pakistan, India, Bangladesh, and Afghanistan—make up 34 percent of American Muslims, according to the polling organization Zogby International. Arab-Americans constitute only 26 percent, while another 20 percent are native-born American blacks, most of whom are converts. The remaining 20 percent come from Africa, Iran, Turkey, and elsewhere.

Muslims have no equivalent to the Catholic pope and his car- 2 dinals. The faith is decentralized in the extreme, and some beliefs and practices vary depending on region and sect. In America, Muslims do not think and act alike any more than Christians do. That said, all observant Muslims acknowledge Islam's "five pillars": faith in one God, prayer, charity, fasting during Ramadan, and pilgrimage to Mecca. Muslims are also united in the way they pray. The basic choreography of crossing arms, bowing, kneeling, and prostrating oneself is more or less the same in mosques everywhere.

The two major subgroups of Muslims, Sunni and Shiite, are 3 found in the United States in roughly their global proportions: 85 percent Sunni, 15 percent Shiite. Ancient history still animates the rivalry, which began in the struggle for Muslim leadership after the Prophet Muhammad's death in 632. Shiites believe that Muhammad intended for only his blood descendants to succeed him. Muhammad's beloved cousin and son-in-law Ali was the only male relative who qualified. Ali's followers became known as Shiites, a derivation of the Arabic phrase for "partisans of Ali." Things did not go smoothly for them.

The larger body of early Muslims, known as Sunnis, a word re- 4
lated to Sunnah, or way of the Prophet, had a more flexible notion
of who should succeed Muhammad. In 661, an extremist assassinated Ali near Najaf in what is now Iraq. Nineteen years later Sunnis killed his son, Hussein, not far away in Karbala. These deaths
permanently divided the aggrieved Shiite minority from the Sunni
majority.

Sunnis historically have afflicted the weaker Shiites, accusing 5
them of shaping a blasphemous cult around Ali and Hussein. At
the Karbala Islamic Education Center in Dearborn, Michigan, a
large mural depicts mourning women who have encountered the
riderless horse of Hussein after his final battle. "You see our history and our situation in this," says Imam Husham al-Husainy, a
Shiite Iraqi émigré who leads the center. In Dearborn, Shiite Iraqis
initially backed the American invasion to depose Saddam Hussein, who persecuted Iraq's Shiite majority. Most Sunnis in Dearborn condemned the war as an exercise in American imperialism.

Sufism, another important strain of Islam, is also present in 6
the United States. Sufis follow a spiritual, inward-looking path.
Only a tiny percentage of American Muslims would identify
themselves primarily as Sufis, in part because some more rigid
Muslims condemn Sufism as heretical. But Sufi ideas crop up
among the beliefs of many Muslims without being labeled as
such. Sufism's emphasis on self-purification appeals to New Age
seekers and has made it the most common avenue into Islam for
white American converts such as Abdul Kabir Krambo of Yuba
City, California. Krambo, an electrician who grew up in a conservative German Catholic family, helped build a mosque amidst
the fruit arbors of the Sacramento Valley, only to see it burn
down in a mysterious arson. Once rebuilt, the Islamic Center
of Yuba City was engulfed again, this time by controversy over
whether Krambo and his Sufi friends were trying to impose a
"cult" on other worshipers.

Although there is a broad consensus that Islam is the fastest- 7
growing religion in the country and the world, no one has prov-
able numbers on just how many American Muslims there are. The
Census Bureau doesn't count by religion, and private surveys of
the Muslim population offer widely disparate conclusions. A study
of four hundred mosques nationwide estimated that there are
two million people in the United States "associated with" Islamic
houses of worship. The authors of the survey, published in 2001
under the auspices of the Council on American-Islamic Relations
(CAIR), a Muslim advocacy group, employed a common assumption that only one in three American Muslims associates with a
mosque. In CAIR's view, that suggests there are at least six million
Muslims in the country. (Perhaps not coincidentally the American
Jewish population is estimated to be slightly below six million.)
Other Muslim groups put the number higher, seeking to maximize
the size and influence of their constituency.

Surveys conducted by non-Muslims have produced much lower 8
estimates, some in the neighborhood of only two million or three
million. These findings elicit anger from Muslim leaders, who claim
that many immigrant and poor black Muslims are overlooked. On
the basis of all the evidence, a very crude range of three million to
six million seems reasonable. Rapid growth of the Muslim population is expected to continue, fueled mainly by immigration and high
birthrates and, to a lesser extent, by conversion, overwhelmingly by
African Americans. In the next decade or two there probably will be
more Muslims in the United States than Jews. Worldwide, the Muslim
head count is estimated at 1.3 billion, second among religions only
to the combined membership of Christian denominations.

American Muslims, like Americans generally, live mostly in cities 9
and suburbs. Large concentrations are found in New York, Detroit,
Chicago, and Los Angeles. But they also turn up in the Appalachian
foothills and rural Idaho, among other surprising places. Often the
presence of several hundred Muslims in an out-of-the-way town
can be explained by proximity to a large state university. Many
of these schools have recruited foreign graduate students, including Muslims, since the 1960s. In the 1980s Washington doled out
scholarships to Arab students as part of a campaign to counter
the influence of the 1979 Iranian Revolution. Some of the Muslim
beneficiaries have stayed and raised families.

In New York, Muslims are typecast as cab drivers; in Detroit, as 10
owners of grocery stores and gas stations. The overall economic
reality is very different. Surveys show that the majority of American Muslims are employed in technical, white-collar, and professional fields. These include information technology, corporate
management, medicine, and education. An astounding 59 percent
of Muslim adults in the United States have college degrees. That
compares with only 27 percent of all American adults. Four out of
five Muslim workers earn at least twenty-five thousand dollars a
year; more than half earn fifty thousand or more. A 2004 survey
by a University of Kentucky researcher found that median family
income among Muslims is sixty thousand dollars a year; the national median is fifty thousand. Most Muslims own stock or mutual
funds, either directly or through retirement plans. Four out of five
are registered to vote.

Relative prosperity, high levels of education, and political 11
participation are indications of a minority population successfully integrating into the larger society. By comparison, immigrant Muslims in countries such as Britain, France, Holland, and
Spain have remained poorer, less well educated, and socially
marginalized. Western European Muslim populations are much
larger in percentage terms. Nearly 10 percent of French residents
are Muslim; in the United Kingdom the figure is 3 percent. In the
more populous United States the Muslim share is 1 to 2 percent,
depending on which Muslim population estimate one assumes. It's
unlikely that American cities will see the sort of densely packed,

volatile Muslim slums that have cropped up on the outskirts of Paris, for example.

America's social safety net is stingy compared with those of Western Europe, but there is greater opportunity for new arrivals to get ahead in material terms. This may attract to the United States more ambitious immigrants willing to adjust to the customs of their new home and eager to acquire education that leads to better jobs. More generous welfare benefits in Europe allow Muslims and other immigrants to live indefinitely on the periphery of society, without steady jobs or social interaction with the majority. Europeans, who for decades encouraged Muslim immigration as a source of menial labor, have shown overt hostility toward the outsiders and little inclination to embrace them as full-fledged citizens. Partly as a result, violent Islamic extremism has found fertile ground in Western Europe. 12

Understanding Meaning

1. What are some of the more striking facts Barrett presents about American Muslims? Would most Americans be surprised to learn that most Muslims in this country are not Arabs and have higher-than-average incomes?
2. How does Barrett explain the difference between Sunni and Shia Muslims? What percentage of American Muslims are Sunni?
3. Barrett states that Muslims have a faith that is "decentralized in the extreme." What basic beliefs do most Muslims share?
4. Why is it difficult to ascertain exactly how many Americans are Muslim?
5. *Critical Thinking:* How is the Muslim-American community different from those found in Western Europe? Does America's history of absorbing diverse immigrant groups create a different environment for Muslims? Why or why not?

Evaluating Strategy

1. How difficult is it to describe a religion objectively? Do you think Barrett is successful? Why or why not?
2. Which facts about American Muslims do you consider the most significant? How can a writer determine which facts are important and which are trivial?
3. *Blending the Modes:* How does Barrett use *definition, comparison,* and *cause and effect* to develop and organize his description?

Appreciating Language

1. Do you think Barrett uses objective and neutral language in describing American Muslims? Can you detect any terms some readers might find insensitive or biased?
2. Barrett states that some Muslims condemn Sufi Muslims as "heretics" trying to impose a "cult" on other Muslims. Look up the words "heretic" and "cult" in a dictionary. What do these words mean? Are these terms objective or subjective?

WRITING SUGGESTIONS

1. Write a description essay that objectively describes a group of people. You might provide details about the residents of your apartment building, coworkers, or members of a sports team. Use neutral language and include factual details.

2. *Collaborative Writing:* Working with a group of students, review Barrett's description and select three facts about American Muslims you think most significant. Which ones would surprise most Americans? Write a brief set of factual statements that might be used on billboards or blogs to educate the public.

Writing Beyond the Classroom

BAYOU PRINTING

1500 Magazine Street
New Orleans, LA 70130
(504) 555-7100
www.bayouprinting.com

JOB ANNOUNCEMENT

Join a winning team!

Bayou Printing, New Orleans's largest independent chain of print shops, needs a creative, dynamic store manager to join our team.

Bayou offers successful managers unique opportunities unavailable in national firms:

- Performance bonuses
- Profit sharing
- Full medical and dental coverage
- Education benefits

Requirements:

- Experience in hiring, training, and supervising employees in a high-volume retail operation.
- Full knowledge of state-of-the-art printing technology.
- Strong leadership and communications skills.
- Proven ability to lower employee turnover and overhead costs.

To apply for this job and join our winning team, email us at www.bayouprinting.com

Understanding Meaning

1. How does the ad describe Bayou Printing?
2. What are the most important requirements for the position?
3. What kind of person does Bayou Printing want to attract?
4. *Critical Thinking:* What are the limits of any want ad? Can a job be fully described in a few paragraphs? Why can't employers address all their interests and concerns?

Evaluating Strategy

1. Why does the ad first describe the job and then list the requirements?
2. How effective are the bulleted points?

Appreciating Language

1. What words does the ad use to describe the ideal candidate?
2. The ad uses the term "winning team." What impact does this term have? What is the company seeking to impress on applicants?

WRITING SUGGESTIONS

1. Write a want ad for a job you once had. Try to model yours after ones you have seen in the newspaper or online. Keep your ad as short as possible.

2. *Collaborative Writing:* Work with a group of students and write a want ad together. Imagine you are hiring a part-time employee to act as secretary for your writing group. Determine the skills needed, the major duties, and how the ad should be worded. If members have differences of opinion, craft more than one ad, and ask other students to choose the most effective ad.

MONICA RAMOS

CONTEXT: *Monica Ramos was born in New Orleans and managed a record store that was heavily damaged during Hurricane Katrina. Realizing that record stores were losing business to the Internet, she went to college to study printing and publishing. Having graduated with an associate's degree, she responded to the Bayou Printing ad reproduced on page (127).*

WRITER'S NOTE: *Ramos includes unrelated work experience to describe her skills and uses bulleted lists of specific accomplishments that are easily read or skimmed.*

The Résumé of Monica Ramos

MONICA RAMOS
1455 Josephine Street #12
New Orleans, Louisiana 70118
(504) 555-6580
ramosm@nola.net

OBJECTIVE	Print Shop Manager
OVERVIEW	Associate Degree in Printing and Publishing. Eight years experience in all areas of retail management, including hiring, training, and motivating staff. Proven ability to lower overhead and increase sales through online marketing. Created new revenue streams for traditional business in declining markets.

EXPERIENCE
2010–Present CORCORAN & BLACKWELL

Executive Assistant in 28-attorney law firm preparing documents and media to be presented in court. Worked 25 hours a week while attending college.

- Personally responsible for printing and assembling documents used in $75 million class-action lawsuit involving 6 attorneys and 9 paralegals.
- Assisted partners in developing new corporate website.

2002–2010 BOURBON STREET MUSIC

Manager of New Orleans's second-largest record store, supervising 35 employees. Reported directly to owners and investors.

- Increased profits 12% in first year through improved training and cost control.
- Worked with local bands to sell CDs and memorabilia at concerts to offset declining in-store sales.
- Created "CD-of-the-Month" club that coupled CD sales with concert tickets and free promotional items to develop new revenue stream.
- Assisted owners in transforming business from traditional retail box store to virtual multimedia enterprise.
- Secured inventory and expedited repairs to help owner re-open within three weeks following Katrina.

EDUCATION	DELGADO COMMUNITY COLLEGE, New Orleans, LA
	Associate's Degree in Printing and Publishing, 2012. Completed courses in editing, photo editing, desktop publishing, marketing, cost accounting, print purchasing, and personnel management.

- Experienced in operating and servicing all major brands of copiers.
- Maintained 3.5 GPA while working 25 hours a week.
- Personally raised $72,000 during alumni fund telemarketing campaign.

VOLUNTEER WORK	GREATER NEW ORLEANS COUNCIL
	Assisted with fund-raising drive to solicit support from corporations and foundations to assist small business owners rebuilding after Katrina. 2005–2008.

References available on request

Understanding Meaning

1. Compare this résumé to the Bayou Printing want ad. Does it address the employer's needs?
2. What skills and experiences does Monica Ramos highlight? What are her important attributes? Why do you think she emphasizes her experience helping a business with "declining sales" when applying to a print shop?

Evaluating Strategy

1. One study revealed that the average executive devotes nine seconds to each résumé on initial screening. Does this résumé communicate its main points in a few seconds? Would it make a reader stop skimming and start reading?
2. How is the information arranged? Is it clear and easy to follow? Do you think the résumé demonstrates the value of Ramos's unrelated experience managing a record store? Why or why not?

Appreciating Language

1. What is the tone of the résumé? How do the words portray the applicant?
2. What device does Monica Ramos use to convey a sense of action?

WRITING SUGGESTIONS

1. Write your own résumé, either a current one designed for student jobs or a professional one if you are graduating this semester.
2. *Collaborative Writing:* Meet with a group of students and have each member supply a résumé. Discuss the merits of each résumé you review. Talk about problems you have encountered. Take notes to improve your own résumé. Your library or placement office may offer guides and computer programs to help you develop your résumé.

Responding to Images

Seattle street kids with gun, 1983

1. Describe your first reactions to this picture. Do you feel anger, disgust, fear, concern? What kinds of young people are drawn to guns?

2. This photograph was taken in 1983. What do you assume happened to the boys in the picture? Where might they be today?

3. How would you describe the attitudes shown by the boys in the photograph?

4. Write a brief story describing these boys' lives or situations. Use dialogue to construct a conversation.

5. *Visual Analysis:* What do the hats, hair, clothing, and demeanor suggest about the two boys?

6. *Collaborative Writing:* Discuss this photograph in a small group. How does each of you react to this picture? What do you see in the eyes of the boy on the left? Work together to create a brief paragraph describing your observations.

Strategies FOR WRITING DESCRIPTION

1. Determine your purpose. What is your goal—to entertain a general audience or to provide information to colleagues, employees, superiors, or customers?

2. Define your role. If you are expressing personal opinion, you are free to add subjective elements by making personal references and writing in the first person. If you are writing as a representative of a larger body, objective language is more appropriate.

3. Consider your audience. Which type of description would best suit your readers—subjective impressions or objective facts? What needs and expectations does your audience have? What details, facts, statistics, or descriptions will influence readers the most?

4. Review the discipline or writing situation. Determine if you should use technical or specialized terminology. If you are writing for a profession, academic discipline, government agency, or corporation, use standard methods of developing ideas.

5. Select key details. Having determined the context, select details that emphasize your purpose, impress your audience, and follow any guidelines in your discipline. Descriptions should have focus. Eliminate details that may be interesting in themselves but do not serve your purpose. What do you want readers to really know and remember about your subject?

6. Organize details in an effective manner. Good description is more than a collection of details. To be effective, your writing should be logically organized. You may organize details spatially by describing a house room by room or a city neighborhood by neighborhood. You may organize details in order of importance. If you use objective and subjective description, these details can alternate or be placed in separate sections.

7. Describe people and objects in action. Include short narratives to demonstrate ideas and use direct quotations to bring people to life and add variety to your text.

Revising and Editing

1. Avoid unnecessary detail or mechanical organization. Descriptions have focus. A description of your apartment does not have to list every piece of furniture, explain how each room is decorated, or provide dimensions. In general, avoid writing descriptions that draw unnecessary attention to mechanical arrangements:

> *On the left-hand wall* is a bookcase. *To the right of the bookcase* is a stereo. *Around the corner of the stereo* stands an antique aquarium filled with tropical fish. *Above the aquarium* is a large seascape painting. Model ships line the windowsill. A cabinet *to the right of the window* is filled with seashells.

2. Examine your paper to determine if you have created dominant impressions that highlight what you want readers to know. A subjective description of a room can focus on a single theme:

> Although I live hundreds of miles from the ocean, my apartment has a seagoing motif. Beneath a sweeping seascape, a large antique aquarium dominates the living room, its colorful tropical fish flashing among rocks and shells I collected in Florida. Miniature schooners, windjammers, and ketches line the windowsill. The

ornate glass cabinet intended for china houses my prized collection of Hawaiian seashells.

3. **Review word choices.** Make sure you explain terms readers may find confusing. Examine words for connotations that conflict with your message or may offend readers.

4. **Determine if your description requires a thesis.** In some essays the facts and dominant impressions will speak for themselves, while others require a clear statement of purpose for readers to understand your point.

Suggested Topics for Descriptive Writing

General Assignments

Write a description on any of the following topics. Your description may contain passages demonstrating other modes, such as comparison or cause and effect. Select details carefully. Determine whether your description should rely on factual, objective support or subjective impressions. In choosing diction, be aware of the impact of connotation.

1. Your first apartment
2. The people who gather in a place you frequent—a coffee shop, store, health club, library, or student union
3. How the recent recession affected a friend, your family, your neighborhood, or a business
4. The most desirable/least desirable place to live in your community
5. The most dangerous situation you have faced
6. The type of man/woman you find attractive
7. A consumer or social trend like online shopping, texting, or speed dating
8. A social problem you are confronting or believe is widely misunderstood or ignored
9. The most interesting or most unconventional person you have met in the past year
10. The best/worst party you have attended

Writing in Context

1. Imagine that your college has asked you to write a description of the campus for a brochure designed to recruit students. Your depiction should be easy to read and create a favorable impression.
2. Assume you write a column for an alternative campus newspaper. Develop a sarcastic description of the campus, the college administration, the faculty, or the student body.
3. Write an open letter to the student body of your high school describing what college life is like.
4. Imagine you are trying to sell your car. Write two brief ads, one designed for a campus flyer and the other for Craigslist.

Student Paper: Description

This paper was written in response to an assignment calling for "a brief description of a person, place, or object."

First Draft with Instructor's Comments

As the nation slowly recovers from the recession, our community is beginning to <u>recover</u> from the record layoffs and foreclosures that devastated it. The parking lots at Mayfair Mall are full, though a number of the landmark stores have closed. Shoppers stroll past the still-open discount stores. Never realizing the colourful murals and banks of glittering TV screens <u>camaflage</u> rows of vacant retail space.

Wordy, repetitive

Sp: camouflage, Fragment,

The food court is busy, giving the mall a sense of activity and noisy liveliness but <u>their</u> shopping bags tell a different <u>tail</u>. Community colleges still have waiting lists as people gear up for new careers. The on and off ramps are still jammed at commuter time, but many of those heading to work are heading to lower paying jobs. Downtown, the eighteen story Regency condo tower stands uncompleted, its work having stopped in 2009 with no one willing to finance its completion or sale. Nearby the new headquarters of Southwest Financial Services looks busy, though the firm only uses the first two floors. The empty offices on the third floor remain dark and unairconditioned to save money.

"rows of retail space"—unclear
Wordy, RUN-ON. What "tale" do the bags tell? Explain. Who does "their" refer to?

Wordy, awkward

In many suburbs the results of the recession are hidden by clever landscaping ~~tricks and designs~~. Vacant and vandalized houses have been torn down and passersby barely notice, assuming the neighboring homes simply have bigger yards. Lots have been graded to create banked flowerbeds or low maintenance rock gardens ~~that require less maintenance and watering~~.

Delete, not needed

Delete wordy phrase

Few visitors realize that almost all the homeowners are underwater they owe more than their houses are worth.

Run-on

Still, there are signs of progess. Grande Boluvard now has six new stores and some kids coming right out of school are getting good jobs. My cousin just came out of City College and got an accounting job paying $47,000. At twenty-two, he feels happy. He is looking to get a brand new condo at half price and his boss is putting him on the track for a promotion. He is lucky, but he is working hard, doing accounting work once done by two older men each making $75,000. We are seeing signs of progress. But still this recession is going to haunt a generation of kids who saw their dad laid off or their mom pack their belongings because they lost the house. Some kids are

sp

Run-on

discouraged and feel there is no use finishing school or going to college because diplomas and degrees did not work out for their parents. Other kids get the opposite message, and they get motivated to work harder, save money, and realize they can't have everything they want.

Revision Notes

You have selected a good topic and present a number of ideas about the recession. At this point, however, it is not really an essay but a list of brief observations. Instead of trying to record everything you have observed, choose one topic.
—Describe how Mayfair Mall or the suburbs camouflage lost stores or homes.
—Describe your cousin's career and what it represents.
—Describe the lasting effects of the recession on young people.

Revised Draft

Vista Del Sol Way

In 2005 an ambitious developer constructed brand-new houses on a brand-new street called Vista Del Sol Way. Before the backhoes broke ground, investors began buying. The 3800-square-foot homes feature vaulted living rooms, granite counter tops, stainless steel appliances, wine cellars, pantries, hardwood cabinets from Sweden, stained glass windows, and marble foyers banked by Greek columns. Sweeping staircases lead upstairs to mammoth bedrooms with walk-in closets. The master suite, larger than most New York apartments, has his-and-hers bathrooms, a dressing room with built-in cabinets, a sauna, a hot tub, skylights and a balcony with a wet bar. The three-car garage includes a toolbay and a game room/gym on the second floor.

The houses sold quickly and resold faster. People in Chicago and LA, eager to get into the frenzy of flipping Vegas proper-ties, bought the houses with no intention of ever moving in. A San Diego divorce lawyer bought three homes and resold them, making ninety thousand dollars in less than three months. One house was sold three times in a single year, its value rising over 20 percent.

Those people who eventually moved in bought the houses with little or no money down and watched their homes skyrocket in value. Suddenly families had a hundred thousand or more in equity. They took out loans against their houses to buy cars and boats, pay country club dues, build swimming pools, and finance vacations. Vista Del Sol Way took on the look of an up-scale neighborhood with new SUVs carrying kids from private schools to soccer practice and towing boats to Lake Mead on weekends.

Then everything changed. In 2008 the real estate market collapsed, and the houses on Vista Del Sol Way lost half their value. The developer declared bankruptcy, leaving half-constructed houses unfinished, their 2 x 4 frames rising like skeletons over newly paved driveways. Now owing more than their homes were worth, families scrambled to make payments. The rash of layoffs and downsizings hit the new neighborhood, and one by one the FOR SALE signs went up. By early 2009 the first foreclosure notices appeared. Realtors lowered prices and hired an actress to host sparsely attended open houses. Upbeat video tours with a bouncy soundtrack attracted few hits on YouTube.

Now all twenty-eight of the cream-and-buff Mc Mansions on Vista Del Sol Way stand empty. College students and laid-off auto workers earn eight dollars an hours to mow the lawns, trim hedges, and water the flower beds. Rent-a-cops in blue sedans and surveillance cameras scan the empty neighborhood to keep the vandals at bay.

A state senator has suggested the government buy these houses and bulldoze them to clear "surplus inventory" and stimulate new home construction. Until that happens Vista Del Sol Way stands as a monument of the Great Recession. Like the ghost towns of the Gold Rush days, the houses are reminders of a boom that went bust.

Questions for Review and Revision

1. How interesting do you find this essay? How can a writer make the description of a place meaningful?

2. How does the student blend objective details and subjective impressions? Which are more important, in your view?

3. What is the student's goal in describing these houses? What does he or she want readers to know?

4. How effective is the ending? Does it sum up the point of the essay?

5. Descriptions do not always have an identifiable thesis statement. How would you state the student's thesis?

6. Did the student follow the instructor's comments? Could you suggest other improvements?

7. Read the paper aloud. Are there any sentences that could be revised for clarity?

WRITING SUGGESTIONS

1. Write a description of your own neighborhood or one you are familiar with. What details would you want to share with readers? What makes this place significant or memorable to you?

2. *Collaborative Writing:* Discuss this essay with a group of students. Have each member volunteer opinions on its strengths and weaknesses. Do members suggest revisions or a need for added detail?

EVALUATING DESCRIPTION CHECKLIST

Before submitting your paper, review these points:

1. Have you limited your topic?

2. Do your supporting details suit your context? Should they be objective, subjective, or a blend?

3. Is your description focused and clearly organized, or is it a random list of facts and observations?

4. Have you avoided including unnecessary details and awkward constructions?

5. Does sensory detail include more than sight? Can you add impressions of taste, touch, sound, or smell?

6. Do you avoid overly general terms and focus on specific impressions? Have you created dominant impressions?

7. Do you *show* rather than *tell*? Can you add action to your description to keep it from being static?

8. Do you keep a consistent point of view?

9. Read your paper aloud. How does it sound? Do any sections need expansion? Are there irrelevant details that should be deleted or awkward expressions that can be revised?

Accompanying English CourseMate Resources

Visit English CourseMate at **www.cengagebrain.com** to find many helpful resources and study tools for this chapter.

Definition: Establishing Meaning

6

What Is Definition?

Definition limits or explains the meaning of a word or idea. As a college student you have probably devoted much of your time to learning new words and their definitions. Fields such as chemistry, psychology, sociology, economics, law, and anatomy have technical terms that you must master in order to communicate within the discipline.

Clearly stated definitions play a critical role in professional and business writing. Employment contracts, insurance policies, business proposals, government documents, and leases often include glossaries so that all parties share a common understanding of key terms. Failing to understand a definition can be costly. A tenant who does not know a landlord's definition of *excessive noise* may face eviction. The car buyer who misinterprets the manufacturer's definition of *normal use* can void the car's warranty.

Definitions are not always precise or universally accepted. To be an effective writer in college and in your future profession, it is important to appreciate the range of definitions.

Types of Definitions

■ **Standard definitions** are universally accepted and rarely subject to change. Words such as *tibia, dolphin, uranium, felony, turbine,* and *rifle* have exact meanings that are understood and shared by scholars, professionals, and the general public. Doctors, nurses, paramedics, and football coaches, for example, all recognize *tibia* as a specific bone in the body.

■ **Regulatory definitions** are officially designated terms and are subject to change. The National Football League, Internal Revenue Service, Federal Aviation Administration, Federal Communications Commission, school boards, labor unions, the Catholic Church, and insurance companies issue definitions to guide policy, control operations, and make decisions. The Internal Revenue Service definition of *deductible meal allowance* can change yearly. Many states have changed their definition of *drunk driving* by lowering the legal blood alcohol content from 0.10 percent to 0.08 percent. Regulatory definitions may be universally accepted, but they can change or be limited to a specific region or discipline. The building codes of New York and San Francisco may have different definitions of what makes buildings *structurally sound*. Federal agencies use different methods to define the term *small business*.

■ **Evolving definitions** reflect changes in community attitudes, social values, governmental policy, and scientific research. In the nineteenth century corporal punishment was a routine feature of public school discipline. Today such *discipline* would be defined as *child abuse*. The term *date rape* defines incidents that generations ago would not have been viewed as criminal assaults. Evolving definitions track social change but rarely shift as abruptly as regulatory definitions.

■ **Qualifying definitions** limit meanings of words or concepts that are abstract or subject to dispute. How does one define an *alcoholic*? At what point do doctors label a patient *obese* or *senile*? Which young people are labeled *juvenile delinquents*? How does one define *genius*? In some fields organizations provide definitions. The American Medical Association may offer a definition of *alcoholism*. But unlike a regulatory definition, physicians and researchers are free to dispute it and apply a different meaning altogether. Some definitions are hotly debated. Researchers, politicians, and social commentators continually argue about whether drug addiction and alcoholism should be defined as *disabilities*, which would entitle people with these conditions to receive government benefits.

■ **Cultural definitions** are shaped by the history, values, and attitudes of a national, ethnic, or religious group. Just as evolving definitions alter over time, cultural definitions differ from group to group. In some countries it is customary to offer cash gifts to officials as a *tribute*. In the United States the same action would be defined as an illegal *bribe*. People around the world embrace freedom, but define it very differently. For most Americans *freedom* is defined in personal terms, meaning freedom of individual movement and expression. In other countries, people may define *freedom* in national terms, as protecting the independence and security of their homeland even if it means censorship and restricted personal liberties.

- ■ **Personal definitions** express individual interpretations of words or ideas. Your concept of a *good parent* would be a personal definition. A writer can frame an entire essay in terms of a personal definition or establish a series of personal definitions at the outset of a narrative or persuasive paper. Writers often use personal definition as a method of stating their opinions.

- ■ **Invented definitions** identify a new or newly discovered idea, behavior, object, situation, or problem. The term *road rage* was invented to identify a situation in which a motorist violently overreacts to a minor traffic incident. Soon after, the word *air rage* was used to define the violent and rude behavior of frustrated airline passengers. The Internet has led to a number of invented definitions, including *chat room*, *malware*, and *cyberstalking*.

The Purpose of Definition

Writers use definition for two purposes.

1. **To provide a common understanding.** In most instances writers define a term to limit meaning and prevent confusion. Before conducting research on terrorism, truancy, or unemployment, writers must establish definitions. What events are considered acts of *terrorism*? How many classes does a student have to miss be counted as *truant*? How many hours a week does a person have to work to be considered *full time*?

2. **To persuade readers to accept a point of view or change their opinion.** To transform public attitudes, writers frequently urge readers to redefine something, to see striking a child as *abuse* instead of *spanking* or to accept graffiti as *street art* and not *vandalism*. Definitions can play a critical role in shaping opinions and making arguments. Drug addicts, for instance, can be defined in legal terms and viewed as *criminals* who should be imprisoned, or defined in medical terms as *patients* needing treatment.

Methods of Definition

Definitions are established using five methods:

1. **Defining through synonyms** is the simplest method of providing meaning for a word. Glossaries and dictionaries customarily use synonyms to define technical terms or foreign words. *Costal* refers to *ribs*. A *siesta* can be translated as a *nap*. A *casement* can be explained as a *window*.

2. **Defining by description** presents details about a subject to give readers a sense of what it might look, feel, taste, smell, or sound like. Defining a *costrel* as *a small flask with a loop or loops that is suspended from a belt* provides readers with a clear picture. Descriptive definitions demonstrate how something operates. An *airbag* can be defined as *a rapidly inflated cushion designed to protect automobile passengers in a collision.*

3. **Defining by example** provides specific illustrations to establish meaning. *A felony* can be defined as *a serious crime such as murder, rape, or burglary*. Examples can establish meaning through identification. Telling a fourth-grade class that an *adjective is a word that modifies a noun* will not be as effective as providing examples children can easily recognize— *red, fast, tall, silly, old-fashioned, hot*. Complex or abstract concepts are easier to comprehend if defined by example. Income tax instructions, for instance, often include numerous examples to define what is and is not deductible.

4. **Defining by comparison** uses analogies readers can understand to give meaning to something unfamiliar. A television reporter covering a space mission defined NASA terminology using comparisons viewers would readily understand. To explain the term *power down*, she remarked that the astronauts were *conserving power by turning off nonessential electrical devices, much like switching off the radio and windshield wipers on a car*. Because they can oversimplify complex ideas, comparative definitions must be used carefully.

5. **Extended definitions** qualify or limit the meaning of abstract, disputed, or highly complex words or concepts by relating a narrative or presenting a detailed example. The biography of one person could illustrate the definition of a *hero* or an *addict*.

Definition in Context

The way writers define subjects depends on context. In defining depression for a marketing brochure (page 169), a psychotherapist directs an explanation to prospective clients:

> Depression is an internal state—a feeling of sadness, loss, "the blues," deep disappointment. *When it is more severe, you may have feelings of irritability, touchiness, guilt, self-reproach, loss of self-esteem, worthlessness, hopelessness, helplessness, and even thoughts of death and suicide.*

This definition is addressed to the reader, using the word *you*, and focuses on personal "feelings" stated in general terms. In contrast, a psychology instructor's website (page 168) offers an objective definition for nursing students:

> **Depression** or **Major Depressive Disorder** (**MDD**), also known as **clinical depression, major depression, unipolar depression** or **disorder,** and **recurrent depression,** is a biopsychological condition characterized by dysphoria (sadness), anhedonia (loss of interest or pleasure), social withdrawal, unexplained guilt, dejection, feelings of worthlessness, despair, and frequently suicidal ideation or attempts.

The inclusion of words such as *biopsychosocial* indicate that this definition is intended for a specialized audience familiar with technical terms.

Writing Techniques: DEFINITION

Definition Statement

Definition essays often include a clear statement summarizing the writer's meaning. Eileen Simpson (page 145) defines *dyslexia* as "the inability of otherwise normal children to read." Sydney J. Harris (page 150) defines a *jerk* as "a man (or woman) who is utterly unable to see himself as he appears to others."

Explaining What Something Is *Not*

To prevent confusion, writers frequently define a topic by explaining what it is not. A teacher defining an *acronym* might tell students that it is a "pronounceable word like NOW or AIM" and *not* simply "an abbreviation like FBI or NASA." A psychology book might inform readers that *schizophrenia* defines a condition in which patients are "split from reality" and *not* "patients with split personalities." Eileen Simpson (page 145) points out that "children whose intelligence is below average, whose vision or hearing is defective . . . may be unable to read, but they cannot properly be called dyslexics."

Using or Revising Existing Definitions

In scientific papers researchers often inform readers that they are accepting an existing definition, such as the American Medical Association's definition of *obesity* or the Social Security Administration's definition of *disability*. Other writers will question, revise, or reject widely used definitions to establish one of their own. Robert Rector (page 164) argues that the government's definition of *poverty* is inaccurate because it only counts family income and fails to include welfare benefits.

Strategies FOR READING DEFINITIONS

In reading the definition entries in this chapter, keep these questions in mind.

Understanding Meaning

1. Which type of definition is the author developing—standard, regulatory, evolving, qualifying, cultural, or personal?

2. What is the author's purpose—to establish or limit the meaning of a word or to persuade readers to change their opinions?

3. What audience is the writer addressing—general readers or specialists? Does the audience need to know the definitions in order to make decisions or guide future actions?

4. What is the nature of the discipline or writing situation? Is the writer working within a strictly regulated profession or the general marketplace of ideas?

Evaluating Strategy

1. How does the writer define the word, object, or concept—through synonyms, descriptions, examples, or comparisons?

2. Is the definition limited to a specific incident or context, or can it be applied generally? Is the writer defining a particular person or a personality trait that could be shared by millions?

3. Does the writer supply personal examples, or does he or she rely on official sources to establish the definition?

Appreciating Language

1. What role do word choice and connotation play in establishing the definition?

2. What do the tone and level of language reveal about the writer's purpose and intended audience?

EILEEN SIMPSON

Eileen Simpson (1918–2002) was a psychotherapist who struggled for years to overcome dyslexia, a reading disorder that affects more than 20 million Americans. She was the author of several books, including *Poets in Their Youth*, a memoir of her marriage to the poet John Berryman. Other books based on her personal experiences explored problems of children growing up without parents. This section comes from her 1979 book, *Reversals: A Personal Account of Victory over Dyslexia*.

Dyslexia

CONTEXT: *Simpson provides a standard definition by examining the term's Greek and Latin roots and then demonstrates the effects dyslexia has on reading.*

WRITER'S NOTE: *Simpson provides numerous examples to demonstrate how people with dyslexia see words.*

Dyslexia (from the Greek, *dys*, faulty, + *lexis*, speech, cognate with the Latin *legere*, to read), developmental or specific dyslexia as it's technically called, the disorder I suffered from, is the inability of otherwise normal children to read. Children whose intelligence is below average, whose vision or hearing is defective, who have not had proper schooling, or who are too emotionally disturbed or brain damaged to profit from it belong in other diagnostic categories. They, too, may be unable to learn to read, but they cannot properly be called dyslexics. | *opens with definition* | *describes what dyslexia is not*

For more than seventy years the essential nature of the affliction has been hotly disputed by psychologists, neurologists, and educators. It is generally agreed, however, that it is the result of a neurophysiological flaw in the brain's ability to process language. It is probably inherited, although some experts are reluctant to say this because they fear people will equate "inherited" with "untreatable." Treatable it certainly is: not a disease to be cured, but a malfunction that requires retraining. | *background*

Reading is the most complex skill a child entering school is asked to develop. What makes it complex, in part, is that letters are less constant than objects. A car seen from a distance, close to, from above, or below, or in a mirror still looks like a car even though the optical image changes. The letters of the alphabet are more whimsical. Take the letter *b*. Turned upside down it becomes a *p*. Looked at in a mirror, it becomes a *d*. Capitalized, it becomes something quite different, a *B*. The *M* upside down is a *W*. The *E* flipped over becomes Ǝ. This reversed *E* is familiar to mothers of normal children who have just begun to go to school. The earliest examples of art work they bring home often have I LOVƎ YOU written on them. | *explains why reading is difficult*

Dyslexics differ from other children in that they read, spell, and write letters upside down and turned around far more frequently and for a much longer time. In what seems like a capricious manner, they also add letters, syllables, and words, or, just as capriciously, delete them. With palindromic words (was–saw, on–no), it is the order of the letters rather than the orientation they change. The new word makes sense, but not the sense intended. Then there are other words where the changed order—"sorty" for story—does not make sense at all.

4
explains
how
dyslexics
see letters

The inability to recognize that g, g, and G are the same letter, the inability to maintain the orientation of the letters, to retain the order in which they appear, and to follow a line of text without jumping above or below it—all the results of the flaw—can make of an orderly page of words a dish of alphabet soup.

5

Also essential for reading is the ability to store words in memory and to retrieve them. This very particular kind of memory dyslexics lack. So, too, do they lack the ability to hear what the eye sees, and to see what they hear. If the eye sees "off," the ear must hear "off" and not "of," or "for." If the ear hears "saw," the eye must see that it looks like "saw" on the page and not "was." Lacking these skills, a sentence or paragraph becomes a coded message to which the dyslexic can't find the key.

6

It is only a slight exaggeration to say that those who learned to read without difficulty can best understand the labor reading is for a dyslexic by turning a page of text upside down and trying to decipher it.

7

While the literature is replete with illustrations of the way these children write and spell, there are surprisingly few examples of how they read. One, used for propaganda purposes to alert the public to the vulnerability of dyslexics in a literate society, is a sign warning that behind it are guard dogs trained to kill. The dyslexic reads:

8

Wurring
Guard God
Patoly

for

example #1
demonstrates
dyslexia

Warning
Guard Dog
Patrol

and, of course, remains ignorant of the danger.

Looking for a more commonplace example, and hoping to recapture the way I must have read in fourth grade, I recently observed dyslexic children at the Educational Therapy Clinic in Princeton, through the courtesy of Elizabeth Travers, the direc-tor. The first child I saw, eight-year-old Anna (whose red hair and brown eyes reminded me of myself at that age), had just come to the Clinic and was learning the alphabet. Given the story of

9

"Little Red Riding Hood," which is at the second-grade level, she began confidently enough, repeating the title from memory, then came to a dead stop. With much coaxing throughout, she read as follows:

> Grandma you a top. Grandma [looks over at picture of Red Riding Hood]. Red Riding Hood [long pause, presses index finger into the paper. Looks at me for help. I urge: Go ahead] the a [puts head close to the page, nose almost touching] on Grandma

example #2 of dyslexia

for

> Once upon a time there was a little girl who had a red coat with a red hood. Etc.

"Grandma" was obviously a memory from having heard the story 10 read aloud. Had I needed a reminder of how maddening my silences must have been to Miss Henderson, and how much patience is required to teach these children, Anna, who took almost ten minutes to read these few lines, furnished it. The main difference between Anna and me at that age is that Anna clearly felt no need to invent. She was perplexed, but not anxious, and seemed to have infinite tolerance for her long silences.

Toby, a nine-year-old boy with superior intelligence, had a year 11 of tutoring behind him and could have managed "Little Red Riding Hood" with ease. His text was taken from the *Reader's Digest's Reading Skill Builder,* Grade IV. He read:

> A kangaroo likes as if he had but truck together warm. His saw neck and head do not … [Here Toby sighed with fatigue] seem to feel happy back. They and tried and so every a tiger Moses and shoots from lonesome day and shouts and long shore animals. And each farm play with five friends…

example #3 of dyslexia

He broke off with the complaint, "This is too hard. Do I have to 12 read any more?"
His text was: 13

> A kangaroo looks as if he had been put together wrong. His small neck and head do not seem to fit with his heavy back legs and thick tail. Soft eyes, a twinkly little nose, and short front legs seem strange on such a large strong animal. And each front paw has five fingers, like a man's hand.

An English expert gives the following bizarre example of an 14 adult dyslexic's performance:

> An the bee-what in the tel mother of the biothodoodoo to the majoram or that emidrate eni eni Krastrei, mestriet to Ketra lotombreidi to ra from treido as that.

example #4 of dyslexia

His text, taken from a college catalogue the examiner happened   15
to have close at hand, was:

> It shall be in the power of the college to examine or not
> every licentiate, previous to his admission to the fellow-
> ship, as they shall think fit.

That evening when I read aloud to Auntie for the first time, I   16
probably began as Toby did, my memory of the classroom lesson
keeping me close to the text. When memory ran out, and Auntie
did not correct my errors, I began to invent. When she still didn't
stop me, I may well have begun to improvise in the manner of this
patient—anything to keep going and keep up the myth that I was
reading—until Auntie brought the "gibberish" to a halt.

Understanding Meaning

1. What basic definition does Simpson provide? What misinterpretation does
   she note can occur if a condition is considered "inherited"? What does she
   explain dyslexia "is not"?
2. How does Simpson summarize controversies in the field of research? What do
   scientists from different disciplines agree on?
3. What is the implication to dyslexics and their parents that dyslexia is "not a
   disease to be cured," but "a malfunction that requires retraining"?
4. *Critical Thinking:* How can this disorder affect a child's development if it is not
   detected?

Evaluating Strategy

1. Why is it effective to provide an etymology of the word *dyslexia* at the opening? Does this help satisfy reader curiosity about a term many people have
   heard but do not fully understand?
2. How does Simpson's introduction of personal experience affect the definition?
   Does this add a human dimension to her definition, or does it detract from
   its objectivity? Would the inclusion of personal experience be appropriate in a
   textbook?
3. Do the examples of dyslexic reading dramatize the effects of this disorder?
   Would a simple explanation impress readers with the crippling effects of a reading disorder?
4. *Blending the Modes:* How does Simpson use *narration*, *description*, and *comparison* to develop her definition? What role can stories or case studies play for
   readers seeking to understand a complex subject?

Appreciating Language

1. Simpson is defining a complex disorder. How does her language indicate that
   she is seeking to address a general audience? Would the vocabulary differ in
   a definition written for psychology students?

2. Simpson cites an example of a dyslexic reading a warning sign as "propaganda." Does the use of this word weaken her argument that dyslexia is a serious condition? Why or why not?

3. How does Simpson define the term "palindromic"?

WRITING SUGGESTIONS

1. Write a concisely worded definition of dyslexia in your own words.

2. *Critical Writing:* Write an essay expressing your view on how students with dyslexia should be graded in college. Should these students be allowed more time on essay tests, be offered special tutorial services, or be given alternative assignments and examinations? Can colleges accommodate students with disabilities while maintaining academic standards?

3. *Collaborative Writing:* Working with several other students, craft a brief explanation of dyslexia to be incorporated into a brochure for parents of children with learning disabilities. Keep your audience in mind, and avoid making negative comments that might upset parents.

SYDNEY J. HARRIS

Sydney J. Harris (1917–1986) was born in London and grew up in Chicago, where he pursued a career in journalism. He wrote a column that was published for over forty years, first in the *Chicago Daily News* and later in the *Chicago Sun-Times*. In addition to collections of his columns, Harris published several books, including *Winners and Losers* (1973) and *Would You Believe?* (1979).

A Jerk

CONTEXT: *In this essay, Harris develops a personal definition of an invented term.*

WRITER'S NOTE: *Harris provides a clear definition statement of "a jerk" in paragraph 6.*

1   I don't know whether history repeats itself, but biography certainly does. The other day, Michael came in and asked me what a "jerk" was—the same question Carolyn put to me a dozen years ago.

2   At that time, I fluffed her off with some inane answer, such as "A jerk isn't a very nice person," but both of us knew it was an unsatisfactory reply. When she went to bed, I began trying to work up a suitable definition.

3   It is a marvelously apt word, of course. Until it was coined, not more than 25 years ago, there was really no single word in English to describe the kind of person who is a jerk—"boob" and "simp" were too old hat, and besides they really didn't fit, for they could be lovable, and a jerk never is.

4   Thinking it over, I decided that a jerk is basically a person without insight. He is not necessarily a fool or a dope, because some extremely clever persons can be jerks. In fact, it has little to do with intelligence as we commonly think of it; it is, rather, a kind of subtle but persuasive aroma emanating from the inner part of the personality.

5   I know a college president who can be described only as a jerk. He is not an unintelligent man, nor unlearned, nor even unschooled in the social amenities. Yet he is a jerk *cum laude*, because of a fatal flaw in his nature—he is totally incapable of looking into the mirror of his soul and shuddering at what he sees there.

6   A jerk, then, is a man (or woman) who is utterly unable to see himself as he appears to others. He has no grace, he is tactless without meaning to be, he is a bore even to his best friends, he is an egotist without charm. All of us are egotists to some extent, but most of us—unlike the jerk—are perfectly and horribly aware of it when we make asses of ourselves. The jerk never knows.

"A Jerk" by Sydney J. Harris was published in Last Things First, by Sydney Harris, Houghton Mifflin Company, 1961.

Understanding Meaning

1. How does Harris define "a jerk"? Can you state this idea in your own words?
2. Harris argues that intelligence plays no role in defining someone as a jerk. How does this differentiate a "jerk" from a "fool" or a "dope"?
3. *Critical Thinking:* Harris states that he began "trying to work up" a definition of the word "jerk" in response to a question. Do we often use words and concepts without clear definitions? Do we assume other people share our definitions of common terms?

Evaluating Strategy

1. How does Harris use a question to set up his essay?
2. Harris shares his thinking process with readers, moving from an "unsatisfactory" definition to a clearer one. Is this an effective device? Does it stimulate critical thinking in readers?

Appreciating Language

1. Harris initially defines a jerk as someone who "isn't a very nice person." Does that loose definition fit many negative words used to disparage people? Why do people use so many words—*idiot, clown, clod, fool*—to express the same idea?
2. *Critical Thinking:* Why does slang, especially insults, change with each generation? Does this reflect changing values and attitudes or simply illustrate people's desire to invent more colorful terms to define the same behavior?

WRITING SUGGESTIONS

1. Write a short essay providing a personal definition of a common term. How would you define an "addict" or a "geek"? What, in your view, is a "dead-end job" or a "no-win situation"?
2. *Collaborative Writing:* Working with a group of students, develop your own definition of *jerk*. Have each member develop a definition statement and provide at least one example.

ELLEN GOODMAN

Ellen Goodman (1941–) was born in Massachusetts and graduated from Radcliffe College. She worked for *Newsweek* and the *Detroit Free Press* before joining the *Boston Globe* in 1967. Until her retirement in 2010, Goodman's column "At Large" was widely syndicated throughout the United States. As an essayist and television commentator, Goodman discussed feminism, changes in family life, sexual harassment, and male and female relationships. Her essays have been collected in several books, including *Close to Home, At Large,* and *Turning Points.*

The Company Man

CONTEXT: *Instead of using a number of illustrations to develop a definition, Goodman presents a single, extended example of a person who fits her personal view of a workaholic.*

WRITER'S NOTE: *Goodman does not provide a definition statement but instead relies on extensive details to establish the meaning of "company man."*

1 He worked himself to death, finally and precisely, at 3:00 A.M. Sunday morning.

2 The obituary didn't say that, of course. It said that he died of a coronary thrombosis—I think that was it—but everyone among his friends and acquaintances knew it instantly. He was a perfect Type A, a workaholic, a classic, they said to each other and shook their heads—and thought for five or ten minutes about the way they lived.

3 This man who worked himself to death finally and precisely at 3:00 A.M. Sunday morning—on his day off—was fifty-one years old and a vice-president. He was, however, one of six vice-presidents, and one of three who might conceivably—if the president died or retired soon enough—have moved to the top spot. Phil knew that.

4 He worked six days a week, five of them until eight or nine at night, during a time when his own company had begun the four-day week for everyone but the executives. He worked like the Important People. He had no outside "extracurricular interests," unless, of course, you think about a monthly golf game that way. To Phil, it was work. He always ate egg salad sandwiches at his desk. He was, of course, overweight, by 20 or 25 pounds. He thought it was okay, though, because he didn't smoke.

5 On Saturdays, Phil wore a sports jacket to the office instead of a suit, because it was the weekend.

6 He had a lot of people working for him, maybe sixty, and most of them liked him most of the time. Three of them will be seriously considered for his job. The obituary didn't mention that.

But it did list his "survivors" quite accurately. He is survived by 7
his wife, Helen, forty-eight years old, a good woman of no particular marketable skills, who worked in an office before marrying and
mothering. She had, according to her daughter, given up trying to
compete with his work years ago, when the children were small. A
company friend said, "I know how much you will miss him." And
she answered, "I already have."

"Missing him all these years," she must have given up part of 8
herself which had cared too much for the man. She would be "well
taken care of."

His "dearly beloved" eldest of the "dearly beloved" children is a 9
hard-working executive in a manufacturing firm down South. In the
day and a half before the funeral, he went around the neighborhood researching his father, asking the neighbors what he was like.
They were embarrassed.

His second child is a girl, who is twenty-four and newly married. 10
She lives near her mother and they are close, but whenever she
was alone with her father, in a car driving somewhere, they had
nothing to say to each other.

The youngest is twenty, a boy, a high-school graduate who has 11
spent the last couple of years, like a lot of his friends, doing enough
odd jobs to stay in grass and food. He was the one who tried to
grab at his father, and tried to mean enough to him to keep the
man at home. He was his father's favorite. Over the last two years,
Phil stayed up nights worrying about the boy.

The boy once said, "My father and I only board here." 12

At the funeral, the sixty-year-old company president told the 13
forty-eight-year-old widow that the fifty-one-year-old deceased
had meant much to the company and would be missed and would
be hard to replace. The widow didn't look him in the eye. She was
afraid he would read her bitterness and, after all, she would need
him to straighten out the finances—the stock options and all that.

Phil was overweight and nervous and worked too hard. If he 14
wasn't at the office, he was worried about it. Phil was a Type A, a
heart-attack natural. You could have picked him out in a minute
from a lineup.

So when he finally worked himself to death, at precisely 3:00 A.M. 15
Sunday morning, no one was really surprised.

By 5:00 P.M. the afternoon of the funeral, the company presi- 16
dent had begun, discreetly of course, with care and taste, to make
inquiries about his replacement. One of the three men. He asked
around: "Who's been working the hardest?"

Understanding Meaning

1. How does Goodman define a workaholic? Why does she assert that Phil's
   heart attack was directly related to his career?
2. What does Goodman's definition imply about the quality of Phil's life?

3. What does she suggest that it was lacking? What, if anything, seemed to have driven Phil?

4. Goodman mentions that Phil provided well for his widow. Is Phil, a hardworking vice-president who cares about his family, an ideal man in the eyes of many women? If Phil were African American or Hispanic, would he be viewed as a "role model"? Would a "company woman" be seen as a feminist?

5. *Critical Thinking*: Americans have long admired hard workers. Benjamin Franklin, Thomas Edison, Henry Ford, and Martin Luther King, Jr. became legendary for their accomplishments. On the other hand, Americans long for more leisure time. Is there a double standard? Do we want to spend more time with our friends and family but expect our doctors, lawyers, contractors, and stockbrokers to work overtime for us, meet our deadlines, and always be a phone call away?

Evaluating Strategy

1. Would Goodman's definition be stronger if she included more than one example?

2. What impact does the final paragraph have? How does this reinforce her point?

Appreciating Language

1. Goodman places certain phrases in quotation marks—"well taken care of" and "dearly beloved." What is the effect of highlighting these terms?

2. What does the term "company man" suggest? Would "church man" or "advocacy man" provoke different responses?

WRITING SUGGESTIONS

1. Develop your own definition of *workaholic*. Can it be defined in hours worked or by the degree of stress a job creates? Does an actor or writer working eighty hours a week to rehearse a play or write a novel fit the category of *workaholic*? Is a mother with young children by definition a *workaholic*?

2. *Collaborative Writing:* Speak with fellow students, then write a short statement in response to the question "What do we owe our employers?"

WILLIAM SAFIRE

William Safire (1929–2009) was born in New York City and attended Syracuse University. An author, columnist, journalist, and presidential speech writer, Safire was best known for his long association with the *New York Times*. His popular column "On Language" examined the history and usage of common and unusual words. In addition to writing books on language and politics, Safire published several novels, including *Sleeper Spy* (1995) and *Scandalmonger* (2000).

Liberal and Conservative

CONTEXT: *In these entries from Safire's* Political Dictionary *(1978) Safire defines the meanings of two common political labels by exploring their roots.*

WRITER'S NOTE: *Safire uses several quotations from famous politicians and philosophers in developing his own definition.*

LIBERAL currently one who believes in more government action 1 to meet individual needs; originally one who resisted government encroachment on individual liberties.

In the original sense the word described those of the emerging mid- 2 dle classes in France and Great Britain who wanted to throw off the rules the dominant aristocracy had made to cement its own control.

During the 1920s the meaning changed to describe those who 3 believed a certain amount of governmental action was necessary to protect the people's "real" freedoms as opposed to their purely legal—and not necessarily existent—freedoms.

This philosophical about-face led former New York Governor 4 Thomas Dewey to say, after using the original definition, "Two hundred years later, the transmutation of the word, as the alchemist would say, has become one of the wonders of our time."

In U.S. politics the word was used by George Washington to indicate 5 a person of generosity or broad mindedness, as he expressed distaste for those who would deprive Catholics and Jews of their rights.

The word became part of the American vocabulary in its earlier 6 meaning during a rump convention of Republicans dissatisfied with the presidency of Ulysses S. Grant, at Cincinnati in 1872. German-born Carl Schurz, who chaired the convention, used the word often. So did the leading journalist-thinker of the rebellion, Edwin L. Godkin of *The Nation*, who began his career in England. The short-lived party born of the convention was called "The Liberal Republican" party.

In its present usage, the word acquired significance during the 7 presidency of Franklin D. Roosevelt, who defined it this way during

SAFIRE'S POLITICAL DICTIONARY by William Safire (2008) Definition of "Liberal" from pp. 388–389. By permission of Oxford University Press, USA.

the campaign for his first term: "Say that civilization is a tree which, as it grows, continually produces rot and dead wood. The radical says: 'Cut it down.' The conservative says: 'Don't touch it.' The liberal compromises: 'Let's prune, so that we lose neither the old trunk nor the new branches.'"

Liberalism takes criticism from both right and left, leading to various terms of opprobrium. Herbert Hoover in a magazine article referred to "fuzzy-minded totalitarian liberals who believe that their creeping collectivism can be adopted without destroying personal liberty and representative government." 8

To its opponents, liberalism and liberals seem to call out for qualifying adjectives expressing contempt. Barry Goldwater, trying to combat the popularity of President Johnson with businessmen, told a U.S. Chamber of Commerce conference, "If you think President Johnson is going to give you any better attention than you have got, you're very, very mistaken. If he's a conservative," said the senator, "I'm a screaming liberal." 9

Sometimes even liberals cannot avoid the temptation to assault the term. Adlai Stevenson, quoting an uncertain source, once described a liberal as "one who has both feet firmly planted in the air." And columnist Heywood Broun, who came to consider himself a radical, wrote: "A liberal is a man who leaves a room when a fight begins," a definition adopted by militant Saul Alinsky. 10

The word has fallen on hard times. In the 1976 presidential primaries, Representative Morris Udall told columnist David Broder: "When a word takes on connotations you don't like, it's time to change the label." Henceforth, Udall said—though he would think of himself as a liberal—he would use the word "progressive" instead because the word "liberal" was "associated with abortion, drugs, busing and big-spending wasteful government." 11

Liberals are variously described as limousine, double-domed, screaming, knee jerk, professional, bleeding heart. 12

CONSERVATIVE a defender of the status quo who, when change becomes necessary in tested institutions or practices, prefers that it come slowly, and in moderation. 13

In modern U.S. politics, as in the past, "conservative" is a term of opprobrium to some, and veneration, to others. Edmund Burke, the early defender and articulator of the conservative philosophy, argued that the only way to preserve political stability was by carefully controlling change and seeking a slow, careful integration of new forces into venerable institutions. In his *Reflections on the Revolution in France*, he wrote: "It is with infinite caution that any man ought to venture upon pulling down an edifice which has answered in any tolerable degree for ages the common purposes of society, or on building it up again without having models and patterns of approved utility before his eyes." Abraham Lincoln called it "adherence to the old and tried, against the new and untried." 14

The philosophy has had some famous detractors as well. Dis- 15 raeli, who was to become a Tory Prime Minister, wrote in his sprightly novel *Coningsby*: "Conservatism discards Prescription, shrinks from Principle, disavows Progress; having rejected all respect for antiquity, it offers no redress for the present, and makes no preparation for the future." Lord Bryce was of two minds about it in *The American Commonwealth*: "This conservative spirit, jealously watchful even in small matters, sometimes prevents reforms, but it assures the people an easy mind, and a trust in their future which they feel to be not only a present satisfaction but a reservoir of strength."

The political origin of the word can be traced to the *Senat Con-* 16 *servateur* in the 1795 French Constitution, and was used in its present English sense by British statesman, later Prime Minister, George Canning in 1820. J. Wilson Croker, in the *Quarterly Review* of January 1830, made the concrete proposal: "We have always been conscientiously attached to what is called the Tory, and which might with more propriety be called the Conservative party." It was soon applied in America to the Whigs, amid some derision: "*The Pennsylvania Reporter*," wrote the *Ohio Statesman* in 1837, "speaking of a probable change in the name of the opposition, from Whig to 'Conservative,' says the best cognomen they could adopt would be the 'Fast and Loose' party."

Today the more rigid conservative generally opposes virtually 17 all governmental regulation of the economy. He favors local and state action over federal action, and emphasizes fiscal responsibility, most notably in the form of balanced budgets. William Allen White, the Kansas editor, described this type of conservative when he wrote of Charles Evans Hughes as "a businessman's candidate, hovering around the status quo like a sick kitten around a hot brick."

But there exists a less doctrinaire conservative who admits the 18 need for government action in some fields and for steady change in many areas. Instead of fighting a rear-guard action, he seeks to achieve such change within the framework of existing institutions, occasionally changing the institutions when they show need of it.

Understanding Meaning

1. How did George Washington define the word "liberal"?
2. According to Safire, how did the meaning of liberalism change in the 1920s?
3. How did Franklin Roosevelt define radicals, conservatives, and liberals?
4. Why do many people now prefer the term "progressive" rather than "liberal"?
5. How did Edmund Burke define conservatives?
6. *Critical Thinking*: Are some policies difficult to label liberal or conservative? Can abortion, censorship, gay marriage, gun control, and capital punishment be supported or opposed applying both liberal and conservative principles?

Evaluating Strategy

1. Safire indicates that meanings of "liberal" have changed over the years. Why is this important?
2. Safire heavily relies on quotations from famous political figures. Is this an effective device? Why or why not?
3. *Critical Thinking*: How difficult is it to discuss opposing viewpoints without bias? What challenges does any writer face in trying to objectively describe something he or she does not believe in?

Appreciating Language

1. Safire uses quotations presenting critical views of liberals and conservatives. Does allowing others to state subjective opinions make the writer appear more objective? Why or why not? Can a writer exhibit bias in selecting quotations?
2. Safire points out that many liberals prefer the term "progressive." Current conservatives appear to embrace their label, often denouncing rivals as not being "true conservatives." What does this suggest about the public perceptions of these terms?

WRITING SUGGESTIONS

1. Write a pair of definitions that limit the meaning of opposing or related terms such as "pro-life" and "pro-choice," "Democrats" and "Republicans," "rap" and "hip-hop," or "prosecution" and "defense."
2. *Collaborative Writing*: Today many Americans identify themselves as "independents." Work with a group of students and, using Safire's entries as models, write a brief definition of "independents." If members disagree, consider creating opposing definitions.

BRUCE BARTLETT

Bruce Bartlett (1951–) was born in Ann Arbor, Michigan, and received a bachelor's degree from Rutgers University and a master's degree from Georgetown University. In 1976 he went to work for Congressman Ron Paul. A year later he worked for Congressman Jack Kemp, focusing on tax and economic issues. Although long associated with Republican policy makers, Bartlett published articles blaming the 2009 recession on the Bush administration. He has written articles for the *Wall Street Journal*, the *New York Times*, the *Los Angeles Times*, and *Fortune* magazine. His books include *The Supply Side Solution* (1983); *Imposter: How George W. Bush Bankrupted America and Betrayed the Reagan Legacy* (2006); and *The Benefit and the Burden: Tax Reform—Why We Need it and What it Will Take* (2012).

Who Counts as "Rich"?

CONTEXT: *In this* New York Times *article Bartlett examines the qualifying definition of the "'rich' in America."*

WRITER'S NOTE: *Bartlett does not provide an exact definition but selects a widely accepted one as being "reasonable," noting that many question its accuracy.*

1   Last week, Catherine Rampell posted a commentary on a new Gallup poll on the question of who is "rich" in America. The median threshold in the poll's responses was that rich is $150,000 a year of income or a net worth of $1 million. Because I have asserted that the rich need to pay more taxes if we are to get out of our fiscal mess, and even Republicans say that government benefits for the rich should be cut off, the question of who is rich is politically important.

2   The first thing to know is that there is no formal definition of who is rich, middle class or poor. Of course, there is an official definition for the poverty rate, but that figure is just a back of the envelope calculation that has simply been increased by the inflation rate since the 1960s. There are many other ways of calculating the poverty rate that could either raise the poverty threshold or reduce it.

3   Another problem is that one's social class is a function of both income and wealth. There are many among the elderly who have little income but may have fairly substantial wealth by, for example, owning a home free and clear. At the other end, there are those with high incomes who are, nevertheless, deeply in debt, perhaps even having a negative net worth.

4   Social class also involves self-identification. According to the General Social Survey at the University of Chicago, which has

been asking people what social class they belong to since 1972, more than 90 percent of Americans put themselves squarely in the middle—belonging either to the working class or the middle class.

Historically, less than 6 percent of people identify with the lower 5 class—well below the poverty rate, which was 15.1 percent in 2010—and about 3 percent with the upper class. Not surprisingly, the economic crisis has increased the ranks of the lower class and working class and reduced the ranks of the middle class and upper class.

Of course, social class is also a question of perception. A fam- 6 ily that has temporarily fallen on hard times might still view itself as belonging to a higher social class than its income justifies. Therefore, it is also useful to look at how people identify their income class. The results are not dissimilar to those above— the vast bulk of people see themselves as being broadly in the middle.

Another factor that might shape people's perceptions of their 7 social class and what, if anything, the government ought to do to improve the distribution of wealth and income is the prevalence of mobility.

Republicans often oppose policies that would equalize incomes 8 on the grounds that today's poor could be rich tomorrow and vice versa. Data from the General Social Survey show, by and large, that people believe they have a pretty good chance of improving their economic condition, but probably less so than Republicans believe.

These data are confirmed by various *New York Times* polls, 9 the latest of which, in October, found that 67 percent of people believe it is still possible to start out poor in America and become rich. Only 32 percent said that it was not possible. The peak of optimism came in February 2000, when 84 percent of people said it was possible for average people to become rich. The stock market peaked a month later. The trough came in January 1983, when only 57 percent of people thought they could become rich. That was right on the brink of an economic boom.

Times polls also cast light on the issue of mobility. In a 2005 10 poll, people were asked about their social class when they were children compared with today. People generally saw themselves as better off today.

Since 1989, the *Times* has asked people whether they think fu- 11 ture generations will be as well off as people today. In October, 26 percent said that future generations would be better off, 22 per- cent said they would be the same and 46 percent said they would be worse off.

The peak of optimism was also in February 2000, when 44 per- 12 cent said future generations would be better off and 27 percent said they would be worse off. The trough came in March 1995, when 16 percent of people thought future generations would be better off and 58 percent said they would be worse off. This was also right on the brink of an economic boom.

When people are asked whether it is the responsibility of gov- 13 ernment to reduce income inequality, they mostly disagree, but not strongly. The data for 2010 show an increase in the percentage of people opposed to income redistribution that may reflect the influence of the Tea Party movement.

The *Times* poll in October, however, found that only 26 percent 14 of people thought the distribution of money and wealth was fair, with 66 percent saying it should be more evenly distributed.

Obviously, the question of who is rich in America is extremely 15 fluid. The commonly used threshold of $250,000 is certainly reasonable, but it is nevertheless questioned by those who have such an income but also have equally high expenses, such as children in expensive Ivy League schools.

Understanding Meaning

1. Why does Bartlett believe it is important to define who is "rich"?
2. What problems do writers encounter when they try to define who is rich? Why is it important to measure both income and wealth?
3. What role does "self-identification" play in defining economic status? Why do both rich and poor prefer to call themselves "middle class"?
4. *Critical Thinking*: Do people tend to view "rich" and "poor" as static groups? Do most people come out of college "poor" because they have low income and a lot of debt, then become middle-class or even "rich" at the peak of their careers, then become "low income" in retirement?

Evaluating Strategy

1. Bartlett opens the essay quoting the results of a poll. How much does popular opinion shape qualifying definitions? Do the meanings of terms like "child abuse," "addiction," "success," or "patriotism" depend on public opinion? Can they change over time?
2. Bartlett concludes his essay stating that "the question of who is rich in America is extremely fluid." Why is this an important admission in shaping a qualifying definition?

Appreciating Language

1. What connotations does the word "rich" have? Why do many wealthy people prefer describe themselves as being "successful" and condemn taxing the rich as "punishing success"?
2. How do you define "social mobility"? Why is this important to Americans?

WRITING SUGGESTIONS

1. Using Bartlett's article as an example, write an essay that tries to define the "middle class." What role does income and wealth play in deciding who is in the middle? Does geography play a role in determining the level of income one needs in order to be considered middle class?

2. *Collaborative Writing:* Working with a group of students, write a definition of whom you consider rich. First, have each member write down an income number they would use as a bench mark. Then compare the results. What do these numbers reveal about our perceptions of the rich? If your group has difficulty determining who is rich, consider writing opposing viewpoints.

Blending the Modes
ROBERT RECTOR

Robert Rector received a bachelor's degree from The College of William and Mary and a master's degree in political science from Johns Hopkins. He has worked for the Heritage Foundation since 1984, where he serves as a senior research fellow. Rector is credited with playing a major role in shaping welfare reform in the 1990s and has testified before Congress on poverty and immigration issues. He is the co-author of *America's Failed $5.4 Trillion Dollar War on Poverty* (1996), which criticized existing welfare policies.

How Poor Is 'Poor'?

CONTEXT: *Rector has frequently asserted that the government overestimates the extent of poverty through inaccurate definitions.*

WRITER'S NOTE: *Rector first presents the widely accepted description of poverty, then questions who should be defined as being "poor." Notice where he uses* comparison, analysis, cause and effect, *and* argument *to develop his essay.*

Yesterday morning, the U.S. Bureau of the Census released its annual report on income and poverty, saying that some 46.2 million Americans—15 percent of the population—were poor in 2011. The poverty rate did not fall from the prior year but remained at a near record high, the agency said. 1

The rise in poverty from 36.4 million in 2006 to 46.2 million in 2011 was due initially to the recession and now to the failure of the Obama administration to restore jobs in the economy. 2

According to the Census Bureau, some 11 million more adults are without work today than before the recession began. This number has been getting worse year by year. Similarly, roughly 8 million fewer Americans work full time through the year. The collapse of jobs sharply increases the total poverty number. 3

But what does it mean to say that 46.2 million Americans are "poor"? For most people, the word "poverty" suggests near destitution: an inability to provide nutritious food, clothing, and reasonable shelter for one's family. However, only a small number of the 46.2 million persons classified as "poor" by the Census Bureau fit that description. 4

Nearly all "poor" persons live in houses or apartments that are in good repair and not overcrowded; in fact, the dwelling of the average poor American is larger than the house or apartment of the average non-poor person in countries such as France and the United Kingdom. By their own reports, most poor persons in America had sufficient funds to meet all essential needs and to obtain medical care for family members throughout the year whenever needed. 5

Some 80 percent of poor adults and 96 percent of poor children 6
were never hungry at any time during the year because they could
not afford food. The average consumption of protein, vitamins,
and minerals is virtually the same for poor and middle-class children and is well above recommended norms in most cases. Some
80 percent of poor households have air conditioning; nearly two-
thirds have cable or satellite TV; half have a personal computer;
43 percent have Internet access; and one-third have a wide-screen
plasma or LCD TV.

Clearly, there is a wide gap between what the average American 7
thinks when he hears the word "poverty" and the actual living conditions of most persons the Census Bureau defines as poor. In part,
this is because the bureau ignores nearly the entire welfare state
when it measures poverty.

The Census Bureau determines that a family is poor if its annual 8
"income" falls below specified thresholds. For 2011, the threshold
for a family of four was around $23,000. But the bureau doesn't
count welfare benefits such as food stamps, public housing, the
earned-income tax credit, and many other programs as "income"
for purposes of determining whether a family is poor.

The federal government runs nearly 80 means-tested welfare 9
programs that provide cash, food, housing, medical care, and targeted social services to poor and low-income persons. In FY 2011,
government spent $927 billion on these programs, not counting
Social Security and Medicare. Roughly one-third of the U.S. population received aid from at least one of these programs, at an average cost of $9,000 per recipient.

But the Census Bureau counts only about 3 percent of this 10
$927 billion as "income" for purposes of measuring poverty. This
missing means-tested welfare spending—taxpayer funds spent
on the poor but not counted by the Census Bureau for purposes
of measuring poverty—exceeds the GDPs of most nations on
earth.

If the Census Bureau's official poverty numbers don't convey ac- 11
curate information about poverty, do they tell us anything useful
at all? The answer is yes. While the bureau does a lousy job of
counting welfare aid, it does a fairly good job of measuring wages
and salaries. This means that it provides a fairly accurate picture
of "self-sufficiency"—the ability of a family to sustain an income
above the poverty level without government welfare assistance.

If the government's "poverty" figures are reinterpreted as "self- 12
sufficiency" numbers, they're actually quite informative. The fact
that the Census Bureau ignores most welfare assistance is irrelevant, because welfare is specifically excluded from the concept
of self-sufficiency.

Although it is misleading to say that 46.2 million Americans were 13
"poor" in 2011, it is accurate to say that 46.2 million lacked self-
sufficiency. They were unable to maintain an income above poverty without means-tested welfare aid.

Paradoxically, promoting "self-sufficiency" was the original 14
goal of President Lyndon Johnson's War on Poverty. Johnson declared that his aim was to eliminate "the causes, not just the consequences of poverty." He sought to increase the incomes of the poor by increasing families' capacity for self-support, not by increasing dependence on welfare. LBJ actually promised to reduce, not increase, welfare dependence. The goal of the War on Poverty, he stated, would be "making taxpayers out of tax-eaters."

Clearly, things haven't worked out as LBJ planned. The U.S. has 15
spent over $19 trillion on means-tested welfare since he launched the War on Poverty. But Americans are no more capable today of supporting themselves through work than they were in the mid-1960s.

The short-term rise in families lacking self-sufficiency is owing 16
to the failure of the Obama administration to restore jobs in the economy. But self-sufficiency had not substantially improved even before the recession. The long-term failure to boost self-sufficiency (and decrease official "poverty") has been caused largely by the welfare state itself, which has eroded the work ethic and severely undermined marriage in low-income communities.

When the War on Poverty began, 7 percent of American chil- 17
dren were born outside marriage; today the number is 42 percent. Single-parent families are four times more likely to be "poor" or non-self-sufficient than are families headed by a married couple with the same level of education.

What can be done to increase self-sufficiency and reduce official 18
"poverty"? In the short term, the number of jobs should be increased by easing the threat of excessive taxes and greater regulation on employers and investors who create jobs. In the long term, welfare must be transformed from a system that discourages work and marriage into a system that promotes both. All able-bodied adult recipients of means-tested welfare aid should be required to work or prepare for work as a condition of receiving aid. And marriage must be incrementally rebuilt in communities where it has all but vanished.

These steps are best for the welfare recipients, for taxpayers, 19
and for society as a whole. They are necessary if we are ever to move toward Johnson's original goal of self-sufficiency for all Americans.

Understanding Meaning

1. According to Rector, what does the word "poverty" suggest to most people? Does this description match the federal definition of poverty?

2. Why is a definition of poverty important?

3. How does the federal government define poverty? Why does Rector believe this measurement is inaccurate?

4. What was the stated goal of President Johnson's War on Poverty? Why, in Rector's view, have anti-poverty programs failed?

5. Rector makes a distinction between "poverty" and "non–self-sufficiency." Can you restate his definition in your own words?

6. *Critical Thinking*: Rector states that many Americans "are no more capable today of supporting themselves through work than they were in the mid-1960s." Are government poverty programs to blame or the lack of well-paying jobs? Has the decline in manufacturing employment made it harder for low-income families to support themselves through work alone?

Evaluating Strategy

1. What evidence does Rector include to argue that the government exaggerates the degree of poverty in the United States?

2. Rector states that when the War on Poverty started 7 percent of children were born out of wedlock and that the current rate is 42 percent. Is he suggesting there is a cause-and-effect relationship? What else could explain this social trend? Are more middle- and upper-class children now born outside of marriage?

3. *Blending the Modes*: Where does Rector use *comparison, cause and effect*, and *argument* to develop his essay?

Appreciating Language

1. What connotations does the word "poverty" have? Could these associations explain why some people prefer the term "low income"?

2. Would working parents who are eligible for food stamps or Medicaid consider themselves "welfare" recipients? Why or why not? Do we associate "welfare" only with the unemployed?

WRITING SUGGESTIONS

1. Develop your own definition of poverty and write a short explanation. What factors in addition to income would you include?

2. *Collaborative Writing:* Working with a group of students, write a short paper defining what group members consider "necessities" without which people would be poor. To start the discussion, have each person answer the following question: A thirty-year-old American has a full-time job that offers health insurance. The wages provide enough money for basic groceries and a one-room apartment with a television and telephone. He or she cannot afford a car but can get to most destinations by bus or subway. By skipping meals, he or she can save thirty or forty dollars a week for an annual vacation. *Would you define this person as being poor? Why or why not?*

Writing Beyond the Classroom

Two Definitions of Depression

Definition is a critical feature of all professional writing. Professionals need common standards in order to communicate and operate efficiently. The way definitions are stated depends on the writer's goal, the audience, and the discipline.

SIOBHAN LEHANE

Siobhan Lehane is a college instructor who teaches clinical psychology to students enrolled in nursing and allied health professions.

CONTEXT: *This definition of depression was written for a glossary posted on Lehane's Clinical Psychology 101 website.*

WRITER'S NOTE: *Lehane explains terms that might be unfamiliar to first year college students.*

School of Nursing and Allied Health

Clinical Psychology 101   **Dr. Siobhan Lehane**
Course Glossary

Depression

General Definition

Depression or **Major Depressive Disorder (MDD)**, also known as **clinical depression, major depression, unipolar depression** or **disorder**, and **recurrent depression**, is a biopsychological condition characterized by dysphoria (sadness), anhedonia (loss of interest or pleasure), social withdrawal, unexplained guilt, dejection, feelings of worthlessness, despair, and frequently suicidal ideation or attempts. Depression may be divided into reactive and endogenous disorders based on precipitants and symptomology. The DSM-IV classifies depression by severity, recurrence, and association with hypomania or mania. MDD is one of the most commonly diagnosed psychological disorders, affecting 3–6 percent of the adult population. The disorder is twice as prevalent in women. MDD is uncommon in children, usually manifesting itself during puberty. MDD is caused by biopsychological, psychological, and social factors. It may or may not be precipitated by a life changing event such as job loss, the death of a family member, divorce, personal crisis, or trauma. It may be caused by or coexist with other mental disorders and chronic drug and/or alcohol dependence.

Diagnosis

Without laboratory testing for depression, diagnosis relies on self-reporting by patients, observations by physicians, family members, and psychiatric examination. To receive a diagnosis of MDD, patients must have experienced daily occurrences of symptoms for at least two weeks prior to evaluation. Professionals must distinguish MDD from normal feelings or reactions to loss or trauma and episodes of transitory moodiness or mild dissatisfaction that are non-disabling and self-limited.

DON D. ROSENBERG

Donald D. Rosenberg is a licensed psychologist specializing in marriage and family therapy, employee assistance, child and adolescent therapy, and substance abuse counseling. He has been the Director of the Family Therapy Training Institute and an adjunct professor in the School of Social Welfare at the University of Wisconsin-Milwaukee and is currently president of a mental health and substance abuse clinic in Milwaukee, Wisconsin.

CONTEXT: *This definition appeared in a brochure distributed in the waiting room of a Milwaukee mental health clinic.*

WRITER'S NOTE: *This text is directed to the general public and seeks to explain the nature of depression to people seeking help for psychological problems they may have difficulty understanding.*

What Is Depression?

Depression is an <u>internal state—a feeling of sadness, loss, "the blues," deep disappointment.</u> *When it is more severe, you may have feelings of irritability, touchiness, guilt, self-reproach, loss of self-esteem, worthlessness, hopelessness, helplessness, and even thoughts of death and suicide.* It may include such other feelings as <u>tearfulness, being sensitive and easily hurt, loss of interests, loss of sexual drive, loss of control in life, feeling drained and depleted, anger at yourself, and loss of the ability to feel pleasure.</u>

It may be accompanied by physical symptoms similar to the sense of profound loss, including:

- *loss of appetite*, often with weight loss, but sometimes we find increased eating
- *insomnia or early morning waking*, often 2–4 times per night, nearly every day, but sometimes we see a need to sleep excessively
- moving and speaking slows down, but sometimes we see agitation
- *fatigue or loss of energy* nearly every day
- *loss of concentration*, foggy and indecisive
- sometimes it includes anxious and headachy feelings and also *frequent crying*

Besides the <u>physical sensations</u> and <u>emotions of depression</u>, depressed people may *withdraw, may brood or ruminate about problems*, have trouble remembering things, wonder if they would be better off dead, and become very concerned about bodily symptoms and pains. They may be grouchy, sulking, restless, and unwilling to interact with family and friends.

Understanding Meaning

1. The website is a reference for nursing students and professionals. What is the purpose of its definition? How does its definition differ from the clinic's definition, which is aimed at the general public?
2. What role does definition play in the treatment of any disorder? How is addressing professionals different from addressing potential patients?
3. Which are the objective statements in this definition and the preceding one? Do both definitions agree on the basic elements of depression?
4. How does the brochure address its readers differently from the website?
5. *Blending the Modes:* What *persuasive* elements are used in the brochure?

Evaluating Strategy

1. The brochure by Don Rosenberg uses italics, underlining, and bulleted points for highlighting. What functions do these have? Discuss their suitability.
2. How does the brochure direct its message to the public and potential patients?

Appreciating Language

1. Does the purpose of the definition dictate the tone of the language in these two examples? Does the website's description focus on objective, observable symptoms? Does the brochure seem to focus on feelings and emotions?
2. Would the language of the website appear cold and unfeeling to a patient seeking help with depression?

WRITING SUGGESTIONS

1. Take a definition from the glossary section of a textbook, and write a version for a general audience of clients, consumers, or students.
2. Using information from the website and brochure, write a definition of depression targeted to college students. Describe symptoms in terms students will readily identify.
3. *Collaborative Writing:* Discuss a common problem or issue with fellow students: job insecurity, lack of sleep, stressful family relationships, child care, or the fear of crime. Select a term you often overhear, and provide a clear definition for it. Have each member of the group list features of this term. Try to incorporate objective elements. Write the definition in two versions: one designed for an "official" publication such as the college catalog or textbook, the other for a self-help website.

Responding to Images

Anti-Gay Marriage Protest In Boston, 2004

JIM BOURG/Reuters/Corbis

1. What is your first impression of this photograph? Do you find this an effective form of protest? Does use of a 1 + 1 = ___ argument make a strong point or does it seem simplistic?

2. How important are definitions in law and public policy? How should our society define concepts such as marriage, stalking, child neglect, obscenity, and discrimination?

3. *Visual Analysis:* Note the wording of the sign. What connotations does the word "preserve" have? Does it imply that traditional marriage is imperiled? Would signs with negative messages be less effective?

4. *Critical Thinking:* Clearly the man in the photograph is holding his sign to the camera. In a visual society, do people feel they must condense their points to something that can be captured on a billboard, website, or bumper sticker? Does it reduce complex ideas to simple phrases and sound bites?

5. *Collaborative Writing:* Working with a group of students, select a current political or social issue and discuss the role definition plays. Identify opposing points of view and write a definition statement that expresses each position. How, for instance, do people who argue over free speech define obscenity? How do people who debate gun control define the "right to bear arms"?

Strategies FOR WRITING DEFINITION

1. **Determine your purpose.** Is your goal to explain a term to prevent confusion or persuade people to change their views?

2. **Define your role.** Is your definition based on personal observation and opinion or standard principles and methods used in a specific discipline or profession?

3. **Consider your audience.** What knowledge base do your readers have? Your definition should offer recognizable examples in language they will understand. Determine how your audience will use your definition. Will readers base decisions on your definition?

4. **Make extended definitions relevant.** Extended definitions depend on examples, illustrations, and narratives. The items you include to explain your topic should be relevant and understandable to your audience.

5. **Review special needs of the discipline or writing situation.** Each discipline can have a distinct history, research methodology, and set of concerns. Make sure your definition respects any special interests and addresses special needs.

6. **Use or refer to existing definitions.** Instead of attempting to create your own definition, you can adopt an existing one. If you accept the American Psychological Association's definition of *obsession*, you can simply restate the definition for readers. In using existing definitions, acknowledge their sources. If you disagree with an existing or official definition, restate it and then demonstrate how your interpretation differs.

Revising and Editing

1. **Make sure you *define* and not merely describe your topic.** Descriptions present information about a particular person, place, object, idea, or situation. Definitions must provide information about a "type" of person, place, object, idea, or situation.

2. **Include a clearly stated definition statement.** Definitions usually have a one-sentence statement that concisely summarizes the author's point: "Dyslexia ... is the inability of otherwise normal children to read." The statement can be placed at the opening or the closing of the essay.

Suggested Topics for Writing Definitions

General Assignments

Write a definition on any of the following topics. Your definition will probably contain other modes, such as description, comparison, and narration. Choose your terminology carefully, and avoid using words with misleading connotations. When defining complex and abstract concepts, consider defining extremes and then working toward the middle.

1. A successful professional in your career; define a good defense attorney, computer programmer, nurse, or teacher
2. A good relationship
3. A social or political movement such as the Tea Party or Occupy Wall Street
4. Addiction
5. The perfect career
6. Terrorism
7. A healthy lifestyle
8. The level of insanity at which a person should not be held criminally liable for his or her actions
9. A social problem or issue such as racial profiling, identity theft, elder abuse, or truancy
10. A hero or role model

Writing in Context

1. Imagine you have been asked to write a brief brochure about college life to be distributed to disadvantaged students at a high school. The principal stresses that she fears many of her students lack independent study skills and the discipline needed to succeed in college. Define the characteristics of a good college student, stressing hard work.

2. You have been asked to participate in a panel on sexual harassment. In preparation, provide two definitions of sexual harassment: one expressing attitudes, feelings, and statements you have observed and heard from males on campus, the other expressing attitudes, feelings, and emotions you have observed and heard from females. Try to be as objective as possible, and state any differences fairly.

Student Paper: Definition

This paper was written in response to the following assignment:

> Invent a definition for a social issue or problem you have experienced. You may support your definition with factual research or personal observation. Make sure your paper clearly defines the subject and does not simply describe it.

First Draft with Instructor's Comments

Fathers are probably the most important people our lives except may be for our mothers. They are supposed to teach us a lot. But my father was kind of a disappointment. *needs stronger opening* — *too general, delete*

Like half the members of my generation, I am the product of what used to be called a "broken home." My parents divorced when I was eight. I lived with my mother all the time and would see my father every other weekend. And every summer my dad took me on a vacation lasting two weeks. *wordy, condense*

My father, like many of his generation, was a Disneyland Dad. He always arrived on time, brought me stuff, and took me to places I wanted. He bought me a lot of clothes and toys and gave me things my mother would not get for me. He was always kind and generous. But I found it disappointing that he gave me things and took me places he never really acted like a real Dad. I think divorced dads can be generous and responsible when it comes to paying bills. I know my dad always came through when my mom told him she needed money for us. When we needed school clothes or had to see to the dentist he sent my mom extra money without any problems.

But even so my Dad never really acted like a real Dad. He could of done so much more. Looking back, I really feel cheated. My dad was there for me, but he never acted like a real father just a Disneyland Dad. *redundant* — *"have"*

REVISION NOTES

This paper is a description, not a definition. A description provides details about an individual person, place, or thing. Definition presents details about a type of person, place, or thing. You call your father a "Disneyland Dad." What exactly is a Disneyland Dad? You need to define that term. You can use your father as an example. Make sure your essay contains a clear definition of a "Disneyland Dad" that readers will be able to understand.

Revised Draft

Disneyland Dads

Like half the members of my generation, I am the product of what used to be called a "broken home." My parents divorced when I was eight. I lived with my mother and saw my father on alternate weekends and for two weeks during the summer.

My father, like many of his generation, was a classic Disneyland Dad. The Disneyland Dad is usually found at malls, little league fields, upscale pizza restaurants, and ice cream parlors. He is usually accompanied by a child busily eating food forbidden by Mom, wearing new clothes, or playing with expensive toys. The Disneyland Dad dispenses cash like an ATM and provides an endless supply of quarters for arcade games. Whether they are motivated by guilt, frustration, or an inability to parent, Disneyland Dads substitute material items for fatherly advice, guidance, and discipline.

While my mother furnished the hands-on, day-to-day parenting, my father remained silent. My mother monitored my eating habits, my friends, my grades, even the programs I watched on television. But without daily contact with my mother, my father found it difficult to make decisions about my upbringing. He was afraid of contradicting Mom. So he showered me with gifts and trips. He expanded my wardrobe, gave me my first pieces of real jewelry, introduced me to Broadway shows, and took me to Disneyland—but he did not help me with school, teach me about the job market, give me insight into boys, or allow me to be anything more than a spoiled consumer.

As I grew older, my relationship with my father became strained. Weekends with him were spent shopping, going to movies, playing tennis, and horseback riding—activities I loved, but activities that limited opportunities for anything but casual conversation.

Like most of my friends, I came to view my father as more of an uncle than a parent. He was a beloved family figure, someone who could be counted on for some extra cash, new clothes, a pizza. And like most of my friends, I was troubled by the gulf that widened between my father and myself. I talked, argued, and made up with my mother as I went through my teens. Both of us changed over the years. But my father remained the same—the generous but distant Disneyland Dad.

The Disneyland Dad is a neglected figure. While books and daytime talk shows focus on the plight of single moms, few people offer advice for the fathers. Men in our society are judged by success and conditioned to dispense tokens of their achievement to their children. We kids of divorce want all the things the Disneyland Dad can offer, but we really need his attention, his guidance, his experience, his mentoring. Someone has to help Disneyland Dads become fathers.

Questions for Review and Revision

1. What tone does the term "Disneyland Dad" have? Is it suitable for a serious essay? What connotations does it have?

2. Does this student really "define" or merely "describe" Disneyland Dads?

3. Does the paper include enough details to outline the qualities of a Disneyland Dad?

4. The student uses quotation marks to highlight certain words. Do you find this an effective technique?

5. *Blending the Modes:* Where does the student use *narration* and *comparison* to develop the essay? Does the final paragraph state a *persuasive argument*?

6. Did the student follow the instructor's suggestions? Do you sense she appreciates the difference between description and definition?

7. Read the paper aloud. Can you detect awkward or vague passages that would benefit from revision?

WRITING SUGGESTIONS

1. Invent a term that defines a personality type, and illustrate it using a parent, friend, or co-worker as an example.

2. *Collaborative Writing:* Discuss this paper with several students and collect ideas for a process paper that offers tips to teenage children on how to communicate with a Disneyland Dad.

EVALUATING DEFINITION CHECKLIST

Before submitting your paper, review these points:

1. Is your purpose clear—to inform or persuade?

2. Do you avoid defining a word with the same word, such as "a diffusion pump diffuses"?

3. Is your level of technical or professional language suited to your audience?

4. Does your definition provide enough information and examples so that readers can restate your thesis in their own words?

5. Are there existing definitions you can use for reference or contrast?

6. Do extended definitions contain illustrations, narratives, or comparisons that readers may either not recognize or misinterpret?

7. Do you state the essence of your definition in a short summary statement that readers can remember or highlight for future reference?

8. Are you really "defining" your subject or merely "describing" it?

Accompanying English CourseMate Resources

 Visit English CourseMate at **www.cengagebrain.com** to find many helpful resources and study tools for this chapter.

Comparison and Contrast: Indicating Similarities and Differences

What Is Comparison and Contrast?

Comparison and contrast answers the question: How are things alike or different? What distinguishes a gasoline engine from a diesel engine? What separates a misdemeanor from a felony? How does a bacterial infection differ from a viral one? What did Malcolm X and Martin Luther King Jr. have in common? How has a neighborhood changed in the last twenty years? What are the advantages and disadvantages of leasing a car? All of these questions can be answered by comparing similarities and contrasting differences.

You have probably encountered essay questions that require comparison and contrast responses:

Compare the industrial output of the North and South at the outbreak of the Civil War. Which side was better equipped to wage a protracted conflict?

How do the rules of evidence differ in criminal and civil proceedings?

Which arrangement offers business owners greater protection of personal assets—general or limited partnerships?

Contrast Freud's dream theory with Jung's concept of the unconscious.

At the end of *The Great Gatsby*, Nick Carraway decides to return to the Midwest because he is too "squeamish" for the East. What differences did Fitzgerald see between the East and the Midwest?

How did the role of the federal government change after World War II?

Comparison and contrast writing is commonly used to organize research papers. You might compare two short stories by Edgar Allan Poe in an English course, explain the differences between methods of depreciation in accounting, or contrast conflicting theories of childhood development for psychology. Comparison and contrast writing is also used by engineers to explain the fuel efficiency of different engines, by real estate developers to explore potential building sites, and by social workers to determine the best method of delivering medical services to the homeless.

The Purposes of Comparison and Contrast

Writers use comparison and contrast for five main purposes:

1. **To draw distinctions between related subjects.** In many instances, comparison is used to eliminate confusion. Many people, for instance, mistake an *optician,* who makes and sells eyeglasses, for an *optometrist,* who performs eye examinations and prescribes lenses. Comparison can pair definitions to show readers the difference, for example, between air-cooled and water-cooled engines, African and Indian elephants, or cross-country and downhill skiing.

2. **To recommend a choice between two things.** Television commercials compare competing products. Political campaign brochures urge voters to support a candidate over his or her rival. Articles in medical journals argue that one drug is more effective than another. Business proposals recommend one product over its competitor. Government studies assert that one air-quality standard is preferable to another. The basic purpose of stating recommendations is to *persuade readers to make a choice.*

3. **To examine advantages and disadvantages of a single subject.** A consumer magazine might contrast the advantages and disadvantages of buying gold, declaring bankruptcy, or operating a franchise. A consulting report could balance the added tax revenue a new factory might bring to a community against the costs of supplying it with water, sewer, and emergency services.

4. **To show how one subject has changed.** A television critic might argue that a TV series lacks the quality shown in its first season. A sportswriter might compare a team's performance this season with last season's. An employee might explain how a company has changed since it was purchased by a multinational corporation. A "before and after" comparison could illustrate how a friend changed following the loss of a job or the death of a family member.

5. **To propose an idea, criticize a change, or make a prediction.** Writers can state an argument by comparing a problem with a proposed solution. A city engineer could describe current traffic jams and parking problems, then explain how widened streets and new parking garages could resolve congestion. A doctor could describe a patient's existing lifestyle as a cause of obesity, and then propose a diet and exercise program as a solution. An environmentalist might predict how climate change will affect the planet by comparing current conditions with those expected in the future.

Selecting Topics for Comparison-and-Contrast Papers

When developing a comparison and contrast paper, be sure your subjects share enough common points for meaningful discussion. You can compare two sports cars, two action adventure films, or two diets. But comparing a sports car to an SUV, an action film to a comedy, or a diet to plastic surgery is not likely to generate more than superficial observations. In addition, comparisons should avoid simply stating obvious details. An essay outlining the general differences between two- and four-year colleges would be less meaningful than one contrasting their tuition or their graduates' job prospects. A comparison essay about two presidents could focus on their foreign policies, their views on taxes, or their relationships with the press.

Organizing Comparison and Contrast Papers

Writers use two basic methods of organizing comparison and contrast papers: **subject-by-subject** (also called the **divided** or **block** method) and **point-by-point** (also called the **feature-by-feature** method).

Subject-by-Subject

The **subject-by-subject** method divides the paper into two sections. Writers state all the information about the first topic and then discuss the second topic, comparing it with the first. In this short paper about two types of life insurance, the writer first explains whole life insurance, then discusses term insurance and draws distinctions between the two types:

Whole Life and Term Insurance

Most life insurance companies offer a variety of life insurance products, investments, and financial services. Two of the most common policy types provided are whole life and term insurance.

Whole life insurance is the oldest and most traditional form of life insurance. Life insurance became popular in the nineteenth century as a way of protecting

---

the buyer's dependents in the event of premature death. A purchaser would select a policy amount to be paid to his or her beneficiaries after his or her death. Payments called premiums were made on a yearly, quarterly, or monthly basis. As the policyholder paid premiums, the policy gained cash value. Part of the payment earned interest like money in a bank account. Insurance served as an investment tool, allowing people to save for retirement and giving them access to guaranteed loans. For a low interest fee, insurance holders could borrow against the cash value of their policies.

Term insurance, introduced in the twentieth century, serves the same basic purpose as whole life insurance, protecting the insured's dependents. Unlike whole life, however, no cash value accrues. In a sense the policyholder is "renting" insurance, buying only a death benefit. The advantage of term insurance is its low cost. Because there is no money set aside for investment, the premiums are lower. This allows a person to afford a larger policy. A term policy for $100,000 could be cheaper than a whole life policy for $50,000.

The type of insurance a person needs depends on his or her income, family situation, investment goals, savings, and obligations. Most investment counselors agree, however, that anyone with a spouse or children should have some form of life insurance protection.

Advantages and Disadvantages The subject-by-subject method is suited to short papers. A twenty-page report organized this way would read like two ten-page papers fastened together. It would be difficult for readers to remember enough of the first subject to appreciate how it differs from the second. This method, however, allows writers to compare abstract subjects with ease, especially when a subject has individual features the other does not share.

Point-by-Point

The **point-by-point** method discusses both topics in a series of comparisons addressing specific issues. In the following paper, the writer compares the history, attractions, facilities, and room rates of two hotels.

St. Gregory and Fitzpatrick Hotels

Campus organizations and academic conventions visiting the city hold special events in either the St. Gregory or Fitzpatrick. Both are large convention hotels, but for many reasons the St. Gregory is more desirable.

Opened in 1892, the St. Gregory is the oldest surviving hotel in the city. The Fitzpatrick is the newest, having opened just last spring. The St. Gregory has a commanding view of State Street. The Fitzpatrick is part of the $200 million Riverfront Centre.

The chief attraction of the St. Gregory is its famed domed lobby, ornamented with carved mahogany and elaborate brass and marble fittings. Admiral Dewey was presented with the key to the city here following his victory in Manila Bay in 1898. In contrast, the sleek Fitzpatrick is noted for its sweeping thirty-story atrium. The open lobby is banked with massive video screens.

The main lounge of the St. Gregory is the Pump Room, a plush, turn-of-the-century Irish bar decorated with gilt-framed paintings of the Emerald Isle. The Fitzpatrick features two bars. Homerun, a sports bar, is popular with local students and young professionals. The Exchange is a smaller, quieter bar that is a favorite of visiting executives. Copiers, fax machines, and computers are available in the nearby executive center.

Both hotels offer a range of room rates. The cheapest rooms at the St. Gregory are $95 a night. Though small, they are comfortable. The Fitzpatrick has only a dozen single traveler rooms for $125. Double rooms at the St. Gregory range from $175 to $250, depending on size and decor. All Fitzpatrick double rooms are identical and cost $195. In addition to convention rates, the St. Gregory offers 20 percent student discounts. The Fitzpatrick does not offer student discounts.

Both hotels provide excellent convention services. Since most professors and academic delegates have access to university computers and fax machines, they prefer the historic elegance of the St. Gregory. Students especially appreciate discount rates and the availability of public transport to the university.

Advantages and Disadvantages The point-by-point method is useful in organizing longer and more technical papers because specific facts, statistics, and quotes appear side by side. Point-by-point organization is helpful when addressing multiple readers who may be interested in only a portion of the paper. As you read the essays in this chapter, you may note that many writers blend both methods to develop their comparisons.

Writing Techniques: COMPARISON AND CONTRAST

Balance

Comparison papers are not always evenly divided between both topics. Although it should provide sufficient details about both subjects, a ten-page report might devote seven pages to one topic and only three to the other. Writing to an American audience, Yi-Fu Tuan (page 185) devotes one paragraph to describing a traditional U.S. home and three paragraphs to explain the less-familiar Chinese house.

Transitions

Paragraph breaks and transitional statements move readers from one topic to another or show a change in time. After describing the American home, Yi-Fu Tuan (page 185) starts the section about Chinese houses with a new paragraph that begins "By contrast...." In "A Fable for Tomorrow" Rachel Carson (page 188) signals a shift from past to present with a paragraph break and the statement, "Then a strange blight crept over the area and everything began to change."

Stating Common Elements to Avoid Repetition

To avoid repeating similar facts, writers indicate what their topics share in common. The student paper (page 215) comparing Ireland and Israel points out that "both…have become affluent high-tech powerhouses with rising per-capita incomes and commanding places in the global economy."

Strategies FOR READING COMPARISON AND CONTRAST

When reading the comparison and contrast entries in this chapter, keep these questions in mind.

Understanding Meaning

1. What is the writer's goal—to draw distinctions, recommend a choice, compare advantages and disadvantages, show how something has changed, or make a prediction?

2. What details does the writer present about each subject?

3. Who is the intended audience? Is the essay directed to a general or a specific reader?

4. Is the comparison valid? Is the writer comparing two subjects in a fair manner? Have any points been overlooked?

5. Does the author have an apparent bias?

6. If the comparison makes a recommendation, does the selection seem valid? What makes the chosen subject superior to the others? What evidence is offered?

Evaluating Strategy

1. What is the basic pattern of the comparison—subject-by-subject or point-by-point? Do variations occur?

2. Does the author use a device to narrow the topic or to advance the comparison?

3. Does the writer make use of transitional statements, paragraph breaks, and visual aids? Are they effective?

Appreciating Language

1. Does the writer use connotations that ascribe positive or negative qualities to one or both of the items? How does the author describe the two subjects?

2. What do the diction, level of language, and use of technical terms reveal about the intended audience?

3. If suggesting a choice, how does the writer use language to highlight its desirability?

YI-FU TUAN

Yi-Fu Tuan (1930–) was born in China and later moved to the United States. He taught geography at the University of Wisconsin, specializing in the cultural differences between America and his native country. Since his retirement in 1998, Tuan has continued to write and give lectures. He published an autobiography in 1999 and *Human Goodness* in 2008. He states that he writes "from a single perspective—namely that of experience." In this article published in *Harper's*, he compares the way people in two cultures view their environments.

Chinese Space, American Space

CONTEXT: *Cultures as diverse as America's and China's have many points of difference. To provide insight into their differences in a brief essay, Yi-Fu Tuan focuses on the concept of space and location. Americans, he asserts, are less rooted to place and are future oriented. The Chinese, savoring tradition, are deeply tied to specific locations.*

WRITER'S NOTE: *Yi-Fu Tuan devotes most of his essay to describing the less familiar Chinese houses and values.*

1 Americans have a sense of space, not of place. Go to an American home in exurbia, and almost the first thing you do is drift toward the picture window. How curious that the first compliment you pay your host inside his house is to say how lovely it is outside his house! He is pleased that you should admire his vistas. The distant horizon is not merely a line separating earth from sky, it is a symbol of the future. The American is not rooted in his place, however lovely: his eyes are drawn by the expanding space to a point on the horizon, which is his future.

American space thesis

American home

2 By contrast, consider the traditional Chinese home. Blank walls enclose it. Step behind the spirit wall and you are in a courtyard with perhaps a miniature garden around a corner. Once inside his private compound you are wrapped in an ambiance of calm beauty, an ordered world of buildings, pavement, rock, and decorative vegetation. But you have no distant view: nowhere does space open out before you. Raw nature in such a home is experienced only as weather, and the only open space is the sky above. The Chinese is rooted in his place. When he has to leave, it is not for the promised land on the terrestrial horizon, but for another world altogether along the vertical, religious axis of his imagination.

Transition

Chinese home

3 The Chinese tie to place is deeply felt. Wanderlust is an alien sentiment. The Taoist classic *Tao Te Ching* captures the ideal of rootedness in place with these words: "Though there may be another country in the neighborhood so close that they are within sight of each other and the crowing of cocks and barking of dogs in one place can be heard in the other, yet there is no traffic between them; and

throughout their lives the two peoples have nothing to do with each other." In theory if not in practice, farmers have ranked high in Chinese society. The reason is not only that they are engaged in a "root" industry of producing food but that, unlike pecuniary merchants, they are tied to the land and do not abandon their country when it is in danger.

Chinese place

Nostalgia is a recurrent theme in Chinese poetry. An American reader of translated Chinese poems may well be taken aback—even put off— by the frequency, as well as the sentimentality, of the lament for home. To understand the strength of this sentiment, we need to know that the Chinese desire for stability and rootedness in place is prompted by the constant threat of war, exile, and the natural disasters of flood and drought. Forcible removal makes the Chinese keenly aware of their loss. By contrast, Americans move, for the most part, voluntarily. Their nostalgia for hometown is really longing for a childhood to which they cannot return: in the meantime the future beckons and the future is "out there," in open space. When we criticize American rootlessness, we tend to forget that it is a result of ideals we admire, namely, social mobility and optimism about the future. When we admire Chinese rootedness, we forget that the word "place" means both a location in space and position in society: to be tied to place is also to be bound to one's station in life, with little hope of betterment. Space symbolizes hope; place, achievement and stability.

4

Final comments on American and Chinese values

Understanding Meaning

1. How does the author see a difference between "space" and "place"?
2. What do the traditional designs of American and Chinese homes reveal about cultural differences?
3. Why do the Chinese honor farmers?
4. What historical forces have shaped the Chinese desire for "rootedness"? How is American history different?
5. What negative aspects does Yi-Fu Tuan see in the Chinese sense of place?

Evaluating Strategy

1. The writer devotes only a single paragraph to describing American concepts of space. Why? Is the essay out of balance? Discuss whether or not a comparison paper should devote half its space to each topic.
2. Is the author objective? Is it possible for a writer to discuss cultures without inserting a measure of bias?

Appreciating Language

1. What words does Yi-Fu Tuan use in describing the two cultures? Do they seem to differ in connotation?
2. Does the word "rootlessness" suggest something negative to most people? How does Yi-Fu Tuan define it?
3. Look up the word "wanderlust." How does a German term suit an essay comparing American and Chinese cultures?

WRITING SUGGESTIONS

1. If you have lived in or visited another country or region within the United States, write a brief essay outlining how it differs from your home. Just as Yi-Fu Tuan used the concept of space to focus a short article, you may wish to limit your comparison to discussing eating habits, dress, attitudes to work, music, or dating practices.

2. *Collaborative Writing:* Ask a group of students about their attitudes toward rootlessness and place. Determine how often students have moved in their lives. How many have spent their entire lives in a single house or apartment? Write a few paragraphs outlining the attitudes expressed by the group.

RACHEL CARSON

Rachel Carson (1907–1964) was a marine biologist known for the literary quality of her writing. She won critical acclaim with her first two books, *The Sea Around Us* (1951) and *The Edge of the Sea* (1955). Then, in 1962, she hit the best-seller list with *Silent Spring*, an exposé of the hazards that insecticides and weed killers were posing to both wildlife and human beings. Her book helped launch the modern environmental movement.

A Fable for Tomorrow

CONTEXT: *Rapid industrialization, both in manufacturing and in agriculture, brought unprecedented material advantages to the developed world throughout the first half of the twentieth century. At the same time, insufficient notice was being taken of the damages industrialization was inflicting on the environment. Although* Silent Spring *is a well-researched book by a reputable scientist, it is intended for a general audience.*

WRITER'S NOTE: *In her preface Carson uses a before-and-after comparison to dramatize her subject.*

There was once a town in the heart of America where all life seemed 1 to live in harmony with its surroundings. The town lay in the midst of a checkerboard of prosperous farms, with fields of grain and hillsides of orchards where, in spring, white clouds of bloom drifted above the green fields. In autumn, oak and maple and birch set up a blaze of color that flamed and flickered across a backdrop of pines. Then foxes barked in the hills and deer silently crossed the fields, half hidden in the mists of the fall mornings.

Along the roads, laurel, viburnum and alder, great ferns and 2 wildflowers delighted the traveler's eye through much of the year. Even in winter the roadsides were places of beauty, where countless birds came to feed on the berries and on the seed heads of the dried weeds rising above the snow. The countryside was, in fact, famous for the abundance and variety of its bird life, and when the flood of migrants was pouring through in spring and fall people traveled from great distances to observe them. Others came to fish the streams, which flowed clear and cold out of the hills and contained shady pools where trout lay. So it had been from the days many years ago when the first settlers raised their houses, sank their wells, and built their barns.

Then a strange blight crept over the area and everything began 3 to change. Some evil spell had settled on the community: mysterious maladies swept the flocks of chickens; the cattle and sheep sickened and died. Everywhere was a shadow of death. The farmers spoke of much illness among their families. In the town the doctors had become more and more puzzled by new kinds of sickness appearing among their patients. There had been several sudden and unexplained deaths, not only among adults but even among children, who would be stricken suddenly while at play and die within a few hours.

There was a strange stillness. The birds, for example—where 4 had they gone? Many people spoke of them, puzzled and disturbed. The feeding stations in the backyards were deserted. The few birds seen anywhere were moribund; they trembled violently and could not fly. It was a spring without voices. On the mornings that had once throbbed with the dawn chorus of robins, catbirds, doves, jays, wrens, and scores of other bird voices there was now no sound; only silence lay over the fields and woods and marsh.

On the farms the hens brooded, but no chicks hatched. The 5 farmers complained that they were unable to raise any pigs— the litters were small and the young survived only a few days. The apple trees were coming into bloom but no bees droned among the blossoms, so there was no pollination and there would be no fruit.

The roadsides, once so attractive, were now lined with browned 6 and withered vegetation as though swept by fire. These, too, were silent, deserted by all living things. Even the streams were now lifeless. Anglers no longer visited them, for all the fish had died.

In the gutters under the eaves and between the shingles of the 7 roofs, a white granular powder still showed a few patches; some weeks before it had fallen like snow upon the roofs and the lawns, the fields and streams.

No witchcraft, no enemy action had silenced the rebirth of new 8 life in this stricken world. The people had done it themselves.

This town does not actually exist, but it might easily have a thou- 9 sand counterparts in America or elsewhere in the world. I know of no community that has experienced all the misfortunes I describe. Yet every one of these disasters has actually happened somewhere, and many real communities have already suffered a substantial number of them. A grim specter has crept upon us almost unnoticed, and this imagined tragedy may easily become a stark reality we all shall know.

What has already silenced the voices of spring in countless towns 10 in America? This book is an attempt to explain.

Understanding Meaning

1. What sort of a world does Carson describe in the first two paragraphs of the essay?
2. Can you tell what had caused the change between the world of the first two paragraphs and the world described next? What does Carson mean when she says the people had "done it themselves"?
3. What is Carson's purpose in providing this fictional account of destruction?

Evaluating Strategy

1. Note each reference to silence. How do all of those references relate to the title of Carson's book, *Silent Spring*?
2. How does Carson use a before-and-after comparison to make her point?

Appreciating Language

1. The first two paragraphs describe the town in almost fairy-tale language. In the remainder of the essay, which specific words help capture the negative atmosphere that Carson is trying to create?
2. Although Carson was a scientist, she used language that would be easily understood by the layperson. Why do you think she made that choice?

WRITING SUGGESTIONS

1. You may have seen specific places go through a transformation of the sort Carson describes. Write a paragraph describing the place as you first knew it, and then write a paragraph describing its current state. Focus on creating dominant impressions.

2. *Collaborative Writing:* Work with a group of students and develop an essay using a before-and-after strategy to describe how people change when they go through a transformation, such as getting married, losing a job, having a child, or buying a house.

SUZANNE BRITT

A native of Winston-Salem, North Carolina, Suzanne Britt holds an MA in English from Washington University in St. Louis. Her work has appeared in *Sky Magazine*, the *New York Times*, and the *Boston Globe*. Her books include a history of Meredith College, where she teaches English, and two essay collections—*Skinny People Are Dull and Crunchy Like Carrots* (1982) and *Show and Tell* (1983). More recently, Britt completed a novel; she is currently writing poetry.

Neat People vs. Sloppy People

CONTEXT: *In this selection, Britt uses humorous exaggeration and fanciful speculation to defend sloppy living habits. Although her statements are not likely to be literally accepted by many readers, they constitute a satirical rebuttal to the notion that cleanliness is next to godliness.*

WRITER'S NOTE: *Britt uses the subject-by-subject method to organize details.*

1   I've finally figured out the difference between neat people and sloppy people. The distinction is, as always, moral. Neat people are lazier and meaner than sloppy people.

2   Sloppy people, you see, are not really sloppy. Their sloppiness is merely the unfortunate consequence of their extreme moral rectitude. Sloppy people carry in their mind's eye a heavenly vision, a precise plan, that is so stupendous, so perfect, it can't be achieved in this world or the next.

3   Sloppy people live in Never-Never Land. Someday is their métier. Someday they are planning to alphabetize all their books and set up home catalogs. Someday they will go through their wardrobes and mark certain items for tentative mending and certain items for passing on to relatives of similar shape and size. Someday sloppy people will make family scrapbooks into which they will put newspaper clippings, postcards, locks of hair, and the dried corsage from their senior prom. Someday they will file everything on the surface of their desks, including the cash receipts from coffee purchases at the snack shop. Someday they will sit down and read all the back issues of *The New Yorker*.

4   For all these noble reasons and more, sloppy people never get neat. They aim too high and wide. They save everything, planning someday to file, order, and straighten out the world. But while these ambitious plans take clearer and clearer shape in their heads, the books spill from the shelves onto the floor, the clothes pile up in the hamper and closet, the family mementos accumulate in every drawer, the surface of the desk is buried under mounds of paper, and the unread magazines threaten to reach the ceiling.

Sloppy people can't bear to part with anything. They give loving   5
attention to every detail. When sloppy people say they're going to
tackle the surface of a desk, they really mean it. Not a paper will
go unturned; not a rubber band will go unboxed. Four hours or
two weeks into the excavation, the desk looks exactly the same,
primarily because the sloppy person is meticulously creating new
piles of papers with new headings and scrupulously stopping to
read all the old book catalogs before he throws them away. A neat
person would just bulldoze the desk.

Neat people are bums and clods at heart. They have cavalier atti-   6
tudes toward possessions, including family heirlooms. Everything is
just another dust-catcher to them. If anything collects dust, it's got
to go and that's that. Neat people will toy with the idea of throwing
the children out of the house just to cut down on the clutter.

Neat people don't care about process. They like results. What they   7
want to do is get the whole thing over with so they can sit down
and watch the rasslin' on TV. Neat people operate on two unvarying
principles: Never handle any item twice, and throw everything away.

The only thing messy in a neat person's house is the trash can.   8
The minute something comes to a neat person's hand, he will look
at it, try to decide whether it has immediate use and, finding none,
throw it in the trash.

Neat people are especially vicious with mail. They never go   9
through their mail unless they are standing directly over a trash
can. If the trash can is beside the mailbox, even better. All ads,
catalogs, pleas for charitable contributions, church bulletins, and
money-saving coupons go straight into the trash can without being
opened. All letters from home, postcards from Europe, bills, and
paychecks are opened, immediately responded to, then dropped
in the trash can. Neat people keep their receipts only for tax purposes. That's it. No sentimental salvaging of birthday cards or the
last letter a dying relative ever wrote. Into the trash it goes.

Neat people place neatness above everything, even economics.   10
They are incredibly wasteful. Neat people throw away several toys
every time they walk through the den. I knew a neat person once
who threw away a perfectly good dish drainer because it had mold
on it. The drainer was too much trouble to wash. And neat people
sell their furniture when they move. They will sell a La-Z-Boy re-
cliner while you are reclining in it.

Neat people are no good to borrow from. Neat people buy   11
everything in expensive little single portions. They get their flour
and sugar in two-pound bags. They wouldn't consider clipping a
coupon, saving a leftover, reusing plastic nondairy whipped cream
containers, or rinsing off tin foil and draping it over the unmoldy
dish drainer. You can never borrow a neat person's newspaper to
see what's playing at the movies. Neat people have the paper all
wadded up and in the trash by 7:05 a.m.

Neat people cut a clean swath through the organic as well as the   12
inorganic world. People, animals, and things are all one to them. They

are so insensitive. After they've finished with the pantry, the medicine cabinet, and the attic, they will throw out the red geranium (too many leaves), sell the dog (too many fleas), and send the children off to boarding school (too many scuff-marks on the hardwood floors).

Understanding Meaning

1. What is Britt's thesis? Can you state it in your own words?
2. What is it that makes sloppy people more moral, according to Britt?
3. Why do neat people come off as the "bad guys" in Britt's essay?
4. *Critical Thinking:* Is there some validity in what Britt says? What are neat people losing out on that sloppy people are not? Is there something worthwhile in the goals of sloppy people, even if they never reach them?

Evaluating Strategy

1. Which organizational method does Britt use?
2. Britt states her thesis bluntly in paragraph 1. What effect does that have?
3. How does Britt inject humor?
4. Why might Britt have decided to end the essay the way she did? What is she suggesting in her conclusion about neat versus sloppy people?

Appreciating Language

1. Which words that Britt chose show her bias in favor of the sloppy? Which show her bias against the neat?
2. What terms does she suggest that neat people associate with children in order to show how insignificant children are to them?

WRITING SUGGESTIONS

1. Write an essay in which you characterize yourself or someone you know as fitting into Britt's description of a neat person or a sloppy person.
2. *Collaborative Writing:* Working with a group of students, develop an essay that compares the characteristics of another pair of opposites: savers and spenders, punctual and unpunctual people, renters and homeowners, or happily and unhappily married people.

MARK TWAIN

Mark Twain (1835–1910) was born Samuel Clemens in Missouri. After working as a newspaper typesetter, Clemens became a Mississippi riverboat pilot. When the Civil War disrupted river traffic, Clemens briefly served in the Confederate army then traveled to Nevada and California to prospect for silver. Failing in this venture, Clemens returned to printing and began writing stories. Adopting the pen name Mark Twain, Clemens became a widely published humorist and novelist. His books include *The Adventures of Tom Sawyer, The Prince and the Pauper, Adventures of Huckleberry Finn,* and *A Connecticut Yankee in King Arthur's Court.* A popular speaker, Twain undertook a worldwide lecture tour in 1895, traveling to Britain, South Africa, India, New Zealand, and Australia.

Two Ways of Seeing a River

CONTEXT: *In this passage from* Life on the Mississippi *Twain recounts how his experiences as a riverboat pilot changed his perceptions of the Mississippi River. In learning how to "read" the water as a riverboat pilot, Twain felt he lost his appreciation of the river's beauty and majesty.*

WRITER'S NOTE: *Twain uses word choices to contrast his two ways of viewing the Mississippi and concludes with the analogy of a doctor examining a patient to reinforce his point.*

Now when I had mastered the language of this water and had 1 come to know every trifling feature that bordered the great river as familiarly as I knew the letters of the alphabet, I had made a valuable acquisition. But I had lost something, too. I had lost something which could never be restored to me while I lived. All the grace, the beauty, the poetry had gone out of the majestic river! I still keep in mind a certain wonderful sunset which I witnessed when steamboating was new to me. A broad expanse of the river was turned to blood; in the middle distance the red hue brightened into gold, through which a solitary log came floating, black and conspicuous; in one place a long, slanting mark lay sparkling upon the water; in another the surface was broken by boiling, tumbling rings, that were as many-tinted as an opal; where the ruddy flush was faintest, was a smooth spot that was covered with graceful circles and radiating lines, ever so delicately traced; the shore on our left was densely wooded, and the sombre shadow that fell from this forest was broken in one place by a long, ruffled trail that shone like silver; and high above the forest wall a clean-stemmed dead tree waved a single leafy bough that glowed like a flame in the unobstructed splendor that was flowing from the sun. There were graceful curves, reflected images, woody heights, soft distances; and over the whole scene, far and near, the dissolving lights drifted steadily, enriching it, every passing moment, with new marvels of coloring.

I stood like one bewitched. I drank it in, in a speechless rapture. The world was new to me, and I had never seen anything like this at home. But as I have said, a day came when I began to cease from noting the glories and the charms which the moon and the sun and the twilight wrought upon the river's face; another day came when I ceased altogether to note them. Then, if that sunset scene had been repeated, I should have looked upon it without rapture, and should have commented upon it, inwardly, in this fashion: "This sun means that we are going to have wind tomorrow; that floating log means that the river is rising, small thanks to it; that slanting mark on the water refers to a bluff reef which is going to kill somebody's steamboat one of these nights, if it keeps on stretching out like that; those tumbling 'boils' show a dissolving bar and a changing channel there; the lines and circles in the slick water over yonder are a warning that that troublesome place is shoaling up dangerously; that silver streak in the shadow of the forest is the 'break' from a new snag, and he has located himself in the very best place he could have found to fish for steamboats; that tall dead tree, with a single living branch, is not going to last long, and then how is a body ever going to get through this blind place at night without the friendly old landmark?"

No, the romance and the beauty were all gone from the river. All the value any feature of it had for me now was the amount of usefulness it could furnish toward compassing the safe piloting of a steamboat. Since those days, I have pitied doctors from my heart. What does the lovely flush in a beauty's cheek mean to a doctor but a "break" that ripples above some deadly disease? Are not all her visible charms sown thick with what are to him the signs and symbols of hidden decay? Does he ever see her beauty at all, or doesn't he simply view her professionally, and comment upon her unwholesome condition all to himself? And doesn't he sometimes wonder whether he has gained most or lost most by learning his trade?

Understanding Meaning

1. How did Twain's mastery of riverboat piloting change his perception of the Mississippi River? What did he lose in the process of learning his trade?
2. Why would a riverboat pilot have to develop a different view of the water than a tourist or passenger?
3. Why does Twain pity doctors?
4. *Critical Thinking:* What does Twain's essay reveal about the perceptual world (see pages 7–9)? How do professional experiences influence people's responses? Do attorneys and judges, for example, view a controversial trial differently than the general public?

Evaluating Strategy

1. How does Twain organize his essay and signal transitions?
2. In the second paragraph, Twain explains how he now looks at the river, placing his comments in quotation marks as if quoting someone else. Is this an effective device to demonstrate his new vision of the river? As a riverboat pilot has he become a different person?
3. How does Twain use the analogy of a doctor examining a patient to illustrate his point?
4. *Critical Thinking:* Twain poses questions in the final paragraph. Is asking a question more effective that making a statement? Why or why not? Can questions prompt readers to consider a writer's ideas, or can they make a writer appear indecisive?

Appreciating Language

1. How does Twain use vocabulary to contrast the two ways of looking at the Mississippi? Why would a riverboat pilot see "a warning" in the water instead of "charm" or "beauty"?
2. Twain uses long compound sentences to describe the river. Are these effective? Would modern readers find his style hard to follow? Does a writer have to consider his or her audience in making decisions about sentence length?

WRITING SUGGESTIONS

1. Write a comparison essay showing different perceptions of the same subject. Contrast how liberals and conservatives view poverty, how realtors and environmentalists look at land use, or the way employers and employees view the minimum wage. Consider the role connotation plays in the way people express their perceptions.
2. *Collaborative Writing:* Discuss Twain's essay with a group of students. Work together to write a short essay about how another experience changes people's perceptions. How does going on a diet change the way people shop or look at menus? How does becoming a parent change the way people drive, spend money, decorate, or celebrate holidays?

CHRISTOPHER B. DALY

Christopher B. Daly (1954–) was born in Boston and graduated from Harvard University with a degree in history. He worked as a reporter for the Associated Press for ten years before becoming a journalist for the *Washington Post*. As a freelance writer, Daly has contributed articles to the *Atlantic Monthly*, the *New England Monthly*, and the *Columbia Journalism Review*. He has taught journalism courses at Harvard, Boston University, and Brandeis. His recent book *Covering America: A Narrative History of a Nation's Journalism* traces the evolution of American journalism from the 1700s to the present.

How the Lawyers Stole Winter

CONTEXT: *In this* Atlantic *article Daly compares his childhood interactions with nature, which involved risk taking, with the safe, controlled environments children operate in today.*

WRITER'S NOTE: *Daly uses a before-and-after comparison of ice skating as evidence of a wider social trend.*

When I was a boy, my friends and I would come home from 1 school each day, change our clothes (because we were not allowed to wear "play clothes" to school), and go outside until dinnertime. In the early 1960s in Medford, a city on the outskirts of Boston, that was pretty much what everybody did. Sometimes there might be flute lessons, or an organized Little League game, but usually not. Usually we kids went out and played.

In winter, on our way home from the Gleason School, we would 2 go past Brooks Pond to check the ice. By throwing heavy stones onto it, hammering it with downed branches, and, finally, jumping on it, we could figure out if the ice was ready for skating. If it was, we would hurry home to grab our skates, our sticks, and whatever other gear we had, and then return to play hockey for the rest of the day. When the streetlights came on, we knew it was time to jam our cold, stiff feet back into our green rubber snow boots and get home for dinner.

I had these memories in mind recently when I moved, with my 3 wife and two young boys, into a house near a lake even closer to Boston, in the city of Newton. As soon as Crystal Lake froze over, I grabbed my skates and headed out. I was not the first one there, though: the lawyers had beaten me to the lake. They had warned the town recreation department to put it off limits. So I found a sign that said Danger. Thin Ice. No Skating.

Knowing a thing or two about words myself, I put my own gloss 4 on the sign. I took it to mean When the ice is thin, there is danger and there should be no skating. Fair enough, I thought, but I knew that the obverse was also true: When the ice is thick, it is safe and there should be skating. Finding the ice plenty thick, I laced up my skates and glided out onto the miraculous glassy surface of the frozen lake. My wife, a native of Manhattan, would not let me take our two boys with me. But for as long as I could, I enjoyed the free, open-air delight of skating as it should be. After a few days others joined me, and we became an outlaw band of skaters.

What we were doing was once the heart of winter in New England—and a lot of other places, too. It was clean, free exercise that needed no Stairmasters, no health clubs, no appointments, and hardly any gear. Sadly, it is in danger of passing away. Nowadays it seems that every city and town and almost all property holders are so worried about liability and lawsuits that they simply throw up a sign or a fence and declare that henceforth there shall be no skating, and that's the end of it.

As a result, kids today live in a world of leagues, rinks, rules, uniforms, adults, and rides—rides here, rides there, rides everywhere. It is not clear that they are better off; in some ways they are clearly not better off.

When I was a boy skating on Brooks Pond, there were no grown-ups around. Once or twice a year, on a weekend day or a holiday, some parents might come by with a thermos of hot cocoa. Maybe they would build a fire (which we were forbidden to do), and we would gather round.

But for the most part the pond was the domain of children. In the absence of adults, we made and enforced our own rules. We had hardly any gear—just some borrowed hockey gloves, some hand-me-down skates, maybe an elbow pad or two—so we played a clean form of hockey, with no high-sticking, no punching, and almost no checking. A single fight could ruin the whole afternoon. Indeed, as I remember it, thirty years later, it was the purest form of hockey I ever saw—until I got to see the Russian national team play the game.

But before we could play, we had to check the ice. We became serious junior meteorologists, true connoisseurs of cold. We learned that the best weather for pond skating is plain, clear cold, with starry nights and no snow. (Snow not only mucks up the skating surface but also insulates the ice from the colder air above.) And we learned that moving water, even the gently flowing Mystic River, is a lot less likely to freeze than standing water. So we skated only on the pond. We learned all the weird whooping and cracking sounds that ice makes as it expands and contracts, and thus when to leave the ice.

Do kids learn these things today? I don't know. How would they? We don't let them. Instead we post signs. Ruled by lawyers, cities and towns everywhere try to eliminate their legal liability. But try as they might, they cannot eliminate the underlying risk. Liability is a social construct; risk is a natural fact. When it is cold enough, ponds freeze. No sign or fence or ordinance can change that.

In fact, by focusing on liability and not teaching our kids how to take risks, we are making their world more dangerous. When we were children, we had to learn to evaluate risks and handle them on our own. We had to learn, quite literally, to test the waters. As a result, we grew up to be savvier about ice and ponds than any kid could be who has skated only under adult supervision on a rink.

When I was a boy, despite the risks we took on the ice no one I knew ever drowned. The only people I heard about who drowned were graduate students at Harvard or MIT who came from the tropics and were living through their first winters. Not knowing (after all, how could they?) about ice on moving water, they would innocently venture out onto the half-frozen Charles River, fall through, and die. They were literally out of their element. 12

Are we raising a generation of children who will be out of their element? And if so, what can we do about it? We cannot just roll back the calendar. I cannot tell my six-year-old to head down to the lake by himself to play all afternoon—if for no other reason than that he would not find twenty or thirty other kids there, full of the collective wisdom about cold and ice that they had inherited, along with hockey equipment, from their older brothers and sisters. Somewhere along the line that link got broken. 13

The whole setting of childhood has changed. We cannot change it again overnight. I cannot send my children out by themselves yet, but at least some of the time I can go out there with them. Maybe that is a start. 14

As for us, last winter was a very unusual one. We had ferocious cold (near-zero temperatures on many nights) and tremendous snows (about a hundred inches in all). Eventually a strange thing happened. The town gave in—sort of. Sometime in January the recreation department "opened" a section of the lake, and even dispatched a snowplow truck to clear a good-sized patch of ice. The boys and I skated during the rest of winter. Ever vigilant, the town officials kept the Thin Ice signs up, even though their own truck could safely drive on the frozen surface. And they brought in "lifeguards" and all sorts of rules about the hours during which we could skate and where we had to stay. 15

But at least we were able to skate in the open air, on real ice. 16
And it was still free. 17

Understanding Meaning

1. What is the principal difference between Daly's childhood and that of the current generation?
2. Why did Daly and his friends skate only on the pond?
3. How, in Daly's view, did risk taking teach children to be cautious? Can the drive to protect children actually make them less able to fend for themselves?
4. *Critical Thinking*: Daly argues that the only people who drowned were newcomers unaccustomed to the climate. Does that not demonstrate the need for signs and regulations to warn people who are "out of their element"? If New Englanders lost a child to quicksand, desert heat, or a poisonous snake in another region of the country, would they be offended if locals suggested they were just "out of their element"?

Evaluating Strategy

1. How does Daly organize his essay?
2. Daly ends the essay with two one-line paragraphs. What impact does this have? Can a writer use too many short paragraphs?
3. Throughout the essay Daly poses rhetorical questions. Is this a good device to promote critical thinking? Can a writer include too many questions? How should they be worded to be effective?
4. *Blending the Modes*: Where does Daly use *narration, cause and effect*, and *argument* to develop his essay?

Appreciating Language

1. Daly states (paragraph 10) that "liability is a social construct; risk is a natural fact." Look up "liability" and "risk" in one or more dictionaries. How are these words defined? Does "risk" suggest recklessness and "liability" responsibility?
2. What does the phrase "out of their element" suggest?

WRITING SUGGESTIONS

1. Write a "before-and-after" essay that compares one aspect of childhood that has changed between generations. Did children eat and exercise differently in your youth? Are television shows and video games more graphic today? How has childhood been changed by social media such as Facebook and Twitter? Do today's children have a better or worse childhood than your generation?

2. *Collaborative Writing*: Discuss Daly's essay with a group of students and compare the advantages and disadvantages of communities limiting liability by reducing risks to the public. Does protecting people from some threats make them vulnerable to other dangers?

Blending the Modes
OSCAR WILDE

Oscar Wilde (1854–1900) was born in Dublin, Ireland, and edu-cated at Trinity College and Oxford University. After graduation, he moved to London to pursue a literary career, writing poems, stories, and essays. Known for his wit, charm, and flamboyant man-nerisms, Wilde became an international celebrity, giving lecture tours in the United States and Canada. Following the publication of his novel *The Picture of Dorian Gray* in 1891, Wilde turned to the stage. His satiric comedies *Lady Windermere's Fan, An Ideal Husband*, and *The Importance of Being Earnest* were highly suc-cessful with critics and the public. In 1895 a highly publicized libel trial exposed his homosexuality and led to his arrest and conviction for gross indecency. Sentenced to two years at hard labor, Wilde emerged from prison in 1897 disgraced and destitute. He died in Paris three years later at the age of forty-six.

Impressions of America

CONTEXT: *Returning to England after his tour of the United States, Wilde recorded his observations and included them in speeches delivered throughout Britain.*

WRITER'S NOTE: *Wilde uses a series of comparative descriptions. He contrasts American and English fashion, language, and customs and tells Britons that Pennsylvania reminded him of Switzerland and that the prairies resembled blotting paper. After noting the difference between teacups in a gaudy San Francisco hotel and a Chinatown restaurant, Wilde compares the Chinese rice paper bill to an artist's etching.*

I fear I cannot picture America as altogether an Elysium—perhaps, 1 from the ordinary standpoint I know but little about the country. I cannot give its latitude or longitude; I cannot compute the value of its dry goods, and I have no very close acquaintance with its politics. These are matters which may not interest you, and they certainly are not interesting to me.

The first thing that struck me on landing in America was that 2 if the Americans are not the most well-dressed people in the world, they are the most comfortably dressed. Men are seen there with the dreadful chimney-pot hat, but there are very few hatless men; men wear the shocking swallow-tail coat, but few are to be seen with no coat at all. There is an air of comfort in the appear-ance of the people which is a marked contrast to that seen in this country, where, too often, people are seen in close contact with rags.

The next thing particularly noticeable is that everybody seems 3
in a hurry to catch a train. This is a state of things which is not
favourable to poetry or romance. Had Romeo or Juliet been in
a constant state of anxiety about trains, or had their minds been
agitated by the question of return-tickets, Shakespeare could not
have given us those lovely balcony scenes which are so full of
poetry and pathos.

America is the noisiest country that ever existed. One is waked 4
up in the morning, not by the singing of the nightingale, but by the
steam whistle. It is surprising that the sound practical sense of the
Americans does not reduce this intolerable noise. All Art depends
upon exquisite and delicate sensibility, and such continual turmoil
must ultimately be destructive of the musical faculty.

There is not so much beauty to be found in American cities as 5
in Oxford, Cambridge, Salisbury or Winchester, where are lovely
relics of a beautiful age; but still there is a good deal of beauty to
be seen in them now and then, but only where the American has
not attempted to create it. Where the Americans have attempted
to produce beauty they have signally failed. A remarkable characteristic of the Americans is the manner in which they have applied
science to modern life.

This is apparent in the most cursory stroll through New York. In 6
England an inventor is regarded almost as a crazy man, and in too
many instances invention ends in disappointment and poverty. In
America an inventor is honoured, help is forthcoming, and the exercise of ingenuity, the application of science to the work of man, is
there the shortest road to wealth. There is no country in the world
where machinery is so lovely as in America.

I have always wished to believe that the line of strength and the 7
line of beauty are one. That wish was realised when I contemplated
American machinery. It was not until I had seen the water-works at
Chicago that I realised the wonders of machinery; the rise and fall
of the steel rods, the symmetrical motion of the great wheels is the
most beautifully rhythmic thing I have ever seen. One is impressed
in America, but not favourably impressed, by the inordinate size of
everything. The country seems to try to bully one into a belief in its
power by its impressive bigness.

I was disappointed with Niagara—most people must be disap- 8
pointed with Niagara. Every American bride is taken there, and
the sight of the stupendous waterfall must be one of the earliest,
if not the keenest, disappointments in American married life. One
sees it under bad conditions, very far away, the point of view not
showing the splendour of the water. To appreciate it really one
has to see it from underneath the fall, and to do that it is necessary to be dressed in a yellow oil-skin, which is as ugly as a mack-
intosh—and I hope none of you ever wears one. It is a consolation
to know, however, that such an artist as Madame Bernhardt has
not only worn that yellow, ugly dress, but has been photographed
in it.

Perhaps the most beautiful part of America is the West, to reach 9
which, however, involves a journey by rail of six days, racing along
tied to an ugly tin-kettle of a steam engine. I found but poor consolation for this journey in the fact that the boys who infest the cars
and sell everything that one can eat—or should not eat—were selling editions of my poems vilely printed on a kind of grey blotting
paper, for the low price of ten cents. Calling these boys on one
side I told them that though poets like to be popular they desire
to be paid, and selling editions of my poems without giving me a
profit is dealing a blow at literature which must have a disastrous
effect on poetical aspirants. The invariable reply that they made
was that they themselves made a profit out of the transaction and
that was all they cared about.

It is a popular superstition that in America a visitor is invari- 10
ably addressed as "Stranger." I was never once addressed as
"Stranger." When I went to Texas I was called "Captain"; when I
got to the centre of the country I was addressed as "Colonel," and,
on arriving at the borders of Mexico, as "General." On the whole,
however, "Sir," the old English method of addressing people is the
most common.

It is, perhaps, worth while to note that what many people call 11
Americanisms are really old English expressions which have lin-
gered in our colonies while they have been lost in our own country.
Many people imagine that the term "I guess," which is so common
in America, is purely an American expression, but it was used by
John Locke in his work on "The Understanding," just as we now
use "I think."

It is in the colonies, and not in the mother country, that the 12
old life of the country really exists. If one wants to realise what
English Puritanism is—not at its worst (when it is very bad), but at
its best, and then it is not very good—I do not think one can find
much of it in England, but much can be found about Boston and
Massachusetts. We have got rid of it. America still preserves it, to
be, I hope, a short-lived curiosity.

San Francisco is a really beautiful city. China Town, peopled 13
by Chinese labourers, is the most artistic town I have ever come
across. The people—strange, melancholy Orientals, whom many
people would call common, and they are certainly very poor—
have determined that they will have nothing about them that is not
beautiful. In the Chinese restaurant, where these navvies meet to
have supper in the evening, I found them drinking tea out of china
cups as delicate as the petals of a rose-leaf, whereas at the gaudy
hotels I was supplied with a delf cup an inch and a half thick. When
the Chinese bill was presented it was made out on rice paper, the
account being done in Indian ink as fantastically as if an artist had
been etching little birds on a fan.

Salt Lake City contains only two buildings of note, the chief 14
being the Tabernacle, which is in the shape of a soup-kettle. It is
decorated by the only native artist, and he has treated religious

subjects in the naive spirit of the early Florentine painters, representing people of our own day in the dress of the period side by side with people of Biblical history who are clothed in some romantic costume.

The building next in importance is called the Amelia Palace, in honour of one of Brigham Young's wives. When he died the present president of the Mormons stood up in the Tabernacle and said that it had been revealed to him that he was to have the Amelia Palace, and that on this subject there were to be no more revelations of any kind!   15

From Salt Lake City one travels over the great plains of Colorado and up the Rocky Mountains, on the top of which is Leadville, the richest city in the world. It has also got the reputation of being the roughest, and every man carries a revolver. I was told that if I went there they would be sure to shoot me or my travelling manager. I wrote and told them that nothing that they could do to my travelling manager would intimidate me. They are miners—men working in metals, so I lectured to them on the Ethics of Art. I read them passages from the autobiography of Benvenuto Cellini and they seemed much delighted. I was reproved by my hearers for not having brought him with me. I explained that he had been dead for some little time which elicited the enquiry "Who shot him"? They afterwards took me to a dancing saloon where I saw the only rational method of art criticism I have ever come across. Over the piano was printed a notice: 16

Please Do not Shoot the Pianist
He is Doing his Best

The mortality among pianists in that place is marvellous. Then they asked me to supper, and having accepted, I had to descend a mine in a rickety bucket in which it was impossible to be graceful. Having got into the heart of the mountain I had supper, the first course being whisky, the second whisky and the third whisky.   17

I went to the Theatre to lecture and I was informed that just before I went there two men had been seized for committing a murder, and in that theatre they had been brought on to the stage at eight o'clock in the evening, and then and there tried and executed before a crowded audience. But I found these miners very charming and not at all rough.   18

Among the more elderly inhabitants of the South I found a melancholy tendency to date every event of importance by the late war. "How beautiful the moon is to-night," I once remarked to a gentleman who was standing next to me. "Yes," was his reply, "but you should have seen it before the war."   19

So infinitesimal did I find the knowledge of Art, west of the Rocky Mountains, that an art patron—one who in his day had been a miner—actually sued the railroad company for damages because the plaster cast of Venus of Milo, which he had imported   20 from Paris, had been delivered minus the arms. And, what is more surprising still, he gained his case and the damages.

Pennsylvania, with its rocky gorges and woodland scenery, re- 21
minded me of Switzerland. The prairie reminded me of a piece of blotting-paper.

The Spanish and French have left behind them memorials in the 22
beauty of their names. All the cities that have beautiful names derive them from the Spanish or the French. The English people give intensely ugly names to places. One place had such an ugly name that I refused to lecture there. It was called Grigsville. Supposing I had founded a school of Art there—fancy "Early Grigsville." Imagine a School of Art teaching "Grigsville Renaissance."

As for slang I did not hear much of it, though a young lady who 23
had changed her clothes after an afternoon dance did say that "after the heel kick she shifted her day goods."

American youths are pale and precocious, or sallow and su- 24
percilious, but American girls are pretty and charming—little oases of pretty unreasonableness in a vast desert of practical common-sense.

Every American girl is entitled to have twelve young men de- 25
voted to her. They remain her slaves and she rules them with charming nonchalance.

The men are entirely given to business; they have, as they say, 26
their brains in front of their heads. They are also exceedingly acceptive of new ideas. Their education is practical. We base the education of children entirely on books, but we must give a child a mind before we can instruct the mind. Children have a natural antipathy to books—handicraft should be the basis of education. Boys and girls should be taught to use their hands to make something, and they would be less apt to destroy and be mischievous.

In going to America one learns that poverty is not a necessary 27
accompaniment to civilisation. There at any rate is a country that has no trappings, no pageants and no gorgeous ceremonies. I saw only two processions—one was the Fire Brigade preceded by the Police, the other was the Police preceded by the Fire Brigade.

Every man when he gets to the age of twenty-one is allowed a 28
vote, and thereby immediately acquires his political education. The Americans are the best politically educated people in the world. It is well worth one's while to go to a country which can teach us the beauty of the word FREEDOM and the value of the thing LIBERTY.

Understanding Meaning

1. What overall impression of America does Wilde give his readers?
2. What principal differences did he observe between American and English life? How, for instance, were inventors regarded in the United States and Great Britain?

3. What differences did Wilde notice between American men and women?

4. Why was he disappointed with Niagara Falls?

5. *Critical Thinking*: What, in Wilde's view, could the United States teach the British?

Evaluating Strategy

1. *Critical Thinking*: Wilde opens his essay with a disclaimer, noting his lack of knowledge about American geography, economics, and politics. Is this an effective way to introduce personal observations? In addition to stating a topic, can it be important for a writer to announce what he or she is *not* going to discuss?

2. How does Wilde organize the essay? Can you tell from its structure that his comments were meant to be delivered orally?

3. *Blending the Modes*: How does Wilde blend *comparison* and *description* throughout the essay? In describing a foreign nation, is a writer likely to rely on comparisons to his or her native country? If you visited China, would you find yourself explaining your observations to Americans by making comparisons to the United States?

Appreciating Language

1. What does the word "impressions" suggest? Does it suit Wilde's purpose? Would a title using words like "definition" or "analysis" create different expectations?

2. What words does Wilde use to describe Americans? Are they positive or negative in your view?

3. Wilde noted that "I guess" was a common American phrase in the 1880s. How often do you hear Americans using it today? What implications does the phrase have?

WRITING SUGGESTIONS

1. Using Wilde's impressions as a model, write an essay that presents a series of comparisons to describe a place you visited or a party, wedding, or concert you attended.

2. *Collaborative Writing*: Wilde toured the United States in 1882. Discuss his observations with a group of students and develop a comparison essay, outlining what has and has not changed in American life. What current customs, traits, and behaviors, if any, would Wilde recognize today?

Writing Beyond the Classroom
PEGGY KENNA AND SONDRA LACY

Peggy Kenna and Sondra Lacy are communications specialists based in Arizona who work with foreign-born employees. In addition, they provide cross-cultural training to executives conducting international business. Kenna is a speech and language pathologist who specializes in accent modification. Kenna and Lacy have collaborated on a series of fifty-page booklets that compare American and foreign business organizations, habits, behaviors, and negotiating styles. Widely sold in airports, these booklets give Americans tips on doing business overseas.

CONTEXT: *This section from* Business Taiwan *contrasts American and Taiwanese styles of communicating.*

WRITER'S NOTE: *In designing their booklets for quick skimming, Kenna and Lacy use charts and bullet points.*

Communication Styles: United States and Taiwan

UNITED STATES

• *Frank*

Americans tend to be very straightforward and unreserved. The people of Taiwan often find them abrupt and not interested enough in human relationships.

• *Face saving less important*

To Americans accuracy is important but errors are tolerated. Admitting mistakes is seen as a sign of maturity. They believe you learn from failure and therefore encourage some risk taking. Americans believe criticism can be objective and not personal; however, all criticism should be done with tact.

• *Direct eye contact*

Direct eye contact is very important to Americans since they need to see the nonverbal cues the speaker is giving. Nonverbal cues are a very important part of the American English language. Americans use intermittent eye contact when they are speaking but fairly steady eye contact when they are listening.

TAIWAN

• *Subtle*

Frankness is not appreciated by the people of Taiwan. They particularly dislike unqualified negative statements.

• *Face saving important*

The Chinese do not like to be put in the position of having to admit a mistake or failure. They also do not like to tell you when they don't understand your point. You also should not admit too readily when you don't know something as it can cause you to lose face.

• *Avoid direct eye contact*

Holding the gaze of another person is considered rude.

- **Direct and to the point**

Americans prefer people to say what they mean. Because of this, they sometimes tend to miss subtle nonverbal cues. Americans are uncomfortable with ambiguousness and don't like to have to "fill in the blanks." They also tend to discuss problems directly.

- **Indirect and ambiguous**

People in Taiwan dislike saying "no." They may not tell you when they don't understand. They often hedge their answers if they know you won't like the answer. If they say something like, "We'll think about it," they may mean they aren't interested. They dislike discussing problems directly and will often go around the issue, which can be frustrating for Americans. The Chinese language (Mandarin) is so concise that the listener needs to use much imagination to "fill in the gaps."

- **"Yes" means agreement**

Americans look for clues such as nodding of the head, a verbal "yes" or "uh huh" in order to determine if their arguments are succeeding.

- **"Yes" means "I hear"**

People in Taiwan do not judge information given to them so they do not indicate agreement or disagreement; they only nod or say "yes" to indicate they are listening to you. The people of Taiwan believe politeness is more important than frankness so they will not directly tell you "no." The closest they will come to "no" is "maybe."

Understanding Meaning

1. What appear to be the major differences between American and Taiwanese methods of communicating?
2. Why is it important for Americans to be sensitive about making direct eye contact with Taiwanese?
3. How do Americans and Taiwanese accept failure?
4. *Critical Thinking:* Why would this booklet be valuable to Americans visiting Taiwan on business? Does such a brief, to-the-point guide risk relying on stereotypes?

Evaluating Strategy

1. How easy is this document to read and review? How accessible would the information be if it were written in standard paragraphs?
2. What does the directness of the document reveal about the intended audience? Would it be suitable for a college classroom?

Appreciating Language

1. What language do the writers use in describing the Taiwanese? Do they attempt to be neutral, or does their word choice favor one nationality over another?
2. Kenna and Lacy suggest that many Taiwanese find Americans to be "abrupt." Is this a good word choice? Does the guide express common prejudices?

WRITING SUGGESTIONS

1. Using Kenna and Lacy's entry as a source, write a short, instructive process paper about how Americans should present an idea or product in Taiwan. Assume you are writing to sales representatives traveling to Taiwan for the first time. Provide step-by-step suggestions for how they should conduct themselves from the moment they enter a seminar room to make a presentation.

2. *Collaborative Writing:* Working with a group of students, discuss the differences between high school teachers and college instructors, then develop a chart contrasting their attitudes toward absenteeism, late homework, tests, and research papers.

Responding to Images

Tea Party Rally, Chicago   *Student Rally, Seattle*

1. What is your first reaction to these signs? What do they reveal about the political values of the protestors?

2. What do the word choices reveal about the demonstrators' views of government? Compare the connotations of "spending" and "investing."

3. *Visual Analysis:* In covering demonstrations, do the media reveal bias by the protestors or signs it chooses to photograph? Are outrageous, humorous, or inflammatory messages more likely to attract attention? Can a rally be unfairly characterized by a handful of extremists? Could an opposition group plant fake protestors to wave offensive signs to discredit a movement?

4. *Critical Thinking:* Do these signs demonstrate conflicting solutions for the nation's fiscal problems – cutting government spending to lower the debt versus investing to spur future growth?

5. *Collaborative Writing:* Discuss these images with a group of students and work to develop a short comparison essay that outlines as objectively as possible liberal and conservative views of the role of government. If members disagree, consider developing opposing essays.

Strategies FOR WRITING COMPARISON AND CONTRAST

1. **Determine your purpose.** Is your goal to explain differences between two topics, recommend one over the other, examine advantages and disadvantages, or show how a single subject has changed? Do you want readers to be informed, or do you wish them to make a choice?

2. **Consider your audience.** Before you can compare two items, you may have to explain background information. For example, before comparing two treatments for arthritis, it may be necessary to explain the nature of the disease and to define basic terminology.

3. **Determine which method would best suit your topic.** A short, nontechnical paper might be best organized using the subject-by-subject method. Longer works with facts and statistics that should be placed side by side are better developed using the point-by-point method.

4. Make use of transitional statements. To prevent confusion in writing comparison, use transitional statements carefully. You may wish to invent labels or titles to distinguish clearly the different subjects you are examining.

5. Use visual aids to guide your readers. Careful paragraphing, page breaks, bold or italic headings, and charts can help readers follow your comparison and prevent confusion.

Revising and Editing

1. Do you provide sufficient comparative details about both topics? Make sure you include enough parallel details about both topics for readers to make informed judgments. Avoid unbalanced comparisons, such as presenting details about one car's engine performance and another's style.

2. Do the introduction and conclusion clearly establish the method of organization and the goal of your essay? Are you informing readers about related subjects, recommending a choice, or stating an argument using a "before-and-after" comparison? Do you provide effective transitions so readers can follow your train of thought?

Suggested Topics for Comparison and Contrast Writing

General Assignments

Write a comparative paper on one of the following topics. You may use either the subject-by-subject or point-by-point method of organization. Clearly determine your purpose. Is your goal to inform or recommend?

1. Advantages and disadvantages of buying a home, owning a business, serving in the military, or living with parents
2. Your best and worst jobs
3. Male and female attitudes on dating/marriage/career/parenting
4. Working for a salary or an hourly wage
5. Two popular situation comedies
6. A sport team's performance this season compared to last season
7. Your favorite and least favorite college courses
8. Your parents' values and your own
9. Something you planned and the way it actually turned out
10. Before-and-after views of how a person, family, neighborhood, company, or social behavior changed over time or after a particular event

Writing in Context

1. Imagine you have been asked by a British newsmagazine to write an article explaining the pro-and-con attitudes Americans have about a controversial topic such as gun control, capital punishment, or health care. Your article should be balanced and objective and provide background information rather than express an opinion.

2. Write the text for a brief pamphlet directed to high school seniors comparing high school and college. You may wish to use a chart-like format.
3. Write a letter to a friend comparing the best and worst aspects of your college, dorm room, community, or job.
4. Examine a magazine or blog on cars, computers, or entertainment. Write a letter to the editor or blogger comparing the magazine or blog's best and worst features.
5. Compare two popular student clubs or restaurants for a review in the campus newspaper. Direct your comments to students interested in inexpensive entertainment.

Student Paper: Comparison and Contrast

This is a draft of a comparison paper a student wrote after reading several articles comparing different cultures. In addition to fulfilling a composition assignment, she considered using these ideas for a talk or display for an upcoming Saint Patrick's Day celebration.

First Draft with Instructor's Comments

Two Countries

At first glance Israel and Ireland would appear to have nothing in common except their small size, but in fact they <u>are just alike.</u> Both countries are small but famous nations. They both have the <u>same kind</u> of history. They share the <u>same history</u> of oppression and a long struggle for <u>independance</u>. Both countries have dealt with terrorism and are important nations when it comes to world politics, culture, and terrorism.

exaggeration— no two countries are "just alike"

SP

Maybe the most striking common thing about these countries is that they have <u>identical</u> histories. Both countries only become fully independent after WWII. Maybe the basic thing these countries have is that the Irish and Jews have so much in common as a people. In fact many Americans are Jewish and Irish and they see these countries as special places that represent the roots of <u>there</u> ancestors. The Jews and Irish both have large communities all over the world and have played leading roles in countries from France and England to Chile and Canada.

Explain in detail, too general, how "identical"?

Words missing?
Run-on
their

Another thing that the <u>counties</u> have in common is the way <u>relgion</u> has uniquely shaped their history and continues to play a role in their modern social dynamics. The same conflict happens in both countries over a range of important social and political issues. Some of these same debates happen in the United States today. Maybe the most striking issue of these two countries is the role that the United States has played a part in trying to resolve long-standing issues that <u>has</u> caused terrorism and other problems. Maybe what is most interesting about these countries is how they went from being poor struggling counties just fifty years ago to having the highest per capita incomes in their regions. They are bound to be winners in the global economy.

countries
Sp

Explain, add detail

have
Add details

REVISION NOTES

You have selected an interesting topic, but to create a meaningful comparison essay, you need to refine points and develop more support.

* No two countries are "just alike." For all the similarities you can draw between Ireland and Israel, readers can list dozens of differences. Admit that both are distinctly different nations with unique histories, then point out striking parallels. Parallel items are similar but not totally identical. Avoid absolute statements like "just alike" or "the same."

* A comparison essay needs to be carefully structured. Create stronger paragraph introductions and transitions beyond saying "another thing." Write a stronger outline and clearly define what each paragraph will be about. Use paragraphs as building blocks that work together to create a coherent essay.
* Finally, in order for this essay to be more than just a list of casual observations, add specific details about each point you address. You might want to conduct some research to identify support.

Revised Draft

Parallel States: Israel and Ireland

Despite obvious historical and cultural differences, Israel and Ireland share striking similarities. Both are small—each has a population of five to seven million—yet significant nations. Israel is a narrow sliver of desert on the Mediterranean, a Middle Eastern country with negligible oil reserves. Ireland, an island on the fringe of Europe, is a neutral nation that played marginal roles in World War II and the Cold War.

Yet these nations have greater profiles than their larger and more powerful neighbors, largely because they represent homelands to vast diaspora populations. More Jews live in America than Israel; more Irish live in America than Ireland. American Jews and Irish were significant supporters of the Zionist and Republican movements that helped establish the modern independent states.

Their recent emergence as sovereign states indicates a shared legacy of oppression and occupation. Although both the Jews and the Irish have cultures thousands of years old, Israel and Ireland did not achieve full independence until after the Second World War. Israel was recognized by the United Nations in 1948. Though partitioned in 1922, Ireland was not officially declared a republic until 1949, ending eight hundred years of British rule.

Since their creation, Israel and Ireland have endured decades of violence and terrorism. Both nations have labored to maintain democratic rights while preserving security for their citizenry.

Both nations have dual identities. On one hand, both Israel and Ireland were founded as Western-style parliamentary democracies. Yet both are religious states. Israel is the Jewish homeland. Ireland is a Catholic nation. The religious authorities—the Catholic bishops and orthodox rabbis—believe citizens should accept their views on marriage, divorce, abortion, censorship, and civil customs. Secular forces, who view the religious orthodoxies as tradition bound and male dominated, champion diversity and tolerance. Issues such as the role of women and gay rights evoke similar debates in Israel and Ireland as both nations struggle to reconcile their political and religious traditions.

In recent years both nations have engaged in a peace process to resolve long-standing conflicts in contested areas. In both Northern Ireland and the West Bank, the populations are split by religious, political, and cultural differences.

In the 1990s the president of the United States, prompted by the large number of Jews and Irish in America, played a pivotal role in stimulating stalled peace talks. Negotiations in both regions were difficult to conduct because Israeli and Northern Irish politicians did not wish to recognize leaders of terrorist organizations.

By first inviting Yasser Arafat and Gerry Adams to the White House, Bill Clinton helped transform their public images from terrorists to legitimate leaders so that other democratic leaders could negotiate with them without appearing to endorse violence.

Despite ongoing tensions in both regions, Israel and Ireland enjoy expanding tourism, particularly from millions of American Jews and Irish who enjoy visiting homelands that represent their heritage.

Economically, Israel and Ireland, both poor struggling countries just fifty years ago, have become affluent high-tech powerhouses with rising per-capita incomes and commanding places in the global economy.

Questions for Review and Revision

1. Is the thesis of this essay too general? Does the paper provide genuine insights or merely list obvious observations? Would it be better to fully develop a single issue, such as the role of religion in the two countries?

2. Would a revised introduction and conclusion provide greater focus?

3. What audience does the student seem to address?

4. *Critical Thinking:* To be effective, does a comparison paper have to accomplish more than merely list similarities? Should there be a greater purpose?

5. How effectively does the student organize the comparison? What role does paragraph structure play?

6. Does the student follow the instructor's suggestions? Is this version greatly improved over the first draft?

7. Read the paper aloud. Do you detect any passages that could be revised to reduce wordiness and repetition?

WRITING SUGGESTIONS

1. Write a 500-word essay comparing two nations, cities, or neighborhoods. Stress similarities of which most readers would be unaware.

2. *Collaborative Writing:* Discuss this paper with a group of students. Ask each member to suggest possible changes. Do they agree on which areas need improvement?

EVALUATING COMPARISON AND CONTRAST CHECKLIST

Before submitting your paper, review these points:

1. Are your subjects closely related enough to make a valid comparison?
2. Have you identified the key points of both subjects?
3. Have you selected the best method of organizing your paper?
4. Is the comparison easy to follow? Are transitions clear?
5. Does the comparison meet reader needs and expectations?
6. Have you defined terms or provided background information necessary for readers to appreciate the comparison fully?
7. Is your thesis clearly stated and located where it will have the greatest impact?

Accompanying English CourseMate Resources

 Visit English CourseMate at **www.cengagebrain.com** to find many helpful resources and study tools for this chapter.

CRITICAL ISSUES

- ► Immigration
- ► The American Dream
- ► America's Role in the World
- ► Privacy in the Electronic Age

CONFRONTING ISSUES

Throughout our lives, we face issues that affect our jobs, our futures, our nation, and the planet we live on. In order to fully understand these issues and respond to them effectively, we need to analyze information, evaluate points of view, and express ideas and opinions clearly and logically. You may already have strong views about many of the topics presented in this book. It is likely that you have heard them debated on television or discussed by family and friends. Good writers, however, do more than simply express what they feel or repeat what they have heard from others. To address complex and often controversial subjects, it is important to move beyond first impressions and immediate reactions.

Learning More About Issues

We are bombarded with information about issues through 24-hour cable news networks, talk radio, and the Internet. These sources, however, generally provide superficial and repetitive accounts of current events. To write meaningfully about issues, it is important to understand background information and appreciate different points of view.

Strategies for Learning More About Issues

1. Get an overall description or history of the issue. Try to get the "big picture" first by learning basic facts. What has been the history of immigration? Can the police legally monitor cell phone calls without a warrant? How much of America's national debt is held by foreign investors?

2. Understand key terms. What is "identity theft"? Are there conflicting interpretations of "the right to privacy"? What is a "green card"? What is the difference between "the deficit" and "the national debt"? What is meant by "upward mobility"?

3. Establish key facts. People often discuss issues using misleading or obsolete data. To evaluate sources and write effectively, try to obtain recent and accurate data. How many immigrants enter the United States each year? How large is the national debt? How many people have a Facebook page?

4. Distinguish objective, widely accepted facts from opinions subject to debate, controversy, or conflicting interpretation. Historians may agree that immigration benefited American society in the past but argue over whether twenty-first-century immigration policies will help or harm in the future. Try to find out what information most experts accept as valid. Determine what events, ideas, situations, or interpretations are debated or contested.

5. Identify leading authorities, organizations, experts, commentators, activists, or participants. Who supports immigration reform? Who

rejects it? What columnists, academics, or government officials have written about online privacy? If there is an active debate about this issue, who is on the pro side? Who are the major figures on the con side? Can you separate objective commentators from those who are paid or sponsored to promote a point of view?

6. **Establish main schools of thought or points of disagreement.** What are the major differences among those who write about immigration? What different approaches do experts advocate to counter cyberbullying? Is there a liberal or conservative point of view on this issue? Is this an argument between science and faith or between different visions of social justice?

7. **Examine sources for errors in critical thinking.** Do writers use statistics without explaining how they were collected or analyzed? Do articles rely on anecdotal evidence, borrowed authority, or false analogies? Do you detect that authors are "filtering" data by only selecting facts that support their views and ignoring others? Are there alternative interpretations of the data writers present?

Strategies for Finding Information About Issues

Although you may not have time to conduct extensive research about each issue you will study in this course, there are sources that will help you become a more informed reader and an effective writer.

1. **Review textbooks.** Textbooks offer overviews of subjects and often include endnotes, bibliographies, and footnotes directing you to additional sources.

2. **Survey encyclopedia articles.** A good encyclopedia will present background information and objective facts that summarize issues. Online encyclopedias have search features that allow you to enter keywords to generate a list of related articles.

3. **Review specialized encyclopedias, dictionaries, and directories.** A general encyclopedia such as *The Encyclopedia Britannica* may offer only brief commentaries on subjects and will not include minor people, events, or topics. The reference room of your library will likely have specialized encyclopedias that may contain multipage articles about a person or organization not even mentioned in general encyclopedias.

4. **Review indexes, databases, and abstracts.** Available in print, online, or on CD-ROM, these are valuable tools in obtaining information. Databases list articles. Many provide abstracts that briefly summarize articles, usually in a single paragraph. Skimming abstracts allows you to review a dozen articles in the time it would take to locate a magazine and find a single article. Abstracts not only list the source of an article but also indicate its length and special features such as photographs or tables. Sources like *Psychological Abstracts* and *Criminal Justice Abstracts*

provide summaries in specific disciplines. Other databases are especially useful because they allow you to read and print entire articles. Many libraries subscribe to online services, such as InfoTrac, which list articles from thousands of general, professional, and scholarly newspapers, journals, and magazines.

5. Conduct an Internet search. In addition to specific databases such as Info-Trac, you can use popular search engines such as Google and Bing to locate online sources. Each of these accesses millions of sites on the World Wide Web. These tools offer Web guides that organize sites by categories such as "arts and humanities," "education," or "news and media." You can also enter key words to generate focused lists. Specialized search engines such as Google Scholar limit searches to academic and professional sources.

6. Refine your search. Students unfamiliar with conducting Internet searches are often frustrated by the overwhelming list of unrelated "hits" they receive. Entering **Martin Luther King Jr.** may generate thousands of sites about **Billy Martin**, **Martin Luther**, and **King George III**.
   Search engines usually provide tools to refine your search.

   - Check the spelling of your search terms, especially names.
   - Make the search words as specific as possible.
   - Follow these directions to narrow your search:

     terrorism AND immigration *or* **terrorism + immigration** will list sites that include one or both words.

     terrorism NOT immigration *or* **terrorism − immigration** will list sites about terrorism that do not mention immigration.

     "Leopold and Loeb" will list only sites that include both names, eliminating documents about **King Leopold** or **Loeb Realty.**

   - If you find it difficult to locate useful sources, ask a reference librarian for assistance.

IMMIGRATION

Rather than changing our society to adapt to existing immigration, it would seem to make more sense to change the immigrant stream to fit our society. This would require significantly reducing the number of immigrants permitted to enter without regard to their skills and their ability to compete in and contribute to American society.

Steven Camarota

From "Our New Immigration Predicament" by Steven Camarota, THE AMERICAN ENTERPRISE, December 2000, p. 26.

I reject the idea that America has used herself up in the effort to help outsiders in, and that now she must sit back exhausted, watching people play the cards fate has dealt them... We have no right to be content, to close the door to others now that we are safely inside.

Mario M. Cuomo

From "The American Dream and The Politics on Inclusion," by Mario Cuomo, PSYCHOLOGY TODAY, July 1986, p. 54.

America is a nation of immigrants. Since its founding, the United States has absorbed waves of new arrivals from around the world. Settled primarily by the English, French, and Dutch in the seventeenth century, America attracted large numbers of Germans in the early nineteenth century. During the potato famine of the 1840s and 1850s, 1,700,000 Irish emigrated to the United States. Near the end of the century, millions more individuals arrived from Italy and Eastern Europe. By 1910, 15 percent of American residents were foreign born.

These immigrants filled American cities, adding to their commerce and diversity. European immigrants provided the labor for the country's rapid industrial expansion. Chinese workers laid the railroad tracks that unified the nation and opened the West to economic expansion.

But immigrants also met with resistance. Groups like the Know-Nothings opposed the influx of Irish Catholics. As late as the 1920s, help-wanted ads in many newspapers contained the statement "No Irish Need Apply." California passed laws denying rights to the Chinese. Ivy League universities instituted quotas to limit the enrollment of Jewish students. Many hotels, clubs, and suburbs were "restricted," excluding blacks, Asians, and Jews. Despite discrimination and hardships, these immigrants and their descendants entered mainstream American society and prospered. Today, some 40 percent of Americans can trace their roots to ancestors who passed through Ellis Island during the peak years of immigration a century ago.

The United States is now experiencing the largest increase in immigration in its history. Between 1990 and 2000 the number of foreign-born residents increased 57 percent, reaching 31 million in 2000. Today's immigrants come primarily from Mexico, Asia, and the Middle East. This new wave of immigration is changing the nation's demographics, so that Hispanics, not African Americans, are the largest minority group. Within decades, Muslims may outnumber Jews, making Islam America's second largest religion.

This flow of immigrants, both legal and illegal, has fueled a debate about whether immigration benefits or hurts the United States. Supporters of immigration argue that immigrants offset a declining birthrate, adding the new workers and consumers needed to expand the nation's economy. Critics contend that the United States has a limited capacity to absorb immigrants, especially unskilled ones. Although immigrants provide employers with cheap labor, they burden the local governments that must provide them and their children with educational and health care services. Because of their numbers and historic ties to the land, Mexicans are changing the cultural fabric of the Southwest. In response, Americans concerned about national identity call for tighter border controls, restricted immigration, and the establishment of English as an official language.

The terrorist attacks of September 11, 2001, led to new concerns about immigration, border controls, and national security. The 2008 recession generated demands to limit both legal and illegal immigration because of rising unemployment. At the same time, economists claimed that the United States was suffering a "brain drain" of talented foreign students who are required to leave the country after completing advanced degrees.

Before reading the articles, consider these questions:

Where did your ancestors come from? Were they immigrants? Did they encounter discrimination when they arrived? Did they struggle to maintain their own language and culture or seek to assimilate into American society?

Should people who entered the country illegally be given legal status? Should amnesty be granted to illegal immigrants who have lived and worked in the United States for several years?

Do wealthy countries like the United States have a moral obligation to accept immigrants? The United States has historically admitted immigrants fleeing war and oppression. After Castro assumed power, 250,000 Cubans fled to the United States. Tens of thousands of Vietnamese refugees entered the United States after the fall of South Vietnam. Does a prosperous nation have an obligation to absorb some of the world's poor?

How should the United States determine the number and type of immigrants allowed to enter the country each year? Should talented immigrants be given priority over the unskilled? Should the number of immigrants be limited during times of recession and high unemployment?

Does admitting immigrants improve the country by adding consumers and workers or weaken it by draining resources and burdening public services?

E-Readings Online

Find each article by visiting the Premium Website, accessed through **CengageBrain.com.**

Find each article by accessing CourseMate at **www.cengagebrain.com.**

Jon Meacham. *Who We Are Now*

The 1965 Immigration and Nationality Act signed by Lyndon Johnson will have profound consequences well into the twenty-first century, when whites will constitute only 47 percent of the population, making them the nation's largest minority group.

James W. Thomson. *The Problem That Refuses to Leave*

Before the immigration act, the vast majority of immigrants were white and European. Today's Hispanic immigrants may change the cultural makeup of the United States, prompting conservatives to warn of social and political discord.

Robert J. Bresler. *Immigration: The Sleeping Time Bomb.*

Although past waves of immigrants have enriched this country, Bresler argues that unless immigration is limited our population could swell to 500 million in less than fifty years, reducing the quality of life for all citizens.

Robert Samuelson. *The Hard Truth of Immigration: No Society Has a Boundless Capacity to Accept Newcomers, Especially When Many of Them Are Poor and Unskilled Workers.*

Samuelson states that immigration reform is needed to stem illegal immigration while granting legal status to illegal immigrants already living in the United States. "The stakes," he argues, "are simple: will immigration continue to foster national pride and strength or will it cause more and more weakness and anger?"

Anna Quindlen. *Undocumented, Indispensable; We Like Our Cheap Houses and Our Fresh Fruit*

Our borders remain porous because, despite concerns about illegal immigration, American employers and consumers benefit from cheap labor.

Joel Kotkin and Erika Ozuna. *America's Demographic Future*

"If attitudes harden against immigration," the authors assert, America would "suffer the loss of a major source of entrepreneurial growth and innovation."

Peter Duignan. *Do Immigrants Benefit America?*

Duignan believes that most of today's immigrants "will be an integral part of a revised American community" but warns that "past success does not guarantee that history will repeat itself."

Lawrence Brunner and Stephen M. Colarelli. *Immigration in the Twenty-First Century*

Viewing the United States as an organization, much like a corporation, Brunner and Colarelli maintain it should admit talented immigrants, like a company recruiting employees.

Vivek Wadhwa. *A Reverse Brain Drain*

Having started 52 percent of Silicon Valley's technology companies and contributed 25 percent of America's global patents, highly skilled immigrants are vital to the nation's economy and their loss threatens our country's future.

Harvard International Review. *Going Home: Illegal Immigration Reverses Course*

Now the twelfth-largest economy in the world, Mexico has an expanding middle class and is enrolling more children in school, decreasing the number of Mexican emigrants.

Ronald Brownstein. *Brown versus Gray: Immigrants in the United States*

America will see a growing conflict between young Hispanics who favor government programs in education, social welfare, and health care and an aging white population concerned about the national debt and skeptical of government spending.

Richard D. Lamm and Lawrence Harrison. *A Bold Plan to Solve America's Illegal Immigration Problem*

Lamm and Harrison argue the United States must secure its borders, reduce all immigration, grant amnesty to most current illegal immigrants, and end multiculturalism as a national value.

Arian Campo-Flores. *Don't Fence Them In*

The birth rate in Mexico has collapsed so dramatically that in the future states like Arizona may suffer from a lack of young immigrants needed to offset an aging population.

Critical Reading and Thinking

1. What do authors see as the major costs and benefits of immigration?
2. What reasons do the authors give for the country's unwillingness to address illegal immigration?
3. What drives immigrants, both legal and illegal, to enter the United States?
4. How will the current wave of immigration change American society?
5. What motivates people to demand restrictions on immigration?

WRITING SUGGESTIONS

1. Write an essay about your own family history. Were you or your ancestors immigrants? When did they arrive? Did they encounter any discrimination or hardships? Did they assimilate into mainstream American society or seek to maintain ties to their native language, culture, and traditions?

2. *Collaborative Writing:* Working with other students, develop an essay presenting your group's views on one aspect of immigration—tightening

border security, giving amnesty to illegal aliens, developing a guest worker program, or prosecuting employers who hire illegal aliens. If members have differing opinions, consider developing opposing statements.

3. *Other Modes*

   • Write an essay that *analyzes* the language used to discuss illegal immigrants, such as "undocumented workers," "illegals," and "illegal aliens." Note the role that connotation plays in shaping attitudes toward illegal immigrants.

   • *Compare* current immigrants with those who entered Ellis Island a century ago.

   • Use *process* to explain how immigrants can obtain citizenship.

   • Write a *division* essay to outline the major problems that recent immigrants face in finding employment, housing, and health care in the United States.

   • Use *classification* to rank suggestions for immigration reform from the most to the least restrictive or from the most to the least acceptable to the public and politicians.

Research Paper

You can develop a research paper about immigration by locating additional sources to explore a range of issues:

• How effectively does law enforcement prosecute companies that hire illegal aliens?

• How has concern about terrorism affected immigration policies? Do immigrants from Muslim countries face greater scrutiny than other immigrants? Has Homeland Security viewed the borders as potential weak spots?

• What does current research reveal about the status of Mexican Americans? Are immigrants from Mexico entering the middle class at a similar rate to that of immigrants from other countries?

• How will the new wave of immigrants influence American society, culture, economy, and foreign policy?

• Examine the impact immigration has had on other developed countries, such as Canada, the United Kingdom, France, Germany, and Italy. What problems, if any, have immigrant populations posed in these nations?

For Further Reading

To locate additional sources on immigration, enter these search terms as Info-Trac subjects:

Immigrants

Subdivisions
- analysis
- behavior
- cases
- civil rights
- economic aspects
- education
- laws, regulations and rules
- personal narratives
- political activity
- psychological aspects
- social aspects
- statistics

Additional Sources

Using a search engine such as Google or Bing, enter one or more of the following terms to locate additional sources:

immigration	green cards
visa lotteries	Ellis Island
citizenship	bilingual education
Mexican Americans	English only

See Evaluating Internet Sources Checklist on pages 480–481.

THE AMERICAN DREAM

... there has been also the *American dream,* that dream of a land in which life should be better and richer and fuller for every man, with opportunity for each according to his ability or achievement . . . . It is not a dream of motor cars and high wages merely, but a dream of a social order in which each man and each woman shall be able to attain to the fullest stature of which they are innately capable, and be recognized by others for what they are . . .

James Truslow Adams, 1931

From THE EPIC OF AMERICA by James Truslow Adams (Boston: Little, Brown & Company, 1931), p. 404.

James Truslow Adams popularized the term "American Dream" during the Depression to describe a country that fostered personal fulfillment free of social and class barriers. In his view this American dream required that the wealthy contribute to the "Great Society" and that the poor strive upward not only economically but culturally:

We cannot become a great democracy by giving ourselves up as individuals to selfishness, physical comfort, and cheap amusements. The very foundation of the American dream of a better and richer life for all is that all, in varying degrees, shall be capable of wanting to share in it. It can never be wrought into a reality by cheap people or by "keeping up with the Joneses."

From THE EPIC OF AMERICA by James Truslow Adams (Boston: Little, Brown & Company, 1931), p. 411.

In the prosperity following the World War II, the public came to view Adams's "richer life" largely in monetary terms. The American Dream was associated with two central ideals—upward mobility and homeownership. Americans celebrated the belief that through hard work anyone could succeed and build a business or obtain a good job. Men and women who had grown up during the Depression witnessed the postwar expansion of a consumer economy based on easy credit, well-paying manufacturing jobs, and an aspirational conviction that children would do better than their parents. The hit song *Only in America* claimed the United States was a country where "a kid without a cent" could "grow up to be President." A key goal was owning a house. In the 1950s and 1960s suburbs mushroomed across the country, and the single-family home became a standard feature of middle-class life.

Popular culture created darker and more decadent visions of the American Dream, suggesting it had been reduced to greedy self-indulgence. Posters for Brian De Palma's 1983 film *Scarface* used the tagline "He loved the American Dream. With a vengeance" to describe Tony Montana's rise from penniless Cuban refugee to cocaine kingpin. The long-running Broadway musical *Miss Saigon* included a song by a Vietnamese nightclub owner praising the American Dream symbolized by a Marilyn Monroe-like blonde sitting astride an oversized Cadillac. Social critics claimed Americans had become "aspirational," obsessed with affluence and consumerism. The American tract home had given way to the ubiquitous "McMansion," often purchased with little or no money down.

Bankers, realtors, immigrants, and politicians embraced the concept of an "ownership society" that promised to provide families with security and improve communities. The 2003 American Dream Downpayment Initiative gave funds to low-income homebuyers for down payment and closing costs. The new program was promoted with a customized bus named the American Dream Express. With rising home prices, real estate appeared a safe investment, and many consumers borrowed to buy houses they could not afford.

The 2008 recession caused millions of Americans to lose their jobs, their homes, and their retirement savings. Facing deficits, state and local governments laid off public employees and cut salaries. New graduates, many of them deeply in debt, faced dismal job prospects. While many economists maintained that the recession, though severe, would, like others, lead to recovery, some insisted that a lower standard of living had to be accepted as "the new normal." Xavier University's Center for the Study of the American Dream found that although most Americans remain confident about their chances of achieving their dreams, they believe it will be harder for them than prior generations.

Before reading the articles, consider these questions:

How do you define the American Dream? What role does money play in your view? Can self-fulfillment and personal freedom lead to happiness without material comfort?

Do you consider owning a home essential to achieving the American Dream? If your parents owned a home, did they tell you stories about building or purchasing it? Are renters made to feel like second-class citizens in your community?

Do most of your friends expect to earn as much or more than their parents? Would they consider it unfair or themselves failures if they made substantially less than their parents?

Has the lingering recession changed students' expectations about their job prospects, future salaries, and lifestyles?

If your ancestors were immigrants, did they come to this country in search of the American Dream? How did they define their dream? Did they, in their view, achieve their goals?

How can the United States rebuild or redefine the American Dream? What role should the government play in helping Americans achieve their goals? Should people learn to succeed based on individual effort with less support from government? Should the government provide education and loans to help people succeed?

Would you consider moving to another country if it offered a better job or a higher standard of living than you could obtain in the United States? Why or why not?

E-Readings Online

Find each article by accessing CourseMate at **www.cengagebrain.com.**

Ronald Brownstein. *Is The American Dream a Myth?*

"Though we venerate the American Dream," Brownstein notes, "studies show that children born to low-income parents in the United States are more likely to remain trapped near the bottom than their counterparts in Europe."

From "Is the American Dream a Myth?" by Ronald Brownstein, NATIONAL JOURNAL, October 16, 2009.

Kristine Springate. *At What Price the American Dream?*

"Confident in the power of the American dream," an ESL teacher discovers that immigrant children benefit from material wealth in the United States which "comes at a high cost—their own isolation and disconnection from their culture."

James W. Thomson. *The American Dream's Death Spiral*

For too long "the American Dream seemed to compel people to set unreasonable goals for themselves, and then encouraged them to use more debt to realize their objectives."

Bob Herbert. *Hiding From Reality*

"However you want to define the American dream," Bob Herbert writes, "there is not much of it that's left anymore." Only when the nation faces how dire its situation is "will we be able to begin resuscitating the dream."

Christopher Caldwell. *Fantasy Politics*

Surveys reveal that immigrants are "among the biggest believers in the American dream" while middle-aged white women in the Midwest are the most skeptical.

David Streitfeld. *Ruins of an American Dream*

Believing that "owning a home is the American dream," developers, consumers, and lenders became reckless, convinced "that this dream could be achieved with no risk, no worry and no money down."

Scott Winship. *Mobility Impaired: The American Dream Must Move From the Bottom Up*

Both liberals and conservatives are troubled by the lack of upward mobility for low-income families, especially minorities. "Two-thirds of black children," Winship notes, "experience a level of neighborhood poverty growing up that just six percent of white children will ever see."

Louis Uchitelle. *A New Generation, an Elusive American Dream*

Watching "America's once mighty economic engine losing its pre-eminence in a global economy," a WWII veteran and retired stockbroker urges his grandson, an unemployed Ivy League graduate, to seek work overseas.

Brook Larmer. *Building the American Dream in China*

Laid off by a New York architectural firm, Daniel Gillen found work in China, where he found opportunities unavailable in the United States, building entire new cities and a state-of-the-art museum that cannot be found in America.

David Brooks. *The Gospel of Wealth*

Religious leaders are redefining the American Dream, rejecting material success for spiritual growth and service to God.

Lauren Sandler. *The American Nightmare*

Despite their good jobs, homes, and children, Americans are increasingly suffering from anxiety and depression. Behavioral researchers reveal that much of people's discontent "seems linked to the unrealistic expectations of the American Dream."

PR Newswire. *Heritage Unveils "Saving the American Dream Plan"*

Edwin Feulner, president of the Heritage Foundation, argues that "America is on the brink of national decline because Congress has been spending beyond its means." To restore prosperity, workers must be given incentives to save, the federal government must be reduced by 50 percent, and the federal budget must be balanced within a decade.

Isabel Sawhill. *Bring Back the American Dream? It's Not That Hard.*

Restoring the American dream requires "an activist government and individual responsibility" to create jobs, reduce debt, improve education, and strengthen families.

Critical Reading and Thinking

1. How do most authors define the American Dream?
2. What role did government policies play in the mortgage crisis?
3. Do writers appear to blame American consumers for lavish spending and reckless borrowing?
4. What factors have slowed upward mobility in the United States?
5. Are Americans reluctant to believe the country contains a permanent underclass? Do they want to believe that poverty is a temporary condition people can overcome with hard work? Do they presume that poverty is lifestyle choice marked by personal decisions such as dropping out of school, engaging in crime, consuming drugs, or having children out of wedlock?
6. What is motivating young Americans to seek success by moving overseas?

WRITING SUGGESTIONS

1. Write an essay defining your vision of the American Dream.

2. Describe a popular book or movie you feel most accurately depicts your view of the American Dream.

3. *Collaborative Writing:* Working with other students, develop an essay presenting your group's observations on one aspect of the American Dream—getting a good job, owning a home, or doing better than previous generations. If members disagree, consider developing opposing statements.

4. *Other Modes*

   • *Compare* your parents' American Dream and your own. What differences, if any, do you see? Do you feel you will have to work harder or wait longer to achieve your goals?

   • *Classify* elements of your vision of the American Dream from most to least important. What do you consider necessary to achieve happiness?

   • Use *process* to explain how individuals can achieve success in a challenging economy or the steps the government needs to take to assist citizens in achieving their goals.

   • Use *narration* to relate the story of someone you know who achieved the American Dream.

   • *Analyze* the meaning of the phrase "American Dream." Does "dream" suggest an illusion, something that is an unrealistic goal? Do Americans assume that everyone deserves to possess a level of success or just the opportunity to pursue it on his or her own? Is widespread poverty acceptable as long as individuals have the ability to achieve great wealth through talent and hard work?

Research Paper

You can develop a research paper about the American Dream by locating additional sources to explore a range of issues.

• Analyze the surveys conducted by Xavier University's Center for the Study of the American Dream (http://www.xavier.edu/american-dream/). What do the polls reveal about Americans' current attitudes?

• How have declining job prospects influenced the actions of graduates? Are many young Americans seeking career and business opportunities overseas? Are fewer foreign students seeking to stay in the United States after they graduate?

• What does current data reveal about the housing market? Can a young working couple with average incomes obtain an affordable mortgage?

• Review websites by the Democratic and Republican parties. Compare and contrast their views on restoring the American Dream.

- Review the epilogue of James Truslow Adams's book *The Epic of America*, which describes his view of the American Dream. Review online book reviews of commentaries written when his work was first published in 1931. Use InfoTrac or other databases and enter "James Truslow Adams" or "The Epic of America" as keywords to find recent articles about the American Dream. How have critics and commentators viewed his 1931 vision of an ideal society?

For Further Reading

To locate additional sources on the American Dream, enter these search terms as InfoTrac subjects:

American Dream

Subdivisions

analysis
economic aspects
evaluation
other
political aspects
portrayals
social aspects
surveys

Additional Sources

Using a search engine such as Google or Bing, enter one or more of the following terms to locate additional sources:

American dream	upward mobility
homeownership	middle class
real wages	foreclosures
mortgage crisis	James Truslow Adams
unemployment	American incomes

See Evaluating Internet Sources Checklist on pages 480–481.

AMERICA'S ROLE IN THE WORLD

Once we cease to distract ourselves . . . we shall be amazed to discover that there is already an immense American internationalism. American jazz, Hollywood movies, American slang, American machines and patented products, are in fact the only things that every community in the world . . . recognizes in common. Blindly, unintentionally, accidentally and really in spite of ourselves, we are already a world power . . . America is already the intellectual, scientific and artistic capital of the world.

Henry Luce, 1941

From "The American Century," by Henry R. Luce in LIFE magazine, February 12, 1941, pp. 61–65.

America will never again experience the global dominance it enjoyed in the 17 years between the Soviet Union's collapse and financial crisis of 2008. Those days are over.

Gideon Rachman, 2011

From "Think Again: American Decline: This Time It's For Real," by Gideon Rachman, FOREIGN POLICY, January-February 2011.

In February 1941 *Life* featured an article by Henry Luce, the magazine's founder. In "The American Century," Luce called upon Americans to play a greater role in international affairs. World War II had been raging in Europe for eighteen months, but the United States remained neutral. Luce challenged Americans to accept their duty and "exert upon the world the full impact of our influence." America, he asserted, was "the powerhouse of the ideals of Freedom and Justice" obligated "to be the Good Samaritan of the entire world." America's material wealth, technical knowledge, and democratic values would create "the first great American century."

Four years later the United States emerged from the World War II the most powerful nation on Earth, with its troops occupying the capitals of its defeated enemies, and the only country with the atomic bomb. For the next half century, the United States' power was checked by the Soviet Union and its allies. To confront the threat of Communism, the United States developed an unparalleled arsenal of nuclear and conventional weapons and sought to influence nations in the "free world" through economic aid.

The collapse of the Soviet Union in 1991 created a "unipolar world" in which the United States stood alone as the richest, most powerful, and most influential nation. With only 5 percent of the planet's population, the United States controlled 27 percent of the world's wealth. No country or group of countries could challenge it militarily. American corporations like Microsoft, Apple, GE, and IBM shaped education, business, and communications around the globe. Hollywood films were shown worldwide, and American words and ideas became standard phrases in foreign languages.

The terrorist attacks of 2001 shocked the nation, tarnishing America's image as an unassailable superpower. The long wars in Iraq and Afghanistan cost trillions of dollars and escalated the national debt. The financial crisis of 2008 caused record foreclosures, unemployment, and business failures. Despite massive government spending, unemployment remained high and corporations reported sluggish growth.

By 2012 the United States had a $16 trillion national debt, its government annually spending a trillion dollars more than it took in. With an aging population requiring more health care, states facing unfunded pension liabilities, continued military operations overseas, and American companies investing abroad, critics began to see the United States as a nation in decline. China now made more cars than any other country in the world, producing eight times as much steel as the United States, and consuming more cement than the rest of the world combined. Shanghai now has twice as many skyscrapers as Manhattan and Macau five times the gaming revenue of Las Vegas. In addition, the rising economies of India, Russia, and Brazil weakened America's hold on the world economy. A Pew survey of fourteen nations found that 42 percent of respondents considered China the world's leading economy, compared to 36 percent who named the United States.

As economists and historians examined America's role in the world, vigorous debates developed between those who saw the United States in an inevitable decline and those who believed that adjustments in fiscal and foreign policy could chart a new course for American preeminence in the world.

Before reading the articles, consider these questions:

Do you think most Americans measure the quality of their country by its status on the world stage or by its economy at home?

Should American leaders accept decline as inevitable and try to manage a peaceful transition to a different world order or seek to maintain American preeminence, even if it requires making tremendous sacrifices?

Should the United States view China as a rival power or a potential partner in a new world order?

Do you think Americans are willing to pay more taxes and accept cuts in Social Security and Medicare to lower the national debt and strengthen the country's standing in the world?

How should a nation's power be measured—by its military power, its capital reserves, or its cultural influence?

Will Americans resist accepting the idea that the United States is destined to become the second most powerful country in the world?

How will America's changing role in the world affect terrorism? If America is perceived to be weaker, will terrorists be emboldened to attack or feel less threatened by the United States? Will a "multipolar" world lead terrorists to target other nations?

E-Readings Online

Find each article by accessing CourseMate at **www.cengagebrain.com.**

Mortimer Zuckerman. *A Second American Century*

In 1998 Mortimer Zuckerman confidently predicted the American economic boom of the 1990s would continue into the twenty-first century because of the nation's entrepreneurial innovation and technical advancements.

Andrew Bacevich. *The American Century Is Over—Good Riddance*

In 2012 Andrew Bacevich, noting the impact of costly wars abroad and the recession of 2008, asserted that the American Century was over. "Among the conjurers of imperial dreams in Washington," he argued, "the American Century might live on. In places like Newark or Cleveland or Detroit, where real people live, it's finished."

Gideon Rachman. *Think Again: American Decline: This Time It's for Real*

Although it survived past challenges from the Soviet Union and Japan, the United States faces a formidable rival in China, which "is now the world's leading exporter and its biggest manufacturer . . . sitting on more than $2.5 trillion in foreign reserves."

Stephen Walt. *The End of an American Era*

"The twilight of the American Era," Walt believes, "is not an occasion to mourn or a time to cast blame. . . . Americans should see the end of the American Era as an opportunity to rebalance our international burdens and focus on our domestic imperatives."

From "The Twilight of the American Era," by Stephen Walt, THE NATIONAL INTEREST, November-December 2011.

Christopher Layne. *The Global Power Shift from West to East*

Like the British a century before, American leaders are striking "a pose of denial" as their nation's ability to influence world events ebbs and new powers rise to challenge their leadership.

Thomas Friedman. *Superbroke Superpower?*

Friedman warns that America, burdened with debt, "is about to learn a very hard lesson. You can borrow your way to prosperity over the short run but not to geopolitical power over the long run. That requires a real and growing economic engine." Unwilling to cut budgets at home, American leaders will be forced to reduce the nation's role overseas.

From "Superbroke Superpower?" by Thomas Friedman, INTERNATIONAL HERALD TRIBUNE, September 6, 2010.

Charles Kupchan. *Is American Primacy Really Diminishing?*

Although United States currently maintains "economic strength and military superiority . . . power is undeniably flowing away from the West to developing nations." America must "husband its many strengths, be more sparing with military force, and rely on judicious diplomacy to tame the onset of a multipolar world."

From "Is American Primacy Really Diminishing?" by Charles Kupchan, NATIONAL JOURNAL, March 15, 2012.

The American Spectator. *Is America in Decline?*

Policy mistakes that have led to American decline can be reversed if future presidents show bold leadership and dramatically reduce federal spending to address the national debt.

Arvind Subramanian. *The Inevitable Superpower*

The future will not be the "multipolar" world many predict but a "unipolar" world with a single superpower, China. By 2030 China will generate twice as much world trade as the United States.

Niall Ferguson. *Let China Do It*

Although China is far more dependent on Mideast oil than the United States is, it "contributes almost nothing to stability in the oil-producing heartland of the Arabian deserts." America, which has spent billions intervening in the Middle East, should reconsider its security priorities.

Thomas Friedman. *Imagined in America*

China provides not only challenges but opportunities to the American economy. Citing security concerns, the United States limits the number of tourist visas granted to the Chinese. However, if the United States accepted as many Chinese tourists as Hong Kong does, it could add over $115 billion to America's resorts, hotels, restaurants, and casinos.

The Economist. *Myths Large and Small: The Economic Waning of America*

The United States may be more able to cope with its economic challenges than Asia or Europe. Problems caused by the 2008 recession are not necessarily indicators of a general decline.

Joel Kotkin. *Undying Creed*

Because of its values and high birth rate, the United States will remain a world power as the aging populations of China and Europe weaken their countries' future growth.

Critical Reading and Thinking

1. What do the authors view as the causes for America's loss of status?
2. Do the writers see American decline as inevitable or reversible? Do any authors view concerns about America's role in the world as unfounded?
3. What roles do demographics play in America's future role? Will the retiring Baby Boom generation weaken the country? Will immigration and a higher birthrate make America more competitive as European and Asian populations age and decline?
4. Would Americans vote for a presidential candidate who claimed the United States had to accept being a lesser power?
5. Will our national debt invariably force the United States to bow to Chinese influence?

WRITING SUGGESTIONS

1. Write an essay defining how a nation's standing in world influence should be measured. Are economic security and energy independence more important than military strength?

2. *Collaborative Writing:* Working with other students, develop an essay presenting your group's views on one aspect of America's role in the world—its national debt, trade with China, immigration, military actions overseas, or the war on terrorism. If members have differing opinions, consider developing opposing statements.

3. *Other Modes*

   • Write a *cause and effect* essay that details the reasons for and the results of America's changing status in the world.

   • Write a *comparison* essay that contrasts different views about American decline. Whose arguments, in your view, are more credible?

   • Use *classification* to rank the most powerful nations in the world. Which rising countries pose challenges to the United States? Which powerful nations could prove to be valuable allies?

   • Write a *process* essay detailing steps American leaders must take to maintain the country's leadership status in world affairs.

   • *Analyze* the social, political, and cultural impact of China becoming the world's largest economy. Will Americans resent becoming the second most influential country in the world? Which political party do you believe is better able to adapt to a change in our nation's status? Will the American people react rationally to this change or will they respond with resentment, denial, and hostility?

Research Paper

You can develop a research paper about America's role in the world by locating additional sources to explore a range of issues.

• Write a paper analyzing predictions about the rise of China. Distinguish between objective facts and subjective interpretations. Which commentators, in your view, appear more credible—those who see China as the inevitable leader of the twenty-first century or those who believe demographic, domestic, and cultural issues will prevent China from replacing the United States as the world's leading superpower?

• Conduct research to determine the lasting economic costs of the wars in Iraq and Afghanistan. How will these costs affect American foreign and military policy in the future?

- Examine the impact the national debt has on other nations' view of American power. Do other countries believe America is bound to lose its leadership status because of its inability to address its deficits?
- The United States is less dependent on oil from the Middle East than it was twenty years ago. Could new sources of fossil fuels in North America and alternative energy make the United States less vulnerable to turmoil in the Middle East and therefore more powerful?
- Determine the current status of America's military force. Is the United States doing enough to defend itself against new threats to its security, such as cyberattacks?

For Further Reading

To locate additional sources on America's role in the world, enter these search terms as InfoTrac subjects:

United States

Subdivisions   analysis
          economic aspects
          economic policy
          forecasts and trends
          foreign policy
          growth
          influence
          international aspects
          international relations
          statistics
          strategic aspects

Additional Sources

Using a search engine such as Google or Bing, enter one or more of the following terms to locate additional sources:

superpowers	China
American decline	national debt
America's role in the world	American power
American trade deficit	American Century
Henry Luce	American era

See Evaluating Internet Sources Checklist on pages 480–481.

PRIVACY IN THE ELECTRONIC AGE

The Internet's greatest impact has been its ability to provide a voice for the many people who have no formal opportunity to speak in the real world.

Thomas A. Workman

From "The Real Impact of Virtual Worlds," by Thomas Workman, THE CHRONICLE OF HIGHER EDUCATION, September 19, 2008.

Two years ago I warned that we were in danger of sleep walking into a surveillance society. Today I fear that we are in fact waking up to a surveillance society that is already all around us.

Richard Thomas

From "Britain's Ranking on Surveillance Worries Privacy Advocate," THE NEW YORK TIMES, November 3, 2006.

The Internet, cell phones, YouTube, Facebook, and Twitter have changed the fabric of modern life. Individuals can now operate corporations from a laptop, conducting business worldwide without the need for an expensive office or support staff. Parents can track children without having to play phone tag. Corporations can keep in touch with employees and customers in real time. Accident victims can summon immediate help by cell phone and be instantly located by GPS. Stolen automobiles and lost pets can be tracked by satellite.

But these conveniences have eroded personal privacy. Cell phone records can reveal a person's location. The average New Yorker is photographed twenty-three times a day by surveillance cameras in apartment lobbies, stores, elevators, and street corners. An embarrassing photograph taken at a party that once might have circulated in a single office or high school can be posted online. Erin Andrews, a sportscaster, was secretly videotaped undressing in her hotel room by a predator. Posted online where it could be viewed, shared, and downloaded by anyone, the video turned a single violation of privacy into a never-ending global personal assault.

Today 70 percent of teenagers have online profiles, which often contain personal information or potentially compromising postings. Few realize that an innocent family snapshot posted on a personal page may reveal a house number or a license plate that could be used by stalkers.

A survey of 500 adolescents revealed that over half had received emails containing inappropriate sexual content. Ilene Berson, a professor of child and family studies, finds that teenagers are especially vulnerable online because for them "the Net is a kind of make-believe world where the regular expectations and rules don't seem to apply. They don't consider that once you turn off the computer, it might spill over into their life."

Employers frequently examine job applicants' online profiles, as do attorneys who screen potential clients and witnesses for damaging or compromising postings. Alarmed that a simple Google search produces unflattering images or comments, many professionals hire companies that specialize in cleaning up online reputations by deleting or burying negative information.

The Internet has raised First Amendment issues. Should high school teachers who post racist comments online or whose Facebook page depicts them drinking or behaving inappropriately be terminated or suspended? Should schools discipline students who slander principals with online parodies they produce at home?

The near-universal use of cell phone cameras and sites like YouTube have created a new global medium that can make anyone a journalist capable of recording a historical event for a worldwide audience. In 2009, cell phones could broadcast images of street demonstrations in Iran that the government tried to block and did not cover on its official media. Sites like YouTube and blogs allowed dissidents to disseminate information and inform the outside world.

These same electronic tools, however, can be used by governments to observe, track, and disrupt dissident movements. Following the demonstrations in Tehran, Iranian security police tracked cell phone accounts and examined online videos to identify demonstrators. In 2011 Syrian intelligence posted fake anti-Assad Facebook pages to lure rebels to websites where spyware and malware enabled the government to track their email, turn on their laptop cameras without their knowledge, monitor cell phone calls, and follow their movements.

Before reading the articles, consider these questions:

Have you posted photographs or personal information on a Facebook page? Have you considered if you have revealed too much of your identity?

Have you observed people taking pictures or videos of others at parties or public events without their knowledge? Would you feel violated if you discovered that someone had posted your picture online without your permission?

Should an employer evaluate applicants based on pictures they may have posted in high school or college?

Would you conduct an online search to locate information about a person before responding to a request for a date or hiring a babysitter?

Do cell phones and the Internet create citizen journalists who can bypass censorship, or do they provide tools to distort events and manipulate perceptions of events?

Does the presence of surveillance cameras make you feel spied upon or protected?

E-Readings Online

Find each article by accessing CourseMate at **www.cengagebrain.com**.

Sami Lais. *No More Secrets?*

With computers recording credit card purchases, GPS devices tracking their movements, and video surveillance cameras taping their behavior, people are daily losing any sense of privacy. More recently, "sexting" has led to blackmail, school suspensions, and prosecutions.

Michael Isikoff. *The Snitch in Your Pocket*

Most of the owners of the nation's 277 million cell phones do not realize their devices can allow authorities to track their movements in real time.

John C. Dvorak. *The Black Box in Your Car Is a Cop in Disguise*

Devices that monitor speed, braking habits, and the use of on-board media promise to lower insurance rates for careful drivers but erode personal privacy.

David Hatch. *Tracking Your Every Move*

ICanStalkU.com, an educational tool, reveals how easily personal data can be compromised online. A teenager's simple Tweet instantly revealed her name, photograph, and current location.

Jeff Gelles. *Web Cams Have Long Concerned Computer Pros*

The widespread use of webcams and increasingly sophisticated remote control software have created threats to privacy and personal safety. Workplace webcams have been hacked by predators to track their victims, and a school-supplied laptop photographed a teenager's bedroom.

Jamie Malanowski. *Big Brother: How a Million Surveillance Cameras in London Are Proving George Orwell Wrong*

Not far from the flat where Orwell wrote his prophetic novel *1984*, thirty-two CCTV cameras run 24 hours a day, creating a "surveillance society" that has eroded privacy but given the public a greater sense of personal security.

Chloe Albanesius and Erik Rhey. *Are You on the Map?*

Online map services like Google Maps, which include street-view images of public buildings and private homes, concern citizens and security experts who fear these images can be used by predators and terrorists to target victims.

Mondaq Business Briefing. *"One of Our Laptops is Missing"—The Risks of Data Loss and How to Prevent It*

Lost or misused data can become a toxic liability for corporations and lead to fines and loss of reputations.

Thomas A. Workman. *The Real Impact of Virtual Worlds*

Students who post videos of themselves participating in risky or outrageous activities should be viewed as engaging in "misdirected recreation rather than purposeful misconduct."

Maria Giffen. *Online Privacy: When Your Life Goes Public*

Seventy percent of high school students have online profiles, and over half have posted their own photos, with little realization how their actions in cyber-space may affect their futures.

Sara Lipka. *The Digital Limits of "In Loco Parentis"*

Online postings of rowdy student behavior vex college administrators. "They know what to do with a drunken student," Lipka notes. "But what about a Facebook photo of a seemingly drunken student?"

PC Magazine Online. *10 Tips for Safe Social Networking*

People can avoid personal and professional embarrassment by posting only items they want everyone to see, realizing that all correspondence is public, and managing privacy settings.

Meredith Bennett-Smith. *Job Interviewer Asks for Facebook Password. Should You Give It?*

Employers who already examine job applicants' public online profiles are increasingly asking potential employees for passwords to examine their private "digital footprint."

Critical Reading and Thinking

1. What do the various authors see as the advantages and disadvantages of electronic devices?
2. How has the cell phone camera changed our notions of privacy?
3. What dangers do young people expose themselves to online?
4. Should teachers be suspended or terminated because their Facebook pages show them partying and drinking away from school?
5. Should attorneys be allowed to introduce online profiles as evidence to discredit witnesses in court?

WRITING SUGGESTIONS

1. Write an essay about one aspect of the electronic age you have observed. Have you noticed anyone posting personal information or photographs on Facebook that you think could have negative consequences? Do young people think before they post?
2. *Collaborative Writing:* Working with other students, write a set of guidelines people should follow before posting items on social networking sites.
3. *Other Modes*
   • Write a *narrative* essay about a personal experience involving a cell phone or the Internet that illustrates the advantages or disadvantages of electronic devices.

- Write a paper that outlines the *effects* of social networking.
- Use *comparison* to identify the advantages and disadvantages of cell phone cameras, social networking sites, or GPS systems.
- Write a *persuasive* paper supporting or criticizing schools that suspend students for posting online parodies accusing principals or teachers of criminal conduct.
- Use *analysis* to study how the concept of privacy has changed in the electronic age.

Research Paper

You can develop a research paper about privacy in the electronic age by locating additional sources to explore a range of issues:

- What cases about online postings have tested First Amendment rights?
- Do employers have the right to monitor employee use of company computers, cell phones, and other electronic devices?
- Have surveillance cameras lowered crime?
- Have terrorists used the Internet to recruit followers, disseminate propaganda, and plan attacks?
- Can police and courts effectively deter online stalking?

For Further Reading

To locate additional sources on privacy in the electronic age, enter these search terms as InfoTrac subjects:

Privacy
Subdivisions:

analysis
beliefs, opinions, and attitudes
cases
political aspects
public opinion
social aspects

Cellular Telephones
Subdivisions:

analysis
laws, regulations, and rules
public opinion

Electronic Mail Systems
Subdivision:

analysis
ethical aspects
laws, regulations, and rules
political aspects
public opinion

Internet

Subdivisions: analysis

                                      beliefs, opinions, and attitudes

                                      political aspects

Additional Sources

Using a search engine such as Google or Bing, enter one or more of the following terms to locate additional sources:

surveillance cameras	GPS systems	Facebook
online predators	privacy	Twitter etiquette
email privacy	identity theft	data mining
YouTube	bloggers	Google

See Evaluating Internet Sources Checklist on pages 480–481.

Analysis: Making Evaluations

8

What Is Analysis?

Analysis moves beyond description and narration to make judgments or evaluations about persons, places, objects, ideas, or situations. A movie reviewer *describes* a new film and then *analyzes* it—critiquing the plot, acting, special effects, and social message. A historian *narrates* an event and then *evaluates* its lasting significance. Marketing executives *summarize* sales reports to *judge* the results of their advertising campaign. A psychiatrist *examines* a patient and then *diagnoses* the individual's mental condition.

Analysis seeks to answer questions. Does aspirin prevent heart attacks? What are Vicki Shimi's chances of being elected governor? Is General Motors' new hybrid car fuel efficient? Does America have too many lawyers? Is addiction a disease? How effective were the poverty programs launched in the 1960s? What is the best way to remove asbestos from a public school? Is a defendant mentally competent to stand trial? Is the central figure of *Death of a Salesman*, Willy Loman, a victim of society or of his own delusions? The answers to all these questions require a careful gathering of information, critical thinking, and a clear presentation of the writer's thesis.

Analysis entails more than expressing an opinion or creating an impression. In an analytical paper, you cannot simply write, "I hated *Death of a Salesman* because it was stupid," or "Welfare programs waste taxpayers' money." Positions must be based on observations and evidence. Why is the play stupid? What facts demonstrate that welfare programs are wasteful? When asked to write analytical papers, students often supply only description and narration, summarizing a short story or describing a social problem. To keep your paper analytical, use the reporter's "Five W's"—*Who? What? When? Where? Why?*—to prompt critical thinking. Questions force you to examine ideas and evidence to provide answers instead of simply summarizing what you read or describing what you saw.

Subjective and Objective Analysis

The way writers develop analytical writing depends greatly on context. In many situations, writers rely wholly on personal observation and experience. Film critics, political columnists, book reviewers, fashion consultants, and social commentators tend to write subjective analysis. **Subjective analysis** is based on close observation and careful interpretation. The writer's points are supported by examples and illustrations he or she has chosen. Robert Reich (page 251) describes reasons why activists oppose Wal-Mart and then analyzes the consumer behavior, including his own, that has made Wal-Mart the nation's largest retailer:

> Bowing to intense pressure from neighborhood and labor groups, a real estate developer has just given up plans to include a Wal-Mart store in a mall in Queens, thereby blocking Wal-Mart's plan to open its first store in New York City. In the eyes of Wal-Mart's detractors, the Arkansas-based chain embodies the worst kind of economic exploitation: it pays its 1.2 million American workers an average of only $9.68 an hour, doesn't provide most of them with health insurance, keeps out unions, has a checkered history on labor law and turns main streets into ghost towns by sucking business away from small retailers. But isn't Wal-Mart really being punished for our sins? After all, it's not as if Wal-Mart's founder, Sam Walton, and his successors created the world's largest retailer by putting a gun to our heads and forcing us to shop there. . .
>
> The problem is, the choices we make in the market don't fully reflect our values as workers or as citizens. I didn't want our community bookstore in Cambridge, Mass., to close (as it did last fall) yet I still bought lots of books from Amazon.com. In addition, we may not see the larger bargain when our own job or community isn't directly at stake. I don't like what's happening to airline workers, but I still try for the cheapest fare I can get.

Objective analysis begins with close observations but seeks to answer questions through factual research. In objective analysis, the writer needs more than personal experience and anecdotal examples to support a position. In "How Television Distorts Reality" (page 264), Benjamin Radford analyzes newscasts to demonstrate that television disproportionately focuses on crime and disasters while paying minimal attention to other issues:

> Another study, this one headed by Syracuse University professor Robert Lissit, found that of 100 newscasts around the country, "nearly 30 percent

of the news time was spent on crime and the courts. Ten percent was devoted to reporting calamities and natural disasters. Only 15 percent of the newscasts were devoted to government and politics. Health and medicine: about 7 percent. Race relations: 1.2 percent. Education: less than one percent." According to Lissit, crime gets a disproportionate amount of coverage not because it is important but because it is easy to cover: "A few shots of the crime scene, a quick interview with a police officer, or someone in the neighborhood, and a quick reporter-on-camera standup. Summary, and that's the end of the story." Noncrime issues such as politics or education require more background and effort and usually can't be wrapped up in such a tidy, quick package.

Objective analysis is not limited to facts and statistics. Writers can balance numbers with interviews, personal examples, and anecdotal accounts. To dramatize the growing number of women who choose not to have children, Jessica Valenti (pages 275–276) includes both statistics and quotations taken from surveys:

> A 2010 Pew Research Center study showed that the rate of American women who did not have children almost doubled since 1976. That's nearly one in five women today.
>
> Laura Scott, the author of *Two Is Enough: A Couple's Guide to Living Childless by Choice,* says the No. 1 reason women give for not wanting children is that they don't want their lives to change. In a two-year study she conducted of child-free women—many prefer to call themselves "child-free" as opposed to "childless," since the latter implies an absence or void— 74 percent said they "had no desire to have a child, no maternal instinct."
>
> The other reasons they gave: loving the relationship they were in "as it is," valuing their "freedom and independence," not wanting to take on "the responsibility of raising a child," a desire to focus "on my own interests, needs or goals," and wanting to accomplish "things in life that would be difficult to do if I was a parent."
>
> "Parenting is no longer the default," Scott told me. "For a lot of people, it's no longer an assumption—it's a decision."

The blending of statistics and personal interviews strengthens the analysis because the conclusions are drawn from more than one source of information. The way writers develop their analytical writing is often influenced by their readers and their discipline. A widely respected restaurant critic will review a new cafe in wholly personal and subjective terms. But an engineer analyzing the structure of a hurricane-damaged bridge will use standard tests and procedures and will only provide conclusions clearly supported by scientific findings and observable detail.

Detailed Observation

Analysis requires close observation, critical thinking, and in some instances outside research. If you have not read Samuel Scudder's "Take This Fish and Look at It" (page 61), you may wish to review it. This essay demonstrates the value of close observation. Good analysis cannot rely on first impressions. Before you can analyze a short story or a poem, you will have to read the work several times. If you are thinking of evaluating how women are depicted in television commercials, you may wish to record two or three evenings' worth of commercials and watch them several times rather than relying on memory. The more closely you examine your subject, the more likely you will move from superficial observation to detecting details you may have overlooked.

Critical Thinking for Writing Analysis

Analytical writing can be challenging. Even the best writers often fall into common traps called *logical fallacies* and make errors in judgment. Following these guidelines can help you improve your analytical writing skills:

1. **Ask questions to avoid summarizing.** The most common error students make is mistaking summary or description for analysis. Asking questions can help you avoid simply retelling the plot of a story rather than analyzing it. For example, before starting to analyze Hemingway's short story "Hills Like White Elephants," you might develop questions. Answering a question such as "Who is the stronger character, the man or the woman?" will guide you toward evaluating the story rather than simply producing a two-page summary.

2. **Limit the scope of your analysis.** Unless you are willing to devote months to research, it will be difficult to gather sufficient material to analyze a subject such as day-care centers fully. You might restrict your topic to day-care centers in one neighborhood or focus on a single issue such as licensing requirements.

3. **Evaluate sources for bias.** If you were analyzing the use of animals in medical research, you would not want to base your judgments solely on information from an animal rights group. When evaluating controversial subjects, you may be unable to obtain objective information, but you can achieve a measure of balance by examining data provided by individuals and organizations with opposing viewpoints.

4. **Apply common standards.** Analyzing data from different sources will be accurate only if all the sources have the same standards and definitions. If you analyze juvenile delinquency, you might face a problem if sources define delinquency differently. Does one study include juveniles who skip school, while another only considers adolescents who commit felonies?

5. **Distinguish between opinion and fact.** Opinions are judgments or inferences, not facts. Facts are reliable pieces of information that can be verified by studying other sources:

> **OPINION:** John Smith is an alcoholic.
>
> **FACT:** John Smith drinks two martinis at lunch and frequents nightclubs on weekends.

The factual statement relies on observation. The writer's opinion of alcoholism is subjective and can be challenged, especially if it is based on limited evidence.

6. **Avoid hasty generalizations.** Generalizations should be based on adequate information, not just on a few instances that you find dramatic or interesting. The fact that two friends had purses stolen in the student union last week does not mean the college is in the grip of a crime wave. You would have to examine several months of police reports to determine whether an actual increase in campus crime has occurred.

7. **Consider alternative interpretations.** Facts do not always indicate what they imply at first glance. A rise in reported cases of child abuse may not indicate increasing violence against children, but instead better reporting. If a school has a low retention rate, does that indicate it is failing to address the needs of students or, instead, that it maintains such rigorous standards that only the best students graduate?

8. **Avoid "filtering" data.** If you begin with a preconceived thesis, you may consciously or unconsciously select evidence that supports your view and omit evidence that contradicts it. Good analysis is objective; it does not simply collect data to support a previously held conviction. The fact that many celebrities dropped out of high school does not disprove the value of a diploma.

9. **Do not assume that parts represent the whole.** Just because one or more patients respond favorably to a new drug does not mean that it will cure all people suffering from the same disease. In an extreme example, the fact that individual men and women die does not mean the human race will eventually become extinct.

10. **Do not assume that the whole represents each part.** If 50 percent of students on campus receive financial aid, it does not mean you can assume that half the English majors receive aid. The student population in any given department may be less or more than the college average.

11. **Avoid reasoning with false analogies.** Analogy or comparison essays often provide weak evidence because they overlook that no two situations are exactly alike. Avoid assuming, for example, that results from a study conducted in Japan provide valid evidence for researchers in the United States. A finding that airbags have been proven to save lives in car accidents does not mean they should be installed in airplanes.

Writing Techniques: ANALYSIS

Questions

Writers sometimes challenge readers with questions. In "Don't Blame Wal-Mart" (page 251) Robert Reich asks readers to evaluate their actions as online consumers before blaming a retail store for the decline of small businesses and well-paying jobs. In "Are All Women Born to be Mothers?" (page 274) Jessica Valenti asks readers to consider why women who decide not to have children are questioned about their choice when "parenthood is the decision that brings another person into the world." Why, she wonders, is having children considered the norm?

Sources and Methods

To be effective, writers have to explain how they examined their subject and the origin of their data. In "How Television Distorts Reality" (page 263) Benjamin Radford demonstrates the disproportionate attention television news devotes to crime by measuring the amount of airtime it receives in contrast to other issues.

Definitions

Writers define terms, especially newly coined words or technical concepts, to explain their meaning and significance. Benjamin Radford (page 265) defines John Ruscio's term "media paradox" as simply, "The more we rely on the popular media to inform us, the more apt we are to misplace our fears." Jessica Valenti (page 274) notes that use of the term "pre-pregnant" reflects a prevailing assumption that defines "motherhood as a woman prioritizing the needs of a child, real or hypothetical, over her own."

Strategies FOR READING ANALYSIS

As you read the analysis entries in this chapter, keep the following questions in mind.

Understanding Meaning

1. What is the author's purpose—to provide a personal opinion or an evaluation based on standard research methods?
2. What discipline is the writer operating in? What kinds of evidence and what analytical methods are presented? Does the writer present sources for his or her evidence? What does the original source of the entry indicate about the intended audience and discipline?
3. What is the most significant conclusion the author draws?

Evaluating Strategy

1. Does the writer rely on close observation, surveys, statistics, or expert testimony? How were the data collected?
2. Does the writer cite sources and supply footnotes?
3. Does the writer consider alternative interpretations?
4. Does the entry appear to be biased?
5. Does the writer present facts to support a preconceived theory?
6. Does the writer avoid logical fallacies?

Appreciating Language

1. Do the author's choice of words and use of connotations indicate bias?
2. What language does the writer use in discussing people or organizations expressing different beliefs?
3. Are terms clearly defined?

ROBERT REICH

Robert Reich (1946–) was born in Scranton, Pennsylvania, and attended Dartmouth College, Oxford University, and Yale Law School. After serving as assistant solicitor general in the Department of Justice, he became director of policy planning in the Federal Trade Commission in 1976. He taught at the Kennedy School of Government from 1981–1992 and served as President Clinton's labor secretary from 1993–1996. In 1997 he became a professor of social and economic policy at Brandeis University. His books include *The Next American Frontier* (1983), *The Work of Nations* (1991), *Locked in the Cabinet* (1997), *Supercapitalism: The Transformation of Business, Democracy, and Everyday Life* (2007), and *Aftershock: The Next Economy and America's Future (2010)*.

Don't Blame Wal-Mart

CONTEXT: *After a real estate developer was blocked from opening a Wal-Mart in 2005, Reich published this editorial in the* New York Times *analyzing attitudes to the nation's largest discount store.*

WRITER'S NOTE: *Reich opens his article listing the reasons people oppose Wal-Mart, then poses a rhetorical question to prompt readers to examine their own behavior as consumers.*

Bowing to intense pressure from neighborhood and labor groups, a real estate developer has just given up plans to include a Wal-Mart store in a mall in Queens, thereby blocking Wal-Mart's plan to open its first store in New York City. In the eyes of Wal-Mart's detractors, the Arkansas-based chain embodies the worst kind of economic exploitation: it pays its 1.2 million American workers an average of only $9.68 an hour, doesn't provide most of them with health insurance, keeps out unions, has a checkered history on labor law and turns main streets into ghost towns by sucking business away from small retailers.   **1** *introductory narrative*

But isn't Wal-Mart really being punished for our sins? After all, it's not as if Wal-Mart's founder, Sam Walton, and his successors created the world's largest retailer by putting a gun to our heads and forcing us to shop there.   **2** *question to readers*

Instead, Wal-Mart has lured customers with low prices. "We expect our suppliers to drive the costs out of the supply chain," a spokeswoman for Wal-Mart said. "It's good for us and good for them."   **3** *direct quotation*

Wal-Mart may have perfected this technique, but you can find it almost everywhere these days. Corporations are in fierce competition to get and keep customers, so they pass the bulk of their cost cuts through to consumers as lower prices. Products are manufactured in China at a fraction of the cost of making them here, and American consumers get great deals. Back-office work, along   **4** with computer programming and data crunching, is "offshored" to India, so our dollars go even further.

Meanwhile, many of us pressure companies to give us even better bargains. <u>I look on the Internet to find the lowest price I can and buy airline tickets, books, merchandise from just about anywhere with a click of a mouse. Don't you?</u>

5
personal example question to readers

The fact is, today's economy offers us a Faustian bargain: it can give consumers deals largely because it hammers workers and communities.

6
thesis presented in one sentence paragraph for emphasis

<u>We can blame big corporations, but we're mostly making this bargain with ourselves.</u> The easier it is for us to get great deals, the stronger the downward pressure on wages and benefits. Last year, the real wages of hourly workers, who make up about 80 percent of the work force, actually dropped for the first time in more than a decade; hourly workers' health and pension benefits are in free fall. The easier it is for us to find better professional services, the harder professionals have to hustle to attract and keep clients. The more efficiently we can summon products from anywhere on the globe, the more stress we put on our own communities.

7

But you and I aren't just consumers. We're also workers and citizens. <u>How do we strike the right balance?</u> To claim that people shouldn't have access to Wal-Mart or to cut-rate airfares or services from India or to Internet shopping, because these somehow reduce their quality of life, is paternalistic tripe. No one is a better judge of what people want than they themselves.

8
question to readers

The problem is, the choices we make in the market don't fully reflect our values as workers or as citizens. I didn't want our community bookstore in Cambridge, Mass., to close (as it did last fall) yet I still bought lots of books from Amazon.com. In addition, we may not see the larger bargain when our own job or community isn't directly at stake. I don't like what's happening to airline workers, but I still try for the cheapest fare I can get.

9

personal example

<u>The only way for the workers or citizens in us to trump the consumers in us is through laws and regulations that make our purchases a social choice as well as a personal one</u>. A requirement that companies with more than 50 employees offer their workers affordable health insurance, for example, might increase slightly the price of their goods and services. <u>My inner consumer won't like that very much, but the worker in me thinks it a fair price to pay.</u> Same with an increase in the minimum wage or a change in labor laws making it easier for employees to organize and negotiate better terms.

10

I wouldn't go so far as to re-regulate the airline industry or hobble free trade with China and India—that would cost me as a consumer far too much—but I'd like the government to offer wage insurance to ease the pain of sudden losses of pay. And I'd support labor standards that make trade agreements a bit more fair.

11

<u>These provisions might end up costing me some money, but the citizen in me thinks they are worth the price. You might think differently, but as a nation we aren't even having this sort of discussion.</u>

12

Instead, our debates about economic change take place between two warring camps: those who want the best consumer deals, and those who want to preserve jobs and communities much as they are. Instead of finding ways to soften the blows, compensate the losers or slow the pace of change—so the consumers in us can enjoy lower prices and better products without wreaking too much damage on us in our role as workers and citizens—we go to battle. I don't know if Wal-Mart will ever make it into New York City.

Reich compares his views with his readers'

I do know that New Yorkers, like most other Americans, want the great deals that can be had in a rapidly globalizing high-tech economy. Yet the prices on sales tags don't reflect the full prices we have to pay as workers and citizens. A sensible public debate would focus on how to make that total price as low as possible.

13 conclusion call for action

Understanding Meaning

1. Why do many Americans oppose the expansion of Wal-Mart?
2. What makes Wal-Mart so popular with consumers?
3. What is the Wal-Mart "technique"? How does it exploit the global economy?
4. Does Reich expose the fact that people want two opposing things at once—high wages and benefits, and discount prices? How does he suggest we balance the "workers in us" with the "consumers in us"?
5. *Critical Thinking*: Reich mentions that he purchases books and plane tickets online to find the lowest prices. Does this indicate that the "consumer in us" is hard to resist? Do those protesting Wal-Mart likely undermine communities and workers by shopping online?

Evaluating Strategy

1. After noting that he shops for bargains online, Reich asks his reader, "Don't you?" Can writers avoid alienating readers by admitting they engage in the same behavior they are criticizing?
2. Reich poses questions throughout his editorial. Is this an effective way to engage readers and prompt critical thinking?
3. *Critical Thinking*: After detailing objections to Wal-Mart's low wages and negative impact on small businesses, Reich reminds readers that the world's largest retailer never forced anyone to shop there. Can fast-food companies and the tobacco industry, both of which have been accused of undermining public health, make the same argument?

Appreciating Language

1. Reich uses the term "Faustian bargain" (paragraph 6) to describe the global economy. Look up the term "Faustian bargain." Is this an effective term?
2. What does Reich mean when he says Wal-Mart is being punished for "our sins." What "sins" is he referring to?
3. Can you detect any biased language in Reich's description of Wal-Mart?

WRITING SUGGESTIONS

1. Write an essay analyzing another "Faustian bargain" facing people today. Do students take on massive debt to gain an education? Are parents pressured to work overtime and spend less time with their children in order to provide them with shelter, day care, and medical care? Does social media provide us with new communication tools yet threaten us with a loss of privacy?

2. *Collaborative Writing:* Imagine that a college organization contacts you to sign a petition or participate in a demonstration against a proposed Wal-Mart near campus. Would members of your group oppose or welcome the retailer? Write a short essay stating your views. If members disagree, consider writing opposing statements.

HAROLD MEYERSON

Harold Meyerson (1950–) was born in Los Angeles and attended Columbia University. His parents were leaders in the Socialist Party of America, and Meyerson was active in the Democratic Socialist Organizing Committee in the 1970s. From 1989 to 2001 he served as the executive editor of *L.A. Weekly*. He has written articles about political, social, and economic issues for the *New Yorker*, *The Atlantic*, *The Nation*, *The New Republic*, and *New Statesman*. He has hosted a radio show and has been a frequent guest on radio talk shows. In 2009 *Atlantic Monthly* included Harold Meyerson in its list of the "50 Most Influential Columnists."

How to Grade Teachers: Lessons from the Teachers Strike

CONTEXT: *This article appeared in* The Washington Post *following a 2012 Chicago teachers' strike that gained national attention.*

WRITER'S NOTE: *Meyerson places his thesis in the last paragraph to give his article a strong ending.*

Here's a bit of advice to America's teachers: If you want the nation's opinion leaders and CEOs to like you, don't congregate in groups. Everyone, it seems, loves teachers individually. But when they get together, they become a menace to civilization. 1

That's one of the clearest take-aways from the just-concluded teachers strike in Chicago. Editorial boards from the right-wing *Wall Street Journal* to the liberal *New York Times* were nearly unanimous in condemning the seven-day strike. The Chicago Teachers Union was depriving the city's children of their right to an education not just during the strike, editorialists argued, but also every day—by refusing to bow down to standardized tests. In the eyes of our elites, such tests have emerged as the linchpin of pedagogy and the best way to measure teacher, not just student, performance. 2

The unrelenting attack on teachers unions has some measurable consequences, too. This is evident from the fact that more than 90 percent of Chicago teachers voted to authorize the strike and that the union's governing body so mistrusted the administration of Chicago Mayor Rahm Emanuel that it took two additional days to go over the proposed contract's fine print. 3

The presumably numbers-driven educational reformers are highly selective when it comes to which numbers they take seriously. For years, many have touted charter schools (which usually are not unionized) as the preferred alternative to (unionized) public schools. But the most extensive survey of student performance at charter schools, from Stanford University's Center for Research on Education Outcomes, found that, of the 2,403 charter schools 4 tracked from 2006 to 2008, only 17 percent had better math test results than the public schools in their area, while 37 percent had results that were "significantly below" those of the public schools and 46 percent had results that were "statistically indistinguishable" from their public-school counterparts.

There's also a good amount of data—including a study of high- 5 performing public schools from the National Center for Educational Achievement—showing that ongoing teacher collaboration and mentoring and using tests for diagnostic, rather than evaluative, purposes produce better outcomes than the reformers' brand of measuring teacher and student performance. The Cincinnati school district, which measures teacher performance chiefly through repeated peer evaluation, has the best student performance of any big Ohio city.

The Century Foundation's Greg Anrig has argued in *Pacific Stan-* 6 *dard* magazine that reducing teacher evaluations to standardized tests amounts to subjecting education to Taylorism—the time-and-motion studies that so entranced corporate managers (and even Lenin) in the early 20th century and that boiled down worker performance to basic, repetitive tasks. A more successful management ethos, Anrig says, has been propounded by W. Edwards Deming, who argued that competitive performance evaluations eroded the social capital and trust successful institutions require. Deming's more collaborative methods were taken to heart in postwar Japan and inform management practices at a range of successful companies, including Ford and Kaiser Permanente. As the example of Cincinnati suggests, they also work pretty well in schools.

There are other data that "educational reformers" would do well 7 to study. Last week, the Illinois political newsletter Capitol Fax commissioned a poll of Chicago voters that showed that fully 66 percent of parents with children in the city's public schools supported the strike, as did 56 percent of voters citywide. The only groups that disapproved of the strike (narrowly) were parents of children in private schools and whites. (Blacks and Latinos supported it.)

Given what we know about the cost of private schools and the 8 demographics of Chicago's public schools (87 percent of students come from households below the poverty threshold), it's safe to say that the school reform movement hasn't converted many outside the upper middle class. I suspect that a number of parents with kids in the city schools may have a more direct understanding of the challenges, both in school and out, that their children confront, as well as a clearer perception of the lack of resources that bedevil the schools.

Teaching, at least in major cities, is also a profession in which 9 minorities are heavily represented; when reformers argue that we need to take down teachers unions to give more opportunity to minority youth, the argument veers perilously close to "We need to destroy the black middle class in order to save it."

As both policy and politics, the demonization of teachers unions 10 is a dead end for improving American education. Working with, not against, teachers is the more sensible way to better our schools.

Understanding Meaning

1. Can you state Meyerson's thesis in your own words?
2. Why did both conservative and liberal newspapers condemn the teachers' strike?
3. What is Meyerson's analysis of charter schools?
4. What educational reforms does Meyerson advocate? Which schools, in his view, should serve as a model for change?
5. *Critical Thinking:* Why do many people, in Meyerson's view, claim to love teachers as individuals but not when they act as a group? Could this be true about other professions?

Evaluating Strategy

1. What evidence does Meyerson include to support his thesis and discredit the solutions offered by those he opposes?
2. Meyerson presents his thesis in the last paragraph. Is this effective? Why or why not?
3. Meyerson supplies the source of the quotations and statistics he uses as evidence. Why is this important?

Appreciating Language

1. How does Meyerson define "Taylorism" (paragraph 6)? Can you think of examples of Taylorism from your own experiences at work or school?
2. Meyerson uses the term "collaborative." Look this term up in a dictionary. How does it differ from "competitive"? Do these terms symbolize different philosophical or political approaches to education?
3. *Critical Thinking*: Meyerson suggests that testing should be used for "diagnostic" rather than "evaluative" purposes. Can you explain the differences?

WRITING SUGGESTIONS

1. Write an analytical evaluation of your high school education. What were your school's strong and weak points? Did it provide students with adequate preparation for the workforce or higher education? What reforms, if any, would you suggest?

2. *Collaborative Writing:* In recent years most of the discussion about schools has focused on schools and teachers. Working with a group of students, write a short essay analyzing the skills and qualities students need to have to succeed. You might refer to John Taylor Gatto's article on page 383 to start the discussion.

FOUAD AJAMI

Fouad Ajami (1945–) was born in Lebanon and came to the United States in 1963. After studying at Eastern Oregon College, he attended the University of Washington, where he received his PhD. He began teaching at Princeton University in 1973 and is currently the Majid Khadduri Professor of Middle East Studies at the School of Advanced International Studies at Johns Hopkins University. A senior fellow at Stanford University's Hoover Institution, Ajami has written articles about the Middle East, Islam, and foreign policy for *The New Republic*, *Foreign Affairs*, and the *Wall Street Journal*. A frequent television commentator, he has appeared on CNN and PBS. His books include *The Syrian Rebellion* and *Dream Palace of the Arabs: A Generation's Odyssey*.

Why Is the Arab World So Easily Offended?

CONTEXT: *Ajami published this article in* The Washington Post *in September 2012 following a series of violent protests against an American-made video deemed offensive to Islam.*

WRITER'S NOTE: *Ajami mentions several previous incidents to place the 2012 protests into a historical context.*

1   Modernity requires the willingness to be offended. And as anti-American violence across the Middle East and beyond shows, that willingness is something the Arab world, the heartland of Islam, still lacks.

2   Time and again in recent years, as the outside world has battered the walls of Muslim lands and as Muslims have left their places of birth in search of greater opportunities in the Western world, modernity—with its sometimes distasteful but ultimately benign criticism of Islam—has sparked fatal protests. To understand why violence keeps erupting and to seek to prevent it, we must discern what fuels this sense of grievance.

3   There is an Arab pain and a volatility in the face of judgment by outsiders that stem from a deep and enduring sense of humiliation. A vast chasm separates the poor standing of Arabs in the world today from their history of greatness. In this context, their injured pride is easy to understand.

4   In the narrative of history transmitted to schoolchildren throughout the Arab world and reinforced by the media, religious scholars and laymen alike, Arabs were favored by divine providence. They had come out of the Arabian Peninsula in the 7th century, carrying Islam from Morocco to faraway Indonesia. In the process, they overran the Byzantine and Persian empires, then crossed the Strait of Gibraltar to Iberia, and there they fashioned a brilliant civilization that stood as a rebuke to the intolerance of the European states to the north. Cordoba and Granada were adorned and exalted in the

Arab imagination. Andalusia brought together all that the Arabs favored—poetry, glamorous courts, philosophers who debated the great issues of the day.

If Islam's rise was spectacular, its fall was swift and unsparing. 5 This is the world that the great historian Bernard Lewis explored in his 2002 book *What Went Wrong?* The blessing of God, seen at work in the ascent of the Muslims, now appeared to desert them. The ruling caliphate, with its base in Baghdad, was torn asunder by a Mongol invasion in the 13th century. Soldiers of fortune from the Turkic Steppes sacked cities and left a legacy of military seizures of power that is still the bane of the Arabs. Little remained of their philosophy and literature, and after the Ottoman Turks overran Arab countries to their south in the 16th century, the Arabs seemed to exit history; they were now subjects of others.

The coming of the West to their world brought superior military, 6 administrative and intellectual achievement into their midst—and the outsiders were unsparing in their judgments. They belittled the military prowess of the Arabs, and they were scandalized by the traditional treatment of women and the separation of the sexes that crippled Arab society.

Even as Arabs insist that their defects were inflicted on them by 7 outsiders, they know their weaknesses. Younger Arabs today can be brittle and proud about their culture, yet deeply ashamed of what they see around them. They know that more than 300 million Arabs have fallen to economic stagnation and cultural decline. They know that the standing of Arab states along the measures that matter—political freedom, status of women, economic growth—is low. In the privacy of their own language, in daily chatter on the street, on blogs and in the media, and in works of art and fiction, they probe endlessly what befell them.

But woe to the outsider who ventures onto that explosive ter- 8 rain. The assumption is that Westerners bear Arabs malice, that Western judgments are always slanted and cruel.

In the past half-century, Arabs, as well as Muslims in non-Arab 9 lands, have felt the threat of an encircling civilization they can nei- ther master nor reject. Migrants have left the burning grounds of Karachi, Cairo and Casablanca but have taken the fire of their faith with them. "Dish cities" have sprouted in the Muslim diasporas of Western Europe and North America. You can live in Stockholm and be sustained by a diet of Al Jazeera television.

We know the celebrated cases when modernity has agitated 10 the pious. A little more than two decades ago, it was a writer of Muslim and Indian birth, Salman Rushdie, whose irreverent work of fiction offended believers with its portrayal of Islam. That crisis began with book-burnings in Britain, later saw protests in Pakistan and culminated in Iran's ruling cleric, Ayatollah Ruhollah Khomeini, issuing a fatwa calling for Rushdie's death in 1989. The protest- ers were not necessarily critics of fiction; all it took to offend was that Islam, the Prophet Muhammad and his wives had become a writer's material. The confrontation laid bare the unease of Islam in the modern world.

The floodgates had opened. The clashes that followed de- 11
fined the new terms of encounters between a politicized version of Islam—awakened to both power and vulnerability—and the West's culture of protecting and nurturing free speech. In 2004, a Moroccan Dutchman in his mid-20s, Mohammed Bouyeri, mur-dered filmmaker Theo van Gogh on a busy Amsterdam street after van Gogh and a Somali-born politician made a short film about the abuse of women in Islamic culture.

Shortly afterward, trouble came to Denmark when a newspa- 12
per there published a dozen cartoons depicting the Prophet Muhammad; in one he wears a bomb-shaped turban, and another shows him as an assassin. The newspaper's culture editor had thought the exercise would merely draw attention to the restric-tions on cultural freedom in Europe—but perhaps that was naive. After all, Muslim activists are on the lookout for such material. And Arab governments are eager to defend Islam. The Egyptian am-bassador to Denmark encouraged a radical preacher of Palestinian birth living in Denmark and a young Lebanese agitator to fan the flames of the controversy.

But it was Syria that made the most of this opportunity. The re- 13
gime asked the highest clerics to preach against the Danish gov-ernment. The Danish embassies in Damascus and Beirut were sacked; there was a call to boycott Danish products. Denmark had been on the outer margins of Europe's Muslim diaspora. Now its peace and relative seclusion were punctured.

The storm that erupted this past week at the gates of American 14
diplomatic outposts across the Muslim world is a piece of this his-tory. As usual, it was easily ignited. The offending work, a 14-minute film trailer posted on YouTube in July, is offensive indeed. Billed as a trailer for *The Innocence of Muslims*, a longer movie to come, it is at once vulgar and laughable. Its primitiveness should have consigned it to oblivion.

It was hard to track down the identities of those who made 15
it. A Sam Bacile claimed authorship, said that he was an Israeli American and added that 100 Jewish businessmen had backed the venture. This alone made it rankle even more—offending Mus-lims and implicating Jews at the same time. (In the meantime, no records could be found of Bacile, and the precise origins of the video remain murky.)

It is never hard to assemble a crowd of young protesters in 16
the teeming cities of the Muslim world. American embassies and consulates are magnets for the disgruntled. It is inside those for-tresses, the gullible believe, that rulers are made and unmade. Yet these same diplomatic outposts dispense coveted visas and a way out to the possibilities of the Western world. The young men who turned up at the U.S. Embassies this week came out of this deadly mix of attraction to American power and resentment

of it. The attack in Benghazi, Libya, that took the lives of four American diplomats, including Ambassador J. Christopher Stevens, appeared to be premeditated and unconnected to the film protests.

The ambivalence toward modernity that torments Muslims is   17
unlikely to abate. The temptations of the West have alienated a younger generation from its elders. Men and women insist that they revere the faith as they seek to break out of its restrictions. Freedom of speech, granting license and protection to the irreverent, is cherished, protected and canonical in the Western tradition. Now Muslims who quarrel with offensive art are using their new-found freedoms to lash out against it.

These cultural contradictions do not lend themselves to the   18
touch of outsiders. President George W. Bush believed that America's proximity to Arab dictatorships had begotten us the jihadists' enmity. His military campaign in Iraq became an attempt to reform that country and beyond. But Arabs rejected his interventionism and dismissed his "freedom agenda" as a cover for an unpopular war and for domination.

President Obama has taken a different approach. He was sure   19
that his biography—the years he spent in Indonesia and his sympathy for the aspirations of Muslim lands—would help repair relations between America and the Islamic world. But he's been caught in the middle, conciliating the rulers while making grand promises to ordinary people. The revolt of the Iranian opposition in the summer of 2009 exposed the flaws of his approach. Then the Arab Spring played havoc with American policy. Since then, the Obama administration has not been able to decide whether it defends the status quo or the young people hell-bent on toppling the old order.

Cultural freedom is never absolute, of course, and the Western   20
tradition itself, from the Athenians to the present, struggles mightily with the line between freedom and order. In the Muslim world, that struggle is more fierce and lasting, and it will show itself in far more than burnt flags and overrun embassies.

Understanding Meaning

1. What historical reasons explain Arab sensitivity to perceived insults from the West?

2. What are Arab children taught in school that leads them to feel injured and hostile to outside influences?

3. Why are American embassies and consulates "magnets for the disgruntled" in the Arab world? Do poor and frustrated people in all nations seek to blame outsiders for their plight?

4. How did President Obama's approach to the Arab world differ from President Bush's? In Ajami's view, what were their assumptions? Were their policies successful?

5. *Critical Thinking*: Ajami notes that politicized Islam is "awakened to both power and vulnerability." Does this ironic blend explain other political or social movements where people sense they have power but face threats? Can you think of other examples?

Evaluating Strategy

1. How effective is Ajami's opening declaration? Might many "pious" Americans be offended by free expression? Can you think of recent examples? Would it more accurate to suggest that modernity requires people to express their objections peacefully rather than tolerate what they consider offensive?
2. What evidence does Ajami provide to support his thesis?
3. How does Ajami use previous incidents to explain the 2012 protests?
4. Can you consider Ajami's final paragraph a warning? Does it make an effective conclusion?

Appreciating Language

1. Ajami repeatedly uses the term "modernity." How would you define it? Why might "modernity" threaten traditional values? Are there Americans who appear uneasy or even hostile to elements of modernity?
2. In paragraph 17 Ajami refers to the "temptations of the West." What does the word "temptation" imply? Would the word "opportunities" suggest a different view?
3. How would you characterize the tone and style of Ajami's depiction of Arab society? Do you detect any bias? What challenges do writers face in describing values and attitudes of another culture?

WRITING SUGGESTIONS

1. Write a short essay that analyzes reactions to a recent event covered by the media. Why does one murder or shooting evoke more response than others? Does it depend on the victim? Does an incident that appears to be part of a greater trend or plays on people's perceptions get more attention?
2. *Collaborative Writing*: Discuss Ajami's article with a group of students. Many websites such as YouTube delete pornography. Should anti-Muslim content that might spark violence be removed as well? Would this be a sign of cultural sensitivity or of self-censorship? Write a short essay stating your views. If members disagree, consider creating opposing statements.

Blending the Modes
BENJAMIN RADFORD

Benjamin Radford (1970–) received a BA in psychology from the University of New Mexico in 1993. He is the managing editor of the science magazine *Skeptical Inquirer* and editor in chief of the Spanish-language magazine *Pensar*, published in Argentina. Radford has published hundreds of articles on urban legends, the media, paranormal events, and critical thinking. His books include *Hoaxes, Myths, and Manias: Why We Need Critical Thinking*, with Robert E. Bartholomew (2003), *Media Mythmakers: How Journalists, Activists, and Advertisers Mislead Us* (2003*)*, and *Tracking the Vampire: Chupacabra in Fact, Fiction, and Folklore* (2011).

How Television Distorts Reality

CONTEXT: *In this essay, Radford argues that television newscasts distort reality by emphasizing sensational events.*

WRITER'S NOTE: *Radford uses objective analysis based on factual reports to support his point of view. Notice where he uses com-parison, definition, and cause and effect to develop his essay.*

1 Television, by its very nature, distorts the reality it claims to reflect and report on. Events are compressed, highlighted, sped up. Thus a person who occasionally watches sports highlights on TV will likely see more home runs and touchdowns than a person who attends local games regularly; television viewers are likely to see more murders than a police detective, more serious car crashes than a tow truck driver, and more plane crashes than a crash investigator.

2 The amount of time devoted to crime coverage is widely dispro-portionate to the amount of crime that actually occurs. Professor Joe Angotti of the University of Miami found that nearly 30 percent of airtime is spent covering crime, courts, and cops. But airtime is fi-nite, of course, and less "sexy" (but more important) topics lose out: Education, for example, got just 2 percent of airtime nationally in the newscasts surveyed. Race relations got just 1.2 percent. Angotti, for-merly a senior vice president of NBC News, says of his findings, "It's unfortunate that body-bag journalism is what local news chooses to focus on at the expense of more important stories." Part of the problem is journalistic laziness. "Crime reporting is easy to do and doesn't require hardly any follow-up. Television journalists have to stand up and say we're here to tell people what they need to know," says Angotti. "Television news has abandoned its responsibility to do serious journalism in favor of sensational video."[1]

---

[1] Terry Jackson, "'Body-bag Journalism' Rules in Broadcast News, Study Says," *Miami Herald*, May 7, 1997.

Another study, this one headed by Syracuse University professor 3
Robert Lissit, found that of one hundred newscasts around the country, "nearly 30 percent of the news time was spent on crime and the
courts. Ten percent was devoted to reporting calamities and natural
disasters. Only 15 percent of the newscasts were devoted to government and politics. Health and medicine: about 7 percent. Race
relations: 1.2 percent. Education: less than 1 percent." According
to Lissit, crime gets a disproportionate amount of coverage not because it is important but because it is easy to cover: "A few shots
of the crime scene, a quick interview with a police officer or someone in the neighborhood, and a quick reporter-on-camera standup.
Summary, and that's the end of story." Noncrime issues such as politics or education require more background and effort and usually
can't be wrapped up in such a tidy, quick package.

Like Angotti, Lissit also dismisses the justification that news 4
directors commonly give for such sanguineous fare: It's what the
public wants. "Market-driven news is giving the viewers what the
stations think they want. Some might ask if that isn't simply representative democracy at work: 'What could be more democratic
than giving viewers what they want?' My answer: What could be
more irresponsible, more cynical, and profoundly wrong?"[2]

Notice that the news media have, in a way, tied their own hands 5
in trying to present "important" stories. Clearly, not everything
that is reported on the news is newsworthy. But because viewers
have been led to believe that what they see on the news *must* be
important, news organizations can't be honest about their vacuous
coverage without making liars of themselves. You'll never hear a
journalist say, "We're still covering this story, but to be honest it's
not very important." Instead, the rules of the profession require
that each story be treated as important and relevant—otherwise
why are they (and we) wasting time on it?

By and large, the news media (and entertainment media, for that 6
matter) seek the broadest possible appeal. This makes sense; the
more diverse the appeal, the larger the audience, and thus the more
profitable a program is. But one side effect of this process is a dumb-
ing-down and homogenizing of content. Programs that are too cere-
bral are doomed, while programs based on the basest instincts and
interests—sex (*Baywatch*), violence (*World's Scariest Police Chases*),
or sex and violence (*Jerry Springer*)—will thrive. Programmers frequently take this too far and insult the viewers' intelligence.

As *Newsweek's* Jonathan Alter wrote, "When news oozes 7
24 hours a day it's not really news anymore. The TV becomes ambi-
ent noise. The newspaper becomes wallpaper. Finding patterns of
importance becomes hard. It's easier—and more profitable—just
to make the consumer gape."[3]

---

[2]"Ditching 'Body Bag Journalism,'" Christian News Archives [online],
www.villagelife.org/church/archives/ucc_bodybagjournalism.html [October 22, 1997].
[3]Jonathan Alter, "In the Times of the Tabs," *Newsweek*, June 2, 1997.

The Media Paradox

Another consequence of the news perspective that contributes to the public's fears is what John Ruscio, a social psychologist at Elizabethtown College in Pennsylvania, calls "the media paradox": The more we rely on the popular media to inform us, the more apt we are to misplace our fears. The paradox is the combined result of two biases, one inherent in the news-gathering process, the other inherent in the way our minds organize and recall information. 8

As Ruscio explains: 9

> For a variety of reasons—including fierce competition for our patronage within and across the various popular media outlets—potential news items are rigorously screened for their ability to captivate an audience.... The stories that do make it through this painstaking selection process are then often crafted into accounts emphasizing their concrete, personal, and emotional content.[4]

In turn, the more emotional and vivid the account is, the more likely we are to remember the information. This is the first element, the *vividness bias*: Our minds easily remember vivid events.

The second bias lies in what psychologists term the *availability heuristic*: Our judgments of frequency and probability are heavily influenced by the ease with which we can imagine or recall instances of an event. So the more often we hear reports of plane crashes, school shootings, or train wrecks, the more often we think they occur. But the bias that selects those very events makes them appear more frequent than they really are. 10

Imagine, for example, that a consumer group dedicated to travel safety established a network of correspondents in every country that reported every train and bus wreck, no matter how minor, and broadcast daily pictures. Anyone watching that broadcast would see dozens of wrecks and crashes every day, complete with mangled metal and dead bodies, and would likely grow to fear such transportation. No matter that in general trains and buses are very safe; if you screen the news to emphasize certain vivid events, accidents will seem more dangerous and common than they actually are. That explains, in part, why many people fear flying even though they know that statistically it's one of the safest modes of transport: Though crashes are very rare, the vividness and emotion of seeing dramatic footage of crashed planes drowns out the rational knowledge of statistical safety. 11

The homicide rate is another example. Many people are surprised to learn that the suicide rate is higher than the homicide rate: Nearly twice as many people die by their own hand than are killed by other people (the murder rate in the United States is 5.9 per 100,000; the suicide rate is 10.3 per 100,000). While murders make news, suicides are frequently ignored unless the victim 12

---

[4]John Ruscio, "Risky Business," *Skeptical Inquirer* (March/April 2000): 24.

is famous. This imbalance in news coverage leads many to believe that homicides are far more common than suicides, when in fact the opposite is true.[5]

The imbalance in media coverage is also due in part to the sen- 13 sational nature of a murder. If a person is found killed by another, the story has only just begun: The police must look for the killer, determine a motive, find the weapon, arrest the killer, put him or her on trial, and so on. But when the killer is the victim, the story is over as soon as it starts. There will be no dramatic arrests or jailhouse confessions, just grief and perhaps memorials or a short quest for motive.

As a society we throw money at things we fear in order to fix 14 them. But when we misplace our fears, we run the very real risk of wasting time and resources on insignificant problems. As author John Ross states," Are we then turning our backs on a raging inferno while we douse the flame of a match?"[6]

The news media do their best to raise alarm, even when no 15 alarm is needed. The death of film director Alan Pakula is a good example. Pakula, director of many notable films, including *All the President's Men* and *Klute*, died in a freak freeway accident in November 1998. A vehicle in front of him ran over a piece of metal, which shot through his windshield, killing him. It was a sudden, horrific, one-in-a-million accident—yet the media reported it differently. While some reporters grudgingly admitted that the accident was very unusual, many others hyped the story. They tried to downplay the rarity of the accident, and rushed to air news segments revealing "hidden dangers on the highway." While trash on the roads is a threat, the number of drivers *ever* killed by road trash compared to, say, the number killed by falling asleep at the wheel or drunk driving in a *single* month is minuscule.

"A single death is a tragedy, a million deaths is a statistic," Joseph 16 Stalin observed. The public and reporters latched onto Pakula's death because it was a single death of someone famous. And it's no accident that single deaths spark more outrage than many deaths. In 1994, more than 800,000 people were killed in genocidal ethnic clashes in Africa. Yet Americans took little notice of the carnage in Rwanda; they (and the news media) were much more interested in the murders of just two people: Nicole Brown Simpson and Ron Goldman.

John Ruscio explains why the news media prefer testimonials: 17

> Producers are aware that a scientific analysis is not as emotionally compelling as one (carefully chosen) individual's personal experience. Why does a television news reporter stand in front of a court-house when sharing a landmark verdict reached earlier that day? Why does a weather correspondent endure frigid temperatures, sleet, and harsh wind on camera to inform us that a severe storm is in

[5]"Mortality," in *Time Almanac 2003* (Boston: Information Please, 2002), p. 132.
[6]John F. Ross, "Risk: Where Do Real Dangers Lie?" *Smithsonian* 26 (1995): 42–53.

progress? Even superficial background elements appear
to add a sense of realism and concreteness to a story.[7]

Note that all this is done to promote the illusion of importance, and
in the process the news media insult their audience's intelligence.
Viewers are smart enough to know that a forecaster doesn't have
to be actually standing outdoors to give them an accurate weather
forecast.

18 Another example of the way in which the media emphasize the
wrong risks is in health care and disease prevention. Though the
news media like to run stories on both real and alleged carcino-
genic dangers lurking in our environments—such as toxic chemicals, cell phones, power lines, and radiation—health experts say
that poor diet may be more likely to cause cancers. At a conference sponsored in part by the National Institute of Environmental
Health Studies, it was reported that a lack of vitamins found in
fruits and vegetables could be damaging people's DNA, increasing their susceptibility to cancer.

19 A California study found that only one-third of California residents reported eating the minimum recommended amount of
fruits and vegetables every day. This can lead to vitamin deficiencies, which has been shown to alter DNA. Bruce Ames, a professor of biochemistry at the University of California at Berkeley, said,
"What is becoming clear is that there is a tremendous amount of
DNA damage in people from not having their vitamins and minerals. People, when they think of cancer, they think of chemicals in
the water or pesticide residue. I just think it's all a distraction."

20 Researchers have found that a lack of folic acid, a vitamin B,
may influence a person's susceptibility to leukemia; vitamin B_{12} de-
ficiency has been shown to damage chromosomes, and still other
research suggests that zinc and iron deficiencies may also result in
genetic damage.[8]

21 These problems can be solved by simply eating well or taking a
daily multivitamin. Yet for the news media, this story isn't interesting.
Telling people to eat right and take a vitamin just isn't eye-catching,
not compared to showing footage of a leaking sewer pipe or pesticide spraying. Certainly there are real dangers from toxic chemicals
and radiation. But the average news viewer has probably seen hundreds or thousands of reports on those dangers, and probably only a
handful reminding them of the importance of eating a balanced meal.

22 The news bias causes us to misplace our fears in other ways as
well. In his book *Creating Reality*, journalist David Altheide notes,

> [D]ifferent news sources produce different stories. Police
> radio monitors, for example, provide crime news involv-
> ing street crimes which frequently involve lower-class and

---

[7]Ruscio, "Risky Business," p. 23.
[8]Maggie Fox, "U.S. Poor Said Damaging Health with Lack of Vitamins,"
Reuters [online],www.thevitamindigest.com/news/2000/oct1900uspoorsaid.htm
[October 19, 2000].

minority group youth. But the story of crime is incomplete if it is only learned about through these sources. The image is presented, albeit unintentionally, that certain kinds of crime are not only committed by certain groups of people, but that this is what the crime problem is about. White-collar crime and corporate rip-offs are not presented via police monitors, even though more money is involved than in dozens of $25–$100 robberies. Thus, the Phoenix media were reluctant to disclose that one of the area's largest banks was being investigated for passing illegal securities. If bank officials *are* eventually indicted, they will be interviewed in their plush offices. In all likelihood we will never see them "drug off" by police officers, handcuffed, disheveled, and looking ashamed.[9]

The white, middle-aged man or woman in a suit you happily sit across a business desk from is perhaps just as likely to rob you as the black youth you might cross the street to avoid—and they're likely to get much more money out of you than a mugger would.

Understanding Meaning

1. How do television newscasts, in Radford's view, distort reality? What stories are disproportionately covered, and which issues are largely ignored?
2. How does the visual nature of television lead broadcasters to select which stories they will cover?
3. What does Radford mean by the term "availability heuristic"? Can you think of examples?
4. Why, in Radford's view, does television news devote so much coverage to homicides even though twice as many Americans take their own lives than are murdered? How does television news give the public distorted perceptions about crime?
5. *Critical Thinking:* Do you think twenty-four-hour cable news channels such as CNN, MSNBC, and FOX NEWS have increased or decreased media distortion? Have competition and expanded broadcast time allowed television to explore more issues and study them in greater depth, or has it increased sensationalism as rival networks seek higher ratings?

Evaluating Strategy

1. What measurements or analytical tools does Radford use in examining television coverage?
2. Radford includes outside sources, including statistics and expert testimony. Does this give his article greater authenticity? Why is it important to include documentation?
3. *Blending the Modes:* How does Radford use *comparison*, *example*, and *cause and effect* in developing his essay? How effective is the conclusion? What impact does it have?

[9]Altheide, Creating Reality, p. 191.

Appreciating Language

1. What tone and style does Radford use in describing the media? Do you detect any bias? Why or why not? Is it important for objective analysis to use neutral language?

2. Radford introduces terms such as "media paradox" and "vividness bias." Does he define these adequately? Can you explain them in your own words? Can you think of examples?

3. Look up the word "sensationalism." What does it mean? Can you think of recent stories that dominated the news that were sensational but had little significance?

WRITING SUGGESTIONS

1. Conduct your own analysis of one or more newscasts. Count the number of stories and use a stopwatch to measure the amount of time devoted to each one. Write an objective analysis of your findings. Which stories received the most coverage? Which stories received the least?

2. *Collaborative Writing*: Discuss the media with a group of students and examine how issues and events are covered by television news. What distortions or biases do students see? Are some stories given greater emphasis than they deserve? Are other issues ignored or given simplistic coverage? Record your comments and use division or classification to organize your group's observations.

Opposing Viewpoints: Motherhood
JENNY ALLEN

Jenny Allen is a writer and performer. Her articles have appeared in *The New Yorker*, the *New York Times*, *New York*, *Vogue*, *Esquire*, *More*, *Huffington Post* and *Good Housekeeping*. She wrote a book of adult fables, *The Long Chalkboard*, which was illustrated by her husband, cartoonist Jules Feiffer. Her one-woman performance *I Got Sick Then I Got Better* recounting her experiences as a cancer patient has been staged in theaters, hospitals, and universities across the country.

I'm a Mom

CONTEXT: *Allen published this article in September 2012 following the Democratic and Republican presidential conventions, which featured speeches by the candidates' wives.*

WRITER'S NOTE: *As a humorist, Allen adopts a dismissive tone to single women without children, telling them to "shoo!" in the first paragraph.*

Are you a mom?   1

No? Then you don't need to read one more word. Go on, shoo!   2
I'm not trying to be mean; it's just that you probably won't understand a lot of what I'm going to say. It's a mom thing. If you're a mom, you know what I'm talking about. Right, moms? Go, us!

I'm not saying that moms are better than other people, but there   3
is, well, something different, something special about us.

When Michelle Obama calls herself Mom-in-Chief, I am, like,   4
"Amen, sister!," because Mrs. Obama knows what we all know: your husband may be a very important person, but who runs the show at home? Not Dad. Mom. But I think Ann Romney carries the day here. Unlike Mrs. Obama, when Mrs. Romney talks so movingly to the women of America, she leaves out the childless gals, and there is a reason for that: they are not moms.

You can sugarcoat that all you like, but Mrs. Romney chose not   5
to, and I say good for her. Because, if you're not a mom, you may not be a bad person, but you are an extraneous person. If there were something great about being a woman who is not a mom, something that added anything to America, if there were even one teeny-weeny example of how the non-moms hold America together the way moms do, Mrs. Romney would mention the childless gals. But she doesn't, because there isn't.

Mrs. Romney says there would not even be an America without   6
moms, and she is totally right about that. We would just be a nation of dads, who, let's face it, don't know a strep throat from a screwdriver and always get the washing machine confused with

the dryer—antics that are funny on sitcoms but have no place in the real America, which is why moms have to do everything.

With just the moms and the doofusy dads, but without the single gals, we would be an even stronger America—there, I've said it!—or, at least, an America with fewer ladies passing their evenings on barstools. And that wouldn't be such a bad thing, would it? 7

Even the word "mom" is great. It's got that cozy *mmm* sound, like "Mmm, mmm, good," which reminds me of Campbell's cream-of-tomato soup, which is the soup I always served my four children, along with grilled cheese sandwiches that I cut into fun shapes with cookie cutters on a frosty winter's day, and which my mom made for me on a frosty winter's day, and which my daughters will make for their children on a frosty winter's day. Because making a thoughtful, nutritious, whimsical lunch is the kind of thing—one of trillions!—that moms do. But not so we can be thanked. No one ever thanks us for anything, and we moms learn to be fine with that, learn that our children's smiling faces, when they take that first sip of hot Campbell's soup and bite into those whimsical sandwiches on a frosty winter's day, are thanks enough. 8

The single gals, the gals who haven't had children, don't understand that. They expect to be thanked for things. But when was the last time your child said to you, "Thank you for taking me to the emergency room," or, "Thank you for writing my history paper for me"? And you know what? They don't have to. Giving is our job. 9

And if you're not a mom you don't understand that. You may understand expensive shoes, and having meaningless, drunken sexual intercourse with men who never call the next day, and trying to cheer yourself up by buying yourself baubles, but you don't understand that it's all about the giving. 10

You know what else I love about being a mom? How we may be a special sorority, but we are not some snobby, exclusive club—not at all. I love how our members come from all walks of life. 11

Like, Ann Romney is a member—and, who knows, she may be our next First Mom!—but so is Snooki. Have you seen the photos of Snooki coming out of the hospital after having her baby? There she is, in a wheelchair, holding baby Lorenzo Dominic, her expression composed, dignified, almost grave, looking straight ahead, as if into her mom future. Unless I'm mistaken, which I never am, Snooki is thinking, I can't believe I just did an episode where I sulked and bitched endlessly in Cancún because I was pregnant and couldn't go out partying with my friends. I can't believe I was such a skanky nincompoop my whole life. Now I must have dignity and grace, for Lorenzo Dominic's sake, and pray to Jesus that MTV never airs reruns during his lifetime. 12

This is what her look says: "I have joined the sisterhood. I'm a mom now. I get it." And today, if Snooki and Mrs. Romney were in a room together, all they would have to say to each other is "How about those contractions?" and they would laugh together in solidarity and be bonded for life. 13

My four children—two girls, two boys—are all grown now, off at college or pursuing their own careers. I've let them go graciously, which is also part of a mother's work, and I speak to each of them on the phone only seven times a day. The boys still send their underpants home to be ironed, and I FedEx sanitary napkins to the girls when they forget their periods, but otherwise they are independent adults, and a credit to their country. 14

I wish I could say the same for Dave, their dad, whom I never asked to do anything to help me, because I knew, frankly, that he would screw it up the way dads always do. 15

I keep him in the basement now, with Sadie, our old, incontinent golden retriever, and that seems to be fine with both of them. I have several unmarried acquaintances, childless women, who have spoken to me about this, saying that they feel it is unkind to Dave. You know what I tell them? I say, Are you a mom? Do you run this country? Do you know the first thing about holding up America? Of course you don't! So go along and scat, and let us moms do the jobs that we women were put on the planet to do. 16

Understanding Meaning

1. In Allen's view, what makes mothers different from other women?
2. Allen states that without "single gals" America would be stronger. What does this statement imply? Is she serious?
3. Allen states in her conclusion "let us moms do the jobs that we women were put on the planet to do." Does this suggest that motherhood is the normal destiny of women? Does it suggest that women without children are abnormal?
4. Allen (paragraph 12) suggests that having a child gave *Jersey Shore* star Nicole "Snooki" Polizzi a sudden look of maturity. Is Allen implying that women automatically become mature and serious by having children? Can you think of examples of immature mothers?
5. *Critical Thinking*: Allen refers to "single gals" as "ladies passing their evenings on barstools" or "having meaningless, drunken sexual intercourse with men who never call the next day." Does this attitude imply a hostility exists between mothers and non-mothers? Would feminists be troubled by divisions between females? Consider her comment that little evidence exists that "non-moms hold America together the way moms do." Can you think of women without children who have contributed to society?

Evaluating Strategy

1. In her opening paragraph, Allen dismisses non-mothers, saying "you probably won't understand a lot of what I'm going to say." Does this strategy risk alienating readers?
2. Allen describes both Michelle Obama and Ann Romney in positive terms. Does this suggest that motherhood trumps politics, and that any rift in society is not between liberal and conservative women but between "moms" and "non-moms"?
3. *Blending the Modes*: Where does Allen use *comparison* and *cause and effect* to develop her essay?

Appreciating Language

1. How would you characterize the tone and style of Allen's essay?
2. Why does Allen say she likes the word "mom"? What does it remind her of?
3. How does Allen describe single women? Do her remarks seem fair?

WRITING SUGGESTIONS

1. Using Allen's essay as a model, write a short essay that celebrates another social role—being a father, homeowner, small business owner, hunter, vegetarian, bike rider, NFL fan, online shopper, Democrat or Republican, Facebook user, veteran, or pet owner.

2. *Collaborative Writing*: Discuss Allen's essay with a group of students and write an opposing essay examining the importance of fathers. Is fatherhood equally celebrated in our culture? Does the large number of single mothers in society marginalize the roles of fathers? If members disagree, consider writing opposing essays.

JESSICA VALENTI

Jessica Valenti (1978–) was born in Queens, New York, and received a master's degree in Women's and Gender Studies from Rutgers University. After working for the National Organization for Women, Valenti founded *Feministing*, an online news source for younger feminists. In 2011 she left the website, stating it should remain a source for the younger generation of feminists. She has written articles for *Ms. Magazine, The Nation, The Guardian,* and the *Washington Post.* Her books include *Full Frontal Feminism* (2007), *The Purity Myth* (2009), and *Why Have Kids?: A New Mom Explores the Truth About Parenting and Happiness* (2012).

Are All Women Born to Be Mothers?

CONTEXT: *In this section from an article published in the* Washington Post, *Valenti analyzes the cultural assumption that all women are destined to become mothers.*

WRITER'S NOTE: *Valenti uses remarks from the 2012 Republican National Convention as a way to set up her analysis of contemporary views of motherhood and the role of women.*

1   These days, "mom" is king. It was perhaps the most frequently used word at the Republican National Convention this past week, where Ann Romney, mother of five, said, "It's the moms of this nation…who really hold this country together." Paul Ryan said his mother is his role model, and Chris Christie all but called himself a mama's boy.

2   Republicans' efforts to woo women have become fever-pitch pandering as the party tries to undo damage from comments such as Rep. Todd Akin's remark that a "legitimate" rape victim can't get pregnant and Pennsylvania Gov. Tom Corbett's advice to women who object to invasive ultrasounds before an abortion: "You just have to close your eyes." But given the GOP's extreme antiabortion platform, which does not include exceptions for rape or incest, focusing on motherhood as a gateway to women's hearts and votes seems misguided. After all, no matter how many platitudes are thrown around, this is the party that wants motherhood not to be a choice, but to be enforced.

3   In a way, Republicans are reflecting American culture, which assumes that all women want to become mothers. And the best kind of woman—the best kind of mother—is portrayed as one who puts her maternal role above everything else.

4   In 2006, the term "pre-pregnant" was coined in a *Washington Post* story about a report from the Centers for Disease Control and Prevention recommending that all women of childbearing age care for their pre-conception health. The agency said all American women—from the time of their first menstrual period until menopause—should take folic acid supplements, not smoke, not

"misuse" alcohol, maintain a healthy weight, refrain from drug use and avoid "high risk sexual behavior."

The CDC was asking women to behave as if they were already 5 pregnant, even if they had no intention of conceiving in the near—or distant—future. For the first time, a U.S. government institution was explicitly saying what social norms had always hinted at: All women, regardless of whether they have or want children, are moms-in-waiting.

Telling women that what is best for a pregnancy is automati- 6 cally best for them defines motherhood as a woman prioritizing the needs of a child, real or hypothetical, over her own.

Rebecca Kukla, a professor of internal medicine and philoso- 7 phy at Georgetown University and the author of *Mass Hysteria: Medicine, Culture, and Women's Bodies* said at a recent seminar, "Do lesbians, women who are carefully contracepting and not interested in having children, 13-year-olds, women done having kids, really want their bodies seen as prenatal, understood solely in terms of reproductive function?"

She noted that this assumption—that all women will be 8 mothers—has led to a "pre-conception" health movement, which "treats the non-pregnant body as on its way to pregnancy." Kukla told me that she experienced this when she once went to her doctor to get an antibiotic for a urinary tract infection, and he asked if she might be pregnant or could become pregnant. Yes, physicians have to ask to inoculate themselves against malpractice lawsuits. But Kukla's doctor wouldn't drop the issue and insisted on a weaker drug that would cause fewer complications during a pregnancy.

"Never mind that I'm a grown woman who is capable of using 9 birth control and would have ended a pregnancy had I become pregnant," she said. "Because I...could become pregnant, I got this other, less effective drug."

This obsession with parenthood as a given doesn't match the 10 reality of women's lives. In fact, most American women spend the majority of their lives trying not to get pregnant. According to the Guttmacher Institute, by the time a woman with two children is in her mid-40s, she will have spent only five years trying to become pregnant, being pregnant or in a postpartum period. So to avoid getting pregnant, she would have had to refrain from sex or use contraception for 25 years. That's a long part of life and a lot of effort to avoid parenthood.

Almost all American women who are sexually active use some 11 form of birth control. The second most popular form after the pill? Sterilization. And women are increasingly choosing forms of long-term contraception. Since 2005, the number of women using an intrauterine device has increased by 161 percent. A 2010 Pew Research Center study showed that the rate of American women who did not have children almost doubled since 1976. That's nearly one in five women today.

Laura Scott, the author of *Two Is Enough: A Couple's Guide to* 12 *Living Childless by Choice*, says the No. 1 reason women give for not wanting children is that they don't want their lives to change. In a two-year study she conducted of child-free women—many prefer to call themselves "child-free" as opposed to "childless," since the latter implies an absence or void—74 percent said they "had no desire to have a child, no maternal instinct."

The other reasons they gave: loving the relationship they were in "as it is," valuing their "freedom and independence," not wanting to take on "the responsibility of raising a child," a desire to focus "on my own interests, needs or goals," and wanting to accomplish "things in life that would be difficult to do if I was a parent." 13

"Parenting is no longer the default," Scott told me. "For a lot of people, it's no longer an assumption—it's a decision." 14

Yet the stigma remains. On Web forums for women without children (I have yet to see such a space for child-free men), the most talked-about topic is the need to constantly justify their decision. The criticisms are so steady and predictable that line of questioning is referred to as "breeder bingo." One contributor even made a bingo card with frequently heard lines, such as "The children are our future!" and "Don't you want to give your parents grandchildren?" On one site, a woman from Virginia wrote that she mostly gets confused looks when she tells people that she doesn't want children. "I suppose it never occurred to them that having kids is a choice," she said. 15

It does seem odd that it's women without children who are most often questioned about their choice. After all, parenthood is the decision that brings another person into the world, whereas being child-free maintains the status quo. 16

And that's what Scott finds truly disturbing. She says she often speaks to women who say they didn't know they had a choice. 17

"I see this a lot—where women are feeling a lot of external pressure and not owning feelings of ambivalence around having children," she told me. "Many of these women end up profoundly unhappy." 18

Indeed, studies show that children who were unintended are raised differently than those who were planned—a disturbing situation, considering that a third of births in the United States are unplanned. 19

American culture can't seem to accept the fact that some women don't want to be mothers. Parenting is simply presented as something everyone—a woman especially—is supposed to do. 20

This expectation is in line with the antiabortion movement and the Republican ethos around women and motherhood. No matter what women actually want, parenthood is perceived as the best, and only, choice for them. In his speech accepting the GOP presidential nomination Thursday night, Mitt Romney said of his wife: "I knew that her job as a mom was harder than mine. And I knew, without question, that her job as a mom was a lot more important than mine." 21

If we really value motherhood—and if it's such a tough, important job—it wouldn't be a given, but a proactive decision. 22

As the Republicans talk about how much they "love women"—as Ann Romney enthused Tuesday—let's remember that love isn't shown by force or coercion. It's based on respect. 23

Understanding Meaning

1. What is Valenti's thesis? Can you state it in your own words?
2. What assumptions about women and motherhood does Valenti examine?
3. How does the attitude that all women will become mothers affect their health care? Is this part of what Valenti calls the "pre-conception" movement?
4. What pressures do women who do not want to have children face?
5. *Critical Thinking*: Valenti notes she has never seen a website dedicated to men who do not want children. Do men face less pressure to become fathers? If so, why? Would a national political convention celebrate "dads"? Why or why not? Does the pro-life movement fail to address the responsibility men have in unplanned pregnancies?

Evaluating Strategy

1. How effective is Valenti's opening? How can positive remarks about motherhood have negative implications for women?
2. What evidence does Valenti provide to support her view that "the obsession with parenthood as a given doesn't match the reality of women's lives"?
3. *Blending the Modes*: Where does Valenti use *comparison*, *cause and effect*, and *argument* to develop her essay?

Appreciating Language

1. Valenti points out that many women prefer to call themselves "child-free" rather than "childless." How do these connotations differ? Does the word "childless" reflect a cultural bias?
2. *Critical Thinking*: Valenti quotes Laura Scott stating that for many people parenting is "no longer an assumption—it's a decision." What is the difference between "assumptions" and "decisions"? Do assumptions imply fundamental values that should not be questioned?

WRITING SUGGESTIONS

1. Using Valenti's essay as a model, analyze another cultural assumption, such as the value of a college degree or owning a home, the benefits of taking vitamins, or the positive impact of "green energy" on the environment.

2. *Collaborative Writing*: Working with a group of students, discuss Allen's and Valenti's articles, then write an essay outlining your group's views on motherhood. Do members believe that motherhood is a "sisterhood" that makes women superior over those without children? Do they believe that being "child-free" rather than being "childless" should not be questioned? If members disagree, consider writing opposing essays.

Writing Beyond the Classroom

Alton Enterprises

CONTEXT: *Professionals use analysis, as in this report, to examine problems and propose solutions.*

WRITER'S NOTE: *Samuel Goldman uses words like "strongly recommend" and "immediate and thorough review" to stress the problems his analysis revealed.*

ALTON ENTERPRISES
www.altonenterprises.com

C O N F I D E N T I A L

Preliminary Security Analysis

Date May 15, 2013
Submitted to Carmen Gonzalez
Submitted by Samuel Goldman

Background

The president of Alton Enterprises requested a preliminary security analysis to determine whether a full security review is required.

Recommendation

Based on personal observations made May 1–3, I strongly recommend a full review of all Alton Enterprises' security procedures to prevent accidents, cancellation of government contracts, and increased insurance premiums.

Examples of Security Lapses Observed May 1–3, 2013

Physical Safety

- On three occasions visitors and family members of employees were allowed to enter work areas, which specifically violates company policy and federal work rules.
- On May 2, only two security guards were present in the main plant. Alton's contracts with the federal government require at least four guards on duty at all times.
- Employee cars were parked in a fire lane on the night of May 2.

Data Security

- Confidential reports were left untended in the copy room.
- Employee laptops containing classified Defense Department specifications were left untended and running in the break room.
- Twenty-two employees are missing security clearance files.

Conclusion

These lapses indicate a clear need for an immediate and thorough review of Alton Enterprises' security policy and procedures.

Understanding Meaning

1. What is the purpose of Goldman's analysis?
2. What evidence does Goldman present to support his conclusion?
3. How could security lapses affect Alton Enterprises?
4. *Critical Thinking*: How could a document like this affect an individual or organization that did not respond to it in a timely fashion?

Evaluating Strategy

1. Why do you think Goldman labeled this report "Confidential"? How could a leak of this document adversely affect the management of Alton Enterprises?
2. How effective is the use of bullet points? Would this analysis have the same impact if written as a standard business letter in traditional paragraphs? Why or why not?
3. Goldman puts the date in large letters. Does this serve to dramatize the fact that all the lapses he observed occurred over three days?

Appreciating Language

1. How would you characterize the tone and style of Goldman's report?
2. Does Goldman's use of terms like "strongly recommend" and "immediate and thorough" suit his purpose? Can a writer use language that is overly dramatic? Can a writer be dismissed as being an alarmist?

WRITING SUGGESTIONS

1. Using Goldman's report as a model, write a short analysis based on personal observations. You might document environmental problems in your neighborhood, list safety and health issues at your job or campus, note the way a company or product is advertised on television, study the way popular blogs or websites address a specific issue, or analyze the strengths and weaknesses of a sports team.

2. *Collaborative Writing*: Discuss this report with a group of students and write a process paper that lists in order of importance the actions Alton Enterprises should take. Why would it be important to generate documents showing that the company is taking immediate steps to address the problems Goldman observed?

Responding to Images

Protester being arrested by Los Angeles police

1. What is your first reaction to this image? Would your reaction depend on how the man being subdued was identified? If a caption described him as a student radical, rabbi, Iraq War veteran, or Islamist, would your view differ?

2. How would the following captions influence the way people view this photograph?

   Police restore order
   Police arrest rioter
   Demonstrator taken into custody by authorities
   Unarmed citizen seized by the government

3. What role do connotations play in shaping the way images are perceived? What words, positive and negative, can be used to describe the figures in the photograph?

4. *Visual Analysis*: The protective helmets and visors obscure the officers' faces, making them depersonalized figures of authority, while the bearded protester appears as a cultural stereotype. Could this image be used as a Rorschach test to examine people's perceptual worlds (see pages 7–9)? Who might identify with the police? Who might identify with the demonstrator?

5. *Critical Thinking*: Because police wear uniforms, helmets, and carry weapons, are they likely to appear as threatening or abusive in images, even when they are preventing violence or protecting public property and other citizens?

Student Paper: Analysis

This paper was written in response to the following assignment:

> Analyze the meaning or significance of a social, educational, or political issue. Your essay should analyze a subject by exploring causes, effects, or deeper meanings. Avoid superficial description.

First Draft with Instructor's Comments

Endless War

When George Bush used the word "war" to describe the fight against terrorism, he created in the mindsets of <u>alot</u> of people that there would eventually be an a final end. So many people are wondering when it will end, what will a victory be? But this war is not like other wars. Because we won WWII and the occupations of Germany, Italy, and Japan created stable democracies people like to see <u>it as a kind of role model.</u>   *Awkward, "a lot"* *Awkward, wordy* *Wordy, unclear, revise statement*

Because the war in Iraq did not turn out like Italy there are <u>alot</u> of questions. Most people don't think Iraq had much to do with 9/11. Osama bin Laden and Saddam had little or nothing in common except maybe a hatred of the United States.   *Awkward, "a lot"*

A war on terrorism is not like other wars. <u>Although it might use armed forces to bomb targets and high tech surveillance equipment like spy satitllites.</u> Most of the conflicts and important battles are fought in secret. Cutting off funding to radical groups and eliminating key personnel, even if that means kidnapping and assassination, is the way terrorism will be fought. It will be a secret war mostly.   *Fragment, sp "satellites"*

The country is not prepared to fight this kind of war. But it is like other things we call wars, like the war on drugs or the war on organized crime. <u>These conflicts go on and on and no one pretends there will be any victory any time soon</u>. So this war against terror will go on and on.   *Add details, explain* *run-on*

Revision Notes

The war on terrorism is a good topic to analyze. An analysis essay, however, must have a clearly defined topic. This paper raises a number of ideas but does not explore them in any depth. An analysis—even a subjective analysis—is more than a collection of random thoughts on a particular subject.

- *Narrow your topic. A short essay cannot address everything you know about a subject. A good way to focus an analysis essay is to ask yourself a question:*
  - *–Is "war" the appropriate term for this conflict?*
  - *–Is military force the best way to counter terrorism?*
  - *–When will anyone declare victory?*
  - *–How will a long war on terrorism change society, civil liberties, immigration?*
- *Because many people do not consider the Iraq war part of the war on terror, you might need to explain your position more clearly.*

Revised Draft

Endless War

Since President Bush declared a war on terror, it is unlikely that any future president will be able to declare victory or even an armistice. The war on terror can never end because billions of people in the world see America as a target. In a global economy, the poor and disaffected, Muslims and non-Muslims alike, see the United States as an imperial power that exploits their people, defames their values, and supports corrupt regimes. All this resentment only has to inspire a handful of fanatics to create a serious terrorist threat. Today's terrorists come from the Arab world. Tomorrow's terrorists could come from the poor of South America, Asia, or even Europe. Today's terrorists wage war to protect their vision of Islam. Tomorrow's terrorists could wage war in the name of the environment, hunger, poverty, or the world's failure to accept their conspiracy theories about UFOs.

Northern Ireland is a small region with the population of Milwaukee County, yet it produced enough IRA terrorists at one point to require 30,000 British troops, metal detectors on the streets, barricades, helicopter patrols, and constant counterterrorism intelligence. A handful of terrorists can paralyze a society and cripple an economy.

As the only superpower and an emblem of what many people in the world fear and resent, America and its interests will always be targets unless there is a major shift in our relationship with people we do not understand, often demonize, and frequently insult through our ignorance.

So the war against terrorism will go on and on. Future presidents may trim funding here and there, but Homeland Security will likely become as American as Social Security because no one can predict when an attack can occur. Lyndon Johnson declared a war on poverty fifty years ago, and no has proclaimed victory yet. You might as well ask when the Urban League and NAACP plan to disband. At what point will African American leaders announce that racism is over? When will NOW declare victory over sexism and go out of business?

Because terrorism does not depend on nation states, mass organizations, or institutional support, it is unpredictable. In 1995 Timothy McVeigh was able to kill 168 people and destroy millions of dollars of property in Oklahoma City with a rented truck and bomb made of fertilizer and diesel fuel. Tomorrow's terrorists will likely have access to nuclear and biological weapons so that the next rental truck that explodes in a city street could kill tens of thousands and contaminate whole neighborhoods for decades. That prospect will keep this war going even if the Arab-Israeli conflict is resolved, democracy and prosperity sweep the Arab world, and America elects a Muslim president. Terrorists in Algeria and Afghanistan have killed thousands of fellow Muslims because they failed to embrace their extremist form of Islam. And it will only take a handful of extremists to stage an attack that will dwarf the events of September 11. No one will dare proclaim victory over terrorism any more than anyone will claim to have won the war against racism, organized crime, or poverty.

Questions for Review and Revision

1. Is the student's thesis clear? Can you restate it in your own words? Does the student provide sufficient proof to support the thesis?
2. How effective are the introduction and conclusion? Would you suggest any changes? Why or why not?
3. The student includes an example about Northern Ireland. Does this provide effective support? Why or why not?
4. The student compares the war on terrorism to wars on organized crime, poverty, and racism. Do you find these comparisons effective? Why or why not?
5. Read the paper aloud. Do you detect any sentences or paragraphs that could be revised for greater clarity?

WRITING SUGGESTIONS

1. Write an essay analyzing a current fad, trend, or common behavior. Include key details, and suggest the cause or significance of your subject.
2. *Collaborative Writing:* Discuss this essay with a group of students, and work together to develop a statement on terrorism. Do they believe any future president will announce that the war on terrorism has ended? Why or why not? Record the group's comments using comparison or division and classification to organize their observations.

EVALUATING ANALYSIS CHECKLIST

Before submitting your paper, review these points:

1. Is the topic clearly limited?
2. Is your approach appropriate for the writing context?
3. Do you present enough evidence?
4. Have you evaluated sources for inaccuracy or bias?

5. Have you avoided errors in logic?
6. Are your research methods clearly explained?
7. Do you clearly present and qualify the results of your analysis?
8. Have you considered alternative interpretations?

Accompanying English CourseMate Resources

 Visit English CourseMate at **www.cengagebrain.com** to find many helpful resources and study tools for this chapter.

Division and Classification: Separating into Parts and Rating Categories

What Are Division and Classification?

Division separates a subject into parts; **classification** rates a subject on a scale. Both are used to make complex subjects easier to understand and help in decision making. Poorly written division and classification, however, can misinform and mislead readers. Division and classification can be based on official and objective designations established by researchers, government agencies, corporations, organizations, or experts. They can also be created by individual writers to express subjective observations and personal opinions.

Division

If you enter a hospital, you will probably see signs directing you to different departments, for example, cardiology, radiology, psychiatry, and pediatrics. Universities consist of separate colleges, such as business and liberal arts. American literature can be divided into courses by historical era (nineteenth- and twentieth-century writers); by genre (poetry, fiction, and drama); or by special interest (women's literature, black literature, and science fiction). Discount stores organize products into housewares, clothing, linens, and other departments. Corporations place personnel into different divisions, such as design, production, maintenance, marketing, sales, and accounting. If you call your cable company's 800 number, a recorded voice may direct you to press one number for billing and another for technical support.

Division makes complicated subjects easier to comprehend and work with. The human body is overwhelmingly intricate. In order to understand how it functions, medical disciplines divide it into systems: digestive, respiratory, nervous, musculoskeletal, reproductive, and others. By studying individual systems, medical students come to a fuller understanding of how the whole body operates. Crime is such a vast social problem that writers discuss it in terms of traditional divisions—robbery, car theft, homicide, fraud, and so on—or invent their own categories, dividing crime by causes: power, greed, identity, and revenge.

The website Depression-help-resource.com uses division to explain different forms of depression:

Types of Depression

Post-Partum Depression—Major depressive episode that occurs after having a baby. Depressive symptoms usually begin within four weeks of giving birth and can vary in intensity and duration.

Seasonal Affective Disorder (SAD)—A type of depressive disorder which is characterized by episodes of major depression which reoccur at a specific time of year (e.g., fall, winter). In the past two years, depressive periods occur at least two times without any episodes that occur at a different time.

Anxiety Depression—Not an official depression type (as defined by the DSM). However, anxiety often also occurs with depression. In this case, a depressed individual may also experience anxiety symptoms (e.g., panic attacks) or an anxiety disorder (e.g., PTSD, panic disorder, social phobia, generalized anxiety disorder).

In contrast, Judith Viorst (page 294) uses division to distinguish seven types of friends she has observed, inventing categories such as "convenience friends" and "part-of-a-couple friends."

Division writing can present a series of descriptions or definitions and organize a set of narratives, processes, or persuasive arguments. Ed Koch (page 316), for example, defends capital punishment by rejecting a list of opposing arguments.

Critical Thinking for Writing Division

Dividing any subject can be challenging. Would it make more sense to explain American politics to a foreign visitor in terms of political parties or specific issues? Would you group used cars by year, by price, or by model? The goal of division is to make a complicated subject easier to understand.

When writing division, follow these guidelines:

1. **Identify whether your division is objective or subjective.** Explain the rationale of your division, stating whether you are using a method established by others or creating one of your own.

2. **Avoid oversimplifying your subject.** You have no doubt seen magazine articles announcing three kinds of bosses, four types of marriages, or five methods of child rearing. Writers often invent descriptive or humorous labels, warning you to avoid "the toxic controller" or advising you how to negotiate

with the "whiny wimp." Although these divisions can be amusing and insightful, they can trivialize or oversimplify a subject. Not all people or situations can neatly fit into three or four types. *When discussing complex topics, inform readers of possible exceptions to your categories.* You can indicate exceptions by simply adding the word "most" to your introduction: "*Most* students belong to one of the following categories…"

3. **Indicate the size of each type or group.** If you write that students pay for college in three ways—by scholarships, loans, and personal savings—many readers may assume that a third of students pay their own way, when, in fact, they may constitute less than 1 percent of the whole. To prevent misleading readers, explain the size of each group. If you cannot give precise percentages, indicate the groups' general size: "The vast majority of students rely on loans, while only a very small minority are able to finance their education with personal savings."

4. **Select a method of division that includes all parts of the whole.** If you divide college students into three types, for example, make sure everyone on campus is included in one of the groups. Eliminate potential gaps. You cannot simply divide students into Protestants, Catholics, and Jews if some are agnostics or Muslims. Every member or part of the whole must be accounted for.

5. **Make sure individual parts fit only one category.** If you were to divide businesses by geographical region—north, south, east, and west—how would you handle a company with operations on both coasts? If most items can fit in more than one category, your method of division is not suited to your subject. It might be better to discuss businesses in terms of their gross sales, products, or size rather than location. If a few items do belong to more than one category, acknowledge them as exceptions.

6. **Avoid categories that include too many differences.** If you were examining people of different ages, it could make sense to write about people in groups from thirty to forty or fifty to sixty. But an age category of sixty to seventy would include both working and retired people—both those still paying into Social Security and those receiving benefits. It might be more accurate to break this group into people who are sixty to sixty-five and those who are sixty-five to seventy.

7. **Indicate possible exceptions or changes.** Divisions may not be hard or fast. After explaining the three ways students pay for college, you might point out that some students start college with enough scholarship money to pay for their freshman year, use their own savings to pay for a later semester, and then rely on loans until graduation. Some students might use all three methods at once—spending personal savings on books, scholarship money on tuition, and loan proceeds on remaining expenses.

Classification

Classification ranks a subject on a scale. Teachers grade exams A, B, C, D, or F according to the number of correct answers. Car insurance companies set prices based on drivers' ages, past accidents, and the value of their vehicles. Fire departments rank fires as one, two, three, four, or five alarms to determine how much equipment to send. Prisons are classified minimum, medium, and maximum security. During the football season, teams are ranked by their wins and losses.

Classification helps people to make decisions and to direct actions. Classifications can set prices, establish salaries, and in some cases save lives. The importance of classification is demonstrated by the use of triage in emergency medicine. When a hospital is flooded with accident victims, doctors place patients into three categories: those who will die with or without immediate medical attention, those who will survive without emergency care, and those who will survive only if treated without delay. The last group is given priority to ensure that doctors do not waste time on the dying or those with minor injuries.

Like division, classification can be objective or subjective. The movie listings in a newspaper may display a number of stars next to an R-rated film. The R rating, officially established by the MPAA (see page 323), is an objective classification that will appear in every newspaper listing, television commercial, theater trailer, poster, and website. The number of stars, however, will vary with each newspaper, reflecting the subjective opinion of a local critic.

The National Weather Service uses the Saffir-Simpson Hurricane Wind Scale, which measures sustained wind speeds of one minute, to objectively rank hurricanes in five clearly defined categories:

Categories of Hurricanes

Category 1 (74–95 mph) *Very dangerous winds will produce some damage.* Large branches of trees will snap and shallow-rooted trees can be toppled.

Category 2 (96–110 mph) *Extremely dangerous winds will cause extensive damage.* Many shallowly rooted trees will be snapped or uprooted and block numerous roads.

Category 3 (111–130 mph) *Devastating damage will occur.* Many trees will be snapped or uprooted, blocking numerous roads.

Category 4 (131–155 mph) *Catastrophic damage will occur.* Most trees will be snapped or uprooted and power poles downed. Fallen trees and power poles will isolate residential areas.

Category 5 (over 155 mph) *Catastrophic damage will occur.* Nearly all trees will be snapped or uprooted and power poles downed. Fallen trees and power poles will isolate residential areas.

In contrast, James Austin (page 303) uses subjective classification to explain his personal view that there are four levels of chance or luck, ranging from "pure blind luck" that benefits anyone to "luck that is peculiar to one person."

Critical Thinking for Writing Classification

Classification requires careful planning. To avoid common problems, follow these guidelines:

1. **Avoid confusing division with classification.** Perhaps the most frequent mistake students make in writing classification papers is simply dividing a

subject into parts. *Classification not only divides a subject into parts but also rates the parts on a scale.*

2. **Establish a clearly defined standard of measurement.** To successfully teach writing, for example, an English professor must provide students with a clear understanding of what distinguishes an A paper from a B paper. Even if you are making up your own categories, each one should be clearly defined so that readers understand what distinguishes one from the other.

3. **Explain whether the classification is objective or subjective.** Inform readers if your classification method is universally accepted or is subject to interpretation. Some classifications may be clearly defined because they are based on precise measurements, such as credit scores. The classification of depression into mild, moderate, and severe levels may be more subjective and less universally accepted. If you are creating your own classification, make sure you clearly explain your method of ranking subjects.

4. **Do not mix standards.** You can classify automobiles, for instance, from the cheapest to the most expensive, from the safest to the most dangerous, or from the most fuel efficient to the least fuel efficient. But you cannot write a classification essay that rates cars as being either safe, fuel efficient or expensive since many cars could be both expensive and fuel efficient.

5. **Arrange categories in order.** Organize the categories so that they follow a ladder-like pattern, such as judging items from the best to the worst, the cheapest to the most expensive, or the newest to the oldest.

6. **Provide enough categories to include all parts of the whole.** If you were to classify cars as being either American or foreign, how would you account for Toyotas produced in the United States or Chryslers assembled in Mexico?

7. **Explain if subjects can change categories.** Not all subjects can be permanently labeled. A student's grade point average can change from one semester to another. A consumer's credit score will rise and fall. The five categories of hurricanes are clearly fixed, but an individual storm will move up and down the scale as a tropical storm gathers enough speed to be officially called a hurricane, then move from category 1 to 2 or 3 as it increases force, then fall back to category 1 as it loses strength, and eventually fall off the chart as it ceases to be called a hurricane and becomes nothing more than an ordinary rainstorm. *Make sure readers do not mistakenly assume that items subject to change have fixed designations.*

Using Division and Classification

In many cases, people use both division and classification to make decisions and explain ideas or actions. A travel guide might divide local restaurants by type—seafood, steak, Italian, or Mexican—and then classify them by quality or price range. A financial planner could present clients with different types of investments—stocks, bonds, and mutual funds—and then classify each by risk or rate of return. A nutritionist designing a diet for a weight loss program would first divide foods into groups, such as grains and vegetables, then classify how many calories a dieter should consume of each. A first aid manual might use division to explain the different causes of burns—contact with heat, radiation, chemicals, or electricity—and then use classification to rank them first, second, or third degree based on their severity. In answering a 911 call, a dispatcher uses division to determine whether the emergency requires a police, fire department, or ambulance response. With further information, he or she might use classification to measure the size or severity of the emergency to determine how many police officers or paramedics to send.

Writing Techniques: DIVISION AND CLASSIFICATION

Introductions

Writers use introductions to announce their topics and explain their method of division or classification. The opening can also provide background information, define terms, and address possible misconceptions. In "Four Sides to Every Story" (page 308) Stewart Brand points out that talks about climate change did not consist of a debate between two positions but a discussion of four points of view. In "Four Kinds of Chance" (page 303) James Austin first defines luck, then explains the four varieties he has identified.

Names and Numbers

Writers help readers follow their train of thought by establishing clear categories and identifying them with names or numbers. Stewart Brand (page 308) classifies climate scientists on a scale from those he calls "denialists" to "calamatists." James Austin uses numbers, ranking the forms of luck on a scale from Chance I to Chance IV.

Degree of Precision

Writers inform readers about the exactness of their categories. Some divisions or classifications are based on easily observed and widely accepted measurements, such as the wind speed of hurricanes (page 290). Other rankings are more subjective. Florence King (page 312) divides the American class system into three levels but admits the categories are imprecise because they rely largely on "self-identification."

Strategies FOR READING DIVISION AND CLASSIFICATION

As you read the division and classification entries in this chapter, keep the following questions in mind.

Understanding Meaning

1. What is the writer trying to explain by dividing or classifying the topic? Does the division or classification help you understand the subject better than a simple description would?
2. Do the divisions oversimplify the subject?

3. Do the classification essays have a clearly defined standard?

4. Do the standards seem fair? Do they adequately measure what they claim to evaluate?

Evaluating Strategy

1. How does the writer introduce or set up the division or classification?

2. How does the author use definitions and examples to create distinct categories?

3. Does the writer use standard divisions and classifications accepted by a particular discipline or profession, or invent new ones?

4. Does the writer use division or classification to explain a topic or as a device to recommend one item over another?

Appreciating Language

1. What does the level of language reveal about the writer's discipline and intended audience?

2. What words does the author use to describe or define standards of classification? Do you detect a bias?

JUDITH VIORST

Judith Viorst (1931–) is a graduate of Rutgers University and the Washington Psychoanalytic Institute. Best known for her children's books, including *Alexander and the Terrible, Horrible, No Good, Very Bad Day* (1972) and *Sad Underwear and Other Complications* (1995), she has also written collections of light verse, including *It's Hard to Be Hip Over Thirty and Other Tragedies of Modern Life* (1970), *How Did I Get to Be Forty and Other Atrocities* (1984), *Suddenly Sixty and Other Shocks of Later Life* (2000) and *I'm Too Young to Be 70 & Other Delusions* (2005). She has also published a novel, *Murdering Mr. Monti: A Merry Little Tale of Sex and Violence* (1994).

Friends, Good Friends—and Such Good Friends

CONTEXT: *Before reading this essay, consider the friends you have had in your life. Did they belong to different types? Were school friends different from neighborhood friends or friends met through relatives?*

WRITER'S NOTE: *Viorst uses both numbers and names to identify each category.*

Women are friends, I once would have said, when they totally love and support and trust each other, and bare to each other the secrets of their souls, and run—no questions asked—to help each other, and tell harsh truths to each other (no, you can't wear that dress unless you lose ten pounds first) when harsh truths must be told. *1* *introduction definition of "friend"*

Women are friends, I once would have said, when they share the same affection for Ingmar Bergman, plus train rides, cats, warm rain, charades, Camus, and hate with equal ardor Newark and Brussels sprouts and Lawrence Welk and camping. *2*

In other words, I once would have said that a friend is a friend all the way, but now I believe that's a narrow point of view. <u>For the friendships I have and the friendships I see are conducted at many levels of intensity, serve many different functions, meet different needs and range from those as all-the-way as the friendship of the soul sisters mentioned above to that of the most nonchalant and casual playmates.</u> *3* *division into types*

<u>Consider these varieties of friendship:</u> *4*

<u>1. Convenience friends.</u> These are women with whom, if our paths weren't crossing all the time, we'd have no particular reason to be friends: a next-door neighbor, a woman in our car pool, the mother of one of our children's closest friends or maybe some mommy with whom we serve juice and cookies each week at the Glenwood Co-op Nursery. *5* *type #1 examples*

Convenience friends are convenient indeed. They'll lend us their
cups and silverware for a party. They'll drive our kids to soccer
when we're sick. They'll take us to pick up our car when we need a
lift to the garage. They'll even take our cats when we go on vacation. As we will for them.

But we don't, with convenience friends, ever come too close or
tell too much; we maintain our public face and emotional distance.
"Which means," says Elaine, "that I'll talk about being overweight
but not about being depressed. Which means I'll admit being mad
but not blind with rage. Which means that I might say that we're
pinched this month but never that I'm worried sick over money."

But which doesn't mean that there isn't sufficient value to be
found in these friendships of mutual aid, in convenience friends.

2. Special-interest friends. These friendships aren't intimate, and
they needn't involve kids or silverware or cats. Their value lies in
some interest jointly shared. And so we may have an office friend
or a yoga friend or a tennis friend or a friend from the Women's
Democratic Club.

"I've got one woman friend," says Joyce, "who likes, as I do, to
take psychology courses. Which makes it nice for me—and nice for
her. It's fun to go with someone you know and it's fun to discuss
what you've learned, driving back from the classes." And for the
most part, she says, that's all they discuss.

"I'd say that what we're doing is doing together, not being
together," Suzanne says of her Tuesday-doubles friends. "It's
mainly a tennis relationship, but we play together well. And I guess
we all need to have a couple of playmates."

I agree.

My playmate is a shopping friend, a woman of marvelous taste,
a woman who knows exactly *where* to buy *what,* and furthermore
is a woman who always knows beyond a doubt what one ought
to be buying. I don't have the time to keep up with what's new in
eyeshadow, hemlines and shoes and whether the smock look is in
or finished already. But since (oh, shame!) I care a lot about eyeshadow, hemlines and shoes, and since I don't *want* to wear smocks
if the smock look is finished, I'm very glad to have a shopping friend.

3. Historical friends. We all have a friend who knew us when ...
maybe way back in Miss Meltzer's second grade, when our family
lived in that three-room flat in Brooklyn, when our dad was out of
work for seven months, when our brother Allie got in that fight
where they had to call the police, when our sister married the en-
dodontist from Yonkers and when, the morning after we lost our
virginity, she was the first, the only, friend we told.

The years have gone by and we've gone separate ways and we've
little in common now, but we're still an intimate part of each other's
past. And so whenever we go to Detroit we always go to visit this
friend of our girlhood. Who knows how we looked before our teeth
were straightened. Who knows how we talked before our voice got
un-Brooklyned. Who knows what we ate before we learned about

6

7

8

9 *type #2
examples*

10

11

12

13

14 *type #3
examples*

15

artichokes. And who, by her presence, puts us in touch with an earlier part of ourself, a part of ourself it's important never to lose.

"What this friend means to me and what I mean to her," says Grace, "is having a sister without sibling rivalry. We know the texture of each other's lives. She remembers my grandmother's cabbage soup. I remember the way her uncle played the piano. There's simply no other friend who remembers those things." **16**

4. <u>Crossroads friends</u>. Like historical friends, our crossroads friends are important for *what was*—for the friendship we shared at a crucial, now past, time of life. A time, perhaps, when we roomed in college together; or worked as eager young singles in the Big City together; or went together, as my friend Elizabeth and I did, through pregnancy, birth and that scary first year of new motherhood. **17** *type #4 examples*

Crossroads friends forge powerful links, links strong enough to endure with not much more contact than once-a-year letters at Christmas. And out of respect for those crossroads years, for those dramas and dreams we once shared, we will always be friends. **18**

5. <u>Cross-generational friends</u>. Historical friends and crossroads friends seem to maintain a special kind of intimacy—dormant but always ready to be revived—and though we may rarely meet, whenever we do connect, it's personal and intense. Another kind of intimacy exists in the friendships that form across generations in what one woman calls her daughter-mother and her mother-daughter relationships. **19** *type #5 examples*

Evelyn's friend is her mother's age—"but I share so much more than I ever could with my mother"—a woman she talks to of music, of books and of life. "What I get from her is the benefit of her experience. What she gets—and enjoys—from me is a youthful perspective. It's a pleasure for both of us." **20**

I have in my own life a precious friend, a woman of 65 who has lived very hard, who is wise, who listens well; who has been where I am and can help me understand it; and who represents not only an ultimate ideal mother to me but also the person I'd like to be when I grow up. **21**

In our daughter role we tend to do more than our share of self-revelation; in our mother role we tend to receive what's revealed. It's another kind of pleasure—playing wise mother to a questing younger person. It's another very lovely kind of friendship. **22**

6. <u>Part-of-a-couple friends</u>. Some of the women we call our friends we never see alone—we see them as part of a couple at couples' parties. And though we share interests in many things and respect each other's views, we aren't moved to deepen the relationship. Whatever the reason, a lack of time or—and this is more likely—a lack of chemistry, our friendship remains in the context of a group. But the fact that our feeling on seeing each other is always, "I'm so glad she's here" and the fact that we spend half the evening talking together says that this too, in its own way, counts as a friendship. **23** *type #6 examples*

(Other part-of-a-couple friends are the friends that came with the marriage, and some of these are friends we could live without. But **24**

sometimes, alas, she married our husband's best friend; and sometimes, alas, she is our husband's best friend. And so we find ourself
dealing with her, somewhat against our will, in a spirit of what I'll
call reluctant friendship.)

7. <u>Men who are friends</u>. I wanted to write just of women friends,
but the women I've talked to won't let me—they say I must mention man-woman friendships too. For these friendships can be just
as close and as dear as those that we form with women. Listen to
Lucy's description of one such friendship: "We've found we have
things to talk about that are different from what he talks about with
my husband and different from what I talk about with his wife. So
sometimes we call on the phone or meet for lunch. There are similar
intellectual interests—we always pass on to each other the books
that we love—but there's also something tender and caring too."

In a couple of crises, Lucy says, "he offered himself for talking
and for helping. And when someone died in his family he wanted
me there. The sexual, flirty part of our friendship is very small, but
some—just enough to make it fun and different." She thinks—and I
agree—that the sexual part, though small, is always *some*, is always
there when a man and a woman are friends.

It's only in the past few years that I've made friends with men, in
the sense of a friendship that's *mine,* not just part of two couples.
And achieving with them the ease and the trust I've found with
women friends has value indeed. Under the dryer at home last
week, putting on mascara and rouge, I comfortably sat and talked
with a fellow named Peter. Peter, I finally decided, could handle
the shock of me minus mascara under the dryer. Because we care
for each other. Because we're friends.

8. <u>There are medium friends, and pretty good friends, and
very good friends indeed, and these friendships are defined by
their level of intimacy.</u> And what we'll reveal at each of these
levels of intimacy is calibrated with care. We might tell a medium friend, for example, that yesterday we had a fight with our
husband. And we might tell a pretty good friend that this fight
with our husband made us so mad that we slept on the couch.
And we might tell a very good friend that the reason we got so
mad in that fight that we slept on the couch had something to
do with that girl who works in his office. But it's only to our very
best friends that we're willing to tell all, to tell what's going on
with that girl in his office.

The best of friends, I still believe, totally love and support and
trust each other, and bare to each other the secrets of their souls,
and run—no questions asked—to help each other, and tell harsh
truths to each other when they must be told.

But we needn't agree about everything (only 12-year-old girl
friends agree about *everything*) to tolerate each other's point of
view. To accept without judgment. To give and to take without ever
keeping score. And to *be* there, as I am for them and as they are
for me, to comfort our sorrows, to celebrate our joys.

25
*type #7
examples*

26

27

28
*levels of
friendship
classified by
intimacy*

29

30

Understanding Meaning

1. What was Viorst's original view of women friends? How did she define them?

2. How do convenience friendships differ from special-interest friendships? Are they both superficial relationships in many ways? Why or why not?

3. Viorst states that she did not want to include men in her article, but her female friends insisted that man–woman friendships should be included. Does this reflect a social change? Do you think women today have more friendships with men, especially in the workplace, than their mothers or grandmothers did?

4. *Critical Thinking*: Viorst writes almost exclusively about female friendship. Do you think that men, too, have the same types of friends—convenience friends, special-interest friends, historical friends, and so on? Are male friendships different?

Evaluating Strategy

1. Viorst divides friends into types rather than classifying them from best friends to acquaintances. Does her approach make more sense? Can friendships change? Can a convenience friend over time become your best friend?

2. Viorst mentions other women in her essay. Does this make her observations more effective? If she limited her commentary to only her friends, would the essay be as influential?

3. *Blending the Modes*: Where does Viorst use *description* and *comparison* to develop her essay?

4. *Critical Thinking*: Viorst wrote this essay in 1977. Since then, has technology created new communities and new friendships? Should online friends be included?

Appreciating Language

1. This essay first appeared in *Redbook*. Is there anything in her word choices or tone that indicates she was writing to a female audience?

2. Consider the words we use to describe people we include in our lives: "friend," "acquaintance," "colleague," "partner," "pal." Do men and women define these words differently?

WRITING SUGGESTIONS

1. Write a short essay about the types of friendships you have developed. Have you maintained many friendships that began in childhood? Why or why not?

2. Write a classification essay categorizing people who only take from friends, those who share with friends, and those who only seem to give in relationships. Provide examples of each type.

3. *Collaborative Writing*: Discuss Viorst's essay with a group of students. Do her comments seem to apply exclusively to women's friendships? Why or why not? Write a brief comparison paper contrasting the different ways men and women develop friendships. Is one gender more competitive? Do men or women seem to have or need more friends?

MARTIN LUTHER KING, JR.

Martin Luther King, Jr. (1929–1968) was a leading figure in the civil rights movement in the 1950s and 1960s. A noted minister, King blended his deeply felt religious values and his sense of political and social justice. He created the Southern Christian Leadership Conference, organized many demonstrations, and lobbied for voting rights. In 1964 he received the Nobel Peace Prize. He was assassinated in 1968.

Three Ways of Meeting Oppression

CONTEXT: *In this section from his 1958 book* Stride Toward Freedom, *King describes three ways oppressed people have responded to oppression.*

WRITER'S NOTE: *King uses division to state an argument, rejecting acquiescence and violence before presenting nonviolent resistance as the best method to counter injustice.*

1   Oppressed people deal with their oppression in three characteristic ways. One way is acquiescence: The oppressed resign themselves to their doom.

2   They tacitly adjust themselves to oppression, and thereby become conditioned to it. In every movement toward freedom some of the oppressed prefer to remain oppressed. Almost 2,800 years ago Moses set out to lead the children of Israel from the slavery of Egypt to the freedom of the promised land. He soon discovered that slaves do not always welcome their deliverers. They become accustomed to being slaves. They would rather bear those ills they have, as Shakespeare pointed out, than flee to others that they know not of. They prefer the "fleshpots of Egypt" to the ordeals of emancipation.

3   There is such a thing as the freedom of exhaustion. Some people are so worn down by the yoke of oppression that they give up. A few years ago in the slum areas of Atlanta, a Negro guitarist used to sing almost daily: "Been down so long that down don't bother me." This is the type of negative freedom and resignation that often engulfs the life of the oppressed.

4   But this is not the way out. To accept passively an unjust system is to cooperate with that system; thereby the oppressed become as evil as the oppressor. Noncooperation with evil is as much a moral obligation as is cooperation with good. The oppressed must never allow the conscience of the oppressor to slumber. Religion reminds every man that he is his brother's keeper. To accept injustice or segregation passively is to say to the oppressor that his actions are morally right. It is a way of allowing his conscience to fall asleep. At this moment the oppressed fails to be his brother's keeper. So acquiescence—while often the easier way—is not the

moral way. It is the way of the coward. The Negro cannot win the respect of his oppressor by acquiescing; he merely increases the oppressor's arrogance and contempt. Acquiescence is interpreted as proof of the Negro's inferiority. The Negro cannot win the respect of the white people of the South or the peoples of the world if he is willing to sell the future of his children for his personal and immediate comfort and safety.

A second way that oppressed people sometimes deal with oppression is to resort to physical violence and corroding hatred. Violence often brings about momentary results. Nations have frequently won their independence in battle. But in spite of temporary victories, violence never brings permanent peace. It solves no social problem; it merely creates new and more complicated ones. 5

Violence as a way of achieving racial injustice is both impractical and immoral. It is impractical because it is a descending spiral ending in destruction for all. The old law of an eye for an eye leaves everybody blind. It is immoral because it seeks to humiliate the opponent rather than win his understanding; it seeks to annihilate rather than to convert. Violence is immoral because it thrives on hatred rather than love. It destroys community and makes brotherhood impossible. It leaves society in monologue rather than dialogue. Violence ends by defeating itself. It creates bitterness in the survivors and brutality in the destroyers. A voice echoes through time saying to every potential Peter, "Put up your sword."[1] History is cluttered with the wreckage of nations that failed to follow this command. 6

If the American Negro and other victims of oppression succumb to the temptation of using violence in the struggle for freedom, future generations will be the recipients of a desolate night of bitterness, and our chief legacy to them will be an endless reign of meaningless chaos. Violence is not the way. 7

The third way open to oppressed people in their quest for freedom is the way of nonviolent resistance. Like the synthesis in Hegelian philosophy, the principle of nonviolent resistance seeks to reconcile the truths of two opposites—acquiescence and violence—while avoiding the extremes and immoralities of both. The nonviolent resister agrees with the person who acquiesces that one should not be physically aggressive toward his opponent; but he balances the equation by agreeing with the person of violence that evil must be resisted. He avoids the nonresistance of the former and the violent resistance of the latter. With nonviolent resistance, no individual or group need submit to any wrong, nor need anyone resort to violence in order to right a wrong. 8

It seems to me that this is the method that must guide the actions of the Negro in the present crisis in race relations. Through 9

[1] The apostle Peter had drawn his sword to defend Christ from arrest. The voice was Christ's, who surrendered himself for trial and crucifixion (John 18:11).

nonviolent resistance the Negro will be able to rise to the noble height of opposing the unjust system while loving the perpetrators of the system. The Negro must work passionately and unrelentingly for full stature as a citizen, but he must not use inferior methods to gain it. He must never come to terms with falsehood, malice, hate, or destruction.

10 Nonviolent resistance makes it possible for the Negro to remain in the South and struggle for his rights. The Negro's problem will not be solved by running away. He cannot listen to the glib suggestion of those who would urge him to migrate en masse to other sections of the country. By grasping his great opportunity in the South he can make a lasting contribution to the moral strength of the nation and set a sublime example of courage for generations yet unborn.

11 By nonviolent resistance, the Negro can also enlist all men of good will in his struggle for equality. The problem is not a purely racial one, with Negroes set against whites. In the end, it is not a struggle between people at all, but a tension between justice and injustice. Nonviolent resistance is not aimed against oppressors but against oppression. Under its banner consciences, not racial groups, are enlisted.

Understanding Meaning

1. Briefly describe the three ways people respond to oppression, according to King. Do you know of a fourth or fifth way? Do people, for instance, respond to oppression by blaming each other?
2. Humility is a Christian value. How does King, a minister, argue that humble acceptance of injustice is immoral?
3. King admits that nations have won freedom through violence, but why does he reject it for African Americans?
4. *Critical Thinking*: King defines the third way as a blend or synthesis of the first two. Why does he argue that this last manner is the most successful? What are its advantages?

Evaluating Strategy

1. Why does King use division to develop a persuasive argument?
2. How does King use his religious values as a way of arguing the desirability of his choice?
3. What transition statements does King use to direct his readers?

Appreciating Language

1. How does King define the difference between "acquiescence" and "nonviolent resistance"?
2. What does King's use of Biblical analogies and reference to Hegelian philosophy reveal about his intended audience?

WRITING SUGGESTIONS

1. Use King's essay as a model to write your own classification paper revealing the way people generally respond to a common issue or problem—the death of a loved one, the loss of a job, the discovery that a partner has been unfaithful, or the experience of being victimized. Rank the responses from the least effective to the most effective.

2. *Collaborative Writing:* Discuss King's classification with a group of students. How many people suffering oppression appear to be following his "third way"? Have a member of the group take notes, then work together to draft a short paper dividing or classifying, if possible, your group's responses.

JAMES AUSTIN

Dr. James Austin (1925–) graduated from Harvard Medical School and is a specialist in neurology. He devoted more than twenty years to research on the brain. While serving as professor and chair of the Department of Neurology at the University of Colorado Medical School, he received the American Association of Neuropathologists Prize. Austin's recent work has focused on the nature of creativity and the impact of meditation. His books include *Chase, Chance, and Creativity* (1978), *Zen and the Brain* (1998), *Zen Brain Reflections* (2010), and *Meditating Selflessly* (2011).

Four Kinds of Chance

CONTEXT: *James Austin has written widely on the role of chance or luck in scientific discovery. In this article, written for the* Saturday Review *(1974), he classifies the four kinds of chance that occur in scientific research. Luck, he explains, is not as simple as drawing a winning hand in poker. As you read the article, consider how many of the varieties of chance you have experienced.*

WRITER'S NOTE: *Austin creates a series of invented definitions, numbering each category and illustrating it with examples.*

What is chance? Dictionaries define it as something fortuitous that happens unpredictably without discernable human intention. Chance is unintentional and capricious, but we needn't conclude that chance is immune from human intervention. Indeed, chance plays several distinct roles when humans react creatively with one another and with their environment. 1

We can readily distinguish four varieties of chance if we consider that they each involve a different kind of motor activity and a special kind of sensory receptivity. The varieties of chance also involve distinctive personality traits and differ in the way one particular individual influences them. 2

Chance I is the pure blind luck that comes with no effort on our part. If, for example, you are sitting at a bridge table of four, it's "in the cards" for you to receive a hand of all 13 spades, but it will come up only once in every 6.3 trillion deals. You will ultimately draw this lucky hand—with no intervention on your part—but it does involve a longer wait than most of us have time for. 3

Chance II evokes the kind of luck Charles Kettering had in mind when he said: "Keep on going and the chances are you will stumble on something, perhaps when you are least expecting it. I have never heard of anyone stumbling on something sitting down." 4

In the sense referred to here, Chance II is not passive, but springs from an energetic, generalized motor activity. A certain basal level of action "stirs up the pot," brings in random ideas that will collide 5 and stick together in fresh combinations, lets chance operate. When someone, anyone, does swing into motion and keeps on going, he will increase the number of collisions between events. When a few events are linked together, they can then be exploited to have a fortuitous outcome, but many others, of course, cannot. Kettering was right. Press on. Something will turn up. We may term this the Kettering Principle.

In the two previous examples, a unique role of the individual   6
person was either lacking or minimal. Accordingly, as we move on to Chance III, we see blind luck, but in camouflage. Chance presents the clue, the opportunity exists, but it would be missed except by that one person uniquely equipped to observe it, visualize it conceptually, and fully grasp its significance. Chance III involves a special receptivity and discernment unique to the recipient. Louis Pasteur characterized it for all time when he said: "Chance favors only the prepared mind."

Pasteur himself had it in full measure. But the classic example   7
of his principle occurred in 1928, when Alexander Fleming's mind instantly fused at least five elements into a conceptually unified nexus. His mental sequences went something like this: (1) I see that a mold has fallen by accident into my culture dish; (2) the staphylococcal colonies residing near it failed to grow; (3) the mold must have secreted something that killed the bacteria; (4) I recall a similar experience once before; (5) if I could separate this new "something" from the mold, it could be used to kill staphylococci that cause human infections.

Actually, Fleming's mind was exceptionally well prepared for the   8
penicillin mold. Six years earlier, while he was suffering from a cold, his own nasal drippings had found their way into a culture dish, for reasons not made entirely clear. He noted that nearby bacteria were killed, and astutely followed up the lead. His observations led him to discover a bactericidal enzyme present in nasal mucus and tears, called lysozyme. Lysozyme proved too weak to be of medical use, but imagine how receptive Fleming's mind was to the penicillin mold when it later happened on the scene!

One word evokes the quality of the operations involved in   9
the first three kinds of chance. It is *serendipity*. The term describes the facility for encountering unexpected good luck, as the result of: accident (Chance I), general exploratory behavior (Chance II), or sagacity (Chance III). The word itself was coined by the Englishman-of-letters Horace Walpole in 1754. He used it with reference to the legendary tales of the Three Princes of Serendip (Ceylon), who quite unexpectedly encountered many instances of good fortune on their travels. In today's parlance, we have usually watered down *serendipity* to mean the good luck that comes solely by accident. We think of it as a result, not an ability. We have tended to lose sight of the element of sagacity, by which term Walpole wished to emphasize that some distinctive personal receptivity is involved.

There remains a fourth element in good luck, an unintentional but subtle personal prompting of it. The English prime minister Benjamin Disraeli summed up the principle underlying Chance IV when he noted that "we make our fortunes and we call them fate." Disraeli, a politician of considerable practical experience, appreciated that we each shape our own destiny, at least to some degree. One might restate the principle as follows: *Chance favors the individualized action.*

10

In Chance IV the kind of luck is peculiar to one person, and like a personal hobby, it takes on a distinctive individual flavor. This form of chance is one-man-made, and it is as personal as a signature...Chance IV has an elusive, almost miragelike, quality. Like a mirage, it is difficult to get a firm grip on, for it tends to recede as we pursue it and advance as we step back. But we still accept a mirage when we see it, because we vaguely understand the basis for the phenomenon. A strongly heated layer of air, less dense than usual, lies next to the earth, and it bends the light rays as they pass through. The resulting image may be magnified as if by a telescopic lens in the atmosphere, and real objects, ordinarily hidden far out of sight over the horizon, are brought forward and revealed to the eye. What happens in a mirage then, and in this form of chance, not only appears farfetched but indeed is farfetched.

11

About a century ago, a striking example of Chance IV took place in the Spanish cave of Altamira.[1] There, one day in 1879, Don Marcelino de Sautuola was engaged in his hobby of archaeology, searching Altamira for bones and stones. With him was his daughter, Maria, who had asked him whether she could come along to the cave that day. The indulgent father had said she could. Naturally enough, he first looked where he had always found heavy objects before, on the *floor* of the cave. But Maria, unhampered by any such preconceptions, looked not only at the floor but also all around the cave with the open-eyed wonder of a child! She looked up, exclaimed, and then he looked up, to see incredible works of art on the cave ceiling! The magnificent colored bison and other animals they saw at Altamira, painted more than 15,000 years ago, might lead one to call it "the Sistine Chapel of Prehistory." Passionately pursuing his interest in archaeology, de Sautuola, to his surprise, discovered man's first paintings. In quest of science, he happened upon Art.

12

Yes, a dog did "discover" the cave, and the initial receptivity was his daughter's, but the pivotal reason for the cave paintings' discovery hinged on a long sequence of prior events originating in de Sautuola himself. For when we dig into the background of this amateur excavator, we find he was an exceptional person. Few Spaniards were out probing into caves 100 years ago. The fact that

13

---

[1]The cave had first been discovered some years before by an enterprising hunting dog in search of game. Curiously, in 1932 the French cave of Lascaux was discovered by still another dog.

he—not someone else—decided to dig that day in the cave of Altamira was the culmination of his passionate interest in his hobby. Here was a rare man whose avocation had been to educate himself from scratch, as it were, in the science of archaeology and cave exploration. This was no simple passive recognizer of blind luck when it came his way, but a man whose unique interests served as an active creative thrust—someone whose own actions and personality would focus the events that led circuitously but inexorably to the discovery of man's first paintings.

Then, too, there is a more subtle manner. How do you give full weight to the personal interests that imbue your child with your own curiosity, that inspire her to ask to join you in your own musty hobby, and that then lead you to agree to her request at the critical moment? For many reasons, at Altamira, more than the special receptivity of Chance III was required—this was a different domain, that of the personality and its actions.   14

A century ago no one had the remotest idea that our caveman ancestors were highly creative artists. Weren't their talents rather minor and limited to crude flint chippings? But the paintings at Altamira, like a mirage, would quickly magnify this diminutive view, bring up into full focus a distant, hidden era of man's prehistory, reveal sentient minds and well-developed aesthetic sensibilities to which men of any age might aspire. And like a mirage, the events at Altamira grew out of de Sautuola's heated personal quest and out of the invisible forces of chance we know exist yet cannot touch. Accordingly, one may introduce the term *altamirage* to identify the quality underlying Chance IV. Let us define it as the facility for encountering unexpected good luck as the result of highly individualized action. Altamirage goes well beyond the boundaries of serendipity in its emphasis on the role of personal action in chance.   15

Chance IV is favored by distinctive, if not eccentric, hobbies, personal life-styles, and modes of behavior peculiar to one individual, usually invested with some passion. The farther apart these personal activities are from the area under investigation, the more novel and unexpected will be the creative product of the encounter.   16

Understanding Meaning

1. What are the four categories of chance?
2. What is meant by "blind" or "dumb" luck? Give some examples from your own life.
3. What is the Kettering Principle? Would Edison's famous trial-and-error experiments to discover a filament for the incandescent light bulb fit this kind of chance?
4. How does the Pasteur principle differ from the Kettering Principle?
5. How did the dog's discovery of a cave differ from "blind luck" or Chance I?
6. *Critical Thinking*: How often have you discovered things by chance? What role has chance played in your career and education? Does understanding Austin's

four kinds of chance enhance your ability to be "lucky" in the future? Can you "make your own kind of luck"?

Evaluating Strategy

1. What principle does Austin use to divide chance into four categories?
2. What examples does Austin use to illustrate each type? Are they accessible by a general audience?
3. Would a chart aid in explaining the four types of chance?
4. *Blending the Modes*: How does Austin make use of *definition* and *narration* in developing his classification essay?

Appreciating Language

1. How much technical language does Austin include?
2. *Critical Thinking*: Is part of Austin's task in this article to invent new terms to create categories of chance? Do most of our words for chance—"luck," "fortune," "lot"—all suggest the same meaning?

WRITING SUGGESTIONS

1. List a number of instances in your life you considered lucky. Using Austin's four categories, write a paper categorizing your experiences. Have you ever gotten past Chance I?

2. *Collaborative Writing:* Discuss the role of chance with a group of students. Do many people use the idea of chance to dismiss the accomplishments of others? Do people use luck as an excuse for not trying? Talk about these issues, and then collaborate on a short paper suggesting how Austin's concept of chance should be taught to children.

STEWART BRAND

Stewart Brand (1938–) was born in Rockford, Illinois, and studied biology at Stanford University. After service in the U.S. Army, Brand studied design and photography in San Francisco. In 1968 Brand helped Douglas Engelbart present emerging computer technologies, including email and the mouse. In the late 1960s Brand edited *The Whole Earth Catalog*, which became a best seller in the 1970s. In 1974 he founded the *CoEvolution Quarterly*, which published articles on natural science, technology, and the arts. Brand's other books include *How Buildings Learn: What Happens After They're Built* (1994), *The Clock of the Long Now: Time and Responsibility* (1999), and *Whole Earth Discipline: An Ecopragmatist Manifesto* (2009).

Four Sides to Every Story

CONTEXT: *Brand published this essay in 2009 following climate talks, which, in his view, revealed a variety of positions.*

WRITER'S NOTE: *Brand invents names for the points of view and classifies them from one extreme to another then divides them into two groups: those driven by politics and those driven by science.*

Climate talks have been going on in Copenhagen for a week now, 1 and it appears to be a two-sided debate between alarmists and skeptics. But there are actually four different views of global warming. A taxonomy of the four:

DENIALISTS They are loud, sure, and political. Their view is 2 that climatologists and their fellow travelers are engaged in a vast conspiracy to panic the public into following an agenda that is political and pernicious. Senator James Inhofe of Oklahoma and the columnist George Will wave the banner for the hoax-callers.

"The claim that global warming is caused by manmade 3 emissions is simply untrue and not based on sound science," Mr. Inhofe declared in a 2003 speech to the Senate about the Kyoto accord that remains emblematic of his position. "CO_2 does not cause catastrophic disasters—actually it would be beneficial to our environment and our economy. . . . The motives for Kyoto are economic, not environmental—that is, proponents favor handicapping the American economy through carbon taxes and more regulations."

SKEPTICS This group is most interested in the limitations of 4 climate science so far: they like to examine in detail the contradictions and shortcomings in climate data and models, and they are wary about any "consensus" in science. To the skeptics' discomfort, their arguments are frequently quoted by the denialists.

In this mode, Roger Pielke, a climate scientist at the University of 5
Colorado, argues that the scenarios presented by the United Nations Intergovernmental Panel on Climate Change are overstated
and underpredictive. Another prominent skeptic is the physicist
Freeman Dyson, who wrote in 2007: "I am opposing the holy
brotherhood of climate model experts and the crowd of deluded
citizens who believe the numbers predicted by the computer
models. . . . I have studied the climate models and I know what
they can do. The models solve the equations of fluid dynamics,
and they do a very good job of describing the fluid motions of the
atmosphere and the oceans. They do a very poor job of describing the clouds, the dust, the chemistry and the biology of fields
and farms and forests."

WARNERS   These are the climatologists who see the trends in 6
climate headed toward planetary disaster, and they blame human
production of greenhouse gases as the primary culprit. Leaders in
this category are the scientists James Hansen, Stephen Schneider
and James Lovelock. (This is the group that most persuades me
and whose views I promote.)

"If humanity wishes to preserve a planet similar to that on which 7
civilization developed and to which life on earth is adapted,"
Mr. Hansen wrote as the lead author of an influential 2008 paper,
then the concentration of carbon dioxide in the atmosphere
would have to be reduced from 395 parts per million to "at most
350 p.p.m."

CALAMATISTS   There are many environmentalists who believe 8
that industrial civilization has committed crimes against nature,
and retribution is coming. They quote the warners in apocalyptic
terms, and they view denialists as deeply evil. The technology critic
Jeremy Rifkin speaks in this manner, and the writer-turned-activist
Bill McKibben is a (fairly gentle) leader in this category.

In his 2006 introduction for *The End of Nature*, his famed 9
1989 book, Mr. McKibben wrote of climate change in religious
terms: "We are no longer able to think of ourselves as a species
tossed about by larger forces—now we are those larger forces.
Hurricanes and thunderstorms and tornadoes become not acts
of God but acts of man. That was what I meant by the 'end of
nature.'"

The calamatists and denialists are primarily political figures, 10
with firm ideological loyalties, whereas the warners and skeptics are primarily scientists, guided by ever-changing evidence.
That distinction between ideology and science not only helps
clarify the strengths and weaknesses of the four stances, it can
also be used to predict how they might respond to future climate
developments.

If climate change were to suddenly reverse itself (because of 11
some yet undiscovered mechanism of balance in our climate system), my guess is that the denialists would be triumphant, the
skeptics would be skeptical this time of the apparent good news,

the warners would be relieved, and the calamatists would seek out some other doom to proclaim.

If climate change keeps getting worse then I would expect de-   12
nialists to grasp at stranger straws, many skeptics to become warners, the warners to start pushing geoengineering schemes like sulfur dust in the stratosphere, and the calamatists to push liberal political agendas—just as the denialists said they would.

Understanding Meaning

1. What are the four views of global warming Brand identifies? Can you describe them in your own words?
2. Do you detect any bias in his essay? How does he characterize the members of each category?
3. Why does Brand view calamatists and denialists as being more political than scientific?
4. If science revealed a cooling trend in climate, how does Brand predict the four groups would respond?
5. *Critical Thinking*: Brand states the two extremes are driven more by politics than science. Does this phenomenon also exist in other debates? Do people argue over charter or bilingual schools based on education or on politics? Are discussions about the deficit more about accounting and economics or political ideology? Can you think of any issue that is free of politics?

Evaluating Strategy

1. Brand uses capital letters and bold fonts to label each category. What impact does this have on an essay? Does it make a classification easier to read and remember? Can too many labels or numbers make an essay appear choppy?
2. Brand finds the "warners" the most convincing but states his personal endorsement in parentheses. What impact does this have?
3. How does Brand use the conclusion to qualify his classification? Why is it important for writers to comment on possible changes to any categories they identify?

Appreciating Language

1. How much scientific or technical language does Brand include in defining his categories? What does this reveal about his intended audience?
2. Look up the word "taxonomy" in a dictionary. Should Brand have included a definition in his essay? Why or why not?
3. Are the names he invents for each category neutral? Do you detect any positive or negative connotations that would express a point of view?
4. Does the term "skeptic" imply critical thinking and judgment and "denialist" suggest a blind rejection of ideas?
5. *Critical Thinking*: How can a writer use connotations in naming categories to influence his or her readers? Would numbering categories be more objective?

WRITING SUGGESTIONS

1. Using Brand's essay as a model, classify views of another topic, such as capital punishment, drug legalization, immigration reform, gun control, Medicare, or abortion.

2. *Collaborative Writing*: Discuss Brand's article with a group of students and develop a similar taxonomy to classify views of the role of government from the most progressive to the most conservative.

FLORENCE KING

Florence King (1936–) was born in Washington, DC, and graduated from American University in 1957 with a degree in history. After teaching history in Maryland and working for the National Association of Realtors, she began writing articles for the *Raleigh News and Observer*. Her column "The Misanthrope's Corner" in *The National Review* gave King a national audience. In addition to writing nonfiction articles, King has published several books, including *Southern Ladies and Gentlemen* (1975) and *Confessions of a Failed Southern Lady* (1985). After retiring in 2002, King returned to writing columns for *The National Review* in 2006.

Stuck in the Middle: How to Understand America's Class System

CONTEXT: *King ranks Americans as being Somebodies, Everybodies, or Nobodies.*

WRITER'S NOTE: *King indicates that Americans, no matter their income, insist they belong in the middle category.*

1 Understanding the American class system is elementary. In *Ruggles of Red Gap*, the striving American wife instructs her new English butler on the duties she expects him to perform for her husband. "I want him to look like somebody," she explains. "Like who, madam?" asks the perplexed servant. "Like somebody," she repeats firmly.

2 There you have it. Our upper class are Somebody, our lower class are Nobody, and our middle class are Everybody. Not for us the traditional middle-class composition of doctors, lawyers, judges, business owners and academics. All of these are Somebody to our rank-and-file middle class, who make the cut simply by self-identification. They might be department heads, office managers, supervisors, policemen, firemen, or highly paid skilled laborers like plumbers and electricians, but ask them where they stand on the social ladder and they will unhesitatingly say, "Oh, sorta middle class, I guess." In the last few years the rank-and-file middle class has expanded to include the first person in one's family to go to college and the first person from a blue-collar family to hold a white-collar job. Even now, in the midst of a dying economy, you are what you call yourself: the American who still has a full-time job of any kind, or three part-time ones, is said to be "clinging to middle-class status."

3 What happened, you ask, to the lower middle class? We don't have one for the simple reason that Americans never call themselves that. The sole partial exception is the South, apart and eccentric as always, where lower-middle-class goes by the euphemisms "shabby genteel" and "too poor to paint but too proud to

whitewash." This is the state of mind that allows Southerners to punch two holes in a can of Carnation evaporated milk and call it coffee cream.

Our undefined middle class is the key to what has happened to our economy. It is by definition the striving class, and when just about everyone insists on placing himself in it, you end up with a nation of unrealistic strivers bent on what C. Wright Mills called "affluence without purpose." 4

The omnipresent American Dream is always put forth as the justification for any and all striving, as is the American Standard of Living (H.L. Mencken: "I'd trade the whole Acropolis for one American bathroom"). The two worked in tandem after the second world war when General Motors became the first giant industry to agree to union demands for cost-of-living raises. This seemed only fair—after all, unionized car workers are middle class too—but unintended (or intended) consequences soon took over. The enormous cost of the new union wages was passed along to consumers via "planned obsolescence" as manufacturers used annual redesigning to make people ashamed of old-looking cars and push them into buying a new car every year to prove their middle-class status. 5

Proving one's middle-class status also required credit cards, so these became easily available, but the real middle-class nirvana was the 30-year mortgage with payments fully deductible on the mortgage holder's federal income tax. These deductions came to billions of dollars every year, so knowing the government as we do, we have to wonder why it would be so eager to divest itself of so much moolah. 6

We don't have to wonder long. Try the protagonist of Sinclair Lewis's 1921 novel *Babbitt:* "When folks own their homes, they ain't starting labor troubles, and they're raising kids instead of raising hell." 7

Or the builder of America's first post-second world war suburb, William J. Levitt: "No man who owns his own house and lot can be a Communist. He has too much to do." 8

He won't give the government any kind of trouble, communist or otherwise, because he has lobotomized himself with his own hoe. Being a "homeowner" transforms him from a thinking reed into a tinkering, puttering, dull, small-minded bore, and that's just the kind of citizen a desperate government wants. Someone so busy-busy that he couldn't possibly start a revolution even if he wanted to. The sacred American homeowner will never take to the streets and mount the barricades because he has to stay home all day waiting for the Johnny-Be-Quick men to come and unclog the toilet. 9

We have used 30-year mortgages as a safety valve against civil insurrection to create a bogus squirearchy with "something to lose" so they will live in dread of losing it. This is peace through distraction and debt and it mounted to a fever pitch in the decade or so 10 before the economic collapse of 2009. Americans' definition of middle class made us sitting ducks for the own-your-own-home push. People completely unqualified to take on a mortgage got them anyway, bolstered by hostile attitudes directed against people who live in flats. There were a lot of sneering references to "a drawerful of rent receipts" as if it were a drawerful of snakes. Every application, no matter how unrelated to one's living arrangements, contained blocks marked "Rent" or "Own" that had to be checked. Some TV shrink even came up with a new disorder called "rental addiction."

I'm happy to report that I have it. And Carnation evaporated   11 milk makes delicious coffee cream.

Understanding Meaning

1. How does King classify Americans economically? Why are the categories difficult to define?
2. Why, in King's view, are so many Americans "stuck in the middle"? Why do people insist on claiming to be "sorta middle class"?
3. Why are Southerners the only ones who admit to having a lower middle class?
4. In King's view, how does homeownership benefit government?
5. How did the American Dream and the American Standard of Living fuel the growth of the middle class?
6. *Critical Thinking:* How difficult is it to define upper, middle, and lower classes? Should wealth or debt be considered along with income? Would an income of $200,000 a year make someone wealthy in a small Midwestern town but middle class in Manhattan or San Francisco?

Evaluating Strategy

1. How effective is King's introduction? Does the reference to a comedy set the tone for her essay?
2. How does King demonstrate the expansion of the middle class?
3. By classifying Americans as Somebodies, Everybodies, and Nobodies, does King suggest that their self-respect or social significance is linked to income?
4. What impact does her final comment have?

Appreciating Language

1. What does King mean by the "striving class"? Is this necessarily negative? Who are "unrealistic strivers"?
2. Consider King's comments about rent (paragraph 10). Does the word "renter" have a negative connotation? What does the word imply to many Americans?
3. King places several terms in quotation marks, such as "planned obsolescence" and "something to lose." How does highlighting phrases affect the way readers respond to them?
4. *Critical Thinking*: What does it mean to "own" a house? Should the term "homeowner" apply only to those who own a house outright? Does anyone with a mortgage really "own" a home?

WRITING SUGGESTIONS

1. Using King's essay as a model, write a classification of another group of people such as sports fans, homeowners, parents, or drivers. What role does self-identification play? Would anyone admit to being a bad or neglectful parent?

2. *Collaborative Writing:* Working with a group of students, write an essay explaining why so many Americans define themselves as "sorta middle class." Does the stigma of poverty lead people to claim they are richer than they are? Do the rich insist on calling themselves middle class to avoid higher taxes or being seen as elitist? Do democratic societies that stress equality and fairness find class differences difficult to explain or accept?

Blending the Modes
EDWARD IRVING KOCH

Edward Irving Koch (1924–2013) was born in the Bronx, New York. After attending City College of New York from 1941 to 1943, he was drafted into the army and subsequently received two battle stars. In 1948 he received his LL.B. degree from the New York University School of Law. After serving for two years on the New York City Council and nine years in Congress, he was elected mayor of New York City in 1977 and served three terms. He wrote twelve books, including four novels. In addition to commenting on politics, Koch was also known for reviewing films.

Death and Justice: How Capital Punishment Affirms Life

CONTEXT: *In this article Edward Koch uses division and persuasion to organize an argument supporting the death penalty.*

WRITER'S NOTE: *Koch reverses the usual process of writing an argument by first stating his opponents' views, then rejecting them.*

Last December a man named Robert Lee Willie, who had been convicted of raping and murdering an 18-year-old woman, was executed in the Louisiana state prison. In a statement issued several minutes before his death, Mr. Willie said: "Killing people is wrong.... It makes no difference whether it's citizens, countries, or governments. Killing is wrong." Two weeks later in South Carolina, an admitted killer named Joseph Carl Shaw was put to death for murdering two teenagers. In an appeal to the governor for clemency, Mr. Shaw wrote: "Killing is wrong when I did it. Killing is wrong when you do it. I hope you have the courage and moral strength to stop the killing." 1

It is a curiosity of modern life that we find ourselves being lectured on morality by cold-blooded killers. Mr. Willie previously had been convicted of aggravated rape, aggravated kidnapping, and the murders of a Louisiana deputy and a man from Missouri. Mr. Shaw committed another murder a week before the two for which he was executed, and admitted mutilating the body of the 14-year-old girl he killed. I can't help wondering what prompted these murderers to speak out against killing as they entered the death-house door. Did their newfound reverence for life stem from the realization that they were about to lose their own? 2

Life is indeed precious, and I believe the death penalty helps to affirm this fact. Had the death penalty been a real possibility in the minds of these murderers, they might well have stayed their hand. They might have shown moral awareness before their victims died, and not after. Consider the tragic death of Rosa Velez, 3 who happened to be home when a man named Luis Vera burglar-ized her apartment in Brooklyn. "Yeah, I shot her," Vera admitted. "She knew me, and I knew I wouldn't go to the chair."

During my 22 years in public service, I have heard the pros and   4
cons of capital punishment expressed with special intensity. As a district leader, councilman, congressman, and mayor, I have rep-resented constituencies generally thought of as liberal. Because I support the death penalty for heinous crimes of murder, I have sometimes been the subject of emotional and outraged attacks by voters who find my position reprehensible or worse. I have lis-tened to their ideas. I have weighed their objections carefully. I still support the death penalty. The reasons I maintain my position can be best understood by examining the arguments most frequently heard in opposition.

1. The death penalty is "barbaric." Sometimes opponents of   5
capital punishment horrify with tales of lingering death on the gallows, of faulty electric chairs, or of agony in the gas chamber. Partly in response to such protests, several states such as North Carolina and Texas switched to execution by lethal injection. The condemned person is put to death painlessly, without ropes, volt-age, bullets, or gas. Did this answer the objections of death penalty opponents? Of course not. On June 22, 1984, the New York Times published an editorial that sarcastically attacked the new "hygienic" method of death by injection, and stated that "execution can never be made humane through science." So it's not the method that re-ally troubles opponents. It's the death itself they consider barbaric.

Admittedly, capital punishment is not a pleasant topic. However,   6
one does not have to like the death penalty in order to support it any more than one must like radical surgery, radiation, or chemo-therapy in order to find necessary these attempts at curing cancer. Ultimately we may learn how to cure cancer with a simple pill. Unfortunately, that day has not yet arrived. Today we are faced with the choice of letting the cancer spread or trying to cure it with the methods available, methods that one day will almost certainly be considered barbaric. But to give up and do nothing would be far more barbaric and would certainly delay the discovery of an eventual cure. The analogy between cancer and murder is imper-fect, because murder is not the "disease" we are trying to cure. The disease is injustice. We may not like the death penalty, but it must be available to punish crimes of cold-blooded murder, cases in which any other form of punishment would be inadequate and, therefore, unjust. If we create a society in which injustice is not tolerated, incidents of murder—the most flagrant form of in-justice—will diminish.

2. No other major democracy uses the death penalty. No other   7
major democracy—in fact, few other countries of any descrip-tion—are plagued by a murder rate such as that in the United States. Fewer and fewer Americans can remember the days when unlocked doors were the norm and murder was a rare and

terrible offense. In America the murder rate climbed 122 percent between 1963 and 1980. During that same period, the murder rate in New York City increased by almost 400 percent, and the statistics are even worse in many other cities. A study at M.I.T. showed that based on 1970 homicide rates a person who lived in a large American city ran a greater risk of being murdered than an American soldier in World War II ran of being killed in combat. It is not surprising that the laws of each country differ according to differing conditions and traditions. If other countries had our murder problem, the cry for capital punishment would be just as loud as it is here. And I daresay that any other major democracy where 75 percent of the people supported the death penalty would soon enact it into law.

3. An innocent person might be executed by mistake. Consider the work of Adam Bedau, one of the most implacable foes of capital punishment in this country. According to Mr. Bedau, it is "false sentimentality to argue that the death penalty should be abolished because of the abstract possibility that an innocent person might be executed." He cites a study of the 7,000 executions in this country from 1893 to 1971, and concludes that the record fails to show that such cases occur. The main point, however, is this. If government functioned only when the possibility of error didn't exist, government wouldn't function at all. Human life deserves special protection, and one of the best ways to guarantee that protection is to assure that convicted murderers do not kill again. Only the death penalty can accomplish this end. In a recent case in New Jersey, a man named Richard Biegenwald was freed from prison after serving 18 years for murder; since his release he has been convicted of committing four murders. A prisoner named Lemuel Smith, who, while serving four life sentences for murder (plus two life sentences for kidnapping and robbery) in New York's Green Haven Prison, lured a woman corrections officer into the chaplain's office and strangled her. He then mutilated and dismembered her body. An additional life sentence for Smith is meaningless. Because New York has no death penalty statute, Smith has effectively been given a license to kill.

But the problem of multiple murder is not confined to the nation's penitentiaries. In 1981, 91 police officers were killed in the line of duty in this country. Seven percent of those arrested in the cases that have been solved had a previous arrest for murder. In New York City in 1976 and 1977, 85 persons arrested for homicide had a previous arrest for murder. Six of these individuals had two previous arrests for murder, and one had four previous murder arrests. During those two years the New York police were arresting for murder persons with a previous arrest for murder on the average of one every 8.5 days. This is not surprising when we learn that in 1975, for example, the median time served in Massachusetts for homicide was less than two-and-a-half years. In 1976 a study sponsored by the Twentieth Century Fund found that the average time served in the United States for first-degree murder is ten years. The median time served may be considerably lower.

4. Capital punishment cheapens the value of human life. On 10 the contrary, it can be easily demonstrated that the death penalty strengthens the value of human life. If the penalty for rape were lowered, clearly it would signal a lessened regard for the victims' suffering, humiliation, and personal integrity. It would cheapen their horrible experience, and expose them to an increased danger of recurrence. When we lower the penalty for murder, it signals a lessened regard for the value of the victim's life. Some critics of capital punishment, such as columnist Jimmy Breslin, have suggested that a life sentence is actually a harsher penalty for murder than death. This is sophistic nonsense. A few killers may decide not to appeal a death sentence, but the overwhelming majority make every effort to stay alive. It is by exacting the highest penalty for the taking of human life that we affirm the highest value of human life.

5. The death penalty is applied in a discriminatory manner. This 11 factor no longer seems to be the problem it once was. The appeals process for a condemned prisoner is lengthy and painstaking. Every effort is made to see that the verdict and sentence were fairly arrived at. However, assertions of discrimination are not an argument for ending the death penalty but for extending it. It is not justice to exclude everyone from the penalty of the law if a few are found to be so favored. Justice requires that the law be applied equally to all.

6. Thou Shalt Not Kill. The Bible is our greatest source of moral 12 inspiration. Opponents of the death penalty frequently cite the sixth of the Ten Commandments in an attempt to prove that capital punishment is divinely proscribed. In the original Hebrew, however, the Sixth Commandment reads, "Thou Shalt Not Commit Murder," and the Torah specifies capital punishment for a variety of offenses. The biblical viewpoint has been upheld by philosophers throughout history. The greatest thinkers of the 19th century—Kant, Locke, Hobbes, Rousseau, Montesquieu, and Mill—agreed that natural law properly authorizes the sovereign to take life in order to vindicate justice. Only Jeremy Bentham was ambivalent. Washington, Jefferson, and Franklin endorsed it. Abraham Lincoln authorized executions for deserters in wartime. Alexis de Tocqueville, who expressed profound respect for American institutions, believed that the death penalty was indispensable to the support of social order. The United States Constitution, widely admired as one of the seminal achievements in the history of humanity, condemns cruel and inhuman punishment, but does not condemn capital punishment.

7. The death penalty is state-sanctioned murder. This is the 13 defense with which Messrs. Willie and Shaw hoped to soften the resolve of those who sentenced them to death. By saying in effect, "You're no better than I am," the murderer seeks to bring his accusers down to his own level. It is also a popular argument among opponents of capital punishment, but a transparently false one. Simply put, the state has rights that the private individual does

not. In a democracy, those rights are given to the state by the electorate. The execution of a lawfully condemned killer is no more an act of murder than is legal imprisonment an act of kidnaping. If an individual forces a neighbor to pay him money under threat of punishment, it's called extortion. If the state does it, it's called taxation. Rights and responsibilities surrendered by the individual are what give the state its power to govern. This contract is the foundation of civilization itself.

Everyone wants his or her rights, and will defend them jealously. 14 Not everyone, however, wants responsibilities, especially the painful responsibilities that come with law enforcement. Twenty-one years ago a woman named Kitty Genovese was assaulted and murdered on a street in New York. Dozens of neighbors heard her cries for help but did nothing to assist her. They didn't even call the police. In such a climate the criminal understandably grows bolder. In the presence of moral cowardice, he lectures us on our supposed failings and tries to equate his crimes with our quest for justice.

The death of anyone—even a convicted killer—diminishes 15 us all. But we are diminished even more by a justice system that fails to function. It is an illusion to let ourselves believe that doing away with capital punishment removes the murderer's deed from our conscience. The rights of society are paramount. When we protect guilty lives, we give up innocent lives in exchange. When opponents of capital punishment say to the state: "I will not let you kill in my name," they are also saying to murderers: "You can kill in your own name as long as I have an excuse for not getting involved."

It is hard to imagine anything worse than being murdered while 16 neighbors do nothing. But something worse exists. When those same neighbors shrink back from justly punishing the murderer, the victim dies twice.

Understanding Meaning

1. Many people oppose the death penalty because of the value they place on human life. How does Koch argue that he favors capital punishment for the same reason?

2. Explain how Koch can dislike the death penalty but insist that it is necessary.

3. Why is the death penalty, in Koch's view, perhaps more necessary in this country than elsewhere?

4. How does Koch respond to the common argument that the death penalty violates the Ten Commandments?

5. Why does Koch believe that an execution committed by the state is different from a murder committed by an individual?

6. *Critical Thinking:* You have probably heard various arguments both for and against capital punishment. Did Koch present any new points or make a more compelling case than others? Did his essay influence your views on the death penalty? Why or why not?

Evaluating Strategy

1. Koch announces his plan for organizing his essay in paragraph 4. Is this an effective strategy? Why or why not?

2. *Blending the Modes*: What *comparison* does Koch use to explain the need for executing those who commit heinous crimes? Why does he say this analogy is not perfect?

3. What support does Koch use? What types of evidence are most effective and least effective in your view?

Appreciating Language

1. How would you describe Koch's tone and style? Is it suited to his topic? Why or why not?

2. Do you detect any emotional language in this essay? When writing about an issue like capital punishment, should writers use emotionally charged words? Why or why not?

WRITING SUGGESTIONS

1. Koch addresses seven arguments against capital punishment. Select one reason and write a persuasive essay supporting or rejecting this argument.

2. *Collaborative Writing:* Discuss the issue of capital punishment with a group of students and have each one write a statement explaining when, if ever, they believe a convicted criminal should receive the death penalty. Write an essay using classification to organize the responses from the strongest advocate to the strongest opponent of the death penalty.

Writing Beyond the Classroom

MOTION PICTURE ASSOCIATION OF AMERICA

The Motion Picture Association of America was founded in 1922 as the trade association of the American film industry. The organization's initial goal was to curb widespread criticism of motion pictures by improving the public image of the movie industry. It established production codes to counter state and local censorship boards that threatened to disrupt film distribution. In 1968 the MPAA, in partnership with theater owners, developed a rating system for motion pictures to alert the public, especially parents, of objectionable content.

CONTEXT: *The Red Carpet Ratings Service emails parents the ratings of newly released films. The announcement on page 323, designed to resemble a movie poster, appeared on the MPAA website.*

WRITER'S NOTE: *Addressed to parents, the ad includes a picture of three families with young children.*

Understanding Meaning

1. Who is the target audience for this announcement?
2. What method of classification does the MPAA use to rate films?
3. *Critical Thinking*: Why does a trade organization representing motion pictures feel the need to rate its own products? Does this strike you as being self-defensive or, instead, socially responsible? Do you think many parents would like to see a rating system for music? Why or why not?

Evaluating Strategy

1. How effective is the design of this announcement? What does the title "Parents: Stay Ahead of the Curve!" suggest to you? What parental concerns does it address?
2. *Critical Thinking:* How might a movie studio executive use this announcement to answer critics of the film industry?

Appreciating Language

1. What does the phrase "Red Carpet" suggest? Do you think it makes an effective name for this service? Why or why not?
2. Do you think the wording of the classifications is clear? What is the difference between "not suitable" and "inappropriate," or between "suggesting guidance" and "strongly cautioning"? Do you think these labels provide accurate information for parents making decisions about what movies their children should and should not see?
3. The MPAA originally used X as its most restrictive designation. It changed the listing to NC-17 in the 1980s. What connotation does *X rated* have? Why would the MPAA want to eliminate this term?

PARENTS : STAY AHEAD OF THE CURVE!

PREMIERING

RED CARPET RATINGS

S E R V I C E

G | GENERAL AUDIENCES
ALL AGES ADMITTED

PG | PARENTAL GUIDANCE SUGGESTED
SOME MATERIAL MAY NOT BE SUITABLE FOR CHILDREN

PG-13 | PARENTS STRONGLY CAUTIONED
SOME MATERIAL MAY BE INAPPROPRIATE FOR CHILDREN UNDER 13

R | RESTRICTED
UNDER 17 REQUIRES ACCOMPANYING PARENT OR ADULT GUARDIAN

NC-17 | NO ONE 17 AND UNDER ADMITTED

Sign up for
RED CARPET RATINGS
a free weekly email service that
will keep you up to date on ratings
for films most currently in release.

RATINGS SENT STRAIGHT TO PARENTS.
IT'S JUST THAT SIMPLE.
Sign up at www.filmratings.com

www.filmratings.com

WRITING SUGGESTIONS

1. Write an essay about your experiences with movie ratings. Did your parents restrict the movies you were allowed to see as a child based on the ratings? If you have children, do you use ratings to select movies? Why or why not?

2. *Collaborative Writing*: Work with a group of students to establish a similar rating system for music. Which artists and groups would your group rate PG or R? If members disagree, develop opposing statements.

Responding to Images

Symbols of three faiths.

1. What is your first impression of this photograph? Could you use this image as a book cover, billboard, or poster? Would it grab attention? What message would it communicate in your eyes?

2. Are there places in the world where a poster like this would be largely accepted and others where it might provoke protest?

3. What does this photograph reveal about the power of symbols? What connotations do these images have?

4. *Visual Analysis:* Does presenting symbols of three religions in a similar fashion suggest equality? Might some people be offended, believing that their faith is superior or correct? Why or why not?

5. Write an essay classifying the ways people might respond to this image.

6. *Collaborative Writing:* Share this image with a group of students and ask each to write a caption before you discuss the photograph. What do the captions suggest? Can reactions to this image reveal people's perceptual worlds? Can a photograph like this serve as a Rorschach test measuring an individual's values? Why or why not?

Strategies FOR DIVISION AND CLASSIFICATION WRITING

1. **Determine which mode you will use.** Which method will best suit your purpose: dividing your subject into subtopics or measuring subtopics against a common standard? Do you need to use both methods to explain your subject?

2. **Select an effective method of division.** If you were writing about improving public schools, for example, it might be more effective to divide the paper by discipline, discussing how to improve math skills, writing ability, and knowledge of geography rather than improving elementary schools, junior high schools, and high schools.

3. **Avoid divisions that oversimplify or distort meaning.** Your paper should aid in helping readers grasp a complex subject without trivializing or misstating the issues. You may wish to qualify your division and explain to readers that exceptions and situations may exist where the division may not apply. Indicate the size or significance of each category and explain if it is possible for a specific item to fit more than one category or change categories over time.

4. **Avoid overlapping categories.** When writing both division and classification, make sure the categories are distinct. Do not separate cars into "domestic, foreign, and antique models," because antique cars would clearly have to belong to the first two groups.

5. **Use a single, clearly defined standard to classify subjects.** Classification relies on a clearly stated standard that is used to measure all the items you discuss. Avoid mixing standards. In some instances you may have to explain or justify why you are using a particular standard.

6. **In classification writing, make sure all topics fit into one category.** In a properly written classification paper, every unit should fit only one category. For example, a term paper is either an A– or a B+. In addition, make sure no items are left over that cannot be logically placed.

7. **Explain whether your division or classification is objective or subjective.** Tell readers who established or uses the division or classification method you are using, or explain the division or classification method you created to express your personal views.

Revising and Editing

1. **Make sure the introduction clearly announces your topic and explains your method of division or classification.** Does the opening paragraph provide needed background information and address possible misconceptions?

2. **Is your essay clearly organized and easy to follow?** Have you used numbers, names, capital letters, bold font, and paragraph breaks to identify and separate categories?

3. **Do you qualify your essay, indicating possible changes and exceptions?**

Suggested Topics for Division and Classification Writing

General Assignments

Division

Write a *division* essay on any of the following topics. Your division may use standard categories or ones you invent. Remember to clearly state the way you are dividing your subject. Each subject or example should be supported with definitions, brief narratives, or descriptions.

1. Methods of looking for a job, finding day care, or obtaining loans
2. Student housing on and off campus
3. Baseball, basketball, or football teams
4. Popular music
5. The ways people cope with a problem, such as a divorce, a job loss, or the death of a family member

Classification

Write a *classification* essay on any of the following topics. Make sure to use a single method of rating the subtopics, from best to worst, easiest to hardest, or least desirable to most desirable, for example:

1. Attitudes about a social issue, recent event, or public personality
2. Student services, including health, police, food, etc.
3. Vacation destinations
4. Bosses or professors you have known
5. Talk radio shows, social media sites, or YouTube videos

Division and Classification

Write an essay that uses both *division* and *classification* on any of the following topics. Make sure you clearly separate your topic into parts and use a clear method of classification.

1. *Divide* SUVs, hybrid cars, or any other product into popular brands, then *classify* price ranges for each.
2. *Classify* students from A to F, and then *divide* each level into types. A students, for instance, could include those who study hard, those who had taken related courses, and those who benefited from parents active in that discipline. F students could include those who never attend class and those who study as hard as they can but fail every test.
3. *Divide* a subject like terrorism or pollution into different types, and then classify the threats of each type from most to least serious.
4. *Divide* television shows into different types, and then *classify* specific shows in each group from your most to least favorite.
5. *Classify* football, baseball, or basketball teams into best, average, and worst by their wins and losses, then use *division* to draw distinctions between teams in each level. Do some winning teams owe their success to one or more star players, skilled coaching, or weak opponents?

Writing in Context

1. Assume you have been asked by a national magazine to write about students' political attitudes. You may develop your essay by division or classification. You can discuss politics in general terms of liberalism and conservatism or restrict your comments on students' attitudes toward a particular issue, such as abortion, capital punishment, or health care.

2. Write a humorous paper about campus fashion by dividing students into types. Invent titles or labels for each group, and supply enough details so that readers can readily fit the people they meet into one of your categories.

Student Paper: Division and Classification

This paper was written in response to the following assignment:

> Write a 500-word paper using division or classification to discuss a current social or political issue. Remember to create clearly defined categories and explain possible exceptions.

First Draft with Instructor's Comments

Entitlements

Entitlements are going to be a major issue for years. They are going to dominate politics for years. How we deal with them is going to <u>effect</u> the economy, taxes, and jobs for years to come. We are going hear about them for a long time, but how many Americans even know what an "entitlement" is and why <u>they</u> are important?   *weak intro*   *affect*   *pronoun?*

The oldest entitlement we have is Social Security. It got started in the Depression of the 1930s. Everyone knows this program because we all have a Social Security number. It is a <u>program</u> <u>not in that much bad shape like the others.</u> People pay a lot into the program, but it is paying out more than it collects. By 2037 it is expected to run out. Next, is Medicare that provides medical care for the old. This program is rapidly expanding for two major reasons. More people are getting old and they are living longer. Also, all the innovations in drugs and surgery that <u>keep old people going</u> are costing more and more each year.   *wordy*   *wordy*   *run-on*   *informal*

Medicaid is another entitlement that is costing more and more <u>for a whole number of reasons</u>. It provides health care for low-income people. Health care is getting more expensive. Plus, in the recent deep recession, more people were eligible because they lost their jobs.   *wordy*

Put together these three programs consume a large part of the federal budget. As the population of old people grows, these programs take on a life of their own, getting bigger and bigger. As a result the government has to tax more, borrow more, or spend less on everything else.

The government made promises with these entitlements and they seem sacred. But they are getting so expensive a lot of people, even liberals who fought hard to create these programs, are wondering how to pay for them.   *run-on*

Entitlements are hard for politicians to debate without controversy. The moment anyone talks about changes, it sounds like <u>they</u> want to punish the poor and the old, the most vulnerable people in our country, people who really need help. People expect these programs <u>to be there</u>.   *pronoun?*   *weak*

Members of their families probably get benefits every month. But at the same time, they get upset when they see how much the government takes out of their paychecks every week.

It is going to take strong leadership to address this growing problem and come up with a fair solution. We are going to hear the word "entitlement" for a very long time.

Revision Notes

1. Significant topic.
2. Before discussing entitlements, you need to provide a clear definition of them.
3. This is the type of topic that requires outside sources. Provide specific numbers to demonstrate to readers the importance of your topic. Remember to document sources.
4. Edit sentences for clarity. Revise vague and awkward phrases.

Revised Draft

Entitlements: The Big Three

Political debates, talk shows, and blogs are increasingly dominated by a single word—"entitlements." Many Americans, however, are confused about what entitlements are and why they are so important.

In his *Handbook of American Government*, Erick Rosen defines entitlements as "federal programs that distribute payments based on fixed formulas to citizens who meet certain criteria, such as the disabled, the poor, or the elderly" (271). Unlike programs like defense or NASA, entitlements do not require annual Congressional appropriations. As more people meet the criteria, by turning 65, for example, the more money the government automatically pays out.

Three large entitlement programs consumed 41% of the 2010 federal budget and are expected to grow dramatically.

Social Security ($708 billion)

Founded in 1935 as a pension program for seniors, Social Security was expanded in 1956 to provide benefits for the disabled. Social Security is funded by a payroll tax of 6.2%, which is matched by employers, so that someone making $100,000 a year is contributing $12,400 to the program. Today 52 million people—one in six Americans—receive monthly Social Security payments. In the next generation, the population of retirees will almost double. Under the current formulas, Social Security will begin paying out more than it collects in payroll taxes by 2015 (Mandel 46).

Medicare ($468 billion)

Created in 1965, Medicare provides health care coverage for Americans over 65, people with certain disabilities, and everyone with end-stage renal disease (Lech 17). Like Social Security, Medicare is funded by a payroll tax of 1.45%, which is matched by employers, so the person making $100,000 a year is contributing $2,900 to the program. The number of Americans entitled to receive Medicare will grow from 47 million in 2010 to 80 million in 2030 (Lech 19). Currently, the payroll tax raises about a third of the money needed each year.

Medicaid ($285 billion)

Medicaid was established in 1965 to provide health care coverage for low-income individuals and families. Unlike Medicare, it is funded by both the federal and state governments, with the federal government paying about 57% of the expenses. Currently two-thirds of nursing home stays and one-third of childbirths qualify for Medicaid payments.

In 2008 nearly 50 million people were eligible to receive Medicaid benefits. With the nursing home population expected to rise with the aging Baby Boom generation, expenses are predicted to increase significantly over the next twenty years ("Medicaid").

In 2010 these entitlements totaled $1.4 trillion. Under the current formulas, expenses are expected to grow rapidly in the future. Nancy Kwan, a budget specialist for a Congressional study group, predicts that health care entitlements alone will "increase from 4% of our GDP in 2007 to 12% in 2050." Her analysis shows that "expenses are increasing not just because the numbers of people becoming eligible for Medicare and Medicaid are growing but because of rising costs per patient."

The burden for taxpayers will also grow. In 1955, Kwan noted, there were nine workers paying into Social Security for every retiree collecting benefits. Now the ratio is 3.9 workers for every retiree. By 2030 that number will drop to 2.4.

Candidates running for office are reluctant to discuss either raising taxes or cutting benefits, but the numbers are getting harder to ignore. It is going to take strong leadership to address this growing problem and come up with fair solutions. We are going to hear the word "entitlement" for a very long time.

Works Cited

Kwan, Nancy. Interview by Joe Scarborough. *Morning Joe*. MSNBC. 9 Feb. 2011. Television.

Lech, Albert. "Budget Realities." *Federal Forum*. Sep. 2011: 15–29. Print.

Mandel, Rachel. "Social Security." *American Dimensions*. Oct. 2011:
  35–53. Print.
"Medicaid." *CNN.com*. Cable News Network, 21 Oct. 2011. Web.
  25 Oct. 2011
Rosen, Erik. *Handbook of American Government*. New York: Scribner,
  2011. Print.

Questions for Review and Revision

1. What is the student's thesis?

2. How does the student define the standard of measurement?

3. What value does this division have?

4. How effectively does the student use outside sources? Are they clearly and smoothly integrated into the text?

5. Is the paper properly documented using MLA guidelines (see pages 483–486)?

6. Read the essay aloud. Can you detect weak or awkward passages that need revision?

7. How effectively did the student follow the instructor's suggestions?

WRITING SUGGESTIONS

1. Using this paper as a model, write a similar division paper that breaks a topic into parts or types. You might divide a football team into offense, defense, and special teams or explain different products or services provided by a local business.

2. *Collaborative writing:* Discuss this essay with other students. Do they think that their peers appreciate the impact entitlement programs will have on their future? Write a classification paper ranking levels of awareness of the issue.

EVALUATING DIVISION AND CLASSIFICATION CHECKLIST

Before submitting your paper, review these points:

1. Have you clearly defined your goal—to write a division, classification, or division and classification paper?

2. Do you make meaningful divisions or classifications, or does your paper oversimplify a complex subject?

3. Are your categories clearly defined?

4. Do you avoid overlapping categories?

5. Do you use parallel patterns to develop categories and items?
6. In division, do you explain the size and significance of each category?
7. In classification, do you use a single standard of evaluation?
8. Do all the parts of your subject clearly fit into a single category? Are there any items left over?
9. Do you explain possible exceptions or changes?

Accompanying English CourseMate Resources

 Visit English CourseMate at **www.cengagebrain.com** to find many helpful resources and study tools for this chapter.

Process: Explaining How Things Work and Giving Directions

What Is Process?

Process **explains how things work** or **gives directions to accomplish a task.** Both types are widely used in college and professional writing.

Explaining How Things Work

The first type of process writing explains how an operation, procedure, or occurrence takes place. Textbooks, magazine articles, and websites explain how the heart pumps blood, how the Federal Reserve sets interest rates, or how a hurricane develops.

Mark Clayton (page 361) describes how hackers supporting the Syrian government used surveillance malware such as DarkComet to infect dissidents' computers and monitor rebel activities:

> Once established, DarkComet gives control of the machine to the hacker who can then order the computer to record keystrokes, capture passwords, or activate the machine's webcam or microphone. Or it can send personal information and e-mail address books back to Syrian authorities.

In writing explanations, it is important to consider the knowledge base of your readers. You may have to define technical terms; use illustrative analogies, such as comparing the heart to a pump; and tell brief narratives so that readers understand the process. Some writers will use an extended analogy, comparing a nuclear power plant to a teakettle or a computer virus to a brush fire. One of the challenges of explanatory writing can be deciding which details to leave out and where to make separations.

Critical Thinking for Writing Explanations

1. **Study the process carefully.** Note principal features that need emphasis. Identify areas that are commonly confused or difficult to understand.

2. **Determine how much background information is needed.** Your readers may require, for example, a basic knowledge of how normal cells divide before being able to comprehend the way cancer cells develop. In some instances, you may have to address common misconceptions. If you were to explain criminal investigation methods, you first might have to point out how actual police operations differ from those depicted on television.

3. **Determine the beginning and end of the process.** In some cases, the process may have an obvious beginning and end. Leaves emerge from buds, flower, grow, turn color, and fall off. But the process of a recession may have no clear-cut beginning and no defined end. If you were to write a paper about the process of getting a divorce, would you stop when the final papers are signed or continue to discuss alimony and child visitation rights? When does a divorce end?

4. **Separate the process into logical stages.** Readers will naturally assume all the stages are equally significant unless you indicate their value or importance. Do not overemphasize minor points by isolating them in separate steps.

5. **Alert readers to possible variations.** If the process is subject to change or alternative forms, present readers with the most common type. Indicate, either in the introduction or in each stage, that exceptions or variations exist.

6. **Use transitional phrases to link the stages.** Statements such as "at the same time," "two hours later," and "if additional bleeding occurs" help readers follow explanations.

7. **Stress the importance of time relationships.** Process writing creates a slow-motion effect that can be misleading if the chain of events naturally occurs within a short period. You can avoid this confusion by opening with a "real-time" description of the process:

> The test car collided with the barrier at thirty-five miles an hour. In less than a tenth of a second the bumper crumpled, sending shock waves through the length of the vehicle as the fenders folded back like a crushed beer can. At the same instant sensors triggered the air bag to deploy with a rapid explosion so that it inflated before the test dummy struck the steering wheel.

The rest of the paper might repeat this process for four or five pages, slowly relating each stage in great detail.

8. **Use images, details, narratives, and examples to enrich the description of each stage.** Give readers a full appreciation of each stage by describing it in details they can grasp. Avoid long strings of nonessential, technical language. Use comparisons and narratives to provide readers with clear pictures of events and situations.

9. **Review the final draft for undefined technical terms.** Use a level of language your readers understand. Include technical terms only when necessary, and define ones your readers may not know or find confusing.

Giving Directions

Directions are step-by-step instructions that show readers how to accomplish a specific goal or task. Recipes, repair manuals, training materials, and consumer guides show readers how to bake a cake, change a tire, install software, treat an injury, buy a car, or improve their credit scores. College instructors use process to explain assignments, experiments, or procedures. Websites use process to show customers how to set up an account, select products, and pay for them. In "Fender Benders: Legal Do's and Don't's" (page 346), Armond D. Budish gives drivers specific instructions on what to do if they are involved in a minor traffic accident:

1. **Stop! It's the Law.** No matter how serious or minor the accident is, stop immediately. If possible, don't move your car—especially if someone has been injured. Leaving the cars as they were when the accident occurred helps the police determine what happened. Of course, if your car is blocking traffic or will cause another accident where it is, then move it to the nearest safe location.

When giving instructions, you may find it helpful to add visual aids such as bold type, capital letters, and underlining, as well as pictures, graphs, and charts. Visual aids are commonly used in documents that must be read quickly or referred to while working. A recipe printed in standard paragraphs instead of lists and numbered steps would be difficult for someone to follow while cooking. Because readers are following steps to complete a task, there is no tolerance for errors or omissions in giving instructions. Transposing letters in a URL will prevent users from downloading software. Forgetting a single turn in driving directions will cause motorists to become lost.

Critical Thinking for Writing Directions

1. **Appreciate your responsibility.** When you give directions, you may assume a legal responsibility. If consumers or employees are injured or suffer losses following your directions, they may sue or claim damages. You cannot defend yourself after the fact by arguing that people should have known about a hazard you failed to warn them about.

2. **Write to your readers.** Determine your readers' current knowledge. They may require background information to understand the process. Readers may also have misconceptions that must be cleared up. Define and explain important terms.

3. **Make sure the directions are self-contained.** Your document should contain all the information needed for readers to carry out the task. Readers should not be directed to another source for information to complete the process.

4. **Alert readers to potential hazards.** Use all capital letters, underlining, or italics to highlight warnings and disclaimers. Warn readers about any dangers to themselves, their property, or the environment. In addition to cautioning people about physical dangers, alert them about potential legal liabilities. Remind readers to check local zoning laws or inspection requirements before remodeling their home, and to refer to a car's warranty before modifying its engine.

5. **Explain the cost of materials or time required to complete the process.** Homeowners thinking of installing a redwood deck might begin a project only to discover they cannot afford all the supplies needed to finish the job. Someone making a dessert for the first time may be unable to judge how much time it will take to prepare. List estimated costs or the time required in a subtitle or the first paragraph so readers can make an informed decision before proceeding. In estimating the time required, remember that a reader performing the process for the first time will take longer than an experienced professional.

6. **Consider using numbered steps.** Readers find it easier to follow numbered steps and can mark their places if interrupted. Numbered steps also allow you to eliminate wordy transitional statements such as "The next thing you should do...."

7. **Emphasize verbs.** Begin instructions with action verbs to dramatize what readers should do: "Set the oven to 350 degrees...." or "Call your supervisor...."

8. **Provide complete instructions.** Readers will be performing this process for the first time and will only have your instructions to guide them. If you tell readers "place the cake in the oven for 30 minutes or until done," they will have no idea what the cake is supposed to look like at that point—should it be evenly browned, or can the center remain soft? When is it "done"? Directions should be precise:

   Bake at 350°F for 35 minutes or until edges are golden brown. (Note: Center of cake may remain soft.)

9. **Alert readers of possible events they may misinterpret as mistakes.** If, during the process, an engine may give off smoke or a computer slow down, readers may assume they have made a mistake or used the wrong or defective materials. Tell readers what to anticipate:

   Attach legs to desk top with screws. (Note: Legs will remain loose until final assembly.)

10. **Give negative instructions.** Tell readers what *not* to do, especially if you know people have a tendency to misinterpret instructions, ignore safety warnings, skip difficult steps, or substitute cheaper materials.

11. **Highlight critical steps, especially those that are commonly overlooked or cause problems:**

    MOST IMPORTANT: Do not file a complaint with central office without approval from TWO supervisors!

12. **Use maps, charts, diagrams, and photographs to help readers visualize directions.**

13. **Proofread carefully.** Make sure the names, dates, addresses, room numbers, websites, and prices you list are accurate. Before distributing instructions that are over a year old, verify that the information is current and correct.

14. **Test directions before distributing them.** Because it is easy to overlook details or write misleading instructions, have other people review your document. Before emailing directions to 500 employees, you might want to send it to 20 employees and ask them if they have any questions. Send follow-up emails or call this test group to see whether there are any corrections or changes that should be made before you distribute the directions to everyone.

Writing Techniques: PROCESS

Introductions

Whether explaining or giving directions, writers use introductions to demonstrate the importance of the process, provide background information, or address misconceptions. Armond Budish (page 346) opens his article "Fender Benders: Legal Do's and Don't's" with a brief narrative demonstrating the error of ignoring a minor traffic accident. Mortimer Adler (page 341), challenges readers' assumptions by telling them that "marking up a book is not an act of mutilation but of love."

Second Person

In giving directions, writers generally use the second person to directly address and guide their readers through a set of instructions. Anne Weisbord (page 350) tells nurses writing résumés to "Describe your background in a few punchy sentences." In "How to Recover From a Bad Interview" Donna Farrugia (page 359) tells job seekers, "If you leave the interview thinking, 'I could have answered that better,' use your thank-you note as an opportunity to recover."

Alternative Directions

In giving instructions, writers often include alternative methods to complete the same task. Drivers reluctant to travel on a busy freeway can be given a different route. Recipes might offer alternative ingredients for vegetarians or people with health concerns. Mortimer Adler (page 344) encourages people to mark up books as they read. Realizing that some readers may still object to writing in books, he offers another method to record their reactions, "How about using a scratch pad slightly smaller than the page-size of the book—so that the edges of the sheet won't protrude?"

Strategies FOR READING PROCESS

As you read the process entries in this chapter, keep these questions in mind.

Understanding Meaning

1. What is the writer's goal—to explain or to instruct?
2. Is the goal clearly stated?
3. What are the critical steps in the process?
4. What errors should readers avoid?

Evaluating Strategy

1. What is the nature of the intended audience?
2. How much existing knowledge does the writer assume readers have? Are terms explained?
3. What are the beginning and ending points of the process? Are these clearly defined?
4. How are steps or stages separated? Are the transitions clear?
5. Does the writer include paragraph breaks, numbers, bold type, or other visual prompts? Are these skillfully used?
6. Are instructions easy to follow?
7. Does the writer demonstrate the significance of the process or the value of his or her advice?

Appreciating Language

1. Are technical terms clearly defined and illustrated?
2. Does the writer use language that creates clear images of what is being explained?

MORTIMER ADLER

Mortimer Adler (1902–2001) was born in New York City. He taught psychology at Columbia University, and then moved to Chicago, where he taught the philosophy of law for more than twenty years. He resigned from the University of Chicago in 1952 to head the Institute for Philosophical Research in San Francisco. His books include *How to Read a Book* and *Philosopher at Large: An Intellectual Autobiography*. Adler became famous as an editor of the *Encyclopedia Britannica* and leader of the Great Books Program of the University of Chicago. This program encouraged adults from all careers to read and discuss classic works. This essay first appeared in the *Saturday Review of Literature* in 1940.

How to Mark a Book

CONTEXT: *Before reading Adler's essay, consider your own reading habits. Do you read with a pen in your hand? Do you scan a work first or simply begin with the first line? Do you take notes? Do you have problems remembering what you read?*

WRITER'S NOTE: *In addition to using numbered steps, Adler offers an alternative method to readers who object to writing in books.*

You know you have to read "between the lines" to get the most out of anything. I want to persuade you to do something equally important in the course of your reading. I want to persuade you to "write between the lines." Unless you do, you are not likely to do the most efficient kind of reading.

1 *introduction*

 I contend, quite bluntly, that marking up a book is not an act of mutilation but of love.

2 *thesis*

 You shouldn't mark up a book which isn't yours. Librarians (or your friends) who lend you books expect you to keep them clean, and you should. If you decide that I am right about the usefulness of marking books, you will have to buy them. Most of the world's great books are available today, in reprint editions, at less than a dollar.

3 *disclaimer*

 There are two ways in which one can own a book. The first is the property right you establish by paying for it, just as you pay for clothes and furniture. But this act of purchase is only the prelude to possession. Full ownership comes only when you have made it a part of yourself, and the best way to make yourself a part of it is by writing in it. An illustration may make the point clear. You buy a beefsteak and transfer it from the butcher's icebox to your own. But you do not own the beefsteak in the most important sense until you consume it and get it into your bloodstream. I am arguing that books, too, must be absorbed in your bloodstream to do you any good.

4 *defines "full ownership"*

<u>Confusion about what it means to own a book leads people to</u> 5
<u>a false reverence for paper, binding, and type—a respect for the</u> describes
<u>physical thing—the craft of the printer rather than the genius of</u> "false
<u>the author.</u> They forget that it is possible for a man to acquire the reverence for
idea, to possess the beauty, which a great book contains, without paper"
staking his claim by pasting his bookplate inside the cover. Having
a fine library doesn't prove that its owner has a mind enriched by
books; it proves nothing more than that he, his father, or his wife,
was rich enough to buy them.

<u>There are three kinds of book owners. The first has all the stan-</u> 6
<u>dard sets and best-sellers—unread, untouched.</u> (This deluded
individual owns wood pulp and ink, not books.) <u>The second has</u> classifies
<u>a great many books—a few of them read through, most of them</u> three types
<u>dipped into, but all of them as clean and shiny as the day they were</u> of book
<u>bought.</u> (This person would probably like to make books his own, owners
but is restrained by a false respect for their physical appearance.)
<u>The third has a few books or many—every one of them dog-eared</u>
<u>and dilapidated, shaken and loosened by continual use, marked</u>
<u>and scribbled in from front to back. (This man owns books.)</u>

Is it false respect, you may ask, to preserve intact and unblemished 7
a beautifully printed book, an elegantly bound edition? Of course
not. I'd no more scribble all over a first edition of *Paradise Lost*
than I'd give my baby a set of crayons and an original Rembrandt!
I wouldn't mark up a painting or a statue. Its soul, so to speak, is
inseparable from its body. And the beauty of a rare edition or of
a richly manufactured volume is like that of a painting or a statue.

<u>But the soul of a book can be separated from its body.</u> A book 8
is more like the score of a piece of music than it is like a painting.
No great musician confuses a symphony with the printed sheets
of music. Arturo Toscanini reveres Brahms, but Toscanini's score of
the C-minor Symphony is so thoroughly marked up that no one but
the maestro himself can read it. The reason why a great conductor
makes notations on his musical scores—marks them up again and
again each time he returns to study them—is the reason why you
should mark your books. If your respect for magnificent binding or
typography gets in the way, buy yourself a cheap edition and pay
your respects to the author.

Why is marking up a book indispensable to reading? First, it 9
keeps you awake. (And I don't mean merely conscious; I mean
wide awake.) In the second place, reading, if it is active, is think- explains
ing, and thinking tends to express itself in words, spoken or writ- need to write
ten. The marked book is usually the thought-through book. Finally, as you read
writing helps you remember the thoughts you had, or the thoughts
the author expressed. Let me develop these three points.

If reading is to accomplish anything more than passing time, it 10
must be active. You can't let your eyes glide across the lines of a
book and come up with an understanding of what you have read. defines
Now an ordinary piece of light fiction, like say, *Gone with the Wind*, "active
doesn't require the most active kind of reading. The books you read reading"

for pleasure can be read in a state of relaxation, and nothing is lost. But a great book, rich in ideas and beauty, a book that raises and tries to answer great fundamental questions, demands the most active reading of which you are capable. You don't absorb the ideas of John Dewey the way you absorb the crooning of Mr. Vallee. You have to reach for them. That you cannot do while you're asleep.

If, when you've finished reading a book, the pages are filled with your notes, you know that you read actively. The most famous active reader of great books I know is President Hutchins, of the University of Chicago. He also has the hardest schedule of business activities of any man I know. He invariably reads with a pencil, and sometimes, when he picks up a book and pencil in the evening, he finds himself, instead of making intelligent notes, drawing what he calls "caviar factories" on the margins. When that happens, he puts the book down. He knows he's too tired to read, and he's just wasting time.

11

But, you may ask, why is writing necessary? Well, the physical act of writing, with your own hand, brings words and sentences more sharply before your mind and preserves them better in your memory. To set down your reaction to important words and sentences you have read, and the questions they have raised in your mind, is to preserve those reactions and sharpen those questions.

12

why write?

Even if you wrote on a scratch pad and threw the paper away when you had finished writing, your grasp of the book would be surer. But you don't have to throw the paper away. The margins (top and bottom, as well as side), the end-papers, the very space between the lines, are all available. They aren't sacred. And, best of all, your marks and notes become an integral part of the book and stay there forever. You can pick up the book the following week or year, and there are all your points of agreement, disagreement, doubt, and inquiry. It's like resuming an interrupted conversation with the advantage of being able to pick up where you left off.

13

<u>And that is exactly what reading a book should be: a conversation between you and the author.</u> Presumably he knows more about the subject than you do; naturally, you'll have the proper humility as you approach him. But don't let anybody tell you that a reader is supposed to be solely on the receiving end. Understanding is a two-way operation; learning doesn't consist in being an empty receptacle. The learner has to question himself and question the teacher. He even has to argue with the teacher, once he understands what the teacher is saying. And marking a book is literally an expression of your differences, or agreements of opinion, with the author.

14

reading as conversation

There are all kinds of devices for marking a book intelligently and fruitfully. Here's the way I do it:

15

1. *Underlining:* of major points, of important or forceful statements.
2. *Vertical lines at the margin:* to emphasize a statement already underlined.
3. *Star, asterisk, or other doo-dad at the margin:* to be used sparingly, to emphasize the ten or twenty most important

uses numbered steps and italics for easy reading

statements in the book. (You may want to fold the bottom corner of each page on which you use such marks. It won't hurt the sturdy paper on which most modern books are printed, and you will be able to take the book off the shelf at any time and, by opening it at the folded-corner page, refresh your recollection of the book.)

4. *Numbers in the margin:* to indicate the sequence of points the author makes in developing a single argument.

5. *Numbers of other pages in the margin:* to indicate where else in the book the author made points relevant to the point marked; to tie up the ideas in a book, which, though they may be separated by many pages, belong together.

6. *Circling of key words or phrases.*

7. *Writing in the margin, or at the top or bottom of the page, for the sake of:* recording questions (and perhaps answers) which a passage raised in your mind; reducing a complicated discussion to a simple statement; recording the sequence of major points right through the book. I use the end-papers at the back of the book to make a personal index of the author's points in the order of their appearance.

The front end-papers are, to me, the most important. Some people reserve them for a fancy bookplate. I reserve them for fancy thinking. After I have finished reading the book and making my personal index on the back end- papers, I turn to the front and try to outline the book, not page by page, or point by point (I've already done that at the back), but as an integrated structure, with a basic unity and an order of parts. This outline is, to me, the measure of my understanding of the work. **16**

If you're a die-hard anti-book-marker, you may object that the margins, the space between the lines, and the end-papers don't give you room enough. All right. How about using a scratch pad slightly smaller than the page-size of the book—so that the edges of the sheets won't protrude? Make your index, outlines, and even your notes on the pad, and then insert these sheets permanently inside the front and back covers of the book. **17**

Or, you may say that this business of marking books is going to slow up your reading. It probably will. That's one of the reasons for doing it. Most of us have been taken in by the notion that speed of reading is a measure of our intelligence. There is no such thing as the right speed for intelligent reading. Some things should be read quickly and effortlessly, and some should be read slowly and even laboriously. The sign of intelligence in reading is the ability to read different things according to their worth. <u>In the case of good books, the point is not to see how many of them you can get through, but rather how many can get through you—how many you can make your own.</u> A few friends are better than a thousand acquaintances. If this be your aim, as it should be, you will not be impatient if it takes more time and effort to read a great book than it does a newspaper. **18**

goal of reading good books

You may have one final objection to marking books. You can't 19
lend them to your friends because nobody else can read them
without being distracted by your notes. Furthermore, you won't
want to lend them because a marked copy is a kind of intellectual
diary, and lending it is almost like giving your mind away.

If your friend wishes to read your *Plutarch's Lives*, Shakespeare, 20
or *The Federalist Papers*, tell him gently but firmly to buy a copy.
You will lend him your car or your coat—but your books are as *conclusion*
much a part of you as your head or your heart.

Understanding Meaning

1. In Adler's view, when do you really *own* a book? What makes a book truly yours? What makes a book like a steak?
2. What does Adler mean by the "soul" of a book? How does respecting it differ from respecting its "body"?
3. Why is it important, in Adler's view, to write as you read?
4. *Critical Thinking*: This essay was first published seventy-five years ago. Are Adler's suggestions any different from the study skills you may have learned in high school or college?

Evaluating Strategy

1. What audience is Adler addressing?
2. *Blending the Modes*: Where does Adler use *comparison, description*, and *classification* in developing this essay?
3. Adler provides seven suggestions that are stated in italics and numbered. If this advice were written in a standard paragraph, would it be as effective? Why or why not?

Appreciating Language

1. The *Saturday Review of Literature* had a general but highly literary readership, much like that of today's *New Yorker* or *Vanity Fair*. Does the tone and style of the article seem suited to this audience?
2. Are there any words, phrases, references, or expressions in this seventy-five-year-old article that need updating?

WRITING SUGGESTIONS

1. Using Adler's seven suggestions, write a brief one-page guide to active reading directed at high school students.
2. *Collaborative Writing*: Adler presents tips for active reading. Work with a group of students and discuss their experiences in studying for examinations. Record your ideas and suggestions, and then write a well-organized list of tips to help new students develop successful study skills.

ARMOND D. BUDISH

Armond D. Budish is an attorney and consumer-law reporter. He practices law in Ohio, where he writes columns on consumer issues for the *Cleveland Plain Dealer*. He has also published articles in *Family Circle* magazine. His books include *How to Beat the Catastrophic Costs of Nursing Home Care* (1989), *Avoiding the Medicaid Trap* (1996), and *Why Wills Won't Work (If You Want to Protect Your Assets)* (2008). A Democratic member of the Ohio House of Representatives since 2007, Budish served as Speaker of the House from 2009 to 2011, and is currently the Minority Leader.

Fender Benders: Legal Do's and Don't's

CONTEXT: *In this* Family Circle *article, Budish advises drivers what to do if they are involved in a minor accident.*

WRITER'S NOTE: *Budish uses numbered steps and bold type to make his directions easy to skim, and warns drivers what* not *to do by giving negative instructions.*

1   The car ahead of you stops suddenly. You hit the brakes, but you just can't stop in time. Your front bumper meets the rear end of the other car. *Ouch!*

2   There doesn't seem to be any damage, and it must be your lucky day because the driver you hit agrees that it's not worth hassling with insurance claims and risking a premium increase. So after exchanging addresses, you go your separate ways.

3   Imagine your surprise when you open the mail a few weeks later only to discover a letter from your "victim's" lawyer demanding $10,000 to cover car repairs, pain and suffering. Apparently the agreeable gentleman decided to disagree, then went ahead and filed a police report blaming you for the incident and for his damages.

4   When automobiles meet by accident, do you know how to respond? Here are 10 practical tips that can help you avoid costly legal and insurance hassles.

5   **1. Stop! It's the Law.** No matter how serious or minor the accident is, stop immediately. If possible, don't move your car—especially if someone has been injured. Leaving the cars as they were when the accident occurred helps the police determine what happened. Of course, if your car is blocking traffic or will cause another accident where it is, then move it to the nearest safe location.

6   For every rule there are exceptions, though. If, for example, you are rear-ended at night in an unsafe area, it's wisest to keep on going and notify the police later. There have been cases in which people were robbed or assaulted when they got out of their cars.

"Fender Bender Do's and Don't's" by Armond Budish as appeared in Family Circle, July 19, 1994. Reprinted by Permission of the author.

2. **Zip Loose Lips.** Watch what you say after an accident. 7
Although this may sound harsh, even an innocent "I'm sorry"
could later be construed as an admission of fault. Also be
sure not to accuse the other driver of causing the accident.
Since you don't know how a stranger will react to your remarks, you run the risk of making a bad situation worse.

   Remember, you are not the judge or jury; it's not up to you 8
to decide who is or is not at fault. Even if you think you caused
the accident, you might be wrong. For example: Assume you
were driving 15 miles over the speed limit. What you probably
were not aware of is that the other driver's blood-alcohol level
exceeded the legal limits, so he was at least equally at fault.

3. **Provide Required Information.** If you are involved in an 9
accident, you are required in most states to give your name,
address and car registration number to: any person injured in
the accident; the owner, driver or passenger in any car that was
damaged in the accident; a police officer on the scene. If you
don't own the car (say it belongs to a friend or your parents),
you should provide the name and address of the owner.

   - You must produce this information even if there are no ap- 10
   parent injuries or damages and even if you didn't cause
   the accident. Most states don't require you to provide the
   name of your insurance company, although it's usually a
   good idea to do so. However, don't discuss the amount
   of your coverage—that might inspire the other person to
   "realize" his injuries are more serious than he originally
   thought.
   - What should you do if you hit a parked car and the owner 11
   is not around? The law requires you to leave a note with
   your name, and the other identifying information previously mentioned, in a secure place on the car (such as
   under the windshield wiper).

4. **Get Required Information.** You should obtain from the 12
others involved in the accident the same information
that you provide them with. However, if the other driver
refuses to cooperate, at least get the license number
and the make and model of the car to help police track
down the owner.

5. **Call the Police.** It's obvious that if it's a serious accident 13
in which someone is injured, the police should be called
immediately. That's both the law and common sense. But what
if the accident seems minor? Say you're stopped, another car
taps you in the rear. If it's absolutely clear to both drivers that
there is no damage or injury, you each can go your merry way.
But that's the exception.

   Normally, you should call the police to substantiate what 14
occurred. In most cities police officers will come to the scene,
even for minor accidents, but if they won't, you and the other

driver should go to the station (of the city where the accident occurred) to file a report. Ask to have an officer check out both cars.

If you are not at fault, be wary of accepting the other driver's suggestion that you leave the police out of it and arrange a private settlement. When you submit your $500 car-repair estimate several weeks later, you could discover that the other driver has developed "amnesia" and denies being anywhere near the accident. If the police weren't present on the scene, you may not have a legal leg to stand on. 15

Even if you are at fault, it's a good idea to involve the police. Why? Because a police officer will note the extent of the other driver's damages in his or her report, limiting your liability. Without police presence the other driver can easily inflate the amount of the damages. 16

6. **Identify Witnesses.** Get the names and addresses of any witnesses, in case there's a legal battle some time in the future. Ask bystanders or other motorists who stop whether they saw the accident; if they answer "yes," get their identifying information. It is also helpful to note the names and badge numbers of all police officers on the scene. 17

7. **Go to the Hospital.** If there's a chance that you've been injured, go directly to a hospital emergency room or to your doctor. The longer you wait, the more you may jeopardize your health and the more difficult it may be to get reimbursed for your injuries if they turn out to be serious. 18

8. **File a Report.** Every driver who is involved in an automobile incident in which injuries occur must fill out an accident report. Even if the property damage is only in the range of $200 to $1,000, most states require that an accident report be filed. You must do this fairly quickly, usually in 1 to 30 days. Forms may be obtained and filed with the local motor vehicle department or police station in the city where the accident occurred. 19

9. **Consider Filing an Insurance Claim.** Talk with your insurance agent as soon as possible after an accident. He or she can help you decide whether you should file an insurance claim or pay out of your own pocket. 20

For example, let's say you caused an accident and the damages totaled $800. You carry a $250 deductible, leaving you with a possible $550 insurance claim. If you do submit a claim, your insurance rates are likely to go up, an increase that will probably continue for about three years. You should compare that figure to the $550 claim to determine whether to file a claim or to pay the cost yourself. (Also keep in mind that multiple claims sometimes make it harder to renew your coverage.) 21

10. **Don't Be Too Quick to Accept a Settlement.** If the other driver is at fault and there's any chance you've been injured, don't rush to accept a settlement from that person's insurance 22

company. You may not know the extent of your injuries for some time, and once you accept a settlement, it's difficult to get an "upgrade." Before settling, consult with a lawyer who handles personal injury cases.

When you haven't been injured and you receive a fair offer to cover the damage to your car, you can go ahead and accept it.   23

Understanding Meaning

1. What problems can motorists encounter if they are careless about handling even minor accidents?
2. What are some of the most important things you should do if involved in a fender bender?
3. Why should you go to the hospital even if you have what appears to be a minor injury?
4. *Critical Thinking*: Should this article be printed as a pamphlet and distributed to drivers' education classes? Have you known anyone who has encountered difficulties that could have been avoided if he or she had followed the writer's advice?

Evaluating Strategy

1. How does Budish arouse reader attention in the opening?
2. How effective are the numbered steps? Would the article lose impact if it were printed in standard paragraphs?
3. How easy is this article to remember? Can you put it down and recall the main points?

Appreciating Language

1. This article was written for *Family Circle*. Does the choice of language appear targeted to a female audience?
2. Why does Budish, who is an attorney, avoid legal terminology?
3. Does Budish's language create concrete images that make strong impressions and dramatize his subject?

WRITING SUGGESTIONS

1. Using this article as a model, provide the general public with a similar list of tips to prevent heart disease, deter muggers, prepare children for school, save money for retirement, or provide tips on a topic of your choice.
2. *Collaborative Writing*: Work with a group of students to provide tips for new students on campus. Use peer review to make sure you do not overlook details in writing your student guide.

ANNE WEISBORD

Anne Weisbord has a master's degree in education and served as director of Career Services at Hahnemann University in Philadelphia before beginning a career as a private career counselor. Widely published, she has appeared on radio and television providing advice on careers, job search strategies, and interviewing. In this article, written for *Nurse Extra*, Weisbord tells nurses how to write effective *résumés*.

Résumés That Rate a Second Look

CONTEXT: *Although directed to nurses, Weisbord's instructions apply to most professionals.*

WRITER'S NOTE: *Weisbord states her directions in the terse, to-the-point language used in most* résumés.

In today's business and professional environment—in which health-care positions can be eliminated STAT—every nurse should have a résumé ready to send to potential employers. 1

The purpose of the résumé is to get you a job interview. Employers use résumés to screen out undesirable, or less desirable, candidates. Your résumé should summarize your skills and experience, and convince employers of the value they will gain in hiring you. It's an advertisement for yourself, and as with all ads, it should generate interest and motivate the reader. 2

Before you prepare your résumé, take a few moments to consider your marketable skills. Identify the strengths and accomplishments that are relevant to the position you are seeking, and present them as succinctly and as clearly as possible. You'll need to organize all of this information in no more than two pages, in an easy-to-read, attractive format. Beyond this, there are really no hard-and-fast rules about writing résumés. 3

Let's look at the standard components of the traditional résumé that presents your relevant nursing background in reverse chronological order. 4

1. **Personal identification.** You need include only your name, degree, and your professional certification, address, and phone number. Omit date of birth, marital status, and health; these can be discriminatory factors in hiring. 5

2. **Career objective.** This is optional. If you know exactly what you want to do, you can use a phrase that describes the type and level of position you are seeking. An objective might be "Nurse Coordinator in Pediatrics," or "Nurse Manager, ICU." However, if you would consider a variety of positions, skip the objective and use only a summary. 6

3. **Summary.** Describe your background in a few punchy sentences. This is the "hook" that will pique the reader's interest in the rest of the résumé. 7

Weisbord, Anne, "Resumes That Rate a Second Look" from Nurse Extra August 1, 1994 by Anne Weisbord. Anne Weisbord, president of Career Services Unlimited in Havertown, PA has a private career counseling practice and conducts career management workshops.

4. **Professional experience.** List names, places, job titles, and dates of employment. Link your experience to your summary or objective. Stress accomplishments and emphasize responsibilities that will impress the potential employer. Use brief phrases with vivid verbs and nouns to describe the skills essential to each position. Omit obvious duties. Emphasize accomplishments with bullets. 8

    As you go back into your work history, present fewer details. When you first became a nurse, you naturally had fewer responsibilities. Devote more space to higher-level, more professional duties. 9

5. **Education.** If you are a recent graduate with little nursing experience, put education before professional experience. Always list the most recent school, degree or certificate program and work backward. Do include honors or academic awards. Don't list high school. If you have a college degree, the employer will assume you earned a high-school diploma. 10

6. **Professional certification(s).** List certifications in reverse chronological order or organize them according to specialty areas. 11

7. **License(s).** List only the state and title of each professional license. Don't give your license number(s). You will be asked to provide them later in the interview process. 12

8. **Activities.** No one will hire you for a healthcare position based on your interest in golf or coin collecting, but volunteer community involvement shows positive personal characteristics. Be careful about listing political or religious activities. Your reader may have biases against your persuasions. 13

    Remember that your résumé serves as a first impression of you. To a potential employer, your coffee-stained copy or your misspellings say something about your attention (or lack of attention) to detail, your neatness, and even your attitude. Also, modesty is not an asset in a résumé. Toot your own horn! 14

Understanding Meaning

1. Summarize Weisbord's key points on résumés.
2. What is the purpose of a résumé? Why does this seemingly obvious fact need to be explained? Do many people have misconceptions about résumés?
3. What information does Weisbord suggest omitting? Why?
4. *Critical Thinking:* What is the context of a résumé? How does this document reflect the roles of writer, audience, and discipline?

Evaluating Strategy

1. How effective is the format of Weisbord's article?
2. Weisbord tells readers "there are really no hard-and-fast rules about writing résumés." Why is this important?
3. How does her article mirror the document she is training readers to write?

Appreciating Language

1. How effective are Weisbord's style and choice of words? Is the article readable?

2. How does Weisbord's emphasis on verbs, "*Describe* your background..." and "*List* names, places..." (italics added), reflect the kind of language found on most résumés?

WRITING SUGGESTIONS

1. If you have not written a résumé, draft one, adopting Weisbord's advice.

2. *Collaborative Writing:* Meet with a group of students and review each other's résumés. Select the best features you discover, and then write a brief process essay explaining step by step how to create an effective résumé.

WALTER C. VERTREACE

Walter C. Vertreace graduated from Howard University and received a law degree from Temple University. For twenty-eight years Vertreace worked for the Hess Corporation, where he was the Director of Corporate Equal Employment Opportunity. Past president of the New York State Advisory Council on Employment Law, Vertreace is now a human resources consultant based in Philadelphia. He has published numerous articles in *The Black Collegian* about searching for jobs, interviewing, and evaluating offers.

Modifying Your Résumé for Computer Selection

CONTEXT: *In this article from* Black Collegian, *Vertreace directs students to make their résumé stand out in an electronic screening process.*

WRITER'S NOTE: *Vertreace includes negative instructions, telling students not to add attachments (paragraph 8), use colored paper (paragraph 10), or insert tabs and bullets (paragraph 12).*

On the road to a new job, freshly printed diploma close at hand, you are as ready as you've ever been for the application and interview process. Your most important tool, your professional résumé, has been prepared, reviewed, and is ready for presentation. You have used the most expensive light blue paper, typed it on your computer in an elegant, classy font, with bullets, highlighting and all the impressive bells and whistles money can buy. You have underlined or bold-faced the most important points, and even included a photograph of yourself to impress the interviewers. Then you faxed it, mailed it or scanned it to anyone and everyone, and you're just waiting for the offers to roll in. And waiting. And waiting.

Still no takers. Why can't they see the star that is waiting to be hired? Perhaps you wrote the right résumé but for the wrong decade. Maybe what you need is a document designed, not to wow the human eye, but to impress the computer system that will get the first crack at evaluating you for the job.

When your mom and dad, or maybe even your big brother or sister, applied for their first professional positions, things were different. They would send a paper résumé through the mail, which would then be reviewed by a human resources representative before being referred to a hiring manager for evaluation. It was important for the document to catch the eye, quickly show that they possessed the necessary skills and highlight the important aspects of their background in prose. This may have been a chronological résumé, showing their experience in inverse date order, a functional document showing the most impressive qualifications first, or some combination of the two.

In today's world, the first one to review your résumé is less likely 4
to be human than it is to be a computer, accessing your information from a database. In most cases, the job-seeker enters and
uploads information independently, to be retrieved later by the
employer as job openings arise. It is now as important to show the
computer what you bring to the table as it is to impress the human
interviewer, who may never get to see your skills if your résumé
does not get past computer screening.

Most large companies, and many smaller ones, now maintain 5
databases of résumés, applications and candidate profiles, either
internally or externally, which they search periodically for individuals
who have expressed an interest in employment. There are several
things you need to consider in making your résumé scannable, so
that it will attract the attention of that "electronic screener."

The Road Map to Your High Points

Database searching is usually done through the use of software 6
that extracts data—in this case data included in your résumé-based
on keywords used in the document. If keywords used in the search
do not match those used in your résumé, chances are your document will not pass the first screening. For this reason, you should
take a hard look at the job description of the position for which you
are applying, and include in your document the words and phrases
that show that you have what they are looking for. That way, when
the recruiter searches the database, your qualifications will pop up.
In addition to the basic skill and abilities common to applicants in
your field, are there professional organizations the company may
be interested in? For example, if you are a newly minted accoun-
tant, and a member of the National Association of Black Accountants, you may want to list both the full name and the abbreviation
NABA, to make sure the membership is found. Are you a CPA,
MBA, CLU, or a person with other impressive alphabet soup after
your name? Include both the initials and the complete title.

Although you can use bold print for your headings, do not use 7
it to identify other important points in your résumé. Your skills and
qualifications, properly listed within the text of the document, will
speak volumes for themselves. Standard headings, such as Education, Experience, etc., will quickly guide the reader to your capa-
bilities without being a distraction.

Do not attach business cards, lists of references, photographs or 8
work samples. If needed, these can be presented at the interview.
Unless specifically requested by the employer, do not fax your résumé. Faxed copies may not scan well, and as a result may be
ignored later during the employer's search of the applicant pool.

Roadblocks

As noted at the beginning of this article, you did several things in 9
the course of résumé preparation that may have looked good, but

stood in the way of the computer selecting your résumé, or even finding it in the first place.

First, reconsider the powder blue paper. Any senior human resources professional has received cover letters and résumés on various colors, textures, and sizes of paper. This may be nice for personal letters, but it can be deadly for business correspondence. Colored paper, as well as paper with watermarks or patterns, will sometimes confuse the software, making the document difficult to read, and eliminating you from consideration before you even get started. And although you can get more information on legal size paper, stick to 8½ x 11 standard stock. 10

You want to stand out, but not in the wrong way. Your computer may allow you to select from numerous font styles, some more decorative and flamboyant than others, but you should restrict yourself to the basics such as Times New Roman or Arial. Also, since some of the older systems may hiccup when confronted by flair, I recommend sans serif typefaces. You have undoubtedly heard the old rule that your résumé should not exceed two pages. That rule still stands, and you should not try to circumvent it by using type that is so small that it cannot be seen by the naked eye. Font size of 11 or 12 points should suffice, although 10 to 14 is the generally accepted norm. You should also make sure your e-mail address presents you as a professional seeking upscale employment; HotAndAvailable@xyz.com may not be the image you want to convey. 11

Bullets and tabs are out. The newest optical character recognition software can recognize them, but why take the chance that the company to which you are applying may not be up to date? Use standard keyboard characters, such as asterisks instead of bullets, to be on the safe side, and use the space bar instead of the tab key. Also avoid vertical lines, underlining and graphics, and especially avoid using your picture. 12

The Fast Lane: Life Beyond Scannable

An improperly formatted résumé forwarded via e-mail, posted on an Internet database or job board, or pasted to an employer's Internet form will not present properly when opened, may not be readable at all, or may be dropped altogether. To ensure that this does not occur, your résumé should also be converted to the ASCII (American Standard Code for Information Exchange) format. Many systems automatically convert your document into ASCII, as long as you have followed the other recommendations contained in this article (plain white paper, simple basic type, no underlines or italics, etc.). 13

The HTML résumé format, sometimes referred to as the Web-Ready Résumé, enables you to publish your résumé to a web page, thereby allowing employers to search for and review your résumé, online, at any time. It also allows you to provide links to work samples, reports, and other pertinent information. However, 14 it also carries with it its own set of potential pitfalls in addition to those discussed above. Interesting graphics, music and type-faces are available in this format but should not be used for most professional positions in industry, outside of the graphic design, entertainment, and related fields. Links to work samples and refer-ences can be provided, and content control is exercised by you, the writer. Be careful, as some employers will not bother to access your résumé when presented in this fashion, and some job boards do not support HTML submissions.

Although the focus of this article has been on electronic   15
submission, scanning, and computer applications to applicant screening, you should still have a high-quality, attractive print résumé for presentation at the interview, or to those employers and agencies who request paper submissions at job fairs, orga-nizations' career days, and campus sessions. Like your scannable document, this résumé should clearly show the skills you possess and their relationship to the position for which you are applying. And always accompany your résumé submission with an attrac-tive cover letter, identifying the position for which you are apply-ing and summarizing the unique talents and positive attributes you bring to the table.

Your road to the position you seek may be shorter and faster   16
when you are equipped with the best and most up-to-date equip-ment to get you there.

Understanding Meaning

1. How has computer scanning changed résumé preparation? What visual effects suitable for printed documents are impediments to electronic scanning?
2. What font sizes and styles should applicants use? Why?
3. What key words should applicants include to make sure their résumés appear during a database search?
4. Which online formats should students convert their documents to?
5. Who might include graphics and music in a résumé? Why?
6. *Critical Thinking*: Does electronic scanning accelerate the job search or does it make it more impersonal? Should job seekers rely on networking and meeting people face-to-face rather than submitting résumés to a computer?

Evaluating Strategy

1. *Blending the Modes*: How does Vertreace use *comparison* to demonstrate how computer scanning has changed the way résumés should be prepared?
2. Vertreace does not use numbered points. Would his article be easier to read and remember if he used numbered steps and bold headings?
3. What impact does the conclusion have? In writing about résumés and the job search, should writers project a positive and encouraging tone? Why or why not?

Appreciating Language

1. Vertreace instructs students to consider their email names. What connotations do email names convey about an applicant? Should students also consider the tone and language of their voicemail greetings? Why or why not?

2. Why do scans and database searches make word choice critical in designing a résumé?

3. *Critical Thinking*: What challenges would someone changing careers face in selecting key words?

WRITING SUGGESTIONS

1. Using Vertreace's article as a model, write suggestions to job seekers how they should revise their Facebook pages, which are often viewed by employers to screen applicants. What words and images should be deleted? What should be added? How can a Facebook page provide information about an applicant that is important but not suitable for a résumé?

2. *Collaborative Writing:* Working with a group of students, share copies of your résumé and discuss how you would convert it for online submission. What visual effects would you change? How would you highlight key words?

DONNA FARRUGIA

Donna Farrugia is executive director of The Creative Group, a specialized staffing firm placing design and marketing professionals on a project and full-time basis. In this position, she manages operations for the firm's locations in major markets throughout the United States and Canada. She has presented at industry events, including the HOW Design Conference and American Advertising Federation National Conference, and has contributed articles on career-related topics to various publications. Farrugia has more than twenty-five years of marketing, business development and management experience and holds a Bachelor of Science in Business Administration from the University of Pittsburgh.

How to Recover from a Bad Interview

CONTEXT: *In this article Farrugia instructs job applicants how to cope following a bad job interview.*

WRITER'S NOTE: *Farrugia uses second person to address readers and organizes the essay by stating problems, then recommending recovery strategies.*

Interviewing for a new job is no easy task, and chances are you've faltered at some point in the process at least once. The list of potential pitfalls is numerous—everything from arriving late to not answering the hiring manager's questions as well as you would have liked to a simple lack of rapport between you and the interviewer. No matter the reason for a bad interview, the result is nearly always the same: a greatly diminished chance of landing the job you'd hoped for and, often, a significant blow to your self-confidence. 1

Can you turn it around? By keeping your cool, you may be able to recover from a poor showing and put yourself back in the running for the position. Consider these situations and ways of handling them: 2

You're running late

You mapped your route beforehand and left home an hour and a half before your interview was scheduled to start to ensure you would arrive on time. But a wrong turn off the highway is jeopardizing your on-time arrival. In situations like this where a bad impression seems inevitable, head it off by calling your interviewer as soon as you suspect you will be late. If you're running behind schedule by more than 15 minutes, offer to reschedule the interview for a different time or day. Apologize for your tardiness and follow up with a written note that conveys the same sentiment. Most—but not all—hiring managers will understand that unforeseen incidents can strike at the least opportune moments and will appreciate your consideration for their schedules. 3

Farrugia, Donna. "How to recover from a bad interview." All Business.com. N.p., 23 May 2005. Web. 16 Dec. 2011. <http://www.allbusiness.com/human-resources/workforce-management-hiring-interviewing/450308-1.html> Reprinted with permission.

You drew a blank

No matter how much time you spent preparing for your interview, 4
sometimes you simply can't think of a good response to a hiring
manager's question. To a certain extent, this should not come as
a surprise. Increasingly, hiring managers are asking applicants puz-
zling brainteasers, which are meant to provide a greater sense of
a potential employee's personality and creative-thinking skills than
standard interview queries alone. Consider a recent survey commissioned by our company that asked executives for the strangest questions they had been asked by hiring managers during interviews.
The responses include such head-scratchers as, "If you could be any
animal, what would you be?," "What did you want to be when you
were 10 years old?" and "What would I find in your refrigerator?"

Of course, even standard questions like "Name your greatest 5
weakness" can occasionally throw you for a loop.

If you leave the interview thinking, "I could have answered that 6
better," use your thank-you note as an opportunity to recover. Don't
rehash any mistakes you made, but use the letter as a method of selling yourself and your skills better than you did during the meeting.
Thank the interviewer for his or her time and reiterate why you think
you are perfect for the position. If possible, key in to a point the hiring
manager made during the interview and tie it to your experience or
background. For example, if the interviewer stressed the company's
commitment to leading-edge technology, include in your thank-you
note details about your involvement in the selection and purchase of
a new accounting software system for a previous employer.

You didn't establish a connection

Often, the cause of a bad interview is a lack of rapport between 7
you and the hiring manager. But not hitting it off with the interviewer doesn't necessarily mean the end of the line for you.

First, consider that a number of factors external to the interview 8
could have affected the hiring manager's behavior. Personal issues
or a looming deadline at work could have caused him or her to
seem distant or distracted. Don't take it personally; you may have
made a better impression than you think. Also remember that
many companies today are ensuring they make quality hires by
asking candidates to interview with more than one individual. You
may have the opportunity to make a stronger connection with a
different person down the road.

Regardless of the reason, if you fail to establish rapport with the 9
interviewer, focus on keeping the relationship alive by following up
occasionally for updates on the status of the opening. You can also
send the hiring manager articles of interest you come across in newspapers and trade publications as a means of remaining in contact.

Occasionally, a bad interview can actually be a good thing. If 10
the situation seemed tense because the interviewer asked inappropriate or irrelevant questions, for example, this may signal a
lack of respect for employees or disorganization in the department

or firm. In this case, these warning signs can help you steer clear of a potentially regrettable move. Remember, an interview is not only an opportunity for a company to judge you, but also for you to evaluate the employer.

Sometimes, despite your best efforts, there's little you can do to recover from a bad interview. Rather than become discouraged, remember that the company thought well enough of you to invite you in. Chalk the incident up to "experience" and focus on what you learned so you can improve your interview skills and make a great impression next time. 11

Understanding Meaning

1. What should applicants do when they realize they are running late for an interview?
2. How can applicants use a thank-you letter to recover from a bad interview?
3. What should applicants keep in mind if the interviewer seems distracted or distant?
4. Why can a bad interview be "a good thing" in Farrugia's view? What can people learn about a company by the way it treats applicants?
5. *Critical Thinking*: Are there other common problems that Farrugia could have addressed in this article?

Evaluating Strategy

1. Farrugia organizes the essay by describing common problems, then suggesting remedies. Is this an effective method? Why or why not?
2. How important is her conclusion? Is she admitting that in many cases there is no way to recover from a bad interview?
3. *Critical Thinking*: Farrugia reminds applicants that an interview is their opportunity to judge the company. Why is this important for job seekers to remember?

Appreciating Language

1. How would you characterize the tone and style of Farrugia's article?
2. How does the use of second person influence the way readers are likely to respond to Farrugia's advice?

WRITING SUGGESTIONS

1. Using Farrugia's article as a model, write an essay advising students how to recover from a bad exam, a poor work performance, a customer complaint, or a rebuke from a superior or instructor.
2. *Collaborative Writing:* Discuss Farrugia's article with a group of students and identify additional problems applicants face. Suggest remedies to overcome them. Place recommendations in easy-to-read numbered steps.

Blending the Modes
MARK CLAYTON

Mark Clayton is a staff writer for *The Christian Science Monitor*. From 1993–2007 he served as the newspaper's Toronto bureau chief, writing about Canadian politics and culture. Beginning in 1997 Clayton also served as the *Monitor's* reporter on higher education. He began covering energy and the environment in 2003 and cybersecurity in 2008.

Syria's Cyberwars: Using Social Media against Dissent

CONTEXT: *In this 2012 article Clayton describes how the Syrian government used fake social media sites to attract dissidents, then used spyware and malware to monitor their online activities and turn their computers into tracking devices.*

WRITER'S NOTE: *To explain this process, Clayton uses* narration, definition, *and* cause and effect. *He adds credibility to his article by identifying the people he quotes (paragraphs 5, 9, 20).*

1 For years, average Syrians were blocked from Facebook, YouTube and other social media by Bashar al-Assad's repressive police-state government. Early last year, however, as the Arab Spring swept through the region, something odd happened: The social media sites that were pivotal to uprisings in other Arab nations were suddenly switched back on.

2 Now we know why: It's easier to track people—and find out who is against you—if you can monitor computer traffic to such sites, or trick visitors into clicking on tainted links that download spyware onto their computers, rights activists and cyber experts say.

3 To a far greater degree than Libya, Egypt or perhaps any other nation in the Arab world, Syria's government has succeeded in flipping activists' use of digital tools and social media to the government's own advantage, cyber experts with an eye on Syria say.

4 A "Syrian Revolution" page showed up on Facebook in March 2011, winning 41,000 fans in just a few days, and 138,000 a few weeks later, a recent report found. By last month, it had 438,000 fans. But frequenting such pages may be potentially hazardous, as well as educational or motivational.

5 "Online social media, which virtually anyone can use from home, played a central role in the Syrian uprising and helped break the decades-old government media monopoly," Amjad Baiazy, a Syrian researcher living in London writes in a new study published last month by MediaPolicy.org, a London-based new media think tank. "But it helped the Syrian government crack down on activists."

6 As bombs fall and bullets fly, dissidents and opposition figures have had their favorite social media tools turned against them, and

their cloak of anonymity pierced by veiled online hackers loyal to Syria's government.

Last fall, the government bought centralized Internet eaves- 7 dropping equipment. But dropping spyware directly onto activists' computers is Syria's newest cyberwar trend.

Luring opposition sympathizers with tainted video links in e-mail, 8 fake Skype encryption tools, tainted online documents, hackers believed to be allied to Syria's government have in recent months deployed an array of powerful spyware with names like DarkComet, backdoor.brueut, and Blackshades. Available on the Internet, these malware are used to infiltrate the personal computers of opposition figures and rights activists and send back information on their friends and contacts as well as passwords, cybersecurity experts say. The impact of this spying is hard to gauge. But even as the physical battle intensifies in and around Damascus, Syria cyber watchers are worried.

The Syrian regime had long blocked access to social media 9 sites, says Richard Zaluski, president of the Center for Strategic Cyberspace and Security Science, a London-based think tank.

"Blocking, however, prevented the tracking down of activists, 10 so the regime ultimately responded by unblocking sites such as Facebook, YouTube, and Twitter," he writes in a recent analysis posted on the group's website. "This move enabled the regime's security apparatus to conduct its internal cyber war against its own people and aided in tracking down the identities of activists."

Alongside open electronic forums, blogs have been used by 11 thousands of Syrians to launch a counteroffensive against the government's curbs on public expression, Mr. Baiazy's study, called "Syria's Cyber Wars," notes. These forums also provide a way for users to share information on how to bypass government website blocking. At least seven Facebook groups provide Syrians with technical means for remaining anonymous while on the Internet.

Even so, social networks and blogs in Syria have not had quite 12 the same impact they have had in Iran and Egypt, according to Baiazy. The Internet is "still accessible by a relatively small portion of the Syrian population, and it is still limited to the elite," he writes. Just 16.4 percent of the Syrian population has Internet access, compared with 47 percent in Iran.

With Syrian activists being detained in large numbers, there are 13 concerns that at least some portion of those are being identified by government-sponsored hackers, says Eva Galperin, with Electronic Frontier Foundation, an Internet rights group.

Human Rights Watch has identified some 20 different torture 14 centers in Syria. So the potential consequences for someone whose computer becomes "infected by malware written by someone in the employ of Syrian security forces are dire," Ms. Galperin says.

"It's clear that the Assad regime has learned lessons from Libya, 15 Tunisia, and Egypt, and that's why they are pursuing this tactic," she says. "Using malware to infiltrate individuals' computers is a characteristic of the Syrian conflict that's not been widely seen in other Arab Spring uprisings."

To watch dissidents' activities online, the Assad government has 16 deployed Branch 225, the secret Syrian communications security department in charge of Internet monitoring, according to both Baiazy's study and Mr. Zaluski. As part of that effort, Syria last year purchased millions of dollars of Internet filtering equipment—much of it made in the United States and Europe—to track communications to Facebook and other sites.

But all that high-tech equipment has proved increasingly less 17 effective since Facebook, Twitter, YouTube, Google and others began encrypting by default communications between their sites and users' computers, Galperin and other experts say.

As a result, Syria's government is resorting to state-supported 18 actors who are launching attacks that take over online accounts without the user knowing it. In other cases it's meant forging fake Facebook pages to steal activists' passwords. Security forces have also used torture against captured opponents to obtain the passwords to their Facebook and e-mail accounts, Baiazy reports.

Amid this turmoil, the Syrian Electronic Army, a hacker militia 19 loyal to the Assad regime, has come to the fore. It is this latter group that infiltrates opposition computers directly that's apparently moving hard after activists' identities by taking spyware available on the Internet and customizing it to be invisible to antivirus security.

"What we've seen in Syria is a campaign targeting activists with 20 surveillance malware," says Morgan Marquis-Boire, a cybersecurity researcher with Citizen Lab, a Toronto-based computer security think tank.

His research, which has involved analyzing malware captured on 21 the hard drives of Syrian activists, has identified 16 separate types of malicious software. All of those have at their core the purpose of delivering into the computer another nasty piece of malware called a "remote access trojan," or RAT. Once activated, the RAT sends information to computers located within Syria's telecom service.

Several RATs are being used. One in particular, called Dark- 22 Comet, is frequently delivered by a compromised Skype account belonging to a trusted friend, Mr. Marquis-Boire says. In that way many are infected.

Once established, DarkComet gives control of the machine to 23 the hacker who can then order the computer to record keystrokes, capture passwords, or activate the machine's webcam or microphone. Or it can send personal information and e-mail address books back to Syrian authorities.

"We have found that Facebook and other forums that carry the 24 comments of pro-Syria liberation groups frequently are seeded with videos of atrocities in Homs that also include malware," Mr. Marquis-Boire says. "It's dangerous to trust too much what you find online."

Understanding Meaning

1. Why did the Syrian government allow citizens to have access to social media after the Arab Spring swept the Middle East?
2. What did the Syrians learn from the revolts in Egypt, Tunisia, and Libya?
3. How does the Syrian government use malware and spyware to monitor dissidents? What can hackers accomplish?
4. Has media coverage focused on military actions by the Syrian government? Are cyber activities invisible to the public and press?
5. *Critical Thinking*: How could security hackers in other countries use the same technology to track American citizens, journalists, and government officials? Could false social media pages be generated for propaganda purposes? Do reporters and the public have reasons to doubt what they see online?

Evaluating Strategy

1. How does Clayton explain the process Syrians use to "flip" digital tools and social media.
2. What examples does Clayton use to illustrate the process?
3. Clayton includes direct quotations as support. Why is it important to identify the source of any testimony provided as evidence?

Appreciating Language

1. How does Clayton define a RAT?
2. What words and phrases does Clayton use to describe both sides in this conflict? Do any connotations suggest a bias?
3. *Critical Thinking*: How would you define "cyber war"? What does it consist of? Could similar tactics be used in political campaigns in democracies?

WRITING SUGGESTIONS

1. According to Clayton, Syria was able to purchase American and European equipment to conduct its cyber operations. Write a process paper proposing how the government or corporations should examine orders from countries accused of human rights violations. Can nations refuse to sell Syria arms but still provide products or services used to oppress its citizens?

2. *Collaborative Writing*: Discuss Clayton's article with a group of students and consider how the same technology could be used by dissidents or terrorists to undermine a government. Could innocent-looking consumer sites or Facebook pages lure government employees to sites that could then monitor their movements and online actions? Write a short process paper how governments, companies, and individuals should protect themselves from hackers.

Writing Beyond the Classroom

As you read these directions about conducting a self-assessment, determine whether you would find them easy to follow. Are they clearly organized and do they provide enough detail?

WRITER'S NOTE: *The opening paragraph uses second person to address clients personally and show empathy for people who have lost their jobs.*

STEIN AND GIOTTA ASSOCIATES
CONDUCTING A SELF-ASSESSMENT

Transitioning to a new career after losing a job can be stressful. You may feel bitter, confused, and anxious. Stein and Giotta specializes in helping displaced professionals find new and rewarding employment opportunities. Before meeting with your assigned consultant, follow these guidelines to identify your strengths and weaknesses. The more you know about yourself, the better prepared you will be to benefit from our services.

1. **Examine your work history and ask yourself these two questions:**
   What three things did I like about my past jobs?
   What three things did I hate?

2. **Identify your strengths and weaknesses:**
   List three of your greatest strengths or abilities.
   List three of your greatest problems or weaknesses.

3. **Create a priority list of the following items you want in a new career. Think carefully and add comments about each one.**
   a. income
   b. job security
   c. the ability to work independently
   d. chance for advancement
   e. personal satisfaction
   f. opportunity to learn new skills
   g. pension and benefits
   h. status

4. **Write a paragraph describing your ideal job.**

5. **List five specific things you will have to accomplish to get this job.**

Understanding Meaning

1. What questions should applicants ask themselves about their past jobs?
2. What items should applicants prioritize in considering their future careers?
3. *Critical Thinking:* The last question asks applicants to list things they will have to do to get their ideal job. Is it useful to ask people to identify these tasks themselves rather than tell them what to do? Do people have to take charge of their own job search even when they seek professional assistance? Why or why not?

Evaluating Strategy

1. Why are numbered steps useful in giving directions?
2. How does asking questions engage readers? Does it force them to take responsibility for their success?

Appreciating Language

1. What does the level of diction and word choice reveal about the intended audience?
2. Do the authors successfully avoid overly technical language that some readers would find difficult?

WRITING SUGGESTIONS

1. Write your own self-assessment, identifying your strengths and weaknesses, what is important to you in a job, and what you will have to accomplish to get your ideal job.

2. *Collaborative Writing:* Using this document as a model, work with a group of students and create an academic self-assessment to help students identify their strengths and weaknesses and what it will take to succeed in college.

Responding to Images

Fotosearch/Getty Images

1. What is your immediate reaction to this photograph? Are you registered to vote? How many times have you voted? If you have not voted, why not?

2. In recent elections as many as half the eligible voters did not cast ballots. Why do people fail to vote?

3. Do you think negative campaign tactics and the emphasis on fundraising alienates voters? If elections were based on reasonable debates instead of attack ads would more people take an interest in politics?

4. *Critical Thinking:* Do you think the voting process could be streamlined? Should citizens be able to vote online? Do people mistrust the accuracy and security of voting machines? Should the nation have a uniform method of voting that is reliable and verifiable? Why or why not?

5. *Visual Analysis:* What impression does the informal style of the banner create? Does it look amateurish or inviting? Why the exclamation point?

6. *Collaborative Writing:* Discuss this photograph with a group of students. Ask each student if they know people who do not vote or who refuse to vote. Write a list of suggestions that would encourage more people, especially young people, to vote.

Strategies FOR PROCESS WRITING

1. Define your goal—to explain or to instruct. Is your purpose to explain how something takes place or to instruct readers how to accomplish a specific task?

2. Evaluate your audience's existing knowledge. How much does your audience know about the subject? Do any common misconceptions need to be clarified? What terms should be defined?

3. Define clear starting and ending points. When does this process begin? What is the end? Readers must have a clear concept of the beginning and end, especially in instructions.

4. Separate the process into understandable stages or steps. To explain a process, it is important to break it down into a chain of separate events that makes the process understandable without distorting it. When giving instructions, do not include too many operations in a single step.

5. Number steps for clarity in directions. Instructions are easier to follow if organized in numbered steps. If interrupted, readers can easily mark their places and later resume the process without confusion.

6. Consider using visual aids. Large print, capital letters, bold or italic type, and underlining can highlight text. Graphs, drawings, diagrams, and photographs can be beneficial to reinforce both explanatory writing and instructions.

Revising and Editing

1. Measure readability of instructions. Instructions, especially directions people will have to refer to while working, should communicate at a glance. Short sentences and wide spacing between steps are used in recipes and repair manuals so a person working in a kitchen or garage can read the text at a distance.

2. Test your writing. Because it is easy to skip steps when explaining a process you are familiar with, it is important to have other people read your writing. Other readers can be objective and easily detect missing or confusing directions.

Suggested Topics for Process Writing

General Assignments

Write a process paper on any of the following topics. Assume you are writing for a general, college-educated audience. You may develop your explanation using narratives, comparisons, and definitions. *Explain* the process as a clearly stated chain of events. Draw from your own experiences.

1. How the university processes student applications
2. The operation of an appliance such as a microwave, refrigerator, or washing machine
3. The process of a disease or disability
4. The way small children learn to talk
5. The method your employer uses in training
6. The stages of childbirth
7. How malware infects a computer
8. The way corporations market a new product

9. The way the body loses fat through diet or exercise
10. How networks select television programs

Write another process paper *giving directions* to complete one of the specific tasks listed. You may wish to write your instructions in numbered steps rather than standard paragraphs. Remember to highlight any safety hazards.

1. How to protect your computer against viruses
2. How to purchase a new or used car at the best price
3. How to improve your credit score
4. How to sell something on eBay
5. How to find a job or prepare for a job interview
6. How to handle sexual harassment on campus or in a job
7. How to prevent identity theft
8. How to operate a drill press, microscope, or other piece of industrial or scientific equipment
9. How to treat a second-degree burn or other injury
10. How to monitor a child's use of social media

Writing in Context

1. Imagine you have been selected to write a section for a student handbook instructing freshmen how to register for classes. Write a step-by-step paper giving complete directions. Include exact room numbers, times, and locations. You may wish to refer to a campus map. When you complete a draft of your paper, review it carefully to see if you have left out any essential information.
2. Select a process you learned on a job, and write instructions for training new employees. Consider how your job may have changed. Give trainees the benefit of your experience, and add tips that might not be included in the standard job descriptions. Warn readers, for instance, about common problems you encountered.
3. Select a process from one of your textbooks and rewrite it for a sixth-grade class. Simplify the language and use analogies sixth graders would understand.

Student Paper: Process

This paper was written in response to the following assignment:

Write a 500-word process paper providing directions to accomplish a specific task. You may include graphs, charts, diagrams, or numbered steps.

First Draft with Instructor's Comments

Home Safety

Use more specific title, "Home Safety" could refer to avoiding accidents in the home.

Homeowners are generally only concerned about security when they plan to take a vacation. When they take off for a week or two to the mountains or down the shore, they install additional locks, set timers, purchase sophisticated monitoring systems, talk to neighbors, and hope their homes will not be robbed while they are enjoying themselves. But the reality is different. Most homes are not burglarized while their owners are thousands of miles away. Most houses are robbed before 9 p.m., often while their owners are near or inside the residence. Your house is more likely to be robbed while you are grilling in the backyard or watching a football game than when you are on a cruise or camping trip. *[Wordy, shorten opening sentences]* *[What do timers do?]* *[Good point]* *[Wordy]*

There are things you can do to make your home burglar proof. The most important thing you can do is to take steps in case a burglary does happen. You will have to prove any loss. So it makes sense to make a list of your valuables. Photograph or videotape each room in your house. Keep receipts of major purchases. Store these in a safe deposit box. Review your insurance to see if special items like furs, artwork, or coin collections are covered. It is also important to identify valuables. Engrave computers, televisions, cameras, stereos, and DVD players with your name or an identifying number. Police often discover stolen property but have no way of contacting the owner. *[Good advice]*

A really important thing to remember is to always lock your doors. Nothing is more tempting to a criminal than an open garage door or unlatched screen door. <u>Lock up even when you plan to visit a neighbor for "just a minute" because that "minute" can easily turn into a half an hour, giving a burglar plenty of time for a burglary.</u> Many people buy very expensive and high-tech security systems but leave them off most of the time because they are so hard to use. A cheap alarm system used <u>24-7</u> is better than one used just now and then. It can also be important to trim shrubbery around doors and windows to keep burglars from having a hiding place. *[Wordy, shorten]* *[Slang, revise]*

It is very important to network with neighbors and let them know <u>what is going on</u>. Let neighbors know if you expect deliveries or *[New paragraph]* *[Revise]* contractors. Thieves have posed as moving crews, casually looting a house and loading a truck while neighbors looked on.

Thieves are usually reluctant to leave the first floor, which usually has a number of exits. They don't like going into attics or basements where they might get trapped, so that is where to hide valuables. And finally, call the police the moment you discover a break-in. If you return home and find evidence of a break in—do not go inside the home. The thieves, who could be armed <u>with weapons</u>, might still be inside. Use your cell phone or go to a neighbor's to call the police. Never attempt to confront a burglar yourself. No personal possession is worth risking death or a disabling-injury.

Delete, not needed

Revision Notes

This is a good topic, but your instructions could be made clearer and easier to follow.

- *Qualify your opening remark. No one can promise to make a home "burglar proof" but you can suggest ways to reduce the risk of break-ins.*
- *Number steps and use titles to highlight each of your suggestions. Stress verbs to highlight actions readers should take. Numbered steps can reduce wordy and repetitive transitional statements like "another important thing is."*

Revised Draft

Securing Your Home

Homeowners frequently think of security only when planning a vacation. Leaving home for a week or two, they install additional locks, set timers to trigger lights, purchase sophisticated monitoring systems, alert neighbors, and hope their homes will not be robbed in their absence. But most homes are robbed before 9 p.m., often while their owners are near or inside the residence. Your house is more likely to be robbed while you are grilling in the backyard or watching a football game in a basement rec room than when you are on a cruise or camping trip.

Although it is impossible to make any home "burglar-proof," there are some actions you can take to protect your home and property:

1. **Document your assets.**
   Make a list of your valuables. Photograph or videotape each room in your home. Keep receipts of major purchases. Store these and other important records in a safe deposit box so you can prove any losses. Review your insurance policies to see if special items like furs, artwork, or coin collections are covered.

2. **Identify valuables.**
   Engrave computers, televisions, cameras, stereos, and DVD players with your name or an identifying number. Police often

discover stolen property but have no way of contacting the owners.

3. *Always lock your doors.*
   Nothing attracts a thief more than an open garage or unlatched screen door. Lock up even when you plan to visit a neighbor for "just a minute." That "minute" can easily become half an hour, plenty of time for a burglary to occur. Don't leave doors open if you are going to be upstairs or in the basement.

4. **Install only security systems you will use.**
   Many homeowners invest in expensive, high-tech security systems that are so cumbersome they leave them off most of the time. A cheap alarm system used twenty-four hours a day provides more protection than a state-of-the-art system used randomly.

5. **Trim shrubbery around entrances and windows.**
   Don't provide camouflage for burglars. Thieves can easily conceal themselves behind foliage while jimmying doors and windows.

6. **Network with neighbors.**
   Let neighbors know if you expect deliveries, houseguests, or contractors. Thieves have posed as moving crews, casually looting a house and loading a truck while neighbors looked on.

7. **Store valuables in attics and basements.**
   Thieves are reluctant to venture beyond the ground floor, which usually offers numerous exits in case of detection. Attics and basements, therefore, provide more security for valuable or hard-to-replace items.

Finally, call the police the moment you discover a burglary has occurred. If you return home and find evidence of a break-in—do not go inside! The thieves, who could be armed, might still be on the premises. Use a cell phone or ask a neighbor to call the police. Never attempt to confront a burglar yourself. No personal possession is worth risking death or a disabling injury.

Questions for Review and Revision

1. The student offers seven directions. Would these be easier to recall if emphasized by the subtitle "Seven Tips to Keep Your Home Secure"? Would it be better to introduce the steps stating that "there are seven actions you can take" instead of "some actions"? Why or why not?

2. What misconceptions does the student address?

3. How important is the final warning?

4. The student writes in the second person, directly addressing the readers. Would the paper be less effective if written in third person? Why or why not?

5. Do the level of language, diction, and tone suit the intended audience?

6. Did the student follow the instructor's suggestions?
7. Read the paper aloud. Is this document easy to read and easy to remember? Could revisions increase its clarity?

WRITING SUGGESTIONS

1. Using this paper as a model, write a set of instructions directed to a general audience about improving the performance of your car, installing a new computer program, planning a trip or a wedding, losing weight, choosing a pet, preparing for a job interview, or another topic of your choice.

2. *Collaborative Writing:* Discuss this paper with other students. Using some of its ideas, work together to write a brief set of instructions on securing a dorm room or an apartment.

EVALUATING PROCESS CHECKLIST

Before submitting your paper, review these points:

1. Is the process clearly defined?
2. Do you supply background information that readers need?
3. Is the information easy to follow? Is the chain of events or the steps logically arranged?
4. Could the text be enhanced by large print, all capital letters, bold or italic type, diagrams, charts, or photographs?
5. Are your instructions complete? Do readers know when one step is over and another begins?
6. Do your instructions alert readers to normal changes they might mistake for errors?
7. Are hazards clearly stated?
8. Do you tell readers what *not* to do?
9. Did you verify that names, phone numbers, dates, prices, and email addresses are current and correct?
10. Did you use peer review to test your document?

Accompanying English CourseMate Resources

 Visit English CourseMate at **www.cengagebrain.com** to find many helpful resources and study tools for this chapter.

Cause and Effect: Determining Reasons and Measuring or Predicting Results

What Is Cause and Effect?

What causes terrorism? How will Hurricane Sandy affect the future of the Jersey Shore? What caused the 2008 recession? How will health-care reform affect the deficit? Would a handgun ban lower street crime? Can a Supreme Court ruling prevent frivolous lawsuits? What causes autism? Will a new school policy prevent bullying? The answers to these questions call for the use of **cause and effect,** writing that seeks either to **determine reasons why something occurred** or **measure or predict results.**

Historians devote much of their time to determining the causes of events. What caused the Civil War? Why did Hitler rise to power? What led to the women's movement of the 1970s? Historians also consider the ramifications of events and policies and speculate about the future. What impact did the growth of suburbs after World War II have on cities? Did a tax cut create jobs? Has a drug treatment program been successful? Will another oil crisis occur? How will a change in American foreign policy increase chances for peace in the Middle East? What will happen in Syria?

Nearly all professions and disciplines engage in cause-and-effect reasoning. Marketers try to determine why a product succeeded. Engineers examine why a test engine failed. Medical researchers measure the results of a new treatment. City planners predict the effect a major earthquake would have on emergency services. Educators consider whether curriculum changes will improve Scholastic Aptitude Test scores. Federal Aviation Administration (FAA) investigators examine wreckage to determine why a plane crashed.

Many of the research papers you will be assigned in college and the email and reports you will write in your future career will be developed using cause and effect. Identifying the reasons why something occurred can be difficult. Determining future outcomes, no matter how much data are examined or how many experiments are conducted, can remain largely guesswork.

Deduction and Induction

Writers often formulate cause-and-effect papers using **deduction** and **induction**. **Deduction** is a form of logic in which a *major premise* or general rule is applied to a *minor premise* or specific instance to reach a conclusion. You may be familiar with this classic example of deduction:

MAJOR PREMISE:	All cows are mammals.
MINOR PREMISE:	Bessie is a cow.
CONCLUSION:	Bessie is a mammal.

This illustration, though famous, fails to show the practical value of deduction. Other examples reveal how often we use deduction:

MAJOR PREMISE:	All full-time students are eligible for financial aid.
MINOR PREMISE:	Sandra Lopez is a full-time student.
CONCLUSION:	Sandra Lopez is eligible for financial aid.

MAJOR PREMISE:	The student health plan is only available to California residents.
MINOR PREMISE:	Amy Kwan is a resident of New York.
CONCLUSION:	Amy Kwan cannot join the student health plan.

Deduction can be used to solve problems and answer questions: Are dental exams deductible on my income tax return? Can I sublet my apartment? Will the college give me a refund if I drop a class in the fourth week? Each of these questions forms a minor premise. The IRS rules, apartment leases, and college policies you consult for answers serve as major premises. Deduction can be used to help determine both causes and effects.

Was a plane crash caused by a defective part?

MAJOR PREMISE:	FAA regulations consider this part defective if three bolts are missing.
MINOR PREMISE:	One bolt was missing from this part.
CONCLUSION:	This part was not defective.

How will an increase in bus fares affect ridership?

MAJOR PREMISE:	Bus ridership declines with fare increases.
MINOR PREMISE:	The city authorized a fifty-cent fare increase.
CONCLUSION:	Bus ridership will likely decline.

Problems occur with deductive reasoning if the major and minor premises are not precisely stated. The statement "All full-time students are eligible for financial aid" might be clearer if it included a definition of who is considered a full-time student: "All students taking twelve credits or more are eligible for financial aid." Other problems arise if the major premise is subject to interpretation. A warranty for snow tires might refuse to cover "improper use." Is off-road driving considered "improper"? How much damage can be considered "normal wear and tear"? Some major premises may prove to be false or require qualification.

Induction, unlike deduction, does not open with a major premise. Instead, it presents and interprets data and then makes a conclusion:

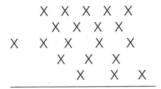

Data or Evidence

X X X X X
X X X X
X X X X X
X X X
X X X

_____

Inductive Leap—Conclusion

The X's in the diagram could represent reports of stolen cars, the number of laptops sold last month, blood tests of patients taking a new fertility drug, satellite photographs, interviews with consumers, or evidence collected at a crime scene. Based on a review of the evidence, a conclusion is drawn: car thefts are increasing in the suburbs, the new fertility drug damages red blood cells, coastline erosion is worse than it was last year, the consumers' major complaint is poor service, or the murder suspect is a Caucasian female with O-positive blood and dyed hair.

As these examples illustrate, effective induction requires a large body of valid evidence to achieve reasonable conclusions. Ford Motor Company would have to interview more than a handful of Focus owners to determine customer satisfaction. Medical researchers must rule out other reasons for damaged red blood cells. As the diagram notes, the movement from specific details to conclusion requires an _inductive leap_. No matter how much evidence is discovered and examined, no absolute assurance can be made that the conclusion is totally true.

The best demonstration of inductive reasoning takes place in a courtroom. In a criminal case, the prosecutor tells members of the jury that if they examine all the evidence they will conclude that the defendant is guilty beyond a "reasonable doubt." The defense attorney will attempt to raise doubt by providing alternative interpretations and by introducing conflicting evidence. He or she will tell the jury that reasonable doubt exists and that not enough evidence has been presented to reach a conclusion of guilt.

Establishing Causes

By the 1920s, surgeons and physicians began noticing that many of their patients with lung cancer were heavy smokers. An observable association was discovered, but there was no clear proof of a cause-and-effect relationship. Not all lung cancer patients smoked, and millions of smokers were free of the disease. Though scientists were concerned, they had no evidence that smoking caused cancer. In fact, throughout the 1930s and 1940s cigarette ads featured endorsements by doctors who claimed that the calming effect of nicotine reduced stress and prevented stomach ulcers. It was not until 1964 that researchers assembled enough data to convince the Surgeon General of the United States to proclaim cigarette smoking a health hazard.

In some instances, causes can be established through investigation and research. Doctors can diagnose an infection as the cause of a fever. Accountants can study financial records to discover why a company lost money. But many controversial issues remain subject to debate for decades. Why are American schools failing to educate children? John Taylor Gatto (page 383) examined the issue, determining that television and schools cause detrimental effects on children's lives:

> Two institutions at present control our children's lives—television and schooling, in that order. Both of these reduce the real world of wisdom, fortitude, temperance, and justice to a never-ending, nonstop abstraction. In centuries past, the time of a child and adolescent would be occupied in real work, real charity, real adventures, and the real search for mentors who might teach what one really wanted to learn.

When evaluating a writer attempting to establish a cause, consider the amount of evidence, the degree of objective analysis, and the willingness to qualify assertions. If General Motors sees an increase in car sales after a major promotional campaign, does it prove the commercials were successful? Could additional sales be attributed to a change in interest rates, easier credit, a price increase in imported cars, or a surge in consumer confidence? It would take careful research to determine if the advertising directly contributed to the sales results.

Measuring and Predicting Results

Measuring results tries to answer a question: what happened? Have the efforts of Mothers Against Drunk Driving changed public attitudes and behaviors about driving under the influence? How has downloading songs changed the music industry? Did an antismoking education program prove effective? Like establishing causes, measuring results requires careful research. Could you measure smoking rates of young people who participated in the program and those who did not? If young people who participated in the program smoked less or began smoking at a later age, would these be considered signs of success?

Predicting results requires careful critical thinking. In 1936 the *Literary Digest* declared that Alf Landon would defeat Franklin Roosevelt in his bid for a second term as president. The editors based their conclusion on a detailed telephone survey. By randomly selecting names from phone books and asking people whom they planned to vote for, the surveyors assumed they would get an accurate prediction. Their responses, from men and women, government employees and business executives, Italians and Jews, farmers and factory workers, and young and old, strongly indicated a preference for Landon. But their research failed to predict the outcome of the election accurately because the survey method did not measure a significant population. In 1936 many Americans could not afford telephones, and these economically deprived voters tended to favor Roosevelt.

Predicting future outcomes can be challenging because evidence may be difficult to collect or may be subject to various interpretations. In addition, numerous unforeseen factors can take place to alter expected events. A school board that determines to close schools because of a declining birthrate may fail to account for an influx of immigrants or the closure of private schools that would place more students into the public system.

Alexander Cockburn (pages 412–413) argues that raising the minimum wage would benefit workers, stimulate the economy, and create more jobs:

> A smart coalition stretching from *American Conservative* publisher Ron Unz to James K. Galbraith says a $12 minimum wage makes good sense as long-term stimulus. As Unz points out, "The minimum wage in Ontario, Canada, is currently well over $10 per hour, while in France it now stands at nearly $13. Even more remarkably, Australia recently raised its minimum wage to over $16 per hour, and nonetheless has an unemployment rate of just 5 percent." Properly enforced, a $12 minimum wage would slow illegal immigration, which is powered by a low-wage economy.
>
> As Galbraith, seizing on Unz's proposal, wrote, "What would workers do with the raise? They'd spend it, creating jobs for other workers. They'd pay down their mortgages and car loans, getting themselves out of debt… Women in particular would benefit because they tend to work for lower wages."

In contrast, Phil Kerpen and Nicole Kaeding (pages 415–416) argue that raising the minimum wage would burden the economy and reduce job openings, especially for women and young people without experience:

> Economists have tried to measure the effects of a minimum wage. Hundreds of studies have been completed, focused primarily on low-skilled and teenage employment. The consensus result has been that for every 10 percent increase in the minimum wage, a 1 to 3 percent decrease in employment is observed, disproportionately affecting low-skilled, mostly young workers.
>
> The last minimum-wage increase was in July of 2009, when the final dollar increase of the legislation passed back in 2007 took effect. Adjusted for inflation, the minimum wage is currently 36 percent higher than the minimum wage of 2006. A study released in June by University of Chicago economist Casey Mulligan estimates that the most recent minimum-wage increase (after adjusting for the effects of the recession) resulted in the loss of 800,000 jobs, mostly by low-skilled and young workers.

When examining writing that predicts future effects, consider the amount of evidence presented, the recognition of other factors that may affect results, and the use of critical thinking.

Critical Thinking for Cause-and-Effect Writing

When writing cause-and-effect essays, avoid these common traps, many of which are known as logical fallacies.

1. **Avoid mistaking a time relationship for a cause** *(post hoc, ergo propter hoc)*. If your brakes fail after you take your car to the dealer for an oil change, does that mean the mechanics are to blame? Can the president take credit for a drop in unemployment six months after signing a labor bill? Because events occur in time, it can be easy to assume an action that precedes another is a cause. The mechanics may not have touched your brakes, which were bound to wear out with or without an oil change. A drop in unemployment could be caused by a decline in interest rates or an upsurge in exports and may have nothing to do with a labor bill. Do not assume events were caused by preceding actions.

2. **Do not mistake an effect for a cause.** Early physicians saw fever as a cause of disease rather than as an effect or symptom. If you observe that children with poor reading skills watch a lot of television, you might easily assume that television interferes with their reading. In fact, excessive viewing could be a symptom. Because they have trouble reading, they watch television.

3. **Do not confuse associations with causes.** For years researchers argued that marijuana use led to heroin addiction. The evidence was clear. Nearly every heroin addict interviewed admitted to starting with marijuana. But since most addicts also drank beer, smoked cigarettes, chewed gum, and attended high school, this association could not alone be considered proof. Associations can be compelling and command attention, but they are not proof of a cause-and-effect relationship.

4. **Anticipate unexpected changes.** Many researchers qualify their predictions with the statement "all things being equal, we can anticipate..." But conditions never remain frozen. An increase in a school's test scores following a curriculum change could be caused by weaker students dropping out, the arrival of gifted transfer students, or increased tutoring, rather than any reforms in the classroom.

5. **Avoid "slippery slope" interpretations.** Do not assume that changes will start a trend that will snowball without restraint. If the government allows euthanasia for the terminally ill, you cannot argue that eventually the elderly and handicapped will be put to death.

6. **Realize that past performance, though an important factor, cannot predict future results.** In early 2008 the price of oil hit $100 a barrel. Production was lagging and the growing energy demand from China assured experts that prices would continue to increase. Throughout the spring oil prices rose, reaching $125 by May. In July oil climbed to $145, and a few analysts predicted oil would soon reach $200 a barrel. High gasoline prices led Americans to drive less, lowering demand. Months later a financial crisis shook world markets as banks collapsed and evidence of a global recession mounted. In February 2009 the price of oil dropped to $34 a barrel. *Past trends cannot be assumed to continue into the future.*

7. **Be aware of unintended consequences.** Policies or actions driven by one purpose may cause something unplanned or unanticipated to occur. The demilitarized zone separating North and South Korea inadvertently created a valuable wildlife sanctuary because for over fifty years humans were prevented from entering the territory. The banning of smoking in hotels for health reasons may have decreased fires caused by the careless use of smoking materials.

Writing Techniques: CAUSE AND EFFECT

Objective and Subjective Cause and Effect

Cause and effect essays can be based on objective facts or subjective observations. Alexander Stille (page 408) uses statistics to explain why the National Archives is unable to adequately process and store the records it receives, noting, "Factoring in for inflation, the budget of the Electronic Records Division has fallen by about 15 percent and its personnel have been cut by ten percent during a period when the volume of new data has increased tenfold." In contrast, Stephen Winzenburg (page 388) relies on personal experiences to measure the effects of social media on student behavior. "Most surprising are the athletes," he observes, "who publicly brag about breaking rules that could cause them to lose eligibility for their scholarships." As with description, cause and effect often blends objective facts and subjective impressions. John Taylor Gatto (page 383), for instance, cites studies revealing the amount of time children spend watching television then lists the effects he has observed in his own students.

Deduction and Induction

Writers frequently use deductive and inductive reasoning to organize cause and effect. In "The Declaration of Independence" Thomas Jefferson (page 418) states a major premise that governments derive their powers "from the consent of the governed" who have the right "to alter or abolish" them when they become "destructive" to life and liberty. He then presents the minor premise of the American colonies with a list of grievances against the King, which leads to his conclusion that the colonies have the right to become "free and independent states." Phil Kerpen and Nicole Kaeding (page 416) use induction, presenting data about teenage unemployment then stating their conclusion that they believe "should gain bipartisan support in Congress: Exempt teenagers from the 2007 legislation increasing the minimum wage."

Qualifications and Admissions

To persuade readers to accept their views, writers may have to qualify their conclusions or acknowledge possible errors and exceptions, missing or questionable evidence, or alternative interpretations. In concluding that the high rate of teenage unemployment is caused by the minimum wage, Kerpen and Kaeding (page 415) also acknowledge that "the overall weak economy is certainly at fault." In "We Can't Wish Away Climate Change," Al Gore (page 393) admits some scientists overestimated the melt rate of glaciers but asserts that "the overwhelming consensus on global warming remains unchanged."

Strategies FOR READING CAUSE AND EFFECT

When reading the cause-and-effect entries in this chapter, keep these questions in mind.

Understanding Meaning

1. Is the writer seeking to establish a cause or to measure or predict results?
2. What is the source of the evidence? A writer opposed to atomic power who cites only studies commissioned by an antinuclear group is not as credible as one who presents data collected by neutral organizations.
3. Are alternative interpretations possible? Does a rise in the number of people receiving food stamps mean an increase in poverty, or does it reflect better government assistance?

Evaluating Strategy

1. Does the writer mistake a result for a cause? A survey revealing that 90 percent of batterers in domestic violence cases are abusing alcohol might lead to a call for more treatment centers. In fact, alcohol abuse and domestic violence may both result from unemployment.
2. Does the writer assume past trends will continue into the future?
3. Does the essay rest on unproven assumptions?
4. Does the writer demonstrate skills in critical thinking?
5. Does the author use narratives or comparisons to demonstrate his or her conclusions?

Appreciating Language

1. Does the author's choice of words indicate bias?
2. How does the writer introduce technical terms? Are definitions supplied? What do the tone and style of the entry suggest about the intended audience?

JOHN TAYLOR GATTO

John Taylor Gatto (1935–) taught in New York City public schools for twenty-five years. He was named the city's Teacher of the Year three times and New York State Teacher of the Year in 1991. Gatto has published several books about public education, including *Dumbing Us Down, The Exhausted School, The Underground History of American Education: A School Teacher's Intimate Investigation into the Problem of Modern Schooling,* and *Weapons of Mass Instruction.* Since leaving teaching, Gatto has become a public speaker, addressing audiences at the White House and NASA's Goddard Space Flight Center. His writings and speeches are available on his website *www.johntaylorgatto.com.*

Why Schools Don't Educate

CONTEXT: *In this section of a speech Gatto presented after receiving an award, he outlines the effects television and schools have on children. As you read his list, consider if there could be other causes for the symptoms he describes.*

WRITER'S NOTE: *Originally delivered as a speech, Gatto's address uses numbered points and repetition to help listeners follow his train of thought.*

Two institutions at present control our children's lives—television and schooling, in that order. Both of these reduce the real world of wisdom, fortitude, temperance, and justice to a never-ending, nonstop abstraction. In centuries past, the time of a child and adolescent would be occupied in real work, real charity, real adventures, and the real search for mentors who might teach what one really wanted to learn. A great deal of time was spent in community pursuits, practicing affection, meeting and studying every level of the community, learning how to make a home, and dozens of other tasks necessary to becoming a whole man or woman. [1] *Thesis*

But here is the calculus of time the children I teach must deal with: [2]

Out of the 168 hours in each week, my children must sleep 56. That leaves them 112 hours a week out of which to fashion a self. [3]

My children watch 55 hours of television a week, according to recent reports. That leaves them 57 hours a week in which to grow up. [4] *Outside objective evidence*

My children attend school 30 hours a week; use about 8 hours getting ready, going, and coming home; and spend an average of 7 hours a week in homework—a total of 45 hours. During that time they are under constant surveillance, have no private time or private space, and are disciplined if they try to assert individuality in the use of time or space. That leaves 12 hours a week out of which to create a unique consciousness. Of course my kids eat, too, and [5] that takes some time—not much, because we've lost the tradition of family dining. If we allot 3 hours a week to evening meals we arrive at a net amount of private time for each child of 9 hours.

It's not enough. It's not enough, is it? The richer the kid, of course, the less television he watches, but the rich kid's time is just as narrowly proscribed by a broader catalogue of commercial entertainments and his inevitable assignment to a series of private lessons in areas seldom of his choice.

And these things are, oddly enough, just a more cosmetic way to create dependent human beings, unable to fill their own hours, unable to initiate lines of meaning to give substance and pleasure to their existence. It's a national disease, this dependency and aimlessness, and I think schooling and television and lessons—the entire Chautauqua idea—have a lot to do with it.

Think of the things that are killing us as a nation: drugs, brainless competition, recreational sex, the pornography of violence, gambling, alcohol, and the worst pornography of all—lives devoted to buying things—accumulation as a philosophy. All are addictions of dependent personalities and that is what our brand of schooling must inevitably produce.

I want to tell you what the effect is on children of taking all their time—time they need to grow up—and forcing them to spend it on abstractions. No reform that doesn't attack these specific pathologies will be anything more than a facade.

1. The children I teach are indifferent to the adult world. This defies the experience of thousands of years. A close study of what big people were up to was always the most exciting occupation of youth, but nobody wants to grow up these days, and who can blame them? Toys are us.

2. The children I teach have almost no curiosity, and what little they do have is transitory; they cannot concentrate for very long, even on things they choose to do. Can you see a connection between the bells ringing again and again to change classes, and this phenomenon of evanescent attention?

3. The children I teach have a poor sense of the future, of how tomorrow is inextricably linked to today. They live in a continuous present; the exact moment they are in is the boundary of their consciousness.

4. The children I teach are ahistorical; they have no sense of how the past has predestined their own present, limiting their choices, shaping their values and lives.

5. The children I teach are cruel to each other; they lack compassion for misfortune, they laugh at weakness, they have ʼtempt for people whose need for help shows too plainly.

ʼren I teach are uneasy with intimacy or candor. They
ʼal with genuine intimacy because of a lifelong habit
ʼing a secret self inside an outer personality made
ʼficial bits and pieces, of behavior borrowed from

6 question to audience

7 effects on children; school and television as causes

8 social effects

9 list of observed effects

Numbered points and repetition to organize ideas for a listening audience

television or acquired to manipulate teachers. Because they are not who they represent themselves to be, the disguise wears thin in the presence of intimacy, so intimate relationships have to be avoided.

7. <u>The children I teach are materialistic</u>, following the lead of schoolteachers who materialistically "grade" everything—and television mentors who offer everything in the world for sale.

8. <u>The children I teach are dependent, passive, and timid in the presence of new challenges.</u> This timidity is frequently masked by surface bravado or by anger or aggressiveness, but underneath is a vacuum without fortitude.

I could name a few other conditions that school reform will have to tackle if our national decline is to be arrested, but by now you will have grasped my thesis, whether you agree with it or not. <u>Either schools, television, or both have caused these pathologies. It's a simple matter of arithmetic. Between schooling and television, all the time children have is eaten up.</u> That's what has destroyed the American family; it no longer is a factor in the education of its own children.

10 restatement of thesis, cause and effect of schooling and television

Understanding Meaning

1. How, in Gatto's view, are television and schools linked in children's lives?
2. How has television affected children's views of the world?
3. Gatto states that schoolchildren are "cruel" and "passive." Can one be both cruel and passive? Can pent-up energy and stunted creativity lead children to express themselves in bursts of selfish violence?
4. Gatto observes that children are materialistic. How much of this is caused by television and how much by the values of their parents?
5. Do Gatto's observations explain why many people advocate school choice and homeschooling?
6. *Critical Thinking:* Gatto remarks that "children live in a continuous present" without a sense of past and future. Is this a natural attribute of childhood or something induced by television? Doesn't television teach children something about history, even if what it teaches is simplified and distorted?

Evaluating Strategy

1. How effective is Gatto's use of numbered steps?
2. All of Gatto's eight points open with "The children I teach …" Is this repetition suited to a speech? Does it help hammer home his ideas to a listening audience? Does it seem less effective in print?
3. What risk does a writer run in criticizing children? How might parents respond?

Appreciating Language

1. Gatto uses the word "ahistorical." How would you define this term?
2. Gatto calls "being devoted to buying things" the "worst pornography of all." Is "pornography" an effective word choice?

WRITING SUGGESTIONS

1. Write your own essay detailing the effects television has had on your generation or your children's. Do your observations match Gatto's?

2. Write a brief narrative about an elementary school experience that truly taught you something. Did it occur in the context of the traditional classroom?

3. *Collaborative Writing:* Discuss Gatto's article with a group of students. Record their observations about school reform. Select the major ideas you come up with and write a letter to the local school board suggesting ways to improve education.

STEPHEN WINZENBURG

Stephen Winzenburg is a communications professor at Grand View College in Des Moines, Iowa, where he teaches radio and television production. Winzenburg has worked as a general manager, producer, talk show host, and reporter at over a dozen radio and television stations in the Midwest and Florida. He has published articles in *Radio World, Inside Higher Ed, Advertising Age,* and *Television Quarterly.* His books include *TV's Greatest Sitcoms* (2004), *TV's Greatest Talk Shows* (2005), and *The Communications Job Search Handbook* (2011).

In the Facebook Era, Students Tell You Everything

CONTEXT: *In this* Chronicle of Higher Education *article, Winzenburg describes the effects social media has had on student discourse and their attitudes about privacy.*

WRITER'S NOTE: *As a college professor, Winzenburg presents himself as a neutral observer and uses comparison to demonstrate how social behavior has changed.*

The impact of Facebook on the college classroom goes far beyond technological innovations and the ability to build relationships. It has led young people to publicly announce intimate personal details without thought of the consequences. And that style of communication has led to some very uncomfortable encounters between students and their professors.   1

The first time it happened to me, the student's words came so quickly that I didn't have time to think about my reaction. A young woman approached me in the hall with a smile on her face, and said, "I won't be in class next week because I have to terminate a pregnancy."   2

I was dumbfounded. How could someone share something so private in a public setting with a professor she barely knew? She had been in my class for only six weeks, and we hadn't really established much of a relationship, so I had no idea how to respond. Was she looking for help? Or should I simply treat it like any other notification of an absence?   3

That incident was one of what has become a series of encounters with students who are so used to social media that they now openly share what was formerly considered private. Posting and tweeting intimate life details are now so normal for them that they think nothing of cavalierly giving too much information to surprised professors.   4

Lest any reader doubt the stories I'm about to tell, let me assure you they all happened as I describe over the past few years. The only facts I've changed are the names of the students involved.   5

Allison walked into my classroom apologizing for missing two   6
weeks of classes by saying she had been in rehab for alcoholism.
Stan's excuse, stated in front of the class, was that drugs he was
taking for a psychological disorder had caused him to oversleep.
Greg said he didn't have his assignment done because he had to
go to court after being arrested for punching a guy in a bar fight.
Carly texted me that she couldn't make it to class that day because
she was in the hospital after having a miscarriage.

A new advisee, Amy, was in tears as she asked if she could shut   7
my office door. It was her first semester, and she had always had a
bright smile on her face in the classroom. But in my office, she told
me her grades were suffering because she was having an affair with
a local married TV reporter.

Such intimate details used to be considered too embarrassing   8
to share. But with Facebook and Twitter, young people think nothing of confiding in strangers. Often the less the students know the
person they are communicating with the more willing they are to
spill. And they do it bluntly, now that they are used to summarizing
life in 140 characters.

Oversharing creates more than a few mixed feelings in the hearts   9
of academics. We know that asking students an innocent question,
making a supportive comment, or giving a comforting hug could all
be easily misconstrued. It's difficult to know how to react, especially
when students announce sensitive circumstances in the classroom.

Bill told a room full of students that he was tired every Wednes-   10
day morning because he was gambling every Tuesday night and
was probably an addict. Becky choked back tears trying to answer
a simple textbook question and then apologized, saying her boyfriend had just broken off their engagement a few hours earlier.
Normally chipper Elliot told the class he was depressed because
of struggles with his live-in boyfriend. One of my student-radio
DJ's got on the air and announced that over vacation he had received psychiatric treatment for his bipolar disorder, detailing how
he needed help after attacking a female shopper at a store where
he was the assistant manager!

Even personal hygiene has become classroom fodder. Kurt an-   11
nounced at the start of one period that he might miss the next
meeting because he was seeing a doctor about a blocked bowel.
Jacob and Carol were platonic roommates but complained in my
class about each other's gross bathroom habits.

It has become normal to hear students proclaim that they have   12
no interest in ever having children, but one senior added that he
planned to get a vasectomy as a graduation gift. I even had a student confess that he paid a prostitute to help him get his mind off
being stressed about midterm assignments.

Most surprising are the athletes who publicly brag about break-   13
ing rules that could cause them to lose eligibility for their scholarships. An underage football player complained as I handed him a
test that he had been up all night getting drunk with teammates.

A runner said that he was unable to complete an assignment after winning a meet and spending the night drinking in celebration.

The most baffling aspect for a faculty member to adjust to is that the same young people who now tell you everything have conversely become much more sensitive about what *you* say to them. An instructor may make an innocent comment, often in response to what is perceived to be open communication, only to have the student take offense.

14

A young woman who spent her entire final semester telling my class about her forthcoming marriage suddenly froze when I asked her one day how the wedding plans were going. I didn't know that her fiancé had recently called it off, and she burst into tears in front of the class. She had changed her status on Facebook and posted numerous public messages about it.

15

In another course, during the first-day icebreakers, students randomly picked out questions from a bowl about things like their hometowns or favorite restaurants. One student, whom I knew from his constant talking in other courses, refused to answer when his turn came and he was asked how many kids he wanted. He said that question was "too personal." Normally gregarious students may turn silent when asked about things that used to be considered innocuous, like family background or colleges they previously attended.

16

One guy who openly talked nonstop about his 2-year-old boy got upset one day before class when I asked how the child was. He gave me a serious look and said, "Don't ever mention my son again." I was stunned and apologized to the student afterward, at which time he revealed he was in a new custody battle with the boy's mother after she moved out of town.

17

I've learned that while Twitter-addicted young adults usually have no problem sharing too much information with strangers, it has to be at their own initiative. They think nothing of sending out personal messages that would make many of us blush but then turn around to perceive seemingly innocuous questions or comments from faculty members as "judgmental" or "disrespectful."

18

In this Facebook age, young people expect everyone to be a "friend" who is willing to accept whatever they "post." As a natural reactor who likes to respond to what students say, I have learned it is important to hold my tongue and show no expression during their startling revelations. I may want to drop my jaw and scream "Why are you telling this to strangers?" but I must remain neutral and act like whatever they say is totally normal.

19

That's how I responded after a student submitted a video assignment on his flash drive because he had difficulties getting it to me online. He just handed me the drive to use for grading his project, but when I later inserted it into my laptop there were no titles on the numbered files. So I clicked on the first file.

20

The dark, grainy footage showed the head of a girl performing fellatio on my student in the front seat of a car. That obviously wasn't the class project.

21

I opened a second file, and they were both naked. I eventually 22
located the correct video to grade but was amazed that he gave
me a drive with such intimate material. When I handed the flash
drive back to him at the start of the next class period, I didn't make
a comment and kept my facial expression neutral. I had learned
that no matter what students share in this Facebook era, sometimes it's wisest not to comment on their status.

Understanding Meaning

1. How, in Winzenburg's view, have social media changed young people's attitudes about privacy and intimacy?
2. Why do students who share so much private information resent questions or comments about their private lives from adults?
3. Winzenburg notes instances of students admitting to activities that violate school rules or laws. What dilemma does this present to instructors and other authorities?
4. Do Winzenburg's observations show a generational difference in social attitudes and behavior? Is this an ongoing process? Were college students in the 1960s more open about their personal lives than students in the 1940s?
5. Do Winzenburg's reactions reveal aspects of his perceptual world and his values? Might other instructors respond differently, even positively, to students speaking openly about personal matters?
6. *Critical Thinking*: Winzenburg implies that "oversharing" is caused by social media. Have there been other cultural influences? Have television programs like *Oprah* and *Dr. Phil* encouraged people to be open about their lives? Is there a difference between privacy and discretion or shame and repression? Have young people been encouraged to admit rather than hide personal issues?

Evaluating Strategy

1. What evidence does Winzenburg present to support his thesis?
2. What role does Winzenburg play in the article? Why is it important for a writer providing personal observations to remain neutral?
3. In paragraph 5 Winzenburg assures readers that the incidents he relates are true. Is this an important declaration for writers to make? What impact does it have?
4. *Critical Thinking*: This article appeared in *The Chronicle of Higher Education*, which is largely read by college instructors and administrators. How does this influence Winzenburg's approach? Would his article be written differently if directed to students or parents? Why or why not?

Appreciating Language

1. How do young people, in Winzenburg's view, now define friends?
2. How would you characterize Winzenburg's tone? How do word choices support his thesis?

WRITING SUGGESTIONS

1. Write an essay describing the way you think social media has affected social behavior. Are there benefits to people being able to link electronically with others? Have some people exposed themselves to risks by sharing too much personal information online? Have texting and phone calls diminished or increased intimacy? Have people lost the ability to sustain long, complex conversations? Does digital media divide our attention? Have you observed people talking and texting at the same time?

2. *Collaborative Writing:* Discuss Winzenburg's article with a group of students and develop an essay outlining what your group considers appropriate discourse for college classrooms. What topics or personal revelations should be restricted to conversations with family and friends? What problems can students encounter later in their careers if they habitually "overshare" personal details?

AL GORE

Al Gore (1948–) was born in Washington, DC, and graduated from Harvard University in 1969. After serving in Vietnam in the US Army, Gore enrolled in Vanderbilt University's divinity school and later attended law school. In 1976 Gore left the university to run for Congress at the age of twenty-eight. He served in the House of Representatives from 1977 to 1985 and the United States Senate from 1985 to 1993, when he was elected vice-president. In 2000 he was the Democratic presidential candidate, losing to George Bush after a protracted recount. Since 2000 Gore has focused on environmental issues. His 2006 documentary film about climate change *An Inconvenient Truth* received an Academy Award. In 2007 he shared a Nobel Peace Prize for his environmental work.

We Can't Wish Away Climate Change

CONTEXT: *In this 2010* New York Times *article, Gore explains the causes and effects of climate change.*

WRITER'S NOTE: *Gore responds to critics of global warming in paragraph 5, admitting that some scientists had published flawed data about Himalayan glacier melt.*

It would be an enormous relief if the recent attacks on the science 1 of global warming actually indicated that we do not face an un-imaginable calamity requiring large-scale, preventive measures to protect human civilization as we know it.

Of course, we would still need to deal with the national security 2 risks of our growing dependence on a global oil market dominated by dwindling reserves in the most unstable region of the world, and the economic risks of sending hundreds of billions of dollars a year overseas in return for that oil. And we would still trail China in the race to develop smart grids, fast trains, solar power, wind, geothermal and other renewable sources of energy—the most important sources of new jobs in the 21st century.

But what a burden would be lifted! We would no longer have 3 to worry that our grandchildren would one day look back on us as a criminal generation that had selfishly and blithely ignored clear warnings that their fate was in our hands. We could instead celebrate the naysayers who had doggedly persisted in proving that every major National Academy of Sciences report on climate change had simply made a huge mistake.

I, for one, genuinely wish that the climate crisis were an illusion. 4 But unfortunately, the reality of the danger we are courting has not been changed by the discovery of at least two mistakes in the thousands of pages of careful scientific work over the last 22 years by the Intergovernmental Panel on Climate Change. In fact, the crisis is still growing because we are continuing to dump 90 million tons of global-warming pollution every 24 hours into the atmosphere—as if it were an open sewer.

It is true that the climate panel published a flawed overestimate 5 of the melting rate of debris-covered glaciers in the Himalayas, and used information about the Netherlands provided to it by the government, which was later found to be partly inaccurate. In addition, e-mail messages stolen from the University of East Anglia in Britain showed that scientists besieged by an onslaught of hostile, make-work demands from climate skeptics may not have adequately followed the requirements of the British freedom of information law.

But the scientific enterprise will never be completely free of mis- 6 takes. What is important is that the overwhelming consensus on global warming remains unchanged. It is also worth noting that the panel's scientists—acting in good faith on the best information then available to them—probably underestimated the range of sea-level rise in this century, the speed with which the Arctic ice cap is disappearing and the speed with which some of the large glacial flows in Antarctica and Greenland are melting and racing to the sea.

Because these and other effects of global warming are distrib- 7 uted globally, they are difficult to identify and interpret in any particular location. For example, January was seen as unusually cold in much of the United States. Yet from a global perspective, it was the second-hottest January since surface temperatures were first measured 130 years ago.

Similarly, even though climate deniers have speciously argued 8 for several years that there has been no warming in the last decade, scientists confirmed last month that the last 10 years were the hottest decade since modern records have been kept.

The heavy snowfalls this month have been used as fodder for 9 ridicule by those who argue that global warming is a myth, yet scientists have long pointed out that warmer global temperatures have been increasing the rate of evaporation from the oceans, putting significantly more moisture into the atmosphere—thus causing heavier downfalls of both rain and snow in particular regions, including the Northeastern United States. Just as it's important not to miss the forest for the trees, neither should we miss the climate for the snowstorm.

Here is what scientists have found is happening to our climate: 10 man-made global-warming pollution traps heat from the sun and increases atmospheric temperatures. These pollutants—especially carbon dioxide—have been increasing rapidly with the growth in the burning of coal, oil, natural gas and forests, and temperatures have increased over the same period. Almost all of the ice-covered regions of the Earth are melting—and seas are rising. Hurricanes are predicted to grow stronger and more destructive, though their number is expected to decrease. Droughts are getting longer and deeper in many mid-continent regions, even as the severity of flooding increases. The seasonal predictability of rainfall and temperatures is being disrupted, posing serious threats to agriculture. The rate of species extinction is accelerating to dangerous levels.

Though there have been impressive efforts by many business 11 leaders, hundreds of millions of individuals and families throughout the world and many national, regional and local governments, our civilization is still failing miserably to slow the rate at which these emissions are increasing—much less reduce them.

And in spite of President Obama's efforts at the Copenhagen 12 climate summit meeting in December, global leaders failed to muster anything more than a decision to "take note" of an intention to act.

Because the world still relies on leadership from the United 13 States, the failure by the Senate to pass legislation intended to cap American emissions before the Copenhagen meeting guaranteed that the outcome would fall far short of even the minimum needed to build momentum toward a meaningful solution.

The political paralysis that is now so painfully evident in Wash- 14 ington has thus far prevented action by the Senate—not only on climate and energy legislation, but also on health care reform, financial regulatory reform and a host of other pressing issues.

This comes with painful costs. China, now the world's largest and 15 fastest-growing source of global-warming pollution, had privately signaled early last year that if the United States passed meaningful legislation, it would join in serious efforts to produce an effective treaty. When the Senate failed to follow the lead of the House of Representatives, forcing the president to go to Copenhagen without a new law in hand, the Chinese balked. With the two largest polluters refusing to act, the world community was paralyzed.

Some analysts attribute the failure to an inherent flaw in the 16 design of the chosen solution—arguing that a cap-and-trade approach is too unwieldy and difficult to put in place. Moreover, these critics add, the financial crisis that began in 2008 shook the world's confidence in the use of any market-based solution.

But there are two big problems with this critique: First, there is 17 no readily apparent alternative that would be any easier politically. It is difficult to imagine a globally harmonized carbon tax or a coordinated multilateral regulatory effort. The flexibility of a global market-based policy—supplemented by regulation and revenue-neutral tax policies—is the option that has by far the best chance of success. The fact that it is extremely difficult does not mean that we should simply give up.

Second, we should have no illusions about the difficulty and the 18 time needed to convince the rest of the world to adopt a completely new approach. The lags in the global climate system, including the buildup of heat in the oceans from which it is slowly reintroduced into the atmosphere, means that we can create conditions that make large and destructive consequences inevitable long before their awful manifestations become apparent: the displacement of hundreds of millions of climate refugees, civil unrest, chaos and the collapse of governance in many developing countries, large-scale crop failures and the spread of deadly diseases.

It's important to point out that the United States is not alone in its inaction. Global political paralysis has thus far stymied work not only on climate, but on trade and other pressing issues that require coordinated international action. 19

The reasons for this are primarily economic. The globalization of the economy, coupled with the outsourcing of jobs from industrial countries, has simultaneously heightened fears of further job losses in the industrial world and encouraged rising expectations in emerging economies. The result? Heightened opposition, in both the industrial and developing worlds, to any constraints on the use of carbon-based fuels, which remain our principal source of energy. 20

The decisive victory of democratic capitalism over communism in the 1990s led to a period of philosophical dominance for market economics worldwide and the illusion of a unipolar world. It also led, in the United States, to a hubristic "bubble" of market fundamentalism that encouraged opponents of regulatory constraints to mount an aggressive effort to shift the internal boundary between the democracy sphere and the market sphere. Over time, markets would most efficiently solve most problems, they argued. Laws and regulations interfering with the operations of the market carried a faint odor of the discredited statist adversary we had just defeated. 21

This period of market triumphalism coincided with confirmation by scientists that earlier fears about global warming had been grossly understated. But by then, the political context in which this debate took form was tilted heavily toward the views of market fundamentalists, who fought to weaken existing constraints and scoffed at the possibility that global constraints would be needed to halt the dangerous dumping of global-warming pollution into the atmosphere. 22

Over the years, as the science has become clearer and clearer, some industries and companies whose business plans are dependent on unrestrained pollution of the atmospheric commons have become ever more entrenched. They are ferociously fighting against the mildest regulation—just as tobacco companies blocked constraints on the marketing of cigarettes for four decades after science confirmed the link of cigarettes to diseases of the lung and the heart. 23

Simultaneously, changes in America's political system—including the replacement of newspapers and magazines by television as the dominant medium of communication—conferred powerful advantages on wealthy advocates of unrestrained markets and weakened advocates of legal and regulatory reforms. Some news media organizations now present showmen masquerading as political thinkers who package hatred and divisiveness as entertainment. And as in times past, that has proved to be a potent drug in the veins of the body politic. Their most consistent theme is to 24 label as "socialist" any proposal to reform exploitive behavior in the marketplace.

From the standpoint of governance, what is at stake is our ability 25 to use the rule of law as an instrument of human redemption. After all has been said and so little done, the truth about the climate crisis—inconvenient as ever—must still be faced.

The pathway to success is still open, though it tracks the outer 26 boundary of what we are capable of doing. It begins with a choice by the United States to pass a law establishing a cost for global warming pollution. The House of Representatives has already passed legislation, with some Republican support, to take the first halting steps for pricing greenhouse gas emissions.

Later this week, Senators John Kerry, Lindsey Graham and Joe 27 Lieberman are expected to present for consideration similar cap-and-trade legislation. I hope that it will place a true cap on carbon emissions and stimulate the rapid development of low-carbon sources of energy.

We have overcome existential threats before. Winston Churchill 28 is widely quoted as having said, "Sometimes doing your best is not good enough. Sometimes, you must do what is required." Now is that time. Public officials must rise to this challenge by doing what is required; and the public must demand that they do so—or must replace them.

Understanding Meaning

1. What causes climate change? What are its effects?
2. Why are the effects of global warming unevenly distributed?
3. Why does the United States play an important role in the world's response to climate change?
4. How have the media, in Gore's view, affected the way climate change is debated?
5. Why does Gore believe that the "cap and trade" approach is currently the best solution for climate change? What do critics, in his view, overlook?
6. *Critical Thinking:* What conflicts do the United States and other nations face in addressing climate change? Do policies limiting carbon emissions require nations to reduce their use of energy and curtail industrial activity? Can nations counter climate change without lowering their standard of living, increasing unemployment, and inflating energy prices?

Evaluating Strategy

1. Gore admits scientists made errors but insists the overwhelming body of evidence indicates climate change is occurring. Why is acknowledging errors important? Can it strengthen or weaken a writer's position?
2. What evidence does Gore include to support his point of view?
3. In the opening paragraphs Gore wishes the climate crisis were an illusion. Why is this important? Do advocates of a cause sometimes raise suspicions that they invent or exaggerate problems for their own ambitions or profit?

Appreciating Language

1. Gore wrote this article for a general newspaper audience. Does he use any scientific terms that require definition or further explanation?

2. What does Gore mean by "market triumphalism"?

3. Use "global warming" and "climate change" as Internet search terms and examine the results. Do you see a difference? Is one more scientifically accurate? Does "climate change" have a different political connotation than "global warming"?

4. *Critical Thinking*: Why is it important for advocates of a cause to establish the correct tone? Can a writer dramatize an issue without appearing to be an alarmist?

WRITING SUGGESTIONS

1. Using Gore's article as a model, write an essay that explains the causes and effects of another issue—the rising cost of health insurance, the national debt, cyberbullying, identity theft, sexual harassment, addictions, divorce, student loan debt, or single parenthood.

2. *Collaborative Writing:* Discuss Gore's article with a group of students and write an essay detailing the causes and effects of the political debate about climate change. Has the issue become so politicized that it has become an ideological rather than a scientific issue?

BRENT STAPLES

Brent Staples (1951–) was born in Chester, Pennsylvania, and graduated from Widener University in 1973. He received a doctorate in psychology from the University of Chicago in 1982. After writing for several Chicago publications, he joined the *New York Times* in 1985 and became a member of its editorial board in 1990. He has also contributed articles to *Ms.* and *Harper's*. In 1994 he published a memoir, *Parallel Time: Growing Up in Black and White*, recalling a childhood of poverty and violence.

Black Men and Public Space

CONTEXT: *In this* Harper's *article Staples recounts the effects he has had on white pedestrians. As a black male, he realized he had the power to cause fellow citizens to alter their behavior by simply walking in their direction.*

WRITER'S NOTE: *Staples uses the word "victim" in the opening sentence to provoke interest and invoke the stereotype of the predatory black male he is writing about.*

1   My first victim was a woman—white, well dressed, probably in her early twenties. I came upon her late one evening on a deserted street in Hyde Park, a relatively affluent neighborhood in an otherwise mean, impoverished section of Chicago. As I swung onto the avenue behind her, there seemed to be a discreet, uninflammatory distance between us. Not so. She cast back a worried glance. To her, the youngish black man—a broad 6 feet 2 inches with a beard and billowing hair, both hands shoved into the pockets of a bulky military jacket—seemed menacingly close. After a few more quick glimpses, she picked up her pace and was soon running in earnest.

2   Within seconds she disappeared into a cross street.

3   That was more than a decade ago. I was 22 years old, a graduate student newly arrived at the University of Chicago. It was in the echo of that terrified woman's footfalls that I first began to know the unwieldy inheritance I'd come into—the ability to alter public space in ugly ways. It was clear that she thought herself the quarry of a mugger, a rapist, or worse. Suffering a bout of insomnia, however, I was stalking sleep, not defenseless wayfarers. As a softy who is scarcely able to take a knife to a raw chicken—let alone hold one to a person's throat—I was surprised, embarrassed, and dismayed all at once. Her flight made me feel like an accomplice in tyranny. It also made it clear that I was indistinguishable from the muggers who occasionally seeped into the area from the surrounding ghetto. That first encounter, and those that followed, signified that a vast, unnerving gulf lay between nighttime pedestrians—particularly women—and me. And I soon gathered that being perceived as dangerous is a hazard in itself. I only needed to turn a corner into a

dicey situation, or crowd some frightened, armed person in a foyer somewhere, or make an errant move after being pulled over by a policeman. Where fear and weapons meet—and they often do in urban America—there is always the possibility of death.

In that first year, my first away from my hometown, I was to be- 4 come thoroughly familiar with the language of fear. At dark, shadowy intersections, I could cross in front of a car stopped at a traffic light and elicit the *thunk, thunk, thunk, thunk* of the driver—black, white, male, or female—hammering down the door locks. On less traveled streets after dark, I grew accustomed to but never comfortable with people crossing to the other side of the street rather than pass me. Then there were the standard unpleasantries with policemen, door-men, bouncers, cabdrivers, and others whose business it is to screen out troublesome individuals *before* there is any nastiness.

I moved to New York nearly two years ago and I have remained 5 an avid night walker. In central Manhattan, the near-constant crowd cover minimizes tense one-on-one street encounters. Elsewhere— in SoHo, for example, where sidewalks are narrow and tightly spaced buildings shut out the sky—things can get very taut indeed.

After dark, on the warrenlike streets of Brooklyn where I live, I 6 often see women who fear the worst from me. They seem to have set their faces on neutral, and with their purse straps strung across their chests bandolier-style, they forge ahead as though bracing themselves against being tackled. I understand, of course, that the danger they perceive is not a hallucination. Women are particularly vulnerable to street violence, and young black males are drasti-cally overrepresented among the perpetrators of that violence. Yet these truths are no solace against the kind of alienation that comes of being ever the suspect, a fearsome entity with whom pedestrians avoid making eye contact.

It is not altogether clear to me how I reached the ripe old age of 7 22 without being conscious of the lethality nighttime pedestrians attributed to me. Perhaps it was because in Chester, Pennsylvania, the small, angry industrial town where I came of age in the 1960s, I was scarcely noticeable against a backdrop of gang warfare, street knifings, and murders. I grew up one of the good boys, had per-haps a half-dozen fistfights. In retrospect, my shyness of combat has clear sources.

As a boy, I saw countless tough guys locked away; I have since 8 buried several, too. They were babies, really—a teenage cousin, a brother of 22, a childhood friend in his mid-twenties—all gone down in episodes of bravado played out in the streets. I came to doubt the virtues of intimidation early on. I chose, perhaps uncon-sciously, to remain a shadow—timid, but a survivor.

The fearsomeness mistakenly attributed to me in public places 9 often has a perilous flavor. The most frightening of these confu-sions occurred in the late 1970s and early 1980s, when I worked as a journalist in Chicago. One day, rushing into the office of a maga-zine I was writing for with a deadline story in hand, I was mistaken for a burglar. The office manager called security and, with an ad hoc posse, pursued me through the labyrinthine halls, nearly to my editor's door. I had no way of proving who I was. I could only move briskly toward the company of someone who knew me.

Another time I was on assignment for a local paper and killing 10 time before an interview. I entered a jewelry store on the city's affluent Near North Side. The proprietor excused herself and returned with an enormous red Doberman pinscher straining at the end of a leash. She stood, the dog extended toward me, silent to my questions, her eyes bulging nearly out of her head. I took a cursory look around, nodded, and bade her good night.

Relatively speaking, however, I never fared as badly as another 11 black male journalist. He went to nearby Waukegan, Illinois, a couple of summers ago to work on a story about a murderer who was born there. Mistaking the reporter for the killer, police officers hauled him from his car at gunpoint and but for his press credentials would probably have tried to book him. Such episodes are not uncommon. Black men trade tales like this all the time.

Over the years, I learned to smother the rage I felt at so often 12 being taken for a criminal. Not to do so would surely have led to madness. I now take precautions to make myself less threatening. I move about with care, particularly late in the evening. I give a wide berth to nervous people on subway platforms during the wee hours, particularly when I have exchanged business clothes for jeans. If I happen to be entering a building behind some people who appear skittish, I may walk by, letting them clear the lobby before I return, so as not to seem to be following them. I have been calm and extremely congenial on those rare occasions when I've been pulled over by the police.

And on late-evening constitutionals I employ what has proved to 13 be an excellent tension-reducing measure: I whistle melodies from Beethoven and Vivaldi and the more popular classical composers. Even steely New Yorkers hunching toward nighttime destinations seem to relax, and occasionally they even join in the tune. Virtually everybody seems to sense that a mugger wouldn't be warbling bright, sunny selections from Vivaldi's *Four Seasons*. It is my equivalent of the cowbell that hikers wear when they know they are in bear country.

Understanding Meaning

1. What is Staples's thesis? What is he saying about race, class, crime, prejudice, and fear in our society?

2. What is Staples's attitude toward the way women responded to his presence? What caused their reactions?

3. Staples reports that both African American and white drivers locked their doors when they encountered him. What is he saying about racial perceptions and fear?

4. How do you interpret the conclusion? Why would people be reassured by a black man whistling classical music? What does this say about prejudice, racial profiling, and stereotyping? What else would make a black man appear less threatening—singing spirituals, carrying the *Wall Street Journal*, walking a poodle? Why?

5. *Critical Thinking:* Would a white man walking through an African American neighborhood produce similar results? Would residents respond differently than if he were black? Would a Hispanic, an Asian, an orthodox Jew produce similar or different results?

Evaluating Strategy

1. What is the impact of the first sentence?

2. Staples shifts the chronology several times. How does he prevent readers from becoming confused? How important are transitional statements and paragraph breaks to maintaining a coherent essay?

3. *Blending the Modes:* How does Staples use *narration* and *comparison* in developing his essay?

Appreciating Language

1. Staples avoids using words such as "racist," "prejudice," and "stereotype" in his essay. Do words like these tend to be inflammatory and politically charged? Would they detract from his message?

2. What does the tone and style of the essay suggest about the response Staples hoped to achieve from his readers? Do you sense he was trying to reach white or African American readers?

WRITING SUGGESTIONS

1. Write an essay narrating your own experiences in public space. You can explore how you cause others to react to your presence or how location affects your behavior. What happens when you cross the campus late at night, drive alone, or enter a high-crime neighborhood? Would the police and public see you as a likely victim or a probable perpetrator?

2. *Collaborative Writing:* Discuss this essay with a group of students. Consider if a white man in shabby clothing or a black man in a business suit would provoke the same or different responses in white pedestrians. Is class or race the defining factor in producing fear? Is age an issue? Has the public been influenced to see young black men as threatening? Would a middle-aged black man provoke different reactions? Why or why not? Develop an outline for a sociological experiment that measures people's reaction to a variety of test figures engaged in the same actions. Write a process paper explaining how your group might conduct the experiment and evaluate the results.

Blending the Modes
ALEXANDER STILLE

Alexander Stille (1957–) was born in New York City and gradu-
ated from Yale University and the Columbia University Graduate
School of Journalism. He has published articles for the *Boston
Globe*, the *New York Review of Books*, the *New York Times*, and
the *New Yorker*. His books include *Benevolence and Betrayal: Five
Italian Jewish Families Under Fascism* (1992); *Excellent Cadavers:
The Mafia and the Death of the First Italian Republic* (1995); and
The Future of the Past (2005). Stille currently teaches journalism at
Columbia University.

Are We Losing Our Memory?

CONTEXT: *In this passage from* The Future of the Past, *Stille explains the causes and effects of a great irony of the information
age. The twentieth century was the most recorded era in history,
yet many of its words and images were stored on obsolete devices
that make material harder to access and more prone to decay.
While newspapers from the Civil War remain readable, videotapes
from the Vietnam War are deteriorating.*

WRITER'S NOTE: *Stille uses* comparison, process, definition, *and*
classification *to develop his essay. In addition, he uses direct quotations from an expert to provide a conversational tone, introduce
evidence, and organize details.*

In a temperature-controlled laboratory in the bowels of the vast   1
new National Archives building outside Washington—nearly two
million square feet of futuristic steel and glass construction—an
engineer cranks up an old Thomas A. Edison phonograph. A cylin-
drical disc begins to turn and from its large wooden horn we suddenly hear the scratchy oompah-pah of a marching band striking
up a tune at a Knights of Columbus parade in July of 1902.

Nearby sits an ancestor of the modern reel-to-reel tape recorder;   2
it's the very machine that recorded President Harry Truman's famous whistle-stop speeches as he traveled the country by train
during his legendary come-from-behind victory in the election of
1948. Instead of capturing sound on magnetic tape, the device
stored its data on coils of thin steel wire as fine as fishline. Now
some of the wire has rusted, and it occasionally snaps when it is
played back through the machine.

This laboratory, in the Department of Special Media Preservation,   3
is a kind of museum of obsolete technology where Archives technicians try to tease information out of modern media that have
long vanished from circulation. But the laboratory is more than a

curious rag-and-bone shop of technologies past; in many ways, it offers a cautionary vision of the future. The problem of technological obsolescence—of fading words and images locked in odd-looking, out-of-date gizmos—is an even bigger problem for the computer age than for the new media produced in the first half of the 20th century.

One of the great ironies of the information age is that, while the late twentieth century will undoubtedly have recorded more data than any other period in history, it will also almost certainly have lost more information than any previous era. A study done in 1996 by the Archives concluded that, at current levels, it would take approximately 120 years to transfer the backlog of nontextual material (photographs, videos, film, audiotapes, and microfilm) to a more stable format. "And in quite a few cases, we're talking about media that are expected to last about 20 years," said Charles Mayn, the head of the laboratory. Decisions about what to keep and what to discard will be made by default, as large portions will simply deteriorate beyond the point of viability.

Mayn is a tall, thin man with gray hair, a soft-spoken, gentle manner, and the neat, understated, conservative dress of a computer engineer of the 1950s—the time of his youth. A self-described "science weenie," he is more comfortable fiddling with the interior of a machine than talking about himself. He plays down his own considerable ingenuity in rebuilding or reinventing many of these machines, rigging up pieces of the original items with modern parts in order to get them to play back intelligible sounds and images. His particular laboratory is dedicated to "dynamic media"—things with moving parts such as audio and visual players. In his spare time, Mayn has been known to scour junk shops and yard sales in the Washington area, looking for old castaway Dictabelts or movie projectors that have been consigned to the dustbin of history.

A short distance down the laboratory workbench from the Edison phonograph are some 18-inch glass discs, precursors of the long-playing vinyl record—rapidly becoming a relic itself. The U.S. Army used the disks to record enemy broadcasts throughout World War II. They play on a machine called the Memovox, which has a turntable that changes speed as the record plays, slowing down to compensate for the quicker rotation of the disc as the stylus approaches the center, so that the needle always moves at a constant speed in relation to the groove in which it sits. It was an ingenious invention, but it didn't catch on, perhaps because it required rather complex internal machinery. A glass disk—marked "Germany, October 24, 1941, 11:55 p.m."—lies shattered on its turntable. "Luckily, the glass generally breaks in fairly clean pieces so we are often able to put them back together," Mayn explained. The Archives possesses some 70,000 of these foot-and-a-half military recordings, each of which has a playing time of about two hours. It would take a researcher who worked without interruption for eight hours a day approximately 48 years to listen to this collection in its entirety. "A lot of them may contain a lot of nothing, airwave noise, shortwave whistles, but you may have to listen to the whole thing to figure that out," Mayn said.

On the wall are the internal organs of a film projector from 7 the 1930s; the old heads have been mounted to play together with modern reels. "Twenty-eight different kinds of movie soundtracking systems were devised during the 1930s and 1940s, trying to improve the quality of sound tracks," Mayn explained. "Most of them are unique and incompatible." This particular one used something called "push-pull" technology, in which the sound signal was split onto two different tracks. The technology was meant to cancel out noise distortion, but the two tracks must play in near-perfect synchrony. "If it is played back properly, it is better than a standard optical track, but if it is played back even a little bit improperly, it is far, far worse," Mayn said. In the mid-1980s at a theater in downtown Washington, he was able to actually use this reconfigured projector to show several reels of push-pull film containing the trials of top Nazi leaders at Nuremberg. And the lab has transferred some 1800 reels of push-pull tape onto new negatives.

Potentially, the computer age appears to offer the historian's 8 Holy Grail of infinite memory and of instant, permanent access to virtually limitless amounts of information. But as the pace of technological change increases, so does the speed at which each new generation of equipment supplants the last. "Right now, the half-life of most computer technology is between three and five years," said Steve Puglia, a preservation and imaging specialist whose laboratory is just down the hall from Mayn's. In the 1980s, the Archives stored 250,000 documents and images on optical disks—the cutting edge of new technology at the time. "I'm not sure we can play them," said Puglia, explaining that they depend on computer software and hardware that is no longer on the market.

In fact, there appears to be a direct relationship between the 9 newness of technology and its fragility. A librarian at Yale University, Paul Conway, has created a graph going back to ancient Mesopotamia that shows that while the quantity of information being saved has increased exponentially, the durability of media has decreased almost as dramatically. The clay tablets that record the laws of ancient Sumer are still on display in museums around the world. Many medieval illuminated manuscripts written on animal parchment still look as if they were painted and copied yesterday. Paper correspondence from the Renaissance is faded by still in good condition while books printed on modern acidic paper are already turning to dust. Black-and-white photographs may last a couple of centuries, while most color photographs become unstable within 30 or 40 years. Videotapes deteriorate much more quickly than does traditional movie film—generally lasting about 20 years. And the latest generation of digital storage tape is considered safe for about ten years, after which it should be copied to avoid loss of data.

Digital technology—based on incredibly precise mathematical 10 coding—either works perfectly or doesn't work at all. "If you go beyond the limits of the error rate, the screen goes black and the audio goes to nothing," Mayn said, "and up to that point, you don't realize there are any errors. Analog technology"—used in vinyl records or electromagnetic tapes—"deteriorates more gracefully. The old wax cylinders of the original Edison phonograph sound faded and scratchy, but that are still audible." Mayn picked up some tiny plastic digital audiotapes that fit neatly in the palm of his hands. "People love these things because they are so small, compact, and lightweight and store tons of data, but as they put larger and larger amounts of data on smaller and smaller spaces, the technology gets more precise, more complex, and more fragile." He bends the little data tape in his hand. "We have a lot of these from the late 1980s and even the mid-1990s that can't be played at all."

The National Archives and Records Agency (NARA) was created 11 during the 1930s on the optimistic premise that the government could keep all of its most vital records indefinitely, acting as our nation's collective memory. Now, as it drowns in data and chokes on paper, the agency is facing the stark realization that it may not be able to preserve what it already has, let alone keep up with the seemingly limitless flow of information coming its way.

The numbers are so huge as to be almost comical. The Archives 12 is currently custodian to four billion pieces of paper, 9.4 million photographs, 338,029 films and videos, 2,648,918 maps and charts, nearly three million architectural and engineering plans, and more than nine million aerial photographs. Storage consumes nearly half its budget so, ironically, the more information it keeps the less money it has to spend on making it available to the public. Because other government agencies are generally not required to hand over their records for permanent storage for some 30 years, the Archives is only just beginning to grapple with the extraordinary explosion of information over the last generation.

Space has been a problem at the National Archives from be- 13 fore it opened on November 8, 1935 in a grand neoclassical structure on Pennsylvania Avenue, down the street from the White House. That building was supposed to have a handsome internal courtyard, but the nation's first archivist had the space filled in for more stacks. These, too, quickly proved inadequate, so the high-ceilinged floors were chopped in half, creating 21 short floors of stacks. An archivist much over six feet tall would risk a concussion navigating this rabbit warren of seemingly identical corridors and shelves. Here you can see the information explosion in tangible terms. Six rows of shelves on a single floor hold all of the documents generated by the U.S. Supreme Court in its first 140 years of life, while it takes the rest of the floor, the equivalent of about half a city block, to house the papers from the last 60 years. One term of the Supreme Court now generates as much paper as 40 years did in the early 19th century.

With nowhere left to store all the paper, the Archives built new 14
headquarters in College Park, Maryland, which opened in 1994.
Although the third-largest government building and about half the
size of the Pentagon, Archives II is already approaching its storage
capacity. Despite predictions some 20 years ago about the paper-
less office, most government agencies are still printing out their
computer files and producing more paper than ever. Each year, on
average, the Archives receives about 1.5 million cubic feet of new
records, of which about one-third are kept for storage.

In theory, computer technology should be more helpful with 15
the storage of textual documents than with the audio and video
records of Mayn's dynamic media lab. But so far, it has only compounded the problem. In 1989, a public interest group trying to
get information about the Iran-Contra scandal successfully sued
the White House to prevent it from destroying any electronic records. The result is that all federal agencies must now preserve
all their computer files and electronic mail. Because government
offices use different kinds of computers, software programs, and
formats, just recovering this material has proved to be a logistical
nightmare. It took the National Archives two and a half years (and
its entire electronic records staff) just to make a secure copy of all
the electronic records of the Reagan White House. And it may take
years more to make most of them intelligible. "They are gibberish
as they currently stand," said Fynette Eaton, who worked at the
Archives' Center of Electronic Records before moving over to the
Smithsonian Institution.

The beauty of digital technology is that it reduces everything to 16
a series of zeroes and ones—a simple, seemingly universal mathematical language—but unless one has the software that gives
meaning to those zeroes and ones, the data is meaningless. The
problem of deciphering Egyptian hieroglyphs may look like child's
play compared with recovering all the information on the hundreds
of major software programs that have been discarded during the
astonishing transformations of the computer revolution.

The losses from the first decades of the digital age are likely 17
to be considerable. The federal government, with its multitude of
departments, agencies, and offices, is a dense thicket of incompatible computer languages and formats—many of them old and
obsolete. Many of the records of the National Military Command
Center are stored in a database management system (known as
NIPS) that IBM no longer supports and that the National Archives
has difficulty translating into readable form. The Agent Orange
Task Force has been unable to use herbicide records written in
NIPS format.

For several years a disturbing rumor circulated that the data from 18
the United States Census of 1960 had been lost. According to the
story, the information lies locked on obsolete 36-year-old computer
tapes that can no longer be read by today's machines. The Archives
continues to reassure the public that the material has been safely

copied to more modern media, but because census data must be kept private until 72 years after its collection, the rumor will probably persist until independent researches can view the material for themselves in the year 2032. Meanwhile, later census surveys are still at risk. "Bureau of Census files prior to 1989 threaten to eclipse the NIPS problem," the Archives reported to Congress a few years go. "The Bureau reported to us…that they have over 4000 reels of tape, containing permanently valuable data, which are difficult, if not impossible to use because they are in CENIO (Census Input/Output) format or because the files have been compressed on an ad hoc basis." Each computer tape can store 75,000 pages of information so that, if the data cannot be recovered, the Census Bureau might lose up to 300 million pages of data.

Because of the problems posed by reconstructing obsolete 19
hardware and software, the Archives issued an order that government agencies were free to print out their email onto paper for permanent storage. The Archives may be faced either with mountains of computer data it cannot interpret or an avalanche of paper of unprecedented volume. But Scott Armstrong, a journalist who helped bring the initial White House email suit, has protested the Archives' directive. "It makes no sense," said Armstrong. "If your basement were flooded, the first thing you would try to do is turn off the flow of water, and then start worrying about mopping up. The Archives are doing the exact opposite. They are already drowning in paper, but they are still telling people to print out their records onto paper. If the government had dedicated the energy it has spent fighting the email lawsuits into modernizing its record-keeping operations, it would have gone a long way to solving its problems."

Although "the era of big government is over," as President 20
Clinton declared, the era of big government data banks is only just beginning. Ken Thibodeau, the head of the Electronic Records Division at the Archives, insisted that Armstrong and others underestimate the immense technological difficulties in trying to recover email from thousands of different government computers. Between 1989 and 1996, the Electronic Records Division took in 25,000 new records. The email from the Reagan-Bush White House suddenly buried it in an avalanche of 200,000 files, just as the State Department prepared to hand over 1,250,000 electronically stored diplomatic cables. And this represents just the tip of the iceberg— the period from 1972 until 1975. Since then, the State Department has been averaging about a million messages a year. Meanwhile, in recent years, the White House has been pumping out an average of six million electronic files a year.

These expected additions could well lead to a crash of the 21
Archives' computer system. "We designed a new system to handle maybe 10,000 messages a year. You cannot scale up our system to deal with a million messages a year," Thibodeau said. His office ran an experiment, trying to copy one single storage tape of the

Clinton email. The Archives' computer churned and ground for some 50 hours but failed to copy the entire tape. "We can normally copy a whole tape with up to 200 megabytes in about ten or 15 minutes," Thibodeau explained. The reason the computer had so much trouble with the White House tape is that email systems are not designed with long-term storage in mind. Given the state of current technology, the computer insisted on treating each individual email message as a single file that had to be opened and closed in order to be copied from one tape to another. It takes far longer to copy 100,000 one-page messages than to copy a thousand 100-page messages even though they may use up the same amount of space on the tape.

Thibodeau said the Electronic Records Division was looking at 22 sophisticated storage devices coming onto the market, but these present problems of their own. "There's a new kind of tape that can hold 200 times the volume as the kind of data tapes we are using, the same plastic cartridge we use," Thibodeau said. "So it would be great in terms of space. But as we talk to people who use this technology, we have not talked to anyone who has successfully taken the tape out of the silo and read it on a different machine." The extreme precision and miniaturization of the new technology is such that each machine produces tapes that are unintentionally customized to fit the particular alignment of the laser beams that encode and read information. It's as if you were stamping a record with grooves that were thousands of times smaller than on an LP and using a stylus that needed to land just right in order to play back the record. "When you get to these highly dense media, your tolerance for error is extremely small," said Thibodeau. "A slight misalignment of the head is sufficient to guarantee that you will never read the tape other than on a machine that has the same misalignment. And if you are in the archive business, if we can't take a tape from another system and read it on ours, then it's no good."

Ironically, the downsizing of government has actually magnified 23 the information crisis. "When a government agency downsizes, usually the first thing they do is get rid of record keepers and clean out the storage closet," Mayn said. "We suddenly get a call telling us to pick up a trailer-sized truckload of records." When the Pentagon closed Northrop Air Force Base, it decided to turn over its huge motion picture storage warehouse to the Archives, doubling in a single stroke the Archives' video holding. At the same time, the Archives is having to do more with fewer resources. Factoring in for inflation, the budget of the Electronic Records Division has fallen by about 15 percent and its personnel have been cut by ten percent during a period when the volume of new data has increased tenfold. The staff of Mayn's dynamic media laboratory has been cut from 16 to nine in the last decade. Everyone seems to want to keep everything, but nobody wants to pay to keep it.

The problem, in Mayn's view, is that nobody inside or outside 24 government is making the tough decisions about what to keep and what to discard. "I'm not a historian, but personally I have my doubts about some of the stuff we are trying to keep," Mayn said. "Do we really need hundreds of different films on the workings of the M1 tank?" he asked. "I can see keeping a few as a sample, but I'm not sure we need the entire collection." At the height of the Vietnam War, the Pentagon routinely sent hundreds of men with cameras out into the jungles and the battlefields to film the combat. "Each of these people was told to shoot hundreds or thousands of feet of film," Mayn said. While much of this film is of genuine historical interest, the total quantity would take several lifetimes for a technician to copy or for a researcher to study. Because much of this material will eventually deteriorate beyond the point of intelligibility, Mayn believes that the choice of what to keep will be made by default. "We will keep those things that researchers happen to have requested and that get copied onto new media," he said.

The sorting out of the information explosion may resemble the 25 process that determined the books we now possess from antiquity. The works of authors such as Homer and Virgil survived intact because of their enduring popularity and the multiple copies that were made at different times. But many of the works we regard as fixtures of our culture (including Plato) were lost for centuries and are known to us only because of a copy or two that turned up in medieval monasteries or in the collections of Arab scholars. Some works of undoubted greatness did not survive at all: Sophocles is known to have written some 120 plays, of which we possess only nine.

There is not likely to be a modern Sophocles in the databases of 26 the Department of Agriculture or the Census Bureau. The greater risk, instead, is of such a vast accumulation of records that the job of distinguishing the essential from the ephemeral becomes more and more difficult. The Archives of the future may resemble the "Library of Babel" that Jorge Luis Borges imagined nearly 60 years ago, an infinite library that contained every conceivable book in the universe. There were books that consisted purely of a repetition of a single letter of the alphabet and others in which all the pages except for one were blank. The discovery of an intelligible sentence was cause for jubilation. Eventually, after many centuries, the librarians of Babel were driven to despair in their unfulfilled quest for a coherent, complete book.

Understanding Meaning

1. What is the great irony of the information age in Stille's view?
2. What has caused the loss of so much data?
3. Why is digital technology more fragile and less durable than older analog formats?
4. What causes some data to be rescued and restored?
5. What challenges do archivists face in accessing and transferring old data to modern storage devices?

6. *Critical Thinking*: Does easy access to information online lead people to assume that data is permanently stored and will be available for future generations? Could cyberwarfare or a massive technical failure erase irreplaceable digital records? Do people assume their computers, flash drives, and online backups will safely and permanently store their records?

Evaluating Strategy

1. How does Stille use descriptions of old film projectors, glass discs, and Dictabelt machines to illustrate the problem of technological obsolescence and data loss?
2. How does Stille use direct quotations from Charles Mayn to provide evidence and organize his article?
3. How effective is Stille's conclusion?
4. *Blending the Modes*: Where does Stille use *comparison, classification*, and *process* to develop his *cause and effect* article?

Appreciating Language

1. What are "dynamic media"? Why do they pose greater challenges than digital forms?
2. Stille uses terms like "rag-and-bone shop" and "dense thicket" to describe the problem of data preservation and storage. Are these effective metaphors to help readers understand an abstract issue?
3. *Critical Thinking*: What is meant by a "cautionary vision"? How does the media laboratory's obsolete machinery provide a warning about the future?

WRITING SUGGESTIONS

1. Write an essay about your experiences with "data decay" or obsolete technology. Does your family have fading Polaroid photos? Have you found vinyl albums, videotapes, or floppy discs belonging to friends or relatives that cannot be played on any device you own? Has a computer crash caused you to lose valuable information?

2. *Collaborative Writing*: Discuss Stille's essay with a group of students and write a short essay suggesting how to avoid the loss of information. Should industry or government standards require greater durability of storage devices? Should technicians work to create greater transferability between old and new technology? Should institutions, organizations, and corporations classify data as it is created so that the most valuable information is given priority for archival or conversion to new storage devices?

Opposing Viewpoints: The Minimum Wage
ALEXANDER COCKBURN

Alexander Cockburn (1941–2012) was born in Ireland and moved to the United States in 1972 to pursue a career in journalism. Working with Jeffrey St. Clair, he edited the political newsletter *CounterPunch*. He also wrote columns for *The Nation* and *The Week* and published articles in *Esquire*, *Harper's*, the *Wall Street Journal*, and the *New Statesman*. He co-edited several books with Jeffrey St. Clair, including *The Politics of Anti-Semitism* (2003), *Serpents in the Garden* (2004), *Imperial Crusades* (2004), *Dime's Worth of Difference* (2004), and *End Times: Death of the Fourth Estate* (2006).

Why We Must Raise the Minimum Wage

CONTEXT: *Cockburn argues that the minimum wage should be raised because it would not only improve workers' incomes but would also stimulate the economy and create jobs.*

WRITER'S NOTE: *Cockburn, a noted liberal, includes comments by conservatives who share his views.*

1   Everyone knows the story of Henry Ford more than doubling his production line workers' pay to $5 a day in January 1914. Ford explained to aghast fellow capitalists that he would be creating customers for his cheap cars, building a new American middle class.

2   Nearly a century later, in 2005, Walmart CEO Lee Scott called on Congress to raise the minimum wage, since "our customers simply don't have the money to buy basic necessities between pay checks." Walmart haters whacked away at Scott for hypocrisy, but he was being perfectly reasonable in identifying what was then and is now America's number-one problem: a huge chunk of the population barely survives on starvation wages. If you adjust for inflation, median personal income hasn't moved for almost half a century. Nearly a quarter of US households have zero to negative net worth. It just takes one unlucky turn of the cards—an illness, an accident, a brush with the law—to put them under.

3   President Obama invokes "the knowledge economy," putatively replete with well-paying jobs demanding advanced skills in all the high-tech arts that can make America great again. But what is the real economy of tomorrow for most Americans? The Bureau of Labor Statistics (BLS) reckons that by 2020 the overwhelming majority of jobs will still require only a high school diploma or less, and that nearly three-fourths of "job openings due to growth and replacement needs" over the next decade will pay a median wage of less than $35,000 a year, with nearly 30 percent paying a median of about $20,000 (in 2010 dollars).

Right now about 50 million Americans are working in: office and   4
administrative support occupations (median wage of $31,250),
sales and related occupations ($24,840), food preparation and
serving occupations ($18,900). Not too much knowledge required.
The growth jobs of tomorrow, according to the BLS: Childcare
workers ($19,430), personal care aides ($19,730), home health
aides ($20,610), janitors and cleaners ($22,210), teacher assistants
($23,220), nonconstruction laborers ($23,460), security guards
($23,900) and construction laborers ($29,730).

So what is the best anti-poverty program? Higher wages for   5
the jobs that are out there. The current federal minimum wage is
$7.25 per hour. Work a forty-hour week for $7.25 and you end up
with $15,080 a year. This is just above the federal poverty line for
an individual ($11,000) but well below the line for a family of four
($22,000). And it's just a bit more than the manufacturer's recom-
mended retail price for the Ford Fiesta ($13,200), Ford's cheapest
car this year. In 1914 an assembly line worker could buy a Model T
with four months' pay.

Even though the cost of living has gone up, the federal mini-   6
mum wage hasn't moved since 2009, when the last of a series of
increases signed into law by George W. Bush kicked in. In 2011
dollars, the minimum wage was more than $10 in 1968, when jobs
and pay were peaking for America's workers.

In November 2008 President-elect Obama promised to "raise   7
the minimum wage to $9.50 an hour by 2011 and index it to infla-
tion to make sure that full-time workers can earn a living wage that
allows them to raise their families and pay for basic needs such as
food, transportation, and housing."

It was a pledge to low-paid workers to give them a 30 percent   8
pay hike. Of all Obama's betrayals, this was one of the bitterest.
He never really tried, skittish with fear that he'd be nailed as an
inflationeer by the Big Business lobbies and their creatures in
Congress. In this cowardice he stands shoulder to shoulder with
Mitt Romney, who in January said at a campaign event in New
Hampshire that he favored raising the minimum wage automatically each year to keep pace with inflation. A couple of whacks
from the *Wall Street Journal* saw Romney flop on the issue at the
start of March.

A smart coalition stretching from *American Conservative* pub-   9
lisher Ron Unz to James K. Galbraith says a $12 minimum wage
makes good sense as long-term stimulus. As Unz points out, "The
minimum wage in Ontario, Canada, is currently well over $10 per
hour, while in France it now stands at nearly $13. Even more re-
markably, Australia recently raised its minimum wage to over
$16 per hour, and nonetheless has an unemployment rate of just
5 percent." Properly enforced, a $12 minimum wage would slow
illegal immigration, which is powered by a low-wage economy.

As Galbraith, seizing on Unz's proposal, wrote, "What would   10
workers do with the raise? They'd spend it, creating jobs for other

workers. They'd pay down their mortgages and car loans, getting themselves out of debt....Women in particular would benefit because they tend to work for lower wages."

Who's fighting for the most vital economic issue in American politics today? Senator Tom Harkin's Rebuild America Act, which he introduced on March 29, calls for raising the minimum wage to $9.80—a 35 percent hike—and pegging the wage to inflation. A day earlier, Ralph Nader flayed Richard Trumka in an open letter to the AFL-CIO president, charging him with giving Obama an "early blanket endorsement," then, among other failures, running a feeble, low-energy campaign for an inflation-adjusted $10 minimum wage law, even though keeping up with inflation for the federal minimum wage "is historically supported by 70 percent of the people....What is the AFL-CIO waiting for?...No wonder [Obama] can get away with giving the trade union movement and unorganized workers the back of his hand."   11

Most progressives watch with complacency the suicidal Republicans heading over the cliff. Let them step back and look at the desperation of millions of Americans today. Will they, like Trumka, stay loyal and inert right through to November?   12

Understanding Meaning

1. What, according to Cockburn, is the "real economy of tomorrow"? What jobs will most Americans have in the next decade?
2. Why does Cockburn call raising the minimum wage the "best anti-poverty program"?
3. What effect, in Cockburn's view, would raising the minimum wage have on the economy?
4. *Critical Thinking*: In analyzing the minimum wage, are other issues just as important as the rate? Does it matter how long workers earn the lowest wage before getting raises? Would a low minimum wage matter if it generally applied only to teenagers and part-time employees? Why or why not?

Evaluating Strategy

1. Cockburn compares America's minimum wage with higher equivalents in Ontario, Canada, and Australia. Are these analogies meaningful only if readers know the cost of living in those countries, such as the price of bread, a gallon of gas, or a hamburger?
2. Cockburn refers to conservatives who support a higher minimum wage. Why is it important for advocates to indicate that their positions are shared by people from an opposing party or ideology?
3. *Critical Thinking*: Cockburn opens his essay referring to Henry Ford paying his workers five dollars a day so they could afford cars. Conduct online research to determine the accuracy of Cockburn's description of the wage offer. Do commentators and historians offer different views? Do writers have to examine events or personalities before using them as evidence?

Appreciating Language

1. Cockburn refers to complacent progressives watching "suicidal" Republicans and "Big Business lobbies and their creatures in Congress." What does this language reveal about his political point of view?

2. Cockburn calls those who agree with him "a smart coalition." Does a writer strengthen or weaken his or her argument by labeling people "smart" or "stupid"? Can this alienate readers the writer is trying to persuade?

WRITING SUGGESTIONS

1. Write a short essay about your own experiences working for minimum wage. Had you received an increase, what changes would you have made in your spending or savings habits?

2. *Collaborative Writing:* Discuss Cockburn's article with a group of students and write an essay about the advantages and disadvantages of raising the minimum wage. Would increasing the wage make it harder for small businesses to afford labor? Would businesses have to pass the added cost to consumers, causing prices to rise? Would increased incomes stimulate the economy? If members disagree, consider writing opposing papers.

PHIL KERPEN AND NICOLE KAEDING

Phil Kerpen is a native of Brooklyn, New York, who now resides in Washington. An advocate of small government and free enterprise, Kerpen was a policy analyst for the Club for Growth and served as Policy Director for the Free Enterprise Fund before becoming vice-president of Americans for Prosperity. He is currently president of American Commitment. Nicole Kaeding is the state policy manager for Americans for Prosperity, currently urging states to opt out of health exchanges proposed by the Affordable Care Act. Her work has appeared in the *Chicago Tribune, The Hill, Daily Caller,* and the *National Review Online.*

A Starter Wage for Teenagers

CONTEXT: *In this* National Review Online *article, Kerpen and Kaeding argue that the current minimum wage is too high for unskilled teenagers, causing many of them to miss the chance to get a first job.*

WRITER'S NOTE: *The writers acknowledge that the primary reason for teenage unemployment is the weak economy but argue that the high minimum wage is "another major factor."*

1   If you're a teenager unable to find a job this summer—or a parent with a teenager hanging around the house—you're not alone. The latest data from the U.S. Bureau of Labor Statistics show that the teenage unemployment rate was at a stubbornly high 24.5 percent in June, and because the unemployment rate only includes people actively seeking work, the true number of teens who cannot find jobs is likely higher. For most of the past two years, the rate has been above 25 percent.

2   While the overall weak economy is certainly at fault, another major factor was the decision by Congress and President Bush to raise the minimum wage over 40 percent in the face of a weak economy, without exempting teenagers—thus pricing teens out of the labor market and denying them crucial work experience.

3   Economists have tried to measure the effects of a minimum wage. Hundreds of studies have been completed, focused primarily on low-skilled and teenage employment. The consensus result has been that for every 10 percent increase in the minimum wage, a 1 to 3 percent decrease in employment is observed, disproportionately affecting low-skilled, mostly young workers.

4   The last minimum-wage increase was in July of 2009, when the final dollar increase of the legislation passed back in 2007 took effect. Adjusted for inflation, the minimum wage is currently 36 percent higher than the minimum wage of 2006. A study released in

June by University of Chicago economist Casey Mulligan estimates that the most recent minimum-wage increase (after adjusting for the effects of the recession) resulted in the loss of 800,000 jobs, mostly by low-skilled and young workers.

The political argument for a minimum wage is that compensation below a certain level is exploitative and inadequate to support a family. We don't agree that a minimum wage is the right solution to this problem, but regardless, that rationale is simply not relevant for teenagers trying to enter the first rung on the employment ladder, get out of the house, and earn some spending money.   5

Thom Hartmann, a leading progressive radio and television host with whom we almost never agree, recently said: "I don't have a problem with saying a minimum wage doesn't apply to people under 18 or somebody who hasn't graduated from high school." So this is not a left-right issue.   6

The Organization for Economic Cooperation and Development (OECD), a group of 34 of the world's most advanced economies, suggested in an April 2010 report that teen unemployment could be reduced by exempting teens from the minimum wage and instead instituting a "sub-minimum training wage." In fact, only half of the OECD countries even have a minimum wage, and 9 of those 17—including many in Europe—have a training wage for teenagers. Larry Summers, the former director of Obama's National Economic Council, has reportedly advocated that the United States create such a wage. We agree.   7

The existing Youth Minimum Wage provisions of the Fair Labor Standards Act are inadequate because of their limited scope and 90-day cap. As the *Wall Street Journal* has correctly observed, the 90-day cap makes employers unlikely to hire at all.   8

It would be great if teens could all find summer work at $7.25 an hour or more. But many teenagers with no job experience can't, and so they end up not working, earning nothing, and missing out on valuable work experience. So here is our modest proposal, which we think should gain bipartisan support in Congress: Exempt teenagers from the 2007 legislation increasing the minimum wage. Let them work for $5.15 an hour—if they want to and that's what an employer wants to pay. Let them gain work experience and move up the wage ladder from there.   9

Understanding Meaning

1. In Kerpen and Kaeding's view, what is the result of a higher minimum wage?
2. How, in their view, would a lower minimum wage benefit teenagers?
3. What do unskilled teenagers receive from a job besides wages? Can work experience and training be more valuable than money? Can it provide young people with a "first rung" to "move up the wage ladder"?

4. *Critical Thinking*: Would a lower minimum wage discourage teenagers from looking for work or even accepting a job offer? Would many teenagers prefer having free time? Would some teenagers work for free in internships that provided valuable experience they knew would stand out on their resumes? How much does money and experience motivate young people seeking work?

Evaluating Strategy

1. What evidence do the authors present to support their conclusions?
2. Should the authors address other reasons for youth unemployment, such as laid-off older workers taking lower-paying jobs normally available to unskilled teenagers?
3. *Critical Thinking*: Kerpen and Kaeding, both conservatives, include comments from a "progressive" radio host who shares their view, then state that a lower minimum wage is "not a left–right issue." Can writers use a single quote from an opponent to declare an issue non-partisan or universally acceptable?

Appreciating Language

1. What does the term "training wage" imply? Should a "training wage" require instruction to increase workers' skills?
2. Kerpen and Kaeding end their article stating "Let them work for $5.15 an hour—if they want to." Does this language suggest that lowering wages grants greater freedom? Could the same word choices be used to argue against other regulations, such as health and safety rules or workers' compensation?

WRITING SUGGESTIONS

1. Using Cockburn's and Kerpen and Kaeding's articles as models, write a short essay stating your own prediction how changes to minimum wage would affect the economy. Do you see a compromise between the progressive and conservative arguments? Could there be a higher standard minimum wage and a lower "starter wage" for teenagers? Why or why not?

2. *Collaborative Writing:* Working with a group of students, write an essay that presents other causes and effects of teenage unemployment. Besides wages, what leads employers to avoid offering jobs to teenagers? How does the lack of work experience affect young people's ability to find employment? What lessons can young people learn from having a job?

Writing Beyond the Classroom
THOMAS JEFFERSON ET AL.

During the hot summer of 1776, the Second Continental Congress met in Philadelphia. Following a call for a resolution of independence from Britain, John Adams, Thomas Jefferson, Benjamin Franklin, Robert Livingston, and Roger Sherman were charged with drafting a declaration. Jefferson wrote the original draft, which was revised by Adams and Franklin before being presented to the entire Congress. After further changes, the Declaration of Independence was adopted and signed.

The Declaration of Independence

CONTEXT: *The Declaration of Independence presents a theory of government greatly influenced by the concept of natural rights espoused by Locke and Rousseau, and then provides evidence that the British have failed to respect these rights.*

WRITER'S NOTE: *Most of the declaration is a list of grievances or causes for the colonies to seek independence.*

In Congress, July 4, 1776. The unanimous Declaration of the thir- 1
teen united States of America,

When in the Course of human events, it becomes necessary for 2
one people to dissolve the political bands which have connected them with another, and to assume among the powers of the earth, the separate and equal station to which the Laws of Nature and of Nature's God entitle them, a decent respect to the opinions of mankind requires that they should declare the causes which impel them to the separation.

We hold these truths to be self-evident, that all men are created 3
equal, that they are endowed by their Creator with certain unalienable Rights, that among these are Life, Liberty and the pursuit of Happiness.

That to secure these rights, Governments are instituted among 4
Men, deriving their just powers from the consent of the governed.

That whenever any Form of Government becomes destructive 5
of these ends, it is the Right of the People to alter or to abolish it, and to institute new Government, laying its foundation on such principles and organizing its powers in such form, as to them shall seem most likely to effect their Safety and Happiness. Prudence, indeed, will dictate that Governments long established should not be changed for light and transient causes; and accordingly all experience hath shown, that mankind are more disposed to suffer, while evils are sufferable, than to right themselves by abolishing the forms to which they are accustomed. But when a long train of abuses and usurpations, pursuing invariably the same Object evinces a design to reduce them under absolute Despotism, it is

their right, it is their duty, to throw off such Government, and to provide new Guards for their future security.

Such has been the patient sufferance of these Colonies; and such 6 is now the necessity which constrains them to alter their former Systems of Government. The history of the present King of Great Britain is a history of repeated injuries and usurpations, all having in direct object the establishment of an absolute Tyranny over these States. To prove this, let Facts be submitted to a candid world.

He has refused his Assent to Laws, the most wholesome and 7 necessary for the public good.

He has forbidden his Governors to pass Laws of immediate and 8 pressing importance, unless suspended in their operation till his Assent should be obtained; and when so suspended, he has utterly neglected to attend to them.

He has refused to pass other Laws for the accommodation of 9 large districts of people, unless those people would relinquish the right of Representation in the Legislature, a right inestimable to them and formidable to tyrants only.

He has called together legislative bodies at places unusual, uncom- 10 fortable, and distant from the depository of their public Records, for the sole purpose of fatiguing them into compliance with his measures.

He has dissolved Representative Houses repeatedly, for oppos- 11 ing with manly firmness his invasions on the rights of the people.

He has refused for a long time, after such dissolutions, to cause 12 others to be elected; whereby the Legislative powers, incapable of Annihilation, have returned to the People at large for their exercise; the State remaining in the mean time exposed to all the dangers of invasion from without, and convulsions within.

He has endeavored to prevent the population of these States; 13 for that purpose obstructing the Laws for Naturalization of Foreigners; refusing to pass others to encourage their migrations hither, and raising the conditions of new Appropriations of Lands.

He has obstructed the Administration of Justice, by refusing his 14 Assent to Laws for establishing Judiciary powers.

He has made Judges dependent on his Will alone, for the tenure 15 of their offices, and the amount and payment of their salaries.

He has erected a multitude of New Offices, and sent hither 16 swarms of Officers to harass our people, and eat out their substance.

He has kept among us in times of peace, Standing Armies with- 17 out the Consent of our legislatures.

He has affected to render the Military independent of and supe- 18 rior to the Civil power.

He has combined with others to subject us to a jurisdiction for- 19 eign to our constitution, and unacknowledged by our laws; giving his Assent to their Acts of pretended Legislation:

For quartering large bodies of armed troops among us: 20

For protecting them, by a mock Trial, from punishment for any 21 Murders which they should commit on the Inhabitants of these States:

For cutting off our Trade with all parts of the world: 22

For imposing Taxes on us without our Consent: 23

For depriving us in many cases, of the benefits of Trial by Jury: 24

For transporting us beyond Seas to be tried for pretended   25
offences:

For abolishing the free System of English Laws in a neighboring   26
Province, establishing therein an Arbitrary government, and enlarg-
ing its Boundaries so as to render it at once an example and fit instrument for introducing the same absolute rule in these Colonies:

For taking away our Charters, abolishing our most valuable   27
Laws, and altering fundamentally the Forms of our Governments:

For suspending our own Legislatures, and declaring themselves   28
invested with power to legislate for us in all cases whatsoever.

He has abdicated Government here, by declaring us out of his   29
Protection and waging War against us.

He has plundered our seas, ravaged our Coasts, burnt our towns,   30
and destroyed the lives of our people.

He is at this time transporting large Armies of foreign Mercenaries   31
to complete the works of death, desolation and tyranny, already begun
with circumstances of Cruelty & perfidy scarcely paralleled in the most
barbarous ages, and totally unworthy the Head of a civilized nation.

He has constrained our fellow Citizens taken Captive on high Seas   32
to bear Arms against their Country, to become the executioners of
their friends and Brethren, or to fall themselves by their Hands.

He has excited domestic insurrections among us, and has en-   33
deavored to bring on the inhabitants of our frontiers, the merciless
Indian Savages, whose known rule of warfare is an undistinguished
destruction of all ages, sexes, and conditions.

In every stage of these Oppressions We have Petitioned for Re-   34
dress in the most humble terms: Our repeated Petitions have been
answered only by repeated injury. A Prince, whose character is thus
marked by every act which may define a Tyrant, is unfit to be the
ruler of a free people.

Nor have We been wanting in attentions to our British brethren.   35
We have warned them from time to time of attempts by their legislature to extend an unwarrantable jurisdiction over us. We have
reminded them of the circumstances of our emigration and settlement here. We have appealed to their native justice and magnanim-
ity, and we have conjured them by the ties of our common kindred
to disavow these usurpations, which would inevitably interrupt our
connections and correspondence. They too have been deaf to the
voice of justice and consanguinity. We must, therefore, acquiesce in
the necessity, which denounces our Separation, and hold them, as
we hold the rest of mankind, Enemies in War, in Peace Friends.

We, therefore, the Representatives of the united States of Amer-   36
ica, in General Congress, Assembled, appealing to the Supreme
Judge of the world for the rectitude of our intentions, do, in the
Name, and by Authority of the good People of these Colonies,
solemnly publish and declare, That these United Colonies are,

and of Right ought to be, Free and Independent States; that they are Absolved from all Allegiance to the British Crown, and that all political connection between them and the State of Great Britain, is and ought to be totally dissolved; and that as Free and Independent States, they have full Power to levy War, conclude Peace, contract Alliances, establish Commerce, and to do all other Acts and Things which Independent States may of right do.

And for the support of this Declaration, with a firm reliance on 37 the protection of divine Providence, we mutually pledge to each other our Lives, our Fortunes and our sacred Honor.

Understanding Meaning

1. What were the principal causes for the Congress to declare independence?
2. Why do Jefferson and the other authors argue that these grievances could not be resolved in any other fashion?
3. *Critical Thinking:* When was the last time you read the Declaration of Independence? Do some items strike you as relevant to current conditions? Should Americans be more familiar with a document that helped create their country and establish its values?

Evaluating Strategy

1. How does the Declaration of Independence use induction and deduction?
2. How much space is devoted to the list of causes? Is enough evidence provided to support severing ties with Britain?
3. The causes are placed in separate paragraphs rather than combined. What impact does this have?

Appreciating Language

1. How does the document refer to the king?
2. This document was drafted in 1776. How readable is it today? How has language changed in two hundred years?

WRITING SUGGESTIONS

1. Write a personal analysis of the Declaration of Independence. What do you think is the most significant feature of the document? What does the phrase "Life, Liberty and the pursuit of Happiness" mean to you?

2. *Collaborative Writing:* Discuss the declaration with a group of students. Does the current government reflect the ideals of Jefferson? How has America changed since 1776? To encourage further discussion, look up the original draft, which contained a passage denouncing slavery, a passage Jefferson had to delete to pacify Southern delegates. Develop a statement with other students expressing your opinion of the Declaration of Independence's importance in the twenty-first century.

Responding to Images

Ashley Cooper/Picimpact/Corbis

Sign showing the former edge of the Exit Glacier in Alaska.

1. What is your first reaction to this picture? Would it make a good illustration for Al Gore's article on climate change (page 392)? Why or why not?
2. Does this photograph dramatize an abstract problem?
3. Could you imagine this image being used in a poster warning about climate change?
4. *Visual Analysis*: Does this image lead people to make assumptions? Does the position of a glacier matter as much as its size or mass? Could global warming skeptics post a photograph of an ice storm in Florida or a blizzard in Memphis to dramatize their claims?
5. *Collaborative Writing*: Discuss this photograph with a group of students and have each one write a caption. What does each person's caption represent? Can a photograph like this serve as a Rorschach test that reveals a person's perceptual world?

Strategies FOR CAUSE-AND-EFFECT WRITING

1. **Determine your goal.** Are you attempting to explain a cause or to measure or predict future outcomes?
2. **Evaluate your reader's needs.** What evidence does your reader require in order to accept your conclusions? Are government statistics more impressive than the testimony of experts? Does any background information or do any definitions need to be presented?

3. **Offer logical, acceptable evidence.** Present support that comes from reliable sources readers will accept. Present evidence in a clearly organized manner. Use brief narratives or analogies to dramatize data.

4. **Qualify assertions and conclusions.** A writer who admits that alternative interpretations or conflicting evidence exists can appear more credible to readers than one who narrowly insists he or she has the only possible conclusion.

5. **Use other modes to organize information.** It may be beneficial to use narration, comparison, extended definition, or division and classification to present your cause-and-effect thesis.

Revising and Editing

1. **Review your use of deduction or induction.** Does your major premise contain unproven assumptions? Is it clearly stated, or is it subject to different interpretations? Does your inductive leap move beyond reasonable doubt? Do you provide enough evidence to support your inductive conclusion?

2. **Evaluate sources.** Do not assume that everything you read is valid. Experts can make errors of judgment. Read books, articles, websites, and studies carefully. Look for signs of bias, unproven assumptions, or mistakes in logic. Do writers support their claims with sufficient and reliable evidence? Do they document their sources? Look for what is missing. Have they overlooked or dismissed contradictory evidence? Collect material from a variety of experts and sources.

Suggested Topics for Cause-and-Effect Writing

General Assignments

Write a cause-and-effect paper on any of the following topics. Your paper may use other modes to organize and present evidence. Cause-and-effect papers usually require research. It is possible to use cause and effect in less formal papers, in which you offer personal experience and observations as examples. However, the more objective facts you can cite, the stronger your writing will be.

Write a paper explaining the cause(s) of the following topics:

1. Teenage pregnancy
2. Sexual harassment
3. Divorce
4. The success or failure of a local business
5. The victory or defeat of a political candidate

Write a paper measuring or predicting the effect(s) of the following topics:

1. The information superhighway
2. Immigration
3. A parent's loss of a job
4. Tuition increases
5. The election of a particular candidate

Writing in Context

1. Analyze a recent event on campus, in your community, or at your place of work. Examine what caused this event to take place. If several causes exist, you may use division to explain them or classification to rank them from the most important to the least important.

2. Write a letter to the editor of the campus newspaper predicting the effects of a current policy change, incident, or trend in student behavior.

3. Imagine a job application that asks you to write a 250-word essay presenting your reasons for choosing your career. Write a 1-page essay that lists your most important reasons. As you write, consider how an employer would evaluate your response.

Student Paper: Cause and Effect

This paper was written in response to the following assignment:

> Write an essay explaining the causes or analyzing the effects of a social phenomenon, technological change, economic problem, or political issue. You might discuss causes for the popularity of a fad, the effect of the Internet on political campaigns, or reasons behind recent protests over immigration policies.

First Draft with Instructor's Comments

Effects of Concussions on the NFL

Football and war have a lot in common, besides strategy and drive. Today doctors and researchers are examining something else. The hallmark injury of Iraq and Afghanistan has been head injuries, mostly repeated concussions, caused by roadside bombs. Protected by armored vehicles and helmets, soldiers still suffer serious brain injury from the sudden impact. Football players, especially retired players, are reporting many of the same systems. New abilities to examine and measure brain activity have given doctors new insight into these injuries.

Delete opening, off topic, focus on causes and effects of sports injuries

Right word?

The National Football League is grappling with short and long term issues about its attempts to address the problems of concussions. After years of denying players suffered long term injuries from concussions, the NFL's retirement board has paid two million dollars in disability payments for brain damage (ESPN). Repetitive brain trauma, doctors claimed, left Pittsburgh Steeler Mike Webster with "signs of dementia" (ESPN). In 2000 a survey of a thousand former players revealed that 26 percent had suffered three or more concussions and reported "problems with memory, concentration, speech impediments, headaches and other neurological problems" (New York Times). Researchers from the National Institute for Occupational Safety found that retired NFL players had a death rate from Alzheimer's and ALS (Lou Gehrig's disease) four times higher than the general population.

Weak opening sentence, revise

See comments about MLA

Good use of supporting detail, see note about MLA documentation

Concerns about concussions have led the NFL to make changes on the field and the bench. Concerns about helmet to helmet hits will lead to more fines and penalties, lessening the intensity of the game and leading teams to win by scoring penalties rather than points. Plus, players who get a hard hit won't be sidelined for a game but weeks until cleared by doctors, meaning teams will have key players out for much of a season.

Short term this will make the games less intense and players less aggressive so fans will find the sport less exciting. Players may be unable to command huge salaries because teams will argue that a concussion could sideline them for a whole season. But then NFL owners are concerned about the long term effects concussions might have on the sport. Boxing was once a major sport in the United States. Heavyweight bouts had the media build up of a Super Bowl game. There were high school and college boxing teams and inner city gyms specialized in prize fighting. Concerns about brain injury led parents to dissuade their sons from boxing and the once popular sport diminished so that fights only appear on cable TV and few Americans can even name the current champions.

Run-on

Run-on

The challenge of the NFL is to cope with the effects of concussions in a way that protects players and keeps the games exciting for fans. Some commentators think the new rule will lead players to engineer helmet to helmet contact, knowing it will lead to a penalty, an automatic first down, and a likely fine against the offending player. Others argue that marginal players fighting to stay on the team or advance to a more secure position will lie about concussions, since most of the assessment by doctors relies on personal interviews. Technicians are at work with new helmet liners that absorb and diffuse impact much like Kevlar vests or inflate like miniature airbags on a car.

Expand ideas and build clearer transitions

The effects of policies to stem concussions will have ramifications, both good and bad, on the sport for years to come.

Revision Notes

You have a very good topic for a cause-and-effect paper, though it can be improved with careful revision and editing.

- Explain the causes and effects of concussions, then detail how they may affect the NFL in the future.
- See MLA documentation rules (pages 483–486). You should list all sources in a Works Cited section. In-text notations should use the author's last name or title of the article, not that of the magazine or website.
- Proofread for spelling and sentence errors.

Revised Draft

Frank Perez   **English 201**

Helmet to Helmet: The NFL and Concussions

After long denying any "causal link" between football injuries and long-term brain damage, the National Football League is now addressing concussions. Players who once were described as being "dinged," "shaken up," or "had their bells rung" are now labeled "concussed."

Concussions or mild traumatic brain injuries (MTBI) occur when a blow or sudden acceleration or deceleration causes the brain to slide against the inside of the skull. The effects of concussion vary and are usually temporary. Victims may lose consciousness and experience dizziness, mental confusion, impaired memory, fatigue, and nausea. Repeated concussions are believed to have a cumulative effect that may have long-term consequences. In 2000 a study of over a thousand former NFL players found that one in four had suffered three or more concussions ("Head Injuries"). Researchers from the National Institute for Occupational Safety and Health found that retired football players have a death rate from Alzheimer's and ALS (Lou Gehrig's disease) that is four times higher than the national average. Their study found that wide receivers, running backs, and quarterbacks were more likely to die of these diseases than linemen who have fewer "high-speed collisions" (Norton). In November 2012 three NFL quarterbacks received concussions in one day. Two months earlier five elementary school students suffered concussions during a single Pop Warner game in Massachusetts (Gregory).

Four thousand former players are now suing the NFL for knowingly disregarding information about concussions and failing to inform them about the potential hazards. During Congressional hearings about brain trauma in professional football Representative Linda Sanchez compared the NFL denials of harm to those of the tobacco industry (Brandt).

The NFL now sees long-term effects from the growing public awareness about concussions. Besides mounting lawsuits and disability claims from retired players, the league fears an erosion of popularity. The number of boys under twelve participating in tackle football has dropped by a third in four years as parents discourage their sons from playing (Gregory). If high schools and colleges see a similar decline in interest over the next few years, the result will be a shrinking pool of future players and a dwindling fan base. Critics glumly remind the NFL about boxing's steady decline as the public lost interest in a sport many deemed brutal and life threatening.

In a cover story for *Time* magazine, Sean Gregory detailed NFL Commissioner Roger Goodell's attempts to address concussions by going after the causes—high-speed collisions on the field, especially helmet to helmet contact. The NFL's stiffer fines and more frequent penalty calls are designed to lessen concussions. In addition, concussed players will be subjected to more rigorous examinations by independent neurologists before being cleared for play. Rule changes about kickoffs may also result in fewer head injuries.

The effects of these policies to reduce concussions are hotly debated by players, team owners, managers, fans, and sportswriters.

Some argue these changes are necessary to safeguard players and the future of the NFL. Others insist that football is by definition a contact sport. Efforts to make the sport less aggressive will make games less exciting. Cynics have argued that some players will engineer helmet to helmet hits, knowing it will result in a penalty against the opposing team, an automatic first down, and a fine against the offending player. Future games may be won not by teams that score the most points but by those that score the most penalties. Owners are concerned that concussed players who were once cleared to play after their immediate symptoms diminished will now be benched for weeks or the remainder of the season to recover.

Whatever the immediate and long term effects of these changes, the NFL will continue to grapple with the challenge of making the game safer for players without reducing the excitement that attracts fans.

Works Cited

Brandt, Andrew. "The NFL's Concussion Conundrum." *ESPN.com.* ESPN, 17 Oct. 2012. Web. 23 Nov. 2012.

Gregory, Sean. "Can Roger Goodell Save Football?" *Time.* Time Magazine, 17 Dec. 2012. Web. 26 Dec. 2012.

"Head Injuries in Football." *New York Times.* New York Times, 21 Oct. 2010. Web. 23 Nov. 2012.

Norton, Amy. "Alzheimer's Death Rate Higher in Former NFL Players." *Reuters.com.* Reuters, 5 Sep. 2012. Web. 23 Nov. 2012.

Questions for Review and Revision

1. What is the student's thesis? Can you state it in your own words?
2. Does the student present enough evidence to support the thesis? What, if anything, could strengthen his essay?
3. How effective is the opening? Does it grab attention and dramatize the student's subject? What changes, if any, would you make?
4. *Blending the Modes:* How does the student use *definition, comparison,* and *persuasion* to develop the essay?
5. Did the student follow the instructor's suggestions? Did he develop an original topic?
6. Read the essay aloud. Do you detect any informal or unclear sentences that could be more clearly stated?

WRITING SUGGESTIONS

1. Using the student's essay as a model, describe the causes of effects of another phenomenon—the popularity of reality television shows, a campus fad, rising consumer debt, the prices of homes in your area, the local job market, or differences between male and female attitudes on a certain subject.

2. *Collaborative Writing:* Discuss this essay with a group of students. What impact do they think rule changes to avoid concussions will have on professional football? Will it lessen fan interest? Will it preserve popularity of the game? Do they know parents who discourage their sons from playing tackle football? Use comparison to organize positive and negative comments in a short essay.

EVALUATING CAUSE-AND-EFFECT CHECKLIST

Before submitting your paper, review these points:

1. Is your thesis clearly stated?
2. Are causes clearly stated, logically organized, and supported by details?
3. Are conflicting interpretations disproven or acknowledged?
4. Are effects supported by observation and evidence? Do you avoid sweeping generalizations and unsupported conclusions?
5. Do you anticipate future changes that might alter predictions?
6. Do you avoid making errors in critical thinking, such as confusing time relationships with cause and effect?
7. Have you tested your ideas with peer review?

Accompanying English CourseMate Resources

 Visit English CourseMate at **www.cengagebrain.com** to find many helpful resources and study tools for this chapter.

Argument and Persuasion

What Is Argument and Persuasion?

We are bombarded by argument and persuasion every day. Newspaper editorials encourage us to change our opinions about immigration, gun control, taxes, or terrorism. Sales brochures try to convince us to invest in stocks or buy life insurance. Fund-raising letters ask us to contribute to homeless shelters or the local symphony. Billboards, online pop-ups, magazine ads, email, and television commercials urge us to buy automobiles and soft drinks. Political candidates solicit our votes. Public service announcements warn us against smoking and drunk driving.

As a student, you have to develop persuasive arguments in essays and research papers to demonstrate your skills and knowledge. After graduation you will need a persuasive resume and cover letter to secure job interviews. In your career you will have to impress clients, motivate employees, justify decisions, and propose new ideas to superiors with well-stated arguments and persuasive appeals.

Purposes of Argument

Writers use argument for four basic purposes:

1. **To persuade readers to accept a thesis, understand a point of view, share an opinion, agree with a proposal, or change their beliefs and attitudes.** Persuasion seeks to influence how people think or feel. A film review denounces an action movie for its violence. A business leader argues a tax hike will hinder job growth. Environmentalists support a policy to combat climate change. Senators endorse or reject a Presidential appointment. A medical researcher argues that a new drug has dangerous side effects. A college research paper proposes that *The Glass Menagerie* should be read as a serious drama about the Great Depression rather than a romantic melodrama. A website presents evidence that a convicted murderer is innocent.

2. **To motivate readers to take action or change their behavior.** Motivation moves beyond influencing how people think to how they act. An email encourages parents to boycott a violent movie. A business leader urges Congress to vote against a tax increase. An article in a medical journal instructs doctors to prescribe less than the recommended dosage of a new drug to avoid side effects. An attorney files a motion requesting a new trial for his client.

3. **To defend a decision or action or respond to criticism.** A director writes an op-ed explaining the historical accuracy of a film criticized for being overly violent. A member of Congress releases a statement justifying her vote on taxes. A drug company runs advertisements in medical magazines supporting its new product. A judge defends a controversial ruling. A prominent commentator or celebrity writes a blog explaining why he or she changed positions on gun control or abortion.

4. **To make readers aware of an issue, change, opportunity, or problem.** Writers use persuasion to arouse interest, state an observation, or raise questions without always proposing a specific solution or course of action. A columnist notes that texting has changed our attention span and use of language. A researcher warns that a green energy source releases less carbon than fossil fuels but poses a threat to the water supply. A doctor questions widely believed assumptions about diet and exercise. The goal for many writers is not to state a thesis or motivate action, but rather to encourage critical thinking, spark further debate, and call for additional research.

Audience

The audience plays a critical role in the way writers shape arguments, especially when they suspect that readers hold viewpoints opposed to theirs or might be prejudiced against them or the groups they represent. In directing an argument to readers, writers often use emotional or dramatic statements that stir people's passions and beliefs. Advertisers use sex appeal to sell everything from toothpaste to cars. Commercials for charities flash 800 numbers over images of starving children to motivate people to make donations. In creating persuasive arguments, you should consider the perceptual world of your readers (see page 7).

Appealing to Hostile Readers

Perhaps most challenging is attempting to persuade a hostile audience: readers you anticipate having negative attitudes toward you, the organization you represent, or the ideas you advocate. Although no technique will magically convert opponents into supporters, you can overcome a measure of hostility and influence those who may still be undecided with a few approaches:

1. **Openly admit differences.** Instead of attempting to pretend no conflict exists, openly state that your view may differ from that of your readers. This honest admission can win a measure of respect.

2. **Responsibly summarize opposing viewpoints.** By fairly restating your opponents' views, you force readers to agree with you and demonstrate impartiality.

3. **Avoid making judgmental statements.** Do not label your opponents' ideas with negative language. Use neutral terms to make distinctions. If you call your ideas intelligent and your readers' ideas naïve or stupid, you will have difficulty getting people to accept your points because in the process they will have to accept your insults as being valid.

4. **Point to shared values, experiences, and problems.** Build bridges with your readers by demonstrating past cooperation and common goals.

5. **Ask your readers to keep an open mind.** Don't demand or expect to convert readers. However, almost everyone will agree to try to be open-minded and receptive to new ideas, so you can suggest that what is needed is a reasonable debate about issues, rather than arguments or accusations.

6. **Work to overcome negative stereotypes.** Play the devil's advocate, and determine what negative stereotypes your readers might have about you and your ideas. Then work to include examples, references, and evidence in your paper to counter negative assumptions.

Persuasive Appeals

Writers traditionally use three basic appeals to convince readers to accept their ideas or take action: **logic**, **emotion**, and **ethics**. Because each appeal has advantages and disadvantages, writers generally use more than one.

Logic

Logic supports a point of view or proposed action through reasoned arguments and a presentation of evidence:

Facts *Observable and verifiable details such as stock prices, rainfall measurements, or the number of cars sold last year*

Historical documents *Records such as trial transcripts, letters, email, government and corporate reports, blueprints, contracts, resolutions, minutes of meetings, laws, and regulations*

Test results *Findings established by experiments or standard research methods*

Statistics *Data represented by numbers and percentages*

Expert testimony *Opinions or statements made by respected authorities*

Eyewitness testimony *Statements by those who experienced or witnessed events and situations*

Polls and surveys *Measurements of public opinion, special populations, or sample audiences*

Logic is widely used in academic, business, and government reports.

ADVANTAGES:	Provides evidence needed for major decisions, especially group decisions. Factual evidence is transferable. Those convinced by research or statistics can share that data to persuade others.
DISADVANTAGES:	Demands a high degree of reader attention, concentration, time, and specialized knowledge. Logical arguments are often complex, and data can be difficult to present in brief messages.

Emotion

Emotion uses images, sensations, or shock appeal to lead people to react in a desired manner. Emotional appeals call on people's deeply felt needs and desires:

Creativity *To achieve recognition through self-expression and originality*

Success *To attain money, fame, status, or fulfillment*

Independence *To be unique; to stand out*

Conformity *To be included in a group; to be "in"*

Endurance *To achieve satisfaction by bearing burdens others could not, or to feel successful by simply surviving*

Fear *To resist, avoid, or defeat threats to the self or society, such as cancer, crime, or terrorism*

Preservation *To save or maintain traditions, values, artifacts, or the environment from loss or damage*

Popularity *To be known, recognized, accepted, attractive, or desirable*

Empathy *To share the feelings of others or be moved by their situation*

Service *To help the disadvantaged, contribute to a meaningful cause, or volunteer to aid others*

Emotional appeals are found most frequently in public relations, political campaigns, marketing, and advertising. Emotional appeals are not logical. Persuasive messages often use conflicting emotional appeals to motivate people. Recruiting commercials simultaneously urge men and women to conform by joining a regimented team and to achieve independence by being "one of the few, the proud, the brave."

ADVANTAGES:	Produces immediate results.
DISADVANTAGES:	Has limited impact, can backfire, and provides limited factual support for readers to share with others.

Ethics

Ethics use shared values to influence people. Ethics may call on reasoning but do not rest wholly on logical analysis of data. Like emotional appeals, ethics reflect deeply held convictions rather than personal motivations:

Religion *The desire to follow the rules and behavior espoused by one's faith, such as to be a good Christian or an observant Jew.*

Patriotism *The urge to place one's country before personal needs: "Ask not what your country can do for you; ask what you can do for your country."*

Standards *The desire to be a good citizen, a good lawyer, or a good parent; to express the higher ideals of a community, profession, or family role.*

Humanitarianism *A secular appeal to help others, protect the weak, or be a "citizen of the world."*

Ethical appeals form the basis of many sermons, editorials, and political speeches.

ADVANTAGES:	Can be very powerful, especially if the writer is addressing an audience with the same value system.
DISADVANTAGES:	Dependent on readers who accept the principles espoused by the writer. A Muslim cleric's appeal, for example, may have little impact on Catholics or atheists.

Blending Appeals

To create effective persuasive messages, writers frequently blend factual details with emotionally charged human-interest stories. A fund-raising email for a children's shelter might use the emotional story of a single child to arouse sympathy; provide facts and statistics to demonstrate the severity of the problem; and then conclude with an ethical appeal for financial support:

Make a Difference

Thirteen-year-old Sandy Lopez will not have to sleep in a doorway tonight. Abandoned by abusive parents, she spent six weeks living in subway stations and alleys before she came to Safe Haven. Today she has a warm bed, clean clothes, and regular meals. She is back in school, making friends, and studying music.

Emotion
human interest story demonstrating a problem

Since 1986 Safe Haven has helped thousands of homeless children find shelter, counseling, and support. Eighty percent of our clients complete high school and almost a third graduate from college.

Logic
factual support presenting a solution

But Safe Haven has only 90 beds and every day has to turn away dozens of the 2,000 homeless children who live in the streets, where they often succumb to drugs, prostitution, and alcohol abuse. To meet the growing need, Safe Haven needs your help to build a new dorm, hire more counselors, and expand its job training center.

Living in one of the richest cities in the world, can we ignore the children who sleep in our streets? Make a difference. Contribute to Safe Haven today.

Ethics
moral call to action

Writing Techniques: ARGUMENT AND PERSUASION

Asking and Answering Questions

Writers use questions to prompt readers to examine their attitudes and behavior. In "Stuff Is Not Salvation" Anna Quindlen (page 438) repeats the question, "Why did we buy all this stuff?" to criticize consumerism. Julianne Malveaux (page 463) presents her position on racial identity by answering the question, "Why are we still celebrating Black History Month?"

Organizing Arguments Using Other Modes

Writers often frame arguments using specific modes to set up a thesis, organize evidence, and persuade readers. Rick Newman (page 446) uses division to outline five reasons why Americans should not fear China. Armstrong Williams (page 461) urges readers to reject ethnic identity by comparing a narrow "cultural I" with a greater and more beneficial "civic we" identity.

Using Connotations to Shape Perceptions

Writers influence readers through word choices that provide positive and negative impressions of ideas, people, and events. Students are often accused of "cheating." Mary Sherry (page 442) accuses teachers of "cheating" by passing students who deserve to fail. Chuck Lane (page 452) denounces warning against offending Muslims as "censorship-by-riot." Rick Newman (page 447) calls Americans who fear China "paranoid." In choosing words, writers have to be cautious to avoid inflammatory language that will alienate readers.

Critical Thinking for Writing Argument and Persuasion

Perhaps no other form of writing demands more critical thinking than argument and persuasion. When using logical, emotional, and ethical appeals, avoid the logical fallacies (see pages 380–381).

Strategies FOR READING ARGUMENT AND PERSUASION

When reading the argument and persuasion entries in this chapter, keep these questions in mind:

Understanding Meaning

1. What is the author's thesis? What does he or she want readers to accept?
2. How credible is the thesis? Does it make sense? Are alternatives discussed?
3. How does the writer characterize those who advocate differing views? Does the writer appear to have an unfair bias?

Evaluating Strategy

1. Which appeals are used—logic, emotion, or ethics?
2. Do the appeals seem to work with the intended audience?
3. Are the factual details interesting, believable, and effective?
4. Does the writer present relevant and sufficient evidence to support his or her thesis?
5. Are emotional appeals suitable, or do they risk backfiring or distorting the issue?
6. Are logical fallacies avoided?
7. Does the writer appear to anticipate rejection or approval?

Appreciating Language

1. What role does connotation play in shaping arguments using logical, emotional, or ethical appeals?
2. What does the author's choice of words suggest about the intended audience?
3. Does word choice indicate a bias? Does the writer use inflammatory or derogatory language to dismiss opposing views instead of debating their merits or offering proof?

ANNA QUINDLEN

Anna Quindlen (1952–) graduated from Barnard College in 1974 and began working as a reporter in New York City. After writing articles for the *New York Post*, she took over the "About New York" column for the *New York Times*. In 1986 she started her own column, "Life in the Thirties." Her collected articles were published in *Living Out Loud* in 1988. She has written numerous op-ed pieces for the *Times* on social and political issues and in 1992 received the Pulitzer Prize. The following year she published another collection of essays, *Thinking Out Loud: On the Personal, the Political, the Public, and the Private*. Quindlen has also written six novels including, *Object Lessons*, *One True Thing*, and *Black and Blue*.

Stuff Is Not Salvation

CONTEXT: *Anna Quindlen published this* Newsweek *article in 2008, when a severe recession caused rising unemployment, foreclosures, and business failures.*

WRITER'S NOTE: *Quindlen repeats the question "why did we buy all this stuff?" to emphasize her argument against rampant consumerism and wasteful spending.*

As the boom times fade, an important holiday question surfaces: why in the world did we buy all this junk in the first place?   *1 opening question*

What passes for the holiday season began before dawn the day after Thanksgiving, when a worker at a Walmart in Valley Stream, N.Y., was trampled to death by a mob of bargain hunters. Afterward, there were reports that some people, mesmerized by cheap consumer electronics and discounted toys, kept shopping even after announcements to clear the store.   *2 dramatic example*

These are dark days in the United States: the cataclysmic stock-market declines, the industries edging up on bankruptcy, the home foreclosures and the waves of layoffs. But the prospect of an end to plenty has uncovered what may ultimately be a more pernicious problem, an addiction to consumption so out of control that it qualifies as a sickness. The suffocation of a store employee by a stampede of shoppers was horrifying, but it wasn't entirely surprising.   *3 consumption as sickness*

Americans have been on an acquisition binge for decades. I suspect television advertising, which made me want a Chatty Cathy doll so much as a kid that when I saw her under the tree my head almost exploded. By contrast, my father will be happy to tell you about the excitement of getting an orange in his stocking during the Depression. The depression before this one.   *4 comparison*

A critical difference between then and now is credit. The orange had to be paid for. The rite of passage for a child when I was young   *5* was a solemn visit to the local bank, there to exchange birthday money for a savings passbook. Every once in a while, like magic, a bit of extra money would appear. Interest. Yippee.

The passbook was replaced by plastic, so that today Americans are overwhelmed by debt and the national savings rate is calculated, like an algebra equation, in negatives. By 2010 Americans will be a trillion dollars in the hole on credit-card debt alone.

6
debt

But let's look, not at the numbers, but the atmospherics. Appliances, toys, clothes, gadgets. Junk. There's the sad truth. Wall Street executives may have made investments that lost their value, but, in a much smaller way, so did the rest of us. "I looked into my closet the other day and thought, why did I buy all this stuff?" one friend said recently. A person in the United States replaces a cell phone every 16 months, not because the cell phone is old, but because it is oldish. My mother used to complain that the Christmas toys were grubby and forgotten by Easter. (I didn't even really like dolls, especially dolls who introduced themselves to you over and over again when you pulled the ring in their necks.) Now much of the country is made up of people with the acquisition habits of a 7-year-old, desire untethered from need, or the ability to pay. The result is a booming business in those free-standing storage facilities, where junk goes to linger in a persistent vegetative state, somewhere between eBay and the dump.

7

question
repeated

Oh, there is still plenty of need. But it is for real things, things that matter: college tuition, prescription drugs, rent. Food pantries and soup kitchens all over the country have seen demand for their services soar. Homelessness, which had fallen in recent years, may rebound as people lose their jobs and their houses. For the first time this month, the number of people on food stamps will exceed the 30 million mark.

8
need
for "real
things"

Hard times offer the opportunity to ask hard questions, and one of them is the one my friend asked, staring at sweaters and shoes: why did we buy all this stuff? Did anyone really need a flat-screen in the bedroom, or a designer handbag, or three cars? If the mall is our temple, then Marc Jacobs is God. There's a scary thought.

9

question
repeated

The drumbeat that accompanied Black Friday this year was that the numbers had to redeem us, that if enough money was spent by shoppers it would indicate that things were not so bad after all. But what the economy required was at odds with a necessary epiphany. Because things are dire, many people have become hesitant to spend money on trifles. And in the process they began to realize that it's all trifles.

10

Here I go, stating the obvious: stuff does not bring salvation. But if it's so obvious, how come for so long people have not realized it? The happiest families I know aren't the ones with the most square footage, living in one of those cavernous houses with enough garage space to start a homeless shelter. (There's a holiday suggestion right there.) And of course they are not people who are in real

11
thesis
example

want. Just because consumption is bankrupt doesn't mean that poverty is ennobling.

But somewhere in between there is a family like one I know in rural Pennsylvania, raising bees for honey (and for the science, and the fun, of it), digging a pond out of the downhill flow of the stream, with three kids who somehow, incredibly, don't spend six months of the year whining for the toy du jour. (The youngest once demurred when someone offered him another box on his birthday; "I already have a present," he said.) The mother of the household says having less means her family appreciates possessions more. "I can give you a story about every item, really," she says of what they own. In other words, what they have has meaning. And meaning, real meaning, is what we are always trying to possess. Ask people what they'd grab if their house were on fire, the way our national house is on fire right now. No one ever says it's the tricked-up microwave they got at Walmart.

*12
example*

final point

Understanding Meaning

1. What is Quindlen's thesis? Can you state it in your own words?
2. What does Quindlen blame, in part, for what she calls an "acquisitions binge"?
3. What does Quindlen mean by the need for "real things"? What things matter, in her opinion?
4. How did credit, in her view, fuel consumption?
5. Whom does Quindlen see as the happiest families? Why?
6. *Critical Thinking:* Consumer spending accounts for 60–70 percent of the American economy. Walmart is the nation's largest employer. Can we cut back on spending without causing more unemployment and business failures? Are we trapped in a vicious circle of credit and spending? What would it take to change our economy?

Evaluating Strategy

1. Quindlen restates the question, "Why did we buy all this stuff," three times. Is this an effective device? Why or why not? Do you think she senses that many of her readers have asked themselves similar questions?
2. How effective is Quindlen's opening example? Does the trampling death of a store employee illustrate her point?
3. What facts does Quindlen include to support her thesis? Are they convincing? Why or why not?
4. *Blending the Modes:* Where does Quindlen use *narration* and *comparison* to develop her argument?

Appreciating Language

1. Quindlen uses words like "stuff" or "junk" to describe people's personal possessions. What impact do these words have? Do you know people who spend money on something "they have to have," only to call it "my junk" or "my stuff" a few months later?

2. For some Americans, is the shopping mall a "temple"? Why or why not?

3. What words does Quindlen use to describe the happiest families she knows?

4. *Critical Thinking:* Consider the words in Quindlen's title. Do many people see "stuff" as "salvation"? Do we buy things because we "need" them or because we think they will make us happy, more popular, or enriched?

WRITING SUGGESTIONS

1. Write a short essay about shopping habits you have observed. Do you know people who purchase items they never use or buy clothes they never wear? Is shopping itself a kind of hobby or social activity? Is "going to the mall" something to do, like going to a movie? Is this behavior normal, or do you see it as something harmful?

2. *Collaborative Writing:* Discuss Quindlen's remark that "meaning, real meaning, is what we are always trying to possess" with a group of students. What do they think this statement means? Do people buy "stuff" because it is easier to attain than something more abstract like love, respect, or happiness? Summarize the students' views in a short essay. If they have differing interpretations, use comparison or division to organize their comments.

MARY SHERRY

Mary Sherry (1940–) writes from her experience as a parent, a writer, and a teacher. She writes articles and advertising copy, owns a small publishing firm in Minnesota, and for many years has taught remedial and creative writing to adults.

In Praise of the "F" Word

CONTEXT: *In this 1991* Newsweek *article, Sherry argues that failing students who do not try would motivate them to take school seriously.*

WRITER'S NOTE: *Sherry, a teacher, uses her own son as an example.*

1 Tens of thousands of 18-year-olds will graduate this year and be handed meaningless diplomas. These diplomas won't look any different from those awarded their luckier classmates. Their validity will be questioned only when their employers discover that these graduates are semiliterate.

2 Eventually a fortunate few will find their way into educational repair shops—adult-literacy programs, such as the one where I teach basic grammar and writing. There, high-school graduates and high-school dropouts pursuing graduate-equivalency certificates will learn the skills they should have learned in school. They will also discover they have been cheated by our educational system.

3 As I teach, I learn a lot about our schools. Early in each session I ask my students to write about an unpleasant experience they had in school. No writers' block here! "I wish someone would have made me stop doing drugs and made me study." "I liked to party and no one seemed to care." "I was a good kid and didn't cause any trouble, so they just passed me along even though I didn't read well and couldn't write." And so on.

4 I am your basic do-gooder, and prior to teaching this class I blamed the poor academic skills our kids have today on drugs, divorce and other impediments to concentration necessary for doing well in school. But, as I rediscover each time I walk into the classroom, before a teacher can expect students to concentrate, he has to get their attention, no matter what distractions may be at hand. There are many ways to do this, and they have much to do with teaching style. However, if style alone won't do it, there is another way to show who holds the winning hand in the classroom. That is to reveal the trump card of failure.

5 I will never forget a teacher who played that card to get the attention of one of my children. Our youngest, a world-class charmer, did little to develop his intellectual talents but always got by. Until Mrs. Stifter.

Sherry, Mary, "In Praise of the 'F' Word" Newsweek May 6, 1991 Reprinted by permission of the author.

Our son was a high school senior when he had her for English. 6
"He sits in the back of the room talking to his friends," she
told me. "Why don't you move him to the front row?" I urged,
believing the embarrassment would get him to settle down.
Mrs. Stifter looked at me steely-eyed over her glasses. "I don't
move seniors," she said. "I flunk them." I was flustered. Our
son's academic life flashed before my eyes. No teacher had
ever threatened him with that before. I regained my compo-
sure and managed to say that I thought she was right. By the
time I got home I was feeling pretty good about this. It was
a radical approach for these times, but, well, why not? "She's
going to flunk you," I told my son. I did not discuss it any further.
Suddenly English became a priority in his life. He finished out
the semester with an A.

I know one example doesn't make a case, but at night I see 7
a parade of students who are angry and resentful for having
been passed along until they could no longer even pretend to
keep up. Of average intelligence or better, they eventually quit
school, concluding they were too dumb to finish. "I should have
been held back" is a comment I hear frequently. Even sadder are
those students who are high-school graduates who say to me after
a few weeks of class, "I don't know how I ever got a high-school
diploma."

Passing students who have not mastered the work cheats them 8
and the employers who expect graduates to have basic skills. We
excuse this dishonest behavior by saying kids can't learn if they
come from terrible environments. No one seems to stop to think
that—no matter what environments they come from—most kids
don't put school first on their list unless they perceive something is
at stake. They'd rather be sailing.

Many students I see at night could give expert testimony on 9
unemployment, chemical dependency, abusive relationships. In
spite of these difficulties, they have decided to make education a
priority. They are motivated by the desire for a better job or the
need to hang on to the one they've got. They have a healthy fear
of failure.

People of all ages can rise above their problems, but they need 10
to have a reason to do so. Young people generally don't have the
maturity to value education in the same way my adult students
value it. But fear of failure, whether economic or academic, can
motivate both.

Flunking as a regular policy has just as much merit today as 11
it did two generations ago. We must review the threat of flunking and see it as it really is—a positive teaching tool. It is an
expression of confidence by both teachers and parents that the
students have the ability to learn the material presented to them.
However, making it work again would take a dedicated, caring
conspiracy between teachers and parents. It would mean facing
the tough reality that passing kids who haven't learned the

material—while it might save them grief for the short term—dooms them to long-term illiteracy. It would mean that teachers would have to follow through on their threats, and parents would have to stand behind them, knowing their children's best interests are indeed at stake. This means no more doing Scott's assignments for him because he might fail. No more passing Jodi because she's such a nice kid.

This is a policy that worked in the past and can work today.   12
A wise teacher, with the support of his parents, gave our son the opportunity to succeed—or fail. It's time we return this choice to all students.

Understanding Meaning

1. What was Sherry's purpose in writing the essay? Does she have in mind certain types of students? Are there students who should be excluded from her plan?
2. When Sherry discusses the adults she works with, what reasons do they give for not doing well in school? How do they feel about their past education?
3. Why are the adult students Sherry teaches motivated to study what they failed to learn when they were younger?
4. Why does Sherry call the threat of failure a positive teaching tool?
5. Why would it take a concerted effort of parents and teachers for Sherry's suggestion to work?
6. *Critical Thinking:* Do you feel that the threat of failure would motivate students to do better in school than they would without that threat? Is Sherry right in thinking that students do not perceive failure to be a real threat? Have things changed since Sherry published this essay in 1991?

Evaluating Strategy

1. Is the title effective in grabbing attention? Why or why not?
2. *Blending the Modes:* How does Sherry use *comparison* and *cause and effect* to develop her argument?
3. How does Sherry establish herself as someone who has a right to express an opinion on this subject? In other words, how does she present a trustworthy ethos?
4. Would students in grades K–12 be able to get past their emotional response to failing and understand its logic? If you failed a course and were told it would be good for you in the long run, would you agree?

Appreciating Language

1. What does Sherry mean when she refers to failure as the "trump card" of education?
2. What does the term "educational repair shops" suggest?
3. Is Sherry's tone and style suited to a news magazine like *Newsweek*? Why or why not?

WRITING SUGGESTIONS

1. Write a short essay that agrees or disagrees with Sherry's argument about failing students.

2. *Collaborative Writing:* Discuss Sherry's essay with a group of students and ask them about the grading policies in their high schools. Were failing grades given routinely or rarely? Were students passed based on attendance or good behavior? Write a short essay organizing the group's observations using division or classification.

Blending the Modes

RICK NEWMAN

Rick Newman graduated from Boston College with a degree in English and economics in 1988. He began working at *U.S. News & World Report* as a fact checker. From 1995 to 2001, he was the magazine's chief Pentagon correspondent, where he was a major contributor of material about 9/11. Currently focusing on economic and business issues, Newman has written about major corporations, demographics, and fiscal policy. Newman has also published pieces in the *Washington Post* and the *New York Times*.

Five Reasons to Stop Fearing China

CONTEXT: *Newman argues that Americans do not need to fear China's emerging economy, because it poses a challenge rather than a threat to America's status in the world.*

WRITER'S NOTE: *Newman uses division to organize his argument and places his five reasons in bold font to emphasize his main points.*

Its economy is going gangbusters, and it barely felt the global recession that has left the world's most advanced nations with a nasty hangover. It has cornered the market on some of the world's most valuable minerals. It has a fancy new stealth fighter, proof that it can turn out world-class technology. And its parents are raising overachieving kids who seem way smarter than the slackers slouching around in America's schools. 1

China is clearly on a roll. President Hu Jintao's recent visit to Washington, replete with a formal state dinner, put China's leader on a par with President Obama and the world's most powerful politicians. Many in China feel it's finally their time to displace America as the world's preeminent power, a turnabout that's on the minds of many Americans, too. In a recent Pew Research poll, an astounding 47 percent of Americans said that China is the world's leading economic power, while just 31 percent felt that the United States is No. 1—a complete reversal of Americans' views just three years ago. As if that's not enough, the new bestseller *Battle Hymn of the Tiger Mother*, by Amy Chua, trumpets the superiority of demanding, Asian-style parenting over the indulgent coddling that American parents prefer. Now that really hurts. 2

China does represent a remarkable story of progress, and since it's technically a Communist country—which relatively few Americans have ever visited—it's not surprising that Americans find it somewhat scary. Still, it's like a mouse tormenting an elephant. "I find it very amusing," says Wei Li, a professor at the University of Virginia's Darden School of Business, who also 3 teaches at the Cheung Kong Graduate School of Business in Beijing. "China has gone through an extraordinary growth period, but it's going to take China a long time to realize American levels of prosperity." He also points out that Americans had similar fears of Japan becoming the world's dominant power in the 1980s— right before Japan went into a 20-year swoon from which it still hasn't emerged.

So the next time you're gripped with fear about the prospect of 4 life under a Chinese boot heel, take a deep breath and keep these points in mind:

China still has a middling economy. China's population is 5 four times that of the United States, yet its GDP is just two-thirds as large. That makes China an important economic power, but hardly the world's most dominant. China's per-capita GDP—which measures the productive capacity of the population as a whole— is just $7,400, which ranks 128th out of 230 nations, according to the CIA World Factbook. (The United States, with per-capita GDP of about $47,000, ranks 11th, after a handful of tiny nations like Qatar and Liechtenstein with concentrated wealth and a minimal underclass.) The number of poor people in China is probably greater than the entire population of the United States. And vast stretches of China's interior remain untouched by the impressive modern infrastructure that makes China's coastal region highly productive.

Given China's size, ambition, and industrial capability, it's inevi- 6 table that China's economy will become the world's largest. But it's worth keeping in mind that 30 years ago, China was nearly as backward as North Korea is today, with little external trade, a population that was mostly poor, and a government that could barely prevent mass starvation. China's progress since then has been unprecedented, but it still has a long way to go before lifting the majority of its people out of poverty and raising overall living standards to anything near western levels.

Paranoid Americans (or Europeans, or Japanese, or Koreans) 7 may think China's goal is to somehow conquer them, but China's leaders are overwhelmingly focused on creating jobs and raising living standards for their own people. Failing to do that could provoke class warfare and open rebellion, one of the biggest fears of China's leaders. That's why China will continue to pursue aggressive economic policies meant to boost growth by 7 to 10 percent per year—for the next 10 or even 20 years. But at some point growth will slow and China will start to resemble a mature western economy—with a lot of economic power, but also the bureaucracy, special interests, and destructive specula- tive behavior that tends to bog capitalism down. China will be no more able to dominate America than America has been able to dominate China.

It desperately needs the United States. China's rapid growth 8 depends on a huge stream of consumers to keep buying the stuff it makes. And Americans are China's best customers. Worries about the U.S. government being too dependent on China to finance its debt are legitimate, since China is the top purchaser of U.S. government securities, with about 21 percent of all holdings. But the real problem is Washington's overdependence on debt, not the portion held by China. It's also true that Chinese officials sometimes overplay their hand, which may be the case with reported restrictions on the exports of rare-earth metals found largely in China, which are key components in many high-tech devices. Still, that kind of maneuvering is standard capitalist fare (commodity traders in New York and London try to corner markets all the time) and China is likely to exploit its own resources just as every other capitalist nation has done.

Alarmists tend to worry that China's self-interested behavior   9
could become a form of economic terrorism. That's a stretch. "The Chinese ideology has changed from Communism to GDPism," says Li. "Nothing matters except that the economy grows." Communist Party officials even earn perks and promotions based largely on their contributions to economic growth. So by that logic, China will carefully cultivate its relationship with the United States as long as it needs our business. Which is likely to be a long time. Long after China becomes the world's largest economy, it will still depend on heavily on trading partners, just as the United States does today. In fact, it's hard to imagine a scenario in which China could get wealthy, or stay wealthy, without the trade that has done far more to lift it toward world-power status than any other factor.

The richer China gets, the more it will buy. During a recent   10
visit to Spain, a key member of China's Politburo pointed out that if every person in China bought one bottle of Spanish wine and one container of Spanish olive oil per year, Spain would run out, with nothing left to offer the rest of the world. The rise of China's consumer class may be the most powerful economic force of the next 100 years, and China won't be the only beneficiary. As Chinese consumers earn more disposable income, they're beginning to covet the same cars, appliances, gizmos, and luxury items as everybody else in the world. Western business leaders are right to demand that China crack down on piracy and welcome foreign-made goods on the same terms that other nations import products made from China. But as China becomes wealthier and more dependent on trade, it has incentives to do just that.

One reason Chinese consumers haven't made much of a mark   11
yet is that they're still some of the thriftiest people on the planet, with a savings rate that's close to 50 percent. (The U.S. savings rate, by comparison, is about 5 percent, up from nearly zero a few years ago.) But Chinese consumers are nearly certain to spend more as credit becomes more commonplace, mass marketers work their black magic, and the first generation of affluent consumers begins

to retire in a few years, which will force them to spend down their savings. Even if those consumers do buy mostly Chinese-made goods, that could divert some of China's exports to internal markets, creating new openings for exports from America and other nations.

China's military might is overblown. If you're worried about a 12
Chinese stealth fighter dropping bombs on your neighborhood, you can relax. The staged leak of recent photos showing a "secret" Chinese-made stealth aircraft generated terrific front-page drama and got the world's defense contractors excited about another arms race. But it was more of an exercise in national pride than in aeronautics. As China becomes richer in coming decades, it could well end up with the world's biggest military budget. But for a good long while, America's military technology will be generations ahead of China's.

The stealth fighter is a good case study. If China did in fact build 13
its own stealth aircraft—without simply reverse-engineering a Russian design—then it's a nice achievement. But the plane's first flight, reported a couple weeks ago, comes more than 30 years after America's stealth program began. During that time, the United States has developed numerous next-generation stealth technologies, established a detailed training regimen, built a global support infrastructure, and learned how to defeat stealth technology if an enemy should ever use it. Rather than sending a threatening message to the United States, China was probably showing off its advanced jet for more practical reasons—like advertising its wares to other countries that might want to buy Chinese-made weapons. And if China does decide to sink vast amounts of national wealth into the world's costliest weapon systems, it could end up diverting resources away from worthier projects that might have a much bigger economic impact, as some critics feel America has done.

China is trying to modernize a military that not long ago 14
was completely obsolete, and it does have modern missiles, submarines, and Russian-made aircraft that make it quite capable of defending itself. And there probably are still some Communist party hardliners who feel that waging a war to reclaim Taiwan would be worth the cost. Americans tend to think of China as a superpower wannabe always focused on Washington, but Michael Swaine of the Carnegie Endowment for International Peace points out that China shares land borders with 14 other countries and has a long history of territorial disputes with truculent neighbors. That makes regional dominance its first national-security priority. Plus, any war would torpedo the economic gains China has spent the last 30 years making. Still, if you're really concerned about Chinese aggression, then worry about cyber-war, not bombs and bullets.

Our biggest enemy isn't China. It's ourselves. Critics tend to 15
describe China as "taking" American jobs, as if a whole variety

of industries rightfully belongs in the United States, in perpetuity. That's not how capitalism works. Jobs always move from place to place, based on who can do the work most effectively at the lowest price. As low-paying jobs migrate away from the United States, it's up to us to replace them with higher-paying jobs that require more skill and generate more innovative products. But that requires a strong education system, effective government policies, the careful use of national resources, citizens willing to sacrifice and work as hard as necessary, and above all, enlightened leadership. If we can't muster that, it's not China's fault. It's our own. And if China or any nation can do better, then maybe they deserve to be No. 1 after all.

Understanding Meaning

1. Why, in Newman's view, is China's emergence not a threat to the United States?
2. Who, according to Newman, is America's "biggest enemy"?
3. How does China's geography limit its ability to play a larger role on the world stage?
4. How might Western economies benefit from China's rising purchasing power?
5. Why is China's new stealth fighter not a threat to American security?
6. *Critical Thinking*: Does Newman's argument rest on unproven assumptions? As China becomes richer, does it follow it will buy more from the West? Might China produce its own goods or purchase them from South Korea, Japan, or India? When Japan was a rising power in the 1980s, it strictly limited American imports. Might American companies find themselves locked out of the world's largest economy?

Evaluating Strategy

1. What evidence does Newman include to support his thesis?
2. Does Newman's use of bold subtitles strengthen his argument and make his train of thought easier to follow? Can special effects like bold, italicized, or underlined text distract readers?
3. *Blending the Modes*: Where does Newman use *comparison, cause and effect,* and *analysis* to develop his argument?

Appreciating Language

1. Newman uses the analogy of a "mouse tormenting an elephant" to describe China's relationship with the United States. Does this seem to exaggerate the situation or place it in context?
2. Newman uses words like "paranoid" to describe those who fear Chinese domination. Is this an effective word? Does it appear to dismiss genuine concerns?
3. *Critical Thinking*: Consider the wording of Newman's title. Persuading readers not to "fear" China does not mean it will not become a superpower. Would

many Americans be comforted with the idea of the United States becoming a secondary nation, provided the leading power did not threaten its security or sovereignty?

WRITING SUGGESTIONS

1. Write a short essay that agrees or disagrees with one or more of Newman's five points.

2. *Collaborative Writing:* Discuss Newman's arguments with a group of students. Do you accept his view that our biggest enemy is "ourselves" and not China? Write a short essay stating your point of view. If members disagree, consider drafting opposing arguments.

Opposing Viewpoints: Free Speech and Censorship

CHARLES LANE

Charles Lane graduated from Harvard University in 1983 and received a master's degree from Yale Law School in 1997. He was a foreign correspondent for *Newsweek* and served as the magazine's Berlin's bureau chief. He was the editor of *The New Republic* from 1997 to 1999. After covering the Supreme Court for *The Washington Post* from 2000 to 2009, he joined the newspaper's editorial staff. Lane has taught journalism at Georgetown University and Princeton.

There's No Place for Censorship-by-Riot

CONTEXT: *Charlie Lane published this* Washington Post *editorial in 2012 following riots that swept the Muslim world in response to an anti-Islamic video posted online.*

WRITER'S NOTE: *To arouse attention and dramatize his view, Lane opens his article describing a magazine's publication of cartoons officials feared might spark violence, then proclaims "one cheer" for the editors publishing "things that other people find objection-able and irresponsible." To highlight an idea he places it in a one-sentence paragraph.*

Charlie Hebdo, a French satire magazine, published Wednesday cartoons that nastily mock the Prophet Muhammad, and European governments immediately feared more violence like the murder and arson at U.S. diplomatic installations that followed the appearance of a crude video about Muhammad. France closed 20 embassies as a precaution; the French foreign minister chided the magazine for pouring "oil on the fire." Germany's foreign minister used the same phrase. 1

I say: One cheer for *Charlie Hebdo*. I doubt that its cartoons are either laudable or responsible. In fact, I'm sure that they are neither. But if free speech means anything, it's the right to say and publish things that other people find objectionable and irresponsible, even blasphemous. Censorship is an affront to freedom, whether imposed by official decree or through a rioters' veto—as the Middle Eastern mobs and those who set them in motion seem to want. 2

That is the legitimate political point that *Charlie Hebdo*'s editors are making, at no small risk to their safety. The publication's offices were fire-bombed last year and have been under police protection since. As the magazine's director told Reuters: "It shows the climate—everyone is driven by fear, and that is exactly what this 3 small handful of extremists who do not represent anyone want—to make everyone afraid, to shut us all in a cave."

There's been too much equivocation about such matters lately. 4

I can understand why the Obama administration, trying to 5 quench a crisis last week, would denounce the trashy and deliberately insulting video "Innocence of Muslims." To their credit, administration officials, the most forthright of whom was Secretary of State Hillary Clinton, said that nothing can justify violence—and tried to defend free speech.

But they couldn't really square the circle. The more official oppro- 6 brium they heaped on the video, the more they implied that the rioters had a valid point—and the more they seemed to reward violence.

I suppose that the U.S. government could try to denounce all 7 potentially Islamophobic expression consistently, regardless of whether it triggers violence, just as the French government has preemptively distanced itself from *Charlie Hebdo's* cartoons.

But that would be an impossible task—even if the government 8 could explain why it condemns mockeries of Muhammad and not, say, Mel Gibson's *The Passion of the Christ*.

Meanwhile, Obama administration actions undermined its words 9 about free expression. The White House contacted Google, which does millions of dollars in business with the federal government, and asked it to reconsider whether "Innocence of Muslims" might have violated YouTube's terms of use. Exercising highly selective prosecutorial discretion, the government rounded up the video's alleged producer for an "entirely voluntary" session with his federal probation officer.

Gen. Martin Dempsey, chairman of the Joint Chiefs of Staff, 10 took it upon himself to call the Rev. Terry Jones, the Islamophobic preacher in Florida, to warn him that U.S. troops would be in danger if he didn't cease his support for the offensive video.

Think about that: The commander of the world's most powerful 11 military machine contacted an American civilian and suggested that his exercise of a constitutional right—and not enemy forces — was putting U.S. lives at risk. But it's not surprising, given that Dempsey's former staff lawyer argued in a recent op-ed that "Innocence of Muslims" is not constitutionally protected speech.

Among the many threats that Islamic extremism poses to the 12 West, censorship-by-riot may be the most insidious. We have been facing it at least since Iran's Ayatollah Ruhollah Khomeini issued a kill-the-apostate decree against British novelist Salman Rushdie in 1989. It arose again in 2006, when Muhammad-mocking cartoons in Denmark prompted the sacking of Danish embassies and death threats against the artist.

Think I exaggerate? No less a pillar of intellectual freedom 13 than Yale University Press decided three years ago not to publish the Danish cartoons in an academic book on the controversy, even though they were clearly relevant. Yale declined to print any images of Muhammad in the book, including a sketch by the

19th-century artist Gustave Doré. Yale said "experts" advised that depicting the prophet might offend some Muslims and trigger violence.

We can't slide one more inch down this slippery slope. Voltaire 14 famously remarked: "I do not agree with a word that you say, but I will defend to the death your right to say it." That must be the West's unequivocal, united answer to those who would exploit the ugly words of a few to justify the violent deeds of a mob.

Understanding Meaning

1. Why does Charles Lane support the publication of cartoons that might lead to violence?
2. Is there a difference between censorship and caution?
3. Why does Lane criticize the Obama administration for condemning a video he sees as "trashy and deliberately insulting"?
4. How does Lane view General Dempsey's call to Reverend Terry Jones? If you had a family member serving abroad who might be the target of anti-U.S. attacks, would you urge the government to caution citizens about taking actions or expressing ideas that might incite violence?
5. Lane compares anti-Islamic cartoons with Mel Gibson's film *The Passion of the Christ*. Would most readers see these works as being equivalent?
6. *Critical Thinking:* Is it easier to be objective about free speech that might offend people from another culture or another country? In the 1970s American Nazis planned to march in Skokie, Illinois, which had a large Jewish community that included a number of Holocaust survivors. Politicians, commentators, and legal scholars had heated debates whether local governments had the right to ban expressions that deeply offended their communities. Can you think of recent controversies over free expression and censorship?

Evaluating Strategy

1. How effective is Lane's opening?
2. Lane bases his article about censorship over satirical cartoons. Does this strengthen his point about free speech? Would some people who might object to the banning of a book be less offended by the banning of a cartoon?
3. *Blending the Modes*: Where does Lane use *definition* and *comparison* to develop his essay?
4. *Critical Thinking:* Lane ends his essay with a famous quotation. Is this an effective way to persuade an audience? Can famous quotes leave readers with something they can remember and repeat to others? Are some famous quotes likely to alienate rather than influence readers?

Appreciating Language

1. What words does Lane use to describe the cartoons and video? Do these words support his argument about free speech?
2. How would you define "censorship-by-riot"?

3. *Critical Thinking*: Lane uses the term "slippery slope." What implications does this term have? Can it be used to warn readers about potential dangers? Can writers reject the most reasonable proposal by arguing it is a "slippery slope" to something dangerous or unacceptable?

WRITING SUGGESTIONS

1. Write a short essay agreeing or disagreeing with Lane's position. Would you defend the publication of cartoons that deeply offended your own beliefs? Why or why not?

2. *Collaborative Writing*: Discuss Lane's article with other students and write an essay stating your group's view on free speech and censorship. If a campus organization invited a controversial speaker whose previous appearances sparked violence at other colleges, would they support banning the speaker, call for additional security to deter violence, or ignore the issue? If members disagree, consider drafting opposing statements.

SARAH CHAYES

Sarah Chayes (1962–) was born in Washington, D.C., and received a history degree from Harvard University in 1984. After serving in the Peace Corps in Morocco, she returned to Harvard and completed a master's degree in history and Middle Eastern studies. She was National Public Radio's Paris correspondent from 1996 to 2002, and covered the fall of the Taliban in 2001. Chayes stayed in Afghanistan, founding a non-profit, and then serving as an adviser to the international military command. In 2010 she became a special adviser to the chairman of the Joint Chiefs of Staff. Chayes has written extensively about the war in Afghanistan and the Arab Spring. In 2006 she published *The Punishment of Virtue: Inside Afghanistan After the Taliban*.

Anti-Muslim Movie May Not Meet Free-Speech Test

CONTEXT: *Chayes asserts that an anti-Islamic video that appeared designed to provoke a physically dangerous reaction, like "falsely shouting fire in a theatre," may not meet the test for protected free speech.*

WRITER'S NOTE: *Chayes develops a legalistic argument using deduction, first stating a major premise defining the limitations of free speech, then presenting the "Innocence of Muslims" as a minor premise, lining it up against the legal tests, and concluding that it is debatable whether the film meets the standard for protection by First Amendment guarantees.*

In one of the most famous First Amendment cases in U.S. history, 1 *Schenck v. United States,* Supreme Court Justice Oliver Wendell Holmes, Jr. established that the right to free speech in the United States is not unlimited.

"The most stringent protection," he wrote on behalf of a unani- 2 mous court, "would not protect a man in falsely shouting fire in a theater and causing a panic."

Holmes' test—that words are not protected if their nature and 3 circumstances create a "clear and present danger" of harm—has since been tightened. But even under the more restrictive current standard, "Innocence of Muslims," the film whose video trailer indirectly led to the death of U.S. Ambassador J. Christopher Stevens among others, is not, arguably, free speech protected under the U.S. Constitution and the values it enshrines.

According to initial media investigations, the clip, whose most 4 egregious lines were apparently dubbed in after it was shot, was first posted to YouTube in July by someone with the user name "Sam Bacile." The Associated Press reported tracing a cellphone number given as Bacile's to the address of a Californian of Egyptian

Coptic origin named Nakoula Basseley Nakoula. Nakoula has identified himself as coordinating logistics on the production but denies being Bacile.

According to *The Wall Street Journal*, when the video failed to attract much attention, another Coptic Christian, known for his anti-Islamic activism, sent a link to reporters in the U.S., Egypt and elsewhere on Sept. 6. His email message promoted a Sept. 11 event by anti-Islamic pastor Terry Jones and included a link to the trailer. 5

The current standard for restricting speech—or punishing it after it has in fact caused violence—was laid out in the 1969 case *Brandenburg v. Ohio*. Under the narrower guidelines, only speech that has the intent and the likelihood of inciting imminent violence or lawbreaking can be limited. 6

Likelihood is the easiest test. In Afghanistan, where I have lived for most of the past decade, frustrations at an abusive government and at the apparent role of international forces in propping it up have been growing for years. But those frustrations are often vented in religious, not political, terms, because religion is a more socially acceptable, and safer, rationale for public outcry. 7

In the summer of 2010, Jones announced his intent to publicly burn a copy of the Muslim holy scripture, the Quran, that Sept. 11. He was eventually dissuaded by a number of religious and government officials, including Secretary of Defense Robert Gates, who called him to say his actions would put the lives of U.S. soldiers in Iraq and Afghanistan at risk. On the Joint Chiefs of Staff, where I worked at the time, consensus was that the likelihood of violence was high. 8

When Jones did in fact stage a public Quran burning on March 20, 2011, riots broke out in Afghanistan, killing nearly a dozen people and injuring 90 in the beautiful, cosmopolitan northern city of Mazar-i-Sharif. Seven of the dead were U.N. employees; the rest were Afghans. 9

In Afghanistan, and in all of the Arab nations in transition, an extremist fringe is brawling for power with a more pluralistic majority. Radicals pounce on any pretext to play on religious feeling. I could pick out the signs of manipulation in Afghanistan—riots that started on university campuses where radicalized Pakistani students abound, simultaneous outbreaks in far-flung places, the sudden appearance of weapons. By providing extremists in Libya and elsewhere such an opportunity, the makers of "Innocence of Muslims" were playing into their hands. 10

As for imminence, the timeline of similar events after recent burnings of religious materials indicates that reactions typically come within two weeks. Nakoula's video was deliberately publicized just before the sensitive date of Sept. 11, and could be expected to spark violence on that anniversary. 11

While many First Amendment scholars defend the right of the filmmakers to produce this film, arguing that the ensuing violence 12 was not sufficiently imminent, I spoke to several experts who said the trailer may well fall outside constitutional guarantees of free speech. "Based on my understanding of the events," First Amendment authority Anthony Lewis said in an interview Thursday, "I think this meets the imminence standard."

Finally, much First Amendment jurisprudence concerns speech explicitly advocating violence, such as calls to resist arrest, or videos explaining bomb-making techniques. But words don't have to urge people to commit violence in order to be subject to limits, says Lewis. "If the result is violence, and that violence was intended, then it meets the standard." 13

Indeed, Justice Holmes' original example, shouting "fire" in a theater, is not a call to arms. Steve Klein, an outspoken anti-Islamic activist who said he helped with the film, told al-Jazeera television that it was "supposed to be provocative." The egregiousness of its smears, the apparent deception of cast and crew as to its contents and the deliberate effort to raise its profile in the Arab world a week before 9/11 all suggest intentionality. 14

The point here is not to excuse the terrible acts perpetrated by committed extremists and others around the world in reaction to the video, or to condone physical violence as a response to words—any kind of words. The point is to emphasize that U.S. law makes a distinction between speech that is simply offensive and speech that is deliberately tailored to put lives and property at immediate risk. Especially in the heightened volatility of today's Middle East, such provocation is certainly irresponsible—and reveals an ironic alliance of convenience between Christian extremists and the Islamist extremists they claim to hate. 15

Understanding Meaning

1. Why does Chayes believe that "Innocence of Muslims" should not be protected by the First Amendment?

2. What is the Holmes test?

3. What role does intent play in Chayes' argument? What actions by the filmmakers does she cite as evidence of harmful intent?

4. How, in Chayes' belief, does the "timing" of expression relate to its constitutional protection?

5. Chayes mentions that lines in the video appear to have been dubbed after filming. Does this detail affect your opinion of the film's value or intent?

6. *Critical Thinking*: Does limiting expression that might prompt violence lead to "censorship-by-riot"? Does this empower violent people or organizations to protect themselves from criticism? If a drug gang announced it will punish anyone who attacks it, would any investigative journalism that might prompt violence against the newspaper, television station, or the public automatically be equated with "shouting fire in a theater"?

Evaluating Strategy

1. How does Chayes use quotations by Oliver Wendell Holmes and Anthony Lewis to construct her argument?

2. Does citing the 1969 *Brandenburg v. Ohio* case, which involved a Ku Klux Klan march, as a precedent strengthen Chayes's argument? Why or why not?

3. Chayes mentions living in Afghanistan for a decade and working for the Joint Chiefs of Staff. Does this add credibility to her position?

4. *Critical Thinking*: Chayes uses the Holmes example of shouting fire in a theater to cause panic as a demonstration of a "clear and present danger." Does this test easily apply to making videos in California that are posted online and incite violence thousands of miles away? Does time and distance play a role in determining intent or immediacy? What challenges does the digital age present to our notion of free expression?

Appreciating Language

1. Chayes uses the word "intent" to describe Terry Jones' proposed Quran burning. How does this term suit her purpose and support her thesis?

2. How would you define "imminence"? Why is this an important concept in determining what constitutes a "clear and present danger"?

3. *Critical Thinking*: How would you define a "clear and present danger" or determine "likelihood"? Are these concepts so vague that they can be interpreted to censor any form of dissent? Does "danger" have to include bodily harm? Could one argue that negative press reports about an industry might lead to unemployment and should be censored?

WRITING SUGGESTIONS

1. Write a short essay persuading people to accept your definition of a "clear and present danger." What expressions or actions, if any, would you argue are not protected by the Constitution's guarantee of free speech? Provide examples to illustrate your thesis.

2. *Collaborative Writing*: Discuss Lane's and Chayes's articles with a group of students and write an essay expressing your views on freedom of expression. If, for example, the president of the United States urged Americans not to distribute material that might offend Muslims, in order to prevent violence against Americans serving in Afghanistan, would they see it as a call for censorship or sensible restraint? If members have conflicting opinions, consider writing opposing statements.

Opposing Viewpoints: Ethnic Identity

ARMSTRONG WILLIAMS

Armstrong Williams (1959–) is a talk show host and columnist who has written on a range of issues concerning African Americans. His books include *Beyond Blame: How We Can Succeed by Breaking the Dependency Barrier* (1995) and *Letters to a Young Victim: Hope and Healing in America's Inner Cities* (1996). Williams is a frequent commentator on cable news programs.

Hyphenated Americans

CONTEXT: *In this column, written during the 2000 presidential campaign, Williams argued against Americans retaining ethnic identities that emphasize separateness and erode allegiance to a common civil society.*

WRITER'S NOTE: *Armstrong develops his argument using comparison, contrasting a narrow "cultural 'I'" identity with a wider "civic 'we'" identity.*

Over the past year, small, trite hyphens have been appearing on the campaign trail: Bush courts the African-American vote; the Muslim-American vote will make the difference in Michigan; Gore simultaneously appeals to California's Asian-American population and New York's Jewish-American community; Nader attempts to tap into the Native-American segment of our voting populace. Like deadly spores, these hyphens are replicating everywhere, supplanting our identities as Americans with a tribal ID card. 1

Hopefully now, our elected president will make a renewed effort to regard the citizens of this country not as rival clans, but as humans. To understand the importance of this issue, follow me for a moment, from the political to the personal. With little cultural debate, much of the country now chooses to define themselves not as Americans, but as the proud embodiments of various tribes. We no longer share this vast country. Instead, there is a nation for blacks and a nation for Asians and a nation for gays and Hispanics, one for Jews and whites, with each tribe pledging allegiance not to a unified nation-state, but to their own subjective cultural identity. 2

So what exactly is a hyphenated-American? No one really asks. They understand only that Americans must not be called "Americans" in this day and age. To do so would be to violate the tenets of political correctness, and to invite disaster—at least at suburban dinner parties. Those who dare find strength in their authentic experiences, rather than always trying to go about things as an American might, are deemed traitors to their tribe and soon 3 find themselves joined to no one. This is the new cultural narrative in America: what matters is not your unique experience as a human-American, but rather your ability to identify with some vague tribal concept.

Of course, there are those who swell with pride at being 4 hyphenated Americans. They would argue that those small hyphens keep intact their unique struggles and heritage. Such people might even point to the important symbolic function that such a hyphen serves: it pushes the hyphenated-American experience into the mainstream, therefore reducing any cultural hangover from America's less tolerant past.

In reality though, the argument for rooting oneself in a tribal 5 identity seems terribly destabilizing to the concept of multicultural unity. To insist that we are all hyphenated Americans is pretty much the same thing as asserting that no one is an American. The major implication: your America is not my America. The idea of civic unity becomes clouded as hyphenated Americans increasingly identify with their cultural "I," rather than the civic "we." The great hope that our civil rights leaders had about getting beyond the concept of warring tribes and integrating to form a more perfect union falls by the wayside of these small hyphens.

I fear that we are reverting from a highly centralized country 6 to a set of clans separated by hyphens. Herein lies the danger: when you modify your identity to distinguish it from other clans, you tend to modify your personal attitudes as well. You make the "others" what you need them to be, in order to feel good about your own little tribe. The best in the other "tribes" therefore becomes obscured, as does any unity of understanding. Instead, we distill the cultural "others" into the most easily identifiable symbols: Blacks as criminals; Asians as isolationists; Italians as gangsters; Muslims as fanatics; Jews as stingy; Latin Americans as illegal immigrants; whites as racists. We perpetuate these stereotypes when we willingly segregate ourselves into cultural tribes, even when we know that in our individual lives, we are so much more than this.

Our cultural prophets once dreamt of achieving a nation not of 7 warring tribes, but of humans. Presently, we fail this vision, and we fail ourselves.

Understanding Meaning

1. What observations did Armstrong make during the 2000 presidential campaign? What troubled him the most?

2. Why does Armstrong view ethnic identities as damaging to the nation and civic society?

3. Do you observe that many people on your campus or in your neighborhood prefer to see themselves as African Americans, Hispanics, Jews, or Irish Americans rather than "Americans"?

4. Does identification with an ethnic heritage always imply a political point of view? Why or why not?

5. *Critical Thinking:* Is an ethnic identity undercut by other associations and influences? Do the poor and unemployed of all ethnic groups have more in common with each other than with middle-class professionals with whom they share a common ancestry? Why or why not? Do New Yorkers have a geographical identity that distinguishes them from people of the same ethnicity who live in Texas or Oregon? Do entrepreneurs, doctors, teachers, police officers, and landlords have shared interests that overcome ethnic identities? Can a highly technological and complex society like the United States really break up along ethnic lines?

Evaluating Strategy

1. Williams opens his essay by observing political campaigns. Is this an effective device? Does it reveal how politicians view the voting public?

2. Can you summarize Williams's thesis in a single sentence? Why or why not? Is his point clearly stated?

Appreciating Language

1. How does Williams define "hyphenated Americans"? How does he define "multicultural society"?

2. Williams uses the terms "tribe" and "clan" to describe ethnic groups and ethnic loyalty. What connotations do these words have? Do some people find terms like "tribal" and "clan" demeaning or offensive?

3. Williams places the word "other" in quotation marks. Many commentators use the term "other" to describe people who are seen as outsiders, enemies, or threats. Look up this word in a dictionary. What does the word "other" mean to you? What connotations does it have?

WRITING SUGGESTIONS

1. Write a short essay explaining the way you choose which political candidates to vote for. Does your ethnic identity influence the way you vote? Are you more likely to support candidates who share your background? Why or why not?

2. *Collaborative Writing:* Working with a group of students, discuss Williams's essay and ask each member if he or she agrees or disagrees with his position on ethnic identity. Write an essay that summarizes your group's views, using classification to organize their views from those who strongly agree to those who strongly disagree with Williams's argument.

JULIANNE MALVEAUX

Julianne Malveaux (1953–) was born in San Francisco. She studied economics at Boston College and later attended the Massachusetts Institute of Technology, where she received a PhD in economics in 1980. She has published articles on economics and social policy in *Ms., Essence, Emerge*, and *The Progressive*. Her books include *Sex, Lies and Stereotypes: Perspectives of a Mad Economist* (1994); *Wall Street, Main Street, and the Side Street: A Mad Economist Takes a Stroll* (1999); and *Surviving and Thriving: 365 Facts In Black Economic History* (2010).

Still Hyphenated Americans

CONTEXT: *Malveaux argues that by maintaining a black identity, African Americans are only celebrating the hyphenated status history gave them.*

WRITER'S NOTE: *Malveaux uses the question "Why are we still celebrating Black History Month?" as a prompt for her response.*

"Why are we still celebrating Black History Month?" the young white 1 woman asks me. Until then, our airplane conversation had been casual, companionable. We'd spoken of trivia for nearly an hour, of changed travel conditions, the flight delay, of the plastic knives we'd been handed. My seatmate, a California college student, was traveling to Washington, D.C., to visit friends, and brimmed over with questions about sightseeing in Washington. Then she lowered her voice just a bit, asked if I minded an "awkward" question, and asked about Black History Month.

I didn't know whether to chuckle or to scream. Seventy-five 2 years after Dr. Carter G. Woodson established Negro History week in 1926, folks are still wondering why we should commemorate black history. We need look no further than the words of one of our nation's most-quoted African Americans, Dr. Martin Luther King, Jr., who wrote, "The mistreatment of the Negro is as old as the most ancient history book, and as recent as today's newspaper." As long as African American life and history are not fully represented on newspaper pages, in the broadcast media, or in the history books, it makes sense to commemorate African American History Month.

The Association for the Study of Afro-American Life and History 3 annually selects a black history month theme. Their website, www .asalh.com, lists themes for the next several years. This year, the theme is The Color Line Revisited: Is Racism Dead? I shared the theme with my young seatmate who assured me that class, not race, is what separates Americans. Rubbing shoulders in the first-class cabin of the plane, she wondered, "You can't honestly say you've been discriminated against in your life, have you?"

Discrimination is an institutional, not an individual phenomenon.   4
How else but discrimination do we explain the differentials between African American and white income, unemployment rates,
and homeownership levels. Those simple statistics make it clear
that African Americans and whites have very different realities. If the
overall unemployment rate were 9.8 percent, as the black rate was in
January, we'd be talking about a depression and designing programs to put people back to work. Instead, President Bush's new
budget cuts employment and training programs from $225 million
to $45 million, a cut of nearly 80 percent. These programs, targeted
to some of our nation's largest cities, provide important training to
high-risk young people, many of whom are African American. To
cut such programs at this time is tantamount to cutting the defense
budget in wartime, but we know that President Bush has done
no such thing. Indeed, while job-training funds are being slashed
by millions of dollars, the President proposes increasing defense
spending by $48 billion more this year.

The nation's indifference to high black unemployment rates   5
speaks to the difference in our realities. Many whites see themselves as Americans, while African Americans are hyphenated only
because our realities are hyphenated. We'll feel like "regular"
Americans when we have "regular" experiences (meaning no
racial profiling, among other things), when our "regular" history is
reflected in our nation's statuary (how many cities literally have no
public monuments to African American people) and libraries.

The unemployment rate difference isn't the only place the color   6
line is drawn. Seventy-one percent of all whites own their homes,
compared to 48 percent of African Americans. The gap is a function
of redlining and discrimination in lending, both of which have been
convincingly demonstrated by contemporary research. But when
a home is the largest asset in most people's portfolio, too many
African Americans are denied the opportunity to accumulate wealth
when they can't buy homes. Restrictive covenants no longer prevent people from owning, but implicitly restrictive lending policies
are as effective today as racist covenants were two generations ago.

To be sure, the color line is fuzzier than it has ever been. Our   7
airwaves frequently broadcast the lifestyles of the black and
beautiful—the Oprah Winfreys, Michael Jordans, Condoleezza
Rices and Colin Powells of the world. As proud as we are of African
American icons, it would be foolhardy to suggest that all black
people share experiences with these icons. At the other end, one
in four African Americans and 40 percent of African American children live in poverty. Is racism real? No question. We commemorate
Black History Month because it is an important way to recognize the
many contributions African American people have made to our nation, because our nation, despite the progress it has made, still fails
to systematically acknowledge black history. Until our textbooks
spill over with stories of the slaves who built our nation's capital,
the African American patriots who fought and died for our country,

and the African American scientists whose inventions have shaped our lives, I will gleefully commemorate African American History Month. I shouldn't be the only one celebrating, African American history is American history! We hyphenated Americans are merely celebrating the hyphen that history handed us.

Understanding Meaning

1. Why does Malveaux argue that Black History Month should be celebrated?
2. What does Malveaux mean by "institutional" discrimination? Why does she reject the idea that social problems are "about class, not race"?
3. When, in her view, will African Americans be able to feel like "regular Americans"?
4. *Critical Thinking:* Malveaux comments on the "black and beautiful" celebrities like Oprah Winfrey, Michael Jordan, and Colin Powell. Do you think the presence of successful African Americans leads people to believe that racism no longer exists?

Evaluating Strategy

1. How does Malveaux use comments of the white passenger to open her essay? Is this a valuable device with which to introduce a controversial issue?
2. What facts and statistics does Malveaux use to support her thesis? Why is factual support important in this essay?

Appreciating Language

1. How does Malveaux define "hyphenated Americans"?
2. Are Malveaux's diction, tone, and style suited for a newspaper column that many people will skim rather than read? What challenges do columnists face in writing about complex and difficult issues?

WRITING SUGGESTIONS

1. Write an essay agreeing or disagreeing with Malveaux's column. Could you argue that other groups, such as Hispanics and Asians, are far less represented in the nation's history books, media, and public institutions?
2. *Collaborative Writing:* Discuss Malveaux's column with a group of students and ask if public schools should teach American history by highlighting ethnic differences, or, instead, by weaving them into a single unified version of our past. Should black history be taught separately? Why or why not? Write an essay summarizing your group's view. If students have differing opinions, use comparison or division and classification to organize their opinions.

Writing Beyond the Classroom

DOCTORS WITHOUT BORDERS

Doctors Without Borders is an international medical humanitarian organization founded by physicians and journalists in 1971 in France as Médecins Sans Frontières or MSF. The organization's mission is to provide "quality medical care to people in crisis regardless of their race, religion, or political affiliation." Doctors Without Borders now operates in sixty countries, serving people threatened by armed conflicts, epidemics, malnutrition, or natural disasters.

Field News

CONTEXT: *On its home page Doctors Without Borders encourages the public to support its operations with donations.*

WRITER'S NOTE: *This web page blends the emotional appeal of a doctor treating patients with the ethical appeal of its mission statement and the logical appeal of its responsible use of contributions.*

Understanding Meaning

1. What is the mission of Doctors Without Borders?
2. How is Doctors Without Borders responding to the epidemic in refugee camps in South Sudan?
3. *Critical Thinking*: The website states that "86 cents of every dollar supports our programs." Why is it important for organizations soliciting contributions to demonstrate how donor funds are spent?

Evaluating Strategy

1. How does this "Field News" report illustrate the work of Doctors Without Borders?
2. Is it important to blend appeals to reach the widest audience?
3. How effective is the visual impact of the web page? Does it communicate at a glance and provide enough detail to inform readers?
4. Do you think this page will motivate people to donate to Doctors Without Borders? Why or why not? What changes, if any, would you suggest?

Appreciating Language

1. Does the level of diction seem appropriate for a mass audience?
2. How does word choice dramatize action?
3. *Critical Thinking*: Is there any text you would add or wording you would change to make this page more effective?

WRITING SUGGESTIONS

1. Develop the text for a fund-raising web page using examples for support. Determine which examples would both dramatize a social problem and demonstrate how the organization works to solve it.

2. *Collaborative Writing*: Discuss this web page with a group of students, and then develop a process essay that explains, step by step, how you would conduct a national fund-raising campaign to draw attention to the work of Doctors Without Borders.

Responding to Images

Sign warning drivers about illegal immigrants

1. What is your initial reaction to this sign?
2. What does a sign like this illustrate?
3. What is your impression of the silhouette figures? Does using visual images avoid having to use words that express a political bias, such as "illegal aliens" or "undocumented worker"? Does the sign only warn drivers about people crossing the highway? Is the notion that these people are "illegal aliens" only implied?

Could the same sign be posted outside a football stadium, beach, or amusement park? Why or why not?

4. Might some people find this sign offensive? Why or why not? Will some compare it to deer crossing signs? Will others think of "Children at Play" signs?

5. *Visual Analysis:* The sign depicts a man, a woman, and child in flight. What were the designers trying to suggest? Would a single figure or a group of adult males arouse different reactions? Why or why not? Does this image suggest most illegal immigrants are crossing the border as families?

6. Write a short essay stating how the United States should handle illegal border crossings.

7. *Collaborative Writing:* Before discussing this image with a group of students, have each person write down an immediate reaction and supply a caption for the photograph. Have each member of the group read his or her response; then, discuss the impact word choice has on meaning. Write an essay describing your group's impressions. If members have conflicting reactions, use comparison or division and classification to organize their views.

Strategies FOR WRITING ARGUMENT AND PERSUASION

1. Determine your purpose. Clearly establish your thesis, and define what ideas you want readers to accept and what actions you want them to take. Do not recommend too many separate actions in one document.

2. Evaluate your readers carefully. Examine the perceptual world of your audience. What objections do you have to overcome to convince readers to accept your point of view?

3. Determine which appeals will be effective. Recognize the advantages and disadvantages of each appeal, and consider using more than one.

4. Craft introductions and conclusions carefully. Opening paragraphs must arouse interest and prepare readers for your argument or appeal. Conclusions should end with a statement that will motivate readers to accept your ideas or take the action you recommend.

5. Present factual detail in ways readers can understand. In presenting facts and statistics, use methods such as analogies and narratives to dramatize their significance.

6. Qualify remarks. Avoid making absolute claims and sweeping generalizations. Acknowledge that exceptions exist and that opponents may have valid concerns and objections.

7. **Verify sources.** Before using as evidence a quote or statistic you heard on television or read online, determine if it is stated accurately and comes from a reliable source.

8. **Do not mistake propaganda for persuasion.** Do not assume that hurling accusations, using questionable facts, or employing shock tactics will make your argument successful. People dislike being manipulated, and often potential supporters will find overstated appeals objectionable and offensive.

Revising and Editing

1. **Review your thesis.** Make sure your thesis is clearly stated and placed where it will have the greatest impact on readers.

2. **Use peer review.** Ask others to read your draft and evaluate your thesis, evidence, and use of appeals. Encourage readers to be critical and identify lapses and weaknesses in your argument.

Suggested Topics for Writing Argument and Persuasion

General Assignments

Write a persuasive argument to a general audience on one of the following topics. You may use one or more appeals. You can frame your paper in the form of an essay, a letter, a website, or an advertisement.

1. Community and police relations
2. The drinking age
3. The way colleges prepare or fail to prepare graduates for the job market
4. Bullying
5. School choice
6. Labor unions
7. Facebook
8. Sexual harassment
9. The federal deficit
10. Credit cards

Select one of the following issues, and craft a persuasive essay targeted to one of the audiences listed.

Issues: Medicare reform, distribution of condoms in public schools, school prayer, bilingual education, recycling, gun control, legalization of recreational drugs

Audiences: Suburban residents, retired schoolteachers, small business owners, an organization of minority police officers, urban health-care providers

Writing in Context

1. Imagine you have become close to a highly respected member of your community. This person is well regarded by your family and may play a key role in your future. He or she invites you to join an organization that actively supports a view on abortion that is opposite to yours. Write a letter persuading this person to accept your reasons for declining the offer. Try to make your disagreement known without creating animosity.

2. Write a letter to the editor of the campus newspaper about an issue that you have heard discussed but that no one else seems willing to raise. Urge the community to pay attention.

Student Paper: Argument and Persuasion

This paper was written in response to the following assignment:

> Write a 500–750-word persuasive essay about a current social or political
> issue. Avoid writing about subjects such as abortion or capital punishment
> unless you can provide a new or unique angle. Document your use of any
> outside sources.

First Draft with Instructor's Comments

This college, like many others, has and needs a Black Student Union. It has nothing to do with what everyone seems to think it has. A lot of people who make these claims have never even bothered to visit the Black Student Union or bothered to check the facts they saw in the paper. *[weak, vague, what does everyone "seem to think"? Revise this paragraph for clarity]*

People say black students are getting paid to run their organization, which is so totally not the case. In fact, the Black Student Union only receives money to operate a study center that, in fact, serves lots of non-blacks because the Acamdemic Support Center. The union received money last year, but most of it went to fix the building, which does belong to the university. *[Wordy, informal] [Sp]*

Many people criticize the Black Student Center for foresting racial discrimination. This is not the case. We live in integrated dorms, attend integrated classes, and play on integrated teams. The few hours a week a student might spend at the BSU hardly threatens to create racial isolation. Other students have specialized centers, and no one seems bothered about that. In addition, people have accused the BSU of being a hotbed of radical politics. I see no evidence of this. *[Right word? unclear] [add specific examples] [Explain, expand]*

Black students need the BSU. Black students are a minority on this campus. It is easy for them to feel alienated and isolated. And they are at high risk for failure. Dean Smith says "Since only one of eight black males entering a university will graduate, it is imperative that we seek remedies to support their academic achievement and professional advancement." And the BSU does just that. Black students have problems finding friends and building positive reinforcement networks that provide needed personal support. Because few of their friends in high school were college-bound, they had to isolate themselves and study on their own. This habit, however, is not always the best strategy in college. Many students benefited from "social promotion" and when they get to college, they discover that their A's and B's were really more equal to C's and D's in better suburban schools. The Black Student Union offers African American students a place to relax, to interact with older students, and work to make the university a more hospitable place to minorities. *[Weak] [Clarify, sources?]*

Works Cited

Smith, Dean. *Black Males in Crisis*. New York: Dial Press, 2009. *Print.*

Revision Notes

You have an interesting topic for a persuasive essay, but you need to make several improvements to produce a truly effective paper.

1. *You mention that the Black Student Union has critics, and refer to the recent newspaper article. Expand this point. Explain the claims and criticisms of those who oppose the Black Student Union, then disprove or discount them point by point.*
2. *Provide additional factual support to counter charges that the Union is getting too much money.*
3. *You need to document the sources fully. You list the Smith book in Works Cited but do not show the page reference for the quote you use. See MLA guidelines (pages 483–490).*
4. *Finally, read your draft out loud. Missing words, awkward sentences, and wordy phrases are easier to hear than see.*

Revised Draft

Bradley Harrison   **English 101**

Why a Black Student Union?

Before any controversial issue can be discussed, there is usually a certain amount of misinformation to deal with. This is clearly the case with the Black Student Union. Many students have voiced concern and written letters to the editor since the college paper revealed that $540,000 was being allocated to the Union (Kane 1). The article stated that $52,000 was going to salaries, making the Black Student Union the only student organization with a paid staff.

First of all, the bulk of the money allocated to the Union is dedicated to renovating the building, which is university property. Constructed in 1962, the building has not had major repairs since 1974. Roof leaks, first reported to the administration three years ago, have led to substantial and costly damage. In addition, it is the only building that was not retrofitted with new heating and air conditioning systems in 1996 (CSU 22). Also, the building still does not comply with the Americans with Disabilities Act. Wheelchair ramps must be installed by court order (CSU 23).

Second, no one at the Union receives a salary for student activities. Five graduate students are paid to tutor remedial classes. Given the lack of space in the cramped Academic Support Center, use of the Black Student Union makes sense and creates more openings in the Center. Many non-black students attend classes and remedial seminars at the Union. Less than half the graduates of the Internet course last semester were African American (Kane 2).

But there are other objections to the Union. Why should blacks have their own facility? Many on campus see the presence of a black student union as a kind of self-imposed apartheid. The Union has also been criticized for being the center of racially hostile militancy.

The Black Student Union hardly threatens to impose a new kind of segregation. We live in integrated dorms, attend integrated classes, participate in integrated sports, and serve on mostly white and Asian academic committees. The few hours a week a student might spend at the BSU hardly threatens racial isolation—any more than the women's center risks ending coeducation or the Newman Center pits Catholics against Protestants. From my own observations, I see little evidence of the radical and extremist politics Union opponents mention. The most popular event the Black Student Union holds is Career Week, when black students line up to meet representatives from AT&T, IBM, US Bank, and 3M. Most students are concerned about academic performance and career options rather than radical politics. True, the Union has sponsored some controversial speakers, but so has the university itself. Much of the "extremist literature" cited in a campus editorial is not distributed by the Union. The Union receives a lot of free literature in the mail, which has been traditionally displayed in the lobby. When it was brought to the attention of the board that some of the pamphlets were anti-Semitic, members took quick steps to screen incoming publications and discard "hate literature."

The real purpose of the Union is to assist African Americans to succeed on campus. Comprising less than 5 percent of the student body, blacks easily feel alienated, particularly those who gradu-ated from predominantly black high schools. According to Dean Smith, "Since only one of eight black males entering a university will graduate, it is imperative that we seek remedies to support their academic achievement and professional advancement" (12). Many black students have difficulty forming friendships and joining organizations. Often there were only a handful of college-bound students in their schools. To survive, they had to isolate them-selves, studying alone to avoid associating with peers resentful of their dedication to academics. Outcasts in high school, these stu-dents find college bewildering. They are not accustomed to par-ticipating in class or working in groups. They often discover that they are woefully unprepared for college. Coming from schools with 50–75 percent dropout rates, many suffered from "social pro-motion." They discover that their A's and B's are only equal to C's and D's in better suburban schools. The Black Student Union offers African American students a place to relax, interact with older students, and work to make the university a more hospitable place to minorities.

Given the history of discrimination and disadvantage faced by African Americans, the Union can be a positive asset. Is it a crutch, an undeserved luxury? No one can deny that black students feel handicapped on campus. No one complains about the cost of wheelchair ramps and elevators which benefit a handful of physically disabled students. Why should we ignore the crippling legacy of racism?

Works Cited

CSU Facilities Report: 2011. California State University Budget Office. California State University, 2011. Web. 5 May 2013.

Kane, Kelly. "BSU Funding Furor." *Campus Times* 1 May 2012: 1–2. Print.

Smith, Dean. *Black Males in Crisis.* New York: Dial, 2012. Print.

Questions for Review and Revision

1. What is the student's thesis?

2. What negative assumptions does the student seek to address? How does he counter them?

3. What audience does the writer appear to address? What appeals does the student use?

4. How much of the paper consists of responses to opponents' criticisms? Is this a useful device?

5. How effective is the conclusion? Does comparing disabled students to African Americans make a valid point? Would you suggest an alternative ending?

6. Read the paper aloud. Are there passages that should be deleted or expanded?

7. Did the student follow the instructor's suggestions?

WRITING SUGGESTIONS

1. Using this paper as a model, write a similar essay taking a position on a current campus controversy. Assume you are addressing a hostile audience. Respond to their objections without criticizing or demeaning those who disagree with your thesis.

2. *Collaborative Writing:* Discuss this paper with a group of students. Have a member record comments by the group. Work together to write a short statement approving or disapproving of the concept of establishing separate student unions. If members disagree, consider writing pro and con versions.

EVALUATING ARGUMENT AND PERSUASION CHECKLIST

Before submitting your paper, review these points:

1. Is your message clearly defined?
2. Does your paper meet readers' needs? Do you provide the support they require to accept your thesis?
3. Do you support your views with adequate evidence from reliable sources?
4. Do you anticipate reader objections and alternative points of view?
5. Do you balance the strengths and weaknesses of logical, ethical, and emotional appeals?
6. Do you avoid overstated, sentimental, or propagandistic appeals?
7. Do you avoid preaching to the converted? Will only those who already agree with you accept your arguments?
8. Do you make it easy for undecided readers to accept your position without feeling manipulated or patronized?
9. Have you tested your argument with peer review?

Accompanying English CourseMate Resources

 Visit English CourseMate at **www.cengagebrain.com** to find many helpful resources and study tools for this chapter.

Appendix A: A Writer's Guide to Documenting Sources

What Is Documentation?

Many of the papers you will write in college require documentation—a method of acknowledging borrowed words and ideas. Academic disciplines, publications, and professions have specific ways of documenting sources. When assigned a documented paper, make sure you understand the style your instructor expects.

Why Document Sources?

Writers document sources for three reasons:

1. **To avoid plagiarism.** Plagiarism (derived from the Latin word for "kidnapping") refers to using the words, ideas, or artistic work of others without giving them credit. Some students find it difficult to believe that copying a few paragraphs from *The World Book* or using statistics found on a website can be considered stealing. But using sources without credit is a theft of intellectual property. Instructors routinely fail students who plagiarize papers. Many colleges expel students who submit plagiarized assignments. As a writer, you can protect yourself from charges of plagiarism by noting sources. Accurate documentation clearly distinguishes your work from that of others so no one can accuse you of cheating.

2. **To support a thesis.** Citing sources not only protects you from charges of cheating but also makes your writing stronger. To convince readers to accept your thesis, it is important to provide them with evidence. In court, lawyers prove cases by presenting eyewitnesses, expert testimony, and exhibits. As a writer, you can persuade readers to accept your point of view if you offer proof. The more controversial your thesis, the more your readers will demand supporting evidence from credible sources.

3. **To help readers learn more.** Citations show readers where they can find additional information by listing periodicals, books, and websites.

When to Document

Students are often confused about what they have to document.

What *Not* to Document

First, you do not have to document all the sources you use. Even if you look up something in an encyclopedia or on a website, you do not have to note its use if the information belongs to what researchers call *the realm of common knowledge:*

1. **Common expressions or famous quotations.** You don't need to list the Bible or your edition of Shakespeare if you simply check the wording of a quotation by Jesus or Hamlet. If you refer to statements readers are familiar with, such as Martin Luther King, Jr.'s "I have a dream" or John F. Kennedy's "Ask not what your country can do for you—ask what you can do for your country," you don't have to note their original source. Conversely, less familiar statements, especially controversial ones readers might question, must be documented.

2. **Common facts not subject to change and available in numerous sources.** You don't have to list *The Encyclopedia Britannica* as a source if you use it to look up where George Washington was born, when *Death of a Salesman* opened on Broadway, when Malcolm X died, the number of counties in New Jersey, or the height of Mount Everest. General facts such as these are not subject to change and are readily available in thousands of books, almanacs, biographies, textbooks, and websites. No one will accuse you of stealing information that is considered standard and widely known by millions of people. Facts subject to change or dispute, such as the population of Denver, the number of people on death row, or unemployment statistics, must be documented.

What to Document

In almost every other case, you must acknowledge the use of sources:

1. **Direct quotations.** Whenever you copy word for word the spoken or written words of others, you must use quotation marks or indented paragraphs to distinguish them from your own text and indicate the source.

2. **Indirect quotations or paraphrases.** Even if you don't copy information, but only restate the author's ideas in your own words, you must acknowledge the source. Changing a few words in a quotation or summarizing several pages into a paragraph does not alter the fact that you are using information taken from another source. Although you don't use quotation marks, you must indicate that you have borrowed material.

3. **Specific facts, statistics, and numbers.** Facts will only be acceptable to readers if they know where they came from. If you state, "Last year eighteen innocent men were sentenced to death for crimes they did not commit," readers will demand the source of this number.

4. **Graphs, charts, photographs, and other visual aids.** Indicate the source of any visual aid you reproduce in your paper. If you create your own graphics based on facts or statistics, indicate their source.

Types of Evidence

The sources you include depend on your paper's thesis, topic, and audience. Because each type of evidence has advantages and disadvantages, most writers use a variety of material.

Primary documents—regulations, contracts, reports, or email created by governments, corporations, individuals, and organizations.

Advantages: provide objective data and serve as a basis to evaluate opinions by critics and commentators.

Disadvantages: may require specialized training to locate or understand.

Criticism—analysis of events, works of art, ideas, problems, or proposals by historians, commentators, critics, or researchers.

Advantages: provides quotations from experienced experts.

Disadvantages: is largely opinion and can be biased. Avoid relying on a single critic. Balance personal opinions with alternative viewpoints or other forms of evidence.

Testimony—statements, comments, or interviews by individuals.

Primary evidence includes statements by eyewitnesses and participants in events.

Secondary evidence includes comments by experts or critics.

Advantages: provides human interest and expert insights.

Disadvantages: may be anecdotal, fragmentary, or biased and should be balanced with other forms of evidence.

Facts and Statistics—objective details and information presented in numbers, such as census data or stock prices.

Advantages: provide objective evidence, which readers expect in research documents.

Disadvantages: can be poorly collected or presented in a biased manner to distort facts.

Research and Experiments—data collected through academic studies or laboratory tests.

Advantages: provide objective evidence that can be verified by other sources.

Disadvantages: can require specialized training to understand. Also, studies may be biased in their design or results misinterpreted.

Polls and surveys—measure opinions and attitudes of the general public or specialized populations.

Advantages: offer insight into past or current attitudes about a person, issue, or event.

Disadvantages: can be highly biased and subject to manipulation.

Media—newspaper, website, television, and magazine reports.

Advantages: provide short, factual stories that are easily read; offer insight into current events.

Disadvantages: written to meet deadlines, media reports can be fragmentary and inaccurate.

Evaluating Internet Sources Checklist

As you search for sources online, determine their value and reliability:

☑ **Source:** What is the domain name of the source? The URL—the site's Internet address—can help you evaluate an online source:

Domain	Source
.com	company or for-profit organization
.edu	college or university
.gov	federal government
.mil	military
.net	Internet provider or individual
.ny.us	New York state government
.org	nonprofit organization or individual

Does a reputable organization sponsor the site? Is this organization likely to be impartial in its examination of the information? Does the organization benefit from persuading you to accept its position? Do you detect inflammatory language that reveals bias or prejudice? If a search leads you to a single posting, examine the organization's home page, which may contain information about its staff, mission, and orientation. Use the name of the organization or author as a search term and examine the responses it generates.

☑ **Authorship:** Does the site mention the author or webmaster? This information is often noted at the bottom of the site's home page, but does not always appear on internal pages. Does the author or webmaster include an email address? An email to the author or webmaster can yield valuable insights.

☑ **Credibility:** If you are able to identify the site's author, can you also determine whether he or she has significant knowledge about the topic? Does the site present objective information or express personal opinion? Does the author include his or her biography or résumé?

- To see if the author has also published books, check your library's online catalog or Amazon.com (**www.amazon.com**), which lists books and often includes reviews.

- Place the author's full name in quotation marks and use it as a search term to locate biographical information.

☑ **Purpose:** Is the site designed to present all available evidence? Does it seem to take a side? Is the site intended to provide information and ideas or sell a product or service?

☑ **Audience:** Is the site directed to the general public or targeted to a specific group of people with shared values and opinions? Does the site present objective evidence or only subjective opinions? Does the site invite further investigation by providing links to reputable sites?

☑ **Language:** Are the tone and style objective and professional? Does the site refute or question opposing views using evidence, or does it attempt to dismiss opponents with inflammatory or derogatory statements?

☑ **Presentation:** Has the site been planned and designed well? Is it easy to navigate? Does the text reflect that careful planning has been devoted to it, including thorough proofreading? Don't allow impressive graphics, sound, and video to substitute for accuracy in the information.

☑ **Timeliness:** Many sites are not dated, making it difficult to determine the currency of the information. If dates do not appear, test links to see if they are still active. Place key terms and phrases in quotations and use them as search terms to determine dates and locate more recent sources.

☑ **Critical Thinking:** Do you detect errors in critical thinking, such as hasty generalizations, dependence on anecdotal evidence, faulty comparisons, false authorities, or attacking personalities?

Using Quotations

Direct quotations should be used sparingly. Remember, the goal of your paper is to express *your* thoughts and opinions, not to present a collection of other people's ideas. There are times, however, when direct quotations can be powerful additions to your essay. Use direct quotations:

1. When presenting a significant statement by an authority or eyewitness

2. When the statement is unique or memorable

3. When the idea conflicts with the mainstream of thought or common knowledge

4. When the original statement is well written and more compelling than a paraphrase or summary

5. When readers may doubt a controversial point of view or question that a certain person made the statement

Direct quotations have to be integrated into the text of an essay in a clear, sensible manner and be documented.

1. **Indicate short direct quotations (one to four lines) by placing them in quotation marks followed by a parenthetical citation:**

    According to Lester Armstrong, "The university failed to anticipate the impact of state budget cuts" (17).

    Indicate long direct quotations (more than four or five lines) by placing them in indented paragraphs without quotation marks. Indent ten spaces on the left side and introduce with a complete sentence that ends with a colon:

    According to Lester Armstrong, higher education suffered greatly during the recession:

    The university failed to anticipate the impact of state budget cuts. As a result, construction on the new stadium was halted. Twenty-five administrators were laid off. Plans to expand the computer labs, bilingual programs, and adult night school were scrapped. The library budget was slashed by 24 percent, and two day care centers were closed. The century-old Main Hall, which was scheduled for an extensive refurbishing, was given only cosmetic repairs and painting. (17)

2. **Link direct quotations with your text. Avoid isolated quotations:**
   Incorrect

   Children are greatly affected by violence on television. "By the time a child graduates from high school, he or she has witnessed over 18,000 homicides on television" (Smith 10). Young people come to view violence, even murder, as a reasonable method of resolving conflicts.

   Blend direct quotations into your text by introducing them:
   Revised

   Children are greatly affected by violence on television. "By the time a child graduates from high school," **Jane Smith notes,** "he or she has witnessed over 18,000 homicides on television" (10). Young people come to view violence, even murder, as a reasonable method of resolving conflicts.

3. **You may edit quotations to eliminate redundant or irrelevant material.** Indicate deleted words within a sentence by inserting an *ellipsis* (three spaced periods). If the ellipsis occurs at the end of the sentence, place three spaced periods after the final period. To avoid breaking across lines, you can use the ellipsis symbol, typically found in the symbols menu on your toolbar.

   Original Text

   George Washington, who was heading to New York to confer with his leading advisors, agreed to meet with Franklin in Philadelphia on June 10.

   Edited Quote

   As Smith notes, "George Washington...agreed to meet with Franklin in Philadelphia...."

   Deletions should only remove unneeded information; they should not alter the meaning of the text by removing qualifications or changing a negative statement into a positive one. It is unethical to alter the quotation "We should, only if everything else fails, legalize drugs" to read, "We should...legalize drugs."

4. **Insert words or other information in brackets to prevent confusion or avoid grammatical errors.** For instance, if a direct quote refers to a Frank Obama by his last name and you are concerned readers will confuse him with President Obama, you may insert his first name, even though it does not appear in the original text.

   Original Text

   Hoping to ease tensions in the Middle East, Obama called for UN peacekeepers to patrol the West Bank.

   Quotation

   "Hoping to ease tensions in the Middle East, [Frank] Obama," according to *Newsweek,* "called for UN peacekeepers to patrol the West Bank" (14).

If you delete words or phrases, you may have to insert words to prevent a grammar error:

Original Text

Poe and other writers of his generation were influential in shaping a new, truly American literature.

Quotation

According to Sydney Falco, "Poe ... [was] influential in shaping a new, truly American literature" (64).

5. **Explain, if necessary, the significance of the person or source you are quoting:**

Maria Gomez, who investigated over two hundred crashes for the FAA, notes that "technology cannot replace human perception in reducing accidents."

Wall Street Dreamers, a twenty-year study compiled by a panel of professors from the Harvard Business School and sixteen investment bankers, claims "speculation can be curbed and channeled but never removed from the market."

Using Paraphrases

Paraphrases are indirect quotes. You must document your use of sources, even when you do not copy the text word for word. If you read two or three pages of a history book and summarize its points in a single paragraph, document your use of that source. Although you did not directly reproduce any words or sentences, the ideas you present are not your own and should be documented:

Original Text

More than 10,000 of New York's 29,000 manufacturing firms had closed their doors. Nearly one of every three employables in the city had lost his job. An estimated 1,600,000 New Yorkers were receiving some form of public relief. Many of those fortunates who had kept their jobs were "underemployed," a euphemism for the fact that they worked two or three days a week or two weeks a month—or, if they worked full time, were paid a fraction of their former salaries; stenographers, earning $35 to $40 per week in 1928, were averaging $16 in 1933; Woolworth's was paying full-time salesladies $6 per week.

Robert Caro, *The Power Broker* 323–324

Paraphrase

The Depression devastated New York City. A third of the manufacturers shut down operations, and over a million and a half New Yorkers were on relief. Those with jobs saw their hours cut and their salaries slashed (Caro 323–324). Conditions in Chicago, Los Angeles, and San Francisco were similar.

Parenthetical references should be placed immediately after the paraphrased material at an appropriate pause or at the end of the sentence.

Using MLA Documentation

The MLA style, developed by the Modern Language Association, is the predominant documentation method used in language and literature courses. In the MLA system, sources are listed alphabetically at the end of the paper in a "Works Cited" list and parenthetical citations are placed after direct quotations and paraphrases.

NOTE: Print and online MLA guides created before 2009 use underlining instead of italics and require inclusion of full URLs. If you have any questions about MLA documentation, refer to the current guide, *The MLA Handbook for Writers of Research Papers,* 7th edition.

Building a Works Cited List

List all sources you refer to under the title "Works Cited" at the end of your paper. Items are listed alphabetically by author's last name or first significant word in the title:

General Guidelines

Print Sources:

Author, last name first: **Twain, Mark**

> Title (in quotation marks for articles and other short works; in italics for books and other long works): **"The Gold Bug";** *The Collected Stories of Edgar Allan Poe*
>
> Name of magazines or newspapers in italics for articles: *Newsweek*
>
> City and publisher for books: **New York: Random** (Words like *House, Books, Publishers,* and *Inc.* are omitted from the names of publishers. University presses are designated with UP: **Ohio State UP.**)
>
> Volume and issue number for magazine articles if available: **121.1**
>
> Date of publication (day, month, and year for newspaper articles: **10 Oct. 2012;** year for books: **2012**)
>
> Inclusive page numbers for articles: **125-134**
>
> Medium: **Print.**

Online Sources:

Author, last name first: **Brown, Nina**

> Title (in quotation marks for short works from a larger work; in italics for independent works): **"Teens in Crisis";** *Issues in Psychology*
>
> Name of website in italics: *Modern Language Association*
>
> Publisher of website (use **n.p.** if none is available)
>
> Date (use **n.d.** if none is listed)
>
> Medium: **Web.**
>
> Date of access (the date you downloaded or printed the website): **12 Mar. 2013.**

Sample formats

A book by a single author:

Smith, John. *The City.* New York: Putnam, 2002. Print.

A book by two or three authors:

Smith, John, and Naomi Wilson. *The New Suburb.* New York: Western, 2001. Print.

> *(Only the first author is listed last name, first name.)*

A book with more than three authors:

Smith, John, et al. *Urban Housing*. Chicago: Chicago UP, 2000. Print.

A work in an anthology:

Miller, Arthur. *Death of a Salesman*. *American Literature 1945–2000*. Eds. Keisha Sahn and Wilson Goodwin. New York: Dial, 2001. 876–952. Print.

An encyclopedia article:

"China." *The World Book*. 2009 ed. Print.

> *(Volume and page numbers are not needed in encyclopedia references.)*

A periodical article with a single author:

Smith, John. "Urban Planning Today." *American Architect* 25 Oct. 2013: 24–29. Print.

A newspaper article without an author:

"Mideast Crisis Boils Over." *The Washington Post* 22 May 2013: 54+. Print.

> *(If an article starts on one page, then skips to others, list the first page with a plus sign:+.)*

A television program:

"Oil Boom." Narr. Morley Safer. *Sixty Minutes*. CBS. WCBS, New York. 27 Jan. 2013. Television.

> *(Include both network and local station with date of broadcast.)*

An online article:

Wilkins, Robert. "Reflections on Milton." *Michigan Literary Review*. Sep. 2011. n. pag. Web. 22 Feb. 2012.

> *(Use **n. pag.** for items without page numbers.)*

An article from an online database:

Miller, John. "The New China." *Time* 5 May 2013 n. pag. *Online Sources*. Web. 10 May 2013.

An email:

Hennessey, Richard. "Re: Urban Planning Conference." Message to Sean Brugha. 22 June 2013. Email.

> *(Provide name of writer; title of message in quotation marks, recipient, and date.)*

An online interview:

McAndrews, Natrelle. Interview by Wolf Blitzer. *CNN.com*. Cable News Network. 4 May 2012. Web. 24 Jan. 2013.

A blog entry:

Hsu, Victor. "Hope in a Time of Crisis." *People and Faith*. n. p., 5 May 2013. Web. 10 May 2013.

Lecture notes posted on Blackboard:

> Henderson, Margaret. "Types of Evidence." English 101, Blackboard. 10 Oct. 2012. Lecture.

> *(Label other items* Microsoft Word file, PowerPoint file, Interview *as needed)*

A Tweet:

> Guron, Ben (Really Virtual). "Mayor releases tax returns." 2 May 2013, 2:48 p.m. Tweet.

In-text Citations

When you include direct quotations and paraphrases in your paper, cite their use with parenthetical notations. These citations should be brief but accurate.

If you mention an author or source in your text, you only need to add a page number:

> Winston Hachner has noted, "The Internet has provided us with a dilemma of choice" (874).

> *(Note: Place the period after the parenthetical citation.)*

If you do not mention the source, include the author's last name or title with page numbers:

> The Internet has given us more choices than we can process (Hachner 874). The sheer volume of information can overwhelm, confuse, and strangle businesses accustomed to defined channels of communication ("Internet" 34–35).

Sources without page references do not require parenthetical notes if cited in the text:

> During a *Sixty Minutes* interview in 2012, Randall Pemberton argued, "A terrorist attack in cyberspace can cripple our economy."

You can avoid long, cumbersome parenthetical notes by citing titles or several authors in the text:

> As stated in the *Modern Directory of Modern Drama,* "August Wilson has emerged as one of the nation's most powerful dramatic voices" (13). Jacobson and Marley view him as a dominant force in shaping the country's perceptions of the African American experience (145–146).

Sources and Sample Documented Essay

Read through the excerpts taken from a book, an article, and a website and note how the student uses and notes these sources.

Book Excerpt

From *How to Survive College* by Nancy Hughes, published by Academic Press, New York City, 2012.

HOW TO SURVIVE COLLEGE
176

Today credit card companies bombard incoming freshmen with credit card offers. Card companies operate on campuses, often in student unions and dorm lobbies. Giving out free hats, T-shirts, coffee mugs, and pizza coupons, they encourage students to sign up for cards. Companies generally issue cards to any student over eighteen whether he or she has a job or not. Faced with the need for books, clothes, computer supplies, and student fees, many students quickly apply for cards and ring up charges. At Northwestern University nearly 10 percent of incoming freshmen had maxed out at least one credit card by the end of their first semester.

Actual purchases, however, are often not the culprit. The ability to use a credit card to get cash from an ATM leads many students to live well beyond their means, getting into debt $40 or $60 at a time. Miranda Hayes, who graduated with $7,500 in credit card debts, had made only $2,000 in purchases. "I charged a computer my freshman year and all my books," she admits. "The rest was all cash from an ATM that went for movies, beer, pizzas, bus fare, my cell phone, health club dues, and interest."

Magazine Article

From "Universities Confront Credit Card Issuers" in *Midwest Business,* May 11, 2013, page 17.

Midwest Business

17

UNIVERSITIES CONFRONT CREDIT CARD ISSUERS

This week representatives from sixteen universities meet in Cleveland to discuss campus credit card solicitations. Prompted by complaints from parents and alarmed by a study released last month by the Wisconsin Institute, college administrators are grappling with the growing problem of student credit card debt.

The Wisconsin Institute's findings revealed that the number of undergraduates holding at least one credit card has risen to over 70%. Student card holders carry an average balance of $3300, with some amassing as much as $12,500 on multiple cards. The study reports that 25% of students have paid late fees. One in eight card holders routinely pays over the limit fees. The majority of students state that they rely on credit cards to pay for books, school fees, tuition, and routine living expenses. The institute's survey of two thousand student credit card holders found that 40% did not know the interest rate they were paying and that 70% were unaware that the widely advertised low rates do not apply to cash advances. A surprising 15% of students graduated with over $7500 in credit card debts.

Universities have allowed credit card issuers to solicit on campus in return for donations and athletic sponsorships. Some colleges have contracted with banks to issue their own cards and earn a percentage every time a card is used. Originally promoted to alumni as an easy way to donate to their alma mater, these cards are now made available to students who are encouraged to charge their books and student union purchases. Parents, already burdened by high tuitions, are increasingly resentful that high-priced colleges are profiting every time their children use an ATM or charge a slice of pizza.

A Website

From "Top Ten Student Money Mistakes" by Blythe Terrell on Young Money, updated at http://www.youngmoney.com/money_management/spending/020809_02, and accessed May 10, 2013.

MAIL   PRINT

Top Ten Student Money Mistakes

By Blythe Terrell, University of Missouri

For many students, college is the first major landmark on the path to independence. Moving away from home means no more curfews, no asking for permission, and no parents looking over their shoulders. It also means that the liberty-seeking college kid is now free to make his or her own mistakes. In such an environment, money management often becomes an issue. Knowing how to avoid these problems is the key to beating them. Here are ten common mistakes students make, and how you can avoid them.

1. **Making poor choices about which credit cards to get.** Credit card companies set up booths on college campuses, offering T-shirts and other items to anyone who will sign up for a card. Although the deals can seem fantastic, students must look into the card's repayment terms carefully. "When students get credit cards, two things can happen," said Stephen Ferris, professor of finance at the University of Missouri–Columbia. "One, they don't read the fine print and see what they're paying. And they're paying a lot. Or they use it until it's maxed out." It is absolutely necessary to pay your credit cards on time each month, added Ferris.

2. **Letting friends pressure them into spending money.** College life is full of opportunities to spend money, finals-week smorgasbords, an evening out with friends, road trips and vacations … Not knowing how to say "no" can cause students to spend money they just do not have. "If you can't afford it, just say no," says David Fingerhut, a financial adviser with Pines Financial in St. Louis.

3. **Not setting up a budget.** If they have a set amount of money, they must plan ahead and know how much they can spend each month. "It has to work on paper before it works in real life," Fingerhut said.

4. **Not seeking out the best bank rates.** Banks offer many different kinds of checking and savings accounts, but some charge fees that others do not. It is essential for students to do research and not simply go with the closest, most accessible bank, Ferris said.

Student Essay

College Students and Debt

Students graduating in debt is nothing new. Few students or their parents have enough money to pay as they go. Even students with scholarships take on debts to pay for living expenses. But in recent years tens of thousands of students have added to their financial burdens by amassing credit card debt. Colleges that allow credit card companies to operate on campus must regulate the way these companies advertise and educate students on managing their money.

student thesis
topic sentence

Arriving on campus, freshmen encounter credit card promoters in student unions and dorms. Offering students free gifts, the various card companies urge students to sign up for credit cards. Card companies will issue cards to any college student who is at least eighteen (Hughes 176). Credit cards have become extremely popular with students. Currently over 70 percent of college students have at least one credit card ("Universities" 17).

Paraphrase facts stating problem Citation showing author and page

Many students are unsophisticated when it comes to using credit. Whether making a purchase or obtaining a cash advance, they rarely calculate how interest charges or ATM fees will inflate their balance. In many cases, students get deep into debt not by making major purchases, but by withdrawing costly cash advances. Many students share the fate of Miranda Hayes, who amassed a $7,500 credit card debt, noting, "I charged a computer my freshman year and all my books. The rest was all cash from an ATM that went for movies, beer, pizzas, bus fare, my cell phone, health club dues, and interest" (qtd. Hughes 176).

Topic sentence

Example supporting thesis Quote within a quote paraphrase

College administrators are considering new policies to regulate credit card promotions on campus ("Universities" 17). But the real service colleges can give students is to prepare them for the responsibilities of adult life by including financial planning seminars that focus on credit cards, budgets, and loans. Stephen Ferris, a finance professor, points out that when students sign up for cards, "they don't read the fine print and see what they are paying. And they're paying a lot" (qtd. Terrell). Students don't consider interest rates, let peer pressure guide their spending, and fail to set up budgets (Terrell).

topic sentence

quote within a quote paraphrase conclusion

Ultimately, students are responsible. Away from home for the first time, they have to learn to manage their time, ignore distractions and peer pressure, and use credit wisely. Parents and colleges can provide information and give advice, but as adults, college students must take responsibility for the decisions they make.

restatement of thesis

Works Cited

Hughes, Nancy. *How to Survive College.* New York: Academic, 2012. Print.

Terrell, Blythe. "Top Ten Student Money Mistakes." *Young Money,* 21 Mar. 2009. n. pag. Web. 10 May 2013.

"Universities Confront Credit Card Issuers." *Midwest Business.* 11 May 2013: 17. Print.

Using APA Documentation

The APA style, developed by the American Psychological Association, is the preferred documentation method used in social sciences, including psychology, sociology, political science, and history. In the APA style, outside sources are listed alphabetically at the end of the paper in a "References" list and parenthetical citations are placed after direct quotations and paraphrases.

For complete details, refer to *The Publication Manual of the American Psychological Association*, 6th edition.

Building a Reference List

List all sources you refer to under the title "References" at the end of your paper. Items should be alphabetized by authors' last names or by the first significant word of their titles if no author is listed.

Understanding the DOI System

Increasingly, scholarly articles include a **DOI number.** Developed by international publishers, the Digital Object Identifier system provides a common identification for electronic articles. Many articles appearing in print will also include a DOI number, typically placed on the first page near the copyright notice:

> Journal of Abnormal Psychology: Copyright 2013 by the American Psychological Association
>
> Addiction and Depression 0278-8787/0879.00 **DOI: 10.8798/0044-897.8.090**
>
> 2011, Vol. 35, No.3, 434-445
>
> ## Self-Medication Among the Unemployed
>
> ### Randi Shaviz
>
> Marquette University

Include DOI numbers whether the article is retrieved in print or online.

General Guidelines

Print Sources:

Author, last name first and initials for first and middle names: **Twain, M.**

Date of publication in parentheses (year, month, and day for newspaper articles; year for books): **Twain, M. (1888).**

Title (in regular font for articles and other short works; in italics for books, journals, newspapers, and other long works, capitalizing only the first word, the first word after a colon, and proper names): **New treatment for bi-polar depression;**

Depression: Disorders and therapies

City and publisher for books: **San Diego, CA: Academic**

Volume number in italics and issue number in parentheses for magazines if available: **10 (4)**

All page numbers for articles preceded by "pp": **pp. 1–2, 33, 78–89.**

Online Sources

Author's last name, initials for first and middle names: **Guron, B. D.**

Date with year preceding month and day in parentheses: **(2012, September 25).**

Title (in regular font for short works from a larger work; italics for independent works capitalizing the first word and proper nouns):

Mayor announces budget; *Chicago Tribune.*

Retrieval source (including full URL):

Retrieved from http://www.princeton.edu/publications/cent.asian.studies.html

Sample formats

A book by a single author:

Smith, J. (2002). *The city.* New York: Putnam.

A book by two authors:

Smith, J., & Wilson, N. (2001). *The new suburb.* New York: Western.

(Both authors listed by last name, initial.)

A book with six or seven authors:

Smith, J., Wilson, S., Franco, W., Kolman, R., Westin, K., & Dempsey, F. (2000). *Urban housing.* Chicago: Chicago University Press.

(All authors listed by last name, initial.)

A book with eight or more authors:

Smith, J., Wilson, S., Franco, W., Kolman, R., Westin, K., Dempsey, F.... Smith, K. (2000). *Urban housing.* Chicago: Chicago University Press.

(First six authors listed by last name, initial, followed by ellipsis [...], followed by last author.)

A work in an anthology:

Miller, A. (2001). Depression in the adolescent male. In J. P. Meyers, J. Reed, & R. Rank (Eds.), *The psychology of youth: Problems and solutions* (pp. 87–99). New York: Dial.

An encyclopedia article:

Depression. (1998). In *The Yale encyclopedia of psychology* (Vol. 13, pp. 324–325). New Haven, CT: University Press.

A periodical article with a single author:

Smith, J. (2013, October 25). Urban planning today. *American Architect.* 24–29.

A newspaper article without an author:

Mideast crisis boils over. (2013, May 22). *Washington Post*, pp. 54, 58, 78, 89–92.

Scholarly article with DOI number

Grant, E. (2012). The Hollywood ten: Fighting the blacklist. *California Film Quarterly*, *92*, 112–25. doi:10.1989/9890-7865.24.2.342

An online article:

Wilkins, R. (2013, March). Reflections on depression. *Michigan Science Review*. *9*, 116–123. Retrieved from http://www.umichigan.edu/scireview.html

A corporate or organizational website without dates:

New York City Health Department. (n.d.). Bioterrorism. Retrieved from http://www.nychd.org/bioterrorism. html

Article on CD-ROM:

Albania. (2012) In *Oxford Encyclopedia of Education*. 3rd. ed. [CD-ROM]. Oxford, UK: Oxford University Press.

A television program:

Paulus, G. (Executive Producer). (2012, January 27). *The mind*. [Television series]. New York: WNET.

A podcast:

Adams, D. (Producer). (2012, October 30). Teen suicide. [Video podcast]. Retrieved from http://www.teensuicide.com/

Lecture notes posted on Blackboard:

Jones, b. (2012). *Intervention strategies* [Lecture notes]. Retrieved from http://blackboard.harvard.edu

(*Label other items* PowerPoint slides, Class Handout *as needed*)

An email:

Email and other correspondence are not included in References but are listed within the text by referring to the writer and date.

In-text Citations

When you include quotations and paraphrases in your paper, cite their use with parenthetical notations listing author and year. These citations should be brief but accurate:

Hachner (2013) noted, "The Internet provides us with a dilemma of choice" (p. 12).

(Note: Place the period after the parenthetical citation.)

Wellman (2012) compares two common therapies for treating depression.

(Note: No page references cited for paraphrases.)

For sources without authors, include the titles in the text or a parenthetical citation:

Psychology Year in Review (2012) presents new theories on addiction. A recent article reveals a genetic predisposition to narcotic dependence ("Genetic Maps," 2012).

(Note: Include only years even if day and month are available.)

If a work has three, four, or five authors, cite all authors by only last names in the first reference:

Bodkin, Lewis, Germaine, and Neimoller (2012) dispute commonly held views of addiction.

In subsequent references, cite only the first author:

Bodkin et al. (2012) found no single factor in determining predisposition to alcoholism.

For works with six or more authors, cite only the first author in first and subsequent references:

Bryant et al. (2012) analyzed census figures to determine demographic changes.

Strategies FOR AVOIDING COMMON DOCUMENTATION PROBLEMS

1. Use sources sparingly. A good essay is not a collection of quotations and paraphrases. The focus of your paper should be your thesis, supporting ideas, and commentary. Avoid using long direct quotations that can be summarized in short paraphrases. The fact that you find many interesting sources in the library or on the Internet does not mean that you should include everything you find in your paper. *Be selective.*

2. Take careful notes and collect documentation information when you locate valuable sources. Copy direct quotations carefully, word for word, and do not distort their meaning by taking ideas out of context. Place direct quotations in quotation marks. If you photocopy a book or periodical, record the author's name and all publication information needed to document the sources. If you print an article from the Internet, make sure you record the full website address and the date. If you cut and paste online material directly into your paper, highlight it in a different color to distinguish it from the rest of your text while writing and editing. After accurately documenting the source, change the color to black.

3. Select sources carefully. Avoid sources that appear biased, outdated, or poorly presented. Remember that all books, periodicals, and websites are created by human beings, who may be misinformed or prejudiced. Avoid basing your entire paper on a single source. Do not assume that all sources are of equal value. Use critical thinking skills to measure the significance of the sources you locate. If you have doubts about the validity of a source, consult your instructor or a reference librarian.

4. Comment on the quality and quantity of sources. Let readers know the results of your research. If sources are limited, outdated, or fragmentary, explain this situation to readers. If you find conflicting evidence or theories, objectively summarize the differences and justify your decisions in selecting sources. Don't assume direct quotations can speak for themselves. Don't insert sources into your essay without commenting on their value and demonstrating how they support your thesis.

5. Clearly distinguish your ideas from those of others. Accurate documentation, transitional statements, and paragraph breaks can help readers understand which ideas are solely yours and which originate from outside sources.

6. Blend quotations and paraphrases into your text to avoid awkward shifts. There should be smooth transitions between your ideas and those of others.

7. Be sure to use the documentation system your instructor expects.

Informal Documentation

Even if an assignment does not require formal documentation, you can add credibility to a personal essay by informally noting sources:

According a recent report on CNN, the number of college students working full time has almost doubled since 2011.

The *New York Times* reports that more consumers paid for major purchases using cash in 2013 than 2012.

Students have repeatedly complained about the online registration system (*Campus Times*).

Appendix B: A Writer's Guide to Revising and Editing

What Are Revising and Editing?

After completing a first draft, you may be tempted to check your essay for misspelled words and missing commas. But before *editing* your paper to correct mechanical errors, you should *revise* your work. Revising means "to see again." Before focusing on details, first look at the big picture. Review your assignment and goal, then revise paragraphs and edit sentences and words.

Revising the Essay

Review the Assignment and Your Goal

Before looking at your first draft, review the assignment and your goal. Read over any instructor's requirements or guidelines. What does the assignment call for? What does your instructor expect? What should your paper accomplish? What does it have to contain? Review your own notes and outline. What is your goal? What do you want to say? What do you want your paper to achieve?

Review the Whole Essay

Read the paper aloud. How does it sound? What ideas or facts are missing, poorly stated, or repetitive? Highlight areas that need improvement and delete paragraphs that are off topic or merely repeat ideas.

- Does your draft meet the needs of the assignment?

- What are the most serious defects?

- Have you selected an appropriate method of organizing your essay? Would a chronological approach be better than division? Should you open with your strongest point or state it in the conclusion?

Examine the Thesis

Does your paper have a clear thesis, a controlling idea—or is it simply a collection of facts and observations? Does the essay have a point?

- If your paper has a thesis statement, read it aloud. Is it clearly stated? Is it too general? Can it be adequately supported?

- Where have you placed the thesis? Would it be better situated elsewhere in the essay? Remember, the thesis does not have to appear in the first paragraph.

- If the thesis is implied rather than stated, does the essay have a controlling idea and a sense of direction? Do details and your choice of words provide readers with a clear impression of your subject?

Review Topic Sentences and Controlling Ideas

Each paragraph should have a clear focus and support the thesis.

- ■ Review the controlling idea for each paragraph.

- ■ Do all the paragraphs support the thesis?

- ■ Are there paragraphs that are off the topic? You may have developed interesting ideas, recalled an important fact or quote, or told a compelling story—but if these details don't directly relate to the thesis, they do not belong in this essay.

Review the Sequence of Paragraphs

While writing, you may have discovered new ideas or diverted from your plan, altering the design of the essay. Study your paragraphs and determine whether their order serves your purpose.

- ■ Should paragraphs be rearranged to maintain chronology or to create greater emphasis?

- ■ Does the order of paragraphs follow your train of thought? Should some paragraphs be preceded by paragraphs offering definitions and background information?

Revise the Introduction

The opening sentences and paragraphs of any document are critical. They set the tone of the paper, announce the topic, arouse reader interest, and establish how the rest of the essay is organized. Because you cannot always predict how you will change the body of the essay, you should always return to the introduction and examine it before writing a new draft.

Introduction Checklist

- ■ Does the introduction clearly announce the topic?

- ■ Does the opening paragraph arouse interest?

- ■ Does the introduction limit the topic and prepare readers for what follows?

- ■ If the thesis appears in the opening, is it clearly and precisely stated?

- ■ Does the language of the opening paragraph set the proper tone for the paper?

- ■ Does the introduction address reader concerns, correct possible misconceptions, and provide background information so that readers can understand and appreciate the evidence that follows?

Revise Supporting Paragraphs

The paragraphs in the body of the essay should support the thesis, develop ideas, or advance the chronology.

Supporting Paragraphs Checklist

- **Does each paragraph have a clear focus?** Does it need a stronger topic sentence stating the controlling idea?

- **Should the topic sentence be placed elsewhere in the paragraph?** Would it be better at the end rather than the beginning?

- **Is the controlling idea supported with enough evidence?**

- **Is the paragraph logically organized?** Would a different structure be more effective for unifying ideas?

- **Are there irrelevant or repeated details that should be deleted?**

- **Do paragraph breaks signal major transitions?** Should some paragraphs be combined and others broken up?

- **Do you make clear transitions between paragraphs or does the body appear choppy and disorganized?**

Revise the Conclusion

Not all essays require a separate concluding paragraph. A narrative may end with a final event. A comparison may conclude with the last point.

Conclusion Checklist

- **Does the conclusion end the paper on a strong note?** Will it leave readers with a final image, question, quotation, or fact that will challenge them and lead them to continue thinking about your subject?

- **Does the conclusion simply repeat the introduction or main ideas?** Is it necessary? Should it be shortened or deleted?

- **If your purpose is to motivate people to take action, does the conclusion give readers specific directions?**

Revising Paragraphs

First drafts often produce weak paragraphs that need stronger topic sentences and clearer support.

First Draft

The automobile changed America. Development increased as distances were reduced. People moved outward from the city to live and work. Highways and bridges were built. Travel increased, and greater mobility led to rapid population shifts, causing growth in some areas and declines in others. Cars created new industries and demands for new services.

Revision Notes

The automobile changed America. Development increased as distances were reduced. People moved outward from the city to live and work. Highways and bridges were built. Travel increased, <u>and greater mobility led to</u> rapid population shifts, causing growth in some areas and declines in others. Cars created new industries and demands for new services.

too vague, needs tighter topic sentence. Improve sentence variety.

explain which areas?give examples

Second Draft

The automobile reshaped the American landscape. As millions of cars jammed crowded streets and bogged down on unpaved roads, drivers demanded better highways. Soon great bridges spanned the Hudson, Delaware, and Mississippi to accommodate the flood of traffic. The cities pushed beyond rail and trolley lines, absorbing farms, meadows, and marshland. The middle class abandoned the polluted congestion of the city for the mushrooming suburbs that offered greater space and privacy. Gas stations, garages, parking structures, drive-in movies appeared across the country. Motels, chain stores, and fast food restaurants catered to the mobile public. Shopping malls, office towers, factories, and schools appeared in the new communities, all of them surrounded by what the cities could not offer—free parking.

Editing Sentences

After revising the main elements of the draft, you can *edit* sentences to eliminate errors and improve clarity. Reading papers aloud can help you hear errors that are easily overlooked during silent reading.

Common Grammar Errors

When editing drafts, look for the following common grammar errors:

Fragments

Fragments are incomplete sentences. Sentences require a subject and a verb and must state a complete thought.

Tom works until midnight.	**sentence**
Tom working until midnight.	**fragment (incomplete verb)**
Works until midnight.	**fragment (subject missing)**
Because Tom works until midnight.	**fragment (incomplete thought)**

Notice that even though the last item has a subject, *Tom,* and a verb, *works,* it does not state a complete thought.

Run-ons and Comma Splices

Run-ons and comma splices are incorrectly punctuated compound sentences. Simple sentences (independent clauses) can be joined to create compound sentences in two ways:

1. Link with a **semicolon** (;)

2. Link with a **comma** (,) + and, or, yet, but, or so

I was born in Chicago, **but** I grew up in Dallas.	correct
I studied French; Jan took Italian.	correct
We have to take a cab my battery is dead.	run-on
Jim is sick, the game is canceled.	comma splice

Subject-Verb Agreement

Subjects and verbs must match in number. Singular subjects use singular verbs and plural subjects use plural verbs.

The **boy** *walks* to school.	singular
The **boys** *walk* to school.	plural
The **cost** of drugs *is* rising.	singular (the subject is **cost**)
Two weeks *is* not enough time.	singular (amounts of time and money are singular)
The **jury** *is* deliberating.	singular (group subjects are singular)
The **teacher** or the **students** *are* invited.	plural (when two subjects are joined with *or*, the subject nearer the verb determines whether it is singular or plural)

Pronoun Agreement

Pronouns must agree with (match) the nouns they represent.

Everyone should cast *his or her* vote.	singular
The **children** want *their* parents to call.	plural

The most misused pronoun is *they.* **They** is a plural pronoun and should clearly refer to a plural noun. Avoid unclear use of pronouns.

Unclear

> Crime is rising. The schools are failing. **They** just don't care.
> (*Who does "they" refer to?*)

Revised

> Crime is rising. The schools are failing. **Residents** just don't care. **They** don't even bother to vote.
> (*"They" clearly refers to the plural noun "residents."*)

Dangling and Misplaced Modifiers

To prevent confusion, modifiers—words and phrases that add information about other words—should be placed near the words they modify.

Rowing across the lake, **the moon** rose over the water.	dangling (who was *rowing?* the *moon?*)
Rowing across the lake, **we** saw the moon rise over the water.	correct
She borrowed the car and drove to school, **which was illegal**, and was fired.	misplaced (what was *illegal*, borrowing the car or driving to school?)
She **illegally** borrowed the car and drove to school, and was fired.	correct

Faulty Parallelism

Pairs and lists of words and phrases should match in form and sentence structure.

Jim is **tall, handsome**, and an **athlete**.	not parallel (list mixes adjectives and a noun)
Jim is **tall, handsome**, and **athletic**.	parallel (all adjectives)
We need to **paint** the bedroom, **shovel** the walk, and **the basement** must be cleaned.	not parallel (The last item does not match with **to paint** and **to shovel.**)
We need to **paint** the bedroom, **shovel** the walk, and **clean** the basement.	parallel (all verb phrases)

Awkward Shifts in Person

Within a sentence, avoid illogical shifts among first person (*I, we*), second person (*you*), and third person (*he, she, it, they*).

We climbed the tower and **you** could see for miles.	awkward shift from *we* to *you*
We climbed the tower and **we** could see for miles.	correct
If **a student** works hard, **you** can get an A.	awkward shift from *student* to *you*
If **you** work hard, **you** can get an A.	correct

Awkward Shifts in Tense

Within a sentence, avoid illogical shifts among past, present, and future verb tenses.

Hamlet **hears** from a ghost, then he **avenged** his father.	awkward shift from present to past
Hamlet **heard** from a ghost, then he **avenged** his father.	correct (both past)
Hamlet **hears** from a ghost, then he **avenges** his father.	correct (both present)

Improving Sentences

As you edit the grammar in your draft, examine the sentences in each paragraph. Read each sentence separately to make sure it expresses the thoughts you intended.

Sentence Checklist

- Does the sentence support the paragraph's controlling idea? Or could it be eliminated?

- Are key ideas emphasized through specific words and active verbs?

- Are secondary ideas subordinated?

- Are the relationships between ideas clearly expressed with transitional expressions?

- Do the tone and style of the sentence suit your reader and the nature of the document?

Be Brief

Sentences lose their power when cluttered with unnecessary words and phrases. When writing a rough draft, it is easy to slip in expressions that add nothing to the meaning of the sentence.

Original:	In today's modern world, computer literacy is essential to entering into the job market.
Improved:	Computer literacy is essential in today's job market.

Phrases that begin with *who is* or *which were* can often be shortened:

Original:	Viveca Scott, **who was an ambitious business leader**, doubled profits, **which** stunned her stockholders.
Improved:	Viveca Scott, **an ambitious business leader**, stunned her stockholders by doubling profits.
Original:	Tim showed up at the wedding wearing a suit **that cost fifty dollars.**
Improved:	Tim showed up at the wedding wearing a **fifty-dollar** suit.

Delete Wordy Phrases

Even skilled writers use wordy phrases when trying to express themselves in a first draft. When editing, locate phrases that can be replaced with shorter phrases or single words:

Wordy

Then you have a lot of students out there with a lot of debt.

Improved

Many students are deep in debt.

Wordy	Improved
at that period of time	then
in this day and age	now
in the near future	soon
winter months	winter
round in shape	round
blue in color	blue
for the purpose of informing	to inform
render an examination of	examine
make an analysis	analyze
started to pack	packed
went to go to work	went to work

Eliminate Redundancy

Repeating or restating words and ideas can have a dramatic effect, but it is a technique that should be used sparingly to emphasize a specific point.

Redundant: The computer has revolutionized education, revolutionizing delivery systems, course content, and teaching methods.

Improved: The computer has revolutionized educational delivery systems, course content, and teaching methods.

Avoid Placing Minor Details in Separate Sentences

Sentences should express ideas, not simply state a minor detail that can be incorporated into a related sentence.

Awkward:

The mayor demanded a new budget. This was on Tuesday.
I bought a Corvette. It was red.

Improved:

The mayor demanded a new budget on Tuesday.
I bought a red Corvette.

Vary Sentence Types

You can keep your writing interesting and fresh by altering types of sentences. Repeating the same type of sentences makes writing monotonous. A short sentence isolates an idea and gives it emphasis, but a string of choppy sentences robs your essay of power. Long sentences can subordinate minor details and show the subtle relationships among ideas, but they can become tedious for readers to follow.

Unvaried: Mary Sanchez was elected to the assembly. She worked hard on the budget committee. Her work won her respect. She was highly regarded by the mayor. People responded to her energy and drive. She became popular with voters. The mayor decided to run for governor. He asked Mary Sanchez to manage his campaign.

Varied: Mary Sanchez was elected to the assembly. Her hard work on the budget committee won her respect, especially from the mayor. Voters were impressed by her drive and energy. When the mayor decided to run for governor, he asked Mary Sanchez to manage his campaign.

Editing Words

Appropriate words make your writing clear and memorable.

Diction Checklist

- **Are the words accurate?** Have you chosen words that precisely reflect your thinking?

- **Is the level of diction appropriate?** Do your words suit the tone and style of the document?

- **Do your words' connotations suit your purpose or do they detract from your message?**

- **Are technical terms clearly defined?**

- **Do you use specific rather than abstract words?**

Use Words Precisely

Many words are easily confused. Should a patient's heart rate be monitored **continually** (meaning *at regular intervals*, such as once an hour) or **continuously** (meaning *without interruption*)? Is the city council planning to **adapt** or **adopt** a budget? Did the mayor make an **explicit** or **implicit** statement?

Your writing can influence readers only if you use words that accurately reflect your meaning. There are numerous pairs of frequently confused words. Here are a few:

allusion	an indirect reference
illusion	a false or imaginary impression
infer	to interpret
imply	to suggest

conscience (*noun*)	a sense of moral or ethical conduct
conscious (*adjective*)	awake or aware of something
principle	a basic law or concept
principal	something or someone important, such as school principal
affect (*verb*)	to change or modify
effect (*noun*)	a result

Use a dictionary to make sure you have selected the correct words.

Use Specific Words

Specific words communicate more information and make clearer impressions than abstract words, which express only generalized concepts.

Abstract	Specific
motor vehicle	pickup truck
modest suburban home	three-bedroom colonial
individual	boy
protective headgear	helmet
residential rental unit	studio apartment
digestive ailment	heartburn
educational facility	high school

Avoid Sexist Language

Sexist language either ignores the existence of one gender or promotes negative attitudes about men or women.

Replace sexist words with neutral terms:

Sexist	Nonsexist
mankind	humanity
postman	letter carrier
policeman	police officer
chairman	chairperson

Avoid using male pronouns when nouns refer to both genders. The single noun *man* takes the single male pronoun *he*. If you are writing about a boys' school, it is appropriate to substitute *he* for the noun *student*. But if the school includes both males and females, both should be included.

Every **student** should try **his or her** best.

All **students** should try **their** best.

By using plural nouns, which take the pronouns *they* and *their*, you can avoid wordy *he or she* and *his or her* constructions.

Avoid Clichés

Clichés are worn-out phrases. Once creative or imaginative, these phrases, like jokes you have heard more than once, have lost their impact. In addition, clichés allow simplistic statements to substitute for genuine thought.

white as snow	back in the day	acid test
perfect storm	in the thick of it	on pins and needles
evil as sin	dead heat	crushing blow
viable option	bottom line	all that jazz
crack of dawn	calm before the storm	dog-tired

Use an Appropriate Level of Diction

The style and tone of your writing are shaped by the words you choose. Your goal, your reader, the discourse community, and the document itself usually indicate the kind of language that is appropriate. Informal language that might be acceptable in a note to a co-worker may be unsuited to a formal report or article written for publication.

Formal: Sales representatives are required to maintain company vehicles at their own expense. (employee manual)

Standard: Salespeople must pay for routine maintenance of their cars. (business letter)

Informal: Remind the reps to change their oil every 3,000 miles. (email)

Slang expressions can be creative and attention getting, but they may be inappropriate and detract from the credibility of formal documents.

Appreciate the Impact of Connotations

Connotations are implied or suggested meanings. Connotations reflect a writer's values, views, and attitudes toward a subject. A resort cabin can be described as a *rustic cottage* or a *seedy shack*. The person who spends little money and shops for bargains can be praised for being *thrifty* or ridiculed for being *cheap*. The design of a skyscraper can be celebrated as being *clean and streamlined* or criticized for appearing *stark and sterile*.

The following pairs of words have the same **denotations** or basic meanings, but their **connotations** create strikingly different impressions:

young	inexperienced
traditional	old-fashioned
brave	ruthless
casual	sloppy
the homeless	bums

unintended landing	plane crash
teenage prank	vandalism
uncompromising	stubborn
strong	dictatorial
free	lawless
enhanced interrogation	torture
tax relief	tax break
clearing swamps	destroying wetlands
homebuilder	real estate developer
gaming industry	gambling interests
public servant	government bureaucrat

Index